# SECONDARY SCHOOL READING:

## PROCESS
## PROGRAM
## PROCEDURE

# SECONDARY SCHOOL READING:
## PROCESS, PROGRAM, PROCEDURE

WALTER R. HILL

*State University of New York at Buffalo*

ALLYN AND BACON, INC.

*Boston   London   Sydney   Toronto*

*Cover photographs by George W. Perkins III.*
*Part illustrations by Andrew J. Hill.*

LIBRARY OF CONGRESS CATALOGING IN PUBLICATION DATA

Hill, Walter, 1925–
  *Secondary school reading: process, program, procedure*
  1. Reading (Secondary education)   I. Title.
LB1632.H54          428'.4'0712          78–13358
 ISBN 0-205-06129-X

Printed in the United States of America.

*Second printing . . . July, 1979*

*For Margaret*

# Contents

## PART III: READING INSTRUCTION

# List of Figures

# Preface

Reading is a critical and pervasive behavior in the upper schools and in our society. The enlightened involvement of all junior and senior high school personnel, according to their abilities and responsibilities, can do much to improve reading and learning in school and life situations. Professional competence in reading utilization and improvement in the upper grades requires more than mere acquaintance with a handful of content area or corrective reading procedures. *Secondary School Reading* was written with this broader goal in mind. Within the limitations of a single textbook, it provides a conceptual framework, consistent in theory, yet practical in instructional application. It should be useful to every secondary school professional, whether his or her primary concern lies in content area instruction, the teaching of English, developmental/corrective reading education, pupil personnel services, or administration.

This book provides ample treatment of instructional and assessment strategy, along with illustrative measures, exercises, activities, and materials pertinent to reading use and development in grades seven through twelve. However, it has been my experience that a grasp of instructional procedure and its appropriate application to school situations is enhanced when rooted in consistent and meaningful theory. Care was taken, therefore, to organize the content of *Secondary School Reading* so that it progresses from (1) an introduction to reading and reading education in the secondary setting, to (2) a description of key characteristics of adolescent readers, to (3) an explanation of the nature of the integral-operational reading act and its essential processes, to (4) an overview of the comprehensive reading program, to (5) a presentation of fundamental principles and strategies for effective utilization of reading in any instructional setting, to (6) a discussion of approaches and techniques for improving targeted secondary reading behaviors, and concluding with (7) recommendations for the development and administration of the comprehensive secondary reading program. Chapters are organized on a topical basis, and thus lend themselves to other course or in-service structures, if preferred.

*Secondary School Reading* supports that planned, vigorous, all-school reading education effort which has been advocated by reading authorities and encouraged by school experience. The rationale for that effort and this text is summarized by the following observations:

- Pupils entering secondary school are developmentally immature readers: some are functionally illiterate, while most lack the interpretive power, efficiency, and flexibility needed to maximize content learning and school adjustment.
- Despite a considerable potential to improve, too many leave secondary school having failed to achieve functional competency, and the large majority fall short of that reading maturity which is so essential to personal fulfillment and the survival of a free, literate society.
- These pupils will make greater progress along the continuum of reading development when provided systematic guidance in the learning and application of upper-level reading behaviors.
- The probabilities of success in this crucial effort are increased dramatically when the secondary

school effects a comprehensive, all–school, multi-level program in reading education.

- The essential components of the comprehensive program consist of planned, sequential experiences for all students in reading evaluation, developmental reading instruction, content area guidance in reading-study application, and the extension of personal reading habits, as well as supplementary reading services for those pupils with special needs.

- All secondary school personnel, and content area teachers in particular, have a vital if different contribution to make to this comprehensive effort.

- This contribution will be enhanced to the degree that each secondary staff member understands the nature of upper-school reading processes, the pupil as a reader, the objectives and operations of the total program, the fundamental principles and general strategies of reading instruction, and the various ways in which reading, learning, and application can be facilitated through better content instruction and school services.

- The dividends from this all-staff investment accrue not only in greater pupil reading development and personal adjustment but in better content learning, teacher job satisfaction, school social climate, and educational accountability.

After several decades of reading-related professional involvement and a few more of reading-related life involvement, a writer hardly knows who has not contributed to his knowledges and processes. I would like to express my particular appreciation to Dr. Walter Petty for challenging me to undertake the manuscript; to Audrey Bard, David Bishop, Dr. Norma Inabinette, Thomas McWhorter, Janet Michalak, and Dr. Peter Pelosi for research survey and reaction pertinent to various topics within the manuscript; and to Andrew J. Hill for graphic consultation and original artwork.

WALTER R. HILL

# I

# READING AND READING EDUCATION

# ONE

# Reading in the Secondary Setting

*The dear people do not know how long it takes to learn to read. I have been at it all my life and I cannot say I have reached the goal.*

Johann Wolfgang Goethe

***Overview*** Chapter One serves as an introduction to the text and to reading in the secondary school situation. Attention is focused upon the significant dimensions of reading, reading development, and reading education as they pertain to pupils in grades seven through twelve. Reading is viewed as an integrated act of learned behaviors which is capable of ongoing development. Such development can be effected by a comprehensive program of secondary reading education that incorporates planned provision for instruction, assessment, and classroom utilization for all secondary pupils. Influences on and notable developments of secondary reading education are reviewed as a means of placing the current status and problems of secondary school reading in proper perspective. The chapter closes with seven arguments for the need for all-staff involvement in the secondary school reading effort.

# READING AND READING DEVELOPMENT

The opening quotation from Goethe, penned in the twilight of a highly productive literary and scientific career, is particularly appropriate for a text treating the nature and improvement of reading in the upper schools.[1] It implies that reading is a complex behavior capable of ongoing refinement, and that the general public usually underestimates this developmental potential of the reading act. Too often, professional educators share this public misconception of reading as a narrow, simplistic process.

Arriving at a valid yet operational concept of reading is no inconsequential task at any school level. But it is particularly critical to the development of theory and practice in secondary reading education. How the school perceives the nature of reading usually is reflected in school decisions and practices related to curriculum, instruction, and evaluation. How the classroom teacher views reading influences the effectiveness with which reading is employed to improve content learning as well as reading performance. How the pupil, shaped by the attitudes of society, the school, and the teacher, comes to view reading will do much to influence his own reading sensitivities and expectations, and thus, his reading processes, products, and rewards.

Developing a useful construct of reading—one which squares with current evidence, which is applicable to secondary school and life circumstances, and which is understandable to those with minimal background in the nature of reading—thus becomes a prior task for this text. In this chapter, attention will be directed to the key functions and major dimensions of reading as needed background for understanding the general patterns of reading development and education in grades seven and beyond. Chapters Two and Three will expand upon the essential conditions and interrelated specific processes of reading as a maturing behavior.

## Reading: Some Essential Characteristics

In the upper school and in life, reading is at the same time a product, a tool, and a process. It is a product in the sense that it is the result of what has been taught and learned by the reader. It becomes a tool when it serves as a means of carrying out the reader's immediate purposes and of satisfying his needs, both utilitarian and psychological. It is a process (more accurately a set of integrated processes) in that the actual act of reading requires an appropriate sequencing of reader behaviors which begins with the reader's readiness to locate and/or to respond to a printed source and uses varied decoding–interpreting responses to arrive at the reader's reaction to the meaning he associates with that source material.

In recent years, reading has been widely and variously investigated as process, product, and tool.[2] The more we investigate the reading act, the more we discover of its amazing natures. As yet, there is little consensus among reading educators, psychologists, linguists, sociologists, neurologists, communication specialists, and other investigators concerning the finite nature of reading. However, we have learned enough about the significant elements of the reading process to determine its most useful and most needed functions in school and life and to enable us to improve the product through better secondary reading education and utilization.[3]

### Reading as Integrated, Purposeful Behavior

*Reading is what the reader does to gain the meaning he needs from textual sources.* Viewing reading as purposeful human behavior provides us with an operational construct of reading's most fundamental condition, as well as a means of understanding how the reader both learns and integrates the varied processes of reading into effective patterns of response to selective stimuli. For reading, especially its mature forms, is dependent upon the simultaneous utilization of a number of behavioral processes. Most secondary school reading situations call for communication behavior, perceptual–symbolic behavior, language-processing behavior, cognitive-reasoning behavior, and content reaction behavior.

***Reading as communication.*** Reading is a process of receptional communication.[4] It may take place only if a writer first has encoded a message from certain information he wishes to share with others not present. The medium by which the writer sends this message is print. The fundamental units of print are symbols (primarily words) which simultaneously represent units of language meaning and experiential referents. In order to gain greater scope, intensity, and/or precision in the meaning of his message, the writer arranges his word symbols in syntactical sentence sequences much as he would extend them in an oral language utterance. Because the writer cannot, like the speaker, make use of pitch, stress, juncture, gesture, and immediate feedback to help his word arrangements carry meaning, he must use certain typographical conventions such as punctuation, textual organization, headings, listings, tables, and the like to provide order and emphasis to his statements of fact, concept, and generalization.

*Communication tasks of the reader.* But all this effort on the part of the writer to capture life—its experiences, its reasoned products, its feelings—in textual language comes to naught unless a reader comes along who can and will breathe life back into those representative typographical forms. Among the most essential learned behaviors or behavioral products which the reader must control to accomplish this end are: (1) a willingness to undertake the reading communicative effort; (2) the ability to perceive letter groupings as symbols which in turn represent experiences and/or language referents; (3) an oral and written language competence which enables the reader to convert the writer's syntactical arrangement of word symbols into such units of reference as concepts and generalizations; (4) a collected bank of experiences upon which the reader can draw to associate meaning with the writer's word symbols and syntactical units of reference; (5) a familiarity with the conventions by which the writer may arrange his message in order to organize the information and ideas into a narration, exposition, or reasoned argument; (6) the capability and motivation to pursue the writer's represented reasoning, stated and implied, and to reconstruct the interrelated structure of ideas and supporting infor-

mation which comprise the larger meaning of the message; and (7) the facility to react appropriately to the writer's message.

*Reading as purposeful behavior.* Effective reading in secondary school and in life should be more than the passive reception of a message laid before the reader. As the reader gains in maturity, his reading should become increasingly purposeful, his approach flexible, and his involvement as dynamic as his need and the message warrant. In addition to satisfying a variety of short-term instrumental or service tasks, we read to satisfy such general motives as gaining respite through escape, relaxation, and other psychological reinforcement; enjoying the content or appreciating the style of the written material; and/or the resolving of real or theoretical problems.[5] Such motives influence the reader's reaction to the message—the type of emotional effect it produces, the degree to which the information is assimilated (learned and retained), and/or the logical or creative application of the content. In any case, the reader who makes a purposeful, dynamic search for meaning in the writer's message is likely to increase his accuracy, efficiency, and personal satisfaction in that reading.

*Reading as personal behavior.* Reading is a very personal behavior. How we read is shaped by our personal characteristics, and how well we read is dependent upon our personal resources or reading potential.[6] The degree of reader potential needed will depend upon the nature of the reading task and written source. Even the least demanding reading situations encountered by youth in school and in life will require certain minimal personal resources in the form of general experiential background; competency in handling fundamental language and reading processes; perceptual-cognitive ability to associate, learn, retain, generalize, and reason; as well as freedom from inhibiting physical and emotional conditions. The fact that mature reading calls for efficient integration of multiple forms and higher levels of behavioral processing places even greater demand upon the personal resources of the reader. Secondary pupils vary in their personal potential for reading.

### An Operational Definition of Reading

To be serviceable in school and life circumstances, a construct of reading must recognize the variety of uses which the maturing reader can make of his reading situation, as well as the reservoir of personal behavior which must be integrated to complete the act. Operationally, *successful reading includes the purposeful integration of reader motivation, personal resources, and learned behaviors necessary to the location of, interpretation of, and reaction to printed sources in their various typographical arrangements.*

This concept of reading implies that appropriate reading behavior may take somewhat different forms, depending upon the reader's purposes, the nature of the written material, the reader's familiarity with the concepts and processes represented in the selection, and the physical and psychological circumstances in which the reading takes place. The better secondary school reader will adapt his reading approach to the reading situation. In this sense, he will be *selective, flexible,* and *efficient* in his location, interpretation, and reaction to printed sources. Above all, the successful reader is concerned with gaining the *meaning* of the written message—that meaning which the writer intended, as analyzed and reconstructed by the reader to meet his specific needs and general well-being.

### Reading Development

Reading is a developmental behavior. It is learned gradually and accumulatively. If the pupil has the potential to learn, if his general and school experiences combine appropriately with his need to learn—then he should progress along a continuum toward ever-increasing reading maturity.[7] Such development includes the mastery of increasingly complex reading behaviors: the ability to cope with higher levels of vocabulary and written structure, greater differentiation and flexibility in interpretive response, functional habits of application, and more sophisticated appreciation.

With the caution that "a given stage in reading development may have characteristics and activities of its own, but it is only a section of a number of continuous growth curves marked off for practical convenience," Russell cites the following six stages as representative of typical progression in reading development: prereading readiness (birth through grade I); beginning reading (grades I and II); initial independence in reading (grade II); transition to basic literacy (grades III and IV); early maturity in applied skills and wider choice of reading materials (grades IV through VI); advanced maturity (grades VII to adult).[8] The timing of these stages is rather idealistic; it is how we would like pupils to progress—and it is how some do learn. However, some secondary pupils are functionally illiterate, and a number of others struggle with the tasks of early reading maturity. Relatively few presently master advanced reading maturity prior to graduation. More pupils could reach higher stages with the help provided by a comprehensive program in secondary reading education.

### Pupil Differences in Reading Development

That pupils vary individually in reading development is a fact quite obvious to reading researchers and observant classroom teachers. Such differences are a product of variance in pupil personal learning resources and the opportunity to learn through formal and informal learning experiences. Pupils enter first grade with differing degrees of readiness to cope with initial instruction, and differences in classroom reading and reading test performance are clearly evident by the end of the first year of instruction.[9] And "between-pupil" differences in reading achievement increase with each successive year of schooling.[10]

Normatively, such differences are continuous; that is, the range of pupil reading performance will extend somewhat equidistantly above and below modal pupil performance at each grade/age level.[11] For example, approximately one-third of the reading test scores of a random sample of ninth-grade pupils will fall within .5 grade norms above and below ninth-grade median performance; scores of the remaining two-thirds range from that typical of average fourth-grade readers up to that characteristic of college freshmen.

Although not as dramatic for comparative purposes, *within-pupil* variations in reading development are as educationally significant as *between-pupil* differences and become more visible when one examines the subtest profiles of individual pupils or when close assessment is made of pupil success on mastery measures of specific reading behaviors.

*Differences in secondary test performance.* Although performance on a single standardized reading test represents only a part of the total picture of individual differences in secondary reading behavior, standardized test norms can provide a ready means of illustrating reading performance differences. The following test data from the *SRA Reading Record* are presented here because they can be manipulated to demonstrate within-pupil variations in reading performance as well as between-pupil differences in reading proficiency. The *SRA Reading Record* is a standardized silent-reading survey test whose total score is accumulated from ten measures of pupil reading performance: rate of reading, comprehension over rate selections, paragraph meaning, directory reading, map-table-graph reading, advertisement reading, index usage, technical vocabulary, sentence meaning, and general vocabulary.[12] The grade equivalents and percentile scores representing total test performance for seven grade levels (six through twelve) of the normative population used in standardizing the *SRA Reading Record* are graphically presented in Figure 1.

**Figure 1** *Reading distributions for normative scores for representative secondary school classes* [*SRA Reading Record*].

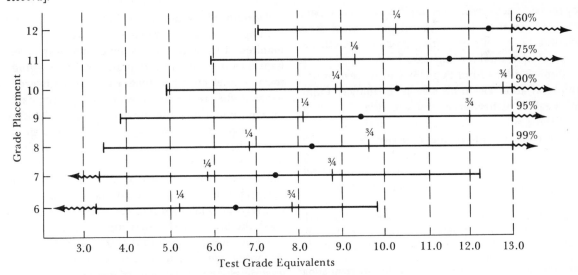

Key:  ◄∿ or ∿► indicates actual pupil scores below or above test norms.
¼ = 1st quartile (25% of class scored below this point).
◆ = Median (50% of class scored above and below this point).
¾ = 3rd quartile (75% of class scored below this point).
60% ∿► = 40% of class reached the top of the given norms.

Total scores on standardized tests at times create a false impression that the performance of an individual pupil is unitary or homogeneous. Within-pupil differences exist as relative strengths and weaknesses in specific reading skills or contributing reading knowledges. As such, they contribute or detract from the composite reading power of the pupil, and they may explain something of a pupil's inconsistent performance on classroom-related reading tasks.

Figure 2 presents hypothetical subtest performance for two ninth-grade pupils obtaining the same total score, the normative average for ninth graders.* As such, the two profiles reveal something of the within-pupil irregularity of specific reading performance.

Pupil A's profile is the less variable of the two, and thus, her total score is more representative of her performance on the various subtests. It might be conjectured that A's middle-range performance in vocabulary, rate, and general contextual reading subtests adds a stabilizing influence to her total reading performance. Although differences this small between individual subtests may be explained by measurement error, this pupil does reveal a pattern of lesser success on technical and applied-type reading tasks while exhibiting greater strength on general contextual reading tasks.†

Pupil B differs from Pupil A, and he reveals notable variation within his own performance. Pupil B's weakest performance occurs in rate of reading and those subtests which assess general contextual interpretation. Pupil B's higher performance on the map-table-graph, directory, and index reading subtests and his lesser difficulty with sentence and word reading suggest that he has relatively greater

difficulty in dealing with continuous written context. But this test profile does not reveal whether such results might be due to specific skills, test attitudes, understanding more abstract reading purposes, or even to inadequate reading rate.

A standardized survey reading test, even one composed of a series of subtest measures, cannot sample all of the reading behaviors in which pupils may differ. A relatively low score on a vocabulary test is the product of a composite performance itself; it does not tell us whether the pupil was weak in understanding word meanings, in word recognition skills, or both. Moreover, standard reading scores usually represent performance in highly structured reading tasks, but they may not assess the pupil's performance on reading tasks where he must develop his own reading purposes and applications. And such test results do not assure us that the better-scoring pupil will bring the power to bear upon a larger or tedious study assignment or upon content materials requiring different backgrounds of information. These, too, are significant aspects of individual reading differences.

*Functional reading differences.* Individual reading differences among secondary pupils are manifested in more directly functional ways. Perhaps no more than a third of a typical tenth-grade social studies class can read a typical tenth-grade social studies text with comprehension acceptable for course learning and application tasks. Another third might do better with a text of eighth-grade readability, and some would need a text of fifth-grade level or lower to independently master the assignment. Some pupils with adequate reading comprehension read nearly all materials in an excessively slow, detailed manner. Other pupils with good literal comprehension are quite unsophisticated in critical analysis of that meaning. Nardelli's evidence suggests that creative reading may be the least developed of the mature reading behaviors.[13] There are very few secondary pupils with balanced maturity in functional reading. Not surprisingly, there are relatively few truly mature readers in the adult population.[14]

---

*Actual *SRA Reading Record* norms are not differentiated into the number of subscores presented in Figure 2, although the differential basis of such scores is present in the test subdivisions!

†In the diagnostic situation, the validity of comparing subtest scores for specific diagnosis and instructional prescription is contingent upon the nature and norming of the test. Ordinarily, the teacher or specialist would verify the reality of such differences with further assessment of a formal or informal nature.

**Figure 2**  *Hypothetical subtest profiles of two ninth-grade pupils achieving the same test grade equivalent of 9.5.*

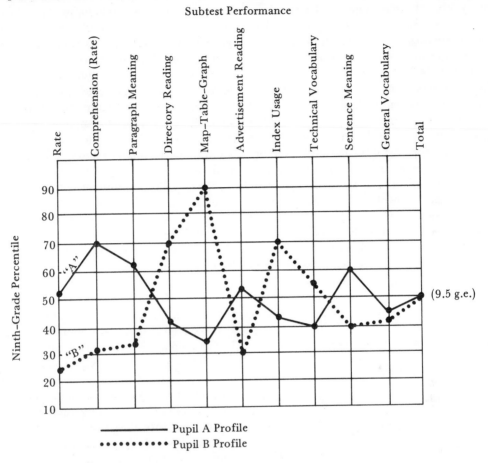

Subtest Performance

Rate · Comprehension (Rate) · Paragraph Meaning · Directory Reading · Map–Table–Graph · Advertisement Reading · Index Usage · Technical Vocabulary · Sentence Meaning · General Vocabulary · Total

Ninth-Grade Percentile

(9.5 g.e.)

——————— Pupil A Profile
•••••••••• Pupil B Profile

## READING EDUCATION

In the broadest sense, reading education consists of those learning experiences which contribute to the individual's reading development — to the reader's present performance and to his potential to read. This includes both in- and out-of-school learning situations, accumulated since birth. Let us consider three major types of learning experience which are necessary to successful reading performance at any school level and which illustrate the interaction of informal with formal learning in reading education.

### *English Language Competency*

Reading is a language behavior, and the effective learning of reading as a receptional English language process will depend substantially upon the pupil's mastery of basic English language competencies — phonemic, grammatical, and semantic. Ordinarily, basic language development occurs through the pupil's interaction with his society in language settings. The family, the neighborhood, the peer group, the electronic media, and the school all make special contributions to the reader's language experiences. Reading, itself, adds to this language background, once the reader starts to read independently.

Pupils whose basic language development is insufficient or is inconsistent with that used in school or by authors are likely to have greater difficulty in reading and learning to read. The school and the teacher can mitigate this difficulty and, in time, can help a pupil overcome general English language deficiencies or differences.[15] Effective reading education usually involves the multiple use of English—in speaking, writing, and listening, as well as in reading. Thus, pupil reading development is influenced by language development; and reading education, in the more formal school sense, contributes to broader language development, while making necessary adjustments to pupil language competency in order to develop reading competencies, as such.

### Experiential Background: Culture Assimilation

The writer draws observations gained from his own accumulated experiential background and commits them to print in the form of representative symbols imbedded in linguistic and textual structure. To understand this written language, the reader must reconvert those symbols into meaning by associating them with their appropriate experiential referents.[16] While it is possible for a reader vicariously to gain experiences through reading, he cannot do this without an experiential basis adequate enough to associate meaning with most of what the writer has encoded. Illustrative here is the rule of thumb used by reading specialists: a reader having difficulty associating meaning with as many as 5 to 10 percent of the words in a selection also will experience serious problems in understanding and personal frustration in reading that selection.

The reader develops an experiential background from direct and vicarious interaction in his cul-

ture(s). From a reading viewpoint, such experience is more useful if it also involves language associations. In any case, experiences which increase the reader's assimilation of the facts, concepts, and generalizations incorporated in his and the writer's culture contribute importantly to reading education. There is direct implication for the school situation here: the teacher may need to select reading materials which are within the probable background experience of the pupil, or she may need to provide the pupil with the necessary experiential background for understanding the assigned selection, or both.

The necessity of adequate background for understanding written sources carries a particular significance for content area teachers. Wendell Johnson once observed, "One cannot write writing any more than one can read reading. One can only write just as one can read—history, or geography, or physiology, or some other subject about which writing can be done."[17] In this sense, the content subjects consist of special segments of our culture. It is not likely that the typical secondary pupil has mastered this background (or why require the course?); thus, he is unlikely to read the content text adequately unless given prior aid with this missing background. On the other side of the coin, when the content teacher contributes to the pupil's background understanding of this special segment of his culture, the teacher adds to the pupil's reading performance potential. It is in this sense that the generalization "All teachers are teachers of reading" is used most accurately. Of course, if the content teacher adds to the pupil's mastery of the technical vocabulary and to the interpretation of the thought processes used by writers in that content area, the generalization is even more appropriate.

### Reading-Process Learning

The third area of critical experience needed for effective reading development is reading-process learning—by which means the reader learns the understandings, skilled responses, and attitudes necessary to the effective use of the reading act for the purposes of utility and personal satisfaction. The pupil profits greatly from planned systematic instruction and practice leading to the mastery of these reading behaviors.

Too often this aspect of reading education is applied in too restricted a manner, i.e., as an intense developmental or corrective period of specific skills instruction in which the learners read silently or orally to answer teacher questions and/or complete exercises. Actually, reading-learning experiences may take place in diverse school situations and may employ a variety of materials, teaching methods, and pupil activities.[18] Most reading education authorities believe that pupils at every school level need structured and informal learning experiences including: (1) specific development of essential reading vocabulary and the operational skills of reading, (2) the guided silent reading of meaningful textual selections, (3) the application of reading to the learning, study, and problem solving of personal reading interests and habits, and (4) the evaluation of status and progress in these areas. Reading instruction, formal and informal, is the central concern of this text, and later chapters will develop its essential conditions and varied forms.

## Secondary Reading Education

Secondary reading education, no less than elementary reading education, draws heavily upon the pupil's language competencies and general experiential background, while attempting to provide those opportunities which the pupil needs to master the necessary behavior of reading itself. Good secondary reading education shares much in common with good reading education at any school level or in any setting. The articulated, system-wide reading program providing continuity in reading-learning experiences from preschool through twelfth or fourteenth grade long has been supported by reading authorities. But secondary reading education is not some imitative aftershadow of the elementary school programs: it must adapt to a different school environment; it has a shorter history and less well defined tradition; it works at reading-learning objectives which include but go beyond those appropriate for elementary pupils; and it faces some unique problems in the organization, administration, and delivery of instruction.

### The Major Goals of Secondary Reading Education

Secondary reading education should be broadly developmental in focus. It contributes to the ongoing mastery of the knowledges, skilled behaviors, and attitudes which the pupil began in the primary grades and brings to the secondary school in various stages of immaturity. Secondary reading education should be integrative in operation. It draws from and contributes to other areas of secondary school learning. Secondary reading is imperative — reading ability is essential to general academic success and school adjustment, and the secondary school provides the last opportunity for most students to obtain guidance in reading proficiency.

For these reasons, secondary reading education needs to give particular attention to meeting three interrelated goals which are developmental, integrative, and imperative in nature:

1. To provide every secondary pupil with sufficient opportunity to develop competency in those reading behaviors required for functional literacy in our society.
2. To help every pupil improve in those reading-study applications which facilitate content area learning and which promote general scholastic success.
3. To assist every pupil to advance as far toward general reading maturity as his capabilities and drive permit.

### The Comprehensive Secondary Reading Program

As we shall see, secondary reading education has been influenced by a succession of instructional emphases and program patterns. Too often, it consists of isolated individual teacher effort, brief instructional exposure, fragmentary curricula, and little broad school transfer and reinforcement. Single- or even dual-emphasis reading instruction lacks the learning balance which McCullough describes as "reading development which does not neglect one essential avenue of learning to read or one aspect of the reading process in favor of another, but maintains an offering which, at any level of instruction, produces the optimal achievement and versatility of the individual reader."[19]

The comprehensive, all-teacher, all-pupil reading program provides the school with its best chance to achieve this balance in learning opportunity.[20] Furthermore, the comprehensive program tends to generate a positive, vital school reading climate which benefits both teacher and pupil—in content learning as well as reading improvement. The comprehensive school reading experience may assume different forms in different school settings. But regardless of the titles of the programs, the departmental affiliation, the delineation of staff responsibilities, the curricular organization employed, or the instructional approaches which prevail in the particular reading educational situation, it provides all pupils with opportunities to learn through five interrelated strands or areas of reading program experience:

1. *Systematic instruction in the essential developmental behaviors of reading*—that is, in those knowledges, skilled responses, and attitudes necessary to effective utilization of conventional materials—which form the foundation for functional reading competency and which enable the development of reading maturity.
2. *Instruction in and effective guidance of reading for content learning* and in the application of content-oriented reading to the satisfaction of school and life tasks.
3. *Extension of independent reading habits* through teacher stimulation of pupil reading interests and appreciations and through opportunity to do sustained reading in a wide selection of printed sources.
4. *Reading evaluation and assessment experiences* of a combined formal-informal nature in order to provide feedback and direction to individual learning as well as to develop a data base for making program decisions of an instructional and administrative nature.

5. *Supplementary reading services* of an instructional, diagnostic, counseling, and/or administrative nature which are targeted for pupils with special needs which are not likely to be met through the first four program strands extended to every pupil.

### *The Evolution of Secondary Reading Education*

Secondary reading education has a relatively short history of forty to fifty years. A look at some of the factors which influenced this development and the patterns which emerged should provide a better understanding of the current status and needs of secondary reading education in this country. This review is necessarily selective. More detailed discussion of the history of reading in the United States is provided by such sources as Smith's *American Reading Instruction*,[21] Harris's "Five Decades of Remedial Reading,"[22] Robinson's *Seventy-five Years of Reading Progress*,[23] and Hill's "Characteristics of Secondary Reading: 1940-1970."[24]

*Cultural shifts and school pressures.* One of the significant conclusions drawn by Smith from her historical research is that reading education in the United States has been susceptible to general social-political-economic conditions which come to bear upon the school. The interaction of external school influences with professional practice is apparent in the emergence and evolution of secondary reading education.

In the largely rural, nontechnical America of the pre-1900s, the formal education of the average citizen often was limited to attending the grammar school—or its later version, the elementary school. Reading materials were not plentiful nor widely available nor were the functions of everyday life highly dependent upon them. The need for most American youth to contribute early to the economic survival of the family by working on the family farm and the ready opportunity to labor in unskilled jobs did not encourage extended school attendance. Fundamental learning in the three R's was deemed sufficient for meeting life needs. The private academy and its later "public" secondary school adaptation were small, selective, and elitist. Traditional academic subject orientation in the selection of secondary teachers firmly established the tradition of a content subject-oriented curriculum in the secondary school. Reading was viewed largely as word pronunciation and oral fluency, a task to be mastered in the grammar-oriented elementary school.

By the time the twentieth century was well underway, the American pattern of life was undergoing changes which were to influence the nature of the secondary school.[25] Among other changes, the United States with its fortunate combination of human and physical resources became a major producer of world goods. Technology advanced, industrialization increased, and the move from the farm to the city was on. Society became more complex, the population grew, and socioeconomic aspiration increased. Abhorrent industrial working conditions, the rise of organized labor, and the need for the average worker and citizen to have better general and technical preparation combined to establish compulsory school attendance through the age of 16 or 18. The first waves of an expanding pupil population and the knowledge explosion began to break upon the secondary school.

Secondary schools began to change. As pupil enrollment grew, classes became larger and instruction less personal. While many of the students brought in by social and legal changes were talented and motivated, others were weak in fundamental school skills, deficient in English language and general experiential background, and minimally motivated toward academic objectives. Wider ranges of pupil differences appeared in every classroom. The pressures on the secondary school increased in other ways. World Wars I and II brought to public attention the fact that a surprising number of American males could not handle the basic literacy demands of military life. The severe economic depression of the 1920s shook public confidence in its economic and educational system and brought a demand for better and more utilitarian school preparation.

The challenge laid out for secondary education by significant national commissions was multidirectional: to extend competency in the functional learnings needed by all youth, to prepare youth for successful vocational life as well as for college, and to improve general learning in the sciences, social sciences, humanities, and the arts. At the same time, academic fields were expanding with additional facts, concepts, and processes. The secondary curriculum broadened, and content courses became more specialized. As content textbooks became more cryptic, encyclopedic, and less readable, the teacher began to rely more and more heavily upon the content textbook assignment as the means by which to deal with greater amounts of content and greater pupil numbers. The critical role of reading-study ability in secondary school learning and adjustment now was fully set, even if its significant, attendant instructional implications went unrecognized.

*Professional influences.* A professional basis for viewing reading and its improvement as something more challenging than teaching children to pronounce letters was initiated early in this century. Eye-movement researchers in this country and Europe developed evidence which revealed reading to be a more complex behavior than commonly thought, that able adult readers read differently than less able and immature readers and in ways not taught in elementary reading instruction, and that the nature of the reading task influenced the nature of reading performance.[26] Such findings suggested a need for reexamination of traditional views of reading and reading education. In this same vein, Huey published his insightful analysis *The Psychology and Pedagogy of Reading* in 1908, which served to stimulate and guide later research into the complexities of reading.[27]

In 1917, Thorndike took then-prevalent practices of reading education to task by publishing the results of a study on paragraph reading which revealed that most upper-grade students in his sample read erroneously, partly because they had been taught to read in a passive, mechanical manner.[28]

The emergence of the objective measurement movement in psychology and education in the 1920s and 1930s provided a vehicle by which evidence was established concerning individual differences in reading performance, the existence of pupil under-achievement in reading, the ongoing developmental nature of reading improvement, and the functional inadequacies of many college and adult readers.

During the second quarter of the twentieth century, a number of significant professional sources appeared that supported the need for reading education at upper school levels. The 1925 yearbook of the prestigious National Society for the Study of Education (NSSE) proposed that reading guidance should be provided in the junior and senior high schools.[29] In 1928, Yoakam published a volume of research and instructional application pertinent to more advanced reading interpretation and study processes.[30] Yoakam's evidence confirmed the findings of Thorndike and others that middle- and upper-grade pupils had considerable difficulty in reading textbook materials with understanding and learning.

The first textbook emphasizing developmental reading instruction in the secondary school—the Bonds' *Developmental Reading in High School*—appeared in 1941.[31] Shortly thereafter, the National Association of Secondary School Administrators conducted a national survey of reading practices in the secondary school and turned up, among other findings, that secondary principals ranked reading performance as a major secondary problem, that only a small percentage of schools offered organized reading instructional opportunity, and that content teachers were not prepared to deal adequately with reading in their instructional settings.[32] With the NSSE 1948 publication, *Reading in High School and College*, the need for secondary school concern for reading and its instruction was professionally established, even if vigorous activity at the school level was yet to appear.[33]

*The emergence of instructional programs.* The first reading program pattern to appear in the secondary school with notable frequency was trans-planted from the elementary school. Advancements in the normative measurement of intelligence and reading achievement produced a concept of under-achievement, the reading version of which was "reading disability." Operationally, reading disability was defined in a number of ways, but when employed by trained professionals it was used to identify pupils encountering unusual difficulty and/or developmental retardation who also were performing significantly below their own mental potential in reading.

The recommended treatment for these pupils consisted of various forms of *remedial reading*, usually in some form of group or individual reading reeducation in deficient areas of reading skills performance. Remedial reading teachers began to take their place in the elementary school during the latter 1930s. It is not difficult to see how such a concept would appeal to secondary school administrators concerned about serious problem learners yet with a teaching staff largely unprepared to deal with such problems. During the 1940s, the most common planned secondary effort in reading education was remedial reading, handled by special reading teachers. It continues as one of the most frequent forms of secondary reading education.

The Bond textbook was followed by a number of professional publications supporting ongoing reading instruction for all pupils, at least at the junior-high level. By the mid-1950s, "developmental reading classes," usually connected with the English program and handled by English staff, became the second established pattern in secondary reading education. In time, the objectives of remedial reading were crossed with the economy of developmental classes, and "corrective reading classes," sometimes offered as a lower-track English course, became yet a third type of reading educational approach appearing in secondary schools.

Secondary reading education drew also from college reading practices. From 1920 to 1960, a growing number of experimental instructional reading laboratories were established in colleges, junior colleges, and universities. These usually served multiple functions: researching reading behavior, providing diagnostic services for public school and college students with reading problems, training the initial ranks of reading specialists, and, significantly, providing instruction for college students who desired to improve their reading-study performance.

The reading laboratory or reading center concept inevitably was transplanted to the secondary school setting. So were some of the methods and materials employed. These included such mechanized instructional aids for improving reading efficiency as tachistoscopes, reading films, and individual reading pacers. A number of textbooks or workbooks in improving college-adult-level reading skills in vocabulary and word recognition, comprehension, and study habits appeared during the 1930s and 1940s. These were extended in content and number by the 1960s. Some of these and their secondary-level variants found their way into secondary school programs. These college reading programs and materials were largely responsible for the appearance of special, often voluntary, classes in reading rate and study improvement at the secondary level—in addition to the reading center concept.

Professional involvement in secondary reading education grew steadily during the 1950s and 1960s. Professional courses dealing with secondary reading instruction were established in many colleges and universities. Professional textbooks relating to secondary reading programs and methods appeared. Several national organizations interested in high school and college instruction were organized, and the *Journal of Developmental Reading* (later the *Journal of Reading*) was established with secondary and college reading as its central focus. Reading instructional materials directed specifically at secondary school learners were published. A growing body of research relating to secondary school readers and programs began to accumulate. Surveys reported a notable increase in the number of secondary schools offering structured reading-instruction activity.[34] As a generous estimate, perhaps no more than one in four schools had some sort of organized program in the early 1950s. By the late 1960s, this estimate had risen to a national average of one in two.

### Current Program Patterns and Challenges

Aided by federal and state funding, growing teacher awareness, and vocal public concern over functional reading difficulty, this decade has witnessed a continued increase in secondary school involvement in reading education. The traditional program patterns of remedial, developmental, and corrective instruction continue to dominate offerings, but are augmented by provisions for disadvantaged pupils, content-oriented reading instruction, and functional reading competency. Although program surveys and individual reports reflect some growing sophistication in secondary reading practices, it is clear that considerable variation in program quality exists from school to school. Notable obstacles remain to be overcome.[35]

*Program frequency.* Regional surveys suggest that the number of schools providing some sort of planned secondary reading education has risen to three out of four, at least in some regions of the country. Lesser frequency of involvement is reported for schools with fewer students, in rural settings, with problems in financial school support, and with conservative administrative and curricular policies.

*Multiple offerings.* There is some evidence to suggest that single-instructional-emphasis programs are evolving into multiple-emphasis programs. Usually this is a combination of developmental reading classes with some form of special help for problem readers, such as remedial or corrective reading. As yet, few schools appear to provide the comprehensive, all-teacher secondary education recommended by the 1948 NSSE Yearbook Committee.

*Developmental reading instruction.* Ongoing instruction in the knowledges, skills, and attitudes necessary to general growth in reading is likely to be provided for most, though not all, pupils at the seventh- and eighth-grade levels. This frequency of offering drops notably at each successive grade level thereafter. Developmental reading instruction usually is provided in class settings, although some schools offer it as individualized work in a reading center. Developmental reading instruction may be handled by trained reading teachers. More often, it is the responsibility of the English staff.

Developmental reading instruction appears in a variety of structures as an English curriculum offering: a developmental reading course, as such, either required or elective; a lower-level or prerequisite English course (often corrective in intent); separate reading units within English courses; one or two periods a week of reading skills practice as part of an integrated course in English language or communication skills; and fused reading skills–literature study instruction. A surprisingly large number of English teachers report little formal professional preparation in the study and teaching of reading as a process, which may account for the evidence that little emphasis is placed even upon the guided in-class reading of literature in English classes.[36] Yet many school administrators assume that the developmental teaching of reading is incidentally fulfilled through traditional English or literature courses.

*Remedial and corrective reading.* In the elementary school, corrective and remedial reading usually are viewed as somewhat different approaches to aiding pupils with different degrees and syndromes of reading difficulty—corrective reading usually taking the form of small-group developmental reteaching of pupils with lesser limitation in reading, and situated in either the regular classroom or in a special setting; remedial treatment more often taking a therapeutic form of highly motivated, individualized instruction for pupils with severe reading learning difficulty in special settings and extending over longer periods of time. Unfortunately, consistent distinctions in classification and practice are not so likely to be made in the secondary school. What is termed "remedial reading" may

be nothing more than corrective group practice sessions for a wide range of problem readers. "Corrective reading," on the other hand, may represent such diverse patterns as lower-track English classes, compensatory programs for disadvantaged pupils, or reading rate improvement. Corrective and/or remedial reading may not be staffed by trained specialists in the secondary school.

Corrective and/or remedial reading provision is reported among the most frequent forms of reading education currently offered by secondary schools. There is a real need for such help, but it is not an adequate substitute for comprehensive secondary reading education. It is most unfortunate that secondary corrective and remedial efforts have not been better planned and executed. In particular, they need to gear pupil selection to the types of learning experiences to be offered; they need to provide for broader reading development beyond that practice in specific skills; and they need to extend corrective-remedial assistance to the pupil with severe content area reading difficulty.

*Reading centers.* The school reading center seems to be an established component of secondary reading education. Reports suggest that half or more of secondary schools with reading programs have a "reading center." The actual facilities will range from a classroom given over to reading instruction for part of the day—to a laboratory containing specialized equipment and centers of instruction—to a center complex containing rooms for group and individual testing, instruction, and counseling, as well as a special library, reception area, and staff offices. A reading center may handle all or most of the school's reading instruction, or it may provide supplementary services of a diagnostic-corrective nature. The reading center may house the school reading program coordinator and reading consultants. In some schools, the reading center serves as the hub of reading program instruction, administration, and in-service education.

*Content area reading instruction.* Perhaps no aspect of secondary reading education has received more professional attention in the last decade than "reading in the content areas." Some differences in theory and practice are represented in publications, college courses, and in-service education dealing with content reading. One common pattern has focused upon bringing content teachers into the developmental reading instructional effort. Another has stressed the content teacher's role as one of assisting the pupil to handle content area classroom reading tasks in a more effective manner. The results to date have been disappointing. Surveys reveal organized approaches to reading instruction within content classroom settings to be the least frequent of all program offerings.[37] Evidence of growth in content area teacher understanding of content reading issues and instruction has been disappointing.[38]

Most authorities feel that active involvement by content teachers in content classroom reading-study usage is crucial if secondary reading education is to exert a significant impact upon the improvement of reading literacy in the U.S. Such involvement is equally critical to the improvement of content area learning. A growing number of states and colleges are requiring at least one course in reading education for secondary teacher certification, and many schools have implemented in-service programs to improve secondary teacher understanding of reading and its instructional use. These efforts are not sufficient to prepare secondary reading teachers or specialists, but they can be helpful to the content teacher sincerely concerned in improving the use of reading as a mode of content instruction. The position taken in this text is that an effective program in secondary reading education and excellence in content area instruction are mutually supportive. The content teacher has an essential role in the development of reading maturity, but as a reading-savvy content teacher not as a developmental reading teacher.

***Reading programs for the disadvantaged.*** Supported by special funding and public pressure, programs for the linguistically, experientially, or socioeconomically disadvantaged pupil represent a more recent addition to the secondary reading educational effort. Perhaps one in ten schools provide such help, often as a part of a multiphase reading program. As might be expected, programs for the disadvantaged are found more often in inner-city or minority-populated schools of larger cities. Rural schools seem not to have taken advantage of such aid. Reading help for the disadvantaged pupil has taken diverse forms, including individual remedial help, content reading tutoring, bilingual reading classes, compensatory reading-language programs, minority-oriented reading units, and socioeconomic support services.

***Evaluation and assessment.*** Better reading tests and assessment procedures have been developed in recent years, and greater attention has been placed upon measurement and evaluation in professional preparation. But the effects are yet to be felt in the assessment of secondary school reading. Most schools do not have a defensible program of secondary reading evaluation. The most common practice is to administer a standardized reading survey test once or twice during the pupil's secondary years. This may be supplemented by diagnostic testing for pupils with severe reading problems. Secondary classroom teachers evidence little expertise in developing and using informal measures to obtain needed information concerning pupil capabilities for classroom reading tasks. The improvement of secondary reading evaluation is essential to improving the secondary reading program.

***Functional reading competency.*** Once again, public concern is voiced over the amount of functional illiteracy among youth and adults. This time the concern appears to be supported by better empirical evidence, professional cognizance, threat of parental litigation, and mandated competency requirements for graduation in some states. It remains to be seen whether this concern for meeting at least minimal functional literacy requirements will be a useful contribution or a disruption to secondary reading education. There always is the danger that overzealous or manipulative administrators will focus all of the school's reading resources into one such program. On the other hand, such a concern with reading competency could do much to provide a realistic basis for all of the present areas of program emphasis: developmental, remedial, corrective, content area-oriented, and disadvantaged. Of course, secondary reading education should not settle for the minimal achievement of a functional competency, but should include it in the broader challenge of developing mature readers.

*Gradual growth amid inhibiting conditions.* An objective evaluation of four decades of secondary reading education reveals definite, if belated, growth in school involvement. On the whole, the quality of instruction has improved, but there is notable variation in quality from school to school. Although we may take satisfaction in the increase in numbers of school programs, what has been gained is hardly sufficient. Many schools provide reading instruction only for certain pupils with notable reading difficulty. And approximately one-fourth of American junior and/or senior high schools make no planned reading educational provision for any of their pupils. The trend from single to multiple phase offerings is promising. However, relatively few schools provide an all-school reading educational attack, and most offer but minimal reading-learning aid at the senior high level. Secondary reading evaluation and assessment practices are sporadic, inefficient, and unsophisticated.

Public and professional awareness of the need for instructional attention to secondary-level reading has never been higher. Particularly during the past decade, progress has been made in secondary reading theory, research, methods, and materials. However, many secondary school reading teacher specialists have but minimal training. And despite a ten-year period of visible concern with content area reading issues, the present status of knowledge and involvement of content teachers in dealing with reading-related content-learning problems has to be rated as inadequate.

Secondary school administrators cite a number of reasons why secondary reading education falls short of desired levels: deficiencies in funding and facilities; lack of trained personnel; conflicts with traditional school curricula; scheduling difficulties; and pressing immediate problems such as overcrowded schools, busing disruptions, pupil social-personal unrest, and teacher unionization.[39] Secondary teachers report such inhibiting factors as lack of professional preparation in reading, minimal administrative support, and unrealistic pressure to meet content area mastery standards.

Although continuing growth in the quality and quantity of school-level provision for secondary reading education seems a defensible prediction, available evidence indicates that much remains to be done before we can be confident that the greater proportion of pupils in grades seven through twelve will receive adequate reading education.

## THE NEED FOR CONTINUING READING EDUCATION

Reading specialists too often take for granted that other secondary school personnel understand why continued reading development is an educational imperative of the first rank. Lest this writer make the same error in assumption, here are seven arguments justifying our common concern.

*1. The opportunity for all youth to master effective skills of communication is a premier educational objective of hallowed precedent.* Tradition is perhaps the weakest of the arguments favoring a vigorous attack upon reading problems in the secondary schools; the criterion of present need should take precedence over antiquated territorial rights in educational matters. The point of precedence is made here only to draw attention to the fact that efforts to implement reading education in the secondary school are sometimes rebuffed by assumptions of historical curricular priority. Much weight of American public educational tradition rests on the side of reading education. No secondary content area predates the Massachusetts Act of 1647, which established reading and writing as the prime concerns of American education. But it is, after all, an extraneous response to a somewhat fatuous argument. The education of youth is not a matter of territorial rights. The function of reading education is to be of service to pupil, teacher, and society in any academic place.

*2. Successful reading is a prerequisite for academic achievement and personal adjustment.* American schools, particularly secondary schools, have been described as reading schools. The textbook, collateral reading assignments, and tests which must be read are basic elements in the instructional strategy of most secondary teachers. Moreover, the pupil needs to draw from a broad experiential background, which is greatly enhanced by wide personal reading. It is not surprising, therefore, that solid empirical evidence associates reading ability with academic success in secondary school and college.[40] Such evidence undoubtedly includes the influence of such concomitant factors as mental ability, cultural background, and motivation. Nevertheless, there is a good basis for accepting reading ability as one of the key factors predicting general success in academic work at the secondary school level.

But reading ability means more than marks in academic settings. Penty's research has provided stark evidence of the relationship which binds reading deficiency to secondary school frustration, truancy, and dropout.[41] Mental health research points to a growing incidence of adolescent neuroses and sociopathic escape. School pressure and frustrations contribute to adjustment difficulties even among some bright students.[42] Reading and study ability are not amulets which successfully ward off school-related failure and maladjustment. But improved reading abilities can facilitate learning and reduce the stress which many secondary students feel. One of the three major goals of secondary reading education is to improve the pupil's chances for academic success and school adjustment.

*3. Functional literacy is a requisite for socioeconomic survival in the United States.* The number of youth and adults in our society who may be classified as functionally illiterate varies with the criteria one employs. In his call for a "right to read," James

Allen cited such statistics as "One out of four students nationwide has significant reading deficiencies," and "About half of the unemployed youth ages 16-21 are functionally illiterate."[43]

If we define functional reading literacy in a broad operational sense as the ability to respond competently to real-world reading tasks, the figures for functional illiteracy, in secondary school and out, may be much higher than previously assumed.[44] Harmon has estimated that over half of American adults, 25 years and older, may be functionally illiterate.[45] Since the newspaper plays a significant role in our socioeconomic well-being. Bormuth's evidence that only 65 percent of middle-class, suburban twelfth graders could demonstrate minimal or better general comprehension of newspaper articles suggests that functional illiteracy may be more pervasive than we think.[46]

Another of the three major goals for secondary reading education is to give every pupil an opportunity to become functionally competent in reading before leaving secondary school. Some pupils with sufficient learning capabilities fall onto the "poor reader's" academic treadmill early in elementary school and never have a chance to get off. A functionally oriented reading reeducation program at the secondary level can provide a new start for these youngsters.

To be able to read always has been important to the individual's self-respect, convenience, and enjoyment. The difference today is that submarginal literacy is more likely to be associated with joblessness and poverty than in the past. Not to be able to participate in the advancing culture results in a much greater suffering than the mere fact of being unable to read would imply. Joblessness and poverty are but two currents of the accelerating whirlpool of illiteracy which catches up one generation after another in the same family.[47]

*4. Sophisticated reading skills are essential to the development of an informed and effective citizenry.* Reading ability is related to critical social issues other than economics and employment. A free nation requires more than gainful employment. Freedom has been defined by MacLeish as an environment in which one has the right to choose.[48] Individuals and groups gain freedom and remain free only when they assume the responsibility for their actions and have the necessary skills to effect their actions. Conversely, the right to choose becomes a distinct threat to freedom unless citizens are capable of making informed choices.

Reading is one of the most essential tools by which citizens become and remain informed.[49] When a society neither proscribes nor prescribes reading material, it becomes crucial that its citizens have the background and skill to critically analyze the differing viewpoints and information which appear in print. When citizens cannot find or interpret contradictory (or supporting) evidence, they become susceptible to all of the factors and techniques which cloud objective decision making.

In a society which encourages free speech and a free press, the ability to identify and absorb accurate information is one of the few avenues through which that society can convert sincere differences to a common working good. Our society and our world have been rife with disruptive dissension. It is significant to note that wherever the conflicts are more severe—between races, between religions, between political philosophies—it is those members of either side with the broadest background of experience who tend to show the most restraint, the most compassion, and the most constructive behavior in the resolution of the situation.

*5. The process and impact of reading shapes the intellectual processes of the individual and the society of which he is a member.* Regardless of whether we utilize logical, psychological, or sociological evidence, it is clear that a high positive relationship exists between reading ability and intellectual processing.[50] Professional and public attention has focused upon the influence which intelligence exerts upon learning to read and upon later reading performance. Equally significant is the influence which reading performance has upon intelligent behavior. Systematic instruction in the reading-thinking skills, along with wide personal reading, enables the individual to amass a fund of terms, concepts, organizational skills, and problem-solving processes

such as judgment, evaluation, and creative application.[51]

The intellectual and emotive impact of reading affects the group as well as the individual. McLuhan argues that the impact of print upon a society goes beyond the influence of the information represented by that print:

> What we've been saying here really is that print in the advent of the Gutenberg era had a rather tremendous effect upon human sensibility and perception.... Methods, techniques of communication, do formulate our modes of thinking, our ways of thinking. Everything we attack, we attack in a certain way which is a result of this technology.[52]

Whether or not McLuhan's hypothesis is accurate in the specific sense has been roundly debated. In the general case, however, we may expect that the society, the societal subgroup, as well as the individual who reads very little, will be psychologically separated from the literate whole—not only by lack of exposure to broad sources of information, but by missing the beneficial mental and emotional conditioning of the mature reading process per se. The third major goal of secondary reading education is to enable all pupils to advance along the developmental continuum of reading maturity.

*6. The ability to read adds to the student's potential for personal fulfillment.* Young adults are faced with a great number of personal decisions and problems to resolve. Yet in the current patterns of our society, many are estranged from or diffident about the use of the adults of their immediate environment as resources for dealing with personally sensitive issues. Reading provides a means whereby the reader can resolve some of the problems which face him. The value gained may be therapeutic, even if not directly applicable to a solution of the specific problem. Through reading, most personal adjustment mechanisms are possible. One may identify with a hero or an antihero. One can experience success and failure vicariously. Reading may provide insight into one's own biases and emotional needs. It can acquaint the reader with choices in strategy. And, as important as any other benefit—it may provide a means of momentary escape or inspiration from which the reader can derive new strength.[53]

Avid readers feel this power which resides in reading, and they never cease to wonder at the fact that others do not share in this. Once established, the habit of personal reading seems to nurture itself. Extensive reading leads to new interests, different solutions, and broader perspectives. Critical interpretation promotes better self-understanding and objective assessment procedures. Those who do not read powerfully develop neither the skill nor the motivation to help themselves through contact with written sources of value. It is important that the secondary school enlarge each pupil's reading power and extend pupil contact with varied reading materials of personal worth. In this, it is important that all teachers serve as sources of stimulation to better reading for students of all levels of ability.

*7. Familiarity with reading and reading strategy contributes to teaching efficiency and satisfaction.* We have emphasized that secondary reading education is of crucial importance to the student reader and, thus, to the school and its social structure. But we should not underestimate its pragmatic value to the teacher as a teacher and sensitive human being.

Most secondary teachers depend rather heavily upon the reading assignment in the textbook or collateral sources as a vehicle for content learning. Available evidence indicates that neither the average nor the better student uses such sources effectively and that the reading assignment falls far short of its potential as a teaching procedure.[54] The less adequate reader poses more serious problems for the content teacher: he learns incorrect concepts through his misreading; he develops negative attitudes toward the subject area and the content teacher; and he becomes a potential source of content classroom disruption and lowered class morale.

The need for content area reading, unlike old soldiers, neither dies nor fades away. The content teacher faces a choice. He can avoid using written sources of information and thus lose a powerful and efficient aid to teaching and learning. He can, in Herber's terms, engage in "assumptive teaching,"

ignore the content-learning consequences, and spend his class time in negative disciplinary action.[55] Or he can improve his understanding of reading-study behavior as it applies to the content-learning situation, improve the use of the reading assignment, and master some readily learned strategies for improving content-related reading performance. Only one of these choices benefits content learning, the pupil, and society, while increasing the teacher's sense of self-worth and teaching satisfaction.[56] The choice is not that difficult to make and even easier to execute.[57]

# REFERENCES

1. Johann Wolfgang Goethe, *Aus Meinem Leben, Dichtung und Wahrheit*, Part IV, 1833.
2. Harry Singer and Robert Ruddell, Editors, *Theoretical Models and Processes of Reading*, Second Edition (Newark, Del.: International Reading Association, 1976).
3. Theodore Clymer, "What Is Reading?: Some Current Concepts," in *Innovation and Change in Reading Instruction*, Sixty-seventh Yearbook, Part II, of the National Society for the Study of Education, Helen Robinson, Editor (Chicago: University of Chicago Press, 1968) p. 12.
4. Edgar Dale, "Reading as Communication," in *Insights into Why and How to Read*, R. T. Williams, Editor (Newark, Del.: International Reading Association, 1976) pp. 3–13.
5. Douglas Waples, Bernard Berelsen, and Franklyn Bradshaw, *What Reading Does to People* (Chicago: University of Chicago Press, 1940).
6. Walter Hill, "Studies of Student Readers," *Research and Evaluation in College Reading*, Ninth Yearbook of the National Reading Conference, D. Causey, Editor (Fort Worth, Tex.: Texas Christian University Press, 1960) pp. 52–64.
7. A. Sterl Artley, "The Development of Reading Maturity in High School—Implications of the Gray-Rogers Study," *Educational Administration and Supervision* 43 (October, 1957) pp.321–27.
8. David H. Russell, "Continuity in the Reading Program," in *Development in and Through Reading*, Sixtieth Yearbook, Part I, of the National Society for the Study of Education, N. B. Henry, Editor (Chicago: University of Chicago Press, 1961) p. 229.

9. H. P. Smith and E. M. Dechant, *Psychology in Teaching Reading* (Englewood Cliffs, N.J.: Prentice-Hall, Inc., 1977) p. 13.

10. Guy L. Bond and Miles A. Tinker, *Reading Difficulties: Their Diagnosis and Treatment,* Third Edition (New York: Appleton-Century-Crofts, 1973) p. 51.

11. James B. Stroud, *Psychology in Education* (New York: Longmans, Green & Co., Inc., 1956) p. 375.

12. G. T. Buswell, *SRA Reading Record* (Chicago: Science Research Associates, Inc., 1954). Revised.

13. R. R. Nardelli, "Some Aspects of Creative Reading," *Journal of Educational Research* 30 (March, 1957) pp. 495-508.

14. William S. Gray and Bernice Rogers, *Maturity in Reading: Its Nature and Appraisal* (Chicago: University of Chicago Press, 1956).

15. John B. Carroll, "Language and Cognition," in *Language Differences: Do They Interfere?* J. Laffey and R. Shuy, Editors (Newark, Del.: International Reading Association, 1973) pp. 173-85.

16. Stroud, *Psychology in Education*, p. 114.

17. Wendell Johnson, "You Can't Write Writing," in *The Use and Misuse of Language*, S. I. Hayakawa, Editor (Greenwich, Conn.: Fawcett Publications, 1962) p. 103.

18. William D. Sheldon, "Reading Instruction in the Junior High School," in *Development in and Through Reading*, Sixtieth Yearbook, Part I, of the National Society for the Study of Education, N. B. Henry, Editor (Chicago: University of Chicago Press, 1961) pp. 305-19.

19. Constance M. McCullough, "Balanced Reading Development," Chapter IX in *Innovation and Change in Reading Instruction*, Sixty-seventh Yearbook, Part II, of the National Society for the Study of Education, Helen Robinson, Editor (Chicago: University of Chicago Press, 1968) p. 320.

20. William S. Gray, "Nature and Scope of a Sound Reading Program," Chapter IV in *Reading in the High School and College*, Forty-seventh Yearbook, Part II, of the National Society for the Study of Education, N. B. Henry, Editor (Chicago: University of Chicago Press, 1948) p. 60.

21. Nila B. Smith, *American Reading Instruction*, Second Edition (Newark, Del.: International Reading Association, 1965).

22. Albert J. Harris, "Five Decades of Remedial Reading," in *Forging Ahead in Reading*, J. A. Figurel, Editor, International Reading Association Conference Proceedings 12, Part 1 (Newark, Del.: International Reading Association, 1968) pp. 25-34.

23. H. Alan Robinson, Editor, *Seventy-five Years of Reading Progress* (Chicago: University of Chicago Press, 1966).

24. Walter Hill, "Characteristics of Secondary Reading: 1940-1970," in *Reading: The Right to Participate*, Twentieth Yearbook of the National Reading Conference, Frank P. Greene, Editor (Milwaukee, Wis.: National Reading Conference, Inc., 1971) pp. 20-29.

25. Ralph L. Pounds and James R. Bryner, *The School in American Society* (New York: The Macmillan Company, 1959) p. 74.

26. Miles A. Tinker, *Bases for Effective Reading* (Minneapolis, Minn.: University of Minnesota Press, 1965) p. 24.

27. Edmund B. Huey, *The Psychology and Pedagogy of Reading* (New York: The Macmillan Company, 1908). Reissued in 1968 by The MIT Press, Cambridge, Mass.

28. Edward L. Thorndike, "Reading as Reasoning: A Study of Mistakes in Paragraph Reading," *Journal of Educational Psychology* 8 (June, 1917) pp. 323-32. Reprinted in *Reading Research Quarterly* 6 (Summer, 1971) pp. 425-34.

29. W. S. Gray, chm., *Report of the National Committee on Reading*, Twenty-fourth Yearbook, Part I, of the National Society for the Study of Education (Chicago: University of Chicago Press, 1925).

30. Gerald A. Yoakam, *Reading and Study* (New York: The Macmillan Company, 1928) p. 502.

31. Guy and Eva Bond, *Developmental Reading in High School* (New York: The Macmillan Company, 1941).

32. National Education Association, "Reading in the Secondary Schools," *Research Bulletin* 20, No. 1 (1942).

33. *Reading in the High School and College*, Forty-seventh Yearbook, Part II, of the National Society for the Study of Education, N. B. Henry, Editor (Chicago: University of Chicago Press, 1948) p. 318.

34. Hill, "Characteristics of Secondary Reading," p. 25.

35. Walter Hill, "Secondary Reading Activity in Western New York," *Journal of Reading* 19 (October, 1975) pp. 13-19.

36. George T. McGuire, *The Teaching of Reading by English Teachers in Public High Schools: A National Survey* (Washington, D.C.: Department of Health, Education and Welfare, 1969).

37. Hill, "Secondary Reading Activity in Western New York," p. 17.

38. L. S. Braam and J. E. Walker, "Subject Teachers' Awareness of Reading Skills," *Journal of Reading* 16 (May, 1973) pp. 608-11.

39. Walter Hill and Norma G. Bartin, *Secondary Reading Programs: Description and Research,* ERIC/CRIER Reading Review Series 30 (July, 1971) pp. 11-23.

40. J. R. Mallard, "Reading Ability and Rank in High School Class," in *Reading and Realism*, J. A. Figurel, Editor, International Reading Association Confer-

ence Proceedings 13 (Newark, Del.: International Reading Association, 1969) pp. 779-84.

41. Ruth C. Penty, *Reading Ability and High School Drop-outs* (New York: Bureau of Publications, Teachers College, Columbia University, 1956).

42. Robert S. Fleming, "Spilling Over: A Further Look at Pressures," in *Children Under Pressure*, Ronald C. Doll and Robert S. Fleming, Editors (Columbus, Ohio: Charles E. Merrill Publishing Company, 1966) p. 65.

43. James E. Allen, Jr., in an address to the National Association of State Boards of Education, September, 1970; also, "The Right to Read," *Phi Delta Kappan* 52 (April, 1971).

44. N. W. Northcutt, "Functional Literacy for Adults," in *Reading and Career Education*, D. F. Nielson and H. J. Hjelm, Editors (Newark, Del.: International Reading Association, 1975) pp. 43-49.

45. D. Harmon, "Illiteracy: An Overview," *Harvard Educational Review* 40 (1970) p. 230.

46. John R. Bormuth, "Reading Literacy: Its Definition and Assessment," *Reading Research Quarterly* 9 (1973-74) pp. 7-66.

47. Walter Hill, "Key Problems in Developing Reeducational Programs for Semi-illiterates," in *Reading and Inquiry*, J. A. Figurel, Editor, International Reading Association Conference Proceedings 7 (Newark, Del.: International Reading Association, 1962) pp. 107-9.

48. Archibald MacLeish, *Freedom Is the Right to Choose* (Boston: The Beacon Press, Inc., 1951).

49. Ralph Preston, "The Changed Role of Reading," *Reading in an Age of Mass Communication* (Chicago: National Council of Teachers of English, 1949) pp. 1-18.

50. D. S. Hage and J. B. Stroud, "Reading Proficiency and Intelligence Scores, Verbal and Non-Verbal," *Journal of Educational Research* 52 (1959) pp. 258-62.

51. B. Harootunian, "International Abilities and Reading Achievement," *The Elementary School Journal* 66 (1966) pp. 386-92.

52. Marshall McLuhan, in *McLuhan: Hot and Cool*, G. E. Stearn, Editor (New York: Signet Books, 1967) pp. 148-49.

53. David Russell, "Contributions of Reading to Personal Development," *Teachers College Record* 61, No. 8 (May, 1960).

54. Walter Hill, "Content Textbook: Help or Hindrance," *Journal of Reading* 10 (March, 1967) pp. 408-14.

55. Harold L. Herber, *Teaching Reading in Content Areas* (Englewood Cliffs, N.J.: Prentice-Hall, Inc., 1978) pp. 191-92.

56. Richard S. Alm, "Goose Flesh and Glimpses of Glory," in *Teaching Reading for Human Values in High School*, James Duggins, Editor (Columbus, Ohio: Charles E. Merrill Publishing Company, 1972) pp. 142-51.

57. Stanley E. Davis, "High School and College Instructors Can't Teach Reading? Nonsense!" *The North Central Association Quarterly* 34 (April, 1960) pp. 295-99.

## SUPPLEMENTARY SOURCES

Freed, Barbara. "Secondary Reading—State of the Art." *Journal of Reading* 17 (December, 1973) pp. 195-201.

Henry, N. B., Editor. *Reading in the High School and College*, Forty-seventh Yearbook of the National Society for the Study of Education, Part II, Chapter I. Chicago: University of Chicago Press, 1948.

Herber, Harold L. *Teaching Reading in Content Areas*, Chapter 1. Englewood Cliffs, N.J.: Prentice-Hall, Inc., 1978.

Hill, Walter. "Characteristics of Secondary Reading: 1940-1970." In *Reading: The Right to Participate*, Twentieth Yearbook of the National Reading Conference, Frank P. Greene, Editor, pp. 20-29. Milwaukee, Wis.: National Reading Conference, Inc., 1971.

Hill, Walter, and Norma Bartin. *Reading Programs in Secondary Schools*, An Annotated Bibliography. Newark, Del.: International Reading Association, 1971. 15 p.

Russell, David H. *The Dynamics of Reading*, Chapter 1. Waltham, Mass.: Ginn-Blaisdell, 1970.

Tuinman, J., M. Rowls, and R. Farr. "Reading Achievement in the United States: Then and Now," *Journal of Reading* 19 (March, 1976) pp. 455-463.

# TWO

# Reading as Pupil Behavior

*Reading, like much human behavior, is a function of the total personality.*

David Russell

***Overview*** As a human behavior, reading is influenced by what is human in the reader. Each specific instance of reading and learning to read is the behavioral product of the reader's motivating forces acting in concert with those personal resources which he brings to bear upon the reading situation. The reader's motivational set is influenced by primary and secondary needs as these are shaped by learning experiences into reading purposes, interests, and habits. The personal resources of the reader comprise the reader's broader reading potential, and include a melding of dynamics emanating from the reader's mental ability, emotional state, and physiological condition, as well as his or her general, linguistic, and reading experiential background. The behavior of the secondary reader, in addition, can be influenced by the conditions of adolescence. Reading and its learning thus are influenced by the totality of the reader's human condition.[1] To understand how reading performance and progress may vary from pupil to pupil, we must understand something of the reader as a human.

### The Major Components of Reading Behavior

Ojemann has suggested that any reasonably complex human behavior is the product of the *motivating forces* influencing the individual and the *available resources* upon which the individual can call to make the responses that are appropriate to the *situation* in which the behavior takes place.[2] We can use these components to form a basic framework for understanding secondary reading behavior.

The reading act is initiated by a state of reader readiness. A key element of this readiness is reader motivation to read. Only when the reader has sufficient drive tension which can be reduced by reading will he undertake the location and/or the interpretation of a printed source. In a positive sense, this drive is generated by certain *motivational forces*, such as needs, incentives, interests, and the like, which the reader, consciously or unconsciously, feels he must satisfy. In the negative motivational sense, the reader needs to be unencumbered by attitudes and emotional states which will inhibit undertaking the act itself, or which will interfere with its accurate and efficient performance. One essential condition of reading for instructional purposes in the secondary school, and one too often overlooked, is that the teacher needs to arouse and shape that state of readiness which will mobilize pupil reading in purposeful, meaningful directions.

The *situation* in which the reading occurs or should occur will involve not only the immediate physical circumstances, including the written source, but also the reader's interpretation of his implied reading setting—e.g., the influence of the personality of the teacher who made the reading assignment or the reader's value judgment of the topic or type of material to be read. The effectiveness with which the reader satisfies the needs of the reading situation will depend upon the *available personal resources* which the reader can bring to bear in that situation. These personal resources, the products of hereditary and environmental conditions, may be classified roughly as the intellectual, physical, social–emotional, and experiential characteristics of the reader. The condition of the reader's resources may exert a negative as well as a positive influence upon reading performance.[3]

Reading requires a human potential beyond the mastery of symbolic, linguistic, and cognitive mechanics. Reading also is an affective behavior. The substance of most writing is the human condition and those issues which influence it. It takes a sensitive reader to feel the emotional impact of that which the sensitive writer has created.

The secondary school reader approaches a prospective reading situation with a particular potential for responding to that situation. This includes a reservoir of reading skills, knowledges, and attitudes which are the products of his formal and informal learning experiences. Whether the reader has mastered specific reading responses appropriate to this situation, whether he can bring those he has to bear upon the material, and what he understands and feels as a result of his interaction with the printed source will be influenced markedly by his larger behavioral condition.

To gain better insight into reading as a human dynamic—into those conditions which influence secondary reader learning and performance and which carry direct and indirect implications for the use and teaching of reading in the secondary school—we need to examine what we have learned about the motivational forces and available resources of the secondary and adult reader.

## READER MOTIVATION

Motivation, conscious or unconscious, instigates complex human behavior. It may come from outside forces (extrinsic) or from internal tensions (intrinsic). Motivation can vary in strength (drive) and in direction (purposes or interests). It can be kicked off by ongoing primary needs, by secondary or learned needs, or by situational stimulation. Usually the motivation which induces human behavior is formed by some combination of these factors. The motivation which activates and directs a reader's responses ordinarily will consist of some combination of the reader's drive level, learned attitudes and interests, prevailing needs of the moment, and the stimulation specific to the reading situation.

## Motivational Factors in Reading

Motivation is essential to reading, as it is to all complex adult behavior. The motivational forces, extrinsic and intrinsic, acting upon the reader, spark the reading act. They comprise a significant part of that state of reader readiness which generates the selective initial location and perception of the printed source. This is no insignificant matter, since the number of adequate secondary readers who don't read school assignments and personal-choice materials is as notable as those who can't read them. Motivational factors also determine the reader's specific reading set; they shape his particular reading purposes and thus influence the processes he will use, the meaning he will gain, and the type of reaction he will make to that meaning. Moreover, the drive strength generated by his reading motivation will influence whether he carries the reading act through to completion—from readiness to reaction.

The child's motivation to learn to read may come from intrinsic sources such as anticipating some of the pleasure he gained from having others read to him, some intrigue with the process, a feeling of independence, or the game-type tasks which accompany instruction. But extrinsic motivational forces also are instrumental in this learning, e.g., pleasing teachers and parents and competing with classmates. When the child masters enough of the reading act to reach early independence, it becomes possible for him to internalize the rewards of reading as reading. As the pupil grows in reading power, the wider his possible sources of reading materials and situations become. If he does read widely, he broadens his potential of intrinsically satisfying reading purposes. The out-of-school adult, with an occasional exception, reads largely to satisfy intrinsic motivation.

The secondary pupil occupies a motivational middle ground where reading is concerned. He must cope with extrinsic reading pressures such as reading tests, literature course grades, reading assignments for content courses, and such devices as teachers use for reading instruction. At the same time, he may draw upon most of the intrinsic motivations of adulthood. Sometimes these conflict, as when too little time forces him to choose between reading an adventure story and the science text assignment. Generally, the adequate secondary reader benefits from both types of motivation. On the other hand, the inadequate secondary reader may find little basis for responding to either type of motivation.

Ideally, the extrinsic motivation of school assignments would draw as directly as possible upon pupil needs and interests. And the pupil, in turn, would develop the facility for finding intrinsic reward in school reading situations. The school reading program, of course, should be concerned with increasing the range of reading experiences with which the pupil finds satisfaction. Some consideration of the effects, habits, and interests of adult and secondary pupil reading should add to our understanding of reading motivation.

### The General Effects of Reading

Psychologists long have recognized the close interdependence of the individual's hierarchy of needs and those rewards which are of value to him. One aspect of this relationship is quite evident: we are most rewarded by those experiences which satisfy our strongest needs. Less evident is the reverse of this relationship, that those experiences which prove rewarding tend to shape our learned need system. Successful interaction with written language can affect the emotional and intellectual makeup of the individual reader or of a society of readers. A teleological phenomenon operates here—the effects of today's reading experiences mobilize the reading effects of tomorrow.

***Primary and secondary needs.*** Motivation and its related effects begin with the primary physiological needs of the individual: hunger, thirst, sex, activity, avoidance of pain and discomfort. Through learning, these are generalized into secondary needs of a psychogenic or socialized nature: security, adequacy, acceptance, recognition, achievement, order, companionship, new experience, activity, freedom and independence, and so on. Each of these may become operational in a particular situation through various incentives. But to satisfy these needs is basically why we read. Moreover, these conditions exert some influence on how we interpret the meaning of material read. As a strategy for improving interpretation and critical analysis, Hill and Eller have recommended that upper-grade pupils be guided in recognizing the needs and motives by which materials appeal to them and which influence their reading responses.[4]

*Reading effects as mobilizers.* An early classification of the effects which reading can have on people (and which thus may serve as potential mobilizers of reading) was developed by Waples, Berelson, and Bradshaw as a part of their investigation of adult reading. The five major effects identified were instrumental (operational purposes), prestige building, reinforcement of attitudes, aesthetic satisfaction, and psychological respite.[5] Russell later reduced this to a four-classification system and added a number of variant patterns of each: (1) *instrumental* (acquisition of information, enrichment of experience, understanding of human relationships, stimulation of creative activity, and extended reading experience and development); (2) *reinforcement* (development of new or modification of old attitudes, strengthening of personal convictions, aid in general adjustment, development of life philosophy); (3) *respite* (escape and relaxation, identification with characters, wish fulfillment, fantasy pleasure); and (4) *aesthetic* (appreciation of style, enjoyment of plot, recognition of author's wisdom, insight, or creative talent).[6]

These classifications suggest a broad range of possible reasons for which mature readers *might* read. It is not at all certain that typical secondary pupils and adults *do* read for all these reasons. These possible effects do reflect a transformation of primary and secondary needs into reading circumstances. For a more pragmatic view of the motivating factors in reading, we need to consider representative findings of studies of reading habits and interests.

### Reading Habits and Interests

In one of the more extensive recent investigations of adult reading habits, Sharon interviewed a national cross-section sample of 5,067 adults, age 16 or older.[7] Sharon's findings confirm that reading is a part of the everyday life of most Americans. (Even those interviewed who could not read expressed a most poignant desire to be able to read.) As an average, these adults spent nearly two hours of a typical day in reading activity. The range is wide; however, 6 percent of the sample read for less than five minutes per day, while another 6 percent read more than eight hours. Most of this reading was done for utilitarian or recreational purposes—newspapers (70 percent of sample), brief-term task-oriented reading (70 percent), magazines (40 percent), and books (33 percent). Reading for instrumental purposes in a wide variety of life or work operational materials (labels, signs, directions, menus, brochures, advertisements, telephone books, TV print, etc.) was reported with high frequency by most of the sample. Socioeconomic, educational, occupational, age, race, and sex differences were significantly associated with frequency of reading, amount of time spent in reading, and type of materials read in both work and recreational situations.

The newspaper figured heavily in personal reading, but in a selective manner. The main page news was mentioned most frequently, followed by local news, comics, sports, society pages, and TV-radio listings. In magazine reading, the order of popularity was general-interest slicks, news and media-oriented publications, women's and homemaking magazines, special-interest publications, religious magazines, and "intellectual" publications (literary, arts, and sociopolitical commentary). The last group was reported mostly by the highest socioeconomic group.

Books were read less frequently but for longer periods of time. The Bible was mentioned most often, followed by general fiction and, with much less frequency, books dealing with natural and physical science, general reference, and hobby-specialty topics. Narrative books mentioned with greater frequency included mysteries, adventure and historical novels, followed by autobiography and biography. Sharon's findings are consistent with those of the larger, less controlled National Literature Assessment Survey. [8]

*Studies of secondary readers.* Like the adult studies, surveys of adolescent reading habits and interests reveal considerable individuality. They tend to reflect some of the same general reading patterns, although secondary pupils reveal somewhat more sophisticated reading tendencies than the average adult reader. Whether this represents the influence of their current school experiences or whether it means that we are making progress toward developing a more mature society of readers is hard to say at this time.

Scharf reported grade level, intelligence level, and sex differences in the reading interests among pupils of an Illinois high school. [9] Males preferred newspapers and magazines to books. Females preferred books. Seniors read more materials on a regular basis than did pupils at other grade levels. Males preferred reading about sports, world events, war, crime, and personalities. Poetry, drama, autobiographies, and novels were more likely read by females. More than one-fourth of these pupils read parts of a newspaper seven days a week; less than one-fifth never read a newspaper. Paperback books were preferred to hardbound books.

In a sampling of reader reaction to short selections by approximately 4,000 pupils, grades seven through ten, Jungeblut and Coleman found notable variation in reading-topic interest at each grade level. [10] In general, folklore, biography, narrative form, social situation behavior, and sports received the highest rating. Degree of interest decreased with each successive lower grade of pupils sampled, and within-interest-area preference differences were as large as between-interest areas. One notable inference was that the writing style may be as important as the topic in determining the reading appeal of an article for these pupils.

Although secondary pupils reported daily reading other than school assignments, Desjardins found both sexes to spend more time in television viewing. [11] Forty-five percent of the girls and 52 percent of the boys read less than one-half hour daily. The school library and personal purchases were the most likely sources of material for those reporting some daily reading.

Sex and grade differences in interest were revealed. Middle and junior high boys preferred sports and car stories; freshmen and senior boys preferred mystery and humorous stories. Girls preferred, in order, romance, mystery, humor, and adventure. Yarlott and Harpin reported somewhat similar patterns of secondary reading preferences. [12] Boys preferred "macho" writers, while girls preferred female and male authors with an understanding of the female personality. In general, fiction was preferred to nonfiction, novels and short stories to poetry and plays, historical novels to historical review, and science fiction to science.

Finally, Sharon's analysis of the reported in-school reading patterns of his secondary subjects reveals some intriguing patterns. [13] The reading of distributed notices and bulletin board materials was reported by 66 percent as their most frequent type of daily in-school reading. Other common types of reading were tests, notes, written assignments, and school papers (reported by only 33 percent). Although tests and written assignments were reported as the most important school reading, the relatively small frequency of daily involvement in reading assignments and other reading-to-learn activities supports the opinion of many that pupil school-oriented reading practices need critical analysis, as do secondary teaching procedures which utilize reading.

### Some School Implications

The significance of motivation in secondary reading performance cannot be stressed too strongly. Motivational factors influence the quality of pupil reading performance and habit. Although considerable differences are reflected in frequency and type of personal reading among pupils and adults, the typical reading patterns reported fall short of that representative of mature reading and the objectives of the American educational system. In effect, the majority of our secondary graduates reflect reading habits and motivations which range from nonreading to utilitarian-recreational reading practices representative of minimal literacy.

The general nature of reading motivation, the broad possible effects of reading, and reported habits and interests in reading have notable implications for the secondary school reading effort. The broadening and raising of student reading habits deserves more all-school emphasis than it receives. Pupil in-school reading patterns and adult reluctance to read quality nonfiction and fiction suggest that something is amiss in our educational goals and/or in our choice and use of classroom reading. Certainly, this would seem to be a good reason for extending developmental reading education through twelfth grade. Analysis of the influence of specific purpose upon reading interpretation is given in Chapter 3. Recommendations for school and teacher improvement in reading motivation are presented in Part II of this text.

## READER RESOURCES

The reader must draw upon many personal resources to implement his reading behavior. To a varying degree of input, all prevailing and momentary conditions of the reader may influence his reading performance. A rather vast literature has accumulated around the research concerning personal reading characteristics.[14] The discussion in this section has been limited to the identification of the more notable of these characteristics, particularly those which may be classified as cognitive, physiological, affective, and experiential factors of known significance. The isolation of such characteristics for discussion purposes does not suggest that reading is anything less than a complex behavior involving the integration of numerous personal

resources. Figure 3 serves as an organizational overview of the reader characteristics and resources treated in the following pages.

### Cognitive Resources of the Reader

Reading is a verbal behavior. Learning to read is highly dependent upon the ability to make and retain associations between verbal symbols (words) and their referents, and to associate meaning with broader concepts and more complex structures as the writer combines symbols to form linguistic statements and ideational arrangements.

Moreover, reading is a thoughtful verbal behavior. The writing of mature writers for mature audiences represents varying degrees of imagery, reasoned processing of ideas, and other abstract operations. The capable reader must be able to transfer and transform meanings gained in one language setting to other language settings. He will need to educe—i.e., to perceive constructs and thought patterns not previously learned—the relationships of items presented by the writer. Depending upon the complexity of the writer's thinking and expression, the reader must deal successfully with connotations, inferences of unstated concepts, and the organization of ideas as represented in creative and expository writing.

It would not be surprising, therefore, to find that measures of the pupil's ability to learn, retain, transfer, and educe symbols and ideas (i.e., tests of verbal intelligence or general academic aptitude) would provide us with useful information about his potential for mature reading performance at the secondary school level. And indeed, they do.

### Measures of Cognitive Ability

The most workable means to evaluate a pupil's cognitive power developed to date has been the test of intelligence or mental ability. An intelligence test samples one or more cognitive processing tasks and converts the result into a meaningful quantitative product, usually the intelligence quotient, mental age, and/or the percentile rank (PR). Most of the intelligence testing carried on in secondary schools is done with group tests. Individual intelligence tests such as the *Stanford–Binet* or the *Wechsler* tests (WISC or WAIS) avoid some of the weaknesses associated with group testing of atypical pupils, but they require trained administrators and take more time; thus, they tend to be employed selectively.

Both group and individual intelligence tests tend

to sample certain behaviors which carry power of predictability for general academic success and reading success in particular: i.e., vocabulary meaning, verbal analogies, symbol classification, quantitative relationship, arithmetic reasoning, and sentence relationships.

***Mental age and intelligence quotients.*** The resulting normative score obtained on an intelligence

***Figure 3*** *Significant secondary reader characteristics and resources.*

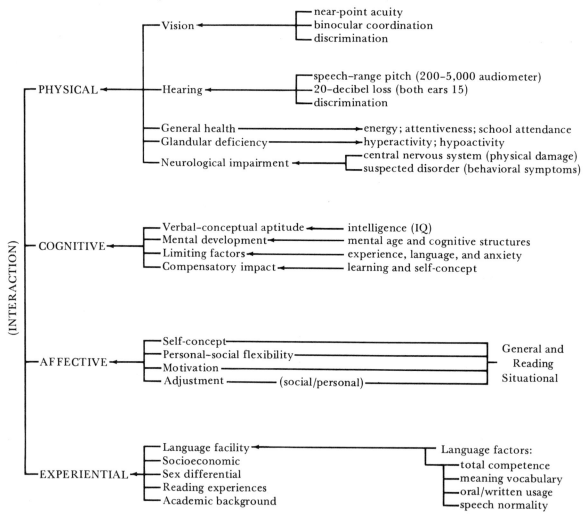

test usually is interpreted as a measure of the mental ability of the examinee in comparison with that representative population upon whom the test was standardized. When the sample population used for standardizing the test norms closely represents the general population, the obtained test score(s) provide us with a relative estimate of the individual's mental performance in comparison with that of the general population.

Two normative products of intelligence tests are used widely in the evaluation and prediction of pupil behavior. One is *mental age* (MA), which is a quantitative measure of mental development of the pupil expressed in age units of years and months. The test MA obtained for an individual indicates his mental development in terms of the chronological age. A boy of 10 CA and who obtains an MA of 12-6 on an intelligence test is considered to perform at the mental level of the mentally average pupil whose chronological age is 12 years and 6 months. Another way of viewing this is that the lad has a mental age which is two and one-half years in advance of pupils of average intelligence who are his own peers (10 years).

Another widely employed normative product of intelligence tests is the *intelligence quotient,* or IQ. The IQ is a product of the following ratio of mental age to chronological age:

$$IQ = \frac{MA}{CA} \times 100$$

The IQ is an index of the pupil's relative brightness as compared with peers of the same chronological age. An IQ of 100 is considered the mathematical average of the distribution of IQs for any age group, half of the peer group stretching above and half below. In the heterogeneous secondary classroom, the range of IQs may run from 75 (slow learner classification) to 135 (gifted learner). Usually, IQs within the 90 to 110 spread are considered in the "normal intelligence range."

### Intelligence and Reading Performance

The relationship between intelligence test scores and reading test scores consistently remains the highest obtained between any single human characteristic and reading performance. The IQ, as an index of relative level of brightness, merits serious consideration in the prediction and analysis of reading success. Intelligence testing, when administered and interpreted in a defensible, professional manner, has served usefully in the general study of reading behavior and in the diagnosis of reading difficulty.

Reading and intelligence are positively correlated variables of human behavior. A correlation coefficient, it will be recalled, is a numerical index of the degree of relationship existing between two sets of measures. Operationally, it provides a way of summarizing the extent to which distributed pupil performance on one measure of variable behavior agrees with the distribution of their scores on another measure of variable pupil performance. Correlation coefficients range between .00 (no agreement) to 1.00 (perfect agreement), and may be negative as well as positive.

The correlation coefficients between the scores obtained on individual intelligence tests and reading performance tests tend to run in the +.60 to +.75 range, which may be described as a moderately high, positive relationship.[15] Correlations between group (written) intelligence tests and reading tests sometimes run higher than +.80, but this probably is the spurious result of the reading required in taking both tests. Correlation coefficients between group "nonverbal" mental test performance and reading test performance usually are lower than verbal intelligence tests and reading, generally falling in the low to moderate positive range.

Reading behavior is a function of the total personality of the reader, and we should not expect intelligence and reading performance to demonstrate a perfect (+1.00) relationship. A correlation coefficient of +.7 between intelligence and reading test results is associated with approximately 49 percent of the possible variance between the two test score distributions. This leaves roughly half of the distribution differences between reading and intelligence test score distributions to be explained by other factors. Although this includes some differences due to testing error, it seems reasonable to assume that other reader resources in addition to mental ability are required of reading performance.

Nevertheless, mental ability, as measured by intelligence tests, does maintain a relatively high, persistent relationship with reading performance. Intelligence test results are among the better predictors of beginning reading success.[16] The relationship between the two improves during the elementary school years, as individual differences in reading performance increase in range, and the relationship continues during the secondary school years.[17] The relationship maintains even among distributions of select populations, i.e., sex, socioeconomic class, race, geographical setting, etc. This pervading tendency of intelligence to relate with reading performance of all pupil populations may be as educationally significant as the size and persistence of reading–intelligence intercorrelations. Of any single reader characteristic measured, only past reading performance provides a better predictive estimate of future growth, at least where groups of pupils are concerned.

*Cautions for individual interpretation.* Considerable caution should be exerted in the interpretation of intelligence test results. No intelligence test is culture free, and intelligence test scores for pupils who are notably disadvantaged in language skills and experiential background may be unfairly depressed. Group intelligence tests which require reading or reading–like ability are particularly suspect for those with reading or language disadvantagement, the disabled, or unusually anxious pupils. The fact that certain intelligence tests may be inappropriate to use with disadvantaged pupils or disabled learners does not refute the conclusion that mental ability is a necessary reader resource or even that such test results can be predictive of the immediate learning and reading success of these pupils in the typical school situation. But the possibility of error in the individual measurement of intelligence should make us cautious in the use of such scores in making generalizations about the long-range read-

ing potential of the atypical pupil. A useful summary of the uses and cautions of psychological assessment as related to reading has been presented by Farr.[18]

### *Development of Cognitive Abilities*

In recent years, psychologists and educators have attempted to ascertain the qualitative nature of intellectual functioning, particularly in the development of cognitive operations and their influence upon school behavior. A number of theories of cognitive development have been formulated.[19] One of the more systematic is that of Piaget.[20]

For Piaget, mental development is the product of continuous adaptive behavior involving the creative activity of the child in his interaction with his environment. This cognitive development is manifested in a series of operational levels which take the individual from the random, diffuse reflexes of the infant to the formal, logical reasoning of adulthood. At each stage, the child's understanding of his world (mental structures) expands, and with the reorganization of this information and the development of new capabilities, it becomes possible to utilize more complex types of reasoning. Key elements in this development include environmental exploration, language acquisition, verbal concept growth, and learning to use mediational thought processes to form generalizations.

The order of succession of Piaget's stages of cognitive development is relatively constant, although the ages at which they are attained may vary with the individual and his environment. As the individual develops from one stage to another, previous mental structures are elaborated and integrated with later mental structures. Each of the three major stages is comprised of developmental phases in the mastery of certain patterns of mental organization.

*1. Sensorimotor operations* (birth to approximately age 2), in which the child grows from mass reflex movement through phases of coordination, intentional goal seeking, experimental and self-adjustment of behavior, as the capacity emerges to respond to nonpresent objects and to invent new means of accomplishing goals.

*2. Concrete operations* (age 2 to age 11 or 12), which includes the successive development of such mental operations (organized internalized actions) as imagery and symbolic functions (2 to 4), elaborated intuitive thought such as comparison and classification in present situations (4 to 7), and conservation, including the principles of constancy and the reversability of operations (7 to 11). In the stage of concrete operations, the child uses logic and reasoning in elementary ways, but his effective application involves the manipulation of concrete objects, rather than the manipulation of verbal propositions.

*3. Formal operations* (ages 11 or 12 to 15 and over), a final stage of mental development in which the adolescent learns to "operate with abstract operations." Characteristic mental development during this stage includes the contraction and internalization of thought language, deductive and inductive reasoning, hypothesis development, simultaneous control of multiple variables, critical thinking, and self-evaluation of thought.

*Cognitive development and secondary reading performance.* The implications of Piaget's theory of cognitive development for language education have stimulated considerable activity.[21] Perhaps the most significant implication for our own consideration is the suggestion that many pupils may not be capable of handling some higher-level processes of abstract reading interpretation until they have moved into the junior-senior high years. Moreover, many will not have developed the related sophistication in language to formulate thoughtful responses for the insight they have developed.[22]

Piaget posits that individual motivation and opportunity to learn are significant factors in mental development. The key implications for us would seem to be: (1) that the secondary school cannot count confidently on the elementary school graduate to have mastered the cognitive processes necessary to mature reading, (2) that reading and other language instruction at the secondary school level is

necessarily intertwined with the maturation of cognitive processes, and (3) that the secondary teacher, in utilizing reading- and content-learning situations, should be aware that the pupils of a class can vary substantially in the level of their mental operations.

The present stage of mental development of the individual pupil should figure in the instructional decisions we make concerning him. Although cognitive functioning is but one of the composite human resources needed for mature reading performance, it well may be among the most crucial.[23] Superior mental ability can compensate somewhat for deficiencies in other reader resources. Limited mental development can hinder reading development even when other reader resources are sufficient. Moreover, the level of cognitive development of the secondary pupil may place a limit on the sophistication of his reading interpretation.

The observed close relationship between mental development and reading development has led reading specialists to employ mental tests as measures of reading aptitude, i.e., as estimates of the level of reading achievement the pupil has the potential to demonstrate at this point in his educational development. From a comparison of the mental age and the reading achievement age of the pupil, the amount of reading underachievement can be estimated. Such estimates, in consideration with other reader and school situational factors, are used in the identification and diagnosis of reading disability, and thus, in decisions concerning the need for and appropriate nature of corrective and remedial reading aid.

## Physiological Resources of the Reader

Reading, like other human behavior, draws upon certain sensory, motor, and general physiological functions as coordinated through the central nervous system. The physical state of the pupil may not exert as much impact upon upper-grade reading performance as mental ability and experiential background. However, it is a factor which has some influence upon the ease with which the young pupil masters the earlier stages of reading, and the secondary school reader is the product of his developmental reading history. Moreover, persistent physiological malfunctions may influence adolescent reading performance efficiency and work–study adjustment.

Considerable research has been expended during the past fifty years in the attempt to identify particular physical conditions or malfunctions that especially hinder reading progress.[24] While no single physical anomaly has been identified as the invariable cause of general reading difficulty, some appear to be more influential than others and figure more frequently in the syndromes of serious reading disability.[25] Such conditions tend to be influential to the greater degree of their malfunction and to the extent to which the learner has not been able to compensate for them in some way. As might be expected, the more critical anomalies are those which inhibit sensory efficiency, neurological functioning, and persistent drive levels of the learner.[26] These anomalies do not occur invariably among problem readers, and can be found even in good readers. Nevertheless, they do appear with greater than chance frequency among the profiles of poorer readers.

## Visual Factors

Secondary-level reading is dependent upon rapid, successive visual processing of printed symbols. Ocular comfort and visual efficiency are of considerable help in a performance that requires continuous, fine discrimination of graphic symbols. Minor visual handicaps can produce some discomfort in the reading act and in certain situations may reduce the efficiency of reading. However, it is not safe to assume that visual anomaly will cause reading difficulty.[27] Visual difficulty and discomfort of a more serious degree can contribute to the learning difficulty of the young pupil, especially if that pupil is being assailed by other resource deficiencies.

Only a few visual deficiencies tend to impede reading performance after the early school years and these to the degree of their severity. The most frequent of these difficulties include hyperopia, binocular focus problems, and underdeveloped visual perception.[28] *Hyperopia* is a refractive condition of the individual eye which produces improper focusing of the entering light rays in such a way that the individual has difficulty seeing clearly with that eye at near point (i.e., at book reading or desk working distance.) *Myopia*, a refractive error which causes difficulty seeing at a distance, has not been significantly associated with reading difficulty, although it is possible that in severe instances, it could prevent the young pupil from accurately viewing the board work of the teacher. A refractive error such as hyperopia in one or both eyes usually is correctable through the use of properly prescribed eye glasses.

Binocular visual difficulties are those which interfere with the precise and simultaneous focus of the two eyes upon the visual target. Three conditions have been identified which contribute to binocular visual problems in reading. These include (1) *strabismus*, or binocular incoordination of the two eyes as a result of eye muscular imbalance; (2) *fusion difficulties*, the imprecise accommodation of the lens focus of the two eyes, which prevents identical retinal images; and (3) *aniseikonia*, a visual condition which results in the production of different or unequal sizes or shapes of ocular images for the two eyes. Binocular visual difficulties are less readily detected in the usual visual screening tests employed by family doctors and schools. Unfortunately, they tend to be more troublesome for the reader than more readily detected visual problems. Though less easily corrected than refractive errors, binocular difficulties can be remediated through lens prescription, corrective exercises, and in more serious instances, through surgery.

Beyond being able to physically see the graphic symbols, the reader will need to perceive fine differences and similarities in complex word symbols. He will need to *perceptually discriminate* and *synthesize* word forms. Problems of perceptual discrimination and synthesis can occur among pupils with adequate vision. Not infrequently, however, difficulties in visual discrimination and synthesis occur as a by-product of earlier or present visual acuity problems. In either case, a functional visual problem exists that deserves diagnostic and corrective attention, especially when pupils evidence unusual problems in word recognition and learning. Correction usually is accomplished through perceptual training by reading or visual specialists.

*Identification and referral.* It is unfortunate that the usual testing procedures employed by schools and general medical practitioners to screen for visual difficulties, such as variations of the Snellen Chart, are not effective in identifying these more crucial patterns of visual difficulty. The use of more sensitive instruments such as the Keystone Telebinocular or the Bausch and Lomb Ortho-Rater, which can detect near-point visual adjustment problems of a binocular nature, would aid the school visual screening effort.

Where such instruments are not or cannot be employed, visual screening and diagnostic assessment may be obtained from a professionally trained specialist. One such specialist is the ophthalmologist, an M.D. with special training in visual problems. An ophthalmologist is prepared to detect and treat visual difficulties of a complex biological nature as well as refractive and coordination problems. Optometrists are specialists licensed to identify refractional visual error and to prescribe corrective eye glasses. Some optometrists provide corrective visual training for difficulties in visual coordination and perceptual discrimination.

School entrance requirements, parental awareness, and the availability of pediatric care are such that gross visual difficulties usually are detected prior to secondary school entrance. This may be less true in large inner-city or smaller rural school settings. Moreover, some visual problems first appear in secondary school as a result of the physical changes of adolescence or as a by-product of more intensive reading-study pressures. Secondary teachers should be aware of some of the more common symptoms of visual difficulty. These include persistent headaches, abnormal eye conditions, awkward head position in close work, facial contortions, excessive restlessness, and frequent loss of place in reading. It is good to remember that these characteristics also may be symptomatic of problems other than vision.

### Auditory Factors

Like visual difficulty, hearing problems tend to exert greater influence upon reading development during the early years of instruction. The reader, especially during the primary grades, draws heavily upon his aural language processes to form meaningful associations with words and to develop independence in the analysis of unknown words. As a broad estimate, perhaps 5 percent of the general population have serious hearing impairment. Such difficulty may contribute indirectly to reading-learning problems. Hearing problems have been associated with speech and language retardation, with deprivation of experiential background, and with lower scores on individual verbal intelligence measures.

Hearing deficiency is associated less frequently than visual deficiency with general reading disability.[29] It does appear in the profiles of some disabled readers, particularly where either the reading disability or the auditory difficulty is severe. It figures more frequently in reading disability among pupils who have been taught to read by instructional programs which emphasize word sounding and oral reading.[30] Hearing problems, like visual problems, are seldom the single direct cause of persistent reading disability. But they can reinforce the reading and school adjustment problems of pupils assailed by other negative learning conditions.

As might be expected, *auditory acuity* problems are more significant in the reading situation when they result in a notable degree of loss within the normal voice range of pitch, roughly 125 to 8,000 cycles of vibration. The usual intensity of voice projection is about 60 decibels. As measured by sensitive instruments such as the audiometer, a hearing loss of 10 decibels of volume should be considered referable. Obviously, such a hearing loss in both ears is of much greater significance than when hearing in one ear is normal.

Auditory acuity problems, those produced by difficulty in sensing the sound stimulus as such, are not the only type of aural difficulty occurring among pupils. Problems of *auditory discrimination* and *generalization*, the inability to perceive fine differences and similarities in word sounds and language nuances, also may inhibit reading development.[31] Ordinarily, these auditory perception problems are of greater influence during the early learning-to-read period, but they can add to the learning problems of the disabled reader in later grades. Like visual perceptual immaturity, deficiency in auditory discrimination and generalization usually responds readily to specific training. Auditory perceptual problems may occur among pupils with adequate auditory acuity; more often, they are a concomitant of more basic hearing difficulty.

*Identification and referral.* Hearing acuity assessment, even for screening purposes, requires more accurate measurement than the commonly used watch-tick or voice-whisper procedures. Impairment is detected more reliably by the use of an accurately calibrated audiometer used by a trained professional. Some reading specialists, school nurses, and teachers of the exceptional child, as well as most speech therapists, are trained in audiometric assessment. Tests of auditory perception usually are included in thorough batteries of reading readiness tests as well as in many diagnostic tests of severe reading and learning disability. For best results, such tests of perception should be administered and interpreted by a psychologist or a specialist trained in reading or learning disability.

As with problems of vision, hearing difficulties may escape detection in the elementary school or may develop during the secondary years as the result of injury. There is some evidence that hearing loss has increased among the adolescent population as a result of the high-decibel barrage of sound projected by electronic rock music groups operating in small rooms. Thus, the secondary teacher should pay some attention to pupils who persistently demonstrate such hearing problem symptoms as frequent earaches, draining ears, reports of buzzing sounds or inability to hear clearly stated directions, and face and body contortions while listening. Since these may be symptomatic of other physical or behavioral adjustment problems, the teacher's best course of action is to refer such pupils to the school specialist for evaluation or referral.

### General Physical Condition

Learning to read and the effective use of reading in learning situations requires ready energy output of a controlled nature. Although pupil learning styles vary, any physical condition which lowers vitality or otherwise interferes with sustained attention and ocular-motor coordination can inhibit reading performance.[32] Also, conditions which cause frequent and extended periods of school absence during the early stages of reading instruction contribute to the learning problems of pupils, especially if those pupils have but modest learning capabilities. Any illness, from extended colds to more complex diseases, can hinder reading progress if the school absence or disabling effects occur over an extended period of time, and if the pupil does not have compensating strengths to counter this special disadvantagement. Malnutrition, drug usage, and inadequate rest are subtle longer-term conditions which detract from learning efficiency and which may occur in any socioeconomic setting. General health problems are not uncommon during early adolescence.

Endocrine imbalance or glandular malfunction have been identified in certain specific cases of reading and learning disability. Since glandular change plays a vital role in adolescent growth, this factor should be considered where reading disability first appears during junior and senior high school. Of the various possible glandular difficulties, thyroid deficiency has been associated more commonly with reading-learning disability. Hypothyroidism is manifested in obesity and behavioral sluggishness; hyperthyroidism with weight loss, hyperactivity and subsequent fatigue, nervousness, and irritability.

*Neurological impairment.* Brain damage and other pathological conditions inhibiting the function of the central nervous system may occur before, during, or after birth. The neurologically impaired pupil sometimes manifests severe difficulty in mastering one or more language functions and related verbal learning in addition to exhibiting general behavioral problems.[33] Fortunately, the presence of overt neurological impairment among school children is quite small. Most authorities are reluctant to estimate incidence of neurological impairment because of the complexity of diagnostic procedure and differences in definition. For comparative purposes, perhaps fewer than one in a hundred school children could be clearly identified by medical specialists as brain damaged or neurologically impaired. The incidence of this type of reading-learning disability among senior high pupils may be even smaller, since the inhibitory effect of central nervous system disorders upon learning often precludes successful competitive participation in the regular secondary school curriculum.

In the past decade, there has been some rebirth in the popularity of ascribing, by soft-symptom association, severe cases of reading and learning difficulty to organic causes, particularly cerebral dysfunction. This position usually is dependent upon the juxtaposition of several assumptions: that minimal brain damage may exist which is undetectable by the usual rigorous medical and psychological diagnoses of neurological impairment, that extreme disability in reading and other learning results from singular areas of causation, and that soft symptoms of brain damage are quite unlike symptoms of emotional disturbance and other causal factors.

This "soft-symptom" theory deserves recognition as such, but, to date, remains unsupported by the bulk of empirical evidence or authoritative opinion. Undoubtedly, there are a few pupils in larger school populations with undiagnosed neurological impairment, and it is possible that this may manifest itself in unusual difficulty in dealing with written language and other printed symbols. Central nervous system dysfunction is not limited ordinarily to such narrow performance areas but influences success in most complex learning tasks. Usually, it is accompanied by such general behavioral characteristics as perseveration, inability to cope with highly stimulating environments, and catastrophic reaction to frustration.[34]

Perhaps the most serious weakness of the generalized "learning disability—therefore, brain damage" hypothesis is that it ignores evidence that severe learning difficulty in reading and other school areas may be the product of other causal factors or combinations of factors which are not appropriately treated by programs predicated on organic malfunction. Under these circumstances, the wiser course for the general teaching professional is to refer pupils with extreme problems in reading and related learning to an appropriately trained source of pupil diagnosis and to resist armchair labeling of such individuals as "brain damaged." Successful reading development clearly is dependent upon the proper functioning of the central nervous system through which graphic symbols are perceived and integrated into appropriate language processes. Where reading is concerned, however, the effective functioning of the central nervous system is dependent, in turn, upon appropriate experience, intellectual capacity, and emotional and general physical well-being.

## Emotional Resources of the Reader

From the 1940s to the mid-1960s, emotional adjustment figured prominently among the research and literature dealing with reading development and reading disability.[35] Personal adjustment is considered no less a vital reader resource today, although it has been overshadowed by professional concern about the impact of social and language disadvantagement upon reading and school success. Most psychologists and reading authorities agree that personal adjustment problems can interfere with initial reading learning and often will confound efforts to remediate reading difficulty, once it has become established.[36]

Spache's evidence of the suppressed or covertly expressed hostility of pupils with reading disability suggests that the relationship between personal adjustment and reading performance may be more subtle and significant than teachers, administrators, and parents realize. [37] Viewed positively, reading and study performance in the secondary school benefit from a healthy self-concept, even where persistent reading disability or abnormal personality patterns are not an issue in the pupil's circumstances. [38]

### Emotional Maladjustment and Reading Difficulty

The incidence of emotional disturbance among disabled readers seems to vary with the criteria employed for identifying either factor. The more stringent the criteria employed in identifying either — that is, the greater the severity of the emotional or reading problem involved — the greater the probability that a relationship exists between the two. From a review of cases of serious reading disability referred to a university reading clinic, Gates reported that nearly three-fourths revealed notable symptoms of maladjustment. [39] Robinson's intensive case study investigation of seriously disabled readers revealed that 54 percent had a psychiatric problem of some kind. [40] Other studies have revealed lower incidence figures as well as shifts of incidence among particular populations investigated. [41] As a general estimate, perhaps half of those pupils with significantly limiting reading disability also display notable personal problems.

*Situational maladjustment.* In all probability, situational maladjustment (personal adjustment difficulty limited to specific settings or situations) of the disabled reader is more prevalent than general maladjustment. An investigation by Witty of 100 ninth graders with notable reading disability revealed that roughly 40 percent evidenced a history of generalized maladjustment. However, nearly 80 percent of this sample manifested serious motivational and adjustment problems where reading and study situations were involved. [42] Especially perti-

nent in this respect are Penty's findings of the felt frustration and related hostility of secondary pupils with limited reading ability toward required reading and those classes where assigned reading was regularly required. [43]

*Causation or association?* Authoritative opinion and research evidence is somewhat equivocal concerning the direction of causative relationship between reading disability and personal maladjustment. [44] The safer generalization is that they have been associated and probably are interrelated. Either condition may lead to the other, particularly when in extreme degree. However, some excellent readers may demonstrate unusual, even neurotic, behavior patterns. And some inadequate readers are very well adjusted, particularly in nonreading situations. Moreover, the relationship is not likely to occur in isolation; where serious reading disability is involved, more than one reader resource deficiency usually appears in the profile. Once the association has been formed, it is very likely to become mutually reinforcing. Successful strategies for treating severe reading disability usually involve special provision for motivation, rebuilding self-confidence, or possibly, therapeutic treatment of the pupil's adjustment difficulties, as well as instructional work with reading performance.

*Possible emotional interference.* In time, emotional problems and reading difficulty involve such an intermingled circularity of interaction that it is difficult to separate cause and effect. It is not impossible to see how certain problems in personal adjustment could interfere with reading development and efficient reading performance.

Learning to read is one of the first serious school learning tasks imposed upon the young pupil. He is expected to pay close attention to instruction and to the printed page for longer periods of time than has been his experience. He is expected to work cooperatively with the teacher and fellow pupils in group learning situations. He is expected to carry out certain tasks of independent learning and practice. And since most pupils encounter some difficulty with these new learning tasks, he must be able to cope with such frustration and to persist in overcoming the difficulty faced.

The insecurity of some pupils causes them to cling to dependency behavior established in infancy. Also, personal anxiety may be manifested in distractability, fatigue, excessive withdrawal, or other behavior not conducive to school learning. Some children become involved in a power struggle with parents and other authority figures; this may be expressed in hostility or passive resistance to structured learning situations such as reading instruction. These and other manifestations of emotional immaturity or maladjustment add to the difficulty of mastering reading learning.[45]

Emotional factors may continue to exert an influence upon reading performance in later school years. Persistent reading failure, itself, serves to reinforce both adjustment difficulty and negative attitudes toward reading and reading instruction.[46]

Emotional resources or the lack of them may influence reading-related behavior in less direct ways and among pupils not traditionally classified as disabled. Personal problems, even though transitional, detract from reading-study concentration and efficiency. For some pupils, the need to erect and maintain strong defense barriers limits interpretive flexibility and open-mindedness and generally prevents critical analysis of positions they favor.[47] Reinforced attitudes about certain subjects can increase difficulty in understanding contrary concepts expressed in text materials, even to the point of misreading the words that represent those concepts.[48] Study-related anxiety among upper-grade pupils increased significantly during the post-Sputnik era and may manifest itself in school and general adjustment problems.

### Reading and Self-Concept

The individual's perception of the *self*, what he thinks himself to be and how he feels about this self-image, is considered to be one of the most crucial components of the personality. A realistic self-evaluation and a full measure of self-acceptance serve as the foundation of healthy adjustment.

Many psychologists believe that the basic self-concept is established during early childhood, although school experiences, particularly those of a persistent emotional flavor or which open the individual's perception of his possibilities, can modify this basic evaluation. Later experiences are likely to contribute to the role differentiation of the self, e.g., the physical self, the social self, the academic self, etc.

Understandably, self-concept as a significant factor of the individual's total development will exert some influence upon relations with others, school adjustment, and reading development. At the same time, reading might be expected to contribute to self-perception. Beyond its own social significance, reading serves as a cornerstone to school success. How the pupil fares in reading and in school achievement is quite likely to influence his self-evaluation. Reading, as a significant source of vicarious experiences, should contribute to self-examination, comparison, and extension of personal horizons. Moreover, reading probably serves a therapeutic function for many people.[49]

Although self-concept has proved to be an illusive phenomenon to pin down through objective instruments of measurement, there is some empirical evidence to support the contention that reading and self-concept are related. Schwyhart's review of the research indicates that pupils with high or positive self-concepts tend toward higher reading achievement in relation to their intellectual potential than do pupils with low self-concepts.[50] This relationship appears to hold, regardless of whether the subjects are primary, secondary, or college-level readers. Moreover, there is some evidence to indicate that improvement in reading through special treatment programs has a beneficial effect upon the self-concept of poor readers.[51]

Selective drive and flexibility are essential to effective reading as a mature process. A positive reading self-concept—the extent to which the individual is willing to extend his conceptual horizons, challenge his aspirations, and adjust his reading attack to meet the opportunities encountered—should benefit reading sophistication even beyond its influence upon basic reading competency. Reading development and effective reading performance draw heavily, though not exclusively, upon the emotional resources of the reader. This includes the creative thrust of a positive self-concept as well as the absence of the debilitating influences of personal maladjustment.

## Experiential Resources of the Reader

We have observed how the conditioning experiences of the individual bear upon the reading act. The reader is dependent upon his broad and specific environmental interactions to develop that body of *referential* and *conceptual understanding* upon which he must draw to associate meaning with the terms and structures of the writer's message. A second and closely related set of experiences consists of those by which the individual comes to master his *language* base and its oral-aural usage, which, in turn, provides the basis for learning and using written language processes. A third crucial set of reader resources involves those formal and informal experiences through which he learns the *processes* of reading itself. Intermingled with these experiences are those of affective or emotional learning which shape his interests and attitudes—about formal learning, the reading act, the writer's topic, and the way the writer uses his language.

### Cultural Membership and Reading

The source of the individual's experiential background is his general and specific culture. The breadth of the person's possible learning experiences is implied in Berelson and Steiner's definition of culture as "that complex whole which includes knowledge, belief, art, morals, law, custom, and any other capabilities and habits acquired by man as a member of society."[52] One's cultural contacts also establish the limits of one's learning experiences.

In a complex society like that of the modern United States, a person may exist in and be influenced by specific cultural experiences as well as by broad, general cultural experiences. Thus, two members of the general culture of American society may be members of different subcultures. A subculture is a division of a total culture set apart by special folkways and mores which have emerged through an extended period of in-group interaction. Subcultures may be formed around various patterns of conditioning experiences, such as geographical setting, age, sex, religion, color, national origin, socioeconomic class, and education. A subculture may be reinforced by certain in-group patterns of oral language known as dialects.

In a multicultural society, the beliefs of the most powerful group (political-social-economic) tend to dominate the reward systems of the general society and thus shape its political, social, economic, and educational institutions as well as its accepted written language patterns. Reading thus becomes a culturally determined and limited behavior. The content and the form of the written message are highly dependent upon the writer's own cultural experiences, which usually reflect mainstream language and cultural reference. Moreover, the instructional setting usually reflects main culture concepts and attitudes. A pupil may be experientially disadvantaged in reading either through lack of necessary learning experiences (*deprivation*) or through conflict of previous learning experiences with those required of the reading situation (*discontinuity*).

### Experiential Differences Related to Reading Success

Subcultural differences provide some insight into how experiential background influences the ease or difficulty with which a pupil masters reading. The three patterns of experiential differences discussed on the following pages have figured differentially in reading performance, are subculturally linked, and represent somewhat different patterns in disadvantagement and discontinuity. The three are *socioeconomic background* differences, *language* differences, and *sex* differences. Obviously, they are not mutually exclusive experiential factors, and their concurrence increases the probability of difficulty in mastering reading.

*Social class differences.* Social stratification involves the ranking of people in a society by other members of the society into higher and lower positions, thus producing a hierarchy of prestige. The basis for such stratification varies with the values of the society. The basic criteria for social classification in the United States accepted by most social scientists include occupation, education, source and size of income, house type, and dwelling area.[53] In general, these amount to indices of power within the society. In the United States, power and prestige are so intermingled with the nature of the individual's or group's economic strength that it has become common to refer to social class position as socioeconomic status (SES).[54] Other and often correlated social class criteria include religion, ethnic origin, family history or reputation, social associates, and community function.

Social class, especially the difference between lower- and middle-class membership, is a factor of critical educational influence.[55] This goes beyond the fact that amount and type of education may be criteria of class membership. Being raised in a particular social class carries with it selective educational opportunities and conditioning experience. For lower-class youth, these differences often manifest themselves in lesser academic achievement, less participation in nonacademic school functions, greater school adjustment difficulty, and earlier and more frequent school dropout. Among other influences, pupils from lower-class homes receive less preparation for initial school experience; are less likely to be exposed to the general experiences, language patterns, and verbal constructs needed as background for school learning; are oriented toward personal interests and vocational choices less dependent upon educational background; have less experiential contact with and motivational support from well-educated models; and generally, display less scholastic potential.[56]

The evidence collected over the past three decades clearly supports the relationship between higher socioeconomic status of the pupil and greater achievement in reading. The impact is felt early; children from lower social-class homes do less well on reading readiness tests at the beginning of school and exhibit greater difficulty in mastering the initial reading act. These differences maintain throughout the elementary and secondary school years and have been associated with differences in reading competency of university freshmen.[57] Social-class background tends to influence reading habits as well as reading proficiency.[58] When the impact of social class upon reading performance is added to the impact of social class upon general academic motivation and conceptual background, the difficulties experienced by many lower-class youth when reading in content area subjects should not be surprising.

### Language Differences

Considerable social and professional concern has been mounted about the differences in oral language patterns used by certain minority groups in the United States — usually those of recent immigrants, ghetto blacks, Puerto Ricans, and Chicanos — and the disadvantagement which those differences may work upon learning-to-read materials couched in standard English. Reading educational concern over these differences is relatively recent, and a flurry of research and exploratory efforts on the matter have produced equivocal results and differing opinions, as might be expected.[59] The sources edited by Laffey and Shuy and by Zuck and Goodman should guide the interested professional in a deeper examination of the problem than space permits here.[60,61]

Language and culture are more than associated behaviors; they form a symbiotic relationship, a highly interdependent social mutualism. The power of this relationship influences attitudes as well as learning and would seem to go to the core of the issue of dialectical and general language differences and their related school learning problems. The anthropologist Sapir observed that the structure of a group's language subtly molds as well as reflects the way in which the members of that speech group perceive the reality around them, and as such, affects their value systems and influences their general behavior.

Languages are more to us than systems of thought transference. They are invisible garments that drape themselves about our spirit and give a predetermined form to all its symbolic expression.[62]

**Dialect, school adjustment, and reading success.** A language, including all dialects of American English, is a workable form of verbal communication containing sufficiently developed rules of the phonetic, grammatical, and semantic systems necessary to that communication. A group of people who use the same speech signals, and thus are able to communicate with each other, constitute a language community. Large, geographically widespread, or socially diverse language communities tend to have subdivisions or dialects. McDavid defines a dialect as "a habitual variety of language—regional or social or both—set off from other such habitual varieties by a complex of features of grammar, pronunciation, and vocabulary."[63]

Social distinctions among dialects are not made on linguistic grounds but on status considerations influenced by political, economic, or cultural dominance. As soon as the dialect of any particular group or region acquires special prestige, it tends to become the standard norm for the general speech community. In time, it becomes incorporated into the institutional workings of that society, including schools, and tends to be learned by speakers of other dialects who have the opportunity and desire to share in the reward systems of the dominant speech group.

Pedagogically, the development of a "proper," major strand form of American English has been accepted as a reasonable, albeit nationalistic, objective since the days of Noah Webster. This has been reinforced by the traditional American penchant for teaching pupils to write English according to Latin grammar school norms.

Although all Americans speak one or more dialects, teachers, writers, and editors usually are members of the dominant English dialectical community, and employ it in their writing, thinking, and feeling. They tend to believe, with some socioeconomic justification, that it is to the pupil's ad-

vantage to learn to do likewise. Even if teachers did not so believe, established curricular patterns, learning materials, and societal sanctions have left very little choice to do otherwise. It is unfortunate, however, that some educators and writers hold misconceptions that minority subcultures are necessarily inferior, that minority dialects are inadequate vehicles of expression and thought, and that pupils from such backgrounds are necessarily incapable of mastering school learning for those reasons.[64]

Many pupils of linguistically different backgrounds do have greater difficulty in mastering, as a second dialect, the "standard" English employed in schools. Their difficulty is even more apparent in developing competency in written English, including reading proficiency. The two problems are related but not identical.

The greater probability of reading deficiency among dialectically different pupils may be traced to some combination of written language discontinuity, experiential discontinuity, and related problems of school adjustment. The mastery of written language behavior usually is built upon the pupil's oral language background. It seems reasonable, therefore, that significant discrepancies in these language modes are likely to make such transfer more difficult. The factor of experiential deficiency seems probable when it is recognized that students of immigrant families or minority backgrounds may not have had an adequate opportunity to amass the referential and conceptual experiences employed by writers and teachers.

Added to this is the observation that pupils with linguistically different backgrounds often face special school adjustment and motivation problems. As Sapir implies, language is more than a mechanic of communication or a means of dealing with cultural referents. It lies close to one's feelings and sense of self-worth. Departing from it can add to one's other insecurities. Being forced to depart from it engenders hostility and learning resistance.

Such difficulties may be reinforced where ethnic conflicts at the school-peer or broader societal level are involved. A hypothesis advanced by some linguists is that much of this adjustment difficulty is caused by or intensified by educators who not only cannot communicate effectively with these pupils in their own dialect, but by statement or action, deal derogatively with the pupil's own language patterns. A variant of this hypothesis is the contention that teachers who mistakenly label the language "miscues" of linguistically different pupils as reading errors, and who belabor these miscues with critical reaction or with well-intentioned but deadly instructional overkill, seriously interfere with the motivation and basic learning success of these pupils in the foundational processes of reading.[65]

Finally, it should be recognized that the phenomenon of individual learning differences obtains for pupils of different language backgrounds just as it does for those raised in dialects which approximate that employed in schools and published materials. It has been observed that pupils who have difficulty mastering their home language patterns and the concepts of their own subculture reveal greater difficulty in mastering the second dialect and school-oriented referents and concepts. Close investigation of those pupils who take this transfer hurdle with greater ease should provide valuable insight about developmental and remedial directions for all pupils with significantly different language backgrounds.

In all probability, the reading difficulties of pupils with differences in language resources may be traced to some combination of these factors. This implies a multidirectional attack upon the problem. To date, no major breakthrough has been achieved, nor is it likely in the near future in view of the complexity of the problem. Considerable progress in social and educational awareness of the problem has been achieved, and in that lies the hope of mitigating these difficulties for future generations of readers.

### Sex Differences

The relatively better performance of girls in reading, other language behaviors, and those school performance areas closely dependent upon them has been observed for over a century in the United States.[66] Concern has intensified about these differences in the past decade.[67] In most situations, the average performance of girls in reading is significantly better than the average performance of peer boys. These differences are notable during the early reading stages, and though they decrease some during the secondary years, they do maintain, are evidenced in college populations, and probably continue throughout life.[68]

This does not imply that all females are superior in reading to all males in any particular population sample, of course. Sex-differentiated school performance distributions overlap, and some of the best readers in a class may be boys. But the general reading performance superiority of girls raises some pertinent questions about the resource characteristics of the reader. The issue becomes operationally significant when we recognize that the incidence of measurable reading disability among boys is approximately twice that of girls, regardless of the criterion of disability employed.

There are several factors which make this matter of sex differences in reading performance pertinent to our discussion of subcultural influence upon reader experiential resources. The first is that we have had little success in tracing the magnitude of these differences to physical, mental, or basic emotional dissimilarities between the two sexes. The second is that these differences tend to vary with the national setting.[69] For example, sex superiority is lessened and even reversed in some countries, such as Germany.[70] A third factor is that sex differences in reading performance seem to hold for nearly every other subcultural division and intensify the learning difficulties imposed by those subcultural differences.[71] Finally, the factors which seem to influence male performance in reading may provide insight about factors which inhibit the reading progress of other subcultural groups with similar conditioning experiences. Since boys and girls within the same socioeconomic and language subgroups are exposed to the same general reading instructional procedures and materials and these differences occur, we need to examine the broader experiences of boys which may condition them to react differently and less successfully than girls to reading instructional situations.

Comparatively speaking, boys are less "ready" for first instruction in reading than girls.[72] They are not as prepared by early conditioning experiences to handle the controlled perceptual and performance tasks of initial instruction. They are not as verbally facile or linguistically as mature as girls. Moreover, they seem to have greater difficulty maintaining attention, suppressing physical activity, and generally adjusting to the controlled routine of instruction. Initial reading success does influence subsequent development; while these differences in learning set are moderated somewhat by school experience, they continue even into the secondary school.

The fact that boys and girls are exposed to the same general instruction in reading does not preclude the fact that traditional procedures and materials are not equally appropriate to the learning proclivities of the two sexes. In the past, at least, such instruction has stressed controlled, passive verbal interaction built around basal reader materials—usually stories of rather innocuous content emphasizing acceptable situations and "nice" behavior. The content of supplementary and recreational reading materials available in classroom and library has reflected a similar lack of virility. There is some evidence to indicate that boys would prefer more "blood and guts," more humor, and less social morality in their stories. Moreover, they evidence greater interest in nonfictional instructional materials requiring active and practical solutions to problems and the creation of projects. While there is no clear evidence that girls prefer the traditional passive, story-oriented patterns of reading instruction, they seem more able to accept those structures. This acceptance may be a significant factor of cultural conditioning, in itself.

While both sexes are exposed to the same general instructional experiences, the nature of teacher interaction with boys may differ in subtle ways from teacher-girl interactions.[73] Accusations of overt discriminatory prejudice upon the part of female teachers are not supported by hard evidence. There is a tendency for both men and women teachers to prefer girls as students; not because they are girls per se, but because they tend to be more cooperative and amenable to controlled instructional situations.

This suggests that boys may encounter a special condition of cultural discontinuity. In their non-school experiences, boys generally are expected to be more active, more physical in their activity, less responsible, more "macho" in their relations with peers. They receive ambiguous indoctrination in regard to acceptance of authority. When they come into the school and classroom situation, society enforces and rewards quite different norms. Some conflict seems inevitable, and the mutual anxieties of both teachers and male pupils may create a set which heightens these adjustment difficulties.

Finally, the early success differential between the sexes in reading and related school achievement probably reinforces these differences, pejoratively for some boys and rewardingly for some girls.[74] There is some evidence to indicate that when the two sexes are separated for elementary school instruction, boys make better progress in reading, make better adjustment to the instructional setting, and prefer to remain in all-boy classes. While girls in all-girl classes achieve as well as in mixed classes, personal competition and social conflict increases between girls, and many prefer to move to the mixed-sex classes. Moreover, teachers may be susceptible to selective perception of boys' reading problems in mixed classes; while the demonstrated greater incidence of male reading disability runs approximately twice as high as that of girls, actual teacher referrals of pupils for reading disability treatment show sex differentials ranging from four boys to one girl, up to ten boys to one girl.

It is likely that sex differences in reading performance may be traced to some combination of the above and other undetected factors. Such differences do demonstrate the selective influence of experiential background and are the more revealing in that these differences are maintained across other subcultural lines as well as across intellectual, physical, and emotional resource patterns. The extent to which sex differences in reading performance may or may not be moderated by in- and out-of-school experiences should provide some realistic insight about the nature and degree to which deficiencies in other experiential resources needed for reading may be accommodated.

## READING AS A COMPOSITE BEHAVIOR

Occasionally one encounters in the general or professional literature certain assumptions of single-factor causality of reading disability. It lies within the realm of possibility that any single human or situational attribute independently may aid or may inhibit, markedly, the reading development of an individual. However, the bulk of our empirical evidence and rational analysis supports multiple-factor interaction and influence upon the reading performance of a secondary reader. With the possible exception of severe mental or neurological disturbance, it is unlikely that single factors exert independent determination of success or failure of the individual reader.

Each of the major reader resource areas discussed may be expected to make some probable contribution to the development of most readers. The extent of that contribution will vary with the particular reader and situation. The following empirically based generalizations serve as appropriate qualifications to observe in the evaluation of causal relationships in reading development.

1. No single anomaly or human resource deficiency invariably appears in all cases of reading disability.
2. Anomalies which have been found in reading disability syndromes also have been identified in good readers.
3. The direction and degree of association between a pupil or situational anomaly have been difficult to ascertain empirically. For example, emotional disturbance may be a cause, an effect, or a concomitant of reading disability.
4. It is possible that a pupil's anomalous condition exerts no direct influence upon his reading per-

formance; the anomaly even may serve as a compensating positive force in reading development.
5. Pupils manifesting greater severity of reading disability tend to exhibit a greater number of personal anomalies than those with lesser or no disability.
6. A notable deficiency in reader resources may be expected to exert greater impact when acting in concert with other inhibiting conditions and when the pupil is unable to make compensatory adjustment.
7. Other factors being equal, anomalies or human resource deficiencies may be expected to exert influence upon reading performance to their greater degree or persistence as an inhibiting condition.
8. Deficiencies or disruptions in the learner's resources may be expected to exert greater inhibiting influence during the formative phase of skill learning or when the demands of reading learning are most exacting.
9. Pupil resource differences associated with reading disability also have been associated with disability in spelling, arithmetic, and other areas of academic skill behavior.

## THE READER AS AN ADOLESCENT

The term *adolescence* is derived from the Latin verb *adolescere*, which means "to grow into maturity." In a modern industrial society, this "coming of age" process is stretched over a considerable period of time. Broadly interpreted, it is kicked off by the prepubertal growth spurt, generally occurring between the ages of 9 and 12 for most girls and 11 and 14 for most boys. *Puberty*, the onset of sexual change, typically is encountered around the twelfth year for girls and about a year later for boys, although the range of its appearance may extend from ages 10 to 20 in a large sample of youth. *Early adolescence*, a period of notable physical and social role change and resulting adjustment, generally is considered to approximate the thirteenth through sixteenth years of life. *Later adolescence*, characterized by a slowing of physical growth and increasing stabilization of behavioral patterns, is assumed to end when reaching legal majority, but this varies considerably with the individual and the situation.

Professional recognition of adolescence was initiated early in the twentieth century by G. Stanley Hall, who described adolescence in the United States and similar cultures as a period of "storm and stress."[75] Since Hall's early analysis, research has been conducted and other theories about adolescence have been published.[76] Not all of these have stressed the physical, social, and psychological awkwardness of the period. Hollingworth viewed it as a positive development thrust, a period of flowering and fulfillment.[77] Erikson includes puberty and adolescence in the fifth of his eight developmental stages of man, a time for establishing a dominant positive ego identity.[78] Anthropologists, notably Benedict and Mead, have emphasized that the positive or negative characteristics of adolescence are influenced by the cultural setting in which it occurs.[79]

Contemporary interpretations of adolescence tend to be flexible and qualified. They stress the presence of wide individual differences among adolescents, the relative impact of the social setting upon the manifestations of adolescence, and the uncertainty of societal change in making predictions about adolescence.[80]

## Some Notable Characteristics of Adolescence

The behavior of an individual may be understood in terms of his motivating forces, his available resources, his situation, and his perception of these factors. With the onset of adolescence, the pupil is faced with some change in these factors. How much of an influence adolescence will have upon general and reading behavior will depend upon how stable a personality structure the individual takes into adolescence, the nature of the changes resulting from his or her genetic structure, how the adolescent's society reacts to this emergence, and how effectively the adolescent has mastered earlier reading, language, and study skills.

### Physical Change

There are two primary and several secondary physiological developments during adolescence which exert a marked impact. The most observable is growth in stature and strength. From the prepubertal spurt to the end of the late adolescent period, the individual rapidly increases in size and weight and more than doubles in strength. The second major factor of physical change during adolescence is puberty or the emergence of reproductive potential and sexual drive. Other related physical developments of early adolescence include the appearance of secondary sex characteristics, glandular shifts and growth of internal organs, and changes in skeletal structure and body shape.

These physical changes often influence the physical and psychological well-being of the adolescent. Structural changes momentarily may set back coordination. Glandular fluctuations instigate irregular bursts of energy which are difficult to predict and control. Growth, itself, exerts a drain upon energy, and when coupled with greater parental and school expectancies, can result in a persistent fatigue condition. Glandular changes, varying energy levels, and anxiety may combine to produce irregular appetites, unusual eating habits, skin disorders, digestive disturbances, and other minor ailments, real or imagined.

### Social Transition and Ambiguity

Adolescence carries important implications for change in status as a member of society. It is a part of our heritage that sexual maturity and greater size and strength signal readiness to take on adult responsibilities and privileges. In earlier times, as in primitive societies, this transition from child to adult status could be of short duration. Moreover, adult status could be readily, if arbitrarily, defined and clearly established. All tribal members were obligated to recognize the symbolical implications of circumcision and other ceremonial versions of the *rite de passage*.

In many modern industrial democracies, the social conditions of adolescence may be imposed as early as age 10 and extend beyond age 21. Within this period, the roles of the adolescent are not well defined. Parents and teachers vacillate in their treatment of the adolescent. Too often they expect the adolescent to assume adult responsibility while accepting the restrictions of childhood. Moreover, these expectations can vary from home to home, from school to school, and from subculture to subculture.[81]

This awkward transition period is extended as the society becomes more complex in technology and commerce. It becomes more ambiguous in societies undergoing rapid cultural transition.

*Self-assessment and self-acceptance.* Maturation, in concert with the reaction of the adolescent, his peers, and adults to that maturation, works no small influence upon the adolescent psyche. Change in physical stature stimulates greater social awareness and self-consciousness. Depending upon the relative timing and degree of pubertal change, the reaction of significant people in the adolescent's life, and the residual self-concept of childhood, this emerging self-perspective may become positively or negatively implanted.

In a relative sense, emotional intensity and lability tend to subside in later adolescence, probably as a result of the stabilizing of physical development, knowledge of role expectancies, and greater self-insight and confidence. However, later adolescence can have its problems. Self-assertive tendencies increase, with greater possibility of thwarting. Resultant anger is more openly expressed. Anxiety related to educational pressures, vocational decisions, and financial dependencies is common among males and is occurring more frequently among liberated females. Early and late adolescence is a critical period of self-reassessment, and the resulting ego product can have far-reaching implications.

### Transition in Personal Relationships

Compared to childhood, adolescence can be both an awkward time of social interaction and a crucial period for social learning and adjustment. Puberty often breaks with sudden discontent into the generally comfortable and stable outward relationships of childhood. Physical changes and related personal problems may spill over into relationships with peers, family, and adults. Disenchantment with the childhood gang and its activities emerges. Sexual antagonism is intensified.

By midadolescence this pattern of interaction undergoes further adjustment. Need for social interaction replaces separation. Resistance to parental authority and friction with siblings increase, and at the same time, conformity with peer practices and peer approval becomes important. Large, impersonal gang involvement narrows to a concern for significant friends and certain cliques. Friendships are more selective and depend upon commonality of interests, abilities, and socioeconomic status. The opposite sex becomes significant, as such, and success in social relations with members of the other sex can be of crucial importance to self-acceptance and prestige within the group.

The later adolescent usually narrows the number of intimates in his or her life, but often broadens the range of group interaction. Resistance to adult authority reaches a peak during this period. Criteria for chums of both sexes are raised, and are likely to include appearance, ability, social status, a pleasing personality, and mutual acceptance. The attraction of specific members of the other sex ordinarily increases, and the forming of liaisons is common during later adolescence. In past decades, the end of adolescence commonly was signaled by marriage, even in complex societies. However, changes in sexual mores, concern with overpopulation, increasing freedom for women, and greater financial dependency may tend to diminish the significance of marriage as an adolescent end game.

### School and Reading Implications

The school is a very important part of adolescent life, and the adolescent influences the nature of the school. The adolescent spends more time in school than in any other institutional setting and will be more involved in school-related matters than in other activity centers. The school is where much of the peer action is. Success and failure with school peer interaction and in academic learning situations exerts a determining influence upon adult life. This is felt increasingly as the pupil moves through adolescence. Adams reports that school-based concerns are reported more frequently by adolescents than any other concern and more frequently by boys than by girls.[82] It is unfortunate that academic pressure is increased just at the time of life when the pupil has more than enough general problems to handle.

*Adolescence and reading.* Adolescence will influence reading behavior. The degree and direction of this influence will vary with the individual. Increasing mental maturity, accumulation of experiences, broadening interests, and school exposure to higher and more vigorous levels of thought should assist the adolescent in making notable strides toward mature reading performance. Unless severe, the usual physical, emotional, and social changes of the period should provide no more than transitional influence upon reading-study performance. Certainly the adolescent who has developed a basic mastery of the reading act should experience no serious setback in this basic mastery. If the school provides the opportunity for further reading development, the pupil can advance along the continuum of reading maturity; a good many will move beyond the reading performance levels of the average adult.

Pupils who have established habits of extensive reading in preadolescent years will continue to read, although reading interests and types of reading experiences will reflect changes in general interest and activities. Greater involvement in social and school activity during later adolescence may reflect a drop in extended personal reading from the more intensive reading activity of the prepubertal and pubertal periods. Newspaper, magazine, and in-strumental effect reading of shorter length usually increases in frequency. The adolescent who has learned to use reading as a therapeutic and information-gaining tool should find reading a considerable help in negotiating the adjustment periods of early adolescence.

But the pupil who has not mastered the fundamentals of reading, who has a history of reading difficulty, is likely to incur some greater adjustment problems in adolescence. He may be frustrated by the amount, intensity, and difficulty of reading-study assignments in the secondary school setting. The stigma of academic difficulty may add to the social adjustment problems of the period. Continuing serious difficulty in reading and related school achievement may intensify anxiety and inhibit self-discovery, realistic vocational choice, and participation in school extracurricular activities. One too-common solution to these problems is to escape from school through day-dreaming, truancy, or early dropout. All adolescents need help and understanding to reduce stress and to increase the self-fulfillment which this time of life offers. For the adolescent with reading and related learning problems, such support is crucial.

Reading is human behavior, and the reader must draw upon his motivational forces and personal resources to effect those reading processes he has learned. The secondary school years coincide with the developmental changes of adolescence. Such changes very likely will exert short-term effects on reading behavior. Whether adolescence exerts long-lasting positive or negative influences upon reading development will depend upon the pupil's earlier stability and how "significant others" react to him as an adolescent. Certainly some very positive forces can benefit reading development during this period. Increased mental maturity, broader experience, the opportunity to learn from stimulating reading and content instruction, and greater power in independent reading—all contribute to the mature reading performance. The nature of the mature reading act is presented in Chapter Three.

# REFERENCES

1. David H. Russell, *The Dynamics of Reading*, Robert Ruddell, Editor (Waltham, Mass.: Ginn-Blaisdell, 1970) p. 3.
2. Ralph H. Ojemann, *Personality Adjustment of Individual Children* (Washington, D.C.: National Education Association, 1954) p. 7.
3. Helen M. Robinson, *Why Pupils Fail in Reading* (Chicago: University of Chicago Press, 1946) pp. 98-101.
4. Walter Hill and William Eller, *Power in Reading Skills* (Belmont, Calif.: Wadsworth Publishing Company, Inc., 1964) pp. 164-76.
5. Douglas Waples, Bernard Berelson, and Franklyn Bradshaw, *What Reading Does to People* (Chicago: University of Chicago Press, 1940) pp. 74-80.
6. James Squire, "Teaching Literature: High School and College," in *The Dynamics of Reading*, pp. 275-76.
7. Amiel T. Sharon, "What Do Adults Read?" *Reading Research Quarterly* 9 (1973-74) pp. 148-69.
8. Simon S. Johnson, "How Students Feel About Literature," *American Education* 10 (April, 1974) pp. 6-10.
9. Anne G. Scharf, "Who Likes What in High School," *Journal of Reading* 16 (May, 1973) pp. 604-7.
10. Ann Jungeblut and J. C. Coleman, "Reading Content That Interests Seventh, Eighth, and Ninth Grade Pupils," *Journal of Educational Research* 58 (May-June, 1965) pp. 394-401.
11. Mary Desjardins, "Reading and Viewing: A Survey," *School Libraries* 21 (Spring, 1972) pp. 26-31.
12. G. Yarlott and W. S. Harpin, "1000 Responses to English Literature," *Educational Research* 13 (1970) pp. 3-11, 87-97.
13. Sharon, "What Do Adults Read?"
14. Ruth Strang, *Reading Diagnosis and Remediation* (Newark, Del.: International Reading Association, 1968) pp. 10-89.
15. James B. Stroud, *Psychology in Education* (New York: Longmans, Green & Co., Inc., 1956) p. 138.
16. Paul R. Lohnes and Marian Gray, "Intellectual Development and the Cooperative Reading Studies," *Reading Research Quarterly* 8 (Fall, 1972) p. 59.
17. Robert L. Thorndike, *The Concepts of Over and Under Achievement* (New York: Teachers College Press, Columbia University, 1963).
18. Roger Farr, *Reading: What Can Be Measured?* (Newark, Del.: International Reading Association, 1969) pp. 186-94.
19. Paul H. Mussen, Editor, *Carmichael's Manual of Child Psychology*, Third Edition, Vol. I, Part III, "Cognitive Development" (New York: John Wiley & Sons, Inc., 1970) pp. 657-1445.
20. Barbel Inhelder and Jean Piaget, *The Growth of Logical Thinking from Childhood Through Adolescence* (New York: Basic Books, Inc., 1958).
21. H. G. Furth, "On Language and Knowing in Piaget's Developmental Theory," *Human Development* 13 (1970) pp. 241-57.
22. David Elkind, "Adolescent Cognitive Development," in *Understanding Adolescence: Current Developments in Adolescent Psychology*, J. F. Adams, Editor (Boston: Allyn and Bacon, Inc., 1968) p. 148.
23. P. Blommers, L. Knief, and J. B. Stroud, "The Organismic Age Concept," *Journal of Educational Psychology* 46 (March, 1955) pp. 142-50.
24. Robinson, *Why Pupils Fail in Reading*, p. 220.
25. Marjorie S. Johnson, "Factors Related to Disability in Reading," *Journal of Experimental Education* 26 (September, 1957) p. 1.
26. Strang, *Reading Diagnosis and Remediation*, pp. 10-34, 42-52.
27. Guy Bond and Miles Tinker, *Reading Difficulties: Their Diagnosis and Correction,* Third Edition (New York: Appleton-Century-Crofts, 1973) p. 113.
28. T. H. Eames, "A Frequency Study of Physical Handicaps in Reading Disability and Unselected Groups," *Journal of Educational Research* 29 (1935) pp. 1-5.
29. J. A. Richardson, "Physical Factors in Reading Failure," *Australian Journal of Education* (1958) pp. 1-10.
30. Guy L. Bond, *The Auditory and Speech Characteristics of Poor Readers* (New York: Bureau of Publications, Teachers College, Columbia University, 1938).
31. Donald Durrell and Helen Murphy, "The Auditory Discrimination Factor in Reading Readiness and Reading Disability," *Education* 73 (1953) pp. 556-60.
32. Albert J. Harris, *How to Increase Reading Ability* (New York: David McKay Company, Inc., 1970) pp. 258-60.
33. H. K. Goldberg and G. B. Schiffman, *Dyslexia: Problems of Reading Disabilities* (New York: Grune & Stratton, Inc., 1972) pp. 43-65.
34. G. Stevens and J. Birch, "A Proposal for Classification of the Terminology Used to Describe Brain-Injured Children," *Exceptional Children* 23 (1957) pp. 346-49.
35. Jack A. Holmes, "Personality Characteristics of the Disabled Reader," *Journal of Developmental Reading* 4 (Winter, 1961) pp. 111-22.

36. Strang, *Reading Diagnosis and Remediation*, p. 67.
37. George Spache, "Personality Patterns of Retarded Readers," *Journal of Educational Research* 50 (February, 1957) pp. 488-93.
38. Walter Hill, "Personality Traits and Reading Disability: A Critique," in *Problems, Programs, and Projects in College-Adult Reading*, Eleventh Yearbook of the National Reading Conference, E. P. Bliesmer and R. C. Staiger, Editors (Milwaukee, Wis.: Marquette University Press, 1962) pp. 174-80.
39. Arthur I. Gates, "The Role of Personality Maladjustment in Reading Disability," *Journal of Genetic Psychology* 59 (1941) pp. 77-83.
40. Robinson, *Why Pupils Fail in Reading*, p. 157.
41. Strang, *Reading Diagnosis and Remediation*, p. 64.
42. Paul Witty, "Reading Success and Emotional Adjustment," *Elementary English* 29 (May, 1950) pp. 289-96.
43. Ruth Penty, *Reading Ability and High School Dropouts* (New York: Bureau of Publications, Teachers College, Columbia University, 1956) p. 55.
44. Strang, *Reading Diagnosis and Remediation*, p. 63.
45. Harris, *How to Increase Reading Ability*, pp. 265-68.
46. Mildred Roebeck, "Effects of a Prolonged Reading Disability: A Preliminary Study," *Perceptual and Motor Skills* 19 (1964) pp. 7-12.
47. Helen J. Crossen, "Effects of the Attitudes of the Reader upon Critical Reading Ability," *Journal of Educational Research* 42 (1948) pp. 289-98.
48. I. Postman, J. S. Bruner, and E. McGinnies, "Personal Values and Selective Factors in Perception," *Journal of Abnormal and Social Psychology* 43 (1948) pp. 142-54.
49. Caroline Shrodes, "The Dynamics of Reading: Implications for Bibliotherapy," *ETC: A Review of General Semantics* 18 (1961) pp. 21-23.
50. F. K. Schwyhart, "Exploration of the Self-Concept of Retarded Readers in Relation to Reading Achievement," doctoral dissertation, University of Arizona, 1967.
51. A. S. McDonald, E. S. Zolik, and J. A. Byrne, "Reading Deficiencies and Personality Factors: A Comprehensive Treatment," in *Starting and Improving College Reading Programs*, Eighth Yearbook of the National Reading Conference, O. S. Causey and W. Eller, Editors (Fort Worth, Texas: Texas Christian University Press, 1959) pp. 89-98.
52. Bernard Berelson and Gary A. Steiner, *Human Behavior: An Inventory of Scientific Findings* (New York: Harcourt, Brace and World, Inc., 1964) p. 646.
53. W. L. Warner, M. Meeker, and K. Eels, *Social Class in America* (Chicago: Science Research Associates, Inc., 1949).
54. W. L. Warner and P. S. Lunt, *The Social Life of a Modern Community* (New Haven, Conn.: Yale University Press, 1941) p. 88.
55. William W. Wattenberg, *The Adolescent Years* (New York: Harcourt Brace Jovanovich, Inc., 1973) pp. 175-91.
56. Stroud, *Psychology in Education*, pp. 30-48.
57. Walter Hill, "Factors Associated with the Comprehension Deficiency of College Readers," *Journal of Developmental Reading* 3 (Winter, 1960) pp. 88-94.
58. H. P. Smith and E. V. Dechant, *Psychology in Teaching Reading* (Englewood Cliffs, N.J.: Prentice-Hall, Inc., 1977) p. 181.
59. Roger W. Shuy, "Nonstandard Dialect Problems: An Overview," in *Language Differences: Do They Interfere?* (Newark, Del.: International Reading Association, 1973) p. 16.
60. James L. Laffey and Roger Shuy, Editors, *Language Differences: Do They Interfere?* (Newark, Del.: International Reading Association, 1973).
61. L. V. Zuck and Yetta Goodman, *Social Class and Regional Dialects: Their Relationship to Reading*, An Annotated Bibliography (Newark, Del.: International Reading Association, 1971).
62. Edward Sapir, *Language* (New York: Harcourt, Brace and World, Inc., 1921) p. 21.
63. Raven I. McDavid, "The Sociology of Language," in *Linguistics in School Programs*, Sixty-ninth Yearbook of the National Society for the Study of Education, A. H. Marchwardt, Editor (Chicago: University of Chicago Press, 1970) p. 94.
64. John B. Carroll, "Language and Cognition," in *Language Differences: Do They Interfere?* J. Laffey and R. Shuy, Editors (Newark, Del.: International Reading Association, 1973) p. 184.
65. Kenneth S. Goodman, "Dialect Barriers to Reading Comprehension," *Elementary English* 42 (December, 1965) pp. 853-60.
66. Dale D. Johnson, "Sex Differences in Reading Across Cultures," *Reading Reasearch Quarterly* (1973-74) pp. 67-86.
67. D. Austin, V. Clark, and G. Fitchett, *Reading Rights for Boys: Sex Role in Language Experience* (New York: Appleton-Century-Crofts, 1971).
68. Walter Hill, "Studies of Student Readers," in *Research and Evaluation in College Reading*, Ninth Yearbook of the National Reading Conference, O. Causey, Editor (Fort Worth, Tex.: Texas Christian University Press, 1960) pp. 9-21.
69. Johnson, "Sex Differences in Reading Across Cultures."

70. Ralph C. Preston, "Reading Achivement of German and American Children," *School and Society* 90 (October 20, 1962) pp. 350-54.

71. L. Eisenberg, "The Epidemiology of Reading Disability," in *The Disabled Reader*, J. Money, Editor (Baltimore: Johns Hopkins Press, 1966) p. 7.

72. W. P. Martenson, "Selected Pre-reading Tasks, Socioeconomic Status, and Sex," *Reading Teacher* 22 (October, 1968) p. 45.

73. Pauline Sears and David Feldman, "Teacher Interactions with Boys and Girls," *National Elementary School Principal* 46 (November, 1966) pp. 30-39.

74. Thomas B. Lyles, "Grouping by Sex," *National Elementary School Principal* 46 (November, 1966) pp. 38-41.

75. G. Stanley Hall, *Adolescence* (New York: Appleton, 1916).

76. Rolf E. Muuss, *Theories of Adolescence* (New York: Random House, Inc., 1964).

77. Leta S. Hollingworth, *Psychology of the Adolescent* (New York: Appleton-Century, 1928).

78. E. H. Erikson, "Identity and the Life Cycle," *Psychological Issues* 1 (New York: International Universities Press, Inc., 1959).

79. Ruth Benedict, *Patterns of Culture* (New York: The New American Library, 1950).

80. Harold E. Jones, "Adolescence in Our Society," in *Adolescence: Contemporary Issues*, A. E. Winder and D. L. Angus, Editors (New York: American Book Company, 1968).

81. I. I. Goldenberg, *Build Me a Mountain* (Cambridge, Mass.: The MIT Press, 1971).

82. J. F. Adams, "Adolescent Personal Problems as a Function of Age and Sex," *Journal of Genetic Psychology* 1 (1966) pp. 240-50.

## SUPPLEMENTARY SOURCES

Artley, A. Sterl. *Trends and Practices in Secondary Reading*, Chapter 2. Newark, Del.: International Reading Association, 1968.

Carroll, John. "Language and Cognition." In *Language Differences: Do They Interfere?* J. Laffey and Roger Shuy, Editors, pp. 173-84. Newark, Del.: International Reading Association, 1973.

Dechant, Emerald. *Reading Improvement in the Secondary School*, Chapters 3 and 4. Englewood Cliffs, N.J.: Prentice-Hall, Inc., 1973.

Karlin, Robert, "What Does Research in Reading Reveal—About Reading and the High School Student?" *English Journal* 58 (March, 1969) pp. 386-96.

Penty, Ruth C. *Reading Ability and High School Dropouts*. New York: Bureau of Publications, Teachers College, Columbia University, 1956. 93 p.

Russell, David H. *The Dynamics of Reading*, Chapters 5 and 8. Waltham, Mass.: Ginn-Blaisdell, 1970.

Wattenberg, William W. *The Adolescent Years*, Second Edition, Chapters 1, 3, and 15. New York: Harcourt Brace Jovanovich, Inc., 1973.

# THREE

# The Integral Reading Act

*Act: a pattern of purposive behavior directed toward a goal*

*Dictionary of Psychology*

*The efficient use of books and other printed materials requires not a single, narrow ability, but a large number of interrelated abilities. It is characterized by an aggressive search for meaning and the utilization of all the abilities involved in reflective thinking.*

Ernest Horn

***Overview*** For the secondary pupil or adult, any meaningful instance of reading consists of a unit of goal-directed behavior—for example, following the directions on a label, understanding the idea structure of a textbook chapter, enjoying a sports editorial, and the like. Because the reader must draw upon and purposefully integrate a number of learned reading functions, such a unit may be described as an *integral reading act*. The nature of the specific reading knowledges, skills, and attitudes which the reader utilizes and the manner in which they are combined may vary from one reading act to another. But the principal functions of the major components of each act are relatively constant: readiness, situational set, decoding, purposeful interpretation, and reaction. Chapter Three presents a schematic survey of the integral reading act, describes the functions of each key component, and outlines the specific skilled behaviors frequently used to implement the reading acts of secondary pupils and adults.

## THE COMPONENTS OF THE INTEGRAL READING ACT

To use printed sources effectively at the secondary school or adult levels, the reader must not only master a variety of individual specific reading behaviors, he must also selectively integrate those needed to satisfy the needs of the situation into a pattern of purposeful behavior.[1,2] We shall call this generalized pattern of reading behavior, which begins with the reader's immediate state of readiness and extends through his reaction to the meaning of the printed source, *the integral reading act*.

A model of the integral reading act is presented in Figure 4. Such a model provides us with a useful instructional overview of the act — a schematic analogy whose function is to identify the significant components and to illustrate their relationships. The model and its associated reader behaviors form the operational construct of reading to which the remainder of this text relates reading programs, instructional strategies, and assessment tactics.

The five key components of this generalized act of reading consist of: (1) *reader readiness*, that composite of personal reader resources and accumulated skills and experiences which prepare the reader to cope with the meaning and produce the behaviors necessary to implement the act; (2) *situational reading set*, that immediate predisposition of the reader — the interaction of his drives, specific purposes, and enabling perceptual processes with the reading environment and the material to be read — which determines the strength and the manner in which the reader undertakes the particular reading act; (3) *decoding*, the conversion of graphic word forms and textual language structures into literal meaning; (4) *purposeful interpretation*, the selective and flexible derivation of the larger and/or deeper meaning of the message as determined by the reader's purposes and enabled through the coordinated use of specific interpretive responses; and (5) *reaction* of the reader to the meaning and style of the message in the form of application, creativity, assimilation, and/or affective involvement.

Each of these components is an essential but flexibly employed segment of the total reading act. Each satisfies an enabling function of reading. The maturing reader will draw upon a number of specific behaviors to implement each component. These component behaviors need to be mastered through instruction and practice in their specific skills and knowledges, as well as through guided combined use in larger reading tasks. The components are separated and placed in linear sequence in Figure 4 to facilitate explanation of the total reading act. In actual reading, the components and their contributing behaviors are continuous, integrated, frequently instantaneous, and multidirectional — for that is how we perceive and react to written language stimuli. It is through guidance in numerous and varied reading situations that the reader learns to master the act and its processes, as well as to employ them selectively to satisfy different purposes.

### Reader Readiness

In its broadest sense, the term *readiness* refers to a general state of individual preparedness to make an appropriate response to a situation. It draws upon those pertinent motivations and those behavioral resources which the individual has available to learn or to perform a particular act or task.[3] Reader readiness as applied to the integral reading act consists of the state of reader preparedness to deal meaningfully with a mature reading task.

#### General Readiness Factors

Reader readiness is composed of general and specific factors. The general factors consist of those broad developmental characteristics and behavioral dynamics which comprise the reader's general potential for dealing with the reading situation. The motivational forces and personal characteristics of the reader — physical, mental, emotional, and experiential — discussed in Chapter Two represent the significant elements of general readiness. The more complex the ideas of the message, the more involved the writer's language and structure, the

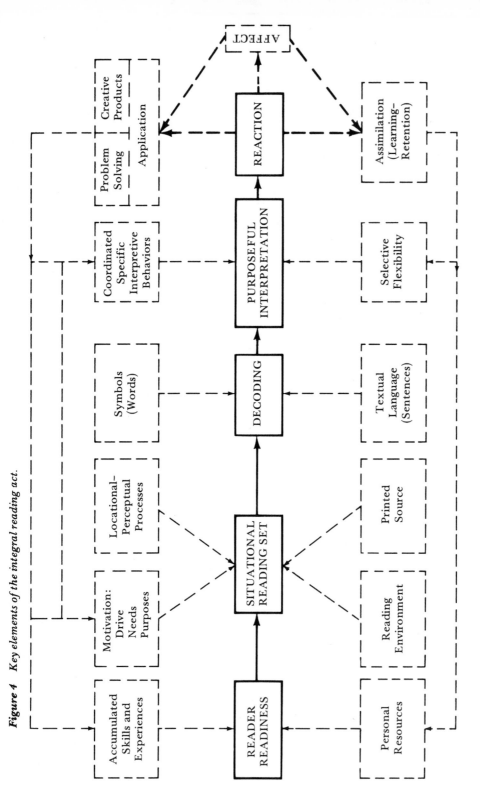

*Figure 4*  *Key elements of the integral reading act.*

more demanding the task of the reader—the more the reader must draw upon this general potential for reading.

What does readiness mean in the particular secondary reading situation? A tenth-grade biology class is assigned a chapter in the text to read. Those with the most adequate general reading readiness—intellectual and social maturity, personal adjustment, general motivation to learn, control of English, broad background in referential experiences, a normal developmental mastery of reading skills and knowledges, etc.—start the chapter with the greater probability of understanding, assimilating, and applying its meaning. But among those with adequate *general* reading readiness in this class, there will be some who lack *specific* readiness, and because of this, either perform inadequately on the assignment or struggle with it in an inefficient and frustrating manner. Of course, those who are inadequate in general reading readiness have a high probability of being deficient in specific readiness for this assignment.

### Specific Readiness Factors

Specific readiness factors consist of those skills and experiences which the reader must command in order to read a particular written selection. Specific readiness usually will include a general understanding of most of the special concepts and processes which figure in the selection, some prior acquaintance with the terminology and explanatory or argumentative format employed, and a mastery of the particular reading skills, knowledges, and attitudes required to meet the predetermined reading purposes or those purposes which emerge during the reading act. The specific readiness needed for a particular selection is determined in part by the immediate general readiness of the reader, in part by the nature of the reading selection, and in part by the objectives to be achieved through reading.

Some of the factors which would bear upon a tenth-grader's specific readiness for the reading assignment of a chapter in a biology text might include: (1) the degree of match between the pupil's level of reading competence and the readability (difficulty level) of the text; (2) the pupil's attitude toward biology, textbook reading, or the teacher; (3) the pupil's familiarity with such text terms as "intrauterine," "embryo," and "cephalocaudal," as well as with such assignment phraseology as "Develop a tabular description which interrelates infant behavior with major growth stages"; (4) the psychophysical state of the pupil at that reading moment, e.g., fatigue from loss of sleep, depression over parental marital difficulties, or discomfort from flu symptoms; and (5) the pupil's understanding of the explanatory organizational structure implied by the writer and the reasoning processes needed to interpret it.

The instructor can do a good deal to improve specific readiness for the particular reading act—for example, by developing interest in the selection, by providing specific purposes for reading, by teaching the technical vocabulary, and by previewing the organizational structure of the selection or chapter. By so doing, the probabilities of pupil success in both reading and related learning are increased considerably. Understanding of the prevailing general state of readiness of the pupil(s) will aid the instructor in the appropriate determination of the reading–learning assignment. Also, an understanding of some of the instructional tactics for readying pupils for the specific reading task will greatly facilitate the reading and learning product. A number of such tactics are presented in Chapters Five through Eight.

### Situational Reading Set

Psychologists consider "set" as a prerequisite for adaptive motor, perceptual, and/or mental responses. A *set* is a condition of the individual which predisposes him to approach a particular situation in a selectively determined manner.[4]

*Reading set*, as a component of the integral reading act, is an extension of specific reader readiness. It is influenced by both general and specific readiness conditions. Reading set serves to focus the readiness state of the reader for the actual reading response; it triggers off the perceptual responses necessary to decoding, interpreting, and reacting to the printed material. To the degree to which it is specified, reading set guides the performance of the mature reader. The flexible mature reader will adjust his reading set or sets as he obtains feedback from his contact with the reading material. Without reading set, it is unlikely the reader will initiate the reading act in a forthright manner, pursue it to interpretation and reaction, or having done so, determine whether his reading responses were satisfactory.

### Reader State: Drive and Purpose

In school or out, the reading act, to be successful, must satisfy some reader need. As early as 1917, Edward Thorndike established that lack of reading purpose was a major factor contributing to erroneous reading performance; the reader needs a set against which he can examine the feedback of meaning produced by his reading activity.[5] Subsequent research has confirmed the crucial importance of reader set for the initiation of the act itself, as well as for the effective pursuit of the writer's meaning.[6,7]

The general affective state of the reader (his needs, interests, and attitudes) will influence his reading drive, and thus will influence the nature of his performance. How the reader feels about the reading situation can exert either a positive or a negative impact upon the strength and direction of his reading thrust. In turn, the nature of this reading thrust becomes a factor in determining the accuracy, efficiency, appropriateness, and enjoyment of reader interpretation.

By the time a pupil reaches secondary school, he has some established attitudes and interests where reading is concerned. A ninth–grade classroom of pupils will reflect a range of basic attitudes toward reading as reading. This could run from the positive few who see any new reading situation as intriguing or challenging to the negative extreme of those few who are predisposed to consider any reading situation as painful or boring. For the majority of the class, attitude toward reading will depend upon the content of the material and the specific reading situation. No doubt there will be some greater preference for fiction material over nonfiction. But even fiction interests and attitudes will vary, as we have seen. Among nonfiction reading, reading interests will vary with the background of the individual, but we should not be surprised that these students favor easier, shorter, more current, and more personalized material.

Likewise, variation in reader set will occur in response to the reading situation itself. Reader attitude is influenced by evaluation of personal competency to deal with anticipated reading circumstances, by interest in and prior knowledge of the reading topic, and by the instructional style of the teacher. Strength of present reading drive will be determined, in part, by previous conditioning experiences in similar instructional situations.

### Purposeful reading.

Reading purpose, well defined in terms of needed interpretation and reaction responses, aids reader set. Such a purpose may be shaped by teacher direction or self-determined by the reader's interest in the topic and conception of the reading task. If the purpose is internalized by the reader, and if it is readily attained through reading the selection, it usually produces better interpretation of the content. This seems to hold not only for that meaning which is most pertinent to the given purposes but also to related content meaning.[8] Definite broad purposes are more likely to produce broad understanding of the material, while specific purposes produce specific understandings. The reader's performance is improved by a sharpening of set, including both general and specific purposes.[9]

The ability to define reading purposes in terms of needed meaning and to connect those purposes with their pertinent interpretive skills is vital to mature reading behavior. The mature reader attempts to determine these purposes as early as possible in the reading act. If the topic and material are somewhat unfamiliar, the mature reader will sharpen and otherwise modify these purposes as he gets a better feel of the actual content. Specific reader purpose is essential to precise interpretation of substantial content. Flexibility in setting purposes and adjusting reading attack to meet those purposes is characteristic of the mature reader.

Precise reading set is a good deal more important to the effective reading and the learning of assigned content than some secondary teachers seem to realize. Many secondary pupils are not mature readers, and thus, such generalized assignments as "Read Chapter Ten for the next class" do little to encourage a positive attitude or to improve precision and efficiency in interpretation and assimilation of meaning. Judicious attention to readiness and to providing specific direction through the reading assignment or reading-study guide can do much to improve the reading act of any secondary reader. It is essential that the faltering or unmotivated reader receive such assistance.

### Initiating Behaviors

Beyond his general drive and specific purposes, the reader must initiate contact with the reading material. How he may do this will vary somewhat with his objectives, the situation, and his learned skills. The mature reader is more selectively efficient in how he opens his reading attack than is the less competent reader. Initial contact utilizes two types of skilled behaviors—locational and perceptual.

**Locational behaviors.** The mature use of the integral reading act is to make purposeful and effective use of printed sources, whatever and wherever they may be. The integral reading act always requires some locational behavior, through larger library search behaviors to locate pertinent sources and/or through specific content search of the sources located. In either case, these locational processes should be purposeful, selective, and as efficient as possible.

Locational reading behaviors, like other reading behaviors, are comprised of learned knowledges, attitudes, and skilled psychomotor responses. The pupil not only must learn what resources the library may contain and how to go about using them, but he should develop attitudes which compel him to do this searching when necessary. Likewise, when he has used the library card catalog or the *Reader's Guide to Periodical Literature* to locate the reading source reasonably pertinent to his need, he now must selectively search (scan, skim-read, or rapidly read) the identified material for the specific information with which he is concerned. Locational behaviors become essential to the targeting of the specific reading act—regardless of whether the pupil must search for books, magazines, or references pertinent to his need or whether he must search in materials provided by the teacher.

### Specific Perceptual Input

*Perception* may be defined as that psychological process by which we select, organize, and otherwise interpret sensory stimulation so that it becomes meaningful. In this definition, we can see the intimate relationship between perception and symbolic behavior. It also becomes apparent that perception is essential to effective reading behavior in the processing of graphic symbols and text to obtain the conceptual meaning represented by those symbols.[10]

A perceptual act begins with selective attention. Out of the host of stimuli which rather simultaneously assail his receptors, the individual must determine those stimuli to which to attend and those to be suppressed. The organization of the stimuli into meaningful patterns and units begins with the selection of word cues, and gestalt should follow closely. The organization of the stimuli into perceptual units requires the efficient and integrated use of three perceptual processes: (1) *discrimination*, detecting similarities and/or differences in stimuli (*house* is not *mouse* or *horse* or *home*); (2) *synthesis*, blending separate stimuli into meaningful whole units (h-o-u-s-e is *house*); and (3) *generalization*, forming classes of highly similar stimuli and responding to any member of the class in a similar manner, e.g., HOUSE, house, HoUsE, *house*, and *house*.

Essentially, this is how the reader comes to deal with written words, the basic graphic perceptual units of reading. By synthesis, discrimination, and generalization, a word becomes a perceptual unit recognized by its individual visual characteristics. But it is not useful in reading until it achieves symbol status, i.e., can evoke its conventional referent meaning in the reader's response. This broader perceptual act of associated meaning draws upon the experiential background of the reader. One can hardly associate meaning with "chandelier" unless he has had a direct or vicarious experience with such a means of lighting. The significance of a rich experiential background to language perception cannot be overestimated.

Unless he is seriously deficient in reading or has serious visual or auditory sensory problems, the secondary school pupil should have achieved a basic mastery of the perceptual processes of discrimination, synthesis, and generalization. It is more likely that some secondary pupils will encounter difficulty with certain reading materials because they lack the experience or language background necessary to associate the appropriate referent meaning with the symbol form. Persistent errors in general perception of word forms call for visual, auditory, and reading diagnosis by those trained in such matters. Efficiency in general perceptual association will be increased by instructional readiness for the needed terms prior to reading and by instructor aid during reading. When a student has persistent difficulty with terms and concepts in a particular reading source, it would be wise to rematch him with a source for which he has better background.

## Reading Situation

A reader's set seldom operates in splendid isolation. It is influenced by the physical or psychological environment in which it occurs. The printed source to be read is a significant aspect of the larger reading situation.

*Reading environment.* General behavior is shaped by the physical setting, objects, and persons which are present, or which the individual perceives to be present, when the behavior occurs. This is no less true of reading behavior. Who of us does not

remember misreading, under the pressure of time or circumstance, a piece of material which we ordinarily could understand? How many times has a confusing exam question become disconcertingly clear—after walking away from the testing place? How much more satisfying and complete the reading of a novel or short story when settled for an hour or two in one's favorite reading place than when read in the dentist's office or when a few minutes are sprung free during a frenetic day's tasks. The reading or content class setting has an influence upon the set of the reader. Whether this set aids or detracts from the reading can be influenced a good deal by the teacher's structuring of the classroom reading conditions and the nature of the teacher-pupil relationship in that setting.

*The printed source.* The material one reads is a critical part of the reading situation as well as the target of one's specific reading processes. Whether the needed source is readily available in the classroom or school library significantly influences the operational success of the reading act. The nature of the material will influence the reader's drive and should shape his specific reading attack. Some materials we look forward to reading; others we read because, like liver, they are good for us. It is possible that one reader's "liver" may be another's cocktail pâté. Our individual reading appetite does influence the sensitivity with which we search content, and the extent of our reading hunger will contribute to the gusto with which we down most any reading material in sight. Moreover, we should not read a science textbook in the same fashion we read a narrative selection, or use a telephone directory with the same analytical attention to concepts and processes as when reading an editorial.

Deficient secondary readers seem to be more dependent on a good reading environment and on appropriate reading material than are adequate readers. Generally, inadequate readers have less reading hunger and less opportunity by which to have educated their reading tastes. A retarded reading development limits both their choice of material to read and the versatility by which they can go about reading in the source. And they are sensitive to reading environment—more easily distracted and more open to ego injury. The anxieties and defensiveness of these youngsters can be changed. But this is not likely if teachers and administrators fail to recognize the power of the reading environment and printed source upon the reading learning and performance of these pupils—and fail to make appropriate adjustments in the school reading situation.

The significance of the reading situation is not limited to the inadequate reader, however. The materials the school makes available, how the teacher aids the pupil in locating materials appropriate to his need, and the way the teacher shapes the environment and the purposes for which the pupil reads will have considerable impact upon whether and how any pupil handles the integral reading act.

## Decoding

Decoding is a decisive component of the integral reading act. In effect, decoding initiates the interpretation process. Through *decoding*, the reader arrives at the literal meaning of the textual statements (words and sentences) constructed by the writer, and literal meaning serves as the vehicle for conveying higher (or deeper) levels of meaning.[11] Decoding in itself seldom satisfies the interpretive purposes of the mature reader, and a narrow fixation on decoding words and sentences can interfere with efficient interpretation of the writer's greater meaning. But the reading act will break down if the reader cannot handle decoding tasks in a satisfactory manner. The following pages of this section discuss the essential processes of decoding: the word-oriented abilities of developing a sight vocabulary, the recognition and analysis of words, the ocular-motor processing of words in context, the reconstruction of the stated meaning of the writer's sentences, and in most situations, processing the literal serial-order meaning of successive sentences in textual language.

### Word Abilities in Reading

In most reading situations, the decoding of words and the decoding of sentences are highly interdependent. Word decoding is essential to sentence decoding, and the form and meaning of sentence context contribute substantially to word decoding.[12] The mature reader usually recognizes the familiar words he encounters by their combined visual cues. He will be aided in this by the sentence structure he perceives and the sentence meaning he has anticipated.[13] When the mature reader encounters an unfamiliar or unknown word, he will fall back upon his slower, more systematic techniques of word analysis.

Decoding is dependent upon the perception, learning, and information processing of printed symbols by the reader. In the language of reading instruction this involves such competencies as the development of an adequate sight vocabulary and the mastery of word recognition and word analysis procedures. Taken together, these comprise the basic word abilities of reading. When combined with sentence reading skills, these word abilities enable the reader to decode the literal meaning of the writer's statements.

Defined briefly, the reader's *sight vocabulary* consists of those words, form and meaning, which he has learned and with which he is so familiar that he perceives their denotative, and usually their connotative meaning, immediately upon encountering them in print. *Word recognition* abilities consist of those learned procedures (skills and knowledges) which enable him immediately to perceive (recognize the meaning of) the words as graphic units—a process necessary to activating his sight vocabulary. *Word analysis* abilities consist of those learned procedures (skills and knowledges) which enable the reader to analyze, rather systematically, the pronunciation and/or meaning of those words with which he is not familiar or which he otherwise fails to "recognize" immediately. It bears repeating that in the successful perception of individual words in context, the reader usually will make use of context meaning clues as well as of individual word perception.

We shall consider instructional tactics for developing word abilities in reading in Chapter Nine. Our concern here is to identify their key characteristics as fundamental reading processes.

*Sight vocabulary.* As indicated above, a sight vocabulary consists of that bank of words which the reader has learned and reinforced through usage so that they are immediately recognizable upon contact in print. A close interdependent relationship exists between word recognition abilities and sight vocabulary. Word recognition techniques are relatively useless unless the words to be recognized have been learned as recognizable units. On the other hand, there is no great advantage in developing a "sight" vocabulary unless the reader can and does use those abilities necessary to recognize immediately the form and meaning of words. Both are necessary to the fluent and flexible pursuit of meaning in the printed context.

In the earlier stages of reading development, the pupil is dependent upon the teacher and controlled instructional materials for associating and reinforcing word forms with meaning or with sound and meaning. As the pupil's reading tasks and contacts expand, it becomes impossible to teach him every word he needs or to limit his reading material to that which uses only words which have been taught. Fortunately, the reader gains increasing independence in word recognition and analysis abilities during his elementary years of instruction. And as he repeatedly comes in contact with new word forms and meaning through his school and personal reading, he adds substantially to his sight-reading vocabulary. He will continue to need help with key unfamiliar words in instructional reading, particularly in content area sources. Of course, review of key vocabulary and the selection of instructional materials with reasonable new vocabulary loads will improve vocabulary learning, interpretation, and content learning.

Decoding involves associating the word form with its appropriate meaning. Thus the development of sight vocabulary must not ignore word meaning. Since some words have more than one referent, appropriate meaning implies that the mature reader's meaning vocabulary should have depth as well as breadth. That is, he should be able to select from several possible meanings that which satisfies the semantic circumstances in which it is employed by the writer.

*Word recognition.* Word recognition behaviors are those which enable the reader to identify the graphic word upon bringing it within perceptual focus. Word recognition involves instantaneous perception; the maturing reader should "recognize" a familiar word in one-fourth to one-fifth of a second. Such perceptual efficiency is necessary to help the reader maintain a fluent and continuous processing of contextual meaning. Word recognition becomes a nearly automatic perceptual reflex once the reader has developed the ability to anticipate meaning, has a sight vocabulary large enough to permit ready use of his word recognition techniques, and can make use of selected recognition cues of the word.

In combination with general meaning and context clues, the mature reader will recognize words by certain individual visual characteristics. These will include certain dominant letters such as ascenders (b or t) and descenders (y or j); small letter combinations (*oo* as in boot or *ain* as in staining); familiar word parts such as known prefixes, roots, and suffixes; and the general configuration of the word. Usually, the reader will employ most of these perceptual cues more or less simultaneously, although he may draw more heavily upon anticipated meaning and word beginnings in uncomplicated context and where the word form is familiar.[14]

*Word analysis.* Those reader behaviors employed to unlock the pronunciation, meaning, or both pronunciation and meaning of unknown or unfamiliar words encountered while reading are classified as word analysis skills. They are an essential part of the resources of the independent reader and are developmentally necessary to attaining maturity in reading. They are utilized heavily during the primary and early intermediate grades when the reader has yet to amass a sizable sight-word vocabulary. Also, word analysis behaviors are needed by the mature reader as a backup for word recognition—to analyze those words which are unknown or on which some recognition confusion has occurred.

The *analysis* of individual words differs from the *recognition* of individual words in three essential ways. (1) Word analysis is necessary for dealing perceptually with unfamiliar words, but it is not required for identifying familiar words. (2) Word analysis usually consists of synthetic left-to-right identification of word parts applied rather systematically to reconstruct the whole of the pronunciation and/or meaning of the unrecognized word. (3) As systematic synthetic procedures, word analysis techniques usually take much longer to arrive at the decoded meaning of the word than word recognition techniques, and hence, are not advisable with familiar words which are quickly identified with word recognition skills.

The reader utilizes enabling skills to arrive at the recognition and/or analysis of words. He employs *phonic* and/or *structural analysis* to attack unrecognized words. The reader makes use of *context* form and meaning clues to support both word recognition and analysis. And he resorts to *word references* when authoritative support is needed in the analysis of pronunciation or meaning.

*Phonic analysis*. Phonic word attack consists of those behaviors necessary to the synthetic pronunciation or "sounding" of the unknown word by vocally or subvocally producing the sounds of the individual letters, phonograms, and/or syllables. Usually these are fused in a left-to-right sequential manner. In the language of linguists, phonic analysis is possible because the reader has learned to make graphemic-phonemic associations and to phonetically synthesize these individual units into the word utterance.[15] Instructionally, "phonics" consists of mastering individual letter form-sound associations, combined letter sound-form associations (phonograms and syllables), and learning certain rules which govern shifts in vowel and combined letter sounds, silent letters, and accent.[16]

Developmentally and operationally, phonic analysis is the most fundamental and least efficient of the word skills. The mature reader utilizes it only when more efficient word recognition or word analysis techniques fail to unlock the unknown word. This should not imply that phonic analysis is foolproof. Many English words are phonetically inconsistent, i.e., the same letter and letter combinations represent different sounds in different words and certain sounds may be represented by different letters and letter combinations. Some otherwise capable pupils have unusual difficulty learning phonics. However, there is enough language consistency to make developmental instruction in phonic analysis useful in the elementary grades.[17]

*Structural analysis*. As its name implies, structural analysis consists of arriving at the pronunciation and/or meaning of an unfamiliar word by analyzing it, then synthetically reconstructing it from such word structure units as prefixes, roots, and endings or suffixes, or, in the case of compound words, by combining the known words. Structural analysis is most applicable where the word is composed of more than one meaning unit which the reader can recognize as such.

Structural analysis (and synthesis) may occur at two different levels: at the word pronunciation level and at the constructed word meaning level. Where mature reading is concerned, the use of structural analysis to arrive at meaning in addition to pronunciation is desirable. For example, a reader encounters for the first time the word *reconstituting* in the context of his reading. By structural analysis he can associate the sound units with each of its major parts (re-constitut(e)-ing) and, blending them together, arrive at the pronunciation of the whole word. This will help, in itself, if the meaning of *reconstituting* is a part of his listening-meaning vocabulary. If it is not, it will be immensely helpful to work out its meaning by structural analysis [e.g., "the act (*ing*) of composing (*constitute*) again (*re*)"]. Because structural analysis is more efficient than phonic analysis for arriving at the pronunciation of words, and because it is useful in the analysis of the meaning of unknown words, it is a more effective word analysis technique than phonic analysis for maturing readers.

*The use of word reference sources.* The text glossary, the dictionary, the thesaurus, and technical word sources are helpful in arriving at the pronunciation and meaning of unrecognized English, foreign, technical, or phonetically inconsistent words. The mature reader needs to know how to locate words efficiently in such sources, as well as how to utilize the special information they provide. Reference sources as a means of word attack suffer two major disadvantages: they take time and thus may interrupt the concentration and interpretive thrust of the reader, and for the immature reader, the written information provided in these sources may be as difficult to read and understand as the unknown word itself. As a means of word attack, reference sources should be utilized as supplementary aids.

*Context clues in word perception.* Using context clues to anticipate word meaning is a most efficient aid to the recognition and analysis of words. Perhaps that is why adults depend upon it more than any other single word ability. Understandably, the mature reader will need to supplement it with some form of individual word perception.

McCullough has identified a number of context clues which will aid the reader in word recognition, word analysis, and the appropriate selection of denotative or connotative meaning.[18] In addition to such general meaning clues as topic, setting, and graphic illustration, these include specific meaning clues provided by the sentence structure: (1) linguistic and life experience clues—"The *injured* dog whined *sadly*"; (2) comparison or contrast clues—"Joe gave up, *but* Bill **persisted**"; (3) synonym clues provided through parallel structure—"The team *not only* wanted to play, they were **anxious** to get underway"; (4) summary of several ideas presented—"*Nothing* moved. *Nothing* grew. It seemed completely **barren**"; (5) mood clues—"The *bright* lights and the sounds of *happy* people began to **elevate** Ann's spirits"; (6) definition clues—"Albert's responses *continued* to be *so angry* that there could be little doubt he was **hostile** to the change";

and (7) familiar expression or idiomatic clues—"As wild as a March **hare**."

Several other classifications of context clues have been published which contain much in common with McCullough's seven basic types. Artley has added topographical clues (e.g., abbreviations, punctuation, parentheses, etc.) as a useful set of context aids.[19] Perhaps the most extensive classification is that of Ames, who identified fourteen patterns of context clues as derived from the study of mature readers: (1) language experience or familiar expression, (2) modifying phrases or clauses, (3) definition or description, (4) connecting or serial words, (5) comparison or contrast, (6) synonyms, (7) tone or mood, (8) referral, (9) association clues, (10) main idea–detail paragraph organization, (11) question-answer paragraph organization, (12) preposition clues, (13) nonrestricting clues or appositive phrases, and (14) cause-effect pattern of sentence and paragraph organization.[20]

Word perception is a critical behavior in decoding. The individual who has substantial difficulty in learning to perceive and symbolically process individual words is very likely to become a problem reader. This does not imply that reading or decoding consists merely of serial association of meaning with isolated words as one encounters them in print. Among other things, the reader must master ocular-motor coordination to sequence rapidly and accurately his perception of visual symbols as they appear in written context in order to support and confirm that larger meaning that he generates from the writer's textual statements.

### Eye Movement Behavior in Reading

Taylor has termed the acquired behavior pattern of the eyes that accompanies visual perception during the reading of continuous context the "fundamental reading skill."[21] This is a finely synchronized response to printed language as demonstrated by mature readers. Eye movement in reading is a product of certain learned ocular-motor responses which are coordinated with that psycholinguistic and information processing the reader employs in the search for meaning in the written material. The interrelationship between efficient ocular-motor behavior and comprehension in reading has been well established.[22] An examination of the fundamental elements of this symbol processing should add to our understanding of the general nature of the reading act.

*Fundamental characteristics.* As early as 1879, Javal determined that eye movement during reading was saccadic, i.e., the reader's eyes jump along a line of print in a series of stop-and-go movements. The "stops" have been labeled *fixations* and the "go" as *interfixative movement.* Total reading time on a particular selection is composed of the sum of the time spent in fixation and in movement. Only the fixations are perceptually useful to the reader; he cannot take in meaningful sensation during the blur of the interfixative movement.

The *duration of fixation* is the length of time the eyes pause to take in perceptual cues. The high school-adult reader spends much more time in fixation than he does in movement. The average fixation lasts about one-fourth of a second for the mature reader, while the average movement time takes about two-hundredths of a second. The interfixative movement is largely a reflexive response; the speed of the interfixative movement is not influenced by reader intent or by training. Training can shorten habitual tendencies in duration of fixation.

Another characteristic of eye movement behavior during reading is the *regression.* A regressive eye movement is a reverse movement the reader makes to refixate on some point of print previously covered. Contrary to general belief, some regressions are natural by-products of the reading act; all readers make regressions. Inadequate readers, however, do regress more frequently than adequate readers, and seriously disabled readers do so excessively — either because of the reading difficulty encountered or as a habit.

Regressions are caused by: (1) reader problems with meaning (e.g., interference with reader attention, rechecking a point not clearly understood, or comparing two or more points in the writer's argument); (2) problems in word recognition; (3) deficiencies in visual acuity or coordination (more often seen in beginning readers or readers with visual or neurological difficulty); (4) poorly learned reading habits; or (5) insecurity as evidenced in anxious or disabled readers.[23] Of these, the regressions caused by issues of meaning plus occasional word recognition difficulty are normally experienced by mature readers an average of once per line of print.

One of the characteristics of symbol perception during reading upon which eye movement research has cast some light is *span of reading recognition,* or the average number of words or word parts which can be perceived during the eye stops (fixations.) Contrary to assumptions of some reading teachers, the visual recognition span during reading is much smaller than the reader's oral phrasing span and smaller than his span of anticipated meaning.

During the early learning-to-read period, the reader averages two fixations per word, giving him an average span of recognition of about half a word. (And these would be smaller, simpler words.) During high school, the reader's average span of recognition increases to approximately one longer word per fixation. The better adult reader seems to have a recognition span ceiling of approximately one and one-half words during continuous reading. Despite the advertising claims of commercial speed reading companies, no solid research evidence has been produced to show that training can increase this maximum in typical prose reading.

*Differences and development.* Individual differences in eye movement efficiency are evident among readers. Some read with fewer fixations, regress less frequently, and/or spend less time in perceptual fixation than other readers. As a consequence, they read a selection more rapidly.

Ordinarily, readers demonstrating greater power of comprehension read with greater eye movement efficiency than those with lesser comprehension. Better readers also reveal greater flexibility in their eye movement performance; that is, they reveal greater adjustment of their perceptual behavior to changes in reading purpose and to changes in the meaning and readability of the material.[24] Efficiency in reading, and thus in eye movement behavior, can be improved through training. However, such improvement is gained more readily and lasts longer when the training is concerned with improving general efficiency of interpretation, rather than isolated training in visual perception, as such.

Individual differences in reading eye movement behavior also are evident in developmental norms. The results presented in Figure 5 were compiled by Educational Developmental Laboratories from data gathered on more than 12,000 cases.[25] The eye movement data included here are for individuals obtaining a reading comprehension score of 70 percent or better. This explains the "rate of comprehension" entry. The rate scores in terms of words per minute should be used advisedly, since rate obtained on relatively short selections read before the camera is not directly transferable to context situations where the reader is free to read selectively. However, the average performance on rate and the specific eye movement behavior are useful in demonstrating developmental growth in these characteristics. The subjects of this survey did not have special training in reading efficiency. The norms change rather notably during the elementary school years and begin to level off during the secondary school years.

*Other findings.* Eye movement research has produced additional useful evidence about perception in reading and the factors which influence it. Among such findings is evidence that visual perceptual behavior is more efficient when reading silently than when reading orally, at least after the reader has mastered the basic mechanics of decoding. Eye movement behavior is less efficient when the reading material is more complex or otherwise presents problems of interpretation, when the purposes for reading are more taxing intellectually, and when the reader feels undue pressure to perform excellently. Finally, eye movement research corroborates other objective evidence that words may be recognized as whole units from certain select perceptual cues and that this is necessary to efficient continuous symbol processing in the reading of context.

### Decoding the Meaning of Sentences

A written sentence is a group of words grammatically and syntactically arranged to constitute a grammatically complete unit of meaning. The basic sentence form is a predicative statement, in that it associates an activator with a related action (past, present, or future). The mature reader usually encounters more complicated sentence forms in his reading. But the minimal structural requirements from which more compound and complex sentences are generated are a noun phrase (activator) and

**Figure 5**   *Averages for measurable components of the fundamental reading skill.* [S. E. Taylor, H. Frackenpohl, and J. L. Pettee, *Grade Level Norms for the Components of the Fundamental Reading Skill,* Research Bulletin 3 (New York: Educational Developmental Laboratories, a Division of McGraw–Hill Book Company, 1960).]

| Grade* | 1 | 2 | 3 | 4 | 5 | 6 | 7 | 8 | 9 | 10 | 11 | 12 | College |
|---|---|---|---|---|---|---|---|---|---|---|---|---|---|
| Fixations/100 words | 224 | 174 | 155 | 139 | 129 | 120 | 114 | 109 | 105 | 101 | 96 | 94 | 90 |
| Regressions/100 words | 52 | 40 | 35 | 31 | 28 | 25 | 23 | 21 | 20 | 19 | 18 | 17 | 15 |
| Average span of recognition (word) | .45 | .57 | .65 | .72 | .78 | .83 | .88 | .92 | .95 | .99 | 1.04 | 1.06 | 1.11 |
| Average duration of fixation (sec) | .33 | .30 | .28 | .27 | .27 | .27 | .27 | .27 | .27 | .26 | .26 | .25 | .24 |
| Rate with comprehension (wpm) | 80 | 115 | 138 | 158 | 173 | 185 | 195 | 204 | 214 | 224 | 237 | 250 | 280 |

*First-grade averages are those of pupils capable of reading silently material of 1.8 difficulty with at least 70 percent comprehension. Above grade 1, averages are those of students at midyear, reading silently material of midyear difficulty with at least 70 percent comprehension.

a verb phrase (action). Obtaining the essential unit meaning of the sentence in its various forms and transformations is a critical task of reader decoding.

*Kernel sentences.* Identifying this basic activator-action or subject-predicate relationship is a first-order task of sentence decoding. Since the subject of the sentence contains a noun or a noun cluster and the predicate contains a verb or a verb cluster, we may diagram this basic structure of the English sentence which the reader must identify as:

$$S \text{ (sentence)} = NC \text{ (noun cluster)} + VC \text{ (verb cluster)}$$

Through oral language experiences, school language instruction, and writing-reading experiences, the reader will repeatedly encounter certain common variations in this basic sentence. In his early publications Chomsky termed these common variations "kernel" sentences.[26] Such kernel sentences probably hold a psychological priority in our interpretive processes.[27]

Four basic (kernel) sentence patterns commonly are identified in linguistic literature. Each consists of a noun cluster and a verb cluster. The kernel sentences vary in their verb forms and/or in the complementary noun or adjectival structure. Each may involve the optional use of an adverb. Some examples for the four basic sentences are presented below.

*1.* The first pattern consists of a subject; a verb form of *to be*; a complement (noun or adjective); and an optional adverb.

| NC | + | VC | | |
|---|---|---|---|---|
| S | | V | C | Adv. |
| The woman | | is | an informer | (today). |
| The man | | will be | a traveler | (tonight). |

*2.* The second pattern includes a subject; an intransitive verb which does not require an object; and an optional adverb.

| NC | + | VC | |
|---|---|---|---|
| S | | Vi | Adv. |
| The waiter | | serves | (reluctantly). |
| The diner | | tips | (minimally). |

*3.* The third pattern involves a subject; a transitive verb needing an object; an object; and an optional adverb.

| NC | + | VC | | |
|---|---|---|---|---|
| S | | Vt | O | Adv. |
| The government | | requires | money | (constantly). |
| A taxpayer | | avoids | payment | (occasionally). |

*4.* This fourth pattern consists of a subject; a copulative verb (linking verb taking a complement); a complement; and an optional adverb.

| NC | + | VC | | |
|---|---|---|---|---|
| S | | Vc | C | Adv. |
| The old man | | seems | better | (today). |
| The elbow | | looks | peculiar | (anytime). |

*Generating other sentence forms.* From such basic sentence patterns, the speaker or writer can generate an infinite number of sentences. He does this by changing the word forms, and/or by utilizing one or more internal sentence operations, called *transformations* — i.e., by combination, inversion, addition, deletion, and substitution. In this way, other sentence patterns may be formed; that is, the kernel string of the sentence may be expanded or changed to interrogative, negative, passive, or imperative form.

In the writing of kernel sentences and in transforming and combining them, the English writer makes use of two sets of grammatical principles — *accidence* and *syntax*. When the reader becomes familiar with these rules, he can internalize them and thus focus directly on following the writer's meaning rather than his form.[28]

*Accidence* consists of those evolved rules of usage by which we alter the form of individual words to fit language uses: (1) changing nouns to and from their singular/plural forms (*man, men*); (2) indicating possessives (*the man's tie*); (3) indicating number and tense in verbs (*I jump, he jumps, I will be jumping*); (4) adjusting the case of pronouns to fit use as subjects, objects, or possessives (*I, me, mine, my*); and (5) changing some adjectives and adverbs to indicate degree (*large, larger, largest/ wonderful, more wonderful, most wonderful*).

*Syntax* consists of the method by which we arrange words in a systematic and meaningful manner. Of primary syntactical significance to the reader is the manner in which language function words are employed to fill out the meaning carried basically by the content or referent meaning words. The basic building blocks of a sentence consist of those words which have *content*, or *referential*, meaning: cat, dog, enemies, peaceful, silent, coexistence. A sentence composed only of content words usually is awkward, austere, and limited in meaning. These content blocks need linguistic filler and cement in the form of grammatical function words:

The cat and dog, once enemies, now live in peaceful if not silent coexistence.

Content words usually carry the fundamental referential meaning of the sentence. Functional words usually serve grammatical meaning purposes.

In traditional language terminology, the content words (or their collocations) are known as nouns, verbs, adjectives, and adverbs. The function words which serve such grammatical purposes as modifying, elaborating, or transposing meaning provide structure cues for the reader. These grammatical function words consist of the articles, auxiliary verbs, prepositions, and conjunctions. Present–day linguists now use a varied terminology to refer to such structural elements.

Smith, Goodman, and Meredith suggest that function words may be further delineated by their language operations. Figure 6 gives their listing of eight operational groupings of the function words with the approximate number of words per group according to Fries.[29]

*Other sentence reading tasks.* A notable advantage of the listener in dealing with a speaker's utter-

**Figure 6**   *Function words in language operations* [From E. B. Smith, K. S. Goodman, and R. Meredith, *Language and Thinking in the Elementary School* (New York: Holt, Rinehart and Winston, Inc., 1970, p. 150).]

| Name | Example | Number |
|------|---------|--------|
| Noun markers | *The* man came. (This group also includes possessives and cardinal numbers used in this slot. It is thus the only open-ended group of function words.) | |
| Verb markers | He *is* coming. | About 15 |
| Negative | He is *not* coming. | 1 |
| Intensifier | He may be *very* tired. | 25 |
| Conjunctions | The man *and* woman are singing *and* dancing. | 9 |
| Phrase markers | They will come *into* the house. | 12 |
| Question markers | *When* will they come? | 7 |
| Clause markers | They will call *before* they come. | 12 |

ances is that the listener is aided by the oral pitch, stress, and juncture by which the speaker conveys intensity, emphasis, breaks, and transitions of thought.[30] Also, the listener is aided by the speaker's paralanguage—the gestures, facial expressions, and body positions used to convey nuances of meaning. The writer may portray these in his accompanying description. More often, the reader, aided by his oral-aural experience, must infer these cues from contextual association and from the writer's use of punctuation and typography.

Other sentence patterns which require reader insight are those which gain meaning through their situational or the linguistic context. Derived sentences are encountered quite frequently in running context. An example of this structure upon sentence meaning is given below, where a pronoun serves meaningfully for a noun through the function of *distribution*.

> The president calmly reacted to the attack. *He* said he understood how the group felt. *He* would consider the problem at first opportunity. *He* hoped the group understood how he felt.

Also, a sentence may be semantically complete in meaning, even though it is contextually incomplete in form. Such a sentence structure is the so-called "incomplete" or elliptical form which is common in oral communication and often appears in narration.

> "When?"
> "Tomorrow, I hope!"
> "What luck!"

This points up an important consideration about sentences and thought: as important as it is for the reader to understand the meaning of a particular sentence, it is not enough! Sentence meaning is not constructed of the linear addition of word meanings, nor is the interpretation of paragraphs and larger typographical units a matter of adding the tandem meaning of the individual sentences. Unless the reader is able to perceive the sentence in its larger language-thought structure—its paragraph unit, its flow of expression, or its expository argument—the individual sentence will provide little more than a literal disjunctive meaning.

### Summary: The Decoding Competencies

Thus, to decode the literal meaning of the writer's statements, the reader will draw heavily upon both word abilities and language processing. He will need to recognize and analyze word forms with their meanings with such competence that their perceived denotative meaning will spring immediately to mind as he encounters them in print. In this he will be aided immeasurably by their language context. If he understands the basic nature of the sentence as it appears in its common variations, he will be able to meld the content and function words the writer has employed to recreate the larger predicative meaning the writer intended.

Decoding shifts subtly into the basic processes of interpretation. The mature reader does not reconstruct the literal meaning of the writer's statement in isolation of the context in which it occurs, except in rare reading situations. Usually he reads text, and the ongoing text will help him anticipate the meaning of the sentence. In recognizing or analyzing the words of the sentence while fitting them into their large predicative statement, he confirms or modifies the meaning he anticipated. Even so, he will hold the product meaning of this sentence as tentative until he has been able to check it against the statements which precede and follow.

A listing of the essential tasks of decoding would include the following:

1. Anticipation of sentence meaning in terms of general contextual setting and meaning of preceding sentences.
2. Word decoding skills, including those necessary to the recognition of familiar words, the analysis of unfamiliar words, and the development of a basic sight vocabulary.
3. Accuracy and fluency in the perceptual–motor (eye movement) behaviors of sentence reading.
4. Identification of noun phrase and verb phrase meaning relationships as they appear in kernel sentence form.
5. Recognition of the kernel structure meaning underlying sentences which have been transformed by the writer through the employment of function words, changes in sentence order, and/or "stringing" (combining) kernel sentences with expanded forms.
6. Tentative selection and modification of the most appropriate meaning for the sentence in terms of its psycholinguistic fit with prior and continuing sentence context.

## Purposeful Interpretation

Purposeful reading interpretation involves *the selective and flexible derivation of the larger and deeper meaning conveyed by the writer's message.* The cluster of behaviors which comprise the component of purposeful interpretation are but part of the closely integrated act of mature reading, which begins with reader readiness and carries through reader reaction. Purposeful interpretation fulfills a most critical function in mature reading. Perhaps more than any other component, it determines the level of sophistication as well as the specific success of the particular reading act. To better understand the functions of purposeful interpretation, we need to consider it as both reading and thought processing.

### Purpose in Reading Interpretation

In mature reading, interpretation is an act of volition; that is, it is intentional, and it is intentionally differentiated according to reader purpose and the reading situation. The selective search for meaning—to satisfy either operational, intellectual, or affective ends—is what distinguishes the function of interpretation from the literal meaning association function of decoding. When successful, the criterion of purposeful functional reading separates the literate from the illiterate and at higher levels of interpretation, contributes to the qualitative differentiation of reading maturity and functional competency. Selective purpose in interpretation is necessary to the negotiation of secondary, college, and life learning tasks.

***Reader–determined purpose.*** The essential connection between reader set and the understanding gained from reading was identified early in this century and has been corroborated by later researchers.[31] Having a purpose usually improves reader interpretation. Moreover, the nature of the reader purpose usually influences the kind of interpretation effected.[32] Ordinarily, the more precisely the reader has defined his reading purpose, the more likely he will obtain the meaning he needs, if it is available in the written material. If the needed information is not included in the material, well-developed purposes will enable the reader to ascertain that fact in a more efficient manner.

The reader may initiate his reading of serious exposition with rather well-defined purposes, and to the degree that he can do so, this will increase his reading efficiency and accuracy. The mature reader attempts to develop appropriate mental questions or hypotheses prior to intensive interpretive involvement with this material. Sometimes he may not have the background or set needed to develop specific interpretive purposes. In such cases, he may have to await some informational feedback from a preliminary overview of the material which has been motivated and guided by more general objectives.

It may be helpful to illustrate how more definite interpretive purposes may emerge during the mature reading act. While casually leafing through a professional journal, a teacher encounters an article entitled "Classroom Study Atmosphere." She starts to read it with a general set—a combination of moderate professional curiosity and a need to pass the time while waiting for a ride to school. Upon reading the introduction and scanning the article subheadings, she finds that the writer intends to make seven recommendations for improving classroom study atmosphere. Now, the teacher adjusts and sharpens her purpose by intending to identify those seven recommendations and to evaluate them in terms of her own professional situation. Sometime after getting into the decoding-interpreting processes necessary to meet these more specific purposes, she encounters two references cited by the writer as excellent sources on teacher-pupil conflicts, a problem with which this teacher has had some reason to be concerned in recent weeks. So, another purpose is added for this reading—to note down the authors, titles, and publisher sources of these two articles for later location and examination.

Of course, it is quite possible that this teacher could arrive at this article or its cited references by other routes. The article "Classroom Study Atmosphere" may have been assigned in a graduate course, say, "The Psychology of Adolescence," and the teacher may have utilized a reading-study approach with the intent to learn and retain the information to pass the summative test for this course.

Or, to write a paper for this graduate course, she may have started with a direct, precise purpose of locating information on pupil-teacher conflict. She arrives at reading "Classroom Study Atmosphere" and the two references dealing with the topic (along with others) by way of using her locational interpretive skills in conjunction with the *Educational Index* and her local professional library.

This teacher's professional reading circumstances serve as a basis for drawing several generalizations about mature reading interpretation: (1) specific reading purposes and their related interpretive behaviors may combine in a variety of ways in a particular reading situation; (2) it is possible to arrive at needed meaning by more than one interpretive approach; (3) depending upon the purpose of the reader, some interpretive approaches are more efficient than others; and (4) the mature reader needs to be flexible in attitude and skill, if she is to adjust her reading attack to meet her emerging purposes and needs.

It is not enough to teach a pupil how to carry out the skilled mechanics necessary to satisfy a teacher-given reading purpose: e.g., how to locate library sources on a topic, how to identify the key ideas of a writer's presentation, how to recognize and appreciate the use of satire, or how to make an outline summary of material read. The pupil also must learn to associate the use of these learned mechanics with those reading circumstances which require their use! It is not enough that the pupil has learned an assortment of interpretive procedures or skills. For mature reading he must be able to identify his own interpretive needs in a reading situation and to selectively draw upon those learned interpretive procedures which are most appropriate to his defined purposes.[33] Unfortunately, content and reading teacher emphasis upon fact-oriented questions has not enhanced pupil versatility and sophistication in developing purposes for reading and learning.[34]

*Interpretive behaviors.* In the interpretation of meaning, the reader may use one or more of a variety of interpretive responses. The most significant of these have been listed in the outline of specific reading behaviors presented at the end of this chapter. The breadth of interpretive possibilities may be inferred from a selected listing of some common tasks in interpretation:

1. Scanning to locate certain facts.
2. Skimming to identify key premise, reading rapidly to determine the basic framework of a selection.
3. Reading in a moderately thorough manner to satisfy emotional needs or to appreciate the writer's craftsmanship.
4. Reading intensively in order to apply written information to operational tasks.
5. Reading analytically to compare the arguments presented in several different sources dealing with the same problem.
6. Reading creatively to pictorially depict a central character in a play.
7. Reading critically to identify the presence of bias in a political handout.
8. Study-reading to learn and retain the information of importance in an assignment.

Even such a selected listing demonstrates the close interaction of the reader's specific purpose, the specific interpretive responses appropriate to that purpose, the type of reading approach (mode of reading) which facilitates the specific interpretive responses, and the implied reaction of the reader. Above all, the variety represented in this brief listing testifies to the need for flexibility in reading attack.

### Flexibility in Interpretation

Reading flexibility generally is defined as *the ability to adjust one's reading behavior to meet the conditions imposed by the reading material, the reader's purposes, and the reading situation.*[35] It is not feasible to attempt to satisfy all possible reading purposes in every reading situation. Even if it were feasible, it would not be necessary or desirable. The secondary reader must be flexible in order to adjust and refine his or her specific purpose-interpretive behaviors to achieve needed accuracy and effi-

ciency. Fact-by-fact learning and memorization of large spans of written material is an archaic academic holdover from those days when materials were few, life was sedately simple, and we knew little of the transiency of verbal learning. The myth of complete mastery of any reasonably sophisticated piece of writing has been exploded by both psychological research and the pressures of a culture changing at an ever-increasing rate.[36]

Reading flexibility necessarily involves *selectivity* in reading purpose, approach, and materials. Reading selectivity is not possible unless the reader is flexible in personal set. Reading flexibility begins with a state of reader mind—a willingness to adapt one's thinking and reading processes to the reading material and situation.

***Reading flexibility and reading rate.*** Some confusion seems to exist about the relationship between reading flexibility and reading rate.[37] One of the advantages of reading flexibility is greater reading efficiency. *Reading efficiency* involves the satisfaction of reader need with the least expenditure of reader time and energy. Quite often, reading efficiency is gained by or results in an improvement in reading rate—the amount of reading material covered per unit of time. But not always! The pupil who rapidly reads a textbook chapter but once, at a fast page-per-minute rate, and who overlooks, misinterprets, or quickly forgets a number of needed key ideas has not read efficiently. Neither has the pupil who takes many hours to memorize a chapter in a detail-by-detail manner and thereby confuses his understanding and debilitates his motivation so that he has no solid grasp of its key concepts and processes twenty-four hours later.

This is not to imply that an inverse relationship exists between reading rate and reading comprehension. They are, in fact, generally related in a positive manner; and the relationship varies with the nature and difficulty of material.[38] The correlation between rate and comprehension probably would be higher if both readers and methods of reading measurement were more selectively flexible.[39] The selective-flexible reader is efficient because he adjusts his reading approach to his material and purpose. When he does so, he usually increases his reading efficiency in terms of needed comprehension per unit of reading time or reading rate of comprehension.

### The Modes of Flexible Reading

Selective reading flexibility involves a state of reader mind, as we have seen. Freedom from personal rigidity and the ability to adjust specific reading purposes to the needed product and situation are essential to *external flexibility*, the determination of the best initial or prevailing reading approach to the entire selection, as well as to *internal flexibility*, the adjustments made in approach while reading the selection. However, reading flexibility, external and internal, is dependent upon whether the reader has learned to use several different general approaches or styles of reading. From these, he can select that approach (or combination of approaches) most likely to meet his specific reading purposes. We will refer to these general interpretive approaches as *modes of flexible reading*. Their general characteristics are described below. They are discussed in greater detail in Chapter Twelve, along with implications for instruction in reading flexibility.

Many high school and adult readers approach all reading with much the same style of attack; quite often, this amounts to attending to every word and line with the same studious attention to detail. They use this approach regardless of their specific purposes, reading circumstances, or the type and difficulty of reading material involved. The flexible mature reader, on the other hand, may employ any of six "modes," or characteristic styles, of reading attack. For some reading aims and materials he may use only one mode; in other reading situations, he may use a combination of these styles. These modes of flexible reading include *scanning, skim reading, rapid reading, personal reading, analytical-evaluative reading*, and *study reading*.

The mature reader will have these modes so under his command that he will slide from one to another in fluid transition as the content, writing style, and interpretive purpose change. However, some modes are more useful with some reading purposes and materials than with others, and the pupil must learn to select consciously the general mode of initial and/or prevailing attack which best meets his needs.

Although pupils will exhibit individual differences in the efficiency with which they use a particular mode, these modes are capable of generating different rate potentials (as determined by amount of material covered per unit of time) for most readers. This difference in rate is the overt difference in the modes most noticed by readers. However, speed or efficiency is only one factor to be considered by the reader in determining the best mode for attacking the material. Each mode implies some difference in technique of reading, and these techniques are geared to satisfying some interpretive purposes better than others, e.g., scanning to locate specific information, rapid reading to make a fast but complete overview of a selection, or analytical reading to make an in-depth study of the writer's bias. The flexible mature reader, in choosing or adjusting to a particular mode, reckons its potential for accuracy and efficiency against his interpretive purposes and the nature of the material!

*1. Scanning.* Scanning is a highly selective locational procedure which is interpretive to the extent that it finds specific information or treatments of data which either answer precise specific questions or which can be subjected to further interpretation through other modes after the target content has been located. Formally defined, scanning involves perceiving or identifying by quickly surveying a surface with the eyes or an electronic device. The reader scans by sweeping his eyes over a page searching for particular cues. Scanning is utilized in association with quick reference to typographical or text aids—headings, italicized words, numbers, outlines of content, indexes, etc.

*2. Skim reading.* Skim reading is a hybrid technique—a combination of scanning with rapid interpretation of selective segments of the reading material as topic sentences, introductions, summaries, and selective serial reading of headings. It focuses upon those elements of the content which carry the most significant information pertinent to the reader's purposes. Skim reading is useful in identifying and interpreting the writer's major generalizations when the detailed information is not of immediate importance to the reader. It may be used effectively to identify the general structure of the writer's argument. Skim reading is valuable in study situations as a preliminary or preorganizational first reading or as a review after more thorough study has been made. It differs from scanning in that it is more interpretational than locational, and it usually is employed in a survey of entire textual segments rather than focusing narrowly upon specific items.

*3. Rapid reading.* Rapid reading occupies a middle ground between the selective reading approaches of scanning and skim reading and the more thorough interpretation of *normal, analytical,* and some *study-reading* approaches. Rapid reading is not intended to result in intensive analysis or long-term retention of information. Rather, it is used to gain general understanding of a selection — its main ideas, their most important supporting details, the general argument, and a general impression of the writer's style and thinking. It is a pragmatic style of reading which accepts the conditions of limited time and the advantages of a broad interpretive set for certain reading purposes.

Rapid reading differs from skim reading in that it employs fairly continuous contact with the textual sequence of the selection. It differs from personal reading and analytical reading in that the reader's set is to satisfy some general interpretive purpose in a highly efficient manner. Ordinarily, one does not rapid-read to enjoy good prose or poetry, to retain detailed information, or to critically analyze the writer's argument. Rapid reading may increase the comprehension of the key ideas of a selection by letting the reader focus continuous and selective attention upon them. It often happens that those who have learned to read rapidly and who continue to use this approach will adapt it to their style of personal reading or will find they can increase the rate of their personal and occupational reading without loss of significant meaning.

*4. Personal reading.* As the name indicates, personal reading is our normal reading style — the one we use when satisfying some short-term functional reading purpose or when we read for relaxation, enjoyment, or general information. Personal reading may employ analytical and evaluative interpretation, but only to the extent which satisfies personal reading purposes. It should be efficient, but not to the extent that it generates stress. Ordinarily, this is the mode which the majority of the general public uses most of the time. Considerable variation in competency and efficiency will be exhibited among the personal reading performance of secondary pupils, of course. Some pupils read personally as if they were analyzing content; others read as if they were rapid-reading. Better readers demonstrate flexibility even in personal reading.

*5. Analytical-evaluative reading.* The serious reader employs some degree of analytical-evaluative reading in most of his reading. However, he is selective in his use of it as a tough-minded, detailed examination of content, for it can absorb both time and energy. Generally, the analytical-evaluative reading mode is used for reading content and purposes which require higher-level reasoning. It consists primarily of the selective utilization of those interpretive behaviors which implement logical/critical analysis of content. As a flexible mode of reading, it may be combined with other reading modes, particularly in study reading. The specific behaviors to be learned to effect this mode are identified later in this chapter, and are instructionally implemented in Chapters Eleven and Twelve.

*6. Study reading.* As used here, study reading is not just any approach to reading which happens to be used for academic purposes. Rather, it is that combination of study and reading which is directed toward the learning and selective retention of essential written content. Consciously employed, it consists of a planned attack, a learned combination of flexible modes and interpretive techniques which systematically coordinate strategies of proved usefulness in reading for understanding, learning, and retention. The most useful of such reader tactics include: (a) determining study-reading purposes,

(b) overviewing the material, (c) raising specific interpretive questions, (d) selective notation, and (e) testing or otherwise making provision for retention of information. A number of specific study-reading systems have been published in the literature. Most of these are identified by their acronyms, which are used as mnemonics and represent steps in the particular system — e.g., PQRST, EVOKER, and PANORAMA. One such system, POINT, is presented in Chapter Six.

### Interpretation as Reasoning

Carroll views reasoning as dependent upon both language and logical system: "Thinking aided by language is called reasoning, and the ability to reason depends largely on the ability to formulate steps in an inferential process in terms of language."[40] The reasoning process involves the manipulation of particulars, concepts, and generalizations in some systematic manner. Generally, this manipulation takes the form of divergent casting or such convergent systems of arrangement as time and event order sequence, induction, deduction, problem solving, and critical evaluation.

Writers seldom develop context which is pure in organizational form or logic. More often, they tend to produce paragraphs and larger units of context with mixed patterns.[41] However, most writers of nonfiction employ these arrangements, however combined, to structure their expositions. The reader needs to understand these organizational patterns, to recognize the reasoning structure of the writer when it is present, to know when it is absent or confused, to follow its implication, and to evaluate its validity.[42]

**Concept formation.** A concept is an implied classification of stimuli (experiences) which have common characteristics. Concept formation is dependent upon the process of classifying or categorizing. To classify, we take individual perceptual units (objects, people, events, etc.) and group them by some similarity in their characteristics, a process which involves generalization. To communicate these formed concepts, the writer or speaker must utilize their language labels, such as "tool," "reptile," "traffic," "parent," "liberal," "play," and "good." As these examples imply, concepts may be formed about objects, animate life, feelings, behavior, ideas, and processes.

Concepts exist at various levels of generality. The "John Smith" that political writers are so fond of using may be a San Franciscan, a Californian, an "American," a world citizen, *homo sapiens*, a primate, or simply another example of life trying to survive on this ecologically disturbed planet. Moreover, a particular unit may fit several classification systems: "The *John Smiths* are *tilting* to the *right*." The fact that concepts do exist at several levels of generality, and that writers do employ examples by way of implied generalization poses additional interpretive problems for the reader; he must "infer" the presence of the concept, pin down the level of generality as precisely as possible, and evaluate whether the writer used the concept in a valid manner.

**Denotation and connotation.** Because concepts usually have word labels, the reader becomes involved with thought processing as soon as he encounters the individual words of a sentence. He will need to identify whether the word is used as a content referent, and if so, he will need to determine whether it is employed denotatively or connotatively. A particular word may have its *denotation*: a certain set of descriptors which form its specific representation — that is, its literal, explicit identifications such as might be found in its basic dictionary definition (*snake*: a scaly, limbless reptile).

A word may also have its *connotation*: a set of generalized feelings and implied associations which it arouses for people who use it (*snake*: a dangerous, distasteful, or sneaky person). Denotations may utilize concepts as descriptors. Connotations usually depend upon an implied classification and thus upon the use of concepts. The ability to differentiate between the denotative and connotative use of terms is a fundamental requirement for careful interpretation of content. In this, the critical reader will be sensitive to the use of *stereotypes* — rigid, biased, overgeneralized connotations of individuals, groups, or beliefs.

*Generalization.* A *generalization* is usefully defined as a statement of the relationship between two or more terms or concepts. Many sentences contain generalizations. Sometimes, the generalization is implied, e.g., "Progress is our watchword." An important task for the reader is to recognize a generalization and to identify the terms or concepts being related, to associate appropriate denotative or connotative meaning with them, and then to pin down as specifically as possible the nature of the relationship between the terms or concepts. This may be a direct task of interpretation, as in recognizing the literal generalization that "Cedars belong to the conifer class of seed-bearing plants." However, when the relationship is implied and the terms are susceptible to connotation, as in "*Progress* (?) is *our* (?) *watchword* (?).", the reader has a more difficult task of *inferential* interpretation, i.e., to identify unstated relationships.

*Divergent casting.* In *divergent casting*, the writer identifies a particular situation and deals with it by relating associated events to it, or he presents a problem and explores several or a variety of associations or solutions. The assumption underlying divergent casting as a reasoning process is that more than one possible response may be appropriate to a situation or that more than one solution may exist for a problem. Frequently, the writer is concerned with exploring new possibilities or new relationships. Examples of divergent casting which the mature reader might encounter would include various forms of creative writing; analyses of individual behavior; reportorial descriptions of an event, person, or object; transcriptions of group interactions; and various forms of "brainstorming" a problem, either by the writer himself or by his recording of the actions of some group or individual.

Divergent casting sometimes is combined with other structures and may serve as a preliminary operation to convergent processes. The preliminary use of divergent casting is encouraged in scientific problem solving as a means of identifying the possible hypothesis(es) to be tested; this may be reflected in science writing and treatments of research.

*Convergent processing.* Convergent operations are more systematic and reductional than divergent casting. In convergent thinking, the writer "closes" on solutions, generalizations, and conclusions in a manner consistent with established definition and logical procedure. By basic nature or by cultural experience, people seem to be goal-oriented. They tend to be seekers of solutions in real or imaginary situations. Consequently, most written expression employs an organizational structure which uses convergence. This may take one or more of several forms, the most common of which are sequence, story, induction, deduction, critical evaluation, and problem solving.

*Sequence.* Although all written content necessarily involves linguistic and typographical sequential arrangement, *sequence* as idea structuring usually conveys a temporal, continuous, or contiguous order of events, things, or concepts. *Chronology,* a direct form of time sequencing, serves as the stated or implied organizational device of such prose forms as fiction, historical writing, biography and autobiography, and news reporting. *Contiguity* refers to physical sequencing, as in the description of the working parts of an operating engine, a report on the seating arrangements of an international conference, or a word picture of a geographical setting. *Continuity* implies a meaningful whole which is composed of a series of related units as represented in the steps in a process—the between- or within-chapter organization of a textbook, the scenario or script of a production, or a plan of operation.

Detection of the writer's use of sequence enables the reader to adjust his reading set to perceive and integrate the elements of that sequence, and to determine when or if the sequence has reached convergence in the form of present status or completion. The reader's interpretation of sequential ordering becomes more difficult when the writer reverses, combines, or otherwise convolutes sequence for purposes of style, argument, or description. Secondary pupils need instruction and practice in interpreting diverse forms of sequencing. This includes the ability to identify and differentiate between constants and variables, a working knowledge of statistical terminology, and an understanding of such concepts as cause–effect, correlation, and concomitancy.

*Story form.* Fictional prose involves more than sequence, of course. While it is not the function of this text to deal with literary interpretation and appreciation as such, prose fiction as story form is a "movable feast" partaken of by most secondary pupils and adults, and fiction does serve reading instructional purposes. Story form as an organizational structure is not as readily grasped by pupils as reading teachers seem to assume.

Parker identifies five structural elements common to most stories and recommends that their various forms should be a part of reading as well as literature education. These include *character*, the actors whose natures and actions influence the development and resolution of incident; *incident*, the dramatic treatment of the theme or plot through a pattern of related episodes which imply causality and inevitability; *time*, the cumulative ordering of the incident; *place*, the historical, geographical, and social setting of character and incident; and *mood*, the emotional tone of the work as shaped by the author's attitude and literary style.[43]

More recently, cognitive psychologists have provided empirical support for the nature of story processing and its related reading difficulties. Bower and others have confirmed that children and adults rely on story structure to understand and remember its meaning. Stories, folk tales, and drama which do not provide the following components are more difficult to interpret than those which do: (1) a setting (characters, location, and time placement), (2) a theme [the main goal of the main character(s)], (3) a plot (a series of episodes each with subgoals and related action designed to facilitate or elaborate the main theme), and (4) a resolution (in which the outcome of the episodes brings the central character or characters to the main goal with its possible outcomes).[44]

As might be expected, episodes are more difficult to comprehend and remember than setting, theme, and resolution. Less mature readers have greater difficulty with understanding the cause of character actions and the reaction of characters to success or failure in goal achievement. Episodes and other story elements further removed from the major theme are more difficult to interpret and remember. The teaching of fiction organization, particularly the basic structure of stories, the selection of stories with complexity of structure appropriate to pupil capability, and the use of guiding questions which recognize the significance of these structural components comprise useful recommendations for reading educational efforts at the secondary level.

*Induction.* Induction is the process by which we arrive at or defend generalizations through a series of subordinate and supporting particulars or examples. Most content area textbook writers make extensive use of statement–support forms of induction to explain generalizations and/or to present significant specific information in its relationship to higher-order data. The basic patterns are:

| (1) | | (2) |
|---|---|---|
| Generalization (supported by) | *or* | Example 1 |
| Particular 1 | | Example 2 |
| Particular 2 | | Example 3 |
| Particular 3 | | Example 4 (leading to) |
| Etc. | | Generalization (unifying the examples) |

In interpreting inductive argument, the reader must be sensitive to the hierarchical weight of generalizations, subgeneralizations, and particulars. Text writers frequently mix the order of presentation and often intersperse the argument with lengthy illustration. And sometimes, the same examples serve to illustrate a very different generalization.

*Deduction.* Deduction is the process by which a conclusion (a generalization) is inferred from the association of a major premise (a generalization) with a specific premise (a subordinate generalization). Only three different terms (referents or concepts) are permitted among the three generalizations employed. The classic example of the deductive syllogism is:

*Major premise:* All men are mortal.

*Minor premise:* Socrates is a man.

*Conclusion:*    Therefore, Socrates is mortal.

The deduction appears in many legitimate and mutilated forms in nonfiction content. The reader needs to be cautious. Of the 256 possible patterns of deduction, only 24 produce valid conclusions.

*Critical evaluation.* *Critical evaluation* involves a cluster of critical thinking processes applied to reading. Consider B. Othanel Smith's classic statement on critical thinking: "Now, if we set about to find out what a statement means and to determine whether to accept or reject it, we would be engaged in thinking, which, for lack of a better term, we shall call critical thinking."[45] This is the nub of the issue. The objective of the critical reader is to ascertain the validity and the pertinency of the written message. In this, the reader will call upon most of the language and thought processes which are necessary to accurate and flexible interpretation. Critical reading will include subjecting the writer and his product to "tests" of authenticity, objectivity, and consistency. However, the critical reader recognizes also that his own emotions and background of information can predispose him to a "reader's bias" in accepting or rejecting the ideas encountered in print.[46] "Critical" reading is the traditional terminology employed for evaluating ideas and processes in printed materials. "Objective" reading would be a more appropriate term.

*Problem solving.* A problem situation exists when either of two conditions exist: (1) the individual recognizes a goal to be obtained, but he cannot determine the means to attain it; or (2) the goal is unclear to the individual, so that even if he has the resources to solve it, he cannot bring them to bear effectively to achieve that goal. In the broadest sense, all reading should be purposeful, and any approach by which the reader satisfies his needs through reading may be considered problem solving. In a more technical sense, "problem–solving behavior" is the term reserved for the "discovery" of responses which satisfy unique problem situations. This may involve the transfer of previously learned responses to new circumstances or the development of new responses to either old or new problem situations. The reader needs to understand the essential conditions and traditional patterns of problem solving (such as the scientific method), to effectively interpret problems in context, or to resolve problems which are generated by printed information. Much remains to be done in developing readers who employ the use of printed material to resolve their in–school and life problem situations.

### Program Implications

The extension and refinement of purposeful reading interpretation falls largely upon the shoulders of the secondary school. It should be evident from the previous discussion that the teaching, practice, and application of this rich body of behaviors is more than the elementary school can accomplish. Also, the learning of many of these sophisticated reading–thinking processes calls for greater mental maturity and broader experiential background than most pupils have obtained by the end of sixth grade.

The responsibility for development of purposeful interpretation should be shared by both developmental reading teachers and content area teachers: developmental instruction providing a systematic scope and sequence in the core processes of interpretation as needed in functional reading tasks and the understanding of conventional materials, and content area instruction assuming the larger obligation in developing those interpretive processes particularly pertinent to content area learning objectives, tasks, and materials.

## Reader Reaction

When the reading of a message has been meaningful, it should produce some reader reaction. In part, reader reaction involves what effect the message has upon the cognitive and affective structure of the reader during and after reading. In part, reader reaction involves what the reader does with the information he has decoded and interpreted. Beyond the immediate reaction of a particular reader to a particular reading experience lies the cumulative impact of reading experiences upon the individual and his society.

Reader reaction may be conscious and overt — as in the application of the interpretation to some specific problem situation, work task, or creative activity. It may be subconscious or semiconscious — as in the satisfaction or modification of the reader's affective condition. Consciously or subconsciously, reaction to any meaningful experience of interpretation will involve some assimilation of that experience.

### Reaction as a Juncture in Reading Experience

Through application or assimilation of the meaning gained by interpretation, reader reaction serves both to terminate one specific reading act and to sow the seeds for succeeding reading acts.[47] The schematic we have been using as a model of reading behavior illustrates this by representing feedback from *reaction* through application, affect, and assimilation to the revision of the reader's set, the improvement of readiness background, and the adjustment of decoding–interpretive processes.

Earlier in this chapter it was stressed that a close interrelationship exists among an individual's motivation, reward system, and reading reaction. We are most rewarded by those experiences which tend to satisfy our strongest and most immediate needs. Broadly speaking, a reader reaction may have one or more effects, which may be classified as: (1) utilitarian (acquiring information for its immediate operational value); (2) affective (finding stimulation, ego support, or respite through reading); (3) aesthetic (gaining new and satisfying present appreciation of literature of merit); and (4) developmental (adding to information background and learning new ways of coping with oneself, with others, and with the general environment). A reader's reward systems not only provide a basis for how he may react to a given source, but they also serve as influences on whether, what, and how he will read further.

### Influence of Personal Reading Experience

It should not be assumed that the effect of reading will necessarily have a benign impact upon the reader. The information gained may be inaccurate, either because the writer's information was inaccurate or because the reader misinterpreted the content. Also, the writer's information and style may disturb the reader's equilibrium, as in reading reports of a tragic occurrence, an argument which runs counter to the reader's treasured biases, or a technical explanation whose complexity threatens the reader's feeling of adequacy. A more critical example is that of the problem reader who views most reading as an unrewarding, if not painful, experience.[48]

What materials are useful to a pupil and how he responds to the content and style of a piece of writing will depend largely upon his learning opportunities as well as his prevailing needs.[49] Varied content and style of materials which elicit diverse intellectual or emotional pupil responses should lead to greater reading development. In the long run, breadth and depth of reading contact and versatility in reader reaction differentiate between the typical and the mature reader. There are significant implications for the secondary reading program and content area curricula and instruction in this. Perhaps fewer than 10 percent of secondary pupils and adults are extensive readers.[50,51]

### Reaction and Literary Appreciation

Classification of the effects of reading and reader reaction include behaviors which relate closely to the appreciation of literature, as such. Many of the goals of the school's program in the study of "literature" coincide with desired reader reaction. From an analysis of authoritative descriptions of literature curricula in secondary schools, Purves grouped pupil objectives under the major headings of (gaining) knowledge, (making) application, (eliciting) response, (improving) expressed response, and (increasing) participation.[52]

Reader personal reaction involves behavioral dynamics which include appreciation of the literary work itself. In a summary of the research, Cooper provides the following useful definitions: "*literature of merit* [means] any work of literature which is honest, original, and powerful; *appreciating* is the act of recognizing literary merit." Cooper adds: "Appreciation, then, is based on understanding.... It is an aesthetic process, involving the evaluation of separate facets of the work."[53]

Thus, the reader's interpretation of content will include a personal by-product of reaction. It would be difficult to explain how certain literature has stirred feelings and sustained interest over decades, even centuries, without accepting that it contains some basic appeal to human emotions. This may involve an appreciation of the writer's craft and/or it may involve something more basic — "blood, sex, and booty," in the words of Jacques Barzun. Shrodes summarizes the interrelationship of reading effect and affect with greater delicacy: "Not only does the eye find what the mind is seeking; the mind finds what the heart is seeking."[54]

### The Social Impact of Reading

The reading act does not end its behavioral chain of interaction with the single reader; it contributes to the collective societal impact of writing upon the knowledge, social processes, and mentality of man. Concerning the general impact of written communication, the historian Breasted states: "The invention of writing and of a convenient system of records on paper has had a greater influence on the uplifting of the human race than any other achievement in the life of man."[55]

One major form of this social impact is the influence of written thought upon the idea content and social processes of the reading society. In summarizing thirty reports of possible social effects of reading, Gray reported likely influence of reading in such areas as beliefs, attitudes and morale, public opinion, voting, and crime and antisocial behavior.[56]

***Reading and mass communication.*** Since the improvement of the printing press, written communication increasingly dominated the way the masses were informed. The development of the electronic or "machine-interposed" media in this century has lessened this singular dominance by the written media, but may not have diminished its crucial role in societal matters.[57] Changes in economic structure and applied science have brought bigness, centralization, and popular appeal to mass communication. These conditions have been accompanied by striking problems in the areas of freedom, balanced representation, truthfulness in reporting, and in the instigation of changes in public mores and tastes. Lazarsfeld and Merton single out three social consequences of the power of electronic mass media: (1) the conferral of legitimate status upon individuals, groups, and ideas; (2) the public confrontation of differences in social norms; and (3) the narcotizing dysfunction of overwhelming amounts of information.[58] The latter may well be a societal defense against yet another social impact of mass communication—increasing rapidity of social change itself.[59]

Written communication may reinforce the social impact of electronic communication. However, it can serve as a modifying influence upon those who read. Preston has identified six highly useful functions of reading in our time. These include: (1) supplying a balance to the selective overstress of electronic media content, (2) providing a needed check on the authenticity of content, (3) augmenting self-respect as an individual, (4) fostering human and social values which are independent of materialistic wealth, (5) facilitating the exercise of language analysis, and (6) preserving mental health.[60]

We would do well to recognize that the cumulative effect of reading written communication may shape the mental and emotional processing of the reader beyond the impact of the ideas contained in the substance of the material read. We are indebted to Marshall McLuhan for the succinct conceptualization of this relationship:"...it is sometimes a bit of a shock to be reminded that, in operational and practical fact, the medium is the message."[61] Concerning print as a medium, McLuhan states that it "had a rather tremendous effect upon human susceptibility and perception.... You can see how print would create an individual person, inner-directed, a kind of person highly self-centered, and very much self-analytical."[62]

The implications for maturity in reading, and the lack of it, are overwhelming. If such effect holds for the individual, then in time it should shape the general psychic patterns of the society and the processes of its institutions. Thus, learning to read and being influenced by a home that is shaped by parents who have been shaped by reading may prepare the individual for acculturation in quite subtle ways.

But what of those millions in the United States who form a minority of illiterates or semi-illiterates in a highly literate culture? Beyond the educational, economic, and social disadvantagement this causes, and which is serious in itself, we must be concerned that the inability to share reaction to societal writing can separate these pupils and adults from their literate fellows—cognitively, experientially, and emotionally.

## THE SPECIFIC BEHAVIORS OF MATURE READING

The components of the integral reading act are implemented through the activation and integration of a number of specific reading behaviors. These behaviors consist of certain skilled performances, understandings, and attitudes related to reading. Most of these need to be taught through developmental instruction, as well as practiced, improved, and extended in content area learning activities. The mature reader selectively draws upon and coordinates these specific behaviors as needed to meet his purposes in the particular reading situation.

As implemented, a reading skill is closely associated with its related understandings and attitudes. For example, the quick location of specific information in a textbook requires an understanding of the general nature and function of the index, specific knowledge of how an index may be organized, and a willingness to implement this through skilled scanning techniques. The "skill" of using an index to locate specific information is a matter of having mastered the behavioral responses necessary to act upon one's understanding of an index and its function. The teaching of a specific reading behavior involves the development of its related understandings and the inculcating of positive attitudes about its use, as well as enough meaningful practice in performing the skill that it becomes accurate, efficient, and selectively coordinated into the larger reading act.

An outline of the more significant skilled behaviors which need to be mastered by secondary pupils if they are to operate at appropriate levels of reading maturity is presented on the following pages. The intent was to identify those behaviors which need to be developed, not to provide a taxonomy suggesting priority of instruction. Such a taxonomy may be useful for instructional and curricular purposes, but it is best developed in reference to the specific school situation and should incorporate consideration of the learning background and abilities of the pupils, the nature of available instructional materials, as well as the broad developmental priorities of skill learning and use.

## A Selective Outline of the
## Specific Behaviors of Mature Reading

I. Decoding Behaviors
   A. Decoding Words
      1. Efficiently recognizing familiar word forms.
         a. Selectively using context clues to anticipate word form, e.g., familiar expression, definition, comparison and contrast, synonym, summary, mood, linguistic structure.
         b. Accurately using individual word-form clues.
         c. Synthesizing whole word forms from perceptual cues.
      2. Accurately analyzing and synthesizing unfamiliar word forms for pronunciation and meaning.
         a. Selectively using context meaning clues [see point I(A)1(a) above].
         b. Phonic analysis: associating and synthesizing letter forms and sounds (consonants, vowels, phonograms, syllables, and pertinent rules).
         c. Structural analysis: associating and synthesizing meaningful prefixes, roots, suffixes, compound words.
         d. Efficiently using word references: dictionary, thesaurus, glossary, etc.
      3. Associating word meanings with word forms.
         a. Making appropriate denotative associations.
         b. Making appropriate connotative associations.
      4. Extending general and special sight vocabularies.
      5. Developing fluency and flexibility in selective use and combination of word-decoding behaviors.
   B. Decoding Sentences
      1. Using textual setting to anticipate general sentence meaning and function.
      2. Gaining accuracy and fluency in ocular-motor perception of words and punctuation as units of sentence meaning.
      3. Recognizing common kernel-sentence forms and meaning.
      4. Utilizing function words and word-order changes to follow meaning of sentence transformations and strings of kernel sentences.

II. Purposeful Behaviors of Interpretation
   A. Mastering the Competencies of Basic Interpretation and Reaction
      1. Extending sentence-reading accuracy and efficiency.
      2. Locating specific needed information within a limited textual segment.
      3. Identifying and understanding basic relationships of textual structure.
         a. Title-content/heading-content relationships.
         b. Topic statements in paragraphs and short selections.
         c. Introductory and summary paragraphs in selections and chapters.
         d. Typical organizational structure of newspapers, magazines, manuals, textbooks, dictionaries, encyclopedias.
      4. Following a stated sequence of meaning units in explanatory materials.
         a. Carrying out a set of directions.
         b. Identifying the steps in a process.
         c. Following the chronology of time- or sequence-related events.
         d. Recognizing simple cause-effect relationships.
      5. Raising questions appropriate to needed meaning in the use of functional materials of school, work, and personal life.
      6. Making meaningful use of operational materials necessary to the tasks of func-

tional literacy, e.g., signs, directions, occupational and governmental forms, directories, maps, charts, recipes, bills and account statements, advertisements and want ads, notices, news articles.

7. Creatively reacting to materials read.
   a. Making brief form notes as memory aids.
   b. Pictorially representing content with diagrams and sketches.
   c. Constructing objects from written directions or description.
   d. Oral reading to communicate essential information to others.
8. Expanding vocabulary and grasp of literal textual meaning toward a minimal goal of dealing adequately (75 percent comprehension accuracy) in materials of approximately eighth-grade readability.
9. Understanding basic story structure.
10. Making recreational use of fiction and nonfiction materials appropriate to independent level of reading mastery.

B. Advancing Competency in Mature Interpretation
   1. Inferring nonstated language relationships.
      a. Recognizing concepts used in written statements.
      b. Recognizing and understanding statements of generalization.
      c. Inferring unstated topic ideas and details of paragraphs.
      d. Identifying topic paragraphs of larger selections.
      e. Differentiating between subordinate and coordinate sentences in a paragraph.
      f. Recognizing main-idea/supporting-detail structure of paragraph.
      g. Discerning the prevailing style or styles of the selection: description, narration, exposition, or argumentation.

   h. Identifying paragraph function in larger written structure: introductory, summary, transitional, illustrative, definitional, descriptive.
   2. Analyzing the writer's structure of ideas and argument.
      a. Identifying specific purpose relationships stated or implied in the content: cause-effect, comparison-contrast, direct- and inverse-order sequence, direct- and reverse-trend patterns, correlation of two or more variables, analogy, classification, evaluation (criteria and/or results).
      b. Extending the understanding of fictional structure.
      c. Recognizing and following inductive argument (inference of generalizations).
      d. Recognizing and following deductive argument (syllogistic reasoning).
      e. Recognizing and following divergent casting.
      f. Recognizing and following material patterned on special organizational structures, e.g., scientific method, historical method, legal procedure, mathematical proofs.
   3. Purposefully recognizing idea relationships.
      a. Abstracting specific statements or data from original context to form such products as lists, summaries, classifications, sequences and processes, quotations to support premises.
      b. Selectively rewriting information contained in original context to form such products as summaries, outlines, questions, commentary.
      c. Creatively reconstructing selected data and ideas to form such products as time lines, pictorial representations, tables and schematics, new narrative or expository text, models.

    d. Deriving information and abstracting data and language from two or more sources to construct a combined argument or to develop a pro-con summary.

4. Evaluating written sources (critical reading).

    a. Maintaining an objective reading set.

      (1) Neutralizing personal predispositions concerning topic, material, or source of material.

      (2) Identifying written use of appeal to personal needs.

      (3) Suspending or qualifying judgment pending sufficient evidence.

      (4) Persistently pursuing needed sources and pertinent evidence.

    b. Determining relevancy of content.

      (1) Determining how directly the content bears upon reading purposes or problem.

      (2) Differentiating between fiction and nonfiction content.

      (3) Separating fact from opinion.

      (4) Identifying whether data are from primary or secondary source.

      (5) Identifying currency of source information.

      (6) Investigating the authoritative credentials of the writer (source) concerning topic.

    c. Ascertaining the validity of content.

      (1) Differentiating between hypothetical constructs and empirical constructs.

      (2) Verifying factual evidence by external authoritative sources.

      (3) Examining factual evidence for internal consistency.

      (4) Examining argumentative procedure for fidelity: adherence to rules of deduction and qualification, adequate and appropriate sampling for inductive processes, delimitation of generalization, appropriate execution of scientific or historical method, and identifying use of implication and conclusion.

      (5) Recognizing the presence of propaganda devices and other slanting techniques.

III. Behaviors of Flexibility and Efficiency

  A. Maintaining a Flexible Mind Set in Reading Attack

    1. Understanding and accepting the nature and need for flexibility in mature reading performance.

    2. Developing proficiency in adjusting reading approach to specific reading purposes and reading material.

    3. Modifying specific reading purposes to the nature of the reading sources where choice is limited, e.g., the course assignment.

    4. Selecting reading materials most appropriate to reading purposes.

  B. Effectively Utilizing the Several General Modes of External and Internal Flexibility

    1. Scanning.

    2. Skim reading.

    3. Rapid reading.

    4. Personal reading.

    5. Analytical reading.

    6. Study reading.

  C. Improving Efficiency of Reading

    1. Developing a total approach to efficiency in reading-related situation, e.g., actual reading of content, daily and weekly scheduling, physical conditions of reading and study settings.

    2. Maintaining an appropriate balance between rate of reading and reading interpretation.

    3. Selecting that mode of flexible reading most pertinent to reading purposes.

    4. Improving efficiency in use of each mode of flexible reading.

IV. Research and Study Behaviors
   A. Mastering Efficient Locational Behavior
      1. Recognizing the potential of locational reading to satisfy many specific reading purposes.
      2. Determining key words or concepts as cues.
      3. Knowing the differentiated functions of book matter and selectively using components of books and magazines as aids to location of in-source information.
      4. Knowing and using general and special reference sources pertinent to areas of reading operations.
      5. Becoming familiar with the library, its operation, and its resources for locating information.
      6. Employing appropriate modes of flexible reading in conjunction with locational purposes, particularly scanning and skim reading.
   B. Developing Effective Notational Behaviors
      1. Understanding the advantages and pitfalls of using notation for appropriate reading tasks.
      2. Accepting the need to employ notation on a selective and flexible basis.
      3. Mastering the common notational forms: marginal notation and underlining in source, listing, outlining, summarizing, abstracting, graphic forms (time-lines, diagrams, graphs, tables, etc.).
      4. Developing an orderly system for organizing notes for learning and retention and for storage and retrieval.
   C. Effecting Behaviors of Learning and Retention of Content
      1. Recognizing the difference between casual reading, reading to learn, and techniques of overlearning for retention.
      2. Avoiding common problems of learning and retention
         a. Recognizing the limitations of a single reading for learning and retention.
         b. Understanding the limitations of rereading as a study procedure.
         c. Knowing the facts about rapidity of forgetting unreinforced learning.
         d. Recognizing the inhibiting influence of negative attitudes and passive set.
      3. Applying learning and retention strategies.
         a. Developing an active and confident set.
         b. Selecting the most important information to be learned and retained.
         c. Providing for strong, clear, original learning.
         d. Relating what is to be learned to what is previously known.
         e. Organizing what is to be learned and retained.
         f. Adapting notational system to retentional needs.
         g. Utilizing immediate recall or review (self-testing).
         h. Utilizing distributed recall or review (reimpression, reorganizing, and self-testing).
   D. Evolving a Personal Reading-Study System
      1. Understanding the component behaviors of an R–S system.
      2. Learning to apply one R–S system effectively.
      3. Learning to adapt the R–S system to type of content.
      4. Modifying the R–S system to fit one's personal style.

V. Reading Reaction Behaviors
   A. Satisfying or Modifying Initial Reading Set and Specific Reading Purposes
   B. Converting Interpretation into Applicational Result or Product
      1. Consciously learning and retaining certain information.
      2. Carrying out an overt operation.

3. Solving a specific problem
4. Reorganizing source(s) data into a notational record.
5. Creating a product (various forms).
6. Meeting certain criteria of outside evaluation.
7. Oral reading or expression to communicate ideas or to share appreciation or information.

C. Assimilating Information or Style
1. Appreciating the aesthetic or operational skill of writer or quality and usefulness of his material.
2. Satisfying emotional needs.
3. Integrating meaning gained into experiential background.
4. Stimulating new reading-learning sets.
5. Developing additional specific reading purposes.

D. Behaviors Related to General Reading Habits and Tastes
1. Developing habits of extensive and varied reading.
   a. Using reading to satisfy, extend, and create personal interests.
   b. Associating reading activity (per se) with enjoyment, personal release, and self-fulfillment.
   c. Expanding reading tastes to include contact with a variety of written sources and literary forms, including such dimensions as: nonfiction-fiction, prose-poetry-dramatic forms, humor-comedy-tragedy, narrative-expository-argumentative, fantasy-reality, modern-classic, regional-national-international.
   d. Developing an effective balance in reading for such effects as entertainment, utility, personal adjustment, and self-development.
2. Appreciating the effective use of fiction, general nonfiction, and technical writing.
   a. Recognizing differences in the writer's objectives for using argumentative, expository, and narrative form.
   b. Appreciating the readability of the writer's style.
   c. Valuing the clarity of the writer's organization.
   d. Sensing the quality of the writer's craftsmanship.

## REFERENCES

1. J. P. Chaplin, *Dictionary of Psychology* (New York: Dell Publishing Company, Inc., 1968) p. 7.
2. Ernest Horn, *A Horn Sampler*, Thelma Peterson, Compiler (Iowa City: University of Iowa, 1957).
3. Lee J. Chronbach, *Educational Psychology* (New York: Harcourt, Brace and World, Inc., 1963) p. 88.
4. Frederick J. McDonald, *Educational Psychology* (Belmont, Calif.: Wadsworth Publishing Company, Inc., 1965) pp. 269-75.
5. Edward L. Thorndike, "Reading as Reasoning: A Study of Mistakes in Paragraph Reading," *Journal of Educational Psychology* 8 (June, 1917) pp. 323-32.
6. E. D. Torrance and J. Harmon, "Effects of Memory, Evaluative, and Creative Reading Sets on Test Performance," *Journal of Educational Psychology* 52 (1961) pp. 207-14.
7. Frederic B. Davis, "Psychometric Research on Comprehension in Reading," *Reading Research Quarterly* 7 (Summer, 1972) pp. 628-78.
8. Eleanor Holmes, "Reading Guided by Questions Versus Careful Reading and Rereading Without Questions," *School Review* 39 (1931) pp. 361-71.
9. M. D. Vernon, "The Improvement of Reading," *British Journal of Educational Psychology* 26 (1956) pp. 85-93.
10. James B. Stroud, *Psychology in Education* (New York: Longmans, Green & Co., Inc., 1956) p. 112.

THE INTEGRAL READING ACT *85*

11. O. J. Mowrer, "The Psychologist Looks at Language," *American Psychologist* 9 (1954) pp. 660-94.
12. Robert Emans, "Use of Context Clues," in *Reading and Realism*, J. A. Figurel, Editor, International Reading Association Conference Proceedings 13, Part 1 (Newark, Del.: International Reading Association, 1969) pp. 76-82.
13. Kenneth Goodman, "The Psycholinguistic Nature of the Reading Process," *The Psycholinguistic Nature of the Reading Process*, K. Goodman, Editor (Detroit, Mich.: Wayne State University Press, 1968) p. 15.
14. Irving Anderson and Walter Dearborn, *The Psychology of Teaching Reading* (New York: The Ronald Press Company, 1952) p. 202.
15. Charles C. Fries, *Linguistics and Reading* (New York: Holt, Rinehart and Winston, Inc., 1963) p. 149.
16. Dolores Durkin, *Teaching Them to Read* (Boston: Allyn and Bacon, Inc., 1970) Chapters 10 and 11.
17. Arthur W. Heilman, *Phonics in Proper Perspective* (Columbus, Ohio: Charles E. Merrill Publishing Company, 1964) p. 7.
18. Constance M. McCullough, "Content Aids in Reading," *The Reading Teacher* 11 (April, 1958) pp. 225-29.
19. A. S. Artley, "Teaching Word Meaning Through Context," *Elementary English Review* 20 (1943) pp. 68-74.
20. W. S. Ames, "The Development of a Classification Scheme of Contextual Aids," *Reading Research Quarterly* 2 (1966) pp. 57-82.
21. Earl A. Taylor, "The Fundamental Reading Skill," *Journal of Developmental Reading* (Summer, 1958) pp. 21-29.
22. Miles A. Tinker, *Bases for Effective Reading Instruction*, (Minneapolis, Minn.: University of Minnesota Press, 1966) p. 12.
23. Evelyn Boyle, "The Nature and Causes of Regressive Movements in Reading," *Journal of Experimental Education* 11 (September, 1942) pp. 16-36.
24. Charles T. Letson, "The Relative Influence of Material and Purpose upon Reading Rates," *Journal of Educational Research* 52 (February, 1959) pp. 238-40.
25. S. E. Taylor, H. Frackenpohl, and J. L. Pettee, *Grade Level Norms for the Components of the Fundamental Reading Skill*, Research Bulletin No. 3 (New York: Educational Developmental Laboratories — McGraw-Hill Book Company, 1960).
26. Noam A. Chomsky, *Syntactic Structures* (The Hague: Mouton, 1957).
27. James Deese, *Psycholinguistics* (Boston: Allyn and Bacon, Inc., 1970) pp. 12 and 44.
28. John Lyons, *Introduction to Theoretical Linguistics* (Cambridge, England: Cambridge University Press, 1968) p. 256.
29. E. B. Smith, K. S. Goodman, and R. Meredith, *Language and Thinking in the Elementary School* (New York: Holt, Rinehart and Winston, Inc., 1970) p. 150.
30. Harold G. Shane, *Linguistics and the Classroom Teacher* (Washington, D.C.: National Educational Association, 1967) pp. 13-17.
31. Francis Robinson, *Effective Study*, Revised Edition (New York: Harper & Row, Publishers, 1961) pp. 18-19.
32. J. Peech, "Effect of Prequestions on Delayed Retention of Prose Material," *Journal of Educational Psychology* 61 (1970) pp. 241-46.
33. Walter Hill, "Evaluating Secondary Reading," *Measurement and Evaluation of Reading*, Roger Farr, Editor (New York: Harcourt, Brace and World, Inc., 1970) pp. 126-53.
34. F. J. Guzak, "Teacher Questioning and Reading," *Reading Teacher* 21 (December, 1967) pp. 227-34.
35. Arthur S. McDonald, "Reading Versatility Twelve Years Later," in *Reading: The Right to Participate*, Twentieth Yearbook of the National Reading Conference, Frank P. Greene, Editor (Milwaukee, Wis.: National Reading Conference, Inc., 1971) pp. 168-73.
36. Alvin Toffler, *Future Shock* (New York: Random House, Inc., 1970) p. 47.
37. Walter Hill, "Applying Research Findings in Rate of Reading to Classroom Practice," in *Forging Ahead in Reading*, J. Figurel, Editor, International Reading Association Conference Proceedings 12, Part 1, (Newark, Del.: International Reading Association, 1968) pp. 620-26.
38. Charles T. Letson, "Speed and Comprehension in Reading," *Journal of Educational Research* 52 (1958) pp. 49-53.
39. Earl F. Rankin, "The Relationship Between Reading Rate and Comprehension," in *Problems, Programs, and Projects in College-Adult Reading*, Eleventh Yearbook of the National Reading Conference, E. P. Bliesmer and R. C. Staiger, Editors (Milwaukee, Wis.: Marquette University Press, 1962) pp. 1-5.
40. John Carroll, *Language and Thought* (Englewood Cliffs, N.J.: Prentice-Hall, Inc., 1964) p. 93.
41. Francis Christensen, "A Generative Rhetoric of the Paragraph," *College Composition and Communication* 16 (1965) pp. 144-56.
42. Robert H. Ennis, "A Definition of Critical Thinking," *The Reading Teacher* 17 (May, 1964) pp. 500-12.

43. Elizabeth A. Parker, *The Teaching of Reading as Fiction* (New York: Teachers College Press, Teachers College, Columbia University, 1969) p. 16.

44. John T. Guthrie, "Research Views: Story Comprehension," *Reading Teacher* 30 (February, 1977) pp. 574-577.

45. B. Othanel Smith, "The Improvement of Critical Thinking," *Progressive Education* 30 (March, 1953) p. 129.

46. William Eller and Judith Wolf, "Factors in Critical Reading," in *The Philosophical and Sociological Bases of Reading*, Fourteenth Yearbook of the National Reading Conference, Eric Thurstone and L. E. Hafner, Editors (Milwaukee, Wis.: National Reading Conference, Inc., 1965) pp. 64-72.

47. S. I. Hayakawa, *Language in Thought and Action* (New York: Harcourt, Brace and Co., Inc., 1940) p. 306.

48. Ruth C. Penty, *Reading Ability and High School Drop-outs* (New York: Bureau of Publications, Teachers College, Columbia University, 1956) p. 75.

49. Isabel Lewis, "Psychoanalytic Points of View," in *The Dynamics of Reading*, Robert Ruddell, Editor (Waltham, Mass.: Ginn and Company, 1970) p. 83.

50. M. M. Hughes and P. Willis, "Personal Reading: A Study of a Seventh Grade," *Proceedings of the Claremont Reading Conference* 29 (1965) pp. 90-100.

51. William S. Gray and Bernice Rogers, *Maturity in Reading—Its Nature and Appraisal* (Chicago: University of Chicago Press, 1956) pp. 77-90.

52. Alan Purves, "Testing in Literature," *Summative and Formulative Evaluation of Student Learning*, B. Bloom, J. Hastings, and G. Madous, Editors (New York: McGraw-Hill Book Company, 1969).

53. Charles R. Cooper, *Measuring Growth in Appreciation of Literature* (Newark, Del.: International Reading Association, 1972) p. 6.

54. Caroline Shrodes, "The Dynamics of Reading," *ETC* 18 (1961) pp. 21-23.

55. Arthur Breasted, *Ancient Times* (Boston: Ginn and Company, 1944) p. 66.

56. William S. Gray, "The Social Effects of Reading," *School Review* 55 (May, 1947) pp. 269-77.

57. John Tebbel, *The Media in America* (New York: Thomas Y. Crowell Company, Inc., 1974) pp. 406-7.

58. Paul Lazarsfeld and Robert Merton, "Mass Communications, Popular Taste, and Organized Social Action," in *The Communication of Ideas*, Lyman Bryson, Editor (New York: Harper & Row, Publishers, 1948).

59. Toffler, *Future Shock*, p. 47.

60. Ralph Preston, "The Changed Role of Reading," *Reading in an Age of Mass Communications* (Champaign, Ill.: National Council of Teachers of English, 1949) pp. 1-18.

61. Marshall McLuhan, *Understanding Media: The Extensions of Man* (New York: Signet Books, 1964) p. 23.

62. G. E. Stearn, Editor, *McLuhan: Hot and Cool* (New York: Signet Books, 1967) p. 148.

## SUPPLEMENTARY SOURCES

Clymer, Theodore. "What Is Reading?: Some Current Concepts." In *Innovation and Change in Reading Instruction*, Helen Robinson, Editor, The Sixty-seventh Yearbook of the National Society for the Study of Education, Part II, Chapter I. Chicago: University of Chicago Press, 1968.

Durkin, Dolores. *Strategies for Identifying Words*. Boston: Allyn and Bacon, Inc., 1976. 139 p.

Gibson, Eleanor J., and Harry Levin. *The Psychology of Reading*, Chapter 12. Cambridge, Mass.: The MIT Press, 1975.

Rankin, Earl F. *The Measurement of Reading Flexibility*, pp. 37-46. Newark, Del.: International Reading Association, 1974.

Russell, David. *The Dynamics of Reading*, Chapter 7. Waltham, Mass.: Ginn-Blaisdell, 1970.

Simons, Herbert D. "Reading Comprehension: The Need for a New Perspective." *Reading Research Quarterly* 6 (Spring, 1971) pp. 338-63.

Tinker, Miles A. *Bases for Effective Reading*, Chapters 2, 4, and 5. Minneapolis, Minn.: University of Minnesota Press, 1965.

# FOUR

# The Comprehensive Secondary Reading Program

*A reading program includes all provisions made by a staff to promote the development of students through reading, to stimulate desirable reading interests, and to increase their reading competence. Some of the steps taken may be integral parts of carefully planned courses; others may occur incidentally as occasion arises in any directed activity.*

William S. Gray

*The solution to the present reading situation must come through the all-school development of basic reading-abilities approach.*

Emmett A. Betts

**Overview** Chapter Four presents an introduction to the comprehensive secondary reading program. It describes the general characteristics of the five component areas of essential pupil experiences which such a program should deliver: (1) reading evaluation and assessment, (2) developmental reading instruction, (3) content-oriented reading learning and utilization, (4) extended independent reading guidance and opportunity, and (5) supplementary reading or reading-related services for those pupils with special needs. The position taken is that the integration of these areas of pupil experience into a composite secondary reading education effort provides the best means of developing mature readers who can meet school and lifelong reading demands.

# ESSENTIAL AREAS OF SECONDARY READING EDUCATION

We have seen how prevailing practices of secondary reading education have reflected the accumulation of a succession of single instructional emphases: remedial, developmental, corrective, and more recently, content area reading and reading for the disadvantaged. Discrete, single-emphasis secondary reading education which produces certain desired changes in the reading performance and development of secondary pupils should be recognized for the good that it does. Moreover, the existence of one or more discrete-function programs in a school can serve as the basis for initiating the comprehensive secondary reading program envisaged by Gray and by Betts.[1,2] But few secondary schools presently provide balanced, comprehensive secondary reading education.[3] And clearly, what has been provided is inadequate in terms of developing functionally competent and mature reading citizens.[4,5]

As noted in the Overview, this chapter discusses five areas of secondary reading-learning experience which should be provided by the comprehensive secondary reading program: (1) reading evaluation and assessment, (2) systematic instruction in the essential developmental behaviors necessary to deal competently and maturely with conventional reading materials and the tasks of youth and adulthood, (3) instruction in and effective guidance in the utilization of reading as a means of content learning and application, (4) guidance and opportunity to extend independent reading habits, and (5) supplementary services for those pupils with special reading needs. This discussion concentrates upon the broad operational nature of these areas and should provide a meaningful structure for the instructional and evaluation-assessment strategies treated in Parts II and III.

These five areas of reading educational experience may be implemented in a number of useful ways. Thus, the comprehensive secondary reading education effort may take different program forms and emphases in different school settings. And it should. The educational structure and pupil maturity of the upper middle and junior high school are not the same as the senior high. The metropolitan inner-city secondary school may need to implement these areas somewhat differently from the secondary school of a small university town. But all of these reading experience areas need attention in all secondary school situations. And the key to the success of the comprehensive secondary reading program lies in the degree to which the whole staff—content teachers, reading teachers, English teachers, guidance counselors, health education personnel, school psychologists, administrators—contribute their special talents to the effort. The components of the comprehensive secondary reading program are depicted in Figure 7.

## Reading Evaluation and Assessment

The most pivotal area of the comprehensive secondary reading program consists of those operations broadly classified as evaluative in nature. Reading evaluation is important to the reading development of every pupil. For what is learned through reading evaluation should influence the nature of other reading-learning experiences provided by the school.[6] The pupil profits directly from reading assessment through improved teacher guidance in reading and content learning activities and through a more realistic understanding of his own behavior. He profits indirectly from the influence such evaluation has upon instructional objectives, curricula, materials, and procedures. Evaluation also serves as a means of identifying those pupils who need special reading services.

### Evaluation, Assessment, Testing, and Measurement

Reading *evaluation*, by definition and function, leads to educational decisions germane to the reading and reading-related behavior of the pupil and of the reading and reading-related experiences which bear upon that behavior. As a school operational entity, it encompasses all means of data gathering, processing, and decision making that pertain

**Figure 7**  *Components of the comprehensive reading program.*

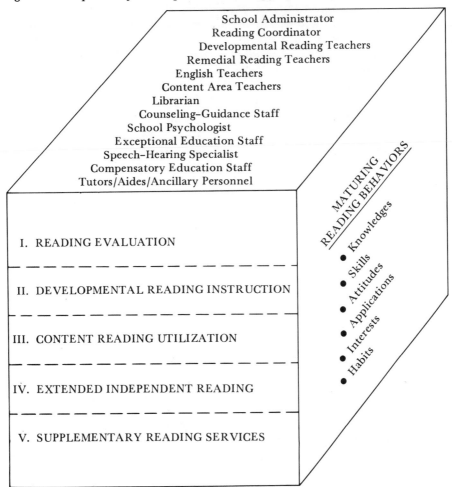

to pupil reading performance and reading program functioning.

Thus, reading evaluation subsumes the functions of reading assessment, reading testing, and reading measurement. Reading *assessment* includes all means of gathering data about the pupil's past, current, or future reading performance. It also includes all means of gathering observations about the functioning of the reading program and its personnel. Reading assessment incorporates reading *testing*, which can be described as any standardized situation, normative or informal, in which the pupil must respond with appropriate behavior to a controlled stimulus (generally written) and where that response is systematically recorded and compared with the performance of others on the same test or evaluated against some predetermined criteria of competent performance. Reading *measurement* consists of that quantification of the observations gathered through reading assessment. Such quantification facilitates the processing and analyzing of the data and encourages greater accuracy and objectivity in evaluative decision making.

Pupil reading behavior and those factors which affect it occupy the central concern of the reading evaluation effort, although evaluation, at times, will need to focus on instructional and administrative practices. Decision making about the pupil or program is dependent sometimes upon pupil characteristics which influence reading development and use. As a consequence, the reading evaluation component of the secondary program may include assessment of pupil reading potential or scholastic aptitude, pupil experience background, language competency, personal and social adjustment, attitudes, and interests, as well as pupil reading performance, as such.

While reading evaluation necessarily involves decision making in terms of the achievement of program objectives, it endeavors to avoid placing individuals in pejorative situations. Reading evaluation is a means to an end, not an end in itself. The major objective of the secondary reading evaluation component is to contribute to the effective development and utilization of reading in school and later life.

Chapter Seven of this text presents strategy, specific tactics, and instruments useful in implementing the objectives and functions of reading evaluation and assessment in the secondary school.

### Significant Contributions of the Reading Evaluation Effort

The reading evaluation effort is useful to the extent that it fulfills essential needs of the reading education effort. Following are eight ways in which reading evaluation contributes to pupil development and program improvement. Effective reading evaluation should:

1. Help to develop precise, realistic ultimate and immediate objectives for the total reading program and classroom reading instruction by determining the current reading needs of pupils and by monitoring the usefulness of present objectives.

2. Improve pupil learning by providing feedback concerning the adequacy of pupil responses in specific reading–learning situations.

3. Audit pupil normative status and progress toward instructional and developmental objectives through systematic appraisal of reading achievement.

4. Identify pupils encountering persistent and significant reading difficulty and provide a diagnostic basis for the treatment of those factors which are inhibiting this reading development.

5. Improve reading program operations through the systematic appraisal of general and instructional content and procedures.

6. Contribute to general professional knowledge about reading behavior and development through the collection of quantified observations.

7. Provide a means whereby the pupil may develop self–acceptance and self–direction in relation to life, academic, and reading goals.

8. Enhance the secondary school curricula and environment by gathering objective evidence of pupil reading performance, thus reducing "armchair" professional decisions.

### Evaluation and Instructional Objectives

A direct, intimate relationship should exist between reading instructional objectives, instructional content, and reading evaluation. Data obtained through reading evaluation enable the teacher or staff to determine whether the objectives are being met. If they are not, evaluation can provide leads concerning why not, whether the problem lies with the instructional programs or with the objectives themselves. If the objectives are being met, evaluation confirms that and aids in the development of the next set of developmental objectives. Unless the reading program or instruction has definite, well-stated objectives, little benefit can come from reading evaluation.

Evaluation can relate most directly and meaningfully to instructional objectives when both are stated in terms of desired pupil behavioral products.[7] *Ultimate objectives* are concerned with final outcomes and usually are stated in broad behavioral end goals of the course or program. An *enabling objective* is concerned with an intermediate goal in pupil learned behavior which is useful in itself, but which also contributes to one or more ultimate objectives. *Immediate objectives* are those which serve as the behavioral target of the short-term instructional sequence. A sort of pyramid relationship exists here. Immediate instructional purposes serve as enabling objectives for intermediate goals, and intermediate goals serve as enabling objectives for ultimate outcomes.

For greatest program efficiency, immediate and intermediate enabling objectives should be derived logically and functionally from accepted ultimate objectives.[8] The outline of reading behaviors presented at the end of Chapter Three illustrates how this is possible. Such a set of interlocked objectives serves as the framework around which reading instructional experiences are built. One does not teach or evaluate an ultimate objective such as "to be able to read in a flexible manner" or a broad intermediate objective such as "to be able to locate information efficiently and accurately" in a direct manner. They are developed through the mastery of a large number of specific, immediate instructional objectives such as: "to be able to locate at least 12 of 15 given topics in a textbook within 5 minutes, using only the index."

Ideally, program objectives should take precedence over evaluation procedures. That is, the data gathered and the way they are processed should be determined as they fit pupil and program needs, not vice versa. Nevertheless, a thorough, long-range program of reading evaluation should provide insight about the nature and validity of the reading program objectives themselves.

## Normative- and Criterion-Referenced Evaluation

Reading evaluation is concerned with the observation of some reading or reading-related behavior, appraising its fitness, and usually, effecting some educational decision as a result of that information. Appraising the fitness of pupil or program performance usually requires some frame of reference or standard upon which that judgment may be based. Reading evaluation, particularly as seen in reading testing, has drawn largely upon two such frames of reference: criterion-based referents and normative-based referents.[9]

### Criterion-referenced reading evaluation. As utilized with tests or other assessment measures, *criterion referencing* involves evaluating actual pupil performance with respect to some predetermined standard of operational performance. Ordinarily, this criterion is specific and definite, and is most useful when described precisely in terms of some reader behavior, as in the statement of behavioral objectives—for example: "(the ability) to use the dictionary to determine the meaning and pronunciation of ten unknown words," or "(the ability) to identify the propaganda technique of 'just plain folks' with 80 percent accuracy when it appears in reading selections," or "(the ability) to carry out five sequential operations with 100 percent accuracy as presented in a set of written directions."

Adequacy, as employed in criterion-referenced evaluation, is judged in terms of the mastery (or degree of mastery) with which the pupil can perform the criterion behavior regardless of how other pupils perform on that task. Criterion-based evaluation is not concerned with determining relative success of one pupil with other pupils, although some such inference may be drawn at times. Rather, its primary purpose is to determine whether a pupil (or group of pupils) has achieved a certain proficiency. The criterion involved may be as specific as the mastery of a certain subskill of reading or as broad as the mastery of a unit of content instruction.

Although widely employed in school reading assessment, a variant form of criterion referencing generally has escaped notice in general discussions of referencing forms and procedures. This is *material-referenced evaluation*. Such a system of assessment referencing recognizes the significance of the writer-reader relationship in reading behavior. Differences in the readability or the reading difficulty of context do exert a notable influence upon reader success. Thus, it is not enough to know that a pupil has an adequate mastery of sight vocabulary; rather, we need to know whether he can handle adequately the words and syntax of a particular paperback novel, the local newspaper sports pages, a high school dictionary, or the eleventh-grade textbook in social problems. Readability is an indirect way of predicting relative difficulty of reading materials. More direct material-referenced reading assessment may be obtained through the use of the *cloze* and the *informal reading inventory* procedures, which are described in Chapter Seven.

*Normative-referenced reading evaluation.* *Normative referencing* involves judgments about the individual's performance in relationship to peer performance on the same test or assessment device. The most familiar form of norm-referenced reading evaluation is the standardized test of reading achievement. Ordinarily, the score or direct product of a normative-referenced measure is meaningful only when compared to the scores obtained by others on that measure, particularly the results obtained by one's grade, age, or ability peers.

A numerical raw score on a standardized test of vocabulary or reading comprehension gains normative reference by comparing that score to the test "norms" (the distribution of obtained scores, running from the lowest to the highest, earned by the random representative sampling of the population on which the test was standardized). The three most useful of these norm scores are percentile ranks, stanines, and standard scores. A *percentile rank* represents the percentage of a reference (peer) group scoring at and below a given raw score. A *standard score* is derived from expressing the raw

test score of an individual in terms of the number of standard deviation units it falls above and below the arithmetical mean score of the reference or norm group. *Stanines* are normalized standard scores through which the pupil's raw score can be placed in one of nine divisions of the total score distribution.

Criterion-referenced measures should provide direct responses to the evaluation of how well a pupil has mastered a particular reading behavior. Normative-referenced measures can provide answers to questions of how well an individual performs in comparison with other individuals or perhaps how well a particular group of pupils performed in comparison with other groups. Both types of referents are useful in the evaluation of secondary reader performance. Both can be useful in the evaluation of secondary reading programs.

### Reading Assessment Sources

Reading *assessment* includes all procedures and devices by which observations of pupil, teacher, or program behavior are collected and organized. Assessment usually implies measurement, although it may limit itself to qualitative description. It encompasses a variety of inquiry sources: cumulative records, interviews, anecdotal records, checklists, electronically derived records, inventories, opinionnaires, projective techniques, self-report procedures such as autobiography, as well as testing procedures of varied nature. Any device or procedure which contributes to a descriptive appraisal of pupil reading performance, pupil reading-related behavior, or school-related reading circumstances qualifies as reading assessment.

Assessment provides the data upon which all succeeding evaluation processes depend. The more thorough the assessment and the more representative its resulting observations of pupil or program performance, the more accurate the related appraisal of that behavior. While human error is an ever-present factor in assessment procedures, such error can be reduced through training and experience with assessment procedures. In any case, reading educational judgments and their related program decisions are likely to be more accurate when adequate observation has been made of the behaviors in question. Within practical limitations, it is the task of reading assessment to collect and process that information necessary to effective reading evaluation.

*Measurement.* While the quantification of observations through measurement will not provide a direct solution to most educational problems, quantification does contribute to the precision and consistency of report about those data pertinent to the problem situation. Measurement also provides a means of critically examining the accuracy of those reported data.

Regardless of the type of assessment procedure involved, reading measurement becomes more effective when three essential operational steps are predetermined. First, the reading behavior or reading program attribute of concern is identified and described as precisely as possible. Second, the mechanics are determined by which this behavior or attribute may be observed—for example, the development of the assessment instrument or procedure. Third, procedures are established for translating the resulting observations into quantitative statements of degree or amount.

## Tests and Testing

Tests are the most common assessment devices employed in schools, and reading tests are among the most frequently used of these. The two categories of testing which figure heavily in reading evaluation are those of achievement and aptitude. If the test measures the degree or nature of proficiency of the examinee's learned knowledges and performance behaviors, it is an *achievement test.* If the test is designed to predict what the examinee could learn to do if he received appropriate learning experiences, it is classified as an *aptitude* or *capacity test.* Tests of *personality* (measures of personal traits or characteristic ways of reacting to personal or social stimuli), *attitude* (predisposition to favor or disfavor something), and *interests*, as well as various tests of pupil *physical resources* (acuity,

sensory perception, and motor coordination), also provide measures pertinent to pupil decisions in reading development.

*Standardized and informal tests.* It sometimes is useful in reading-evaluation circumstances to differentiate between "standardized" and "informal" testing. In one sense, any test worthy of the name is standardized: i.e., the procedures for administration of the stimuli and the elicitation and recording of the subject's response are controlled and followed in a systematic manner. In common professional parlance, however, a *standardized test* usually refers to one which utilizes normative referencing to give it meaning. "Normed" subjects have been organized into descriptive distributions of pupil results. In this way, the test score of a particular examinee can be accorded a relative meaning by comparing it with the performance of others, as we have seen, through the use of percentile ranks, stanine placements, grade equivalents, and standard (deviational) scores.

Although the development of better standardized tests pertinent to secondary school use is much needed, a considerable assortment of normative tests are available for purchase and use. Those standardized reading tests most commonly used in present secondary assessment consist of the vocabulary and/or reading comprehension subtests which are a part of the larger achievement test battery published for annual or biennial school surveys. Another commonly employed standardized reading test consists of those independent reading survey tests which provide total reading test scores plus the scores on one or more of such subtests as vocabulary, paragraph comprehension, rate of reading, and directed reading or work-type reading tasks. Other useful standardized "reading" assessment measures include tests and inventories of work-study skills, study habits, reading interests and attitudes, word skills, reading rate, reading flexibility, and critical thinking.

An *informal test* usually refers to a non-normed test. Many teacher- or school-constructed classroom tests are "informal" in that they are not normed, although they could be. Teacher- or school-developed tests may be "criterion-referenced" tests and, as such, need not be normed. When teacher or school measures are used to rank or otherwise compare performance among pupils, they should receive the same careful consideration in construction, refinement, and treatment of results which is given to the construction of commercial "standardized" tests.

Classroom and clinical use of reading testing encompasses a wide variety of controlled stimulus-response patterns involving specific competencies as in criterion referencing. Group and individual "inventories" or cloze test procedures can be used to assess pupil performance on different levels of instructional materials. Teachers may assess specific reading behaviors through worksheets or informal tests of word recognition and meaning, word analysis skills, oral reading performance, varied specific interpretive tasks, rate and flexibility, and study knowledges and skills. Illustrative patterns of these tests and other assessment measures appropriately employed in the secondary school situation will be discussed in Chapter Seven. An annotated list of secondary reading assessment measures appears in Appendix A.

### Reading Evaluation Problems in the Secondary School

Reading evaluation and the total school reading educational effort are mutually dependent.[10] It is not surprising, therefore, that prevailing secondary reading evaluation and assessment practices have proved inadequate in at least three significant ways. First, the secondary school has not recognized the significant place of evaluation in the improvement of the reading education effort. Relatively few secondary schools, for example, have initiated reading program development with thorough school-wide assessment of all-pupil reading status and appraisal of need. Moreover, the secondary school, as a rule, has not developed a plan for systematic, ongoing evaluation of reading and instructional performance.

A second deficiency is reflected in the absence of good, updated standardized tests constructed particularly to meet the needs of the secondary schools, tests which provide easily gathered and interpreted normative assessment of reading competencies, yet which are realistic and pertinent to the reading situations of secondary pupils and young adults. Since test publishers, like book publishers, tend to market those products for which the schools have created a demand, the responsibility for the limited number of highly useful secondary reading tests must be shared by teacher educators, state and local school administrators, secondary school professionals, and reading educators.

The third area of notable weakness in secondary reading evaluation consists of a prevailing deficiency in the development and use of informal classroom procedures for assessing pupil performance on competency-based and/or material-referenced measures. The use of teacher-constructed assessment tools for guiding day-to-day reading development is essential to realistic classroom instruction and to reading evaluation. This weakness reflects lack of professional preparation in both reading and educational measurement.

Some progress is being made toward the improvement of secondary reading evaluation and its assessment. More will be made when the training of secondary teachers, reading and content, includes greater stress upon reading evaluation and assessment. To this end, Chapters Five and Seven of Part II of this text consider a number of specific strategies and tactics of secondary reading assessment useful to both reading and content area teachers.

### Guidelines for the Reading Evaluation Program: A Summary

Like any other operational structure, an effective program of secondary reading evaluation does not emerge and function efficiently by happenstance. It must be guided by principles or objectives to develop and maintain pertinent supporting services, consistent administration, and creative solutions to problems of instruction and evaluation itself. The following guidelines to be observed in the organization and administration of the reading evaluation program implement concepts and functions of secondary reading evaluation discussed earlier.

The secondary reading evaluation program:

1.  Should consider the improvement of secondary reading, as a personal behavior and tool for learning, to be the fountainhead of its activity; all operational decisions and activity of reading evaluation ultimately must be judged by this criterion: Did they facilitate individual and/or group reading development?

2.  Should be an integral daily element of both reading and content area instruction, as well as a dispassionate means of periodically appraising the products of the instruction program.

3.  Should reflect the general and specific objectives of the reading educational program; this would include clarification and modification of objectives, as well as appraisal of pupil accomplishment.

4.  Should make use of a variety of assessment instruments and related procedures to observe the reading related performance of the pupil, teacher, and program.

5.  Should provide continuous and systematic input of evaluative data to avoid bias in sampling and to evaluate long–term development, as well as immediate pupil and program need.

6.  Should follow an organizational plan which coordinates the evaluative input of classroom teachers, administrators, pupils, and parents, as well as specialists.

7.  Should process gathered information in such a manner that it is available to, can be interpreted by, and can therefore be utilized by all pertinent personnel in effecting educational decisions.

8.  Should draw upon and combine criterion–referenced and normative–referenced measures in such a way that the evaluative strengths of each are maximized and the evaluative weaknesses of each are minimized.

9.  Should be administratively staffed by professionals trained and experienced in reading instruction and diagnosis as well as in the general techniques of educational measurement.

10. Should be a complementary function of the school system's general program of educational evaluation.

## Systematic Instruction in Essential Reading Behaviors

Instruction, in various forms, planned and executed to produce the learning of a scope and sequence of essential reading behavior, comprises the hard core of the reading educational effort at any school level. Broadly interpreted, any of a variety of structured educative acts which contributes rather directly to the improvement of reading performance should be classified as reading instruction. McDonald considers instruction as "the educative act," the major components of which are: (1) formulating learning objectives (desired pupil behavioral outcomes or changes), (2) developing the instructional strategy (the plan of activities) for producing these changes, (3) teaching behavior (making and acting upon decisions) within this strategy so that the learner becomes engaged in situations where he can be guided and reinforced in making the responses to be learned, and (4) evaluating the pupil's behavioral product in terms of the objectives for that instruction.[11] In Chapter Eight we shall see how these components may be adapted to form a generalized model for reading instruction.

All reading instruction would benefit from the satisfaction of these instructional conditions. Yet the scope and nature of such a reading educative sequence can vary. It may correspond to a topical unit of instruction. It may parallel the comparative study of several articles, chapters, or volumes. It could encompass the library researching of a problem or theme. It may involve the intensive analysis of a particular reading selection. Or it may focus on the mastery of a particular skill. It could extend the length of a semester or transpire within a single class period. And reading instruction may occur in a number of secondary reading settings—content area classrooms, remedial learning centers, library orientation sessions, developmental reading classes, for example. Any "educative act" which broadly fits McDonald's characteristics and which produces targeted changes in reading behavior meets our general criteria for systematic reading instruction.

### Developmental Reading Instruction

In a learning sense, all useful secondary reading learning is developmental in that it aids the pupil to progress along the continuum of reading maturity. The phrase "developmental reading instruction," as used in a curriculum or program, denotes planned, organized school efforts to facilitate progress toward reading maturity. Kennedy indicates how such sequential guidance bears upon the issue of reading development:

> Developmental reading can be defined as an instructional approach designed to teach systematically, and in order, all the basic skills and competencies needed for effective reading in conventional materials.... Since developmental reading is concerned with teaching all the skills necessary for acquiring proficiency in general reading ability, it is not restricted to any given program or specific kinds of materials.[12]

**Characteristics of developmental reading instruction.** Four characteristics of developmental reading instruction should be emphasized for its school implementation. (1) Developmental reading instruction takes the reader at his present level of reading competency, and by giving direct and priority attention to mastery of a continuing hierarchy of reading behaviors, enables him to cope successfully with increasingly difficult materials and more complex reading tasks in a more sophisticated manner. (2) In the long run, this is accomplished most effectively through a planned program of instruction—a systematic series of instructional sequences—rather than by whim or chance emergence of reading activity. (3) Such instruction can be accomplished with different general approaches, teaching strategies, and instructional materials, and is most likely to succeed when these are selected and combined judiciously to meet the objectives of the instructional circumstance. (4) Developmental

reading instruction is needed, and thus is justified, throughout the secondary school years, or until a pupil has demonstrated clearly that he has reached reading maturity. Since relatively few college undergraduates and adults demonstrate maturity in this higher reading power, it is assumed that most secondary pupils can benefit from continuance of developmental instruction.[13]

**The continuing functions of developmental reading instruction.** There is a too-common tendency to consider developmental reading instruction at any school level as a collection of skills practice sessions. Although the primary emphasis of developmental reading instruction is on the *how* of reading, narrow and meaningless drill is avoided. Also, developmental reading instruction involves more than instruction and practice in the specific skills of reading. The skilled reading behaviors are learned more efficiently and applied more meaningfully when taught as a part of a realistic spectrum of reading instructional activity. The ten continuing functions recommended for developmental reading instruction are:

1. To contribute to ongoing reading development by providing guidance in increasingly sustained purposeful reading in materials of "instructional"-level difficulty.
2. To extend independence in the decoding processes by increasing sight vocabulary and by improving word- and sentence-reading competencies.
3. To develop those specific, comprehensional, applicational, and assimilative behaviors of reading which lead to functional reading competency in life and work-oriented reading tasks.
4. To deepen understanding of the writer's meaning by increasing sophistication in the various analytical interpretive behaviors of reading.
5. To improve flexibility and efficiency in purposeful reading interpretation and thoughtful reaction to effect study learning, problem solving, and creativity.

6. To contribute to ongoing reading development by providing opportunity to engage in sustained independent reading in materials of "independent"-level difficulty.

7. To expand the pupil's range of reading interests and to establish habits of extended personal reading.

8. To develop sensitivity to and appreciation of honest and powerfully written sources which add to the reader's insight, inspiration, and fulfillment.

9. To contribute to the general mastery of language usage.

10. To promote self-understanding and adjustment and to increase understanding and acceptance of others, of reading, and of school and other work-learning situations.

*Designated reading instruction.* For several decades it has been a common practice for many secondary schools to designate instructional situations where the functions of reading development may receive direct and priority attention. The most common of these are developmental reading classes, as an independent offering or as an English class. Other instructional situations structured purposefully for developmental learning in reading include individual or group reading-center programs; English class reading instructional periods or units; and core combinations of reading with English composition, literature, social studies, or other content areas. Longer-term "corrective" reading classes may serve usefully as adjusted developmental reading instruction.

Secondary reading classes may appear in any of a number of curricular settings under disparate titles, for divergent groups of pupils, with different specific objectives, and utilizing a variety of instructional procedures and materials and any number of organizational structures.[14] They are found in the majority of middle and junior high schools and with lesser frequency at each succeeding senior-high grade level. At present, relatively few school systems provide a sequence of designated reading classes which spans seventh through twelfth grades.

In the secondary school, reading classes and courses provide an instructional-administrative convenience—a means of finding a curricular place for reading instruction in a school structure in which the instructional staff is organized by content departments and which has a curriculum composed of discrete courses and assigned daily time periods. The notable advantages of designated reading classes are that they free the teacher to give priority attention to the development of reading competency, as such, and they are relatively efficient in delivering instruction to larger numbers of pupils. The major disadvantage is that this approach has encouraged the mental and curricular "pigeonholing" of reading instruction—separating reading development from the instructional objectives and activities of other courses, and thus, from the conscious responsibility of the teachers of those content area courses. This disadvantage may be overcome with a comprehensive school reading plan and an effective program of in-service education.

The advantages of designated developmental reading instruction for all secondary pupils far outweigh its disadvantages. As a general rule of thumb, every pupil should receive a required *minimal* equivalent of five periods of systematic reading instruction per week in seventh and eighth grades, three periods weekly in ninth grade, and one weekly instructional period in grades ten through twelve, plus elective courses in reading flexibility and/or study reading at the senior-high level. Decrease in systematic instruction in essential behaviors should be compensated for by increased hours of systematic and content area-oriented reading and study application. Pupils making less than normal progress (in terms of their individual potential) should have an opportunity to receive additional instruction.

Systematic development of essential reading behaviors may be implemented by a number of reading instructional strategies and tactics. Parts II and III of the text describe a number of principles, approaches, and procedures which have proved useful in effecting the reading educative act. These same chapters also identify a wide range of written materials which can be utilized for reading instructional purposes. Commercial materials and programs useful in teaching essential reading behaviors are presented in Appendix D.

### Guidance in Content Reading

We have observed that the processes of reading, the content of the writer's message, and the reader's purposeful reaction to that message are not sensibly separated. The reading act can only function meaningfully in terms of the substance of the message, i.e., understanding the particular referents, concepts, generalizations, and processes the writer has used, as well as the way he has arranged them into associative or logical structures. At the same time, the writer's literal and deeper content remains typographically inert unless the reader can use his decoding-interpretive processes to convert the content into meaning. And neither the reading act nor the writer's message comes to anything unless the pupil or adult does something with it, e.g., immediately applies it in carrying out a process or in solving a practical or theoretical problem, learns and retains it for later problem solving or creative use, and/or is emotionally uplifted by the experience. It is in this broad sense of the reading act that all teachers of reading become teachers of content, and all teachers of content may contribute to reading development.

### *The Need for Content-Related Reading Education*

The extent to which the pupil independently integrates effective reading-study procedure with content reading learning varies with the pupil and the content situation. As a rule, fewer pupils manage this integration than most secondary teachers realize. Perhaps the best of our pupils achieve such an integration in most of the content areas they study. But the majority of secondary pupils do not use reading in content classrooms in a manner which advances either reading development or content learning. The problem here may be one of reading deficiency, content area deficiency, pupil

personal characteristics, teaching approach, or some combination of these factors.[15] The problem can be lessened by the way in which reading is handled in content area situations.[16]

In recent years, both reading and content educators have appeared to be more and more convinced that the secondary school must take definite steps to facilitate this interaction.[17] There are a number of reasons why this should become a professional commitment at the secondary level. The most immediate, practical reason is that content area proficiency is suffering because pupils cannot make good use of reading to learn or to apply content area substance. Closely related is the tendency for content area reading problems to cause or to be associated with content teacher and pupil frustration and teacher-pupil conflict. A third reason is that content area learning situations provide an excellent opportunity to transfer reading behaviors to fairly realistic learning and problem-solving tasks. The content area classroom also provides some unique occasions to develop certain reading applicational behaviors which would be difficult to contrive in the developmental reading situation. In fact, many advanced reading and study objectives of secondary reading education coincide with content area skills learning objectives. Finally, there is a growing realization that even a daily period in developmental reading instruction cannot provide, by itself, all of the reading learning experiences needed by most pupils to develop reasonable maturity in reading.

### *Views of Content Area Reading*

At least five general patterns of content area reading usage are suggested in the professional literature.[18] The least demanding from the content teacher's viewpoint is that the content teacher's role consists of using the textbook and related assignments in a more effective manner. A somewhat larger interpretation of content teacher responsibility for content area reading consists of implementing those classroom conditions which facilitate pupil use of all reading for any learning or application purposes in the classroom setting. It should be noted that any instruction in reading behaviors conducted in these two approaches is largely incidental to the content-learning reading emphasis. These two patterns would seem to be little more than good content teaching, i.e., as it should be taught by content methods courses.

The remaining three patterns recommend some degree of content teacher responsibility for teaching the behaviors of reading as such. One of these argues for the content teacher to develop those decoding-interpretive-study behaviors which are unique and necessary to the learning and use of that particular content area. Sometimes recommendations of this type include responsibility for facilitating content implementation and sometimes they focus on skills development, as such. A fourth pattern would include responsibility for teaching those unlearned conventional reading-study behaviors, not necessarily unique to the course, but which are necessary to the learning activities of the course.

The fifth pattern, and one which appeals to secondary school administrators for its rather obvious pragmatic attraction, is that all secondary reading instruction—developmental included—should be handled within the content classroom setting. This last recommendation seems quite unrealistic in view of the present state of content area teachers' preparation in reading and its instruction, the unnecessary conflict in instructional emphasis this would cause for content area teachers and departments, and the likely negative overreactions against the secondary reading effort this would engender among content field educators. Moreover, those holding such a position grossly underestimate the extent of classroom effort and time that it would take to do an adequate job of teaching, practicing, and implementing all of the maturing reading behaviors.

### Reading education and the content teacher.

Secondary reading education involves more than content course reading and more than the content teacher, individually or collectively, can accomplish and still attain content field objectives. But content reading and reading instructional support from content teachers are necessary to the comprehensive secondary reading program.

How the content teacher is brought into the secondary reading team deserves careful consideration. Operationally, content teachers should receive training in those reading-related strategies which they are expected to carry out, assuming that the content teacher has not had formal preparation in reading education. This training should start with a few procedures easily implemented, instructionally rewarding, and readily adapted to the different content areas. Classroom consultant help from a competent and affable secondary reading specialist should be available as desired. Gradually, as the content teacher's proficiency in content-related reading techniques is expanded, theory and practice in teaching those developmental reading behaviors may be included in the training.

But experience has made it clear that it is neither wise nor necessary to ask the secondary content teacher to be a reading teacher per se. The content teacher does not have to choose between teaching the content area substance and processes and the teaching of reading. There is much which can be done that promotes pupil competency in both.

A more realistic position, and one which avoids the "either reading *or* content mastery" conflict, is one which sees the content area teacher as contributing to the reading education effort by improving pupil reading as it relates to content area tasks. This is more than mere administrative compromise. It is well within the purview of good content area instruction, as such, and can be accomplished readily through effective preservice or in-service teacher education. The notable exception here is the English or content teacher who carries assigned responsibility for developmental reading instruction; in such circumstances, the teacher must function and be adequately trained as a developmental reading teacher in such assignments.

As viewed in this text, the secondary content area teacher is an essential but adjunctive member of the reading education team. Provided the content teacher has access to necessary professional preparation, it is not too much to ask that eventually he or she should understand the nature of secondary readers and secondary reading processes. In addition, the teacher should be familiar with those instructional strategies that will help pupils both to understand the written materials of the content area and to make purposeful and reasonable reaction to the sources of the content area, including the extension of personal content area reading habits and interests. One of the major objectives of this text is to promote such preparation. It is hoped that earlier chapters have provided some understanding of the secondary reader and the integral reading act. All later chapters present information on instructional and assessment strategies which are useful in the content classroom. Chapters Five and Six are addressed to issues particularly pertinent to content area reading instruction and utilization.

### Content Reading and Reading Education

Five ways in which successful content reading experiences, in and out of the classroom, contribute to pupil reading development are summarized below. They demonstrate the vital contribution which content reading education can make to the comprehensive secondary reading program.

*1.* Content area reading education can facilitate transfer of learning through activities which enable the application of reading to the learning of content, the solution of problems, the creation of a product, the appreciation of literature, etc. A good part of this effort can focus upon providing both opportunity and guidance in transferring previously learned reading behaviors to content area tasks. Some pupils can effect such transfer on their own. The majority do not, especially when the transfer calls for a combination of processes, specialized reading usages, or complex content processes.

*2.* Content reading experiences contribute to pupil reading development by providing additional practice in learned reading behaviors and by stimulating the learning of additional reading behaviors. Content-related reading instruction is not responsible for developing basic reading proficiency, as such, but it should not neglect opportunities to reinforce needed reading behaviors.

*3.* A vital aspect of content-related reading education involves helping pupils to handle the textbook and to learn ways to deal, adequately and independently, with substantial sources of written information utilized in the content area of study. One means to this end is to guide pupils through the reading of content-learning selections. Another is to teach them reading-study systems leading to greater flexibility in purposeful learning. A third is to provide meaningful collateral reading assignments under such conditions that pupil success is maximized.

*4.* The content study situation and the content field teacher, in particular, occupy a vantage point in extending pupil reading interests and contacts. Wide personal reading in interesting content field sources not only adds to the pupil's background of content understandings, but also strengthens pupil attitudes about and proficiency in reading, as such.

*5.* Finally, the general climate of content area reading experiences can be adjusted so that pupils have an optimal chance of being and feeling successful in content reading and learning, regardless of their ability. This calls for no deep technical finesse on the part of the content teacher. Rather, it consists of one part teacher concern about pupils and their learning progress, one part basic understanding of reading behavior, and one part implementation of general strategies common to good instruction of any type.

### Extended Independent Reading

The development of reading competence and maturity requires more than skills instruction. Reading, like any other complex human behavior, needs to be used—frequently, independently, continuously, for varied purposes in a variety of materials and reading situations, and with personally satisfying effect. One must read to learn to read. One must read extensively to learn to read well. Reading which satisfies leads to favorable attitudes toward reading and growth in reading skill.[19]

We cannot assume that most secondary pupils automatically will read in a sustained, extensive manner or that they will develop broad tastes and deep reading interests. The extension of independent reading benefits from individual teacher support and special reading programs. But to exert a lifelong impact upon the reading habits of secondary pupils will require school-wide attention in the form of teacher stimulation and guidance plus the availability of materials. This area of pupil reading experience must be the shared responsibility of many elements of the school program: developmental reading, English and/or literature classes, content field instruction, the school library and its staff, and supplementary reading services, among others.

The reading experiences which comprise the major thrust of extended independent reading components fall into two major patterns: (1) sustained individual reading in a variety of collateral sources to implement classroom-oriented learning or problem-solving activity, and (2) personal fulfillment reading to satisfy individual needs, to widen the reader's interests, and to deepen his appreciation of significant writing. Both contribute to the development of reading maturity by increasing the amount of the pupil's reading contact time and by reinforcing flexible and efficient interpretive behaviors to satisfy a variety of reading or reading-learning purposes. While extended reading and personal reading contribute to the same developmental end and sometimes may be achieved through the same reading activity, each generally has its own particular thrust and useful conditions. The pupil needs both types of experiences.[20]

### Guided Sustained Reading

The major functions of extended reading include: (1) adding to the pupil's collective instructional- and independent-level reading-learning experiences, (2) bringing the pupil into contact with the widest possible range of instructionally related materials while reading purposefully, and (3) developing the pupil's capacity to read in a sustained manner to pursue and satisfy longer-term or broader-scope problems of an academic or operational nature. Guided sustained reading also con-

tributes to broader pupil development: among other things, it should facilitate class-related learning, add substantially to the pupil's general education, and provide a means of exploration whereby the pupil can discover written sources and ideas of immediate and future use.

Guided independent reading helps to polish the integral reading act until it becomes an accurate and efficient personal behavior. The more the individual reads, the greater his opportunity to encounter new terms, concepts, and thought processes. Thus, the pupil builds his reading and meaning vocabulary and adds vicariously to that bank of experiences which provide the necessary background for future learning and reading. The more he reads, and the more he reads in varied sources and on varied topics, the more opportunity he has to encounter and learn the patterns of reasoning processes employed by writers and in different areas of content and different textual forms.

The underlying tone of guided sustained reading is instrumental, and this is what differentiates it from personal reading. It goes beyond short-term practice exercises, and may take varied form. Mc-Cracken has recommended a drill called the SSR (Sustained Silent Reading) which involves mandated silent reading of increasingly larger amounts of time.[21] The several reading and rereading phases of the guided developmental reading lesson contribute to the extended reading experience. So does directed or guided reading of the content textbook. Broader school-oriented, sustained reading activity would include the reading of collateral source assignments, various forms of library research projects, the use of reading-study systems, independent reading activities necessary to carrying out learning units or projects, and background reading for creative production.

Extended reading activities are more valuable when the pupil can cope meaningfully with the materials, and when the pupil accepts the purposes for such reading as personally satisfying and meaningful. Sustained reading for school learning purposes benefits from teacher guidance. It should be a planned aspect of both reading and content instruction. It is not likely to take place for most pupils without teacher intervention and control. Guided sustained reading of an extended independent nature need not be heavy-handed, however. Through indirect and informal interaction, the adroit teacher can broaden the reading perspective of pupils and can encourage them to assume a larger personal responsibility for voluntary reading involvement of a sustained nature which goes beyond in-class learning exercises. Suggestions for structuring broader and more continuous reading for both developmental and content-related learning purposes are presented in Chapters Six, Eight, and Twelve.

### Personal Reading

Wide personal reading contributes to reader development in several essential ways: (1) it helps to associate reading with personal satisfaction and pleasure; (2) it forms an essential link in building a lifelong habit of reading; (3) it adds to the pupil's collective extended reading experience; and (4) it enhances the pupil as a feeling-thinking person.[22]

For reading to become a personal way of life, it must give the pupil something—it must reward him. An examination of the types of effect reading has upon readers was made in Chapter Two. These effects also serve to identify the likely "mobilizers" of personal reading activity, since motivation and reward are closely related phenomena. The specific reasons for which the pupil engages in personal reading are numerous, but they are likely to fall into one or more of the following major patterns: (1) gaining information which can be used instrumentally to solve practical problems or satisfy utilitarian needs, (2) deriving ego support, (3) appreciating a vicarious experience either for the substance or quality of the writing, and (4) gaining psychological and physical respite through escape and relaxation.

Developmentally, independent personal reading gets off to a slow start in the early elementary grades because of pupil immaturity in reading and self-direction and a lack of interesting materials at appropriately low reading levels in the school and public libraries. This is somewhat compensated for by being read to by others. Frequency and breadth of personal reading increase gradually during the intermediate grades and tend to reach a peak in the late middle school and junior high school years when pupil leisure time, growing reading ability, broadening background, and appetite for vicarious experiences coincide with the availability of interesting and readable materials. Personal reading habits tend to decrease some during the later secondary school and college years, probably because of greater participation in school activities, greater social interaction, and job responsibilities. However, pupils who form personal reading patterns early tend to maintain them.

Unfortunately, some secondary pupils have not developed even modest personal reading habits. Often, these pupils come from homes where little personal reading occurs. In other cases, this is a product of the pupil's current reading inadequacy or developmental immaturity. Reluctance to read may result from negative attitudes associated with school reading instructional experiences. It is ironic that without special provision for reading stimulation, the less able reader is not likely to do that which would most enable him to overcome his difficulty—to read and to read a lot. One of the major tasks here is finding materials at his reading level which deal with his interests and do not insult him with their simplicity.[23]

Many reasonably able readers are restricted in reading interests and engage in a rather limited pattern of personal reading. Such limited personal reading is not enhanced by ready availability of other recreational sources and activity outlets in our abundant culture. Nor is it improved through benign school neglect—a combination of curricular intensification since Sputnik and a traditional belief that pupil personal reading will emerge naturally as a by-product of literature program experiences and pupil interests. Tactics for stimulating wider reading involvement are suggested in Chapter Twelve. A bibliography of higher-interest reading lists is presented in Appendix B.

*Personal reading and literature study.* It is unfortunate that the study of literature, as such, has been confused with personal extended reading at both the elementary and secondary school levels. The study of literature has many worthwhile objectives of its own. It tends to emphasize the understanding and appreciation of literary sources and modes. Surely such study should include the stimulation of personal reading in these and associated literary sources. But students also need guidance to improve levels of literary understanding and appreciation.[24] Too often, the study of literature neither provides for teaching how to read literature nor results in voluntary pupil reading of literature.[25]

In any case, personal extended reading may or may not include sources which fit criteria for literature study. The key criteria for materials of personal reading will be reasonable ease of interpretation and the satisfaction of pupil interests and needs.

While the teacher of literature can do much to stimulate wider and deeper patterns of personal reading, other members of the secondary staff have similar opportunities and share this responsibility. The developmental reading and the content area teacher can do much to acquaint pupils with new and different reading adventures. Directly and indirectly, the school library staff has a notable impact upon pupil personal reading opportunities. And in some schools, the development of personal reading is considered significant enough to warrant special facilities and services.

## Supplementary Reading Services

The fifth pattern of reading experiences provided by comprehensive secondary education are services which supplement the basic program. While each of the four components treated earlier represents facets of reading which *all* pupils should experience rather continuously through regular, ongoing program functions, the fifth component is composed of somewhat shorter-duration experiences for selected pupils. The supplementary reading services component of the reading program permits the secondary school to: (1) provide for special pupil needs in the most direct, efficient manner; (2) adjust to emerging educational conditions without disrupting the general developmental thrust of the broad reading effort; (3) encourage provisional, creative efforts to stimulate pupil reading development in special settings; and (4) recognize the legitimacy of special reading services as an important adjunct of the comprehensive reading program, rather than a substitute for the comprehensive program.

While supplementary reading services are not offered to all pupils at any given moment, they are made available to pupils on the basis of greatest need or expressed interest. Special reading services should not be limited to one type of activity or selected to fit the needs of only one ability level of pupils. In addition to being undemocratic, the narrow targeting of supplementary services can produce negative associations and labeling which may generalize and hinder other school reading efforts. Any pupil may benefit, directly or indirectly, from some function of the special services program sometime in his secondary years.

### A Broad Spectrum of Program-Related Activities

Supplementary reading services cut across and support the other components of the program. Some special services, such as remedial reading, compensatory programs for disadvantaged readers, and reading counseling, reinforce developmental reading education. Short-term study-skill labs, voluntary or referred, contribute to content area reading prowess. "Great books" clubs and library-based recreational reading programs help to extend personal reading. Special services which contribute to or draw upon the evaluation component include referral diagnostic services, case study investigations of problem readers, and school-based research projects centering upon the reading-related issues. Various teacher in-service reading education activities can be made available through this supplementary services phase of the comprehensive reading program.

As the above examples imply, the operations and functions of the special services component include a broad sampling of diverse activities. Further illustrations picked at random from school observation or published report would include voluntary reading-rate improvement courses; voluntary lunchtime English vocabulary building sessions (conducted, in one report, by the Latin teacher); a special collection of highly readable sports and adventure stories located in the athletic equipment room; voluntary college preparatory reading-study minicourse for upper classmen; an "authors" club of students interested in creative writing that uses a current literary publication as the focal point for each group meeting; an action research group of reading and content faculty investigating the hypothesis that "concentrated instructional units treating key elements of critical reading-thinking in ninth-grade content classes will produce notable and significant improvement in pupil critical reading-thinking behavior." A perusal of articles in the professional journals of the past five years and the sources given at the end of this chapter will reveal a wide spectrum of school reading program offerings.[26]

Too often, supplementary reading services are considered the professional responsibility of the school reading specialist and thus become viewed as "specialist" services. Certain of the functions of the supplementary services component, e.g., aiding the problem reader or implementing in-service educational activities, do call for specialist guidance. But it is neither logistically possible nor philosophically wise for either the reading specialist or the general faculty to view the supplementary reading service component as the territorial imperative of reading teachers. Many faculty members have particular interests and talents which can be utilized here, and this provides a good means for developing greater faculty involvement in the secondary reading effort.[27] The support of other secondary school professionals is quite essential to some supplementary services—particularly the contributions of the school psychologist, the counseling and guidance staff, the general evaluation services personnel, the curriculum director, and the school administrator, as well as various teaching faculty.

Supplementary reading services do encompass the important diagnostic, remedial, and compensatory provisions for pupils with persistent reading difficulty; but as viewed in this text, these services reflect a variety of activities which support the other experience areas of the program and which increase the influence of the program upon the general reading development of pupils. Many of these activities consist of instruction and other direct interaction with pupils. Others involve faculty or staff interaction and development and contribute indirectly to pupil growth in reading and general school adjustment. The supplementary services component is a useful organizational-administrative device to facilitate planning innovation and flexibility in the secondary reading program without disrupting the effective ongoing contributions of the other program components. The broad range of experiences provided through these supplementary services parallels the desired scope of the all-school secondary reading effort.

## GUIDELINES FOR EVOLVING PROGRAMS

In many secondary schools, the initial provision for reading education occurred without much forethought—the "product" of some fortuitous circumstance, some strong personality, some governmental funding, or some state regulation. More than likely this took the form of a limited-objective reading effort rather than a broad, multipurpose program. Viewed over a forty-year span, secondary reading programs reflect growth in size and expansion of function.[28] Although some secondary reading efforts have remained single-strand programs, there has been a general tendency during the past decade for secondary schools to effect dual- or multiple-phase functions. Nevertheless, in many schools, secondary reading education has, like Topsy, just grown.

Programs, like instruction, need an articulated plan by which those professionals involved can determine direction, motivate and synthesize effort, make decisions, assign resources, implement activity more efficiently, evaluate performance and progress, and make necessary adjustments. The most effective secondary school reading efforts are guided by such a plan.

The following guidelines are recommended for the consideration of secondary school personnel involved in establishing, evaluating, and modifying reading program efforts in the direction of comprehensive reading education. Chapter Fourteen extends these concepts and suggests how they can be refined and implemented as an operational plan.

The emerging secondary program:

1. Recognizes reading to be one essential element of the secondary pupil's total language competency, learning behavior, and school adjustment and, as such, requires professional planning, sufficient financial support, and adequately trained personnel.

2. Considers its collective thrust to be developmental, i.e., enables all pupils to become functionally literate and to progress beyond this along the continuum of reading maturity, as their potential permits.

3. Assumes that effective program development and instruction are dependent upon an accurate, ongoing data base as implemented by planned reading evaluation.

4. Provides for five areas of essential reading-learning experiences for pupils — reading evaluation and assessment, content reading instruction and utilization, extended independent reading, and reading evaluation as supplemented by selective reading–related services for pupils with special reading needs and concerns.

5. Coordinates horizontal interaction among these reading–learning experiences within the secondary school as well as vertical continuity between the secondary school reading program and the larger school system reading effort.

6. Accommodates the existence of individual pupil differences in capacity, achievement, and motives through differentiated curricula, instruction, materials, and services.

7. Interprets secondary reading education to be the shared responsibility of all secondary school staff members and educates and encourages the contribution of each according to his or her capabilities and opportunities.

8. Contributes to the larger secondary school product by facilitating content area learning, improving pupil adjustment and motivation, providing needed services, and generally enhancing the school climate.

9. Accepts the challenge of evolving status — that only through continual evaluation and adjustment will the secondary reading program move toward needed comprehensiveness and dynamic flexibility.

10. Realizes that it must persuade administrators, faculty, pupils, parents, and the general public of its virtues through information, services, and personal contact.

## REFERENCES

1. William S. Gray, "Nature and Scope of a Sound Reading Program," in *Reading in the High School and College*, Forty-seventh Yearbook, Part II, of the National Society for the Study of Education, N. B. Henry, Editor (Chicago: University of Chicago Press, 1948) p. 46.

2. E. A. Betts, *Foundations of Reading Instruction* (Cincinnati, Ohio: American Book Company, 1957) p. 568.

3. Walter Hill, "Secondary Reading Activity in Western New York: A Survey," *Journal of Reading* 19 (October, 1975) pp. 13-19.

4. A. Sterl Artley, "The Development of Reading Maturity in High School — Implications of the Gray-Rogers Study," *Educational Administration and Supervision* 43 (October, 1957) pp. 321-28.

5. Louis Harris, *A Study of Functional Reading Ability in the United States* (Washington, D.C.: National Reading Center, 1971).

6. Roger Farr, *Reading: What Can Be Measured?* (Newark, Del.: International Reading Association, 1969) Chapter 6.

7. Diane Lapp, *The Use of Behavioral Objectives in Education* (Newark, Del.: International Reading Association, 1972) pp. 24-27.

8. E. F. Lindquist, "Preliminary Considerations in Objective Test Construction," in *Educational Measure-*

*ment,* E. F. Lindquist, Editor (Washington, D.C.: American Council on Education, 1951) p. 121.

9. Frank B. Womer, "What Is Criterion Referenced Measurement?" in *Measuring Reading Performance,* W. B. Blanton, R. Farr, and J. J. Tuinman, Editors (Newark, Del.: International Reading Association, 1974) pp. 34-44.

10. Walter Hill, "Evaluating Secondary Reading," in *Measurement and Evaluation of Reading,* R. Farr, Editor (New York: Harcourt, Brace and World, Inc., 1970) pp. 131-34.

11. Frederick J. McDonald, *Educational Psychology* (Belmont, Calif.: Wadsworth Publishing Company, Inc., 1965) pp. 43-47, 80.

12. Eddie C. Kennedy, *Methods in Teaching Developmental Reading* (Itasca, Ill.: F. E. Peacock Publishers, 1974) p. 25.

13. William S. Gray and Bernice Rogers, *Maturity in Reading: Its Nature and Appraisal* (Chicago: University of Chicago Press, 1956).

14. Walter Hill and Norma Bartin, *Secondary Reading Programs: Description and Research,* ERIC/CRIER Reading Review Series 30 (Indiana University, 1971) p. 25.

15. Leonard Courtney, "Are We Really Improving Reading in the Content Fields?" in *Current Issues in Reading,* N. B. Smith, Editor, International Reading Association Conference Proceedings 13 (Newark, Del.: International Reading Association, 1969) pp. 18-34.

16. Harold Herber, *Teaching Reading in Content Areas* (Englewood Cliffs, N.J.: Prentice-Hall, Inc., 1978) Chapter 2.

17. Thomas H. Estes and Ralph C. Staiger, "IRA Project CONPASS: An overview," *Journal of Reading* 16 (April, 1973) pp. 520-24.

18. Leo Fay and Lee Ann Jared, *Reading in the Content Fields,* An Annotated Bibliography (Newark, Del.: International Reading Association, 1975) 19 p.

19. James Squire, "Teaching Literature: High School and College," in *The Dynamics of Reading* (Waltham, Mass.: Ginn-Blaisdell, 1970) p. 287.

20. Arthur Heilman, "Developing Reading Tastes in the Secondary School," *High School Journal* 49 (April, 1966) p. 323.

21. Robert A. McCracken, "Initiating Sustained Silent Reading," *Journal of Reading* 14 (May, 1971) pp. 521-24.

22. B. C. Appleby, "The Effects of Individualized Reading on Certain Aspects of Literature Study with High School Seniors," doctoral dissertation, University of Iowa, 1967.

23. Daniel Fader, *The New Hooked on Books* (New York: Berkley Medallion Books, 1976).

24. Bertha Handlan, "The Fallacy of Free Reading," *English Journal* 25 (March, 1946) pp. 182-87.

25. James R. Squire, "Reading in American High Schools Today," in *Reading and Inquiry,* J. A. Figurel, Editor, International Reading Association Conference Proceedings 10 (Newark, Del.: International Reading Association, 1965) pp. 468-72.

26. Walter Hill and Norma Bartin, *Reading Programs in Secondary Schools* (Newark, Del.: International Reading Association, 1971).

27. Sheldon N. Russell, "Crucial Problems Facing Secondary Education," *Journal of Reading* 17 (May, 1974) pp. 600-3.

28. Walter Hill, "Characteristics of Secondary Reading: 1940-70," in *Reading: The Right to Participate,* Twentieth Yearbook of the National Reading Conference, Frank P. Greene, Editor (Milwaukee, Wis.: National Reading Conference, Inc., 1971) pp. 20-29.

## SUPPLEMENTARY SOURCES

Artley, A. Sterl. *Trends and Practices in Secondary Reading,* Chapter 3. Newark, Del.: International Reading Association, 1968.

Duffy, Gerald G., Editor. *Reading in the Middle School,* Part II. Newark, Del.: International Reading Association, 1974.

Early, Margaret J. "What Does Research in Reading Reveal—About Successful Reading Programs?" *English Journal* 58 (April, 1969) pp. 534-47.

Gray, William S. "Nature and Scope of a Sound Reading Program." In *Reading in the High School and College,* N. B. Henry, Editor, Forty-seventh Yearbook of the National Society for the Study of Education, Part II, Chapter IV. Chicago: University of Chicago Press, 1948.

Henry, N. B., Editor. *Development in and Through Reading,* Sixtieth Yearbook of the National Society for the Study of Education, Part I. Chicago: University of Chicago Press, 1961. See especially William D. Sheldon, Chapter XVII, "Reading Instruction in the Junior High School," and Guy L. Bond and Stanley B. Kegler, Chapter XVIII, "Reading in Senior High School."

Walter Hill and Norma Bartin, *Reading Programs in Secondary Schools* (Newark, Del.: International Reading Association, 1971).

Rauch, Sidney J. "Administrators' Guidelines for More Effective Reading Programs." *Journal of Reading* 17 (January, 1974) pp. 297-300.

# II

# READING IN THE SECONDARY CLASSROOM

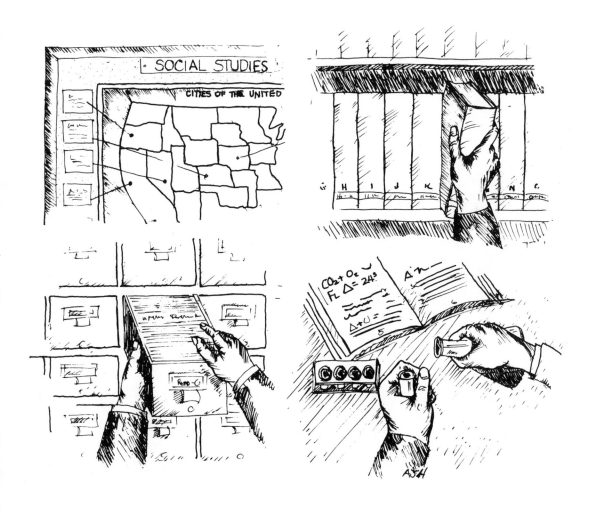

# FIVE

# Utilizing Reading for Content Learning

*The act of reading provides the student with a tool by means of which written records are made accessible.... Reading in the school must be a means toward an end and not an end in itself.... If reading leads to the mastery of ideas and the using of ideas in controlling conduct, it then justifies itself.*

Gerald Alan Yoakam

***Overview*** Reading and content area instruction are mutually supporting concerns of secondary education. The improvement of content area reading is not as difficult nor as esoteric as content teachers have been led to believe. The eight broad strategies suggested in this chapter for improving content learning through more effective utilization of content classroom reading are ready evidence that the task is neither difficult nor inappropriate.

The chapter is directed to the concerns of the content teacher, but it may serve the interests of developmental reading teachers, as well. Reading is not the only tool of learning and study employed by the versatile classroom teacher of the substantive subjects, of course. However, it is used with considerable frequency by most secondary teachers as a major source of content learning and classroom activities and/or as the vehicle of assigned collateral or independent study. Beyond its immediate utility in instruction, the development of lifelong proficiency in using content-related written sources is an important classroom objective in its own right. As Yoakam indicated nearly a half century ago, the justification for employing reading as a learning aid depends upon whether teachers and pupils make effective use of it in the mastery of the concepts, constructs, and processes which comprise the learning objectives of that content subject.[1] The issue is not whether reading has an important place in the content classroom, but *how* it can be employed with efficiency and maximal positive effect.

## READING AND
## CONTENT AREA INSTRUCTION

A two-way relationship exists between reading and content area instruction. We have seen that the processes of reading cannot be separated meaningfully from the facts, concepts, generalizations, and processes which the writer encodes into his written message. Similarly, reading as a process cannot be ignored if content area instruction expects to make use of written materials as vehicles of content learning. The pupil who can handle the reading–thinking–study processes pertinent to a content course has the best opportunity to learn in that course. On the other hand, when a pupil gains a broader and deeper background through content area instruction, he becomes a more powerful reader through this reservoir of potential interpretive associations.

### Toward Reality in
### Content Reading Usage

Reading can be a powerful tool of instruction. How useful it may be depends not only upon the pupil's reading ability, but also upon how it is utilized by the teacher. The content teacher certainly is capable of improving content reading and, thus, content achievement.[2] There are a number of instructional strategies, such as those presented later in this chapter, which are readily employed to improve content reading and content learning. But whether, once aware of them, content teachers make use of them will depend in good part upon whether the content teacher is ready to accept a realistic view of content reading and the instructional situation.[3]

### *Reading and Content "Mastery"*

A continuing state of frustration is a symptom that something is wrong — with the individual or with the situation. Many dedicted content area teachers live with some persistent degree of professional frustration or related malaise.[4] The performance of their pupils simply does not meet the expectations which the teacher uncritically accepts on the basis of curricular tradition or academic indoctrination. At issue here is something beyond defensible societal and professional expectations that pupils should make reasonable progress in the learning, application, and appreciation of the significant and useful concepts and processes attendant to the content area.

The source of this frustration may be incorrectly or but dimly perceived. A graduate teacher in one of the writer's classes put it this way: "I am relieved every Friday and depressed every Monday. Why? Because I know they [her pupils] are not 'mastering the course content', and I feel responsible and guilty." This teacher, an emotionally stable and dedicated professional, did not immediately recognize how accurately her complaint captured the core of the problem: that she may have been responsible for this condition, but not in the way she assumed. At issue, of course, was her unquestioned assumption that "mastery of course content" was a reasonable professional goal.

The position taken in this text is that the traditional and vague goal of "content course mastery" is inconsistent with available evidence and logic, is questionably motivated, and contributes unnecessarily to faculty frustration, inappropriate instruction, and pupil failure. Let us be straight about this! The question is not whether pupils should be expected to "learn well" in terms of developing competency in important content area objectives — but whether it is possible to "learn all" facts, concepts, generalizations, and processes which can be construed as pertinent to any content subject.

Perhaps there was a time in the dim past, when we knew so little of our accumulated societal wisdom or when our technology was so minimally developed, that we might assume that teachers and pupils could and should "master" all that could be taught. A half century of empirical evidence indicates that most pupil performance does not support this assumption. Probably pupils never did, if Plato can be believed. Certainly, if any modern teacher, curriculum maker, or textbook writer believes this objective is more realistic today, he is wonderfully uninformed about what has been happening in the nuclear age and is certainly due for some "future shock."[5]

The teacher's or administrator's argument that their emphasis upon content mastery is simply a device to get pupils to work harder at learning probably involves some rationalization. In any case, it runs contrary to the facts of learning. Moreover, it is how the teacher behaves instructionally which influences pupil performance, not vague curricular aspirations. A lack of realism about content mastery is very likely to lead to ineffective instruction. Herber has argued persuasively that attempts to "cover" the course content (or its textbook substitute) lead to recitation procedures and other forms of "assumptive" teaching.[6] Among these are assumptions that secondary pupils can learn effectively from lecturing and from extensive, unguided reading assignments in the textbook and similar content materials. A more realistic selection of concepts and processes as content objectives makes it possible for the teacher to change pupil cognitive and affective behavior rather than to frantically and superficially inform. Such realism is conducive to more serviceable use of reading to support content area learning. Selecting the most significant content concepts, generalizations, and processes for learning objectives should produce better long-term content learning and application.

### Textbook Reading as Learning

The content textbook serves as the basic and perhaps singular source of information for many content classrooms, and the undifferentiated, unguided assignment of chapters is a quite common practice for using these textbooks. Generally, such a practice assumes that secondary pupils can learn effectively the necessary and significant concepts and processes of a content area simply by reading independently in the textbook or similar technical sources. There are, at least, three questionable dependent conditions which are subsumed by the textbook master concept. One is that the textbook presents all or much of the currently viable, needed information pertinent to the course or unit objectives and that this information is valid today and

will be tomorrow. Another is that absorption of information, even viable and appropriate information, through undirected reading will produce the learning, thinking, and application behaviors which should be a part of content course learning.

However, we are concerned here with a prior third issue: Can most members of a typical content area class satisfactorily *understand* the important meanings presented in a typical general textbook assignment? Research evidence indicates that most secondary class members do not adequately comprehend and remember content textbook information under undifferentiated, undirected assignment conditions.[7]

A number of factors contribute to this lack of success in textbook reading.[8] One is that textbook writing is not very readable even for better readers.[9] A second is that textbooks carry a heavy concept density per page, owing to their prevailing tendency toward encyclopedic summary. A third is that pupils, even those who are adequate general readers, do not know how to read a textbook selectively and flexibly in order to organize the significant data presented for learning, retention, and application. A fourth factor is that many pupils often do not even make a serious attempt to study the textbook — because of attitudes toward the subject, past negative experiences with textbook reading, or reaction to extensive and unclear assignments.

Whatever the factors, it seems clear that the content teacher cannot assume that the textbook plus a general direction to read it (or study it) will produce needed content understanding and learning. The intent here is not to denigrate the secondary textbook as one source of content information, although most could stand some improvement in that regard. Rather, the implication lies in how it is used. Assuming that the textbook will continue to be the most available content area reading source in most secondary classrooms, the effectiveness of textbook reading can be improved by better selection, assignment, teacher guidance, and development of study skills — as we shall see. But unless the teacher makes such adjustments, the textbook may be more of a hindrance to content learning than a help.[10]

## Reading and Content Processing

Too frequently, pupils and teachers assume that reading with a dedicated general intent "to understand" is synonymous with content study reading and automatically will evoke those learning, retaining, and reasoning behaviors necessary to effective content usage. The extent to which content reading produces *effective* thinking, learning, retention, and/or transfer will depend upon a number of factors—not the least of which are how one reads and what mental operations one uses in/or beyond reading to gain general understanding. To see why general adequacy in reading, in itself, may not satisfy content reading tasks, we need to review briefly the essential but somewhat different conditions of several content-related processes.

### Reading and Content Area Reading

We have defined *mature reading* broadly and operationally as the effective, purposeful use of printed sources. This includes the general abilities required to locate, decode, interpret, and react to the meaning of the content. This broad, operational view does subsume the functions of thinking, learning, retaining, and transfer. However, these functions are used more precisely and efficiently when the pupil has learned how to control them, when they are incorporated into the reader's purposes, and when adjustments are made in reading-study processes to achieve those purposes.

The difficulties of content reading for perhaps half the pupils in secondary classes are intensified by their lack of general proficiency in reading. No more than a few pupils in early secondary content area classes will be mature readers, and unless an effective, ongoing, school-wide developmental program has been directed to this end, this is likely to be true for later secondary content classes, too. But even the better readers may not utilize their reading power in content situations, because they have been conditioned to feel that the reading of a content assignment is not safely taken into their own control—it is something to be passively followed, rather than selectively, purposefully, and flexibly searched for meaning, enjoyment, and power.

For a number of reasons then, content reading often turns out to be no more than an unstructured attempt to "cover the pages" of the assignment. Some pupils will do this more efficiently and with more understanding than others; but, unless the teacher provides better direction, the likely focus will be to work rather mechanically at learning *all* of the material—whether it amounts to ten paragraphs, ten pages, or ten chapters. Like getting to heaven, it is hoped that by these good works (these conscious attempts to read the content) proper rewards will be forthcoming—learning, remembering, and passing tests. Unfortunately, even such a humble vision of educational paradise is likely to be lost.

A general, undifferentiated understanding of content does not automatically evoke higher-level mental operations. To be effective, content area reading must break its association with passive assimilation or mechanical memorization of literal meaning. To do so, it needs to incorporate that broader operational definition—*the purposeful use of varied printed sources as employed in the mature reading act.*

### Reading and Content Area Thinking

Curriculum statements for the various areas of content study usually recommend the development of reasoning processes pertinent to those areas. It is usually assumed that pupils should be capable of *assimilative thinking*, i.e., to draw inferences and to follow the organization and argument of the key informational sources for that field. At a somewhat higher level, most statements of content area curricula include as objectives that pupils should develop and employ *critical thinking* and *creative thinking*—the objective analysis and restructure and utilization of content information to solve problems and to create original products.

The nature of thought as a fundamental process of reading and its place in mature reading were discussed in Chapter Three. Decoding, it will be recalled, involves the processes of associating literal meaning with the writer's statements. It amounts to the gaining of information in an unqualified manner and corresponds to the lowest rung of most hierarchies of cognitive processing.[11] The analytical and evaluative interpretive behaviors of the mature reading act correspond to and are dependent upon the assimilative and critical thinking processes. It is the further combination of "interpretive" and "reaction" processes which brings the reader to transformational thinking behaviors.

Not all pupils in a secondary content classroom are capable of decoding the literal meaning of the content textbook and similar materials. More significantly, many more do little beyond decoding. Teachers whose reading assignments, class discussions, tests, and grading practices place priority upon verbalization — the literal parroting of written statements — unwittingly discourage the development and utilization of higher levels of reasoning in the content area.

Thus, it cannot be assumed that the typical content area reading assignment encourages content area thinking or that secondary pupils will utilize reasoning processes when reading the content area materials. Whether content area reading activity does contribute to content-related thinking will depend upon whether the content teacher is willing to build interpretive- and reaction-level tasks into content reading assignments and to guide pupils in the questioning-thinking processes needed to satisfy those assignments. At the very least, it would help if they did not discourage pupils from utilizing those assimilative, critical, and transformational thinking processes they have already mastered.

### Reading, Content Learning, and Retention

While specific definitions vary, most psychologists agree that *learning*, generally, consists of the acquisition of any relatively permanent change in behavior as the result of experience. The behaviors learned may be covert as well as overt. The behaviors to be changed relative to school learning, including content area experiences, usually are described in terms of understandings, attitudes, and skilled performances, as we have seen. The significant conditions of learning include learner readiness, active mental involvement, and strong meaningful association between the situation and the response to be learned. Learning typically is assessed in immediate terms by such tasks as recognition, recall, and reproductive or enactive performance.

Retention is the positive counterpart of the phenomenon we usually describe as "forgetting." Defined more directly, *retention* is the persistence of learning after a period of intervening experiences. The confirmation of retention usually draws upon delayed versions of the procedures used to confirm learning — recognition, recall, reproductive and enactive performance — as well as determination of relearning efficiency or ease. While retention of a behavior subsumes that it has been learned, learning cannot presume retention. Strong original learning usually enhances retention. Generally, learned responses must be reinforced (used and rewarded) periodically to retain their effectiveness. This is particularly true for academic learning.

***Some educational implications.*** Several observations may be made pertinent to content area reading as it relates to learning and retention. The first is that reading assignments are not the most appropriate vehicle of learning and retention of some content area behaviors; some broad and complex relationships may be better learned through iconic devices (such as models, filmstrips, and diagrams), and some performance behaviors are learned best through execution or guided enaction. Second, the teacher cannot be confident that pupils who have read an assignment, even if they have gained a reasonable immediate grasp of its meaning, have acquired a relatively permanent change of specific behavior(s) as a result of that experience. Third, a single reading or rereading of such material, even if understood and learned, generally is limited to short-term retention. If the content teacher is concerned about learning and/or retention beyond understanding, she will need to make instructional provision for it. The pupil can help in this if he is brought to understand these differences, particularly if he is taught some procedures to effect better understanding, learning, and retention of concepts encountered while reading.

If the reading assignment is to produce better understanding, learning, thinking, and retaining of concepts, principles, and processes of the content field, certain reading–related instructional conditions will need to be effected. Reading teachers as well as content teachers will need to teach pupils to read an assignment in a purposeful, flexible manner to satisfy a variety of interpretive tasks. Both teacher and pupil will need to understand the difference between general-purpose reading and that study reading that facilitates reading learning, retention, and transfer of meaning. Also, the content teacher will need to provide pupils with assignments geared to effect the important content objectives. This presumes judicious selection of the concepts to be mastered and the cognitive processes to be emphasized. And it supposes that the content teacher will implement these operations with general strategies for effective utilization of reading in any content learning situation.

## Content Reading and the Content Teacher

How effectively reading is utilized in classroom learning activity will be influenced by a number of conditions. Some of these conditions are larger school factors—its socioeconomic setting, educational philosophy, social and emotional climate, organizational patterns, and administrative policies, among others. Some are closely related to curriculum patterns and available instructional resources. Another important set of conditions are those generated by the motivation and personal resources of the pupils who compose the class membership. But in the long run, the effective use of reading in a secondary classroom will depend heavily upon the teacher of that class.

Four teacher characteristics seem particularly critical to improving reading and learning through reading in the content classroom setting. The first consists of *a positive but realistic teacher attitude*—

about pupils and pupil differences, about teaching, about the content field, and about reading. The teacher who accepts that all class members, regardless of differences in present reading and learning capabilities, deserve to profit as much as possible from this class usually will find ways to improve the learning use of reading in the content class.

The second key teacher factor consists of *general teaching proficiency*—the relating of instructional methodology to course objectives and content area substance. Content area reading supports content learning and, thus, is dependent upon the general learning structure of the course setting. Effective use of reading will improve the learning product in any classroom situation. However, reading cannot compensate satisfactorily for a largely deficient learning environment, particularly where average or below-average readers are concerned. Reading seems to be used most effectively in those classrooms with well-planned and executed instruction. This is hardly surprising. The effective use of reading is but an element of good instruction. Competency in general methodology and competency in reading strategy are interdependent qualities.

A third factor of significance is the teacher's *understanding of the nature and nurture of reading behavior*. Insight about the way reading develops and functions augurs for realistic planning of pupil reading-learning activity. In addition, understanding of reading behavior provides the basis for the effective decision and adjustment of the reading setting when individual or group reading-study problems arise. Part I of this text addressed itself to presenting a basic background about reading and the reader.

The fourth of these teacher characteristics consists of *familiarity with general and specific strategies for the effective utilization of reading in any school setting*. There are a number of sensible instructional procedures which any teacher, content or reading, should find helpful in facilitating pupil use of reading for understanding, learning, and application. Whether, once learned, these strategies are employed will depend much upon whether the other three teacher characteristics are operant.

The instructional-learning advantages of structuring the content setting should not be underestimated. Both learning and reading development benefit from attention to such methodology as suggested on the following pages.

## IMPROVING READING IN THE CONTENT CLASSROOM

Content area reading implementation and developmental reading instruction differ primarily in instructional emphasis and choice of materials. The major concern in content area reading is to use reading and its instruction to achieve the content area objectives; the written content sources are selected primarily for their contribution to these goals, although the goals are more readily achieved if the materials are readable and the pupil is aided in his reading of them. The major concern of developmental reading instruction is the improvement of reading abilities which can be generalized to a wide variety of reading circumstances, including content field and technical situations; the instructional materials are selected primarily because they facilitate the development of reading competency or power.

It would be a mistake, however, to assume that content area reading and developmental reading employ quite different reading behavior or that the instructional strategies useful in the one situation are not useful in the other. The remainder of this chapter treats some recommended general strategies for improving reading in the content classroom. They do not call for expertise in specific reading instruction. Yet the developmental reading teacher is likely to find them as appropriate as the content teacher.

This text does not presume that the content teacher should function as or like a reading specialist. But it does recognize that content teachers can profit from a number of principles and strategies which reading teachers have found useful. Chapter Six describes several general approaches for guiding pupil reading of larger selections. These approaches are equally as useful to the improvement of content understanding, learning, and thinking as to the development of reading skills. Chapter Eight focuses upon the fundamentals of reading instruction, and again, this is information which applies to the teaching and use of reading in any setting—content classroom, developmental reading situations, corrective reading groups, or individualized remedial reading. Even Part III, which presents ways of improving specific reading behaviors, provides information which the content teacher can readily employ, e.g., developing technical vocabulary and teaching crucial reading-thinking skills. To reiterate, much that is instructionally applicable in one school reading situation can be usefully employed in another.

### Eight Fundamental Strategies for Improving Content Reading

Listed below and discussed on the following pages are eight broad instructional procedures which can lead to notable improvement in reading in the content classroom (and are equally useful in the developmental reading situation). Each is effected through certain supporting procedures. Some of these strategies are discussed in detail in this chapter. Others are summarized and their supporting tactics presented in later chapters. For these, the reference chapters are identified, in case the teacher wishes to explore those tactics more immediately.

1. Identifying pupil reading performance characteristics (supporting detail presented in Chapter Seven).
2. Facilitating the use of classroom sources.
3. Coordinating the reading of sources: unit study.
4. Improving the reading assignment.
5. Guiding the reading of text. (Chapter Six details strategies and tactics for aiding pupils in the interpretation of instructional materials.)
6. Developing class-related specific reading behaviors (supporting detail presented in Chapters Eight through Twelve).

7. Extending independent content reading habits and interests (see also Chapter Twelve).

8. Adapting content instruction for poorer readers (see also Chapter Thirteen).

### 1. Identifying Pupil Reading Performance Characteristics

In Chapter Two, we observed that reading potential combined with learning experiences fashion substantial ranges of general reading performance levels among secondary pupils. Content area reading performance also is influenced significantly by the reading resources the reader brings to the page. Such reading differences will exist even if administrative steps have been taken to achieve greater classroom homogeneity. The classroom instructor needs to know the typical reading performance levels and skills for each of his pupils. Information about key pupil resources which influence reading development and behavior often proves useful, as well. With such information, the teacher can be more realistic in the determination of learning objectives and in the planning and execution of group and individual learning activities.

The assessment and evaluation of secondary reading behavior is something less than a perfect science. While it is not realistic to expect the content classroom instructor to become a diagnostic specialist, there are a number of ways in which useful information about pupil reading performance may be obtained by teachers. Four immediate sources of such reading information are: pupil reading-learning history as contained in school records, the results of standardized reading tests, observation of classroom reading performance, and information provided by the school's secondary reading specialist.

*Cumulative pupil records.* The cumulative pupil record (CPR) can be a useful source of background information about pupil reading and learning development. It will be more helpful if pertinent data from the elementary school are included. As a pupil information source, the value of the CPR will depend upon whether significant educational and personal events in the pupil's school experience have been systematically observed and reported.

Past reading performance serves as one of the better predictors of future performance, assuming that no unusual intervening circumstances occur. A history of serious reading difficulty not only will presage present difficulty in content interpretation, it often can serve to warn the teacher of pupil predisposition to reading motivational problems. An effective system of cumulative records should contain useful information with regard to previous learning success in various subject areas, history of school or personal adjustment problems, socioeconomic background and other influential family-related factors, language ability, general academic aptitude, learning-related physical abnormalities, as well as the nature and results of special reading educational experiences.

*Standardized test performance.* A growing number of secondary schools administer reading survey tests, and the normative results and/or related analysis of findings are available for each pupil. Often, these results are obtained on an annual or biennial basis as part of the regular administration of achievement test batteries. In addition, some schools administer supplementary group reading tests. These may be locally or state-developed tests. In some schools, results of diagnostic tests of specific reading competencies have been obtained on pupils exhibiting special reading needs.

There are notable limitations to the valid, yet useful information that standardized reading tests can provide for daily instructional decisions at the classroom level.[12] However, they do provide a normative basis for estimating relative pupil performance which involves general silent-reading proficiency. Standardized reading-test batteries sometimes include subtests which assess performance on reading vocabulary (the ability to recognize the form and meaning of words in simple context); reading comprehension (usually a total score obtained on questions about specifics and generalizations, and, to a lesser degree, about organizational structure contained in paragraph or multiparagraph selections); and certain reading-study skills (particularly dictionary usage, use of an index, and the interpretation of graphs and tables).

Many standardized tests of content area achievement require the examinee to read test selections and answer items which relate rather directly to content area topics or which are typical of content area reading. These can provide some intimation of the pupil's ability to understand content-related context. Standardized tests of language usage and tests of mental ability provide data on pupil attributes which contribute to reading potential and performance.

The normative results of standardized reading and general achievement tests must be treated with some caution. Nevertheless, standardized test results may be helpful if employed as their makers intended. When normed over broad pupil populations, the results permit the teacher to obtain relative comparisons between the performance of a particular pupil with other pupils, a general idea of performance differences within a pupil or class profile, the relative reading strength of the class as a group, and with proper caution, to compare individual reading-test performance with test results of learning aptitude and other areas of achievement performance. Most testing authorities feel that the percentile rank—the test score translated into percent of peer group (norms) surpassed by that score—provides a more accurate basis of performance comparison than generalized and extrapolated conversions of the test score into grade equivalents.

*Classroom reading performance.* There are a number of ways in which the classroom teacher may obtain pupil reading performance information through in-class reading assessment. These informal procedures may lack the rigor of professionally developed tests. Nevertheless, the resulting observations can be more functionally useful if they provide information directly related to course objectives and classroom learning activities. Classroom reading assessment is necessary to gain a more complete picture of the pupil's reading strengths and weaknesses and to gain information for operational and instructional decisions at the classroom level.

Classroom assessment procedures and instruments of use to the content instructor include readability assessment of the relative difficulty of textbooks and assigned collateral reading materials; group informal reading inventories and cloze reading tests to observe pupil ability to cope with the difficulty of content-learning sources; informal tests of specific reading interpretation, study, and application behaviors pertinent to classwork; and analysis of performance on reading-related assignments. Also, checklists, questionnaires, and personal histories can be used to obtain information on pupil reading-study habits, reading attitudes, interests, and self-perceived reading-study problems. The development and use of such assessment measures will be discussed in Chapter Seven.

*The secondary reading specialist as a source of pupil reading information.* Many secondary schools now have one or more reading specialists on the staff, and one of the common activities of the specialist is to serve as a consultant to the classroom teacher. The reading specialist can supply the teacher with supplementary reading assessment measures as well as help in the development of measures applicable to specific class situations. Where serious pupil reading problems are suspected, the specialist can develop a diagnostic profile of the pupil or share such information as previously gathered. The specialist can help the teacher determine appropriate classroom reading-learning activities for problem readers.

## 2. Facilitating the Use of Classroom Reading Sources

A teacher usually can improve the effectiveness of pupil reading and learning simply by improving the working conditions under which pupils may use their present reading abilities. One way to do this is to acquire pertinent materials with easier readability and to promote a closer match between a pupil's functional reading level and the reading difficulty of the source. One can also acquaint pupils with the written materials of the course and provide easier pupil access to the instructional materials.

***Improving the readability match between pupil and source.*** The widespread use of the course textbook and other required reading is based upon the assumption that the pupil will learn and retain the information he reads. This presumes that the pupil can decode and interpret those instructional materials. Unfortunately, collected evidence indicates that the mismatch between the readability of instructional materials and pupil reading and learning capabilities is quite prevalent.[13] Improving the readability match between pupil and the assigned written materials of instruction should reap immediate profit in textbook interpretation and learning. In time, the indirect dividends of this effort will include pupil growth in reading ability, stronger motivation to read assigned material, and a more positive attitude toward the area of content instruction.

*Required reading and reader flexibility.* The traditional major concerns in the selection of the course textbook and other instructional materials have been the validity of the content information presented and the extent to which that content supports the learning objectives of the course.[14] The wisdom of making content pertinency the singular concern in the selection of instructional materials may be questioned—if a sizable proportion of the class cannot understand these materials, or worse, if they misinterpret the facts, concepts, and procedures presented.[15]

The required reading assignment does restrict the reader's choice of material and approach, and this loss of flexibility interferes with the natural reader-writer dynamic. In the general or free-reading situation, the reader can adjust to the focus and difficulty of the written material through self-selection—either in the choice of source or in the choice of what and how he attends to the content of that source. This self-choice does increase the likelihood that the reader can understand the material chosen.

Such reader flexibility is necessarily delimited by practical circumstances in the case of instructional assignments. Most seasoned teachers have discovered that pupil immaturity and the paucity of appropriate learning sources easily available to pupils argue for teacher selection, collection, and/or coordination of instructional materials. However, in assuming this control over the reading-study sources, the teacher has limited the pupil's range of personal adjustment to the difficulty of those sources. Therefore, it seems reasonable, if not imperative, that the classroom instructor also assume responsibility for selecting materials among which the class members can find reasonable choices in interest and interpretive difficulty.

*General and functional readability.* Teachers and textbook selection committees are giving greater consideration to *general readability*, i.e., the broad learning support provided by instructional materials. In this respect, checklists for the evaluation of instructional sources usually assign higher ratings for such items as typographical devices, such as headings and summaries; graphic and pictorial content; suggested learning activities; supplementary exercises; recommended readings; the attractiveness of format; the interest level of examples; and the general appropriateness of vocabulary and prose style. These factors contribute to general readability of the text in the sense that they contribute to its potential as a learning tool.

*Functional readability*, or how well the individual pupil can interpret the prose, itself, can be a somewhat different problem of textbook selection and assignment. There are two notable obstacles to the effective match of reader ability with written instructional materials. The first is the substantial range of pupil instructional reading levels present in most content area classes. In the nonrestricted classroom circumstance, this range may be equivalent to seven or eight reading grade levels. Even in the more homogeneously arranged classes, the reading-level spread seldom is less than three or four reading grades. The teacher cannot expect to completely mitigate such differences by instructional manipulation and textbook choice. But the mismatch between pupil capabilities and material difficulty can be greatly lessened by the use of multiple instructional sources of varying difficulty and by teacher utilization of a wider choice of supplementary or collateral course reading materials!

The second difficulty reinforces the first: the written prose of most texts is too difficult for the average reader of a content class. As a rough estimate, only the top third of the readers of most classes can cope adequately with the textbook designated by publisher, adopted by the school, or chosen by the teacher as appropriate for that class level. Moreover, without considerable instructional support with text reading and study, the proportion of class members who "read" the text with adequate understanding will be even smaller.

When we consider the functional readability of the written prose of the text, we are concerned with the ease, fluency, and accuracy with which the student can decode and interpret the text for his instructional reading purposes. From this viewpoint, written content is "instructionally" appropriate when the reader: (a) finds the material challenging but not frustrating, (b) can recognize readily 95 percent of the running words, and (c) can answer at least 75 percent of questions on an immediate recall or recognition-type test over the selection.[16] These criteria are deemed adequate only if it is assumed that with teacher assistance (through preparation, guided reading, etc.) the pupil will read the material even more fluently and with better understanding. If the pupil were expected to read this material "independently" for enjoyment or study purposes, the needed accuracy figures for word accuracy should be raised to 98 or 99 percent and to 90 percent for interpretation.

***Broadening the selection of instructional materials.*** The problem of textbook reading difficulty has been recognized for some time, and during the last decade, there has been a tendency for publishers to develop textbooks and other commercial learning materials which are more "readable." Most instructional texts and related source materials presently available in the secondary school tend toward the upper ranges of pupil reading ability, however. It remains for the classroom instructor to lessen this disparity by whatever means available.

The collection and utilization of multiple learning sources will be of considerable help, especially if attention is given to obtaining materials of easier readability as well as finding and using a wider variety of materials for instructional purposes. It may prove challenging to find easier materials which satisfy specific learning objectives, but instructional viability and reader interest should be improved by increasing the selection of instructional materials to include cartoons, magazine articles, government brochures, advertising copy, bus schedules, editorials, telephone directories, distributors' catalogs, song books, original editions, plays, pupil-written material, and teacher-rewritten materials.

The instructor will be aided in the search for more readable textbooks and other sources of continuing textual use by knowledge of the relative difficulty of these materials and by assessment of the general level of material the members of the class can comprehend with moderate effort. Familiarity with the use of an efficient readability formula or graph will help with the assessment of relative difficulty levels of texts. Knowing how to construct and administer an informal reading inventory (IRI) or a cloze reading test produces reasonably good approximations of the level of material at which the particular pupil can satisfy "instructional" or "independent" performance criteria. With this information, the teacher can make use of bibliographies of graded source materials such as those listed in Appendix B. Explanation of the use of readability measures, informal reading inventories, and the cloze procedure is presented in Chapter Seven.

Of course, the teacher can do a good deal to lessen the reading difficulty of a reading selection by the way she prepares her pupils for and guides them through the reading and study of a selection. Many of the suggestions given in the remainder of this chapter serve that end.

***Acquainting pupils with the basic written sources of the course.*** Whatever his present state of reading development, the pupil can make better use of classroom instructional materials if he has gained insight into their nature and function. Many teachers overestimate the sophistication of their pupils for dealing with the reading resources of the class. Some direct attention given to familiarizing the class with the sources which play a vital role in the course learning activities will enhance the learning opportunities of all pupils. Such help is essential to the less able readers and learners. Among other values, this concern can do much to create a more cooperative learning dynamic—between pupil and the instructional materials and between pupils and teacher.

*Early introduction and continuing guidance.* Generally, it is advantageous to provide this help early in the course or semester. One approach is to develop it through an introductory class project or to give it a major place in an introductory unit to the course. Elements of such a unit which should benefit most pupils include a systematic guided examination of the basic text; an overview (or review) of basic library research skills needed for study activities in this class; guidance in the location and examination of key supplementary course references; and an explanation of how the instructor plans to use these written sources during the course.

Many pupils will need continued guidance beyond an introductory unit in order to develop independence in the use of course sources. Some teachers find it valuable to review the most pertinent of these learnings at the beginning of each course unit, along with the presentation of sources of particular use for reading and study during that unit. Follow-up practice in the use of the most significant content or general reference sources can be provided by means of worksheets, study guides, or individual or team assignments. The poorest readers and learners will benefit from personal guidance by the instructor—as individuals or in special groups—throughout the period of instruction. Such attention pays off in enhanced learning and attitude.

*Textbook and library usage.* A number of things can be done to help the pupil gain familiarity with the textbooks and other basic sources utilized in the course which do not require extensive time or complex preparation. Explaining the functions of the various parts of the textbook and how they may be used in dealing with particular course tasks will be helpful. Another aid is to show pupils how to vary the reading of a chapter to meet different reading-study purposes. Mentally walking pupils through a short chapter or a longer section of a chapter, with the teacher or a panel of better readers indicating how they use the textbook aids and identifying what they consider to be important concepts and generalizations, can be very revealing to inadequate readers and learners. If study guides or other reading-study aids are to be employed regularly as a method of teaching, the instructor should demonstrate how they are used most effectively. Another technique which is immediately meaningful to many pupils involves the teacher's explanation of how test questions are developed from the textbook assignment.

A sizable proportion of junior high pupils and many senior high pupils do not know how to make effective use of the library and its resources. A conducted class or group tour of the school library or learning resource center can serve as a useful beginning. Major items for consideration in a library study unit would include the location, explanation, and trial use of general references; introduction and practice with library locational aids and systems; and the identification and location of specific library sources pertinent to the content of the course in question. Such introductory learning may be reinforced by a library study assignment checklist or group study guide through which the pupil must make working contact with the most useful library references. Less able pupils may be teamed with more able students for such an assignment. In many high schools, the librarian will work cooperatively with the classroom teacher to provide library education activities. Too often, the librarian is overlooked as a potential member of the reading education program.

*Ready access to essential materials.* It serves no useful purpose to involve pupils in reading-related content learning and research tasks if the pupils cannot find the materials necessary to these ends. For many pupils, simply encountering some difficulty in locating those materials aborts their fulfilling the assignment. How much the teacher provides access depends upon the personal and reading maturity of the pupils. The more mature high school junior or senior can be expected to dig out needed references from the school, public, or home library. Moderately mature junior and senior high readers will benefit from a special library reference shelf of sources set aside for their class. For the less able reader and reluctant learner, the teacher may check out library sources which are especially pertinent to the current topic of study and place them in the classroom. Of course, the teacher should endeavor to build a classroom or departmental library of those sources frequently useful in content study: dictionaries, an encyclopedia, a variety of textbooks, and other individual materials of pertinent content.

There are a variety of other ways in which the enterprising teacher can help students make better use of content reading-learning sources. Some of the suggested procedures of this and other chapters contribute to this end.

### 3. Coordinating the Reading of Sources: Unit Study

The reading and study of content sources becomes more meaningful when the pupil can understand the function of this content in terms of learning objectives, when the sources make sense in terms of the instructional procedures employed, and when the pupils, collectively and individually, may share in the determination of pertinent content objectives and sources.

The unit approach to instruction has been employed for decades as a means of integrating substance and process in content area learning. Units may vary in label (research, study, activity, problem-centered, resource, etc.) and size (one period to a semester). Generally, an instructional unit is a meaningful segment of the content curriculum in which learning activities are organized around objectives related to a particular theme, topic, or a process.[17] Often, it is patterned on the basic research approach of question raising-data gathering-question answering, and it may culminate in the compilation or construction of a project.

The specific steps in unit teaching vary from one authoritative source to another, but the following general procedures are common to most: (a) *planning the unit*, in which learning objectives are determined and stated, pertinent content structure is identified, pertinent pupil data assessed, and needed resources identified; (b) *introduction* of the unit through activities which motivate, assess, provide background, and operationally prepare pupils for subsequent learning activities; (c) *development* of the unit by means of learning, research, and problem-oriented activities; and (d) *culmination* of the unit by means of pupil-centered solution of problems, creative activity, and individual, group, or product evaluation.

Although content unit study utilizes a variety of media, usually it draws heavily upon directed and. independent pupil reading and research. How effectively the teacher makes use of pupil reading will bear significantly upon the success of unit study.[18] The content unit provides an excellent framework for structuring reading-to-learn activity. In this respect, the following outline of teacher responsibilities related to pupil reading activities in unit study should be helpful.

I. Planning the Unit
  A. Determine the reading levels and abilities of students.
  B. Identify suitable materials for reading.
   1. Select materials in harmony with unit objectives.
   2. Use a systematic method of estimating the difficulty of materials.
   3. Make readily available a variety of materials, including reference and supplementary sources of different levels of difficulty, interest, and substance.
  C. Provide a suitable environment for reading.
   1. Plan both group and individualized reading experiences.
   2. Plan suitable physical conditions for reading.

II. Introducing the Unit
   A. State concretely the purposes for reading and for preparatory activities to reading, relate the purposes to student experience, and help students formulate their own purposes for group study and individual reading.
   B. Explore and clarify the experience background of students pertinent to the content and processes of the unit through class discussions, pretests, autobiographies, conferences, special reports, etc.
   C. Extend and enrich the background of students through the judicious use of instructional aids such as illustrative flat pictures, projected still pictures, films, tapes and records, educational and commercial television, oral reading, field trips, etc.
   D. Discuss with students the location of materials and the use of reference aids to guide wide reading activities.
   E. Suggest the use of appropriate general methods of reading, text signals, and other more specific aids for researching the content field pertinent to unit study topics.

III. Developing the Unit
   A. Aid students in locating materials and using library aids effectively.
   B. Develop a series of reading-study guides to structure pupil independent reading and learning activity related to unit subtopics.
   C. Assist students in adjusting their method of reading to varying purposes, materials, and abilities.
   D. Help students practice organizing, remembering, and applying what they read through the use of such techniques as intent to remember, self-recitation, outlining, making summaries and précis, and the use of the whole-part-whole approach to reading.
   E. Continue those activities suggested above in "Introducing the Unit" as they are needed.

IV. Concluding the Unit
   A. Provide for both student and teacher evaluation of the effectiveness of the learning activities.
   B. Encourage students to apply the results of their learning to new problems, activities, and situations.[19]

Finally, the content unit should be recognized as a convenient link between the content objectives of the course and specific reading-to-learn structures. Most of the approaches suggested in this and the following chapter for improving the reading of specific selections should serve to implement the specific reading-learning activities of the content unit.

### 4. Increasing the Effectiveness of the Reading-Study Assignment

The assignment of specific textbook segments or collateral sources as independent reading-study activity is a hallowed instructional strategy in the American secondary school. The reading assignment is a defensible tool of learning when properly employed. Unfortunately, the reading assignment is susceptible to careless use. Excepting the most capable, self-directed pupils, the direction "Read the next chapter for tomorrow" is not likely to produce effective reading and learning, even if seriously carried through by the pupil. When the generalized, undirected assignment becomes a teacher litany, poor readers sink deeper into their educational coffins, and better students cynically sigh in restive boredom. For most pupils, the success of reading as a class-oriented learning activity hangs heavily upon the nature of the teacher's assignment.

*General conditions of the meaningful assignment.* The effective assignment is more than an imperative to cover a certain number of pages with the implication that the pupil must learn and retain all significant facts and generalizations contained therein. The reading-study assignment should be a direct implementation of unit or course learning objectives. It will take into consideration the reading and learning differences among the class members.' It strikes a reasonable compromise between needed systematic reinforcement of skills and concepts and needed motivation through innovation and variety. It provides varying degrees of structure to guide and support pupils in the interpreting, learning, and application targets of the assignment. The effective assignment is a potent learning activity in itself, and it deserves careful teacher consideration and involvement.

*Teacher preparation.* Ideally, major-emphasis course assignments—those which deal with important learning objectives and which involve more than momentary, incidental learning-study activity—will be based in teacher activity which anticipates the actual communication of the assignment to the pupils. Assignments which begin with teacher familiarity with pupil differences in reading and study capabilities are likely to be more realistic and, thus, more successful in pupil acceptance, reading involvement, and learning product. Useful assignments often entail more than the use of a single text. When this is the case, the necessary sources need to be located and made available. These sources will include textbooks of varying difficulty and topic emphasis, collateral nontext readings, nonprose resources (tables, graphs, etc.), as well as general library research references.

*Improving assignment structure.* Because of differences in ability, background, or personality, some pupils need more structure for carrying out reading-related assignments than do others. Typically, secondary teachers underestimate the degree of structure needed by most pupils in their class. Pupil, teacher, and the content learning product benefit from specific guidance in how to fulfill the assignment.

In addition to specific teacher direction and informal teacher-pupil interaction, structure may be built into the assignment itself by various means.[20] Some teachers require the systematic use of a pupil notebook for recording the assignment and its related activity as a means of providing useful structure. Others find that the use of assignment handout sheets conveys a feeling of definite significance to the assignment and increases accuracy and effi-

ciency in assignment direction and interpretation. Directions requiring a product response usually provide more structure to pupils than directions to perform some general act. For example, "Write a list of six advantages and five disadvantages mentioned by the author concerning the..." will produce better response than "Read to identify the advantages and disadvantages of...." Varied levels of sophistication in reading-thinking skills can be incorporated through differentiated group assignments. A multilevel assignment sheet or study guide in which the sequence of response priority is designated, and where individual pupils carry out those study tasks which are most pertinent to their needs and ability, is another way of increasing assignment structure without ignoring individuality.

Structure may be provided by the form of the reading assignment questions or problems. Recognition of a correct response among several choices usually is easier than recall. Designating the location of answers to questions is easier and usually takes less time than the reconstruction of the information by the pupil. But learning may be less effective. Structure also can be provided by delimiting the target area of the printed material needed for carrying out that specific study task, e.g., "The first five questions deal with the topic of..., which is considered on pages 67 to 73 of...."

Shortening the assigned study task and limiting the length of the reading content covered by the assignment usually will facilitate pupil completion and accuracy. In many instances, three assignments covering six pages each will be more fruitful than one assignment of eighteen. Many teachers seem unaware of the prohibitive length of reading assignments. Grob reveals that secondary pupil reading-study differences in time needed to prepare for a chapter test in history can range from two to ten hours, while differences in time taken to read a novel such as *Great Expectations* may run from five to over forty hours.[21] The gravity of these differences is that less able readers are encountering this problem in all their reading-related classes. They simply cannot maintain the pace, and thus, they frequently stop giving their best effort to any reading assignment. Perhaps for one-half or more of the typical secondary class, the well-intentioned long and rigorous assignment fails in its basic objective — to increase pupil learning.

***Guidelines for the effective content reading assignment.*** The following suggestions for improving the reading assignment have emerged from collected classroom experience and research.

*a. The effective reading assignment begins with the instructor's identification of the learning objectives to be accomplished.* Where possible, these should be stated in terms of expected change in specific pupil behaviors.[22] Teacher objectives (how the assignment contributes to content learning) may not be the same as pupil-perceived immediate assignment tasks, and the teacher should be conscious of these differences. Immediate assignment outcomes in terms of pupil product (e.g., making a comparative listing of statements of fact and of opinion contained in an editorial pertinent to the topic of content study) often serve as the enabling means to general course objectives (e.g., the assimilation of certain content concepts and the improvement of critical reading performance). The content course objectives should shape the form and substance of the assignment and should guide the evaluation of both the pupil product and the value of the assignment itself.

*b. The effective assignment involves teacher preparation activity.* Such preparation includes familiarity with the content of any key sources employed; the identification, location, and collection of sources which will require use by pupils; the development of the assignment sheet, study guide, or related tests and worksheets; as well as attending to any administrative details upon which the assignment activity depends (e.g., arrangements to use library, audiovisual equipment, and changes in classroom physical conditions).

*c. Pupil readiness for the assignment should be developed.* Key vocabulary and essential concepts required by the assignment will need to be taught. Reading and study skills to be employed in the as-

signment should be reviewed, and, if necessary, taught or retaught. Films, recordings, trips, speakers, and other instructional devices employed for introductory activities are useful for kicking off longer assignments. Most importantly, the place and value of the assignment in the course schema and its relationship to the course learning objectives should be meaningfully conveyed to the pupils. Developing pupil readiness for an assignment, in itself, can be a fruitful opportunity for instruction and learning.[23] However, some caution must be exerted not to destroy pupil initiative or enthusiasm for discovery, particularly where the reading material is quite readable and intrinsically interesting.

*d. Assignments should be planned with consideration for pupil capabilities.* Most of the reader characteristics discussed in Chapter Two can exert some influence upon the success of the reading assignment. Some will need greater consideration than others, depending upon the nature of the assignment: general reading performance level, language and study skills proficiency, pertinent background of experience, motivation, and social-emotional maturity should be given particular attention. The amount of time needed by most students to successfully negotiate the reading assignment should be reduced wherever possible. Pupil differences in dealing with reading assignments are sizable, and the teacher should plan adjustments to meet these differences through individualized assignment, ability and interest groupings, multilevel study guides, or compensatory pairing of peers.

*e. The assignment should be communicated in a clear, positive manner.* Ineffective results and operational confusion often can be traced to the fact that the teacher did not take adequate time in the initial presentation of the assignment or did not make sure that the necessary elements of the assignment were understood. A careful, patient presentation that includes an opportunity for pupil questioning will prove efficient in the long run. Last minute, end-of-the-period assignments should be avoided. If the teacher does not make use of duplicated assignment sheets, the requirement of an assignment notebook is recommended. The effectiveness of assignment communication will be improved by a regular, ongoing assignment routine.

*f. The assignment should include all the essential information needed to facilitate pupil independence in effecting it.* The amount of assignment detail provided should be determined by the least able and least mature pupil expected to do that assignment. Depending upon the specific form and objectives of the assignment, the following types of information usually prove valuable: (1) identification of reading sources needed, including the targeting of specific sections or pages within the source; (2) the form of the response expected of the pupil; (3) deadline for the completed assignment; (4) the recommended procedure for accomplishing the assignment, including order of priority if the assignment has a logical or operational sequence; (5) how the assignment product will be evaluated and the weighting given in course evaluation; and (6) how the pupil should obtain help if he encounters difficulty. Stating the assignment in the form of specific questions to be answered or tasks to be accomplished is an aid to most secondary pupils.

*g. Make provision for guidance in initiating the assignment activity and in crucial or difficult operations.* Many teachers find it valuable to plan the assignment operation so that pupils begin work on it in class immediately after the assignment has been made. This permits the teacher to deal personally with individual or group confusions at the time they are most likely to arise. It also primes the pupil's study pump at the time he most needs motivational aid. A study guide form of assignment in which written direction on how to carry out the assignment activity is built into duplicated pupil materials is another means of accomplishing this end.

*h. Divide larger assignments and those involving sequential or progressive operations into intermediate stages.* Assignment activity tends to bog down when there is excessive delay in concrete results. The use of shorter, divide-and-conquer assignments is particularly practical when employed with unit study. Longer-range learning strategies often are valuable at the secondary level. Unfortunately,

most secondary pupils have not developed college-level research discipline and independence. Thus, it may be useful to organize the longer reading-study assignment into a series of intermediate steps, each with its own outcomes. Time and opportunity for teacher-pupil interaction should be integrated with these shorter-term assignments.

*i. As pupil experience and maturity permits, increase pupil input in the planning and administration of the assignment.* Beyond the fact that pupils can add new dimensions to course-related concepts, pupil participation in developing the assignment will increase teacher insight about pupil needs and interests. Such involvement often adds to the intrinsic motivation of the group. Moreover, pupil responsibility for assignment development contributes directly to maturity and independence in learning and problem solving. It helps to accomplish one of our major objectives—to turn the dependent "pupil" into an independent "student."

*j. Provide evaluative feedback about the assignment.* Response to one's efforts is a human need as well as a valuable tactic in improving learning. Positive reinforcement is more effective than negative, but lack of reinforcement neither aids learning proficiency nor motivates new learning efforts. It may be impractical for the secondary content teacher to give extensive individual feedback to every pupil on every assignment. But some form of group or individual feedback can be arranged for most assignments (even if it is nothing more than posting the assignment answer key on the bulletin board). The problem is lessened further by the differentiation of levels and degrees of feedback according to the importance of the objectives of the assignment. If the reasons for this differentiation of assignment levels and how feedback will be geared to them are shared with pupils, the teacher can avoid the "busy work" attitudes toward short-task self-evaluation assignments.

## 5. Guiding the Reading of Content Area Text

Perceptive professionals have realized for many years that judicious teacher guidance in the reading of instructional materials improves pupil understanding of content and enhances development of decoding–interpretive processes.[24] Research efforts have identified and contributed to the refinement of teacher intervention procedures. Teacher-guided reading as a broad approach to reading instruction is of such value that many elementary and some secondary commercial reading-instructional programs incorporate such guidance into their materials. At least two professional textbooks in reading have been developed around such procedures.[25, 26]

A number of procedures for guiding the reading of texts have emerged during the past half century. They tend to fall into four, somewhat overlapping patterns: (a) immediate, specifically targeted direction, such as helping pupils use text-implanted reading aids or providing advanced organizers and/or structured overviews; (b) personal, systematic teacher interaction and direction of pupil reading of larger textual selections; (c) indirect guidance of pupil reading through worksheets or study guides; and (d) teaching pupils reading-study systems whereby they can develop independence in structuring their own reading-study attack upon a content selection. Chapter Six presents specific information on the nature and use of representative strategies for guiding pupil reading of text.

## 6. Developing Class-Related Reading Behaviors

Paul Roberts, among others, reminds us that fifty years ago, secondary content teachers assumed substantial responsibility for improving pupil communication and study skills.[27] Although the circle is far from closing, the last decade has seen increasing recognition that the content setting has particular advantages for teaching and reinforcing reading behaviors pertinent to the area of study. Certainly another important way in which the content reading of pupils can be advanced is to help them learn the vocabulary, interpretive, and reaction behaviors they need to use the content sources of written information.

Some general dimensions for providing this aid in the content classroom are suggested in the following discussion. Considerably more detail about the teaching of specific reading behaviors is provided in Chapters Nine through Twelve.

*Expanding pupil grasp of course-related vocabulary.* The special terminology and technical vocabulary of a content field symbolically represent the key concepts of that area of learning. Thus, recognizing the printed terms and associating them with their referents and concepts closely intertwines with mastering the facts, generalizations, and processes which comprise a most essential part of content mastery.

A control over content area vocabulary is essential to effective independent study in that area. Key terms appear frequently and in critical places in textbook assignments and related course reading and study tasks. If a pupil has substantial difficulty with reading the vocabulary of the text—i.e., misreading as many as one word out of ten in running context—the pupil's comprehension of that material can drop below that needed for understanding and learning.

Moreover, the improvement of pupil proficiency in dealing with vocabulary contributes to general reading power, and that, in turn, contributes directly and indirectly to content area learning. Utilizing a variety of approaches in an experimental program of vocabulary improvement, McDonald and Pauk were able to produce significant increases in general reading interpretation as well as in vocabulary knowledge and academic marks.[28] Other lines of evidence support the crucial role of word understanding in tasks of reading interpretation at all levels.[29]

Content classroom aid with vocabulary can be given by several different means. One is in the selection of content materials to be used as basic sources of content study. The teacher can select texts which have used some restraint in their vocabulary-concept load and/or have given attention to clarifying technical terminology through context or special aids. Second, the teacher can provide general and technical dictionaries, glossaries, and other lexical aids and can help pupils learn to use them independently to resolve their word problems. And as a third means of vocabulary assistance, the teacher can make teaching the vocabulary and concepts of the course a basic staple of class operation.

Immediate advantages in content learning, as well as in longer-range improvement in content reading power, accrue from giving direct attention to the development of this special vocabulary of the course. A vital aspect of this instruction involves teaching and reinforcing the *meaning* of the key terms by expanding the specific experiential background of the pupil which is represented by such terms. Also, this instruction should involve the active association of the meaning of the term with its written (graphic) form and its use in context. Thus, when the pupil encounters the word in a printed source, he can accurately and quickly fit its meaning into that context. Equally important to word learning is reinforcement through clear and repeated association of the term with its referent object or meaning. How much reinforcement is needed varies with the term and the pupil. Similar concepts and those which appear often in the pupil's general language experience (e.g., *pressure*) usually need less reinforcement than unfamiliar and complex terms (e.g., *curvilinear*). Less capable readers and learners need more reinforcement of key vocabulary than able students. Most pupils will master vocabulary more readily if the number of new terms to be learned in one session is kept within their vocabulary learning rate.

*Developing reading skills needed for course learning.* The development of reading skills in a content area classroom is a matter of instructional pragmatism. A substantial number of pupils in most content area classes will be unable to use some of the reading skills necessary to interpret assignments and related classroom reading tasks. Because of this, they are easily bored or defensive and are prone to classroom disruption. Direct, short-term instruction in the needed skills is a positive strategy of classroom administration as well as a means of increasing intrinsic interest in content-learning tasks.

Beyond this, some interpretive and application skills are developed best in situations where the utilization of that reading-study behavior is usefully employed. Content area reading also provides an excellent vehicle for transferring skills learned in developmental reading settings to functional application. The content reading situation holds great potential for bridging the gap between reading skill learning, as such, and reading skill as a means of learning or problem solving. Finally, it is simply not realistic to assume that all the crucial reading interpretive behaviors can be mastered through developmental reading classes alone; it will require a rather constant contribution from all secondary teachers to produce the sort of mature readers needed in our increasingly complex society.

It is not crucial that the content area teacher be familiar with the tools and techniques of the reading specialist in order to aid pupils in the development of essential content-related reading skills. What he or she needs to know is what reading-thinking manipulations the pupil should make with the concepts and concept structure of the area. After this, the most essential steps of the skill-teaching process involve: (a) determining pupil competence in the use of the skill, (b) explaining and demonstrating how the skill or process should be performed, (c) providing immediate guided practice in using the skill and aiding those pupils having difficulty with it, (d) providing independent practice in the application of the skill to the content learning tasks of the course, and (e) periodically reinforcing the skill learning through use in content assignments.

## 7. Extending Independent Content Reading Habits and Interests

We have seen how extended reading, both study and personal in orientation, can contribute to the development of conceptual background, reading proficiency, and broader interest and personal adjustment. These are significant contributions to the content area classroom, and the content teacher does no small thing when he turns a pupil "on" to the satisfaction of extended reading in some aspects of the content subject.

Many able, as well as most deficient, readers have restricted reading interests and engage in a rather minimal amount of personal reading.[30] Encouraging more frequent and extended independent reading behavior deserves serious attention in curricular planning and instructional operation. Three prerequisites would seem essential to the successful expansion of pupil reading habits: (a) the availability of reading sources—varied as to type, topic, and difficulty; (b) the planned opportunity to read to satisfy purposes of independent learning and personal fulfillment; and (c) the stimulation of and guidance in expanding pupil reading interests through interaction with the faculty and peers.

The content area teacher can make a very useful contribution to this effort. She is in a unique position to bring students in contact with the choice writers and sources of reading material pertinent to her area. She can capitalize on the greater and deeper specification of interests which characterizes middle and later adolescence. Moreover, she may provide a particularly valuable bridge to personal reading among pupils who are temporarily surfeited with general fiction or who never have found fiction to be their cup of reading tea.

One way in which a teacher of content subjects can broaden pupil contact with personal reading sources is to obtain a ready selection of interesting, informative materials on pertinent topics and on varying levels of difficulty. It is best if such materials can be brought into the classroom on a permanent or at least temporary basis. Another approach is to enlist the librarian's aid in collecting such materials on certain library shelves that are readily available to pupils. Also, multiple copies of an annotated bibliography of recommended personal reading sources for the class can be made and handed out to pupils.

Another means of encouraging wider content-related reading is to make time for independent reading within the content instruction period. Some teachers make this a part of the instructional period—either as an extended reading component of the assignment or as a personal choice activity. Others prefer to set aside a class session once every week or two weeks for browsing in the library or reading in the classroom. A common practice is to permit students to do personal-choice reading during any class period after they have completed the study tasks for that session. One notable disadvantage of the latter approach is that the less able readers and learners, those who need such an opportunity to expand personal reading, are the least likely pupils to complete their assignments in time. Quite understandably, many content teachers are loath to relinquish classroom time which could be used for instruction and practice. However, personal-choice reading in materials pertinent to the area of study can contribute to content background, to changed content study attitudes, and to variety in classroom procedure.

For many reluctant or narrow-interest readers, the provision of materials and time to read them will not be enough. They will need some particular stimulation to whet their reading appetites—to set their personal reading habits in motion. Perhaps the most direct way of handling this problem is to make the reading of related content sources a course requirement. Such an approach is acceptable to many students and may even contribute to broader reading contacts. There are several drawbacks to assigned personal reading, however. One of the major objectives of personal choice reading is to build intrinsic interest in reading, and the use of extrinsic pressure may confound that goal. Also, the objective is to establish ongoing habits of wide reading; too often, extrinsically motivated behavior is discontinued when the outside pressure is removed or the goal awarded. Even so, required personal reading loses some of its onerous overtones if the teacher permits fairly free choice among materials of varied substance and difficulty and accepts any reasonable and honest pupil feedback on that reading as a valid effort. Generally, it is preferable to use collateral reading (required extended reading serving direct learning purposes) as a course requirement and to encourage personal reading as a free-choice option.

There are more personal approaches to stimulating pupil reading interests, assuming that the teacher-pupil relationship is generally positive. Many students are curious about the teacher as a person. Brief, pungent observations drawing upon the teacher's own personal reading can widen students' horizons. This approach need not be limited to course-related reading. It can be most revealing to immature minds to find that an athletic coach enjoys poetry, that the literature teacher subscribes to *Popular Mechanics*, and that the history teacher is a mystery buff. But when the content teacher can comment with feeling and insight upon current and classical sources which relate to his field of study, it can stimulate pupil reading in a most natural manner and add new dimensions to the study of that content field.

Pupils usually have a curiosity about the nonpublic side of their peers, and some pupil reading tastes and habits can be stimulated by encouraging such interaction. Formal oral reporting on personal choice reading in the area may assure a minimal level of interaction, but it carries with it the artificiality and passive resistance with which adolescents seem to regard such pressure. Encouraging pupils to contribute observations drawn from personal reading or to read excerpts from sources as a part of group discussion of a study point is a more effective way of accomplishing the same goal. There are a number of instructionally related tactics by which the secondary content teachers can stimulate extended and independent reading. Illustrative are those presented in Chapter Twelve.

## 8. Adapting Content Instruction for Poorer Readers

Problem readers are not always inadequate learners nor do the less able learners of the class invariably consist of the poorest readers. But the relationship between reading ability and learning performance in most secondary reading classes generally is a close one. Moreover, the relationship between reading disability and attitudes toward those content subjects which draw heavily upon past and present reading performance is largely negative. [31]

Owing to his history of reading difficulty, the inadequate reader has accumulated a poor experiential background, both general and academic. Because he has had difficulty mastering the decoding skills, he very likely will be deficient in flexible use of purposeful interpretation. Because he is deficient in both decoding and interpretation, he may not have developed the attitudes, skills, and habits of study and scholarly practice which were dependent upon satisfactory use of reading. He comes to the content area course as a three-way loser — in motivation, in necessary background, and in currently functioning skills. For many of these pupils the secondary classroom is an academic "Catch 22." Sometimes they rebel. Sometimes they escape. It is amazing that more of them do not.

Frankly, it is not realistic to assume that one teacher can turn this situation around. The remediation of serious reading disability is a full and long-term effort. But the classroom teacher can avoid contributing to the problem, can make some contribution to the pupil's reading and learning development, can help him accomplish the more realistic objectives of the course. And in the process of doing this, class life may become more fulfilling — for the less able reader, for his classmates, and for the teacher.

Most of the suggestions made earlier in this chapter to improve the reading of all pupils should be of particular aid to the less competent reader. But he needs more help than his classmates in these matters. Recommendations concerning the general program for aiding the disabled secondary reader are given in Chapter Thirteen. Some fundamental considerations for improving content classroom productivity of poor readers are presented below:

*a. The teacher's personal reaction to poor readers and learners is the key to what can be accomplished in the classroom learning setting.* Prejudice and defensiveness concerning the poorer learners and their sometimes antagonizing compensatory actions prevent the development of a good working relationship. Acceptance of the poor reader for what he can do now and what he can learn produces better results and more enjoyable relationships than either an adversary or an overprotective stance.[32] While dramatic, immediate changes in performance and motivation are rare, many poor readers respond positively when they feel the teacher is sincere, fair, and helpful.

*b. Identification of reading strengths and weaknesses is particularly important for aiding the problem reader.* The objective here is not for the classroom instructor to develop a remedial program, but rather to identify problem readers and bring them to the attention of the reading specialist, in case they have not been identified and aided at an earlier point, and to determine what they can handle for reading-related learning tasks. In particular, it will be helpful to discover which level of course materials can be read with instructional and which with independent ease, which word skills can be used to unlock the pronunciation and meaning of unknown words, and how much control has been obtained over interpretive and study skills emphasized in the course.

*c. The general recommendations for improving reading-study operations which were given earlier in this chapter need to be observed more diligently in the case of poorer readers.* This holds particularly for finding and matching instructional materials with their performance capability. Where assignments and directed classroom reading activities are concerned, the disabled reader will profit from greater preparation, shorter reading tasks, more specific direction, and more frequent interaction with the instructor to obtain guidance and encouraging feedback. Where the development of vocabulary and course-related reading skills are concerned, the classroom teacher should be realistic about the number of vocabulary words and degree of skill proficiency which can be mastered by the problem reader within a limited time. Once learned, these words and skills will require greater provision for retention than is needed by more able learners.

*d. Developing wider reading habits and greater interest in reading is a priority need for less able*

*readers.* Knowing the pupil's interests and establishing an easy working rapport with him form a useful beginning. The school reading specialist should be able to locate or recommend reading sources on the pupil's reading level. The use of the graded reading bibliographies listed in Appendix B also will serve this end.

*e. The use of nonreading learning activities to supplement reading-based learning activities provides welcome variety for all pupils. But it may be essential to provide these for the poorer readers.* Teacher oral explanation and class discussion will help but can be overdone. Many pupils do not listen as effectively as they read, and unfortunately, poor readers cannot be counted upon to have developed compensating listening skills. The use of film strips, overhead projections, motion pictures, visits, projects, diagrams, video and audio tapes, etc., whenever they meet legitimate learning objectives, should give the poor reader a better opportunity for grasping basic concepts.

*f. Finally, the teacher should try to avoid placing the poor reader in embarrassing reading circumstances.* Unprepared oral reading before the class is perhaps the worst offense. Disparaging labels and confrontations over assignment deficiencies in front of class members seldom improve reading performance and can reinforce hostility toward the teacher, the content area, and the school learning situation, in general. Work and study group membership can be rearranged according to interests, background experiences, or self-selection to avoid separating less able readers from general class interaction. Many less able readers have capable minds and special talents. The teacher who can make use of the contributions of these pupils will enhance the total learning atmosphere of the class as well as provide a bridge over troubled reading waters.

## THE CONTENT TEACHER AND THE COMPREHENSIVE PROGRAM

The content area teacher plays a key role in the comprehensive (all-school) secondary reading education effort as projected in this text. Symbolically and operationally, the battle for secondary readers and improved secondary education will hinge, in good part, upon the extent to which the content teacher steps into this long-neglected breach.[33]

The position taken in this text is that secondary pupils will benefit from any constructive effort at reading education and utilization by any staff member. And the implementation of the recommendations presented in this and later chapters by the classroom teacher amounts to a significant contribution to pupil reading development and adjustment, in itself. Nevertheless, the secondary school is not likely to make a significant thrust toward mature reading behavior unless it mounts a coordinated total program attack.

Beyond his own classroom adjustments, the secondary teacher can contribute to the total school reading education effort in a number of ways. He can:

1. Press for and contribute to a more complete reading evaluation program.
2. Encourage his department to examine its objectives, materials, and procedures in the light of pupil reading abilities and needs.
3. Identify and refer pupils with serious reading problems to the school reading specialist.
4. Develop a cooperative interaction with the school reading consultant to meet their common concerns.
5. Request and participate in in-service professional programs in reading education.
6. Become a contributing member to working committees and groups which have pertinency for reading development and utilization — curriculum revision, textbook selection, library, pupil advisement, etc.

In general, the classroom teacher needs to think positively and act supportively concerning the broad reading improvement effort in the secondary school. Good programs develop from provisional tries. They are not created overnight. They emerge from the varied talents and interests of the total staff, not from executive decree or the isolated efforts of the reading specialist. Moreover, good reading programs are dynamic, everchanging. The vitality and success of the secondary reading program is highly dependent upon prevailing staff attitude.[34] The active concern which the classroom teacher exerts for the improvement of the broad school-reading-education effort usually pays dividends — in pupil reading, in total school climate and production, and in teacher fulfillment.

## REFERENCES

1. Gerald A. Yoakam, *Reading and Study* (New York: The Macmillan Company, 1928) p. 1.
2. Stanley E. Davis, "High School and College Instructors Can't Teach Reading? Nonsense!" *The North Central Association Quarterly* 34 (April, 1960) pp. 295-99.
3. Homer Carter and Dorothy McGinnis, "Some Suggestions Growing Out of an Evaluation of Reading Instruction by Secondary Teachers and Their Students," in *New Concepts in College-Adult Reading*, Thirteenth Yearbook of the National Reading Conference, E. L. Thurstone and L. E. Hafner, Editors (Milwaukee, Wis.: National Reading Conference, Inc., 1964) pp. 40-50.
4. Arthur Jersild, *When Teachers Face Themselves* (New York: Bureau of Publications, Teachers College, Columbia University, 1955).
5. Alvin Toffler, *Future Shock* (New York: Random House, Inc., 1970).
6. Harold Herber, *Teaching Reading in Content Areas* (Englewood Cliffs, N.J.: Prentice-Hall, Inc., 1978) Chapter 1.
7. Yoakam, *Reading and Study*, Chapter 8.
8. Samuel Weintraub, "Research: Reading of Textbooks," *Journal of Reading* 21 (December, 1967) pp. 283-85.
9. J. G. Beard, "The Comprehensibility of High School Textbooks: Association with Content Area," *Journal of Reading* 11 (December, 1967) pp. 229-35.
10. Walter Hill, "Content Textbook, Help or Hindrance: Research for the Classroom," *Journal of Reading* 10 (March, 1967) pp. 408-13.
11. Benjamin S. Bloom, Editor, *Taxonomy of Educational Objectives* (New York: Longmans, Green, & Company, Inc., 1956).
12. Roger Farr, *Reading: What Can Be Measured?* (Newark, Del.: International Reading Association, 1969) p. 214.
13. Hill, "Content Textbook, Help or Hindrance," pp. 408-13.

14. Ivan R. Waterman, "When You Choose a Textbook," *Phi Delta Kappan* 33 (January, 1952) pp. 267-71.

15. John S. Simmons and Juanita Cox, "New Grammar Texts for Secondary Schools: How Do They Read?" *Journal of Reading* 15 (January, 1972) pp. 280-85.

16. Marjorie Johnson and Roy Kress, *Informal Reading Inventories* (Newark, Del.: International Reading Association, 1965).

17. Richard S. Alm, "What Is a Good Unit in English?," *English Journal* (September, 1960).

18. Jean Fair, "Materials for the Unit Plan in Social Studies," in *Materials for Reading*, Supplementary Educational Monograph 86, H. Alan Robinson, Editor (Chicago: University of Chicago Press, 1957) pp. 158-62.

19. T. H. Harris, "Making Reading an Effective Instrument of Learning in the Content Fields," in *Reading in the High School and Colleges*, Forty-seventh Yearbook, Part II, of the National Society for the Study of Education (Chicago: University of Chicago Press, 1948) pp. 133-34.

20. Richard A. Earle and Peter L. Sanders, "Individualizing Reading Assignments," *Journal of Reading* 16 (April, 1973) pp. 550-55.

21. James A. Grob, "Reading Rate and Study-Time Demands on Secondary Students," *Journal of Reading* 13 (January, 1970) pp. 285-88, 316-17.

22. Diane Lapp, *Use of Behavioral Objectives in Education* (Newark, Del.: International Reading Association, 1972).

23. Maurice Williams and Sylvia Black, "Assignments: Key to Achievement," *Journal of Reading* 12 (November, 1968) pp. 129-33.

24. Emmett A. Betts, *Foundations of Reading Instruction* (Cincinnati, Ohio: American Book Company, 1957) Chapter 22.

25. Russell G. Stauffer, *Directing the Reading-Thinking Process* (New York: Harper & Row, Publishers, 1975) p. 366.

26. Herber, *Teaching Reading in Content Areas.*

27. Paul Roberts, "The Improvement of Writing," *Understanding English* (May, 1963) p. 1.

28. Arthur McDonald and Walter Pauk, "Teaching College Freshmen to Read," *Phi Delta Kappan* (December, 1956) p. 53.

29. Robert L. Thorndike, "Reading as Reasoning," *Reading Research Quarterly* 9, No. 2 (1973-74).

30. A. Sterl Artley, *Trends and Practices in Secondary Reading* (Newark, Del.: International Reading Association, 1968) pp. 85-98.

31. Ruth Penty, *Reading Ability and High School Dropouts* (New York: Bureau of Publications, Teachers College, Columbia University Press, 1956) p. 29.

32. Jersild, *When Teachers Face Themselves*, Chapter 1.

33. Margaret Early and Harold Herber, "Redefining the Right to Read," *Journal of Reading* 14 (January, 1971) p. 220.

34. Walter Hill, "Characteristics of Secondary Reading: 1940-1970," *Twentieth Yearbook of the National Reading Conference*, Frank P. Greene, Editor (Milwaukee, Wis.: National Reading Conference, Inc., 1971) pp. 20-29.

## SUPPLEMENTARY SOURCES

Aukerman, Robert C. *Reading in the Secondary School Classroom*, Chapters 5 and 6. New York: McGraw-Hill Book Company, 1972.

Crescuolo, Nicholas P. "An Interdisciplinary Approach to Reading." *Journal of Reading* 19 (March, 1976) pp. 488-93.

Fay, Leo and Lee Ann Jared. *Reading in the Content Fields*, An Annotated Bibliography. Newark, Del.: International Reading Association, 1975. 19 p.

Herber, Harold. *Teaching Reading in Content Areas*. Englewood Cliffs, N.J.: Prentice-Hall, Inc., 1978.

Piercey, Dorothy. *Reading Activities in Content Areas*. Boston: Allyn and Bacon, Inc., 1976.

Schleich, Miriam. "Groundwork for Better Reading in Content Areas." *Journal of Reading* 15 (November, 1971) pp. 119-26.

# SIX

# Guiding the Reading of Text

*Belonging may be thought of as the seeing of relation-
ship...; when relationships are perceived, effect-produc-
ing behavior follows and learning takes place quickly.*

James B. Stroud

*A theory of instruction must specify the ways in which a
body of knowledge should be structured so that it can be
most readily grasped by the learner through a sequence of
statements and restatements of a problem or a body of
knowledge that increase the learner's ability to grasp,
transform, and transfer what he is learning.*

Jerome S. Bruner

***Overview*** Chapter Six continues the presentation of broad instructional strategies
for improving content or developmental reading. Structure benefits reading instruction in two significant ways: it provides the teacher with an efficient framework for the
organization of instructional specifics, and it aids the pupil in selectively perceiving
and organizing the meaning of the writer's message. Four patterns of structuring reading for content understanding are suggested: (1) teacher adjunct aiding procedures
such as using typographic clues, questioning, cognitive organizers, and structured
overview; (2) the guided reading lesson; (3) reading-study guides; and (4) reading-
study systems.

### Structuring Reading and Study

Too often, developmental and content reading experiences consist of short, disparate, unguided episodes. Pupils need structured experiences in the reading of text, particularly larger textual selections. Structure helps the pupil perceive the "belonging" of the writer's organized meaning—that hierarchy of details, concepts, principles, and related processes which comprise the "content" of expository writing—of a textbook chapter or of a collateral reading assignment.[1] The thoughtful manipulation of this first structure, it will be recalled, serves as a major objective of the decoding, interpretation, and reaction components of the integral reading act, particularly when employed in the instructional setting.

The second meaning of reading "structure" refers to the organization of reading-related instructional procedures as planned and activated by the teacher.[2] It involves teacher determination and sequencing of learning activities to facilitate the developmental mastery of the decoding, interpretation, and reaction processes in reading, as well as to facilitate the utilization of those present reader processes to deal with the content reading-learning task at hand.

The following pages suggest four approaches to providing structure for the reading of longer prose selections. Each approach contributes to the effective use of the *integral reading act* in developmental or content-study reading situations. The rather direct relationship of the two holistic strategies, the teacher-guided reading lesson and the pupil independent reading-study system, is illustrated in Figure 8. The use of the reading-study guides, as a variant of the guided reading lesson, facilitates the

**Figure 8** *Some related functions of the major components of the integral reading act, the guided reading lesson, and the POINT reading-study system.*

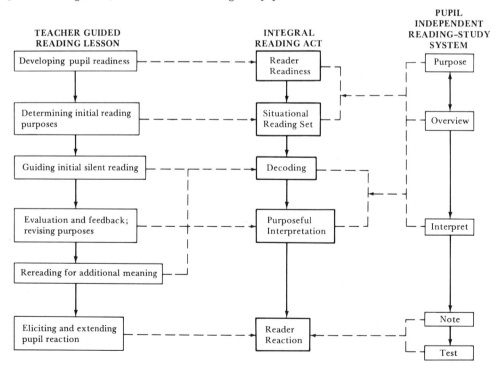

purposeful interpretation phase of the act, as do the shorter intervention strategies of questioning and typographical aids. The contribution of advance organizers and structured overviews to reader readiness and situational reading set is readily observed.

## USING ADJUNCT AIDS TO IMPROVE INTERPRETATION

Making better use of adjunct interpretive supports, such as typographical aids, questioning procedures, cognitive organizers, and structured overviews can facilitate reading in most classroom settings. They may be employed independently or in concert to emphasize the concepts or processes germane to a particular segment of difficult material, or applied over broader ranges of text for less able readers.

The relative superiority among these four procedures or over other such strategies has not been established to everyone's satisfaction.[3,4] As with most instructional procedures, the value of these approaches varies with the conditions operating in their employment—e.g., the teacher's expectations; the nature of the materials to be read; the number and ability of the pupils involved; the amount of time the teacher has for planning, preparing the materials, and direct interaction with pupils; and the role of the reading assignment in the broader instructional setting.[5-7] However, we need not be concerned with whether one of these is of more value than another. Of primary concern here is that each (1) is a useful way to improve the pupil reading-learning product, particularly in comparison to the typical absence of supporting structure for secondary classroom reading-learning activity; (2) provides an opportunity to add variety to reading-related instructional activity; and (3) contributes to the developmental goal of more purposeful, more flexible, more thoughtful pupil behavior.

### Using Typographic Clues

The implanting of organizing or targeting devices within the running text of written material to aid the reader's perception and enjoyment can be traced to the illumination of manuscripts during the Middle Ages. In the modern secondary textbook, such typographical devices have been expanded in an attempt to shape reader interpretation and learning. These writer-publisher structuring devices take such common forms as introductory previews and final summaries of varied form (written précis, abstracted generalizations, outlines, lists of key concepts or terms; illustrations; headings and subheadings; and isolation targeting devices (underlining, italics, and boldface type). Iconic devices such as tables, charts and diagrams may be included as such aids, although they consist usually of substantive conceptual representation patterns which deserve direct instructional attention as such.

The guidance and feedback values of these aids seem almost self-apparent—to writers, editors, and teachers. They may not be so to pupil readers! Empirical investigation has produced rather disappointing evidence of the power of these devices to improve the reading interpretation and retention of students, particularly those with modest reading ability. Moreover, adequate students at the secondary and college level do not reveal marked improvement in understanding and retention when such aids are made available to them.[8,9] Why should this be, especially since publishers have improved upon the quality of textbook aids in the last several decades? One plausible factor is that textbook content is too difficult to understand for a good proportion of pupils even with aids.[10] Another inhibiting influence is the inflexible approach to reading pupils seem to learn in elementary school and fail to escape in the upper grades.[11] Certainly the aids themselves are of potential use, as studies of auditory presentation of the aid reveal.[12]

At least three implications for reading and content instruction arise from this evidence. One is that teachers cannot assume that pupils will make effective independent use of typographical structural aids just because they are textually available. (We shall see that this carries to the use of questions or other adjunct reading structuring devices!) Another is that textual format, although a potential factor for improving textbook readability, may not be able to overcome the linguistic and conceptual confusions of pupils dealing with textbooks whose general readability is significantly above their functional (instructional) reading level. A third implication is that both reading and content teachers need to increase pupil awareness of the advantages of using textual aids through direct and forceful instruction. The latter should be accomplished more easily if the concept and skilled behavior of purposeful-flexible reading have been well established.

### Increasing Pupil Use of Typographical Aids

Assuming that a reasonable match has been made between the difficulty of the selected instructional material and the pupil's instructional reading level, there are a number of ways in which the teacher can increase pupil perception and utilization of such aids. Emphasizing the importance of these aids by giving them direct instructional attention will help. Greater success will be realized if such attention employs the systematic strategy of skills instruction: (1) identify aid-related behavior to be developed (e.g., use of chapter summaries); (2) assess present competence for use; (3) develop readiness in terms of interest and conceptual background; (4) demonstrate-explain functional aspects of the aid; (5) immediately guide practice in using the aid; (6) provide independent practice by means of practice sheets, tests, or creative tasks; (7) identify individual or group difficulties in use, and reteach; and (8) provide delayed practice.

A number of tactics can be employed to improve awareness and use of textual reading aids. The following are illustrative. After appropriate readiness, divide the class in half and give group 1 a content selection with no textual aids and group 2 one with aids. Time the reading of the selection and give a test emphasizing the significant ideas (identified by the textual aids). A variation of this would be to have the two groups take a timed test to locate information within the selection. Another procedure would involve pupil construction of their own textual devices on a mimeographed content selection on which the aids are absent; or groups could

be formed to improve upon the aids of a particular chapter. Teaching the use of textual aids as a part of a larger use of a guided reading lesson or reading-study procedure (the overview or summary step, particularly) is another possibility. And as a last resort, the content teacher can reinforce the use of textual aids in a direct operational manner simply by announcing that 50 percent of the questions on the test over the chapter (assignment, unit, etc.) will reflect terms, concepts, and generalizations which are identified by the several reading-study aids provided by their text or collateral reading.

### Questioning Procedures

Interrogation appears essential to definitive communication and cognitive development. Used effectively, the question can motivate the learner, clarify the learning objective, structure the learning task, and verify and reinforce the learning product. As a classroom tool, it can be a fairly efficient operation. It is not surprising that questioning procedures—from tribal catechism through the more sophisticated procedures of Socrates, John Dewey, and B. F. Skinner—have established a solid place in the history of instruction. Questioning continues to be a major form of teacher behavior.[13] There is reason to believe that it could be used more effectively—in both reading and general classroom instruction.[14]

### Expanding the Foci of Teacher Questions

One of the continuing raps upon the use of questioning in the educational setting is that question type, target, and form have been too narrow and repetitive. This applies to teacher use as well as to standardized test practice. Illustrative is Betts' admonition several decades ago that questioning in reading-learning situations tended to be dominated by the teacher, the factual content of the material, and short, immediate responses of a recall nature.[15]

In his cogent little volume *Classroom Questions*, Sanders defines a question as "any intellectual exercise calling for a response; this would include both problems and projects."[16] This broader focus suggests that teachers need to encourage pupil *use* of information for a variety of cognitive operations which go beyond the *retention* of specific information. Sanders believes that pupils can be led to use information in the manner suggested by Bloom's classification of thinking through teacher questions which call for responses of the following types:

1. *Memory*: The student recalls or recognizes information.
2. *Translation*: The student changes information into a different symbolic form or language.
3. *Interpretation*: The student discovers relationships among facts, generalizations, definitions, values, and skills.
4. *Application*: The student solves a lifelike problem that requires the identification of the issue.
5. *Analysis*: The student solves a problem in the light of conscious knowledge of the parts and forms of thinking.
6. *Synthesis*: The student solves a problem that requires original, creative thinking.
7. *Evaluation*: The student makes a judgment of good or bad, right or wrong, according to standards he designates.[17, 18]

### Questioning in Reading

Sanders' concern with expanding the range of pupil cognitive response is as applicable to reading as it is to any other area of instruction. When employed for reading instruction or reading utilization purposes, a question consists of a language stimulus, in stated or implied interrogative form, which requires an answering response based upon the effective use of printed sources. It may be presented in either oral or written form—before, during, or after pupil reading activity. It may be adjunct to the reading selection or source—imposed by the teacher or the exercise constructor—or it may be an integral part of the writer's exposition or narrative. It may be initiated by the reader, himself; indeed, the internalization of instructional questioning and its related thought processing by the learner is its most significant ultimate outcome.

The prominence of questioning in reading instruction may be readily observed. Along with auditing the oral reading performance, a comprehension check of content meaning serves as a primary means of evaluating the success of pupil performance. The importance of questioning in structuring reading learning increases as greater stress is placed upon silent reading of more complex materials. The question form may be employed to develop pupil readiness, to determine purposes for initial reading, to guide and evaluate the initial reading and rereading of the selection, and to elicit and extend pupil interpretation and reaction to the selection.

The use of questioning procedure as a means of structuring the learning and use of content concepts and processes presented in textbooks and other learning materials merits careful consideration by both reading and content teacher. Auckerman stresses the role of questioning in both teacher planning for and the actual form of the assignment which involves reading.[19] The reading and reasoning (study) guide procedure, as conceived by Herber, is considerably more than the usual listing of assignment questions.[20] Nevertheless, it is doubtful if study guides could function at any level without the use of direct or indirect questioning as broadly defined in this discussion. The decisive function of question raising in one form or another is an integral element in most versions of independent reading study procedures (e.g., SQ3R, PQRST, and POINT).[21] Actually, it is difficult to see how any of the approaches to structuring learning through reading presented in this chapter could function successfully without questions, stated or implied, so necessary are they to communication and cognitive processing.

Considerable research concerned with the effectiveness of questioning in reading has been generated. To a large extent, this research has been concerned with the general effectiveness of questioning, the most effective positioning and pacing of questioning, and the differential influence of question condition upon immediate and delayed recall and upon relevant (question–related) and incidental learning.[22-24] Generally, the use of adjunct questions improves pupil understanding of written materials. The superiority of such questioning is most clearly demonstrated where immediate recall of question-relevant information is desired, and when questioning procedures are compared either to undirected reading and rereading of information or to adjunct statements, headings, and like textual aids interspersed with content. It is hardly surprising that adjunct questions, like other instructional support procedures, are more likely to enhance immediate understanding than delayed retention of pertinent information; longer-term retention usually requires overlearning and periodic reinforcement beyond initial understanding.[25]

***Placement, pacing, and patterning.*** The placement and pacing of questions can influence the type of understanding gained and the amount of information retained. Prereading questions are helpful to the extent that they prepare (motivate and structure) the reading of the pupil. But too much stress upon prereading and content-interspersed questions directed toward the mastery of specific content can interfere with broad interpretive understanding and inhibit the retention of incidental (nonrelevant and nonexplicit) information. Immediate postquestioning is less inhibiting upon general understanding and retention of incidental information, *when* it can be assumed that the pupil does read the material and does utilize the postquestions. Delayed postquestioning is not superior to reimpression when initial reading has not produced retention of essential information.[26] Content-intervening questions (either adjunct or text-inserted) can facilitate understanding of question-relevant contiguous information, but intervening questions offered too frequently can interfere with reader motivation, fluency, and understanding of larger ideas. Combined pre- and postquestioning facilitates better understanding than pre- or postquestioning alone, particularly where the questions are coordinated to emphasize the type of understanding desired—i.e., using prequestions to motivate the reader and to guide him in identifying the general argument and key ideas of the content and using intervening and postreading questions to recognize important specific data and to guide rereading for higher-level interpretation and reaction.

The appropriateness of questioning as a reading support strategy is dependent upon reader ability and other variables which bear upon reading behavior. While we have a good deal to learn about these interactions, some generalizations may be advanced. Pupils with limited backgrounds and/or with general reading deficiency ordinarily need more frequent questioning support aimed at literal-level meanings. Monotony in question form should be avoided. The questions asked should support the desired outcomes of that reading activity and contribute to the objectives for the unit or course. The questions and questioning procedure should take the type of material into consideration. For example, detailed prequestioning can interfere with the personal enjoyment and appreciation which should be experienced in the first reading of a good story or *belles lettres*. Judicious use of teacher-pupil and pupil-pupil interaction can improve both question product and related reasoning. Teaching pupils how to use given questions and how to develop questions for independent reading purposes holds considerable potential for improving the effect of questioning as a reading-learning strategy.

Some promising evidence has emerged concerning question types and their reading behavioral products. The nature of the question asked does have an influence upon the type of understanding gained and retained by the reader. Decoding-oriented questions improve understanding of specific, literal meaning, and therefore are useful where the retention of factual information is desired. Questions leading to better grasp of specific and literal meaning are helpful to pupils with reading problems, but they are of lesser value to average or better readers and can stifle both the motivation and cognitive development of these pupils. Interpretation/reaction-oriented questions, on the other hand, improve understanding of broader argument, the interrelationship of facts and ideas, and the evaluation and application of information.

### Reading Instructional Use of Questions

Perhaps the simplest system for providing assistance in the reading and learning of content is for the instructor to develop questions which focus pupil attention upon the significant concepts and processes of the material and to use these questions to guide pupil reading through the selection. There are any number of ways in which this can be done, and some variety is valuable in maintaining motivation. The number and type of questions should be adjusted to pupil ability, the nature of the content, and the type of thinking processes and concept manipulation the teacher wishes to develop or reinforce.[27] As in-class structuring of reading, greater impact is realized when the teacher and pupils share in the question raising and answering process. Among other advantages, this provides a basis for an emerging pupil-teacher, pupil-pupil interaction which can contribute notably to motivation and concept learning.

*A reductional questioning strategy.* One useful pupil-teacher reading/questioning procedure includes the following elements: (1) the teacher and pupils skim-read the selection to identify the entry question, which usually attempts to capture the central theme and/or scope of the selection (other questions which emerge as part of this interaction are listed also on the board or overhead projector for later clarification and search); (2) the pupils and teacher are encouraged to clarify the meaning of the question or questions raised (and this provides an excellent opportunity to clarify key related concepts); (3) the pupils read selectively to discover the answer or answers to the question; (4) as tentative answers are suggested by group members, these are examined, clarified, and converted into supporting structure questions; (5) the process is repeated until the teacher and pupils feel they are ready to construct their own hierarchy of questions for independent study of that selection; and (6) the strategy culminates in a group-developed summary based on the questions raised and investigated.

In time, pupils gain sophistication in this question raising-resolving process — ask better questions and become less dependent upon the teacher. The teacher should attempt to establish a cooperative "brain-storming" type of climate rather than an ego-involved catechismic atmosphere. Some questions should encourage divergent thinking. Not all

questions need have "correct" answers in the material; open questions provide opportunities for clarifying concepts and processes which run beyond the question itself. Since the members of the group or class have some freedom in developing their personal hierarchy of reading-search questions, differences in viewpoints will occur and stimulate useful debate about the significance of concepts and details presented in the selection.

*The reciprocal questioning procedure.* Manzo has researched an instructional procedure to improve pupil questioning behaviors and reading comprehension.[28] Known as the Re Quest Procedure, it was designed for one-to-one remedial instruction, but can be modified to provide another approach to structuring in-class reading of content for groups of pupils. The basic elements of the reciprocal questioning procedure include: (1) The teacher and pupil each read the first sentence of a selection. (2) The pupil asks the teacher as many questions as he wishes, and the teacher responds. (3) The teacher, in turn, asks questions of the pupil. (4) This reciprocal questioning is repeated for successive sentences until the pupil can provide a reasonable response to the question "What do you think is going to happen in the rest of the selection? Why?"—after which the pupil reads to determine whether his prediction was accurate.

For better reading groups, the first unit for reciprocal questioning might consist of the first paragraph, and each pupil might be limited to one question not previously asked. Questions of a particular type might be stressed. A pupil could serve as secretary for the group and write the questions raised on the chalkboard, after which the group works together (or individually) to answer them. Another variation would involve pairing pupils of like (or unlike) reading abilities.

One of the objectives of the Re Quest Procedure is to improve the quality of pupil questioning. The teacher can serve as a good example in this, by asking good questions herself and by helping pupils rephrase their questions to increase precision and interpretive insight. Where instructional groups are involved, the teacher should strive to get the group to accept this responsibility for sharpening question form.

There is good reason to believe that pupils tend to assimilate the questioning patterns and related thinking processes utilized by their teachers.[29] A major implication is that reading and content teachers alike need to utilize a wider variety of questions in all instructional settings, particularly for average and better readers, to include questions which stress higher level interpretation and reaction to the content of one or more sources.[30]

The outline of reading behaviors presented in Chapter Three, as well as the illustrative questions presented in the following discussion of the guided reading lesson and in the chapters dealing with specific instruction and assessment, should provide some direction in forming reading questioning procedures beyond the decoding aspects of comprehension. The sources written by Herber,[31] Hunkins,[32] and Viox[33] also present useful illustrations of reading-related questions.

## Cognitive Organizers and Structured Overviews

In the broad sense of the term, most of the strategies discussed in this chapter may be classified as cognitive organizers, inasmuch as they usually help the reader to structure his perception, thought, and learning. However, the concept has a more specific connotation which will be employed in the present discussion. A *cognitive organizer* as used here refers to any adjunct graphic or symbolic presentation whose purpose is to mobilize, clarify, and structure the concepts a reader needs to understand and learn information contained in a particular piece of written discourse. Psychologically, the cognitive organizer is an operational implementation of Ausubel's theory of cognitive organization, which holds that learning is facilitated when the learner's structural framework (hierarchy) of factual items, concepts, and generalizations pertinent to the learning task are clear, stable, and organized.[34]

### Cognitive Organizers

From various research presentations, Blanton and Tuinman assembled the following descriptive summary of the most common form of cognitive organizer.

An advance organizer:
1. Provides a brief summary of the more detailed material contained in the learning passage and relates particular content to the learner's existing knowledge.
2. Presents in narrative expository paragraphs the key concepts of the discipline which are to be explained in detail in the unit.
3. Defines the key concepts in simple rather than complex language.
4. Illustrates the key concepts with examples which will be further developed and enlarged in the unit.
5. Introduces the key concepts, with supporting definition and rational material, in the sequence which the concepts are developed in the unit.
6. Arranges the narrative sequence to develop key concepts on the basis of generality and subsumption.[35]

Although these elements were assembled with a research orientation, they identify conditions which the teacher may seek to satisfy in employing cognitive organizers to enhance pupil reading learning. It may not be possible to meet completely all of the above conditions in one organizer, of course. The key question is: Does the organizer help the pupil to understand and relate desired facts, concepts, and generalizations of the learning task to each other (internally) and externally to the larger cognitive framework to which it belongs?

### Varied forms and findings.

As extended by other researchers and practitioners, a cognitive organizer may take any form, typographical, oral, or electronic, as long as it meaningfully employs the concepts and their interrelationships relevant to the cognitive structure of the selection. The most common forms used by teachers and researchers include a brief prose passage, tape recordings, a flowchart, an outline, or a diagram of terms. These may be presented before, during, or after the reading of the learning unit.

A cognitive organizer in the Ausubel sense differs from the usual pre- or postcontent summaries of the reading selection in that it does not intend to selectively abstract and reinforce the statements of the material itself, but rather to place the cognitive structure of the material in a framework of higher-level "generality, abstraction, and inclusiveness" than the selection itself.

Over a decade of research on the use of cognitive organizers with upper-grade and college readers has produced evidence which confirms their general and differential value. Like other adjunct structuring tools, they are more beneficial to immediate comprehension than for delayed retention. Expository, prose-form organizers appear to function more effectively for pupils with lesser background. Comparative-contrastive organizers are more useful for pupils with better informational background. The evidence does not reveal any distinct advantage to the timing of the organizer (advanced or delayed). The mixed results concerning the influence of organizers upon pupils of differing reading ability suggest that interactions of the difficulty and the conceptual structure of the passage with the nature of the organizer need further investigation.

Evidence of the comparative superiority of cognitive organizers (Ausubel type) to other reading structural aids is inconclusive. This may be of more concern to researchers than to reading educators who recognize the need for a variety of useful instructional approaches. Of perhaps greater interest is why fifteen years of research and report has generated so little classroom use of the cognitive organizer. Possibly, this is explained by the fact that the effective use of the cognitive organizer requires the precondition that the teacher thoroughly analyze and structurally organize the internal and external framework of generalizations, concepts, and facts which appear in the textbook chapter or collateral reading exercise!

## The Structured Overview

Estes, Mills, and Barron describe a structured overview in the following manner:

> A *structured overview* may be described as a visual and verbal representation of the key vocabulary of a learning task in relation to more inclusive and subsuming vocabulary concepts that have previously been learned by the student.[36]

If this sounds a good bit like the use of a vocabulary version of an advance cognitive organizer, it is because they do have a good deal in common; both utilize a symbolic diagram to mobilize and clarify the relevant subsuming concepts of the selection to be read (the learning task), to place them within their larger conceptual framework, and to relate them to the learner's existing conceptual mass.

The structured overview differs from the advanced organizer in one very important way! In its traditional form, the advanced organizer is an adjunct structuring aid to be utilized independently by the reader. The structured overview, on the other hand, is utilized to facilitate explanatory instruction by the teacher. In the words of Barron:

> This vocabulary may be depicted through a diagram or outline (iconic representation) so that the relationships between words and the relative importance of each word are highlighted. A verbal discussion (symbolic representation) of the diagram should take place in conjunction with its presentation. This *visual and verbal* presentation is termed a "structured overview.[37]

Earle has described the following set of directions to aid teachers in devising a structured overview of a study unit, although it may be readily adapted to a textbook chapter or reading selection. With appropriate adjustments, the steps serve usefully in the development of other approaches for providing structure for reading learning tasks.

1. Select every word that you intend to use in this unit that you think is necessary to the kids' understanding.
2. Take the list of words...and arrange them and rearrange them until you have

a diagram which shows the relationships which exist among the ideas of the unit, as well as their relationship to the semester's work and to the content area itself.

3. On the first day of the unit, write the diagram that you've made on the chalkboard. While you're doing this, explain why you have arranged the words as you did and get the kids to contribute....

4. Throughout the unit, as it seems appropriate and comfortable, refer back to the Structured Overview.... The object here is to aid the student in his attempts to organize the information in a meaningful way.[38]

Too little research utilizing the structured overview has been reported to hazard conclusions about its effectiveness relative to pupil ability and materials. It would seem to be a useful tool for combining readiness with continuing clarification of concepts. It is possible that the conceptual background net can be cast too widely for less capable students when attempt is made to relate reading selection concepts to an entire conceptual structure of a content field. However, the structured overview provides yet another approach by which teachers can provide supportive help in pupil attack on reading-learning tasks. It would seem to have particular value as an introductory strategy—to a course, to a unit or topic, or to a textbook chapter fulfilling a similar role.

### Concluding Comment

The reiteration of several points seems useful in closing this treatment of adjunct aids to textual interpretation. The first is that most secondary pupils can profit from any additional help teachers can provide for "teaching" the textbook and collateral sources. The second is that the usual approaches employed in secondary content and developmental reading classes tend to fall into rather monotonous patterns; the varied use of these adjunct aids and strategies for teacher intervention should contribute to more spritely pupil involvement in learning. Finally, these adjunct devices should not be considered as isolated instructional techniques; they are usefully combined with each other, and can be used to implement any of the other guiding structures for reading interpretation and content learning.

## THE GUIDED
## READING LESSON

The *guided reading lesson* (GRL) is one of several forms of a general strategy which combines many of the fundamental tasks of reading instruction with pupil reading of moderate-length selections. Known variously as the "directed reading activity," "teaching the reading selection," or "guiding the reading lesson," it consists of a series of sequential instructional phases by which the teacher structures pupil reading of the selection.[39] With appropriate adjustment, the GRL also can be used effectively with such varied written content as textbook segments or chapters, magazine articles, scientific reports, newspaper editorials, a manual of operations, an advertisement, or even with workbook or filmed reading exercises.

The GRL strategy has several notable advantages for reading and content instruction. (1) It places instructional emphasis upon rather continuous pupil reading activity to understand and react to written text of various types for a variety of reader purposes. (2) The strategy facilitates ongoing reader development—especially when (a) the reading materials are selected to provide a gradual sequencing in general reading difficulty, and (b) these materials are fitted to a developmental or meaningful larger learning sequence. (3) It provides the instructor with a convenient, efficient structure for incorporating many of the continuing objectives of content and/or reading instruction. (4) The strategy makes sense to most secondary pupils and facilitates cooperative teacher-pupil planning and execution of the activities of the reading session. (5) It correlates with the essential processes of the maturing reading act, and thus, the strategy itself can be learned by the pupil and transferred to a personal system of reading-study attack.

The functions and tasks of the seven phases of the GRL are discussed on the following pages. While each of these phases makes a contribution to successful reading and learning, it is not assumed that the use of the GRL would require rigid adherence to the sequence. In some circumstances, it may be more efficient or more natural to integrate some of these phases. In this manner, a written study guide might be employed to combine certain operations of phases 4 through 7 into a single instructional activity. Sometimes certain phases may be telescoped or inverted. For example, it may fit the instructional circumstances to have the pupils identify specific interpretational purposes after a first skim reading of the selection. Some phases may be omitted or deemphasized: e.g., a prior reading selection or learning activity may provide sufficient readiness for reading a story or may stimulate useful initial purposes for the reading of this selection. Generally, the functions represented by these seven phases should be accommodated in the order suggested.

### The Major Phases of the GRL

The major phases of the GRL in their usual instructional sequence consist of the following.

1. Teacher self-preparation for guiding the reading of the chosen selection and for organizing and guiding its accompanying learning activities.
2. Developing specific pupil readiness for the reading lesson, including such preparation as necessary to assure that performance on the initial reading of the selection will meet "instructional-level" criteria.
3. Determining or helping pupils determine useful purposes for the initial silent reading of the selection.
4. Guiding the initial reading of the selection so that pupils (a) obtain an adequate general understanding of the content, and (b) satisfy any special predetermined purposes for reading the selection.
5. Monitoring and otherwise evaluating the initial reading of the selection to provide immediate instructional feedback for (a) clarifying under-

standing of the content, (b) improving pupil reading performance, and (c) developing refined purposes for further reading.
6. Guiding the rereading of the selection to develop deeper understanding of the selection and to extend competency in flexible interpretation.
7. Eliciting and extending pupil reaction to the selection, including the development of specific skills.

### 1. Teacher preparation

The GRL integrates teacher and pupil involvement with the content of the reading selection and its accompanying learning activities. The more effectively the teacher prepares the GRL, the more likely the lesson will be executed with minimal waste motion and that pupils will become actively involved in its reading and learning activities. The specific nature of teacher preparation for executing the GRL will vary with the nature of the reading selection and the general and specific learning objectives to be achieved beyond a successful general reading experience. Certain functions of teacher preparation common to most uses of the GRL may be identified, however.

a. Teacher preparation begins with identifying the contribution this particular GRL (the selection and its related learning activities) should make to pupil reading and/or content learning and its place in the instructional flow of the curriculum. If the selection is a part of a published set of instructional materials, the guide or manual to those materials should be reexamined. Otherwise, the selection should be chosen to meet particular program objectives or pupil needs.

b. The teacher should read/reread the selection to become familiar with its concepts, organization, and its instructional possibilities.

c. The selection should be evaluated for its general reading difficulty and its appropriateness for pupils in the class or reading instructional group. Difficult concepts, vocabulary, and processes necessary to successful pupil reading of the selection are identified for needed development in the readiness phase. Instructional procedures will be anticipated for adjusting the selection to likely "instructional-level" performance for the majority of pupils involved. From this assessment, the teacher may decide to subdivide or individualize the group for certain phases of the GRL. The teacher may decide that the selection is too difficult or too easy for certain members of the class to profit from participating in the GRL, and alternative procedures or reading selections will be chosen for those pupils.

*d.* The most meaningful purposes to guide the pupils' initial silent reading and rereading phases of the GRL will be anticipated. In this, the teacher will be influenced by the nature of the selection and the reading behaviors or content concepts to be learned. The anticipation of such purposes should be viewed as preparatory, not final, rigid decisions. (Teacher-pupil interaction during the readiness and later phases of the GRL may reveal that some of the anticipated reading purposes were not functional. Others may emerge from pupil interest or need.)

*e.* The objectives to be met in the readiness phase should be determined, and instructional activities or tactics should be identified which serve these objectives. As is the case in any phase of the GRL where instructional activities are to be implemented, the teacher will wisely prepare at least twice as many activities as are likely to be employed.

*f.* Supplementary instructional materials should be located and/or developed which will be helpful in the learning or practice of specific skilled reading behavior. (The basic reading selection is used as a means of reinforcing or transfer of learning for these skills and knowledges.) Attention should be given to locating or making practice exercises which can be employed with subgroups or individuals even when general group practice activities are provided in commercial sets of instructional materials.

*g.* Prearrangements should be made for special facilities and equipment (e.g., library, laboratories, bus, and audiovisual equipment) profitably used in readiness, instructional, or follow-up activities.

*h.* Group and/or individual follow-up activities to encourage pupil reaction in the form of critical analysis, problem solving, or creative response to the reading selection or its concepts should be anticipated.

*i.* Correlated reading selections which cater to or extend pupil individual reading interests and/or which amplify the topic or significant processes of the core reading selection may be identified, located, and, if possible, brought to the reading instructional setting.

*Teacher preparation* is an essential phase of the guided or directed reading activity.[40] Busy teachers may be tempted to bypass it, particularly if they have taught the selection previously. Even when the set of instructional materials provides supplementary exercises and teaching suggestions, additional teacher preparation is the instructor's readiness phase and should get the teacher "up" for the reading selection and the pupils. Pupil motivation receives a solid assist from teacher enthusiasm and familiarity with the selection. Pupil emotional security and involvement in learning activity are enhanced by the pervading, if subtle, instructional climate of a teacher who knows what he or she is doing.

## 2. Developing Reader Readiness

The essential nature of reader readiness in the performance of successful mature reading was emphasized in Chapter Three. From the instructor's viewpoint, the major goals of the *reader readiness* phase of the GRL are to facilitate the pupil's use of his existing general readiness and to develop such specific readiness as will be needed to read the selection in an instructionally satisfactory manner and to benefit from its related reading-learning activities.

The teacher must decide upon the amount of readiness needed and whether the instructional group should be subdivided for this phase. The emphasis placed upon readiness activities should be adjusted to pupil need and the nature of the reading selection. Too much readiness can inhibit the reader's sense of self-discovery, especially where the content involves narrative or reader solution of a problem. On the other hand, the readiness phase provides the teacher with an opportunity to set the learning directions of the GRL and, within limits, is a means of bringing the general reading difficulty of the selection within the instructional reading performance levels of the less adequate readers. Other things being the same, the easier the selection and the more intrinsically motivated the reader, the less will be the need for extensive readiness activity.

*Motivation.* Motivation is a prerequisite for any reasonably complex behavioral action. The motivation a pupil brings to an instructional reading selection will be compounded of such factors as (a) physical and emotional conditions of the moment, (b) general intrinsic drive to learn, (c) past reading success and enjoyment, (d) interest in or felt need associated with the topic of the selection, (e) personal relationship with the teacher, and (f) the effect of the specific preparational activities of the readiness phase. The teacher's own interest in the selection and the nature of the readiness activities are of greater importance where the other dimensions of pupil motivation and readiness are of modest strength. In general, activities designed to enhance pupil motivation to read and learn are concerned with: (a) tying the topic or its significant components to group or individual interests or concerns, (b) creating a general set of expectancy or entertainment, (c) setting up a group or personal challenge in the form of problems to be solved, and (d) developing pupil understanding of learning objectives. Of course, any readiness or instructional procedure which lessens anticipated or experienced reading difficulty will enhance reader drive, particularly among less secure readers.

*Background.* The successful reading act is dependent upon the degree to which the reader can bring his background of experience to associate meaning with the textual language the writer has used. It also is dependent upon the ability of the reader to use the reading-thinking processes set up by the writer's sentences and larger organization. In some instances, the readiness task is to bring to immediate awareness those concepts, terms, and processes needed for the selection which the pupil previously has learned. In other cases, the teacher will need to develop background concepts and teach vocabulary and reading processes needed to profit from the selection. When this occurs, the readiness phase plays a significant role in the development of reading vocabulary and skilled reading behavior, while the reading of the selection and the related follow-up activities serve to reinforce this learning.

*Activities.* A wide range of readiness activities are useful in the GRL. The following are illustrative:

a. Using audiovisual equipment and other resources to motivate and build background: viewing films/film strips; listening to tapes/recordings; inviting speakers or visiting places which deal with the central topic, key concepts, or the author of longer sources or reading selections.

b. Discussing and group sharing of impressions of the meaning of the title (anticipating the content).

c. Taking a pretest over the vocabulary or reading processes needed for the selection.

d. Reading and discussing an "advanced organizer" or structured overview of the selection.

e. Presentations by individual pupils or a committee selected to preview the selection to identify interesting and/or difficult concepts.

f. Teacher oral reading of a short selection related to the topic, of excerpts from the selection or of another source by same author, followed by teacher-pupil discussion.

g. Locating the meaning of key vocabulary in a glossary or dictionary.

h. Participating in an instructional or review session on specific skilled reading behaviors needed to understand the selection.

i. Scanning or skim-reading the selection for some identified purpose.

j. Creative activity concerning central figures or situations in the selection; writing words or sentences with first impressions to be verified or disproved by later reading of the selection.

### 3. Setting Purposes for Initial Reading

The benefits derived from purposeful reading to satisfy certain needs or to answer specific questions have been established in earlier discussion. Purposeful reading improves mental precision and concentration and thus usually results in better reading interpretation, flexibility, and efficiency.[41] This phase of the GRL should reinforce pupil habits of purposeful reading and should enhance reading performance of the selection at hand.

*General and specific purposes.* In the instructional setting, a continuing general purpose for first reading is to enjoy a broad basic understanding of the selection as a whole. However, most pupils usually will benefit from additional direction for reading. The teacher and/or pupils may determine definite general purposes for initial reading. Such purposes should be geared to the nature of the content, to pupil ability, and to those decoding interpretive behaviors which the pupils need to learn.

When the selection is lengthy or is a bit too difficult for the pupils to handle, the setting of purposes will reflect instructional operations. For example, the first reading may consist of answering in serial order a set of questions which parallel or correspond to the sequential development of the plot or argument. Sometimes, broad topical or theme-related questions will be useful: e.g., "Do you think the author was in favor of slavery or against it?" or "Which of the general types of humor that we have studied does this short story illustrate?" The size of the segments to be covered by the questions can be adjusted to the ability of the pupils. Quite often, the teacher will set initial general purposes to prepare for or to dovetail with more complex purposes or specific questions anticipated as part of a second reading (rereading) of the selection.

*Teacher-pupil responsibility.* The major responsibility for the nature and quality of purposes set for initial reading (and rereading) is assumed by the teacher. If purposes or questions are recommended in the instructional materials, the teacher should examine these critically to see whether they meet the needs of the reading group. Perhaps additional or more pertinent purposes can be developed in terms of the ongoing learning plan and needs of this class. The opportunities provided in this phase for preparing, instructing, or practicing interpretive skills and the importance of achieving a first successful reading of the material are too great to permit it to become a routine procedure or to be determined solely by someone quite remote from the particular reading situation.

The pupils should be brought into the purpose-setting process as often as is practical. By so doing, the teacher: (a) adds vitality to the first reading, (b) gains insight concerning pupil thinking processes, (c) makes better provision for individual differences in the first reading of the selection, and most importantly, (d) encourages maturing readers to accept greater responsibility for directing their own reading.

Pupil purpose input may arise as a natural consequence of reading readiness activities; indeed, setting purposes is an adjunct of broader readiness activity. Pupil purpose setting, like the teacher's, will be improved by some first-hand knowledge of the material. Unless the readiness activity includes preliminary overviewing of the material by the pupils, the more penetrating pupil input may come later when setting or modifying individual or group purposes for rereading.

The teacher must assume final responsibility for purpose setting as for the other phases of the GRL. But the teacher should be flexible enough to depart from plan when pupil interest or need warrants such modification. Moreover, the adroit teacher can bring pupils to set those reading purposes which will serve their own best learning interests. It is in this sensitivity to and the encouragement of a cooperative teacher-pupil dynamic that the teacher turns the "directed" reading activity into a "guided" reading lesson!

*Notable conditions and illustrative purposes.* While the purposes or questions employed to guide the initial reading of the selection will occupy a more restricted range than those set for guiding a second reading, some effort should be made to prevent the purpose or question form from becoming routine and monotonous. The teacher will be aided in vitalizing initial reading purposes by the substance of the material, the author's style of writing, and by past and ongoing teacher–pupil classroom dialogue. Despite the fact that the initial purposes for reading a selection under the GRL procedure are influenced largely by the primary goal of guiding pupils to a successful first reading to gain general understanding and satisfaction, some variation in type of initial reading purposes is possible. Pupils may read for such supporting initial purposes as locating specified needed information, answering questions, making comparisons, verifying ideas or facts, recognizing the writer's tone or bias, determining the sequence of events, following steps in an argument or directions, reacting to central characters or figures, and making aesthetic evaluations.

The setting of initial reading purposes must give consideration to the fact that it contributes to the remaining phases of the GRL. In order to keep the first reading from bogging down in mechanics or specific interpretive difficulties, the number of independent purposes set for the initial reading should be restricted in number and adjusted to pupil ability. A teacher's use of judicious, open-ended, general questions such as the following combine the stimulation of pupil discussion with the implementation of revised reading purposes and reader reaction in later phases of the lesson.

> After reading the selection (story, chapter, etc.) to satisfy your general understanding of its content:
> a. Identify the two most important characters (in this story) and write a sentence or two presenting the reasons for your choice. *or*
> b. Write a new title for the selection which you feel is more descriptive of the content than the original title. *or*
> c. Determine what major steps are used in the development of this product (described in the selection) and put them in their proper sequence. *or*

> d. Identify the two sides of the argument presented in this editorial. Which do you feel the writer really favors? *or*
> e. Write down the five questions whose answers will provide the best summary of this article. *or*
> f. Decide whether the basic style of writing in this article was humorous, angry, or simply straight reporting. *or*
> g. Locate those parts of the writer's presentation which were confusing and need further explanation.

## 4. Guiding the Initial Reading of the Selection

During this phase of the GRL, the pupil reads the selection silently and the teacher provides structured or incidental support as needed. From the pupil's viewpoint, the two major tasks are to gain an adequate understanding of the basic content of the selection and to satisfy any supplementary purposes or answer any questions which were set earlier or which arise while reading.

**Silent reading for meaning.** Since the 1930s, the emphasis in reading instruction has been placed on silent reading for meaning. This is especially true at upper-grade levels. There are a number of reasons why the initial reading of the selection should be silent rather than oral.[42] Silent reading is: (a) more realistic in terms of life reading usage, (b) more facilitative of accuracy and fluency in gaining meaning, (c) more versatile in meeting various reading purposes, (d) more conducive to reading lesson and general classroom management, and (e) less anxiety arousing—particularly for the less adequate reader.

One reads silently to understand and to learn; he reads orally to communicate and to enjoy the sound of language. Oral reading deserves instructional attention, but should not figure prominently in the initial reading of a selection. A pupil may be asked to read a word, sentence, or paragraph aloud to gain diagnostic insight concerning some difficulty he is having or to assess his ability to cope with the selection, perhaps. But except for occasional special usage in the rereading or reaction phases, the GRL stresses silent reading for meaning.

***Attention according to need.*** If the reading selection is instructionally appropriate in difficulty for the pupil, and if sufficient attention has been given to readiness and purpose setting in the previous phases, the average and better reader should handle the tasks of initial reading with reasonable ease. This should give the teacher an opportunity to assist less competent readers. Or, if the class is divided into several reading instructional groups, the teacher can attend to instructional activities with another group during this phase.

Guiding the silent reading of pupils with persistent reading problems usually calls for more continuous teacher attention in individual or small group situations. For such pupils, the teacher should plan more time for this phase. Dividing the reading selection into a series of shorter units, each with its key or guiding question to be answered, is a useful procedure. If necessary, this can be implemented by face-to-face teacher-pupil contact — the teacher giving the question orally and the pupil(s) reading silently to discover the answer. This approach has the advantages of immediate identification and resolution of reader difficulty and the security of close teacher support. But when used in large groups, it slows the better readers in the group and may lead to inattention and group management difficulties.

An alternative technique for heterogeneous groups is to provide a worksheet with the guiding questions listed for each meaningful part of the selection. Pupils read at their own rate in answering the questions and are free to ask for teacher help if encountering difficulty. For poorer readers, the teacher should read and discuss the questions so that all of the group understands them. But the teacher should remain available to problem readers, since they have a tendency to get bogged down, to lose motivation, and to drift into other mental sets or activities.

Close teacher direction may hinder the best readers in a class, on the other hand. For such pupils,

the teacher may find it useful at times to combine phases 4, 5, and 6 of the GRL. The use of a structured reading guide sheet or a worksheet may take the place of personal teacher guidance, evaluation, and the setting of rereading activities. The better readers should not be neglected, however. They, too, need feedback, teacher stimulus, a chance to respond and be rewarded, and to get help when encountering difficulty. Better readers profit from freedom to work independently, but they do need instructional attention to extend skills and knowledges, and should not be shuttled off regularly with the worksheets, study guides, or library assignments.

### 5. Monitoring and Evaluating for Feedback

As handled by the experienced reading teacher, many of the adjacent phases of the GRL are fused together so well that it is difficult for an inexperienced observer to distinguish them. This is particularly true of phases 4 and 5, where guiding the initial silent reading, monitoring individual and group operations, evaluating pupil performance, and providing feedback can be coordinated effectively. Nevertheless, phase 5 does represent important functions in reading instruction which deserve the definite attention of the teacher, regardless of whether they are handled as a separate instructional action or as a rather smooth transition between initial reading and interpretive rereading of the selection.[43]

***The significance of feedback.*** Psychologists have established that feedback is an important, and probably an essential, condition in most learning. Human learning usually takes place when the individual makes a response to a stimulus situation in order to satisfy some motivating condition. The association between the learner's response and the stimulus situation is formed more readily and more firmly if he ascertains that the response was appropriate. The more immediate this reinforcing feedback, the better. If the response was appropriate, early reinforcement strengthens the learned association. If the response was incorrect, early feedback of a correcting nature inhibits the incorrect association and facilitates the correct association.

In basic life learning situations—where the learner's need is strong and the relationship between this need, the stimulus situation, and the response is clear and direct—the learner may be able to determine the adequacy of this response by the extent to which it satisfies his felt need. But in upper-school learning situations—where motivation often is indirect and muted; where the relationship between motivation, stimulus, and response is academic rather than functional—the learner usually needs feedback from some external agent such as the teacher, fellow pupils, a teaching machine, or a keyed worksheet.

*Feedback and evaluation.* Feedback usually is dependent upon evaluation, by self or external source. The better reader usually knows when he is having unusual difficulty with meaning, but he may not be aware of missing specific interpretive points. The poor reader may not be able to determine when he has missed the greater meaning. Thus, the teacher usually must provide some evaluative guidance with the tasks of the first silent reading of the selection for all members of the instructional group. Primarily, this evaluation will focus upon the adequacy of pupil response in: (a) gaining an accurate overall, first-level understanding of the writer's meaning (grasp of main ideas, plot sequence or organizational structure, key concepts, terms, supporting facts, writer's stated purpose, etc.), (b) satisfying the predetermined supplementary purposes for initial reading, (c) demonstrating fluency in the use of silent reading processes required for these tasks, and (d) developing positive attitudes.

The teacher may employ various assessment procedures in arriving at this evaluation: observation of reading reaction to content during initial silent reading, pupil responses and personal reactions during the discussion of the selection, performance on comprehension check tests, purposeful oral reading performance over short segments of the selection, and pupil self-evaluation.

*Instructional redirection.* From the monitoring/evaluating operations pertinent to the initial silent reading of the selection, the instructor should confirm or modify the next appropriate instructional operation. One such decision is whether the GRL group should remain intact or whether subgroupings or differentiated assignments are warranted. If the silent reading tasks are accomplished without notable difficulty, the group or individual will move into the next GRL phase—rereading to extend interpretation. However, if the group or certain members of the group encounter some notable reading problems with the silent reading of the selection, the instructional feedback may take the form of providing additional readiness to read the selection, redefining the purposes for initial reading, or rereading the difficult segments of the selection for initial purposes under close teacher guidance.

Under certain circumstances, the feedback decision may involve revising the remainder of the GRL activity. Now and then, pupil involvement with the initial reading and related discussion of the selection may be so thorough or fulfilling that further rereading or reaction would be superfluous or affectively deadening. The teacher therefore may elect to skip one or more of the remaining phases. And occasionally, pupil emotional reaction to selection content is so negative or pupil difficulty with it so frustrating that it is wiser to terminate the GRL at this point and initiate a different instructional activity. This will occur less frequently—if the earlier functions of the GRL have been properly effected and the selection reasonably matches the pupil instructional reading level.

## 6. Rereading to Extend Flexibility and Interpretation

Rereading has four major values as an operational phase of the GRL. (a) It enables the pupil to derive different and/or deeper levels of understanding from the selection. (b) It may serve as a reinforcing agent for retaining significant concepts and generalizations. (c) It makes use of the reading selection for additional practice of the general reading act; and since the previous GRL activities most likely have smoothed out reader problems with vocabulary and basic comprehension, this rereading can be practiced as a fluent, flexible process. And (d), it provides a vehicle for introducing, teaching, or practicing the specific interpretive skills of flexible reading performance.

***A search for additional meaning.*** Rereading as an instructional procedure requires teacher judgment. It should not become an unvaried routine of going through the same operations or answering the same form questions. Sometimes the teacher may decide to dispense with the rereading phase: the content of the selection may not warrant extended analysis, or pupil motivation may be served by a change in procedure or by moving on to personal reaction or the next selection. The use of rereading should be consistent with the nature of the material; e.g., it makes more sense to reread a selection describing how to build a sailplane to summarize the steps in this process or to make a list of needed materials than to critically analyze the author's purpose.

Above all, rereading should be purposeful; and unless notable difficulty was encountered in the first reading, the purposes for rereading profitably vary from those which guided the original reading. Rereading "just to reread" tends to be mechanical and detracts from meaningful reading habits. Unless the meaning of the material was minimally understood upon first reading or largely forgotten, undirected rereading contributes very little new meaning or retention.[44] However, when rereading efforts are directed toward more precise analysis or stimulate and guide the pupil to higher levels of thinking, new perceptions are gained, additional associations are formed, and interpretation and retention of learning may be involved.[45]

***Increasing flexibility.*** The rereading phase of the GRL provides an excellent opportunity to practice reading flexibility—the adjustment of reading attack (rate and mode of reading) to meet different reading purposes for different reading materials.

Thus, rereading may be more selective and more varied in the reading mode utilized—e.g., scanning, skim reading, rapid reading, critical reading, or even selected use of oral reading. On the other hand, if the first reading of the selection involved some sort of selective overview of the selection, then rereading to gain a more thorough and detailed understanding of the content would be a logical and useful general purpose for second reading. This may be followed by a third reading to satisfy selective and advanced interpretive tasks.

***Illustrative rereading tasks.*** Interpretive tasks emphasized in the GRL rereading phase should be determined by the nature of the selection, the present mental and reading capabilities of the pupil, and the interpretive skills targeted for development in the reading curriculum. Any decoding or interpretive behaviors of mature reading performance presented in Chapter Three can be adapted readily to rereading purposes. The following rereading purposes are illustrative and assume that the interpretive skills required have been introduced at some previous lesson.

a. Skim-read the selection to identify the six basic steps of the process described.
b. Rapidly reread this selection to locate the writer's use of three propaganda techniques, then read these critically to identify their general type and the bias they serve.
c. Reread the selection ("Working in America") to identify what special relationships the writer believes to exist between (personality) and (lifework). Find three examples in the selection which illustrate such relationships.
d. Scan the selection to locate which table or chart presents information which best answers each of the following five (factual) questions. Note the number of that chart or table, then study that table or chart and answer the related question.
e. Each of the four major characters which figure in this story is a symbol. Reread to identify the concept or generalized idea each character represents.
f. We have agreed that this short story poignantly captures the feelings which

two young people hold for their parents. Reread the dialogue in the story to find several examples of how the writer made good use of words and phrases to imply but not directly state the nature of these feelings.

g. Reexamine the list of seven special terms we studied before reading this selection. Scan the selection to locate one denotative and one connotative use for each term.

h. The topic sentences of the six paragraphs of this selection make up an inductive (statement-support) argument. Locate these topic sentences and rewrite them to form a major generalization-supporting argument paragraph.

Rereading can be guided in a number of ways. The group may read individually under the teacher's personal supervision with pupil response taking the form of informal discussion. Rereading may be an independently structured task. Since the basic understanding of the content will have been secured in the first reading, most pupils can work individually on rereading activities through the use of study guides, worksheets, or taped directions to guide the reading tasks.

Rereading may be done as an out-of-class assignment, whereas initial reading generally should be an in-class phase. Even so, the teacher should go over the directions and the form of this out-of-class rereading activity much in the manner of preparing pupils for any independent learning or study assignment. Through the use of subgrouping or differentiated assignment, phase 6 rereading activity presents a good opportunity to provide greater adjustment of basic instruction to individual need.

## 7. Eliciting and Extending
## Pupil Reaction

The essential place of reader reaction in the integral reading act was discussed in Chapter Three. Any meaningful reading should produce a reader reaction. Consciously or subconsciously, it should change the reader in some way—as a reader, as a thinker, as a creator, as a feeling person.[46] Too often, content and developmental reading instruction fails to stimulate and extend pupil personal involvement and self-fulfillment in the use of the skills, concepts, arguments, and tone pertinent to the reading selection. Inhibition occurs when pupil reading response is terminated with the answering of teacher questions for rereading, as important as these may be.

*Objectives and related activities.* One of the primary objectives of this phase (7) is to stimulate and provide a vehicle for pupil personal reaction to the material as a thinking-feeling person. Hopefully, the personal dynamic existing between the teacher and the instructional group is such that any member would feel free to express insights and feelings about the topic, substance, and style of the selection during appropriate moments at any stage of the lesson. However, some students are reticent to express such personal views, and sometimes, classroom management curtails the opportunity to encourage individual or small-group reaction. Such opportunity can be provided in phase 7. Pupil responses may be solicited in a variety of ways: teacher-class informal discussion, setting up small-group "rap" sessions, pupil free-response written reaction, completing a rating sheet over the selection developed earlier by the teacher and class, etc. The adroit teacher can keep such sessions from becoming a generalized "ain't life awful," but the arousal of even strong negative reaction to written material should be recognized as normal, of therapeutic value, and a response which can be used for further learning and adjustment.

A second goal for this phase is to encourage the pupil to transfer the interpretive result of the selection reading experience to productive action in the form of practical application, problem solving, and creative activity. Three benefits accrue from this: interpretation is improved through new insight, creative and applicational interests and abilities are extended, and reading as a life activity gains greater and broader significance for the pupil.

Such creative language activities as the following lend themselves easily to reaction activity and also contribute to language development: (a) writing a new ending to the story read, (b) developing and taping a skit built around one of the characters in the play read, (c) holding a debate on a contemporary issue presented in the reading selection (e.g., the need for prison reform), (d) writing a newspaper advertisement or television commercial about a product explained in the reading selection, and (e) summarizing the major events of a reading selection about an historical happening or a contemporary incident into a press correspondent's 100-word telegram.

Other modes of creative reader reaction are useful and should be stimulated by the instructor: (a) drawing a cartoon to illustrate a personality discussed in an article, (b) building a model of a product described in a selection, (c) making a map or frieze of an area (room, house, yard, village) in which the story or a described event was centered, (d) making a time line of the events which occurred in a biographical selection, (e) rearranging the verbal data presented in the reading selection to develop equations, tables, charts, models, or figures, (f) using the evidence presented in a selection to solve prior problems posed by the group, and (g) conducting a demonstration or experiment using the data and/or processes presented in the selection.

The third objective of this last instructional phase of the GRL is to extend and polish reading performance as such. One form of this activity will involve corrective feedback concerning performance on the interpretive rereading tasks of phase 6. Another will consist of providing additional needed practice on reading behaviors introduced in this lesson or which were identified as deficient in the earlier phase of the lesson by means of skills or content exercises.

A fourth objective is to use the selection and its related reading experiences to stimulate further personal reading—for example, on topics presented in the selection, in the original source from which the selection was taken, in other works by the writer, in similar types of writing, or in materials which present confirming or contrasting evidence. The act of reading is essential to reading improvement. One of the overall strengths of the GRL as a

reading instructional strategy is that it involves the pupil in a considerable amount of such reading activity. Even so, this is not enough in itself. The developing reader must read more than instructional materials in the basic instructional setting. Using the GRL to sow seeds for further reading is one way we can contribute to this personal and independent reading. The extension of individual reading is discussed in greater detail in Chapters Twelve and Thirteen.

### *Concluding Comment*

Instructionally, a number of advantages accrue from employing the guided reading lesson as a reading instructional strategy. It helps the pupil perform better in actual reading, which benefits both his learning and his attitude. It helps the teacher organize the varied learning activities of basic reading instruction into a systematic instructional plan. It can be adapted to most any reading selection of reasonable substance. Teachers with little experience in reading instruction can find security in the practicality of this strategy. Experienced teachers will find it amenable to creative variation in instruction.

The GRL is compatible with both mature reading behavior and learning theory, but it is no reading instructional palliative. It does require teacher time and effort, and it does not guarantee pupil success in reading the selection or in improving skilled reading behavior. However, it increases the probability that pupil reading and learning will be successful, and it helps the teacher make the most of time and energy invested in reading and content instruction.

## READING–STUDY GUIDES

The use of a reading-study guide provides yet another way to combine acceptable reading practices with a structure for improving the understanding and learning of text. Although study guides have received greater attention as a content instructional technique, they also can be employed effectively in secondary developmental reading situations. When utilized within a larger teaching structure, the study guide provides indirectly some of the reading-content learning direction given more directly by the teacher in the guided reading lesson. Thus, Vine et al. describe the basic study guide as "a paper-and-pencil version of the type of inductive thinking through which you might take an entire class in an oral discussion. However, the study guide allows each individual to react each step of the way at his own rate."[47] Earle states this a bit differently: "A study guide, as the name implies, guides a student through a reading assignment, focusing his attention on major ideas and directing his use of the necessary reading-thinking processes."[48]

### Guides as "Within Lesson" Structure

The reading and reasoning guides described by Herber meet many of the conditions desired in the effective assignment and reading-related learning activity.[49] Herber equates the use of reading-reasoning guides with "within lesson" structure, and recommends that they be employed as part of a larger "instructional framework." This instructional framework roughly parallels the teaching of any unit of work and includes three major parts: (1) *preparation* (motivation, background, and review; anticipation and purpose; direction, and language development); (2) *guidance* (skills and concept development); and (3) *independent use* (application of skills and concepts). The reading and reasoning guides are an important means of effecting the guidance and independent use of parts of this framework.

The goal of the reading-study guide is to develop pupil reading-thinking processes concomitantly with the learning of content concepts. It works best when pupils have had previous instruction in the reading behaviors needed to handle the tasks in the guide, and when pupils have been taught how to use the reading-guide procedure. Although the form and processes vary with the instructional situation, the base pattern calls for reading-reasoning tasks at three levels: *literal comprehension* and

recall of selection data, *interpretive manipulation* of concepts of the selection, and *applied use of concepts* in transformation activities or problem solving. The guide can be used for out-of-class study, but it often works better with direct teacher assistance. The guide can be of a differentiated nature, constructed so that students of different abilities may work at different levels of reading-reasoning tasks.

***Related instructional procedures.*** A cogent analysis of the instructional procedures involved in the use of reading-study guides has been described by Earle and is summarized here.[50]

1. Analysis of assignment (reading selection) content in terms of instructional objectives to determine the most deserving aspects of content to be emphasized, as guided by content area significance, present and future utilization, and student interest.
2. Analysis of assignment for process—in particular, identifying the reading–thinking skills necessary for acquiring, interpreting, evaluating, and applying the content information contained in the assignment.
3. Analysis of the degree and nature of pupil assistance needed in terms of the content and process tasks, and the competency of pupils to deal with them.
4. Construction of the physical (paper-pencil) form of the study guide in view of these decisions. The form may vary considerably to accommodate differences in learning objectives and pupil abilities.
5. Use of the study guide within the framework of the planned lesson or unit, including provision for teacher-pupil interaction to motivate, provide, or review necessary background, set study purpose, direct reading-study activity, and implement reaction.

### Reading-Study Guide Forms

Most reading-study guides will employ questioning in the broad sense used by Sanders—a cognitive exercise calling for a response, including problem solution and creative tasks. There can be notable differences in the effectiveness of questioning, and the reading-study guide should not be equated with typical use of worksheet exercises, although their forms may have some similarity. Perhaps the effective integration of questioning procedure with the best strategies of the reading assignment, as recommended in Chapter Five, provides a more defensible parallel with the recommended use of study guides.

The study guide counters some of the notable weaknesses of question-form assignments as commonly used in classroom settings.[51] It incorporates teacher determination of essential content and process of the reading assignment as it relates to unit or course objectives. It considers pupil differences in ability and development. It incorporates a meaningful structure for direct and/or indirect teacher guidance of the reading-learning activity. And it provides for active interpupil and pupil-teacher reaction through in-class discussion of the guides. Herber suggests that this interaction is so beneficial to the extension of concepts and processes that the best questions may be those with more than one defensible answer.

It will be observed that this broader yet more directed structure of the study guide has much in common with the guided reading lesson discussed earlier in the chapter. The difference lies not in the differential emphasis between reading skills and content learning, since both the GRL and the reading-study guide are capable of accommodating (and should accommodate) both. Perhaps the key difference is operational; it depends upon the extent to which the teacher wishes or needs to provide a closer personal step-by-step reading-study guidance for the pupil or pupils, or whether he feels the reading-learning task is accomplished more efficiently by greater pupil independence and perhaps differentiation of reading-study activity. In any case, the sound reading and learning principles of the GRL and the "instructional framework of the study guide" emanate from the same established antecedents. It is these common principles, rather than specific tactical differences, which will best serve the teacher in the long run.

## READING-STUDY SYSTEMS

Another way in which the classroom instructor can improve the reading efficiency and learning effectiveness of assignments and related content reading is to help the pupil develop a system for independently attacking such content. A reading-study system can aid in the structuring of pupil reading in two ways. During the in-class teaching of the system, the teacher guides pupil reading and understanding of the content. Later, when the student has assimilated the system, he should be more capable of guiding his own reading and learning of significant content.

### The Nature of Reading-Study Systems

A reading-study system is a coordinated sequence of reading-learning behaviors for handling significant content materials when the pupil's task includes the thorough analysis, retention, and/or transformation of the writer's information and argument. A number of such systems have appeared in the literature. Most systems are identified by acronyms which serve as mnemonic aids to improve learning the recommended sequence and to aid the recall of the individual steps of that sequence. The following are illustrative: SQ3R,[52] OK4R,[53] PQRST,[54] PANORAMA,[55] POINT,[56] and EVOKER.[57] The first four of these are rather stable sequences for dealing with expository material, like most reading-study systems. EVOKER was developed primarily as an aid to the interpretation and study of literature. POINT is modeled on the nature of the integral reading act. Reading-study systems should be taught consistently with the concept of reading flexibility in mind. Thus, they may be generalized to use with most study materials as well as adapted to a teacher-directed procedure for guiding group reading of a developmental or content selection.

*Common elements.* Most reading-study systems are the products of rational sequences of reading-learning procedures which experience and research have revealed to be effective in reading-study situations. The better-known systems employ some common components or conditions. These include: (1) a goal-directed or purposeful reading-study attack; (2) a quick skim-reading preview or overview of the content; (3) pupil-determined specific reading or study questions; (4) a combination of multiple readings of the content, geared to the necessary interpretive/retention tasks of the reader; (5) a selective, efficient system of note taking; and (6) some provision for overlearning, such as self-testing, purposeful rereading, reorganization or restatement of key information, or some application of information gained.

*Advantages and disadvantages.* Learning the use of a reading-study system provides the pupil with certain learning/retentional/applicational advantages. Depending upon the system and the way it is taught, it increases the pupil's understanding of and flexibility in study-type reading. Since it is a planned method of attack, it motivates the pupil; it gives him a positive method for getting started and carrying out longer assignments. Evidence indicates that it produces better learning results than random study or nonpurposeful reading and rereading. Used flexibly, it is more efficient than typical pupil memory-oriented emphasis of specifics. It has an identity and therefore can be more readily taught and applied than a collection of independent reading study skills. Some systems lend themselves to teacher-guided group instruction of significant content selections. Such instruction is useful in itself, and provides a natural way for transferring the system to the pupil as an independent-study procedure.

The disadvantages of a reading-study system stem largely from poor selection and/or misuse of the materials on the part of the teacher. Some systems are rather narrow in application, and the pupil can learn to use them in too rigid and mechanical a manner. Too often, they are presented to pupils as formulas to be memorized, but are not taught as a process to be used. Teachers have a habit of teaching reading-study systems in a superficial, incidental manner. As a result, the pupil does not master this approach and is "turned off"— he does not immediately increase his test scores as promised. Most of the disadvantages of a reading-learning system can be avoided by informed and serious instruction, stressing the system's selective and flexible use.

A surprising number of high school pupils do not understand the relationship between reading and study, have little insight into the techniques of study reading, and receive little vigorous instruction in reading-study techniques. Reading does not necessarily produce learning and retention. And "study" in the sense of successful learning, retaining, and applying selected important information involves more than reading and rereading. Yet surveys reveal that the most popular forms of study amount to some variation of reading and rereading, reading-underlining-rereading, intermittent single reading and memorization, and reading-underlining-memorization. Such approaches are better than no study whatever or simply reading once, but they are not very efficient, tend not to differentiate between significant and insignificant data, and do not support longer-term retention.

## POINT:
### A Reading–Study System

POINT [58] is a fairly typical reading-study system which has been devised to combine certain reading and study procedures into a systematic attack on longer reading selections or assignments. It differs slightly from other systems in that it stresses flexible adaptation by the user to the reading task, once the system has been learned. POINT is useful particularly when the task is to read a number of pages of serious content—to understand thoroughly the writer's argument, to learn the important ideas and facts, and to overlearn the most important content so it will be remembered for tests and other later use. Since this is the type of reading-study task which composes two-thirds of high school and college learning assignments, POINT can be of frequent aid to most students.

POINT consists of five overlapping steps or stages — one for each letter of the key term. This is simply a mnemonic device to aid memory while learning the system. The cue words for the five basic steps are:

P = Purpose
O = Overview
I = Interpret
N = Note
T = Test

These are the five *basic* steps or stages, and they represent the elements which researchers of the study process have found to be most crucial. It is important to understand that this series of steps is not a rigid one. Each step can be adjusted to meet different study situations, and in some cases, a step may be omitted altogether. However, in the beginning, it is best to teach the five steps of the system as they are presented. Each contributes something to most reading-study assignments.

The five steps are explained briefly on the following pages. The questions given for each step serve as a checklist of operations which the teacher and pupil should find useful in learning that stage of the system. The explanation and questions for each step are directed at the user of the system.

### Step 1: Purpose

Recognition of purpose can add two important dimensions to our behavior. One of these is *drive*, or the force with which we will act. The other dimension of purpose is *direction*, or how we go about achieving our goal. Being able to convert the energy of "drive" into constructive "direction" is essential to successful performance. Knowing one's direction also can have a positive effect of building drive. Some pupils feel defeated by study assignments because they have no effective way to deal with them in the time available or because they have no confidence in their methods of study.

If it is to be efficient, the Purpose step must be directed toward the goals of the specific study assignment. The student should determine the specific things he wants to achieve in his study reading of the material. He should consider three sources in setting his study goals: the purpose of the instructor in making the assignment, the purpose of the writer of the material, and, of course, his own needs and interests which the material may satisfy. Reading and learning are more effective when the student can turn these general purposes into specific questions for which he can seek answers. For example, learning can be more efficient when guided by the specific question "What are the five basic steps in the scientific method?" than when guided by the vague purpose "to know more about science." Specific study questions or purposes may not be provided by the instructor or directly stated by the textbook author. When they are not, the student must develop his own "working questions."

The following questions will help set the POINT system into operation. They serve as a checklist of key aspects of the Purpose step. In learning to use the system, these questions should be studied and rigorously applied to the assignment. After the system is mastered, use of the questions becomes rather automatic and selective.

1. *What do I know now about the content of this assignment?* What have I read or learned about this topic? What is its relationship to previous assignments in terms of content or method?

2. *What do I need to gain from this material?* What was the instructor's purpose in making the assignment? What are the most important ideas presented? How does the content relate to recent class lectures or demonstrations? What new terminology is used? What processes are described? Which facts are most crucial to the writer's argument?

3. *How well do I need to understand this material?* A quick, general impression? Fair understanding of the main ideas? Careful investigation of certain parts? Thorough understanding of the entire content? Overlearning to the point of memory recall?

4. *How shall I adapt the POINT system to this assignment?* [This question relates closely to the answers determined for question (3).] Which steps should receive emphasis? Can some steps be omitted? How shall I "overview?" Which kind of reading "interpretation" is more effective? Are notes necessary?

5. *Am I ready to make a positive attack?* Are the necessary materials handy? Are study conditions reasonable? What degree of attack: *blitzkreig* or *divide-and-conquer* tactics? Shall I set a time limit for completing the assignment? What is the next step?

### Step 2: Overview

The second step or stage in the POINT system involves getting a quick, general understanding of the material to be read and studied. In a sense, this consists of a mental scouting of a written territory. The specific nature of the Overview will vary some with different purposes and materials. In some situations, the Overview may be more thorough than in others. Generally, it involves a brief and selective reading survey of the material assigned. When very little is known about the material to be read and/or the purposes of the assignment, it may be necessary to reverse steps 1 and 2—first to overview the material and then determine general and specific purposes. But the Overview does not substitute for setting purposes for reading–study attack!

The Overview may fulfill varied functions. It may involve screening the material quickly to locate specific needed data. It may be a general survey of the content to obtain a feeling for the author's writing style or to see if the content contains any new or different information.

Where the typical reading–study assignment is concerned, the Overview is a selective first reading step. It helps to turn broad study purposes into specific questions for reading study. It identifies the author's key ideas and the organizational pattern which he uses to support and explain those ideas. It helps to decide how thoroughly the content must be read and studied.

The Overview may require one or more of several reading techniques or styles. It may involve using a locational aid such as the index or table of contents. It may call for a locational *skimming* of the chapter headings or other typographical aids. If the location of specific terms or facts is what is needed, a *scanning* approach may be most useful.

Overviewing the typical textbook assignment will call for a combination of skim-reading and locational reading techniques. This approach includes: (1) surveying the major topics of the chapter presented in the table of contents; (2) rapidly but thoughtfully reading the author's introduction to the chapter as well as his concluding summary, if one is presented; (3) scanning through the chapter, locating the main sections into which the chapter is divided, and rapidly reading the topical headings into which each section is divided; (4) skim-reading for the topic sentences of the paragraphs in any section whose major ideas seem vague; and (5) taking several minutes to think over the content to decide if and how a more intensive reading of the material might be useful.

Some questions which may be raised to guide the Overview include:

1. *What type of Overview best fits my purpose?* Brief sampling of author's writing style? Locational scanning for specific answers to questions? Skim-reading to identify main ideas? A solid survey which prepares for thorough study?

2. *Which content will be most useful?* Table of contents? Review of previous chapter or assignment? Review of class notes? Book index or preface? Introduction to chapter? Chapter summary? Topical headings and other aids such as discussion questions raised by the author? Other reference sources such as the encyclopedia or dictionary?

3. *Does the Overview modify my reading-study purposes?* Does this content satisfy my purposes? Can I sharpen my purpose by raising more specific questions? How thoroughly do I need to study this material? Shall I cover this assignment in one study session or divide it into several?

*4. Which of the remaining steps of POINT should be emphasized?* Which approach to interpretive reading will be most functional? Are notes needed? If so, which form is most efficient? Does this content deserve to be overlearned through testing?

## Step 3: Interpret

The interpret stage of the POINT system usually combines reading and learning actions. An analysis of the specific content will be added to the understanding of the broad framework gained in the Overview. How thorough the approach to reading should be will depend upon the specific purposes for the assignment. In the typical study assignment situation, this will call for fairly intensive activity. When the material is familiar and not complex, a rapid reading for broad understanding will do. However, when the selection contains a number of new concepts or processes or when the author's organization is detailed and complex, a shift toward more careful analysis and a slower rate is recommended.

Thus, the specific reading procedures or styles employed also will vary with the specific goals to be achieved through interpretation. There are four likely patterns here. Taken somewhat in order of the time and effort required, they are: (1) *rapid reading* to gain a general impression or to verify the major ideas and structure of the selection; (2) *selective reading and study* to find specific information to answer questions or to apply to problems; (3) *critical analysis* of the information presented to determine its accuracy and pertinency or to distinguish its emotional appeal from its factual evidence; and (4) *organizational reading* to carefully and thoroughly identify the author's idea structure so that it may be remembered as well as understood.

Some questions which will help determine the type of approach useful in the Interpret step are:

*1. What are the definite questions or problems for which I should locate information?* What signifi-cant processes are described? What major generalizations can be drawn, what concepts supported?

*2. Will my purpose and the material permit a rapid reading?* To gain a general impression? To verify the key ideas and structure? As a second reading prior to careful analysis?

*3. Have I identified the most important ideas?* Do I understand them? What major generalizations did the writer use? What concepts were used to make these generalizations? What facts are absolutely essential to the writer's argument?

*4. Can I reorganize or restructure this content in a more meaningful or useful way?*

*5. Does this material require careful, critical analysis?* What were the writer's purposes? Does this material deal with emotional issues? Is the content "slanted" toward some point of view? Do I have a personal bias toward this material or topic? Need I be concerned with style and quality of the writing as well as with the content?

*6. Does this content require a "retentional" reading approach?* Which content needs detailed understanding? Must this content be remembered as well as understood? Is the content extensive enough to require a "whole–parts–whole" study?

*7. Shall I combine the Interpret and Note steps?*

## Step 4: Note

The making of notes contributes to study learning in several ways. First, if done selectively, it should improve understanding of the content, because it should encourage the identification of the most significant information presented. Second, the very process of noting causes us to rethink and restate the important ideas, and this aids retention. A third value is that noting provides a convenient and familiar source of important content for later review.

Hardly any student doubts the usefulness of notes. Yet he may be concerned about the time and energy the process takes. Noting does take more time and energy than reading alone. Some of this effort, however, can be credited to a more detailed understanding of the material than would be gained by a rapid but general reading. Unfortunately, some students resist taking notes because they are neither efficient nor selective in note taking. They take verbatim notes, regardless of whether this exactness is required. And they are reluctant to omit anything which could be of the slightest possible use. The immediate result is thirty pages of notes over a twenty-five page chapter. The eventual result is to become discouraged with note taking.

Notes are more useful in some study situations than in others. That is why the Note step of the POINT system may be optional and should be used in a flexible manner! It is better to take a few useful notes and continue to profit from the other steps of the system than to drop the entire system because one resents taking notes. There are several ways to make notes, and the student should select his note system to fit his study purposes, his study circumstances, and his personal needs of the moment.

Four notational systems are recommended for possible use in the POINT system: (1) verbatim recording of data when exact quotation is necessary: (2) rewriting key points to reinforce the most important ideas; (3) underlining or checking of key points in the text when speed is essential; and (4) marginal outlining to combine efficient use of time with the benefit of a thorough interpretation and useful study cues.

Following are some questions which will aid in determining how a noting system might fit the particular needs of a study situation:

1. *Is a noting system necessary to meet my study purposes?* For improved understanding? For recall? For later review?
2. *Which noting system best meets my purposes under the conditions I face?* Verbatim recording for quotation? Rewording selected ideas for test review purposes? Underlining? Marginal outline?
3. *Will my notes make sense when they are "cold"?* Clear writing? Organization evident? Source of information included?
4. *Do I have a systematic filing system in which to keep these notes?* Notebook section? Card file? Envelope for related course materials?
5. *How can these notes be related to lecture notes and related sources of information?* Combined under a topical system of organization? A cue system of pages on which related points are found? A "split-page" lecture note-comment approach?

### Step 5: Test

The final step of the POINT procedure is called Test. "Test" in this case means something much broader than "taking a test," although that might be included in this last step of the process. "Test," in this situation, refers to evaluation—a self-analysis—of the content read and studied, and of the study process itself. It also includes any necessary application of the information gained in the form of problem solving.

In terms of the content read or assignment studied, the Test step will serve one or more of four functions: (1) to determine whether the original purposes for reading study have been met, and, if not, what to do about satisfying them; (2) to clarify any serious confusion in the understanding of the content study-read; (3) to aid in the overlearning (review) of those ideas which are important enough to retain for later use; and (4) to determine what application, if any, should be made of the information gained.

The actual form the Test step takes will vary from situation to situation, and should be adjusted to what has been done in the preceding steps. The Test step may be short-term or of an extended nature. When the assignment is open-ended—for example, a set of chapters to be studied for a later examination—the Test stage may be extended by periodic review until the exam has been taken. On the other hand, some assignments require little overt Test action, such as in an assignment to read several short stories in order to catch the mood of a period being studied in a history class.

If only a general understanding of certain key concepts is required, the Test step might consist of skim-reading the marginal notes or the underlined parts of the text. Other Test step activities might include the developing of hypothetical exam questions; rapidly rereading to turn all headings into questions and checking on answers; comparing reading notes with lecture notes; writing a summary; developing a list of key words or ideas to be reviewed; performing the experiment described; or creating a product based on the description given. The important element in all of this is. that the student reacts appropriately to the content, perhaps by "overlearning" (additional learning of information to enhance remembering), through mental activity of one sort or another, perhaps by taking creative action, perhaps by just enjoying.

Some questions for determining the nature of Test-step activities might include:

1. *What were my general and specific purposes for this reading-study assignment?* Is general understanding and appreciation of the content sufficient for this situation?
2. *Do I have need of the Test stage?* Did I satisfy my purposes for reading the material? Do I understand the ideas in the material? Do I need to overlearn the content? How can I apply this information to personal or vocational problems?
3. *What form of review is most efficient for my needs?* Summarizing? Rereading to develop and answer questions? Self-testing over terms, definitions, equations, etc.? Mentally rewriting ideas according to marginal outline?
4. *How shall I adjust my review testing to the course examination?* Thorough review of important ideas of all content for true-false and multiple-choice tests? Intensive self-testing for completion and short-answer tests? Practice application for problem-solving tests? Outlining answers for likely questions for essay examinations?
5. *How shall I time my review testing?* Can I get in three reviews? One immediately upon completion? A second within a week? A third within a month?

6. *Need I and can I react to the material in some meaningful manner?* Carry out some action? Solve related problems? Transform the information into different products?

## Teaching a Reading–Study System

Whether utilized as one means of structuring in- and out-of-class reading of larger school assignments or as a practical life behavior, the nature of study reading and how to use a reading-study system deserve definite and careful attention in the secondary school. It should be taught meaningfully; pupils should understand the nature and differences of reading, learning, and retention, as well as how the reading-study system aids in these matters. It should be taught realistically; pupils should understand that it takes effort to learn to use a system effectively, and that even then, the system is no magic carpet to "A-land." It should be taught systematically with opportunity for guidance and practice in applying it to different study tasks. If possible, one system should be taught throughout the secondary school. It might be wise not to use any system taught at the elementary school level, since pupils seem to have some holdover confusion and negative attitudes about systems taught at the elementary level.

Some illustrative activities for teaching a reading-study system are given below.

*1. Readiness activities.* In the broadest sense, readiness for the learning and use of a study system is served when those specific reading behaviors utilized in a reading-study system are taught as a part of developmental or content-oriented reading. The use of the component sequence in teacher-guided reading instruction also contributes essential readiness. Some specific readiness activities include the following:

*a.* Checking pupil understanding of study systems by means of a questionnaire. Some pupils will have been taught previous systems. Usually this has been inadequately learned, is remembered in a confused manner, and seldom used.

*b.* The class may conduct a school sample survey on study and reading-study systems. First a questionnaire should be developed which is short, inoffensive, and objectively marked. This may take the form of an interview check list. Major divisions of the instrument might include: How do you study? When do you study? What attitudes do you have about study? Each pupil would be responsible for interviewing five to ten school acquaintances. Both the development and the analysis of the results can serve as effective learning procedures.

*c.* For demonstration (not research) purposes, the teacher may pick five pupils of adequate or better reading ability and work with them independently on mastering a reading-study system. Then the entire class is assigned a reading-study task over a short selection or a ten-page segment of a text chapter. The teacher can give either a series of questions to answer and have each pupil mark the amount of time it took to complete them, or a comprehension test to assess learning over the material. Class analysis of results can clarify the system used. This approach can be expanded into basic instruction by forming groups and having each pupil in the original group serve as leader of one group and teach or aid these pupils in learning the system.

*d.* Many pupils are test conscious, and anticipating the teacher's questions is considered a matter of vital significance. The use of overview, the identification of significant ideas, and role playing in question making—all contribute to the ability to anticipate questions, as well as to general interest in study approaches. Getting several content teachers to develop typical practice test questions over selections adds a note of reality to pupil practice and provides variety in feedback.

*2. Three general approaches to instruction.* Three approaches to developing pupil understanding and use of a reading-study system have been reported.

*a.* The first is to develop the system inductively—each component independently and over extended periods of time. Later, these are brought together to form a system. Thus, the value and uses of setting purposes is developed or reviewed as a specific read-

ing behavior, including practice exercises and applications. Each of the other components is developed independently in its turn: making a skim-reading overview, interpreting as guided by specific reading purposes, developing varied and efficient notational systems, and learning the varied uses of self-testing and review. When the teacher feels that most students have a sufficient grasp of the individual components, she brings them together, teaches them as a system, provides practice and application of the system as such, and then guides the pupil in developing flexibility and efficiency in the use of the system.

*b.* The second approach is to teach the system as a problem-solving technique. Actual instruction in the system is organized on a whole-part-whole basis in the solution of a series of study problems. First, a need for a reading system is developed, and the concept, the acronym, and the most significant aspects (nature and uses) of each component are learned as such. Next, the teacher guides the group or class through the procedure as applied to a specific study assignment. Instruction and practice is provided on specific components as demonstrated by pupil need or as the study task provides an opportunity to add to the sophistication or flexibility of component use. Except where serious difficulty occurs, instruction in component use is related to the particular study assignment or problem. In this way, the teacher guides the group or class through a series of such problems, each calling for a different application, a more challenging problem, and/or a greater independence in the use of the system by the pupil.

*c.* The third approach, in effect, teaches the whole and the parts of the system to pupils as a group instructional procedure. That is, the teacher takes the class through the system (without a name) once or more each week under teacher guidance, much like the GRL, with an apparent objective of mastering the content of the text assignment, story, or reading selection. When most pupils have shown that they can handle the processes under guidance, the teacher begins to assign certain components for independent activity. Eventually, the teacher has a session on the nature and values of study systems and elicits from the group the similarity between the general nature of the study systems presented and the group reading instructional procedure which they have been using. The teacher and class can identify the essential components of their procedure, identify key words, and develop their own acronym (or arrive at that which the teacher had in mind from the beginning). From this point on, the teacher may intersperse pupil independent use of the system for study purposes with class-directed use of the system for in-class instructional purposes.

*3. Developing efficiency and flexibility in the use of study systems.*

*a.* It is most important that pupils should learn to adjust a reading-study system to their own needs and the problem at hand. Pupils should enjoy forming variants on the procedure—e.g. (using POINT as a base), POT, PIT, PON, PINT, and PIN—and pairing them with their appropriate reading study tasks.

*b.* To increase efficiency in the use of the reading-study system, pupils may keep a record or chart of how long it takes them to complete approximately equivalent reading-study assignments administered once or twice a week. This also provides nicely for reinforcing the system in its early stages of learning.

*4. Application.* It is most important that the use of a reading-study system be kept realistic. In some schools, the same system is taught by the developmental reading teachers to a volunteer group of content teachers. After discussing how the system might be varied in each different classroom setting, each content teacher agrees to employ it in illustrations and assignments after the developmental teacher passes the word that initial general instruction in the system has been completed.

## REFERENCES

1. James B. Stroud, *Psychology in Education* (New York: Longmans, Green & Company, Inc., 1956) p. 341.

2. Jerome S. Bruner, *Toward a Theory of Instruction* (Cambridge, Mass.: Harvard University Press, 1967) pp. 41 and 49.

3. Ronald P. Carver, "A Critical Review of Mathemagenic Behaviors and the Effect of Questions upon the Retention of Prose Materials," *Journal of Reading Behavior* 4 (Spring, 1972) pp. 93-119.

4. W. E. Blanton and J. J. Tuinman, "Ausubel's Theory of Meaningful Verbal Learning: Implications for Reading Research," *Reading World* 12 (March, 1973) pp. 202-11.

5. Marvin L. Cohn, "Structured Comprehension," *The Reading Teacher* 22 (February, 1969) pp. 440-44.

6. J. P. Parker, "Some Organizational Variables and Their Effect upon Comprehension," *Journal of Communication* 12 (1962) pp. 27-32.

7. Samuel Weintraub, "Teacher Expectation and Reading Performance," *Reading Teacher* 22 (March, 1969) pp. 555-59.

8. C. M. Christensen and K. E. Stordahl, "Effect of Organizational Aids on Comprehension and Retention," *Journal of Educational Psychology* 46 (1955) pp. 65-74.

9. W. Hershberger, "Self-Evaluational Reading and Typographical Cueing," *Journal of Educational Psychology* 55 (1964) pp. 288-296. *See also* K. L. Leicht and V. M. Cashen, "Type of Highlighted Material and Examination Performance," paper presented at the American Educational Research Association Conference, New York, February, 1971. ERIC ED-050-155.

10. Walter Hill, "Content Textbook: Help or Hindrance," *Journal of Reading* 10 (March, 1967) pp. 408-13.

11. William G. Perry, "Students' Use and Misuse of Reading Skills: A Report to the Faculty," *Harvard Educational Review* 29 (1959) pp. 193-200.

12. E. Z. Rothkopf, "Variable Adjunct Question Schedules, Interpersonal Interaction and Incidental Learning from Written Material," *Journal of Educational Psychology* 63 (1972) pp. 87-92.

13. N. A. Flanders, *Analyzing Teaching Behavior* (Reading, Mass.: Addison-Wesley Publishing Company, Inc., 1970).

14. Meredith D. Gall, "The Use of Questions in Teaching," *Review of Educational Research* 40 (December, 1970) pp. 707-21.

15. Emmett A. Betts, *Foundations of Reading Instruction* (Cincinnati, Ohio: American Book Company, 1957) pp. 503-6.

16. Norris M. Sanders, *Classroom Questions* (New York: Harper & Row Publishers, 1966) p. 2.

17. Sanders, *Classroom Questions*, pp. 3-5.

18. Benjamin S. Bloom, Editor, *Taxonomy of Educational Objectives* (New York: Longmans, Green & Company, Inc., 1956).

19. Robert C. Auckerman, *Reading in the Secondary School Classroom* (New York: McGraw-Hill Book Company, 1972) pp. 87-89.

20. Harold L. Herber, *Teaching Reading in Content Areas* (Englewood Cliffs, N.J.: Prentice-Hall, Inc., 1978) pp. 55-58.

21. Walter Hill, *POINT: A Reading-Study System* (Belmont, Calif.: Wadsworth Publishing Company, Inc., 1970) pp. 12-17.

22. Harold Ladas, "The Mathemagenic Effects of Factual Review Questions on the Learning of Incidental Information: A Critical Review," *Review of Educational Research* 43 (Winter, 1973) pp. 87-92.

23. L. T. Frase, "Questions as Aids to Reading: Some Research and a Theory," *American Educational Research Journal* 5 (1968) pp. 319-332.

24. Samuel Weintraub, "The Question as an Aid in Reading," *The Reading Teacher* 22 (May, 1969), pp. 751-55.

25. H. F. Spitzer, "Studies in Retention," *Journal of Educational Psychology* 30 (1939) pp. 641-56.

26. A. M. Sones and J. B. Stroud, "Review, with Special Reference to Temporal Position," *Journal of Educational Psychology* 31 (1940) pp. 665-76.

27. Sanders, *Classroom Questions*, pp. 155-63.

28. Anthony V. Manzo, "Re Quest Procedure," *Journal of Reading* 13 (November, 1969) pp. 123-26.

29. Willavene Wolf and Bernice D. Ellinger, "Teaching Critical Reading: An Observational Study," *Critical Reading*, Martha L. King, Bernice D. Ellinger, and Willavene Wolf, Editors (Philadelphia: J. B. Lippincott Company, 1967) pp. 434-45.

30. George B. Henry, *Teaching Reading as Concept Development: Emphasis upon Affective Thinking* (Newark, Del.: International Reading Association, 1974) p. 84.

31. Herber, *Teaching Reading in the Content Areas*.

32. Francis P. Hunkins, *Questioning Strategies and Techniques* (Boston: Allyn and Bacon, Inc., 1975).

33. Ruth G. Viox, *Evaluating Reading and Study Skills in the Secondary Classroom* (Newark, Del.: International Reading Association, 1968).

34. D. P. Ausubel, *The Psychology of Meaningful Verbal Learning* (New York: Grune & Stratton, Inc., 1963).

35. Blanton and Tuinman, "Ausubel's Theory of Meaningful Verbal Learning," pp. 202-11.

36. T. H. Estes, D. C. Mills, and R. H. Barron, "Three Methods of Introducing Students to a Reading-Learning Task in Two Content Subjects," in *Research in Reading in the Content Area: First Year Report*, Herber and Sanders, Editors (Syracuse, N.Y.: Reading and Language Arts Center, Syracuse University, 1969) p. 41.

37. Richard F. Barron, "The Use of Vocabulary as an Advance Organizer," in *Research in Reading in the Content Area: First Year Report*, p. 32.

38. Richard A. Earle, "Use of the Structured Overview in Mathematics Classes," in *Research in Reading in the Content Area: First Year Report*, pp. 50-51.

39. Betts, *Foundations of Reading Instruction*, p. 491.

40. Eddie C. Kennedy, *Methods in Teaching Developmental Reading* (Itasca, Ill.: F. E. Peacock Publishers, 1974) pp. 130-32.

41. Russell G. Stauffer, *Directing Reading Maturity as a Cognitive Process* (New York: Harper & Row, Publishers, 1969) p. 43.

42. Betts, *Foundations of Reading Instruction*, p. 513.

43. Ruth Strang, *Diagnostic Teaching of Reading* (New York: McGraw-Hill Book Company. 1964) pp. 10-11.

44. Francis P. Robinson, *Effective Study*, Revised Edition (New York: Harper & Row, Publishers, 1961) p. 14.

45. Weintraub, "The Question as an Aid in Reading," pp. 751-55.

46. David Russell, *The Dynamics of Reading* (Waltham, Mass.: Ginn-Blaisdell, 1970) Chapter 8.

47. Harold A. Vine et al., "Guiding Reading Achievement," *Manual Ten, Teaching Reading in Secondary Schools* (Syracuse, N.Y.: Reading and Language Arts Center, Syracuse University, 1967) p. 277.

48. Richard A. Earle, "Developing and Using Study Guides," in *Research in Reading in the Content Area: First Year Report*, p. 72.

49. Herber, *Teaching Reading in Content Areas*.

50. Earle, "Developing and Using Study Guides," pp. 71-80.

51. Vine et al., "Guiding Reading Achievement," p. 293.

52. Robinson, *Effective Study*.

53. Walter Pauk, *How to Study in College* (Boston: Houghton Mifflin Company, 1962).

54. George Spache and Paul Berg, *The Art of Efficient Reading* (New York: The Macmillan Company, 1966).

55. Peter Edwards, "PANORAMA, A Study Technique," *Journal of Reading* 17 (November, 1973) pp. 132-35.

56. Walter Hill and William Eller, *Power in Reading Skills* (Belmont, Calif.: Wadsworth Publishing Company, Inc., 1964); Hill, *POINT: A Reading-Study System,* 1970.

57. Walter Pauk, "On Scholarship: Advice to High

School Students," *The Reading Teacher* 17 (November, 1963) pp. 73-78.

58. Hill, *POINT: A Reading-Study System*, pp. 11-27.

## SUPPLEMENTARY SOURCES

Bruner, Jerome S. *Toward a Theory of Instruction*, Chapter 3. Cambridge, Mass.: Harvard University Press, 1967.

Herber, Harold. *Teaching Reading in Content Areas*, Chapter 9. Englewood Cliffs, N.J.: Prentice-Hall, Inc., 1978.

Herber, Harold, and Peter Sanders, Editors. *Research in Reading in the Content Areas: First Year Report.* Syracuse, N.Y.: Reading and Language Arts Center, Syracuse University, 1969.

Hunkins, Frances P. *Questioning Strategies and Techniques.* Boston: Allyn and Bacon, Inc., 1972. 146 p.

Robinson, Francis P. *Effective Study*, Revised Edition, Chapters 1-4. New York: Harper & Row, Publishers, 1961.

Stauffer, Russell. *Directing the Reading-Thinking Process*, Chapter 2. New York: Harper & Row, Publishers, 1975.

# SEVEN

# Assessing Reading for Classroom Use

*Consistent and balanced growth in reading proficiency is fostered by appraisal. It must be a continuing program.... If the data obtained in the appraisals are evaluated and used, the teacher will be able to select appropriate materials and shape the instructional program to take care of the individual needs that are disclosed....*

Miles A. Tinker

***Overview***  The place of reading evaluation in the secondary reading effort was presented in Chapter Four and the content teacher's need for reading assessment data was developed in Chapter Five. This chapter focuses upon the uses and the procedures of assessment in the developmental or content instructional setting. The chapter identifies the basic functions, conditions, sources, and uses of reading assessment as an instructional tool, and suggests ways in which assessment data can be organized to improve understanding and application. A number of procedures and instruments are identified for collecting operational data through such classroom assessment concerns as surveying the pupil's reading attributes, assessing reading-study habits and attitudes, utilizing normative measures of reading achievement, estimating the readability of instructional materials, and identifying pupil reading level and instructional needs through material-referenced assessment and classroom reading tests.

# CLASSROOM READING ASSESSMENT

Productive reading education presumes effective reading evaluation, and reading evaluation is dependent upon adequate and efficient collection of data—primarily, the description and measurement of pupil reading performance status and progress toward school and instructional objectives.[1] Reading evaluation is of such educational importance that it serves as a major component of the school reading program and also as a significant strand of the school evaluation program. Classroom reading evaluation—developmental, corrective, and content area—should be an important part of this effort. Reading assessment data gathered in the classroom not only should aid classroom instruction in an immediate, direct manner, but, collectively, should be a vital assessment source for the school evaluation program. This is only appropriate. The central purpose of secondary reading assessment is to contribute to the effective development and utilization of those reading competencies which are needed by the secondary pupil—now, in later schooling, and in adult life.

In this chapter, discussion is focused primarily upon those first-line, assessment strategies which are readily effected and immediately applicable to instruction in the content classroom as well as in the developmental reading setting. Procedures for more specific evaluation of particular skilled reading behaviors are presented in Chapters Nine through Twelve. The improvement of the larger school reading evaluation program is discussed in Chapters Four and Fourteen. To supplement the discussion of reading evaluation and assessment in Chapter Seven, a bibliography of upper school measures is presented in Appendix A. For more complete surveys of the published sources of reading tests and instruments, the reader may wish to consult Buros, *Reading Tests and Reviews*[2]; Farr, *Reading: What Can Be Measured?*[3]; and Farr and Summers, *Guide to Tests and Measuring Instruments for Reading.*[4] In addition, three service bulletins published by the International Reading Association provide practical information about approaches to secondary reading assessment: Blanton, Farr, and Tuinman, *Reading Tests for the Secondary Grades*[5]; Johnson and Kress, *Informal Reading Inventories*[6]; and Viox, *Evaluating Reading and Study Skills in the Secondary Classroom.*[7]

## General Functions and Conditions of Classroom Assessment

The functions of reading evaluation as implemented through school or classroom reading assessment are neither narrow nor mechanical. Reading assessment as the key component of reading evaluation becomes a vital cog in classroom instruction and the secondary educational effort as a whole. Russell captures the essence of this challenge:

> In reading, as in other parts of the school program, evaluation is an attempt to discover how well the objectives of instruction are being realized. Since the aims of the reading program have been enlarged beyond mere literacy..., it follows that a modern evaluation program in reading deals not only with reading skills but with more general competencies....[8]

### *The Basic Functions of Classroom Reading Assessment*

There are a number of ways in which classroom assessment may contribute to the immediate and general instructional climate. Seven of the most important functions of classroom reading assessment are presented below:

*1. To help establish and modify instructional objectives.* It is the prerogative of society to establish the ultimate objectives of the school. Intermediate instructional objectives should follow logically from these statements of the general needs of youth in our culture. But to be useful, objectives must be realistic. And they must be translated into specific developmental and content-learning tasks. Once-pertinent statements of ultimate and related intermediate objectives may no longer be consistent with current evidence of pupil needs and abilities or appropriate to changing school circumstances. One of the key functions of evaluation is to improve instructional objectives; to ascertain the usefulness of present objectives, and to contribute to the formation of viable new general and specific objectives for the instructional program.

2. *To determine the achievement status of the individual pupil at planned intervals and to appraise that achievement in terms of progress made, specific criteria met, and/or relative success in comparison with other pupil achievement or with the pupil's own aptitude.* The planned periodic pegging of pupil performance by valid and reliable measures of assessment provides the empirical data base for making key decisions about pupils, individually and collectively, as well as about the instructional program. This function is implemented best by a combination of assessment procedures. However, it remains particularly dependent upon the systematic report of teacher observation and testing which complements the administration and interpretation of appropriate standardized normed tests and test batteries. Systematic appraisal of progress also serves to motivate and reward pupils and staff and provides an initial means of identifying those pupils needing special instructional attention.

3. *To aid in the development of effective instructional content and procedure.* The mandate of the instructional program is to achieve its objectives where these objectives have been determined to be realistic. An effective program of evaluation provides the basis for identifying discrepancies between actual pupil performance and that performance described by the instructional objectives. The evaluation program thus triggers school attention to needed instructional change. Following this, the evaluation process provides the means of determining the effectiveness of those changes which are made in curriculum, instructional materials, and teaching procedure. Reading evaluation becomes essential to the continual shaping and improvement of successful reading program development.

4. *To improve pupil learning by providing immediate feedback concerning the adequacy of provisional attempts in specific learning situations.* In this way, effective responses may be reinforced and ineffective responses may be discouraged or modified. This function of evaluation is activated, largely, through pupil-teacher instructional interaction. The cumulative effect of the thousands upon thousands of such interactions during the pupil's school years comprises a large part of what we term "an education."[9] In the long run, this evaluative feedback during current learning situations is the most crucial function of classroom reading assessment. In effect, good specific instruction and ongoing, day-by-day teacher observation and testing cannot be separated.[10]

5. *To contribute to the general welfare of the individual pupil and to his in- and out-of-school adjustment.* The evaluation effort is concerned with the whole pupil, not just the cold appraisal of his standardized or classroom test achievement. Reading evaluation should include assessment of pupil reading capabilities, interests, habits, and felt needs. There should be a place for qualitative reaction by pupils to classroom reading situations, the school reading program, and to those general school circumstances in which reading is a pivotal condition. Even the use of achievement assessment in reading evaluation should work to the pupil's advantage — by improving instruction and by developing more realistic objectives. Moreover the relationship between pupil reading difficulty and school maladjustment, attrition, and in- and out-of-school delinquency is well known. Through evaluation, reading difficulty may be identified and analyzed and remedial treatment intelligently planned. Beyond this, reading evaluation should contribute to the school's general counseling effort.[11]

6. *To work toward the continuing improvement of the reading evaluation program, itself.* Measurement is less than a perfect science. It might be added that educational evaluation is less than a perfect art. While the theory and practice of reading evaluation are better established than some critics recognize, classroom reading assessment, particularly, has a continuing need to improve upon the validity, reliability, and practicality of its

procedures. It does this by checking and cross-checking its own products, by developing a broad base of assessment input, and by maintaining a certain degree of skepticism about the accuracy of any assessment tool for any particular pupil.

7. *To contribute to the collective professional knowledge about pupil learning, academic performance, and general behavior.* In the immediate school situation, it is the responsibility of classroom reading assessment to complement the total school program of evaluation as well as to provide direct interpretive feedback to teachers and pupils about specific performance. Certain key classroom assessment data should be shared with the faculty. These data should provide and analyze illustrative samples of individual or group pupil behavior which will advance teacher understanding of pupil reading and study behaviors in that setting. In addition, the evaluation program carries a responsibility to share significant new data obtained on pupil reading behavior or on innovative instructional procedures with parents, school patrons, and the teaching profession as a whole. What we know and do not know today about secondary reading behavior, its development, and its utilization is the product of past evaluation. Inasmuch as our knowledge of maturing reading behavior is incomplete, it remains a key function of reading evaluation to continue to push toward professional and public enlightenment in these matters.

### Some Criteria for Classroom Assessment

Instruction in the secondary classroom will benefit from a more systematic gathering and use of pupil-related reading information. Certain criteria regarding how those data are gathered and used in instructional settings need to be observed, however. (1) The frequency and form of reading-related assessment should be determined by whether it *facilitates pupil learning through instruction.* (2) Pupils gain insight about their reading and learning performance through *assessment which is accompanied by explanatory feedback.*[12] (3) Classroom reading assessment *should be balanced in form and type;* testing should be supplemented by other forms of appraisal and observation; and testing patterns should be varied. (4) Reading *assessment should be purposeful;* the time for appraisal and the form it takes should be decided by the type of information needed or instructional objective to be achieved. (5) Classroom assessment should be *a continuing concern.* Although some greater amount of assessment may be needed in the initial weeks of the class or course, classroom assessment should be *extended and integrated* with instruction over the spread of the course. (6) Classroom reading assessment, particularly testing, should be *conducted within a positive learning dynamic,* and should avoid pejorative implication wherever possible. (7) Finally, the data gathered *should be utilized;* reading testing and related appraisal results which are collected and "dead-ended" in the files of the teacher, principal, or reading specialist constitute an indefensible use of reading assessment.

### Classroom Assessment and Instruction

The close relationship between assessment and instruction is captured by the maxim that developmental instruction consists of a teach-test-reteach-retest relationship. The "testing" here refers to whether the pupil has mastered the behaviors taught; and if not, why not. It makes a good deal of sense to recognize that effective instruction in skilled behavior is more likely to follow a diagnostic paradigm than a didactic one.[13] This assessment-instruction relationship needs planning and conscious implementation. For this, the developmental reading or content teacher should be alert to the available standardized and informal sources for gaining such data, should determine the priority instructional uses for which to gather pupil data, and should organize the data gathered for interpretation and use.

### Sources of Instructionally Useful Reading Data

In Chapter Five, several common secondary school sources of pupil reading performance information available to the content teacher were identified. These are equally useful for the teacher of reading classes, developmental or corrective. These *general* sources included: cumulative pupil records; standardized reading, language, content achievement, and intelligence test performance; the secondary reading consultant or reading specialist; and classroom reading performance.

The classroom teacher can generate his own reading data. In this sense, the *specific* sources of reading assessment available for the teacher's own classroom use are limited only by the teacher's knowledge and motivation. Perhaps the most functional of these is (1) continuous and *informed teacher observation* of pupil behavior, aided perhaps by a checklist of objectives or performance criteria and an efficient system of summarizing and recording those observations for instructional use. Other classroom-initiated tools and techniques of reading assessment may include: (2) *supplementary standardized tests* of reading, study skill, or content reading nature; (3) *informal classroom tests* of general comprehension, vocabulary, specific skills, or applied reading; (4) pupil reading-study habits and attitude data obtained through *questionnaires, opinionnaires, interviews, autobiographies, word association games,* and *sentence completion forms;* (5) *pupil self-assessment* procedures; (6) instructional materials evaluation, including the use of *textbook criteria checklists* and *readability estimates;* (7) material-referenced performance measures obtained through the *cloze procedure* or group/individual *informal reading inventories;* (8) applied classroom reading performance on *assignment products, study guides,* and *worksheets;* and (9) if more intensive investigation is warranted—an intensive *individual reading case study,* supported by the classroom teacher under the guidance of the reading consultant, counselor, or school psychologist.

## Organizing Reading Data for Instructional Use

The teacher will need to convert obtained pupil data into a form or forms which will organize that information so that it is readily accessible, provides a survey view of class or group performance patterns, provides a summary of individual pupil capabilities and/or instructional needs, and systematizes ongoing evaluation and record keeping. The developmental reading teacher can be expected to keep more detailed records of pupil reading performance data than the content area teacher, of course.

*Record keeping.* Perhaps the easiest way for the classroom teacher to keep essential pupil reading data accessible for reference and consideration is to enter the most significant data in the traditional *teacher's grade/attendance record book* by utilizing columns for such pupil information as percentile rank or stanine score obtained on most recent standardized tests of reading comprehension, vocabulary, intelligence, and pertinent content achievement; the optimal "instructional" reading level; a (+) or (−) rating of proficiency in the use of library and reference sources; (+) or (−) rating on ability to utilize a reading-study system; a (+) or (−) rating on independent, in-class reading-study attitude and habits; and an identification of class group to which pupil belongs for differentiated study guides or small-group instructional sessions.

To record more extensive data, the teacher may wish to develop a separate *class reading-study data summary sheet* which lists each pupil (alphabetically or by ranked overall reading-study proficiency) along the rows and provides labeled entries by columns for such items of reading competency as listed at the end of Chapter Three. Another method is to develop an *individual reading-study checklist* for each class member. Such a checklist could be divided into five parts: one part for recording available test scores and related assessment products; one part for identifying the specific course-related reading competencies targeted for achievement by the normal-progress pupil; one part for writing in those additional fundamental reading-study competencies on which this pupil is in particular need of help; one part for brief, anecdotal teacher observation related to pupil reading-study performance during the course or term; and one part for end-of-the-term-or-course general summation of teacher appraisal of pupil status and progress.

Publishers of reading instructional programs sometimes provide reading competency checklists which relate to the objectives of those programs. The slavish use of such programs and related data assessment guides is not recommended, since such programs seldom provide the breadth of developmental or content reading experience needed by pupils. If such commercial programs are used as part of class instruction, the provided rating sheets and competency checklists can be modified or used as a base for tailoring the record keeping to the total course experience. Other sources of assessment checklists and recording systems include the manuals of workbook series, the manuals of diagnostic reading batteries, and instrumental statements of cognitive and affective taxonomies of educational objectives.[14]

*Graphic representations.* Quite often a teacher needs to get a group perspective of the interpupil reading performance patterns of the class to use as a reference in planning assignments, to identify pupils who need special referral or help, for classroom grouping purposes, or as an aid in other classroom operations. A quick way to do this is by *ranking* standardized reading test scores or cloze or IRI *instructional* reading levels by listing pupils (name and score or level) from highest to lowest and marking off the list at different levels to find the best combination of pupils composing two, three, or four groups of reasonably common performance levels.

Another approach is to construct a simple *histogram* or *line graph* (frequency polygon) of pupils with similar reading performance levels. Essentially, the process entails choosing an appropriate test score interval which marks off all class members' scores in the number of groupings which seems useful. These data are converted into a graph by marking the score interval along the horizontal axis and the frequency (total number of pupils) falling into that performance interval along the vertical axis. Figure 9 represents a histogram of a class of thirty-three ninth-grade pupils by instructional reading level. Such a graph can be rather revealing to a teacher who plans to use a single text whose readability converts into a ninth-to-tenth-grade instructional reading difficulty.

Sometimes a teacher can improve this perspective of class or group reading performance by graphically comparing it with comparable pupil data, e.g., reading scores with intelligence scores, reading levels with listening levels, reading achievement scores with content area achievement scores, or reading comprehension scores with reading rate scores. Constructing a *scattergram* provides a way of depicting this paired relationship. The scattergram consists of a double-entry charting of the scores of two tests or two variables for each individual in the group. The procedure for doing this is described in most basic texts of educational measurement or elementary statistics. For general descriptive-comparative purposes, scores of the two tests can be converted and plotted as percentile ranks, stanines, or other comparable measures. (To be statistically accurate, the distributions of each score or variable should be marked off in normatively comparable intervals, preferably in terms of standard scores or deviations from the mean.)

Figure 10 presents a scattergram which displays the distribution of a tenth-grade class where pupil data are entered for results on an intelligence test (*Lorge-Thorndike*) and a reading survey test (*Tests of Academic Progress*). Pupil A, for example, earned percentile ranks of 85 in intelligence and 32 in reading. Assuming that the test scores are reasonably accurate, the teacher can begin some analysis of her class. The six pupils who place high in quadrant I probably are the most able readers and learners and seem capable of the most challenging and most independent assignments. The thirteen pupils who are grouped around the median consist of the norm achievers in the class. The two pupils placing in quadrant IV probably can be added to this group for assignment purposes,

**Figure 9**  *Distribution of "instructional" reading levels for a ninth-grade class.*

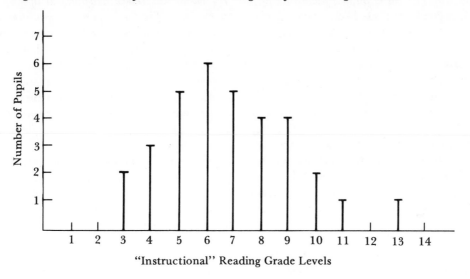

"Instructional" Reading Grade Levels

**Figure 10**  *Scattergram of reading and intelligence distribution for a tenth-grade class.*

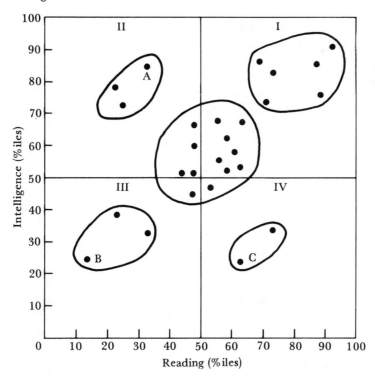

since it is likely that their intelligence scores are erroneously low. The three pupils, including pupil A, falling into quadrant II are likely underachievers in reading and should be referred for diagnostic assessment and possible supplementary remediation. For class purposes they may be treated as an instructional group or grouped with the three pupils falling into quadrant III, the least capable readers and learners in the class. If resources are available, the pupils in the A, B, and C groups should be retested with individual reading and intelligence tests to confirm the accuracy of their group test results. Scattergram comparisons are improved when both tests are normed on the same population, as is the case with the Lorge-Thorndike and the TAP.

*Individual pupil folders.* Many teachers find it useful to develop individual folders for each pupil in the class or group into which pupil assessment data are collected: tests, checklists, questionnaires, representative assignment products, teacher anecdotal appraisals, etc. Individual folders are particularly recommended as a means of organizing the pupil data gathered in developmental or corrective reading instructional situations. They are essential in remedial situations. Summary data sheets and criterion progress checklists can be stapled inside the front cover for ready access and review.

Some reading teachers provide a second set of individual folders in which each pupil may keep his current work. The pupil is encouraged or required to keep his own progress charts and his own appraisal of his mastery of targeted competencies. The teacher regularly reviews these folders as a means of individualizing instruction. Basic or supplementary reading assignments are placed in the folder, and upon entering the reading instructional setting, the pupil obtains his folder and sets to work on the new or uncompleted reading tasks or assignments.

### Fitting Assessment to the Purpose

The use of secondary reading assessment espoused in this text is a pragmatic one: *any approach, instrument, or technique which facilitates the valid and relevant appraisal of pupil reading behavior or program operation qualifies as reading assessment.* Some approaches, instruments, or techniques are better than others—that is, they are more useful for the functions they serve. Figure 11 presents some common reading and reading-related assessment approaches (pertinent instrument or procedure) and the reading assessment purposes to which they make major or complementary contributions.

It should be noted that the results produced through one approach may contribute to more than one purpose function, and that several approaches may contribute to the same function. The figure is illustrative, not exhaustive. It is concerned with secondary reading assessment, not in-depth diagnosis. No attempt was made to appraise the relative value of the assessment approach other than whether it is likely to contribute directly and/or notably to the function (a major source possibility) or whether it contributes indirectly and/or modestly to the function (a complementary source).

## ASSESSING PUPIL READING USE AND REACTION

One of the first things the classroom teacher needs to know about a pupil's reading behavior is how he makes use of his present reading competency. The content teacher will profit from knowing how the pupil applies reading to the learning situation. Can he carry out directed reading tasks? Has he mastered a reading-study system for dealing with larger reading assignments? Does he exhibit any notable deficiencies in supportive study research knowledges and skills appropriate to the content area and level of instruction? In addition, the reading teacher benefits from knowing how the pupil feels about reading and reading instruction and what his personal reading habits are.

No single test or assessment procedure adequately provides the diverse sorts of information needed to answer these questions. The teacher can put together a reasonable understanding of the

**Figure 11**  *Implementing reading assessment–evaluation purposes.*

*Reading Assessment Purposes*

| Assessment Approach (Tool/Procedure) [a] | Achievement status: normative | Interpupil comparison | Developmental reading progress | Mastery: criterion behavioral objectives | Instructional feedback: specific tasks | Readability estimation (material) | Match reading material with pupil ability | Profile: reading/study behaviors | Related behavior assessment | Identify persistent reading difficulty | Identify persistent reading disability | Prognostic/diagnostic evaluation | Enhance motivation/self-direction | Evaluation: program/instruction |
|---|---|---|---|---|---|---|---|---|---|---|---|---|---|---|
| Standardized achievement battery | × | × |  |  |  |  |  | • | × | • | • |  | • | × |
| Standardized reading achievement test (survey) | × | × | × |  |  |  |  | • |  | • | • |  | • | × |
| Standardized reading battery (multiple subtests) | × | × | × |  |  |  |  | × |  | • | • |  | • | × |
| Standardized vocabulary test | × | × | × |  |  |  |  | • | • | • | • |  |  | • |
| Standardized test of reading rate (efficiency) | × | × | × |  |  |  |  | • |  | • | • |  | • | • |
| Standardized word skills test/battery | × | × | × |  |  |  |  | × |  | × |  | × | • | • |
| Standardized language skills test | × | × | × |  |  |  |  |  | × | • | • | • |  | × |
| Standardized work-study skills test | × | × | × |  |  |  |  | • | • |  | • |  |  | • |
| Criterion reading test (school/program/class) |  | • | • | × | × |  | • | • |  | × |  | × | × | × |
| Criterion reading checklist (school/program/class) |  | × | × | × | × |  | • | × |  |  | • | × | × | × |
| Informal tests of specific skills (varied) |  | • | • | • | × |  | • | • | • | • | • | × | • | × |
| Teacher observation (emergent/anecdotal) |  |  | • | • | × |  | × | • | • | • | • | • |  |  |
| Pupil self-evaluation (checklist/rating sheet/chart) |  |  |  | • | • |  | • | • | • |  |  | • | × |  |
| Readability estimation (charts/graphs/formulas) |  |  |  |  |  | × | × |  |  |  |  | • | • | • |
| Cloze reading test procedure |  | • | • |  |  | × | × |  |  | • |  | • | • | • |

[a] ×, major contribution;  •, secondary or complementary contribution.

*(continued)*

**Figure 11**  *Implementing reading assessment–evaluation purposes* [*continued*].

Reading Assessment Purposes

| [Assessment Approach (Tool/Procedure)] [a] | Achievement status: normative | Interpupil comparison | Developmental reading progress | Mastery: criterion behavioral objectives | Instructional feedback: specific tasks | Readability estimation (material) | Match reading material with pupil ability | Profile: reading/study behaviors | Related behavior assessment | Identify persistent reading difficulty | Identify persistent reading disability | Prognostic/diagnostic evaluation | Enhance motivation/self-direction | Evaluation: program/instruction |
|---|---|---|---|---|---|---|---|---|---|---|---|---|---|---|
| Oral reading tests (normed) | • | • | • | • | • | X | • |  |  | • |  | • | • |  |
| Informal reading inventory (IRI) |  | X | • | • | • | X | X | X |  | X | • | X | • | • |
| Informal word inventory (IWI) |  | • |  | • | • | • | • |  |  | • |  | • |  |  |
| Diagnostic reading battery (normed) | X |  | • | • | • |  | • | X | • | X | X | X |  |  |
| Study habits inventory/questionnaire |  | • |  |  | • |  |  | • | X | • |  | X | • | • |
| Intelligence tests (group) |  | X |  |  |  |  | • |  | X |  | • | • |  |  |
| Intelligence tests (individual) |  | X |  |  |  |  | • |  | X | X | X | X |  |  |
| Listening ability tests |  |  |  |  |  | • | • | • | X |  | X |  |  |  |
| Personality/adjustment measures |  |  |  | • | • | • | • | • | X | • | • | • | • | X |
| Attitude surveys |  |  |  |  | • |  | • | • | X | • | • | • | X | • |
| Interest inventories |  |  |  |  | • |  | • | • | X | • | • | • | X | • |
| Language usage survey |  |  |  | • | • |  | • | • | X | • | • | • |  | • |
| Basic literacy test | X | • |  | X | • |  | • | • | • | • | • | • | • | • |
| Objectives checklist |  |  | • | X | X |  |  | X | • | • |  | • | X | X |

[a] X, major contribution; •, secondary or complementary contribution.

174

pupil's school uses and personal reactions to reading by forming a composite picture drawn from a combination of assessment sources: standardized tests or subtests of work-study skills and/or directed reading skills, inventories of reading-study habits and attitudes, interviews or questionnaires obtaining pupil reactions to school and personal reading situations and of course, in-class observation of reading behavior and work habits and performance on reading assignments and study guides.

## Published Sources of Assessment

### Standardized Tests of Work-Study Skills

Generally, these tests measure pupil performance on applied or directed reading tasks, locational reading skills, interpretation of graphic sources, and knowledge and use of the library and common sources of reference. Normative scores usually are provided in terms of percentile ranks, stanines, and/or standard scores. These tests only sample representative study or work-type reading skills, of course. For example, few assess pupil ability to handle larger study assignments, and none test the pupil's ability to read and study a text chapter—the most common unit of high school assignment. They do tend to measure those reading-related study skills which can be measured readily in an achievement test and which figure frequently in schoolwork activities (e.g., using an index, dictionary, tabular data, maps, etc.). Several tests of library skills and usage have been published which assess similar areas of behavior.

Several available tests of upper-grade work-study and library skills and the areas they measure are presented in Appendix A.3.

### Study Habits and Attitudes

Published measures of reading-study habits and attitudes usually involve self-analysis of study-related practices in the form of Likert rating scales (never, seldom, often, always), questionnaires, or checklists. They are highly dependent, therefore, upon the pupil's understanding of the item and the validity of his subjective response. Many students

are wary of revealing their school-related weaknesses and idiosyncratic methods of study. Such measures get at reading and study practices in a secondhand way, and thus are safer indicators of the pupil's knowledges of study procedures than of his actual habits. Study habits and attitude inventories came to the high school from colleges where they enjoyed modest success in college orientation classes and college counseling centers. The greater maturity, objectivity, and career orientation of college students probably enhance their validity in these settings. Interpreted with caution and followed by a personal interview, they can provide some insight into the secondary pupil's broader understanding of the psychology of study and learning. They may serve nicely as an initial activity in an instructional unit or a set of counseling sessions dealing with the improvement of reading-study skills. Several published study-habit measures developed for upper-grade use are identified in Appendix A.3.

### Reading Attitude Assessment

Professional interest in the affective domain of reading has quickened in recent years.[15] A major aspect of this attention has focused upon pupil attitudes toward reading, in general, and toward reading instruction in particular.[16] An attitude may be defined as learned, emotional predispositions or sets to respond favorably or unfavorably to things, people, or situations.

Implicit in this concern are the assumptions that positive attitudes toward reading and reading instruction are associated with more effective reading learning and with more effective use and enjoyment of reading. The teacher may be concerned with reading attitude assessment to gain a broader view of the reading characteristics of the class or individual, to discover specific attitude patterns among the group which deserve positive reinforcement or change, and to identify any negative attitude patterns which may contribute to individual reading and/or school learning problems.

Attitude assessment is usually an indirect and imprecise operation.[17] Attitude assessment procedures may take different forms: rating scales in which the individual responds to cue statements on an agree-disagree basis or in the Likert pattern; semantic differential scales in which the individual associates objectives or makes card sorts of word stimuli; open-ended questionnaires such as sentence completion tests; projective tests; observations of pupil behavior in particular situations; and structured interviews.

## Informal Assessment of Reading–Study Behaviors

The teacher or reading specialist may draw upon one or more of several informal or classroom approaches to assessing pupil reading-study habits and/or attitudes. Systematic observation over a reasonable period, guided by a checklist of key behaviors, is one viable technique. Pupil study concerns can be solicited through class discussion, individual written reports, or taped small-group sessions on study problems. Perhaps the most satisfactory approach is the teacher-pupil interview. This approach benefits from a good rapport between teacher and pupil and should be guided by a questionnaire, checklist, or inventory. The following items have been quite helpful for use in an initial survey interview of reading-study habits and difficulties.

---

### PERSONAL READING–STUDY INTERVIEW*

Name _____ Grade _____ Date _____

1. How would you describe yourself as a reader? What makes you think so? _____
   _____
   _____

2. How often do you read for fun? (Try to get some idea of the extent of the student's personal reading per week. Is he a nonreader, a minimal reader, an average reader, or an extensive reader?) What would you rather do than read? _____
   _____
   _____
   _____

3. What do you prefer to read, when you read? (Pursue for types and levels of material and interest areas, e.g., Which magazines? Which parts of the newspaper?) _____
   _____
   _____
   _____

*For best results, the interview should be conducted in a relaxed, unhurried manner and preferably in a relatively private setting. The teacher should explain that the purpose of the interview is to get ideas on how to help the pupil or to improve the class or program and that responses are confidential. Take only as many notes as necessary to capture the sense of the response.

4.  What topics or subjects do you like to read about? _____

_____

_____

5.  How do you prepare for a course examination? _____

_____

_____

6.  Do you have any special difficulty with school assignments? (How much and how often?) _____

_____

_____

_____

7.  What do you think is the cause of this difficulty? _____

_____

_____

_____

8.  Do you have difficulty in concentrating on your reading or study assignments? (Try to identify whether this happens in just certain subjects, how often it happens, and whether it seems to be related to any physical, attitudinal, or adjustment problem.)

_____

_____

_____

_____

9.  Which subjects give you the most difficulty in reading? (Why these?)_____

_____

_____

10. What could these teachers (of difficult subjects listed in question 9) do to help you read and understand the subject better? _____

_____

_____

_____

11. What is the difference between reading and studying or an assignment? (Try to get the student to personalize this response.) _____

_____

_____

_____

12. When the teacher assigns a chapter in the textbook, how do you go about reading and studying it? (Look for student's awareness of a taught system; also whether he practices a particular technique, e.g., underlining, outlining, writing notes, etc. Also check on use of book locational skills—skimming, index, etc.) _____

_____

_____

_____

13. What study references other than textbooks and workbooks do you use regularly (e.g., dictionary, encyclopedia, almanac, etc.)? Try to determine whether the pupil mastered the techniques of using these._____

_____

_____

14. How do you find needed materials in the library? (Look for typical patterns, e.g., asks for help, random search, card catalog, etc.)_____

_____

_____

15. Describe a typical day of personal reading and study. _____

_____

_____

16. When was your last visual exam? Physical check-up? How would you rate your physical condition? Energy level? _____

_____

_____

_____

17. Have you had any special instruction or individual testing in reading? _____
When? _____ What? _____

_____

_____

18. Would you like to have some special help with reading and study techniques? _____
What kind of help do you feel would do you the most good? _____

_____

19. What do you plan to do when you leave high school? _____

_____

Would you like to have some career counseling? _____

20. How would you describe your personal strengths or talents? (The purpose here is to end the interview on a positive tone, but the response frequently provides insights concerning the pupil's life-style and self-acceptance.) _____

_____

_____

_____

**Interview Summary**

*a.* Attitude and notable behavior during interview (validity of pupil responses):

_____

_____

*b.* Previous history of reading-study difficulty: _____

_____

_____

*c.* Current areas and types of school reading-study problems: _____

_____

_____

*d.* Personal reading habits; type and level of material; frequency: _____

_____

_____

*e.* Attitudes toward school reading and desire for additional help: _____

_____

_____

*f.* Recommendations for reading instruction or assessment: _____

_____

_____

*g.* Need for counseling about school adjustment difficulty or career planning:

_____

_____

## STANDARDIZED READING ACHIEVEMENT TESTS

Standardized reading achievement tests may be classified according to the way they were developed: (1) those which are components (tests or subtests) of a standardized achievement battery which provide separate reading achievement scores and which may or may not be purchased for independent use as reading tests, and (2) those which were developed expressly for purchase and use as independent standardized tests of reading achievement. The first two sections of the test bibliography presented in Appendix A identify commonly employed standardized reading tests of both types.

As standardized group tests of silent reading, the two have a great deal in common. The central measure employed in both (often the only measure in the achievement battery subtest) consists of silent comprehension: the examinee's ability to read a number of content passages (such passages ranging in length from single, short paragraphs to multi-paragraph selections) and to answer questions dealing with the meaning of the passage (usually multiple-choice recognition items which immediately follow the passage). The passages ordinarily sample prose writing of an expository nature from conventional literature or from varied content areas—content which is neither specifically familiar to the examinee nor so narrowly technical that it requires highly specialized background to understand it.

Most of these tests are built on a "power test" format; the passages and their questions progress gradually from easier to more difficult readability and interpretation as the examinee works his way through the test. Although the comprehension items over the passages tend to sample the examinee's grasp of literal meaning as well as ability to use varied interpretive processes, each test usually produces one total raw score of the number of items correctly answered on all passages read within the time limits. By the use of the norms established by the test developers, this raw score may be converted into normed scores for comparative interpretation, i.e., into standard scores, stanines, percentiles, or age or grade equivalents. These normed scores may be used selectively to describe the pupil's general and relative reading comprehension performance; to make comparative reading assessments between individuals, between classes or schools; to compare the performance of the same pupil across different achievement areas; and/or to determine progress made between periodic testings with alternative forms or levels of the test.

## Achievement Battery Reading Tests

The reading tests of standardized achievement batteries are developed to comply with the construction and standardization of the achievement battery as a whole. As a consequence, the mechanics of measurement and norming typically are quite defensible. Direct comparisons of reading achievement scores with scores on other achievement area tests of the battery (e.g., vocabulary, mathematics, science, etc.) are therefore permissible as long as the appropriate type of norm is employed (e.g., stanines and PR's) and the error of measurement factor for the two or more tests being compared is taken into consideration. Perhaps the single major advantage of the reading achievement subtest is its ready availability to personnel of those many secondary schools which regularly administer such batteries on an annual or biennial schedule. It serves well as a first-level, broad screening measure in the secondary reading evaluation program.

## Tests of Academic Progress: Reading Test

The *Tests of Academic Progress* (*TAP*) achievement battery includes a better-than-average example of a general reading achievement test[18] — a separate, 60-minute silent test of reading which represents rigorous, albeit typical, silent-reading test construction, grades nine through twelve. It consists of twenty-two multiparagraph reading passages representing a spectrum of topics within various content areas and arranged in a gradient of increasing complexity of language and concepts. The examinee reads the eleven or twelve passages appropriate for his grade placement and answers the multiple-choice questions following each selection. The test authors constructed these questions to sample collectively four types of interpretation behaviors: (1) identification (location and recognition) of explicitly stated facts and relationships in specific segments of the passage, (2) comprehension (coordination and translation) of details and relationships within the total passage, (3) application, by drawing conclusions and inferring meanings not stated, and (4) evaluation of the general theme or author's intent.

The *TAP Reading* test produces a single total score representing composite reading interpretation which may be converted into a standard score or into a percentile rank. The reading test score may be compared to such other *TAP* achievement test results as social studies, composition, science, mathematics, and literature. Although separate scores are not provided for each of the four types of reading interpretation reflected in the test questions, the teacher may make some tentative rational analysis of the pupil's relative strengths and weaknesses in these by utilizing the item classification key provided in the *TAP Teacher's Manual.*

*The Silent Reading Comprehension Test* of the *Iowa Tests of Basic Skills*[19] includes reading achievement tests for use in grades three through nine which are comparable lower-level forms of the *TAP Reading* test. Since it sometimes is useful to compare a pupil's reading achievement test performance with a measure of his general academic aptitude, it is useful to know that the *Lorge-Thorndike Intelligence Tests* (verbal and nonverbal) have been normed on the same population as were the *TAP* and the *Iowa Test of Basic Skills*. The *TAP Reading* may be purchased singly and may be machine- or hand-scored. It produces standard scores and percentile ranks for each grade level.

## Independent Reading Achievement Surveys

Independent reading achievement survey tests generally are constructed by reading specialists for reading evaluation purposes. They tend to be longer than most achievement battery reading tests and thus may sample reading behavior more thoroughly. Independent reading tests usually measure reading vocabulary and reading comprehension. Some independent tests provide a subtest measure of reading rate or rate of comprehension, and a few have subtests directed at measuring different interpretational behaviors. The comprehension subtest of most of the independent reading tests attempts to sample a variety of literal and inferential reading behaviors, e.g., accuracy of factual recall, recognition of key ideas, identification of passage organization, inference of unstated particulars or generalizations, and critical evaluation.

Some independent reading achievement tests suffer from less rigor in test construction and standardization. It should be recognized, however, that the within-type differences in nature and quality of these two types of published standardized tests of silent reading may be greater than between-type differences, and in this writer's opinion, some independent standardized tests are superior in development and product than some achievement battery reading tests. Those who plan to purchase or use either type should give careful attention to the accompanying test manual for a description of test construction and norming procedures as well as to the general sources of reading evaluation listed at the beginning of this chapter.

Independent standardized reading tests may be utilized for a school-wide, first-level, normative

evaluation of reading achievement, but they suffer from lack of direct comparison with the scores from similarly normed tests of other areas of achievement. They are most effective as a second-level reading achievement assessment selectively used to confirm or extend the information gained from the school-wide achievement battery reading test. They are particularly useful as part of the initial assessment effort in developmental, corrective, and remedial settings, and the use of alternative forms of these tests provides a means of objective pre- and postinstructional assessment of progress.

### *The Iowa Silent Reading Tests*

The 1973 revision of the *Iowa Silent Reading Tests (ISRT)*[20] is an exemplary, independent silent-reading achievement test. For this reason, and because it utilizes a representative variety of silent-reading testing patterns, it is discussed here in some detail. Other independent standardized silent-reading tests are identified in Appendixes A.1 and A.2.

Standardized on nearly 80,000 pupils in 31 states, including representative urban populations, the *ISRT* is published in two equated forms at each of three levels. Level 1 is intended for use in grades six through nine and for high school students reading below grade level. Level 2 is designed for grades nine through twelve, with norms differentiated according to post-high school plans. Level 3 is appropriate for academically accelerated eleventh and twelfth graders. Levels 1 and 2 involve approximately 90 minutes working time; level 3 takes 56 minutes.

The *ISRT* produces standard scores, percentile ranks, and stanines for five reading measures for the first two levels and four measures at the third. The five measures gained from levels 1 and 2 are Reading Power, Vocabulary, Reading Comprehension, Directed Reading, and Reading Efficiency. Level 3 does not test Directed Reading. The Reading Power score consists of a special norming of the pupil's combined accuracy on the vocabulary test (50 items) and Reading Comprehension test (50 items).

***Vocabulary test.*** The Vocabulary test of the *ISRT* was designed to measure precision, breadth, and depth of word knowledge. It uses a typical reading vocabulary format—a stimulus word presented in isolation followed by four words from which the examinee is to choose the word closest in meaning to the stimulus. A selection of five items from the vocabulary tests of level 1 (grades 6-9) and level 2 (grade 9-community college) which approximate the range of difficulty of each of the two levels (easiest to hardest) are presented below. These items also illustrate how the choice of response words increases the sampling and exerts notable influence on the difficulty of vocabulary items.

*Level 1* ( *Test 1—Level 1—Form E*)*

| 1. *collect* | 2. *spectator* | 3. *myth* | 4. *accurate* | 5. *option* |
|---|---|---|---|---|
| (a) count | (e) worker | (a) drama | (e) complete | (a) choice |
| (b) gather | (f) onlooker | (b) biography | (f) reasonable | (b) basis |
| (c) dig | (g) speaker | (c) legend | (g) similar | (c) opinion |
| (d) pack | (h) suitor | (d) essay | (h) correct | (d) comparison |

*Level 2* ( *Test 1—Level 2—Form E*)*

| 1. *prolong* | 2. *gratifying* | 3. *eccentric* | 4. *malicious* | 5. *impromptu* |
|---|---|---|---|---|
| (a) inspect | (e) surprising | (a) wicked | (e) jealous | (a) offhand |
| (b) extend | (f) pleasing | (b) wary | (f) frantic | (b) occasional |
| (c) establish | (g) puzzling | (c) odd | (g) brazen | (c) easy going |
| (d) manage | (h) inspiring | (d) ignorant | (h) spiteful | (d) uninteresting |

*Reproduced from the *Iowa Silent Reading Tests.* Copyright © 1973 by Harcourt Brace Jovanovich, Inc. Reproduced by special permission of the publisher.

***Reading Comprehension*** (*general*). The Reading Comprehension test of the *ISRT* is composed of two parts producing one total score. Part A requires the student to answer multiple-choice questions over six short selections, much in the manner of most standardized reading tests. Part B consists of one relatively long essay over which the pupil answers a multiple-choice test of immediate recall and interpretation—without opportunity to reread the selection after seeing the questions. The test questions are designed to measure: (1) grasp of literal meaning, (2) inference and reasoning in reading, and (3) evaluation and appreciation.

***Directed Reading.*** The Directed Reading test of the *ISRT* samples the pupil's ability to handle work-study reading skills and knowledges. Part A measures proficiency in dictionary use, ability to use library sources, and knowledge of sources of information. Part B presents a two-page encyclopedia form article complete with charts, tables, and other typographical aids and asks questions which require the pupil to scan, skim, and rapidly read to locate specific information, much as he might neeα to do in an actual study situation.

Illustrative items from level 2 of the Directed Reading test appear on the following pages.

## TEST 3: DIRECTED READING, PART A*

DIRECTIONS: Below you see part of a page from a dictionary that contains made-up words. Since you have never seen the words before, you will have to use this dictionary and the Pronunciation Key in order to answer questions 1 through 9.

---

**lemopital**                          772                          **lentise**

**le·mop·i·tal** [lə·mop′e·təl] *n.* 1. Any literary work of considerable length. 2. The reading of a literary work of considerable length. 3. *Music* Any musical work of a length equal to, or longer than, an opera or a symphony. 4. *Anthropol.* A basic belief held by the peoples of an ancient culture.

**lem·or·ate**[1] [lem′ôr·āt] *v.* To allow another person to use something belonging to you.

**lem·or·ate**[2] [lem′ôr·it] *adj.* 1. Of, or having to do with,

**len·ga·le·sure** [*n.* len′gə·lē′zhûr; *v.* len·gal′ə·shŏŏr] *n.* 1. A long period of freedom for the people of a given nation. 2. Anything allowed to grow to its maximum size. 3. The maximum length of anything. 4. *Archaic* Boredom. — *v.* 1. To grant freedom to a people. 2. To win one's freedom. 3. To measure the length of anything. 4. *Archaic* To bore or otherwise tire someone. — **to lengalesure one's words** 1. To think carefully before speaking. 2. To speak slowly and clearly.

---

> *Pronunciation key:* add, āce, câre, pälm; end, ēqual; it, īce; odd, ōpen, ôrder; tŏŏk, pōōl; up, bûrn; ə = a in *above*, e in *sicken*, i in *possible*, o in *melon*, u in *circus*; yōō = u in *fuse*; oil; pout; check; ring; thin; this; zh as in *vision*.

1. Which one of the following words appear on page 771 of this dictionary?
   - (a) lemurse
   - (b) lemoop
   - (c) lenn
   - (d) lentiss

2. *Lemorate* means to—
   - (e) use
   - (f) lend
   - (g) belong
   - (h) return

---

> Suppose that you are starting your research for a paper that will deal with changes in the political opinions of American voters. Questions 10 through 15 present typical tasks that you might face in locating information for a paper of this kind. Read each question, and then decide which one of the four possibilites is the best source for the information you need.

### What Is the Best Source for Finding:

10. An account of New Deal policies under Franklin D. Roosevelt?
    - (e) *World Atlas*
    - (f) *World Almanac*
    - (g) An unabridged dictionary
    - (h) An encyclopedia

11. A detailed account of the life of the Vice President of the United States?
    - (a) Card Catalog: Author Card
    - (b) *Current Biography*
    - (c) *New York Times Index*
    - (d) *World Almanac*

---

*Reproduced from the *Iowa Silent Reading Tests.* Copyright © 1973 by Harcourt Brace Jovanovich, Inc. Reproduced by special permission of the publisher.

> Questions 16 through 24 test your general knowledge of
> sources of information. If you finish before time is called,
> go back to check your work on pages 11 through 13 only.

20. What abbreviation might be used in a bibliography entry to indicate that a book has more than one author?

    (e) etc.        (g) ed.

    (f) i.e.        (h) *et al.*

21. A news story labeled *Chicago* (*AP*) indicates that —

    (a) the story was released by a news service whose main office is in Chicago

    (b) the story was written by a Chicago columnist whose initials are A.P.

    (c) the story is an exclusive, appearing only in Chicago newspapers

    (d) the story, concerning an incident in Chicago, was released by a news service

*Part B.* This part of the Directed Reading test consists of a two-page article of encyclopedic format complete with headings, subheadings, contextual discussion, diagrams, graphs, footnotes, and related references. The directions advise the examinee to read the article selectively as directed by the questions. The items selected below are illustrative of the twenty questions presented on the Level 2, Form E selection, which deals with pearls — their history, cultivation, marketing, and care. The article source and type of interpretation required to answer the question has been added after each item. Other items, not shown here, require the ability to locate and interpret the topic main idea, graphs, and tabular material, as well as the ability to draw general conclusions through reskimming the entire article.

### TEST 3: DIRECTED READING, PART B*

1. Which one of the following is *not* a major heading?

    \_\_\_\_"History of Pearls"

    \_\_\_\_"Selection and Care of Pearls"

    \_\_\_\_"Recovery and Pearl Growth"

    \_\_\_\_"Marketing Pearls"

(Typographical structure of article headings)

*Reproduced from the *Iowa Silent Reading Tests.* Copyright ©1973 by Harcourt Brace Jovanovich, Inc. Reproduced by special permission of the publisher.

*3.* During which stage of pearl cultivation are cryptomeria branches used?

\_\_\_\_Spot collection        \_\_\_\_Harvesting

\_\_\_\_Oyster growth        \_\_\_\_Seeding

(Context — locational interpretation of subheadings and stated detail)

*5.* Which book cited as a source of information on pearls was published most recently?

\_\_\_\_*The Cultured Pearl*

\_\_\_\_*Our Oriental Heritage*

\_\_\_\_*The Book of Pearls*

\_\_\_\_*The Oxford History of India*

(Footnotes — location and interpretation)

---

*Reading Efficiency.* The *ISRT* Reading Efficiency test is designed to provide a general indication of how quickly and accurately a student can read material of moderate difficulty. The test consists of a series of six interpretive cloze-form passages, such as the one from level 2 partially reproduced below. The reader has four minutes to respond to modified cloze-procedure items on the passages. The number of items answered correctly is used to obtain normative standard scores, percentile ranks, and stanines. In addition, this test also yields a unique index which combines speed (the number of items attempted) and accuracy (the number answered correctly) by means of a special table. This index is particularly helpful in identifying inefficient readers of two types: those who read accurately but too slowly and those who read fast but inaccurately.

---

## TEST 4: READING EFFICIENCY *

DIRECTIONS: As you read through each of the passages below, you are to mark the space to the left of the word that best fits the passage. Work as QUICKLY and as ACCURATELY as you can.

SAMPLE: This test tells how quickly and accurately you

\_\_\_\_ speak.        _X_ read.        \_\_\_\_ walk.

  A. Thousands of years ago, pictures were carved on the rock ledges of Oregon's Columbia River. Today, the ledges form an unusual art gallery high above the

\_\_\_\_ city.        \_\_\_\_ river.        \_\_\_\_ ocean.

Archeologists believe that these pictures were carved on the rocks by members of some ancient American

\_\_\_\_ culture.        \_\_\_\_ club.        \_\_\_\_ church.

*Reproduced from the *Iowa Silent Reading Tests*. Copyright © 1973 by Harcourt Brace Jovanovich, Inc. Reproduced by special permission of the publisher.

***Supplementary data: functional reading levels.***
*ISRT* test booklets are reusable. The tests may be hand-scored, machine-processed locally, or scored through the Harcourt Brace Jovanovich Scoring Service. In addition to these normative and test-related scores, the *ISRT* also provides the teacher with some qualitative evaluative information. Two high-quality and very useful interpretive aids are a part of the *ISRT* test package—a *Manual of Directions* and *Guide for Interpretation and Use*.

One of the more illuminating of these aids is Table 9 (reproduced here as Figure 12) from the

***Figure 12*** *Recommended reading grade level of materials for pupils in the level 1 ISRT Reading Power (Vocabulary plus Reading Comprehension) stanine groups.* [From the *Iowa Silent Reading Tests.* Copyright © 1973 by Harcourt Brace Jovanovich, Inc. Reproduced by special permission of the publisher.]

| *National Reference Group* | *Reading Power Stanine* | *Reading Grade Level of Instructional Materials* | *Reading Grade Level of Independent Materials* |
|---|---|---|---|
| Level 1 | 7, 8, 9 | 8–10 | 7–8 |
| Grade 6 | 4, 5, 6 | 5–7 | 4–5 |
| | 3 | 4–5 | 2–4 |
| | 2 | 3–4 | 2 |
| | 1 | 2–3 | a |
| Level 1 | 7, 8, 9 | 9–11 | 8–9 |
| Grade 7 and | 6 | 8–9 | 7–8 |
| age-controlled | 5 | 6–8 | 5–6 |
| (13-year-olds) | 4 | 5–6 | 4–5 |
| | 3 | 4–5 | 2–4 |
| | 2 | 3–4 | 2 |
| | 1 | 2–3 | a |
| Level 1 | 7, 8, 9 | 10–12 | 9–10 |
| Grade 8 | 6 | 9–10 | 8–9 |
| | 5 | 7–8 | 6–7 |
| | 4 | 6–7 | 5–6 |
| | 3 | 5–6 | 4–5 |
| | 2 | 4–5 | 2–4 |
| | 1 | 3–4 | 2 |
| Level 1 | 7, 8, 9 | 11–12 | 10–11 |
| Grade 9 | 6 | 10–11 | 9–10 |
| | 5 | 8–9 | 7–8 |
| | 4 | 7–8 | 6–7 |
| | 3 | 5–6 | 4–5 |
| | 2 | 4–5 | 2–4 |
| | 1 | 3–4 | 2 |

[a] These pupils probably need diagnosis in the fundamental reading skills; they would probably have difficulty reading independently.

*Guide for Interpretation and Use* for level 1.[21] It provides a means of *estimating* independent and instructional functional reading levels from the stanine placement on the *ISRT*. The table serves to reinforce two points previously emphasized: (1) grade equivalent scores on standardized reading tests are not equivalent to pupil reading levels, and (2) the performance range within each grade is wide and overlaps that of other grade placement pupils.

## Uses and Limitations of Standardized Reading Tests

When selected and interpreted in an intelligent manner, group standardized tests of reading achievement serve the reading evaluation program very well for those purposes for which they were intended. Most provide equated alternative forms for comparable retesting at successive levels and multiple grade norms so that consistent sequential comparisons may be made over the pupil's school tenure. Because they are mass-produced and can be administered in reasonably sized groups, they are relatively economical and efficient to administer. Most tests provide a manual to aid the professional in understanding the nature of the test and its results.

Any assessment device has its limitations, and standardized reading achievement tests are no exception. Because these tests are built to be administered at low cost within school time schedules, they tend to sample short-span reading passages which are rather atypical of the higher school and life reading tasks of secondary pupils. Even though the test authors attempt to establish reasonable time limits for these tests, the tests do tend to place the slow but accurate reader at a disadvantage, and to that extent, are rate-dependent.

Some limitations of standardized reading tests are accentuated by school misuse.[22] Standardized reading achievement tests best measure general reading performance, as their authors intended, and are not appropriately applied or adapted to the evaluation of specific curricula or atypical school populations. The broad population sampling employed in standardizing most of these tests tends to produce norm scores for inner-city school populations which are test-valid but relatively low. This is hardly the fault of the test, which is supposed to detect achievement differences. Test publishers would do well to publish specific as well as general norms for such populations.

The misuse of grade norms is another example of test consumer deficiency. Grade norm scores (provided usually to satisfy administrator and teacher demand) are extrapolated from median grade-level performance and statistically are not as reliable as standard scores, percentiles, or stanine scores. Grade score results should not be used to identify reading-material levels; they usually measure frustrational reading performance and typically overestimate the level of reading material which the pupil can handle in independent or instructional situations.

### Criterion Behaviors and Diagnostic Potential

A criticism currently leveled at standardized reading survey tests is that their format and norm products do not measure mastery of criterion behaviors or specific skills. A second, and closely related criticism, is that they do not lend themselves to direct (and simple) diagnostic interpretation.[23] It is true that most achievement battery reading tests produce a single normative score representing general or global reading interpretation, and thus provide little direct help in evaluating mastery or in forming individual profiles of specific-criterion reading skills. Independent standardized reading tests are more likely to produce some differential subtest scores, but these also tend to be assessments of combined behaviors. Of course, most currently published standardized reading achievement tests did not consider teacher use of differential diagnosis of individual skills to be a high-priority objective. Future editions of these tests may make a more direct effort to incorporate criterion referencing in their construction.

However, arguments that tests can be referenced to measure certain skills—that they must be before they are instructionally valid—are open to question. We have had relatively little success in isolating pure strains of measured reading performance.[24] Surely, assessing how well pupils can understand passages taken from sources used or comparable to those read in school or life situations may be a more readily transferable general school reading reference for secondary pupils than the mastery of isolated skills tests. The substantial and significant positive degree of correlation consistently demonstrated between standardized reading achievement test results and content-related reading test results, content achievement test results, or school grades suggests that this form of reading test does incorporate a substantial amount of empirical validity, even if most do not evaluate specific reading skills mastery. At any rate, specific competency is best assessed directly with locally developed criterion tests.

*Diagnostic functions.* It seems somewhat naive to assume that any test, standardized or nonstandardized, can be "diagnostic" in itself.[25] Diagnosis is a human behavior—an analytical problem-solving process not unlike the scientific method. Tests and other reading assessment procedures are employed to supply information concerning the questions or hypotheses developed by the diagnostician. Any source which contributes to this procedure lends itself to "diagnostic" use. No single assessment measure is likely to provide all of the information needed in diagnostic case analysis. Standardized reading achievement tests do provide the bases for answering such questions as: Does this pupil exhibit notable reading difficulty in comparison with his peers? Is he a reading underachiever in comparison with his mental ability or with his listening achievement? Moreover, some standardized achievement tests provide valid and reliable subtest measures of differential reading performance, e.g., vocabulary, general reading comprehension, work-type reading tasks, and rate of comprehension.

Finally, an examination of the specific error pattern even on tests of general reading comprehension can provide the teacher with some insight about the pupil's individual reading performance: Does he have relatively greater difficulty with items calling for inference than factual recall? Did he make random errors throughout the various difficulty levels of the passages, or were his errors notably influenced by the complexity of certain passages read? Is he a slow but reasonably accurate reader? Such observations will need more specific confirmation and may lead to further diagnostic hypotheses—but that, of course, is the heart of the diagnostic method.

Used appropriately, good standardized achievement tests do contribute at the entry or screening level of reading diagnosis. They provide objective, normative measures of the pupil's generalized ability to interpret the meaning of words and textual selections. In this way, valid inter- and intrapupil comparisons can be made of reading achievement status and growth. If they provide additional insight concerning the pupil's differential reading strengths and weaknesses, that is a bonus.

It must be assumed that the effective second reading evaluation effort will supplement standardized achievement tests with other tests and assessment procedures. Just as the administration of an independent standardized reading achievement test may confirm and extend the information gained from the achievement battery reading test, so classroom observation and informal reading assessment procedures are needed to evaluate more specific reading behaviors, the mastery of instructional objectives, and reading-related personal and instructional factors. Certainly, defensible reading diagnosis would make use of a number of reading assessment tools, and the standardized reading survey would be one of these.

## Standardized Vocabulary Tests

Standardized vocabulary achievement tests supply a normative measure of the pupil's composite ability to read words. Also, they correlate in a moderately positive manner with total reading power. With proper caution, vocabulary test scores can be useful, in addition, in making four types of reading analysis: (1) comparing the reader's vocabulary power with that of peers, (2) determining the pupil's growth in vocabulary (if alternative forms and levels of the same test are administered on a periodic basis), (3) comparing the pupil's reading vocabulary performance with his sentence, paragraph, or other specific comprehension performance, and (4) comparing his differential vocabulary strengths, if the test provides scores or subscores based on vocabulary samples from different disciplines or content areas.

### Typical Format and Normative Scores

The usual format for vocabulary tests is to present a series of multiple items, generally in direct progression of difficulty and sometimes in some rotational sequence of difficulty, as in the *ISRT* vocabulary test. The stem consists of the stimulus word presented in isolation or in simple context, and the examinee is to select from four or five choices that word which is most synonymous with the stimulus word. The raw score consists of the total correct identifications, possibly with some correction for error (e.g., $R - 1/4W$), and is converted into standard scores, percentiles, stanines, grade equivalents, etc. through the use of norms. Single-word stimulus items cover a wider range of word uses. Stimulus words presented in context tend to assess more definitive uses of the word and involve some basic ability to read simple context. Items which require more than the recognition of word meaning, such as the analysis of word roots or solving analogies, are not vocabulary items in the usual sense, and are better classified according to their specific function as word analysis tests or verbal reasoning tests.

### Two General Functions

Although highly similar in form and drawing upon common response behavior, standardized vocabulary achievement tests may be classified by the primary function they were intended to serve — as measures of reading behavior or as measures of conceptual knowledge. Reading vocabulary tests are constructed with the intent to assess pupil ability to read (recognize and understand) printed words. The concern in selecting the word sample in "reading vocabulary" tests is that they provide a range of familiarity and difficulty appropriate to usage in general reading materials. In vocabulary "knowledge" tests—such as those which are identified with a particular content area or as a separate test of vocabulary in a general achievement battery—the words are chosen because they sample representative concepts or pertinent referents, and they become silent word-reading tests simply because that is the most efficient vehicle for group testing.

Because content and reading process are highly interrelated, both types of vocabulary tests may be helpful in reading assessment. The caution to be observed is that the vocabulary knowledge test may be significantly influenced by the pupil's understanding of concepts in a particular area or areas of knowledge. This is helpful in assessing reading power in that or those areas, but it may underestimate the pupil's broad capabilities in recognizing and understanding words.

### Caution in Interpretation

Thus, the analysis of a pupil's score on a group standardized vocabulary test should be done with caution. Although it appears to render a score of particular behavior, a score on a vocabulary test reflects something of the pupil's composite word power. High scores generally indicate that the pupil has this composite behavior well in hand. Low scores may indicate deficiency in composite word power, or they may reflect the seriously inhibiting influence of any of its several components: deficiency in word meaning due to limited mental ability, experience background, or both; restricted sight vocabulary resulting from minimal personal reading activity; inadequate word recognition and analysis skills; or even slow rate of reading, since most vocabulary tests are timed.

The use of group (silent-reading) vocabulary scores to estimate mental ability should be avoided.

It is true that the vocabulary subtest of intelligence tests does correlate in a high positive manner with total results on verbal intelligence tests. However, the vocabulary items on those tests are selected specifically for that purpose. Also, group intelligence tests, vocabulary or otherwise, require reading, and, thus, tend to underestimate the intelligence of normal or bright pupils with reading deficiency.

## ESTIMATING THE READABILITY OF INSTRUCTIONAL SOURCES

Until recently, constructive action by educators and publishers concerning the readability of secondary school instructional materials has been minimal. As a consequence, most secondary texts and other required reading sources vary widely in readability. Too many are more difficult than their school placement suggests and too difficult for the typical secondary pupil to read and understand readily.[26,27] As long as the textbook in conjunction with the independent reading assignment continues to be pivotal to learning success in the secondary school, improving the match between pupil reading ability and the readability of instructional materials is essential. Knowing something of readability and how to estimate the relative reading difficulty of printed sources thus becomes a useful element of reading assessment procedure.

### Readability

Readability is an operational construct and, hence, means different things in different settings. Broadly, readability refers to the condition of the written or printed source which exerts a notable influence upon the performance of the reader. Klare concludes from his review of the research literature that the term "readability" has come to be used in three ways: (1) to indicate legibility of either handwriting or typography; (2) to indicate ease of reading due to either the interest value or the pleasantness of writing; or (3) to indicate ease of understanding or comprehension due to style of writing.[28] It is reader ease and/or success in dealing with written language which concerns us in this discussion.

Klare has identified five "principles of writing readably" which he distilled from the literature on readability.[29] While he is careful to note that quality writing is a creative talent and that following a formula does not guarantee excellence or even understanding, these principles serve nicely to identify some of the major factors which influence readability and which have figured in its measurement. Paraphrased, these principles consist of: (1) identifying and writing to the purpose which the material is to fulfill (e.g., to instruct, to entertain, to indoctrinate, etc.); (2) identifying the nature of the prospective reader and writing to meet such characteristics as his educational level, experiential background, interests, and anxieties; (3) selecting words which the reader encounters frequently and which are likely to be within his meaning and reading vocabulary; (4) constructing sentences which, generally, are brief and concise; and (5) using, when appropriate, a style of writing which is personal or person-oriented.

Each of the major factors associated with these principles contains diverse elements, and none is without its exceptions. Word selection and sentence construction have figured heavily in the measurement of readability and need some amplification. While words encountered frequently in oral and written expression usually lead to familiarity and thus to reading ease, this presumes reasonably adequate language and reading ability on the part of the readership. Other qualities of word readability include those words which are learned early, are shorter, have Anglo-Saxon origins, have general rather than technical or special meanings, and have concrete rather than abstract referents.

Obviously, not all sentences which are short are easily understood and not all long sentences are difficult to understand. Compare: "Cognizance engenders mobility." with "Once upon a time, a very young boy decided to visit the zoo which was located on the far side of the city." Even brief statements composed of short, familiar words can carry an implied conceptual complexity beyond the apparent level of literal readability, e.g., "No man is an island." Despite these exceptions, shorter sentences usually are more readable than longer ones, especially those which contain numerous prepositional phrases and/or have complex, compound, or compound-complex constructions.

It should be added that readability involves more than writer style. Other significant elements of written material which influence reader success include format, organization, and density of conceptual content. However, content, format, and organization have proved difficult components on which to obtain facile, valid, and applicable measurements, and as a consequence, have not figured significantly in educational practices of predicting readability.

The literature on readability is extensive. Only the high points of the nature of readability and its measurement are touched here. In addition to G. R. Klare's *The Measurement of Readability,* interested students will find excellent general references in J. S. Chall's *Readability: An Appraisal of Research and Application,*[30] Seels and Dale's annotated bibliography, *Readability and Reading,*[31] and more recently, Klare's *Reading Research Quarterly* article, "Assessing Readability."[32]

## Ratings and Functional Performance

The use of readability formulas to predict reading ease of materials is the most widely recognized, and perhaps most viable, means of assessing readability. It is the one to which most attention is given in this discussion. However, there are other general approaches to assessing readability in addition to the use of formulas. Three, in particular, should be identified. They can be useful in themselves, and they have served as the means by which formula ratings have been developed and validated.

*Reader ratings.* The first of these nonformula approaches involves some sort of subjective reaction of readers to the materials of concern—either by the pupils who use them or who typify the pupils who will use them, or by a panel of authorities (teachers, reading scholars, etc.). Such judgments usually are improved by having the pupils or panel use a checklist or a classification system for rating individual materials or by having them develop a relative readability ranking among the materials of concern.

*Reader performance criteria.* The second approach consists of measuring directly some aspect of reader performance on the materials of concern. The most common practice is to measure comprehension of a selective norm group or groups by means of an objective test. The materials may be ranked relatively by group mean score or can be evaluated according to some preset criteria of reading ease. For multiple-choice tests, the early practice was to use 50 percent accuracy as the criterion of minimal ease. The use of 75 percent comprehension accuracy as the criterion of instructional ease seems to be gaining in popularity.

Another recent trend has been the use of the efficient *cloze* testing procedure as a measure of reader ability to cope with a selection. Since cloze testing is more demanding, the criteria for acceptable accuracy under cloze procedure generally is placed at 35 to 40 percent accuracy. Cloze testing procedure and other material-referenced assessment procedures will be discussed in the next section of this chapter.

A variant means of the reader performance approach to assessing readability involves measuring the relative reading efficiency (rate of reading) with which a selected group of readers negotiates representative selections. Yet another is the identification of word difficulty, either by noting errors in oral reading or by having readers underline or otherwise identify the words which gave them either recognition or meaning problems as they read silently. Those representative passages which produce the greater number of word problems represent the more difficult reading materials.

The use of measures of reading rate and word accuracy as indicators of readability has both empirical and rational justification. The contribution of word factors to total reading power has been demonstrated by a variety of research. Word counts have been used as a single estimation of readability. The relative time it takes to read various selections correlates very well with relative measures of comprehension over those selections. Rate seems to summate the various influences which the material exerts upon the reader, just as lack of word facility tends to exert the greatest single influence. Obviously, these are better indicators of the reader's general reading ease than of his specific interpretive prowess.

***Performance on criterion materials.*** The third nonformula approach to assessing the readability of written materials involves a combination of the two approaches previously mentioned. This involves: (1) the use of reading testing to establish a criterion set of reading selections (which then represent successive levels or ratings of readability), and (2) the assessing of the readability of any other materials of concern by matching or otherwise comparing them with the criterion selections of labeled readability. Perhaps the best known of such materials are the McCall-Crabbs *Standard Test Lessons in Reading,* a set of graded reading test selections which have been used to calibrate and validate a number of the most prominent of the readability formulas.[33] The stability and consistency of basal reader materials makes it possible to use them for comparative estimation of materials up to eighth-grade levels.[34]

Nonformula assessment of readability is subject to both the advantages and disadvantages of reader-based performance. Such methods can provide a more realistic estimate—being based on direct assessment of reader response. This places substantial onus upon the appropriate selection of the reader sample and the degree of consistency or reliability of the reader judgment or performance. Perhaps the greater limitation of these approaches is their operational inconvenience in school use. They take both teacher and pupil time and require sufficient copies of the materials in question. Moreover, there is an obvious operational advantage to being able to *predict* the reading ease of materials prior to decision to purchase or to use them and to do so in a reasonably efficient manner. In general, the use of predicted readability for initial purchase or screening of instructional materials combined with the use of direct material-referenced assessment for individual pupil or group assignments presents the most reasonable solution to a difficult instructional problem.

## Readability Formulas and Graphs

A readability formula is a predictive device that provides quantitative estimates of the reading ease of written materials, usually through some weighted combination of the measurement of language elements. Longer selections, chapters, and books can vary in readability. Like other measures of readability, the use of formulas therefore requires the sampling of representative selections within the material upon which the assessment formula is applied. Most formulas indicate the recommended minimal number of samplings necessary, and if wide variation occurs, suggest that the passage samples be increased until the variation stabilizes.

The formula components considered vary a bit from formula to formula. Most often, they involve assessment of just two language elements, usually word counts and sentence counts. The most common word counts used are word length, word familiarity, or word difficulty. The latter two generally are determined by some known word list, e.g., the *Dale List of 3000 Words* (by word frequency/familiarity) and Thorndike's *Teacher's Word Book of 20,000 Words* (by word usage/difficulty). Counts by word function—e.g., prepositions, personal referent words—have been used less frequently.

Sentence counts usually have been made in terms of length (average number of words or syllables per sentence) and less frequently in terms of complexity (number or type of phrases and clauses) or function (declarative, imperative, etc.). No great advantage has been demonstrated by utilizing complex formulas, especially in school applications. There may be some advantage to using more complicated formulas for research purposes if one has a computer programmed to handle the necessary manipulations.[35]

Nearly fifty different readability formulas or their variant functions are available for possible use. Klare has provided an excellent summary of those published to 1960[36] and has updated this listing in 1974.[37] Four formulas will be described and one readability graph will be presented which are pertinent for the range of reader levels for secondary pupils. They are representative of the general patterns of readability assessment for classroom purposes.

### The Dale-Chall Formula

The Dale-Chall formula[38] is considered one of the more precise of the formulas available for upper-grade and adult level materials. Published in 1948, it was recalculated for greater accuracy in 1958.[39] To facilitate determination of the Dale-Chall readability scores, Koenke published a graphic computation method in 1971,[40] and Williams recently has developed a table for rapid determination of revised Dale-Chall scores.[41] Several computer programs are available for computing the Dale-Chall.

The Dale-Chall utilizes a number of specific rules but is based on just two counts: (1) average sentence length, and (2) percentage of unfamiliar words (i.e., those not appearing on the Dale List of 3,000 words) plus a constant (3.2672). The revised formula is based on a criterion of grade-level scores for a group of pupils obtaining 50 percent minimal accuracy on questions at pertinent levels of the 1950 McCall-Crabbs Standard Test Lessons.

$$X_{c_{50}} = .1155x_1 + .0596x_2 + 3.2672$$

where $X_{c_{50}}$ = reading grade score of a pupil who could answer one-half of the test questions on passage of that level

$x_1$ = Dale score (percentage of words not on Dale list)

$x_2$ = average sentence length in words

The Dale-Chall raw score can be converted into corrected grade-level scores which range from approximately third grade to twelfth grade, and which should be interpreted with due consideration for measurement error. The rather extensive list of rules and the Dale-Chall list of words are available in published form.[42]

### The Flesch Formulas

Rudolf Flesch has developed a number of readability formulas[43] in his pursuit of more readable writing. His Reading Ease (RE) formula has been one of the most frequently employed in evaluating materials for mature readers and is considered among the most accurate for formulas not requiring a special word list. It has been used as the basis for the development of a number of variant formulas. Flesch's Human Interest (HI) formula attempts to assess a more evasive quality of reading—its appeal to the reader through more personal word referents (e.g., first person) and personalized sentences (e.g., dialogue, anecdotes). Both the RE and HI formulas involve the systematic sampling of 100-word samples. The two formulas (the RE formula as recalculated on the 1950 McCall-Crabbs materials by Powers, Sumner, and Kearl) are presented below:

$$RE = -2.2029 + .0778sl + .0455wl$$
$$HI = 3.635pw + .314ps$$

where $wl$ = number of syllables per 100 words

$sl$ = average number of words per sentence

$pw$ = number of personal words per 100 words

$ps$ = number of personal samples per 100 sentences

Students interested in using these Flesch formulas will be aided by the explanation and rating charts presented in the article cited above or in his many other writings.

### The Fry Readability Graph

The Fry Graph[44] is more accurately described as an application aid than a formula. However, its two-dimensional plotting of word length and sentence length counts performs the same functions as a two-component formula. The directions and chart are presented here because the graph provides a highly efficient means of determining readability levels for materials in the secondary-grade range, like major readability formulas, and correlates highly with the Dale-Chall (.94), the Flesch (.96), and with tenth-grade student comprehension scores (.93). Like formulas which employ sentence- and word-length measures as indicators of writing difficulty, the Fry graph tends to underestimate the reading difficulty of those materials, such as simplified texts and technical articles, which use a large percentage of short sentences and one-syllable words but utilize unfamiliar or technical word concepts.

The directions for using the Fry Graph are as follows:

1. Select one 100-word passage from near the beginning, middle, and end of the book. Skip all proper nouns. Use several additional samples if wide variability is found in sentence or syllable counts.
2. Count the total number of sentences in each 100-word passage (estimating the nearest tenth of a sentence). Average these three numbers.
3. Count the total number of syllables in each 100-word sample. Average the total number of syllables for the three samples.
4. Plot on the graph [see Figure 13] the average number of sentences and the average number of syllables per 100 words. Perpendicular lines mark off approximate grade-level areas. Most plot points fall near the heavy curved line.

### SMOG Grading

Another formula delivering a general estimate of readability which requires no external word lists and requires very little time is McLaughlin's SMOG grading.[45] Like other quick and practical readability formulas, it samples word and sentence length. By some adroit mathematical manipulation, McLaughlin has reduced the procedure to four steps, given below, which are based upon polysyllabic word count: the SMOG grade = 3 + the square root of the polysyllable count! As might be expected, SMOG estimates are better employed with more sophisticated literature. The SMOG grade is a rough approximation of readability placement. Its author indicates that it will predict the grade difficulty of a passage within one and one-half grades in 68 percent of cases.

The directions for SMOG grading are as follows:

1. Count 10 consecutive sentences near the beginning of the selection to be assessed, 10 in the middle, and 10 near the end. Count as a sentence any string of words ending with a period, question mark, or exclamation point.
2. In the 30 selected sentences count every word of three or more syllables. Any string of letters or numerals beginning and ending with a space or punctuation mark should be counted if you can distinguish at least three syllables when you read it aloud in context. If a polysyllabic word is repeated, count each repetition.
3. Estimate the square root of the number of polysyllabic words counted. This is done by taking the square root of the nearest perfect square. For example, if the count is 95, the nearest perfect square is 100, which yields a square root of 10. If the count lies roughly between two perfect squares, choose the lower number. For instance, if the count is 110, take the square root of 100 rather than that of 121.
4. Add 3 to the approximate square root. This gives the SMOG grade, which is the minimal reading level needed to understand the selection assessed.

### Summary: Readability Formulas

Readability formulas provide a quick, objective, and inexpensive means of anticipating the reading ease of written materials. They are not exact predictors of reading difficulty, of course. Generally, they sample only one dimension of writing—the difficulty imposed by lexical and syntactic complexity of style. They are better at estimating the relative difficulty among different materials or in identifying broad reader population ranges than in pegging a particular grade level.

***Figure 13*** *Fry Graph for estimating readability.*

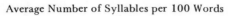

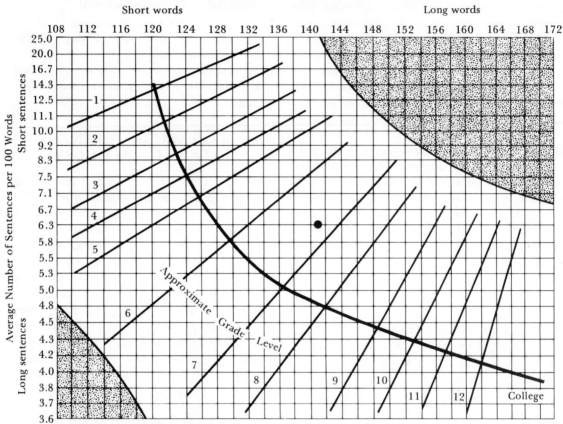

DIRECTIONS: Randomly select three 100-word passages from a book or article. Plot the average number of syllables and the average number of sentences per 100 words on the graph to determine the grade level of material. Choose more passages per book if great variability is observed and conclude that the book has uneven readability. Few books will fall in the gray area, but when they do, grade–level scores are invalid.

| EXAMPLE: | | Syllables | Sentences |
|---|---|---|---|
| | 1st Hundred Words | 124 | 6.6 |
| | 2nd Hundred Words | 141 | 5.5 |
| | 3rd Hundred Words | 158 | 6.8 |
| | Average | 141 | 6.3 |

*Readability*: *7th Grade* (see dot plotted on graph)

Formulas standardized upon a 50 percent criterion of comprehension tend to yield higher placements than those with 75 percent criterion. The better formulas provide grade placements with ± one-half to one grade level error. However, even this assumes the mythical average reader for the grade or that the teacher has a stable, accurate assessment of the instructional or independent level of reading material a particular pupil can handle.

Nevertheless, readability formulas do provide relatively accurate predictions; and if this seems like faint support, one only has to examine the gross errors of readability judgment which publishers, educators, and librarians have made for decades when not employing formulas. Perhaps the greatest value of their use will be the accumulative pressure exerted upon publishers to produce more readable instructionally related materials and upon teachers and librarians to make sure the most readable learning materials are made available in their schools.

### Other Considerations in Book Selection

Readability formulas or graphs function best when supplemented by the consideration of such other, more qualitative assessment factors as the following:

1. The nature of the format: attractiveness, type legibility, use of organizational aids and instructional directions, illustrations and other graphic aids.
2. The length of total source and the size of reading unit (longer articles, selections, or chapters are more taxing to reader motivation and performance).
3. The density and difficulty (or familiarity) of significant concepts employed per page or per selection.
4. The extent to which the material appeals to pupil needs or interests, or satisfies specific learning objectives.
5. The appropriateness of the language and referents used for readers with linguistically different backgrounds.

6. The appeal of the particular writer's style and literary form (e.g., short story, essay, technical explanation, etc.) of the material.
7. The reactions of a few pupils with known reading abilities and/or with varying degrees of reading motivation.
8. Pupil criterion word accuracy or selection comprehension performance on samples of the material.

## MATERIAL–REFERENCED READING ASSESSMENT

We have observed that reading interpretation, fluency, and attitude are influenced by the extent to which the reader can cope with the complexity of the material to be read. This is one of the major reasons secondary school personnel need to be concerned with readability estimation.

More direct assessment of the match between reader ability and complexity of written sources may be accomplished through material-referenced reading testing. Such testing procedures can be employed to: (1) determine how well the people can handle a specific source (e.g., the required eleventh-grade biology text or Paton's *Cry, the Beloved Country*), or (2) identify approximate generalized levels of material at which the reader should be able to function for various purposes. In this section, three approaches to material–referenced reading assessment are considered—the word inventory, the *cloze* reading test, and the informal reading inventory (IRI). The classroom application of these three procedures is tied closely to the concept of "functional reading levels."

### Functional Reading Levels

If other factors are held constant, increases in the complexity of language-thought structure of reading materials are associated with poorer reader performance as manifested in more frequent inaccuracy or hesitation in word recognition, lower comprehension scores, reduction in silent speed and oral fluency, as well as in greater reader stress or discomfort. Thus, if a series of reading passages is arranged in a power gradient of difficulty, from easiest to most complex in language structure, we should be able to locate the levels of reading materials at which that pupil "functions" best for different purposes. And if we do this often enough under controlled conditions with an appropriate sample of pupils, we should be able to determine some objective criteria for determining when a particular selection is appropriate or inappropriate for instructional or personal reading purposes.

Four designations of functional reading levels carry particular meaning for the reading professional and content teachers. From easiest (lowest material level) to most difficult (highest material level) designation, these are: (1) basal, (2) independent, (3) instructional, and (4) frustrational reading levels. For normal-progress upper-school readers, oral word recognition accuracy lessens somewhat in importance, while silent-reading interpretation, both literal and inferential, increases in significance. Applicable criteria for the general run of secondary readers for these designations are given below[46]:

*1. Basal.* The highest level of reading material at which the pupil reads with oral and silent fluency, perfect accuracy on literal and inferential interpretation questions, no word recognition hesitancies or errors, and no indications of personal stress while reading. The basal level is a classification useful primarily for theoretical purposes, since good readers make chance errors in word recognition and no comprehension check can assume perfect reliability.

*2. Independent.* The highest level of reading material at which the pupil reads with no more than 1 to 2 percent oral-reading word recognition error, no less than 90 percent accuracy on silent or combined oral-silent interpretation, with optimal oral fluency and silent-reading speed, and no notable evidence of personal discomfort. The "independent" level serves as a guide to the optimal difficulty of materials for extended reading, both personal and assigned, for which the pupil receives little preparation or teacher aid while reading.

*3. Instructional.* The highest level of reading material at which the pupil demonstrates approxi-mately 95 percent oral word recognition accuracy, approximately 75 percent accuracy on silent-reading interpretation, and reasonable silent-reading rate and/or fluency in oral reading. Instructional reading level indicates that level of material which the reader can handle for classroom learning purposes when given instructional preparation and guidance by the teacher. The pupil should be challenged by this material but have little serious anxiety about his performance on it. The pupil's instructional performance should improve with good preparation and classroom guidance. Thus, less stringent criteria may be used when the teacher plans to provide considerable personal attention; i.e., 90 to 95 percent word accuracy and 65 to 75 percent comprehension may be adequate.

*4. Frustrational.* The level of material at which the reader's performance is too inadequate and/or too stressful even when given a substantial aid by the teacher. In effect, it is the next highest level beyond the maximal (or highest) instructional level with which the pupil can cope. The criteria often associated with "definite" reading frustration are less than 85 percent word recognition accuracy, less than 50 percent comprehension accuracy, and/or consistent evidence of serious psychological discomfort or anxiety while reading.

These, of course, are generalized levels; they are pertinent for most pupils, for most reading materials and situations, much of the time. Variations do occur in a reader's functional performance—from day to day, with changes in the style or topic of the material, and with the reader's psychological ups and downs. Because he can handle higher or more difficult materials, the better secondary reader's spread of functional levels—basal to frustrational—will be wider than the functional spread of lesser readers. There will be a considerable overlap in reading levels from reader to reader, as was illustrated earlier in the stanine-functional reading levels data presented in Figure 12.

Poorer secondary readers of high intelligence and conceptual background sometimes demonstrate unusually wide and inconsistent functional spreads, failing to read fluently and recognize words accurately on lower-grade materials, but having the intellectual potential to handle comprehension tasks at much higher (more difficult) materials. Highly anxious pupils of adequate reading ability sometimes manifest the same pattern. In this connection, it should be noted that while readers often are consistent in the levels at which they demonstrate breakdown in their criteria performance, this is not invariably the case. The examiner or teacher will need to use judgment in deciding where fluency, accuracy, comprehension, and personal stress—in combination—indicate the most reasonable materials or approximate functional levels for the pupil.

### Material– and Level–Referenced Word Inventories

Word recognition difficulty is a fairly consistent symptom of the literal reading difficulty a reader has, or is likely to have, with a written source. A word recognition test of a representative sample of words from a particular article or book can provide a quick screening check of whether or not a pupil is likely to encounter unusual problems in reading that source. Material-referenced word recognition tests thus provide a quick way to make a provisional match between a pupil and a particular source. When the test is composed of word samplings from successive levels of difficulty (i.e., a power test), an estimate of his functional reading levels may be obtained. By providing a means of recording pupil responses, such a word test also can supply insight into the pupil's specific word recognition and/or word analysis tendencies.

### *Informal Word Inventory Format and Procedure*

The format for an individual word recognition test usually follows this pattern:

| | Pupil Response | |
|---|---|---|
| *Stimulus Word* *(card or tachistoscope)* | *(Flash)* *Recognition* | *(Untimed)* *Analysis* |
| 1. would | ✓ | |
| 2. consist | ✓ | (1)              (2) |
| 3. procedure | 0 | pro-ducer/pro-ced-ure |
| 4. sampling | sapling | sam-pling |
| 5. etc. | | |

The test is administered individually, each stimulus word being exposed (by flash card, tachistoscope, or by sliding a masking sheet of paper off/on the word) for approximately ⅓ second or less to prevent studied analysis. The subject responds by orally pronouncing what he has seen. If correct, the teacher marks a ( ✓ ); nonresponse is recorded with a (0). If an incorrect recognition, the teacher writes in the incorrect response, phonetically if necessary, and then exposes the word for approximately 5 to 15 seconds to see if and how the pupil analyzes the word, given time to do so. Since quick word recognition is a better indicator than studied analysis of how readily the pupil can handle a given level of material, the initial correct/incorrect responses on the word *recognition* column are given priority in estimating reading level. The recorded pupil errors provide supplementary evidence concerning recognition/analysis processes and whether the pupil can use analysis techniques to improve his word reading performance. However, a strong analysis performance may be considered in placing a pupil in materials where he demonstrates borderline recognition success.

Acceptable performance criteria tend to vary for informal word recognition tests. Absence of recognition errors is a good indication that the pupil can handle that level of material. Performance as low as 90 percent accuracy may be acceptable if the pupil is intellectually able and/or receives considerable instructional aid in reading the material and/or has a strong desire to read that material. In the secondary content situation, choices of appropriate instructional material are sometimes limited. Hence, the performance on a word recognition test may serve only to make relative decisions among those materials available and to alert the teacher to the pupil's need for special help in using such a source.

*Sampling.* The sampling of words used in a word recognition inventory is important. The best rule is to choose the sample randomly from a representative pool of words and to sample as many words as time or situation permits. It helps if the text or manual provides a glossary of key terms or a list of the new vocabulary introduced in that book (as many reading instructional materials do). If the teacher is concerned with whether the pupil can read a particular content textbook, a test sample may be developed by taking fifteen to twenty-five words, randomly or at systematic intervals, from the index, plus an equal-sized sample of every tenth running word from the context of a representative page located approximately in the middle of the text.

If the sample is to be part of a power-levels recognition test, the sample should be drawn from successive levels of materials which have been developed with progressive and representative vocabulary complexity (such as basic reading instructional series or units). To keep the multiple-levels inventory from becoming tedious, the total sample at each level will need to be limited to ten or twenty words. Since reading series often introduce new vocabulary in order of progressive difficulty within each text, it may be necessary to systematically sample the words in the order in which they are introduced in the text. Thus, if a sample of 20 words were to be taken from a sequential order list of 1,200 new words introduced in the text, one would choose every sixtieth word for the test ($1,200/20 = 60$). Where no appropriate reading series is available, an indirect source of power-level material-referenced words may be found in such vocabulary sources as the EDC Core Vocabulary List, published by McGraw-Hill.[47] This vocabulary consists of two lists of words (grades 1-8 and 9-12), indexed by frequency of use in published materials.

### The San Diego Word Assessment Inventory

A graded word list has been developed by LaPray and Ross.[48] Commonly called the *San Diego Quick Test*, it consists of a list of ten words at thirteen different levels (preprimer through grade 11) and has proved to be a particularly efficient screening device for estimating "independent," "instructional," and to a lesser extent, "frustrational" functional reading levels for elementary, middle, or junior high pupils, as well as for high school pupils and adults experiencing notable difficulty with reading.

The authors suggest starting with that list which is two years below the pupil's grade placement. The lists in which the pupil misses no more than one of ten words represent independent reading levels. Two errors per list indicate instructional level of difficulty. The list may be mimeographed to facilitate recording of number and type of errors. Typing each list of ten words on a separate index card for the pupil to read improves administration and avoids unnecessary distraction. The San Diego Graded Word List is presented, by permission of the authors, on page 200.

| PP | Primer | 1 | 2 | 3 |
|---|---|---|---|---|
| see | you | road | our | city |
| play | come | live | please | middle |
| me | not | thank | myself | moment |
| at | with | when | town | frightened |
| run | jump | bigger | early | exclaimed |
| go | help | how | send | several |
| and | is | always | wide | lonely |
| lock | work | night | believe | drew |
| can | are | spring | quietly | since |
| here | this | today | carefully | straight |

| 4 | 5 | 6 | 7 | 8 |
|---|---|---|---|---|
| decided | scanty | bridge | amber | capacious |
| served | certainly | commercial | dominion | limitation |
| amazed | develop | abolish | sundry | pretext |
| silent | considered | trucker | capillary | intrigue |
| wrecked | discussed | apparatus | impetuous | delusion |
| improved | behaved | elementary | blight | immaculate |
| certainly | splendid | comment | wrest | ascent |
| entered | acquainted | necessity | enumerate | acrid |
| realized | escaped | gallery | daunted | binocular |
| interrupted | grim | relatively | condescend | embankment |

| 9 | 10 | 11 |
|---|---|---|
| conscientious | zany | galore |
| isolation | jerkin | rotunda |
| molecule | nausea | capitalism |
| ritual | gratuitous | prevaricate |
| momentous | linear | risible |
| vulnerable | inept | exonerate |
| kinship | legality | superannuate |
| conservatism | aspen | luxuriate |
| jaunty | amnesty | piebald |
| inventive | barometer | crunch |

## The Cloze Reading Test

Another efficient approach to material-referenced reading assessment is to convert representative passages from the material under concern to the *cloze* testing format as developed by Taylor.[49] The usual procedure for doing this is to select 250-word passages and to substitute an underlined blank of ten spaces for every fifth word, producing a fifty-item test. The pupil's task is to fill in the missing word. Only responses identical to the deleted words (not synonyms) are accepted as correct—which makes scoring much easier and creates no significant loss of assessment value. Misspellings of the correct (exact) word replacement are disregarded as long as the intended word can be recognized.

An optional procedure is to leave the first and/or last sentence intact, although Bartoo's research results suggest that the use of preparational contiguous sentences or contextual paragraphs has little effect on cloze results.[50]

Cloze reading test scores tend to correlate in a moderately high positive manner with scores on standardized reading tests, multiple-choice test scores over the same passages, readability formula results, and informal reading inventory results.[51-53] Evidence rather consistently reveals that cloze test percentage of accuracy (2 times the number of correct word gestalts in a 50-cloze-item passage) falls lower than the percentage of accuracy on multiple-choice items for the same passage. It is not surprising, therefore, that lower cloze criteria scores are associated with functional reading levels than those for comprehension question accuracy. The relationship of cloze to other reading and readability measures is summarized below.

| Cloze Score (%) | M-C Score (%) | IRI Functional Level | Readability Placement |
|---|---|---|---|
| 38 | 50 | | |
| 40 or less | | Frustrational | |
| 44 | 75 | | (Fry) |
| | | | (Dale-Chall) |
| 40-55 | | Instructional | |
| 57 | 90 | | |
| 60 and above | | Independent | |

Cloze tests may be used to determine the general or literal comprehension of a particular selection. They have not been particularly useful in assessing specific interpretive behaviors.[54,55] They may be used for determining the readability of selections — if a representative or random sample of readers is employed and if the median-most cloze passage of the multiple-passage samples taken is used as the criterion passage for each source. A considerable amount of research and discussion has focused on the cloze procedure since Taylor introduced it in 1953. Robinson has compiled a useful annotated bibliography on the nature and use of *cloze* procedure.[56]

An example of a cloze test selection, with the first sentence intact, is given on page 202 and serves to illustrate some of the generalizations made earlier about comparative reading assessment. The article from which this test selection was taken had a style and content representative of social science literature. It was placed at a low eighth-grade readability using the Dale-Chall formula. The cloze test passage was administered to a random group of tenth graders from a school whose pupils consistently perform above average on state reading and math achievement tests. The average percentage of accuracy obtained by this tenth-grade sample on this cloze passage of eighth-grade readability was 42 percent or at the lower end of the instructional spread. The range of cloze scores for this sample ran from a low of 22 percent (clearly frustrational) to a high of 56 percent (nearly independent level).[57]

## CLOZE TEST

While New York and Boston were still struggling villages, Port Royal had many of the features of a great metropolis. Rich houses, as elegantly _furnished_ (1) as any on earth, _were_ (2) jammed along Queen's Street, _where_ (3) real-estate prices were higher _than_ (4) in central London. Although _their_ (5) charges were astronomical, the _town_ (6) supported silversmiths, goldsmiths, wigmakers, _and_ (7) dealers in choice goods _and_ (8) wines.

Contemporary descriptions of _life_ (9) in Port Royal varied _according_ (10) to the prejudices of _the_ (11) speaker. One writer likened _it_ (12) to "a continual fair," _while_ (13) another found it "a _den_ (14) of all filthiness." Since _pirates_ (15) were creators of the _great_ (16) prosperity, and big spenders _as_ (17) well, everything catered to _their_ (18) tastes. It was estimated _that_ (19) there was one tavern _for_ (20) every ten inhabitants. After _a_ (21) particularly profitable raid at _sea_ (22), a pirate might scatter _as_ (23) much as two or _three_ (24) thousand pieces of eight _for_ (25) a single evening's entertainment.

_Dueling_ (26) was common and murders _were_ (27) frequent. Occasionally a pirate _would_ (28) be brought to trial, _but_ (29) since other pirates were _usually_ (30) on the jury, no _more_ (31) than a few minutes _were_ (32) needed to get a _not guilty_ (33) verdict. Street-corner evangelists warning _that_ (34) the city was doomed _got_ (35) no more than laughter _from_ (36) the pirates.

Even after _England_ (37) signed a peace treaty _with_ (38) Spain and agreed to _outlaw_ (39) piracy, Port Royal continued _as_ (40) the richest city in _the_ (41) New World. Then the _prophesied_ (42) doomsday arrived. June 7, _1692_ (43), dawned clear, bright, hot. _Then_ (44) about 11:30 the ground _began_ (45) to move and the _earthquake_ (46) began. It caused such _great_ (47) destruction that most of _the_ (48) survivors were eventually prompted _to_ (49) leave and found a _new_ (50) city called Kingston.

## Informal Reading Inventories

Informal reading inventories (IRI) are, in effect, power reading tests which sample silent and/or oral reading performance on targeted materials. Like the cloze test, they are constructed upon selections from specific or representative sources, and it is this referencing which gives them notable usefulness in reading assessment. In its usual form, the IRI consists of one or more strands of reading passages (plus associated questions) drawn from successive levels of a developmentally sequential set of readers, workbooks, or textbooks. One major purpose of the IRI is to identify the pupil's most realistic functional reading levels (independent, instructional, frustrational) according to the criteria identified earlier. A second purpose is to use the reading and question response performance to gain insight concerning specific instructional needs. The IRI format and procedure also can be used to determine how well the pupil can cope with particular content textbooks.

### Diagnostic Uses

When used as a diagnostic tool, the IRI usually is administered individually and consists of a silent reading strand of test selections and a parallel strand of equivalent oral-reading test selections. Sometimes an abbreviated IRI is performed using oral passages read without prior preparation. Unless the specific purpose is to obtain some supplementary insight about how the pupil deals with words in context (recognition, analysis, and fluency), one should be wary of using the isolated oral test with adequate or better secondary pupils. It does not provide a realistic assessment of the pupil's silent reading performance with upper-level materials. Moreover, most normal-progress secondary readers will have developed reasonable mastery of context, word skills, and oral fluency. The use of oral-reading-passage performance to supplement silent-reading-passage performance does make it possible to use the word recognition criteria to identify functional reading levels as well as to supplement the comprehension check on the silent passages with that on the oral passages.

For greater diagnostic insight, one or two additional parallel strands of reading passages may be utilized: one to assess functional listening level (the highest level the pupil can listen to and answer approximately 75 percent of content questions accurately); another for rechecking results, to further analyze specific weaknesses, or to determine how well the pupil handles the selection when instructionally prepared for it. Comparison of the pupil's listening level with his instructional level, derived from performance on the silent-reading passages or from combined oral and silent reading performance, produces an operational estimate of how well the pupil's reading achievement approaches his functional reading potential. This assumes that the listening-level measure is a valid indication of the pupil's receptive language potential, of course. When multiple strands are used for combined or comparative assessment, it is essential that the parallel passages be of equivalent readability or difficulty as well as representative of materials of that level.

### Basic Procedure

The key steps in the procedure for developing and using an individual silent-oral IRI are presented below. More detailed information is provided by Johnson and Kress,[58] and in the sources identified in the annotated bibliography by Johns et al.[59]

*1.* Meaningful reading passages, 100 to 250 words in length, are taken from approximately the middle of each reading source, so that a string of passages is formed representing successive reading difficulty over the span that seems useful. Passages ranging from third- through twelfth-grade level comprise a reasonable span for most secondary assessment purposes; an IRI used for diagnosing secondary problem readers might utilize passages from first- through eighth-grade readers. Additional sets of sequential passages (e.g., for assessing oral reading or listening performance) should be of parallel, equivalent difficulty; the use of contextually contiguous passages from each source usually is an efficient way to achieve consistency in parallel passages.

*2.* Ten to fifteen questions over the meaning of the passage and which draw equally upon literal and inferential interpretive behaviors should be developed. The questions for parallel-level passages should be of equivalent form and difficulty. Questions for higher-level materials should sample higher reasoning processes. For individually administered inventories, short-answer and brief-analysis questions are practical. Group silent inventories will find true-false and multiple-choice comprehension items more feasible. A general purpose or question for directing the initial reading of the selection and one or two questions for assessing rereading are optional. A tryout and revision of passages and questions often improves the long-range validity of the inventory.

*3.* Reproduction of the passages, questions, and a summary rating sheet will facilitate the recording of results by teacher or examiner. Reproducing the passages read by secondary pupils is acceptable if the reproduction is of good legibility, and permission is gained from the copyright holder. Some specialists prefer the pupil to read the actual copy. This can be done by machine duplicating (with author/publisher permission) or by removing the passages from the original source, mounting them on oak tag or in acetate, and placing them in a looseleaf binder. Group silent IRI's and questions probably will need to be retyped and reproduced, and care should be taken that the type is readable and the copy quite legible.

*4.* The usual procedure for administering the individual IRI is first to administer the listening strand intact, if a listening level ("reading capacity") is to be determined. The examiner reads aloud each passage and its comprehension questions and records the pupil's response to the comprehension check. It is better to begin listening test passages at a level where the pupil is quite likely to achieve 100 percent success and move up to the level where he does no better than 75 percent accuracy (on two successive selections, if in doubt). After the listening level is established, the silent-reading passage at the level assumed to be independent reading for the pupil is given, followed by the oral-reading passage

of the same level. This pairing of silent and oral passages of the same level is continued until independent, instructional, and frustrational functional-level identifications have been made.

*5.* Recording and analysis for the silent-reading selections consists of assessing correct responses and determining the percent of accuracy ($10 \times$ number correct, if ten questions are used). Determining the rate of silent reading is an optional procedure (words in the selection divided by the seconds of reading time multiplied by 60 equals the words per minute); it can be a useful additional measure of comparative difficulty. Most upper-grade pupils read faster silently than orally, and a reversal of this tendency may be symptomatic of reading problems. Also, one would expect rate to decrease gradually after the pupil reaches instructional reading level and drop noticeably when he reaches frustrational-level reading. If it does not, one might suspect either inflexible reading habits or lack of attention to meaning and purposeful reading. The examiner can note unusual reader symptoms of stress, vision problems, etc. while the pupil reads silently. Comparison of the pupil's comprehension error patterns (e.g., details, main ideas, literal-inferential, analytical reading) over those passages above independent level, but below frustrational level, may reveal specific interpretive tendencies and needs.

*6.* Recording for the oral-reading selections consists minimally of (a) checking or drawing a line through each word mispronounced (proper nouns excluded); (b) determining the comprehension accuracy over the ten questions; (c) calculating the word accuracy (e.g., 12 word errors on a 120-word passage would produce a 90 percent word accuracy score, i.e., $108/120 = .90$, or 90 percent), and (d) determining the oral reading rate over the selection as in determining silent rate (e.g., $120 \div 30$ seconds $\times 60 = 240$ wpm).

Reading specialists and experienced teachers often prefer a more detailed marking system and use a code such as the one given on page 205. A summating of error patterns over the selections read thus can be made an analyzed for instructional significance.

H = brief hesitancy, but pronounced correctly

*P = pronounced word for pupil after 5-second block

*~~conceit~~ = mispronunciation (response written phonetically) [*sin/kit* written above]

*roman~~(ing)~~ = omission of word or part of word

*ready ~~in~~ time = substitution of word or word part [*any* written above]

Jump boys! = reversal of word

the gang = repetition [*R* written above]

thirt~~y~~ = self-correction (cross out response corrected) [*thirteen* written above]

above/the/ground = phrasing markers, e.g., word-by-word reading

*As a rule, only definite word recognition difficulties are counted as errors in determining the percentage of passage word accuracy.

7. An example of a marked oral-reading passage is presented below. This is an eighth-grade selection on which the pupil has performed with instructional-level competency: eight countable word recognition errors = 158/166, or 95 percent word accuracy and a comprehension accuracy (four half-errors) of 80 percent. The countable word errors are numbered. It will be noted that all variant responses are recorded for analysis of patterns, but only those definite errors in word recognition (excluding proper nouns) are counted to determine functional reading level.

The equivalent-level silent reading or listening selection would take similar but unmarked form. Indeed, if care is taken to select highly similar parallel passages for the oral, silent, and listening strands, they can be used interchangeably. However, some professionals find it advantageous at upper-grade levels to use somewhat shorter selections and more factual recall comprehension items for the oral-reading passages and longer selections with questions which place greater stress on interpretive reasoning for the silent selections.

## OPERATION SUNSHINE

The Arctic ocean/is an/ice-covered/body/of water, five times/the size of/the Mediterranean Sea,/lying ~~atop~~ our planet./Unlike the/Antarctic area/which is mostly solid earth covered/ by ice and snow,/the Arctic/is completely fluid. The Arctic ice-pack/covering the ocean/is not/a totally/solid layer/of ice,/as generally pictured,/but rather/it is composed/of huge chunks/and floes,/varying greatly/in size/and thickness,/grinding/one/upon the/other,/ creating the effect/of a/solid/mass. Here and there/are leads,/or cracks/in the ice,/and ~~polynyas,~~/or fairly large/open stretches,/sometimes/referred to/as Arctic ~~lagoons.~~ The ice-pack/is/in/almost constant ~~motion,~~ and in winter time,/in sub-zero weather,/it reaches/far down the coast/of Greenland on the eastern side,/and the Bering Strait/on the western side.

It is a de~~solate,~~ cold,/barren,/inho~~spitable~~/place,/which for decades/has ~~fascinated~~/ explore~~rs,~~/adventure~~rs,~~/and more recently,/defense experts.

**Comprehension Check**

MI*  ½X. What is the central topic of this passage? (" Arctic and Antarctic areas.")

SD    2. Where is this land area located? (" It is above Canada — Arctic is the far north.")

SD    ½8. What is the main difference between the Arctic area and the Antarctic area? ("Ice. The Antarctic is mostly solid earth, and the Arctic is mostly ice and water.")

V    ½X. What does the word "leads" mean in this story? (" Paths in the ice.")

V    ½8. What does the word "polynyas" mean in this story? ("Open lagoons — water area.")

SD    6. Is there anything in this passage that tells you how large the Arctic Ocean is? ("It is bigger than the sea. It is five times the Mediterranean Sea.")

SD    7. Who has been interested in the Arctic Ocean? (" Adventurers, scientists, and army - military.")

Inf.    8. What kind of personality should a volunteer have to live in the Arctic? ("Someone tough - physically and a hermit type - someone interested in trying something different — maybe in studying it.")

*MI, main idea; SD, stated detail; V, vocabulary; Inf., inferential interpretation; Anal., analytical interpretation.

Inf.     9. Why isn't Greenland always located in the Arctic pack? *("It moves, floats; it goes back to the warmer weather.")*

Anal.   10. What is the purpose of this selection—a scientific analysis, a description, or to tell a story?

*(" Description.")*

(4 ½-errors = 80% accuracy)     Grade eight level     Total words = 166

---

*8.* The resulting data are analyzed and summarized. Figure 14 is a partial summary sheet for George R., a tenth-grade male who established an independent level at the sixth-grade level, instructional at the eighth, and frustrational at the tenth. However, his listening level was established on eleventh-grade material, suggesting that he may be underachieving in reading by two or three years.

*Summary comment.* George seems to encounter a number of unfamiliar words at levels 7 and up. He has difficulty dealing with these and also makes some recognition errors on familiar words. He frequently is able to correct these errors after analysis. His oral and silent comprehension difficulties seem to be associated with difficulty with word concepts more than with any particular reasoning

---

*Figure 14*   *Summary of IRI results.*

Test form: ___H Series___     Student: ___George R.___

Grade placement: ___10th___     Date: ___10/4/75___

| Passage Level | Listening Comprehension (%) | Silent | | Oral | | | Functional Level |
|---|---|---|---|---|---|---|---|
| | | Comprehension (%) | Rate | Comprehension (%) | Word (%) | Rate | |
| 12 | 60 | | | | | | |
| 11 | 80 | | | | | | Listening |
| 10 | 80 | 60 | 108 | 50 | 83 | 140 | Frustrational |
| 9 | 90 | 70 | 195 | 70 | 92 | 175 | Instructional (max.) |
| 8 | 100 | 70 | 210 | 80[a] | 95[a] | 180[a] | Instructional |
| 7 | | 80 | 230 | 80 | 97 | 185 | Instructional (easy) |
| 6 | | 100 | 280 | 90 | 98 | 195 | Independent |
| 5 | | 100 | 310 | 100 | 100 | 215 | |

[a] Results obtained on "Operation Sunshine" selection.

processes. He tends to become overly cautious in his attack and more literal in his interpretation as he encounters some word difficulty with a passage. George comes from a family of minimal educational background and does very little personal reading. He likes wrestling, cars, and girls. The results suggest that George is underachieving in reading by two or three years and is capable of improvement with special help on vocabulary-related concept development, recognition accuracy, and a program of wider reading. George is more likely to understand and learn from textbooks at seventh- and eighth-grade levels and will need considerable teacher preparation and guidance if the texts are ninth grade or higher in reading difficulty. (*Note:* This summary is based upon the analysis of all selections read.)

### Group Silent IRI for Assigning Materials and Comprehension Analysis

Secondary teachers, particularly those teaching content classes, are more likely to make use of a group silent IRI. A group IRI consists of a collection of passages and related sets of questions such as in any silent-reading survey test, except that each passage is material-referenced—being drawn from either the instructional sources available for that class or drawn from content area materials or differentiated reading levels. These test selections in reproduced form are administered to all the members of the class or group. Sufficient time to read and answer the questions is necessary. An additional vocabulary test consisting of ten words for and representing each passage level of difficulty adds further substance to the assessment.

From such data, the teacher can gain an initial idea of the range of text difficulty levels needed by the class as well as an identification of those pupils who will need considerable help with reading assignments. If the IRI includes comprehension questions representative of the reading-thinking tasks of the class, it may help the teacher identify those skills for which the pupils will need instructional preparation.

## IMPROVING CLASSROOM OBSERVATION AND INFORMAL ASSESSMENT

Charting the status and developmental patterns of pupil reading behavior improves with frequent observation, assessment, and descriptions of varied pupil reading performance, habits, attitudes, and interests. Classroom observation and informal assessment can provide many useful data concerning these matters.

### Fulfilling Particular Assessment Functions

Classroom assessment should not take the place of the careful, objective, and normative measures of achievement provided by standardized reading tests. Rather, its purpose is to complement standardized survey assessment by contributing description and measurement of pupil specific reading skills and knowledges, of pupil progress toward short-term objectives, of pupil mastery of criterion behaviors, and of pupil application of reading to functional learning tasks. While classroom observation and assessment should emulate the professional qualities of standardized testing, it need not try to duplicate its functions.

Observation and assessment of classroom-related reading behavior presents the teacher and reading specialist with a good opportunity to add specific information about the day-to-day performance of the pupil. It is, perhaps, the most valid source of data about how the pupil copes intellectually and emotionally with classroom reading-study situations, with extended reading assignments, with the effect of instruction upon short-term improvement in reading-study-thinking behaviors, how well he learns concepts and processes by instructional media other than reading, and about his differential content area reading performances.

### Conditions Influencing Classroom Assessment

Classroom observation and assessment incur some limitations for reading evaluation which should be recognized and hedged against. One key factor here is the degree of teacher preparation. Accuracy and pertinency of resulting data are dependent upon the extent to which the teacher understands reading behavior, is personally objective, makes systematic observations, and develops some mastery in constructing reasonably valid and reliable assessment measures.

Reading performance is often situation-oriented. Although highly competent students and emotionally stable readers seem able to perform consistently well in most school reading circumstances, the performance of less capable readers, borderline students, and pupils with high anxiety levels or motivational problems can be inhibited by the classroom environment, the teacher's personality, or even the textbook employed. Even adequate readers are susceptible to difficulty in reading content for which they have minimal background understanding of related concepts and processes. It is useful to note when reading-study difficulties seem to occur only in certain classroom settings. Unless repeated observations provide evidence that these problems occur with other textbooks and in other instructional situations, one should be wary of drawing general conclusions such as: "This pupil has a serious reading problem" or "Reading disability is a major cause of this pupil's classroom learning difficulty" or even "This pupil lacks motivation to do work-study reading." Such statements would be more defensible and more useful if they were qualified by "as revealed in this classroom" and "Observation in this reading-study situation suggests...."

### Collective Staff Effort

Classroom observation and assessment of reading behavior in most secondary school situations is in need of considerable improvement. After securing sincere teacher interest in the problem, probably the most helpful step is for the staff, individually or collectively, to engage in formal or in-service training in the process, instruction, and evaluation of reading and the development and use of class-room assessment procedures. Accuracy in description and evaluation improve with the number and variety of assessment observations. Observation improves when it is guided by specific purpose and example.

***Developing a school reading checklist.*** To this end, the reading coordinator (reading committee or a department faculty) might develop a basic checklist or rating scale by which each classroom teacher would be aided in the types of reading-study behavior deserving special attention, workable means of observation or assessment, and encouragement to assess reading-study performance on a systematic basis. Each teacher or department could develop additional items which reflect reading-study behaviors needed for the particular content area.

Such checklists greatly enhance pupil evaluation in course-learning achievement and progress and provide the teacher with substance for making pupil referrals for special help and for contribution to team study of pupil cases. By systematically collecting and collating these checklists, the reading specialist, school counselor, or designated adviser can develop a broad source profile of the pupil's classroom reading-related performance and behavior.

## Improving Classroom Tests of Reading

A *test* may be defined broadly as any controlled situation in which a stimulus is presented to the subject with the intent to elicit a response which is systematically recorded and evaluated against predetermined functional or normative criteria. Although teachers may not think of classroom tests in these terms, they do have many opportunities to structure such assessment situations. No classroom test should attempt to meet all of the reading evaluation functions of the program. Nor is it likely that a particular test content and format will lend itself equally well to the assessment of all reading behaviors or evaluative functions. Thus, it is important that the classroom teacher first determine the general purpose and specific objectives of the test and then construct or select the test form and items which will best meet that purpose and those objectives.

As we have seen, reading tests may be used to compare the performance of more than one pupil (normative-referenced) or to determine the pupil's mastery or degree of mastery of a particular reading behavior or knowledge (criterion-referenced). Classroom-developed reading tests are more likely to be criterion-referenced, although there is no reason why a criterion-oriented test cannot be used to compare the performance of different pupils. Whether criterion or normative in referent use, the teacher would do well to emulate published standardized tests in their pursuit of accuracy, efficiency, validity, and reliability.

### The Various Forms of Classroom Tests

A classroom reading test can take any of a number of forms, depending upon its purpose(s). With reasonable control and appropriate structure, the following serve to illustrate the range of acceptable formats for classroom reading tests: a dictionary usage worksheet; a quiz over the meaning of selected prefixes; writing a one-paragraph personal interpretation of the meaning of a poem; matching a list of restated topic sentences with a given set of paragraphs; sorting a set of sentence cards according to the topics they support; locating and reading orally the sentences or passages which answer certain questions; listing the pages upon which selected topics are explained in a text; completing a crossword puzzle of key vocabulary and definitions; filling in an incomplete outline of the organization of a selection read; and carrying out a list of written directions.

Since secondary school reading and its instruction tends to be concerned with the understanding of material read silently in group situations, the most common pattern for classroom tests of reading interpretation is some variation of the "reading passage followed by questions" pattern illustrated by the standardized reading test sources noted

earlier. The questions can precede the selection if one is concerned with the selective location of meaning. The questions may follow the selection in such a way that the examinee cannot reread the material, if the purpose is to assess recall as well as understanding of meaning. The statement of the question can determine the type of thinking-interpretative process to be assessed. The relationship of instructional question form to reading interpretation was discussed in Chapter Six.

### Improving Question Construction

A checklist formulated by Selltiz et al. will be helpful to teachers concerned with improving reading test questions.[60]

1. Is this question necessary?
2. Is the point already sufficiently covered by other questions?
3. Should the question be subdivided?
4. Does the question adequately cover the ground intended?
5. Does the question contain difficult or unclear phraseology?
6. Could unintended emphasis on a word or phrase change the question meaning?
7. What type of question—multiple-choice, true or false, etc.—is most suitable?
8. Is the form of response easy, definite, uniform, and adequate for the purpose?
9. Do earlier questions create a set that might influence this particular question?
10. Do preceding questions aid the recall of ideas that bear on this question?

The teacher should vary the mode of pupil reading test response. Oral and written free and structured response questions sample accuracy of larger recall and permit insight into the reader's qualitative thinking, affective response, and expressive language power. Usually, reading test questioning takes an objective form, employing multiple-choice, true-false, or matching-type item responses. The objective pattern of tests lends itself to broader survey of multiple behaviors or knowledges; permits greater precision of control of the specific interpretive thinking the reader needs to employ; is less dependent upon the reader's proclivity to verbatim recall; is more efficient per unit of time; is less confounded by the subject's writing difficulty or hesitance; may be scored more efficiently by pupil, teacher, or aides; and provides additional opportunity to assess and reinforce the central behavior of concern—silent-reading interpretation. The fact that objective reading tests are by nature print-referenced material helps them avoid those common pitfalls of content tests, such as overemphasis of recall, mastery of lesser details, and abstract verbalization.

Some direct consideration of the relative values of different test-item types will aid in test construction. The following suggestions offered by Noll are representative of those presented by texts in educational measurement.[61]

*Multiple-Choice Items:*
1. Probably the most important skill in making multiple-choice items is in the framing of alternatives. One choice must be clearly the best, but the others must appear plausible to the uninformed.
2. A multiple-choice item should not have more than one acceptable answer.
3. The choices in an item should come at or near the end of the statement.
4. The best or correct answer should be placed equally often in each possible position.
5. Choices should be in parallel form wherever possible.
6. Choices should fit the stem grammatically.
7. The length of the item and the length of choices should be determined by the purpose of the item.
8. The number of choices in multiple-choice items should be at least four; the generally preferred number is five.

*Short-Answer Questions:*
1. Select and state the questions in such a way that they can be answered with a word or a short phrase.
2. Select and phrase short-answer questions so that only one or a very small number of answers will be correct.
3. The item should consist of a rephrasing of the idea or point being tested, or an entirely original statement of it.
4. Short-answer questions are useful primarily in testing knowledge of facts and quite specific information.

*Completion Questions:*
1. Omit only significant words from the statement.
2. Avoid negative statements wherever pos-enough clues to enable the competent person to answer correctly.
3. In scoring short-answer and completion items it is generally most satisfactory to allow one point credit for each blank, unless the item requires several words or a phrase.

*True-False Items:*
1. Do not include more than a single idea in one true-false item, particularly if one idea is true and the other is false.
2. Avoid negative statements wherever possible.
3. An approximately equal number of true and false items should be used.
4. Avoid long, involved statements, especially those containing dependent clauses, many qualifications, and complex ideas.
5. Use the true-false form only with statements or ideas which are clearly and indubitably true or false as stated.

### Fitting Question Form to Reading Assessment Purpose

The reading test should employ that structure and item type which best suits its purposes. True-false items should be limited to the understanding of particular significant facts and generalizations explicitly stated and considered true (at least within the context of the reading selection). Short-answer items are better restricted to specific verbal or numerical answers, and thus are efficient means of assessing skimming, scanning, and other locational-type reading skills. Matching items are most useful when the association to be made is direct and unambiguous.

Matching items that involve three- or four-way comparison will prove confounding to pupils with lesser mental ability and should be avoided unless that is the reasoning behavior to be assessed. Multiple-choice items lend themselves to the widest range of interpretive and assessment functions of the objective-response items. The "best answer" multiple-choice item lends itself to evaluative, inferential, and critical reading interpretation. Essay-response items, those requiring a response of one or more sentences, lend themselves to the assessment of the abilities to respond creatively, organize, reconstruct, or reorganize information and recall with minimal aid. Essay-responses are enhanced or restricted by the pupil's verbal and writing skill and are more susceptible to subjective evaluation and thus to lesser reliability.

Test construction is not a simple skill. The serious teacher becomes competent in it through training and practice. Reading and content teachers alike should consult basic sources on classroom test construction, if their professional training has not included specific experiences in this activity.[62] Examples of classroom reading tests pertinent to the evaluation and instruction of specific reading behaviors are presented in Chapters Nine through Twelve.

# REFERENCES

1. Miles A. Tinker, *Bases for Effective Reading* (Minneapolis, Minn.: University of Minnesota Press, 1965) p. 254.
2. O. K. Buros, *Reading Tests and Reviews* (Highland Park, N.J.: Gryphon Press, 1968).
3. Roger Farr, *Reading: What Can Be Measured?* (Newark, Del.: International Reading Association, 1969) pp. 225-99.
4. Roger Farr and Edward Summers, *Guide to Tests and Measuring Instruments for Reading* (Bloomington, Ind.: ERIC/CRIER-USOE, 1968).
5. W. Blanton, R. Farr, and J. J. Tuinman, *Reading Tests for the Secondary Grades* (Newark, Del.: International Reading Association, 1972).
6. M. S. Johnson and R. A. Kress, *Informal Reading Inventories* (Newark, Del.: International Reading Association, 1965).
7. Ruth G. Viox, *Evaluating Reading and Study Skills in the Secondary Classroom* (Newark, Del.: International Reading Association, 1968).
8. David H. Russell, "Evaluation of Pupil Growth in and Through Reading," in *Reading in the Elementary School*, Forty-eighth Yearbook, Part II, of the National Society for the Study of Education, Nelson Henry, Editor (Chicago: University of Chicago Press, 1949) p. 284.
9. B. F. Skinner, *About Behaviorism* (New York: Alfred A. Knopf, Inc., 1974) pp. 47-48.
10. M. A. Tinker and C. M. McCullough, *Teaching Elementary Reading*, Third Edition (New York: Appleton-Century-Crofts, 1968) p. 340.
11. Ruth Strang, *Reading Diagnosis and Treatment* (Newark, Del.: International Reading Association, 1968) pp. 63-75.
12. Eugene Jongsma, *The Cloze Procedure as a Teaching Method* (Newark, Del.: International Reading Association, 1971) p. 18.
13. Ruth Strang, *Diagnostic Teaching of Reading* (New York: McGraw-Hill Book Company, 1964) p. 4.
14. N. S. Metfessel, W. B. Michael, and D. A. Kirsner, "Instrumentation of Bloom's and Krathwohl's Taxonomies for the Writing of Educational Objectives," *Psychology in the Schools* 6 (July, 1969) pp. 227-31.
15. Irene Athey, "Reading Research in the Affective Domain," in *Theoretical Models and Processes of Reading*, H. Singer and R. Ruddell, Editors (Newark, Del.: International Reading Association, 1976) pp. 352-80.
16. J. E. Alexander and R. C. Filler, *Attitudes and Reading* (Newark, Del.: International Reading Association, 1976).
17. L. Ball, *Assessing the Attitudes of Young Children Toward School* (Washington, D.C.: Department of Health, Education and Welfare, 1971).
18. D. P. Scannell et al., *Tests of Academic Progress: Reading* (Boston: Houghton Mifflin Company, 1964).
19. H. F. Spitzer et al., *Iowa Every-Pupil Tests of Basic Skills, Test A: Silent Reading Comprehension* (Boston: Houghton Mifflin Company, 1964).
20. Roger Farr et al., *The 1973 Iowa Silent Reading Tests* (New York: Harcourt Brace Jovanovich, 1973).
21. Farr et al., *ISRT: Guide for Interpretation and Use*, Level 1, p. 36.
22. Wayne Otto, "Evaluating Instruments for Assessing Needs and Growth in Reading," in *Assessment Problems in Reading*, W. MacGinitie, Editor (Newark, Del.: International Reading Association, 1973) pp. 14-21.
23. W. H. MacGinitie, "An Introduction to Some Measurement Problems in Reading," in *Assessment Problems in Reading*, W. MacGinitie, Editor, pp. 1-8.
24. F. P. Davis, "Psychometric Research on Comprehension in Reading," *Reading Research Quarterly* 7 (Summer, 1972) pp. 628-78.

25. Robert L. Thorndike, "Dilemmas in Diagnosis," in *Assessment Problems in Reading*, W. MacGinitie, Editor, pp. 57-68.

26. J. G. Beard, "The Comprehensibility of High School Textbooks: Association with Content Area," *Journal of Reading* 11 (December, 1967) pp. 229-35.

27. George R. Klare, *The Measurement of Readability* (Ames, Iowa: Iowa State University Press, 1963) pp. 222-47.

28. Klare, *The Measurement of Readability*, p. 1.

29. Klare, *The Measurement of Readability*, p. 18.

30. Jeanne S. Chall, *Readability: An Appraisal of Research and Application* (Columbus, Ohio: The Ohio State University, 1958).

31. Barbara Seels and Edgar Dale, *Readability and Reading* (Newark, Del.: International Reading Association, 1971).

32. G. R. Klare, "Assessing Readability," *Reading Research Quarterly* 10, No. 1 (1974-75) pp. 62-103.

33. W. A. McCall and L. M. Crabb, *Standard Test Lessons in Reading* (New York: Bureau of Publications, Teachers College, Columbia University, 1925, 1950, 1961).

34. R. D. Powers et al., "A Recalculation of Four Readability Formulas," *Journal of Educational Psychology* 49 (April, 1958) pp. 99-105.

35. John R. Bormuth, "Readability: A New Approach," *Reading Research Quarterly* 1 (Spring, 1966) pp. 79-132.

36. Klare, *The Measurement of Readability*.

37. Klare, "Assessing Readability."

38. Edgar Dale and Jeanne Chall, "A Formula for Predicting Readability: Instructions," *Educational Research Bulletin* 27 (February, 1948) pp. 37-54.

39. R. D. Powers et al., "A Recalculation of Four Readability Formulas," *Journal of Educational Psychology* 49 (April, 1958).

40. Karl Koenke, "Another Practical Note on Readability Formulas," *Journal of Reading* 15 (December, 1971) pp. 203-8.

41. R. T. Williams, "Table for Rapid Determination of Revised Dale-Chall Readability Scores," *The Reading Teacher* 26 (November 1972) pp. 158-65.

42. Dale and Chall, "A Formula for Predicting Readability: Instructions."

43. Rudolf Flesch, "A New Readability Yardstick," *Journal of Applied Psychology* 32 (June, 1948) pp. 221-33.

44. Edward B. Fry, "A Readability Formula That Saves Time," *Journal of Reading* 11 (April, 1968) pp. 513-16, 575-78.

45. G. H. McLaughlin, "SMOG Grading—A New Readability Formula," *Journal of Reading* 12 (May, 1969) pp. 639-47.

46. Emmett Betts, *Foundations of Reading Instruction* (New York: American Book Company, 1957) pp. 443-54.

47. S. E. Taylor et al., *A Revised Core Vocabulary*, Bulletin No. 5 (New York: EDL Laboratories/McGraw-Hill Publishing Co., 1969).

48. Margaret LaPray and Ramon Ross, "The Graded Word List: Quick Gauge of Reading Ability," *Journal of Reading* 12 (January, 1969) pp. 305-7.

49. Wilson S. Taylor, "Cloze Procedure: A New Tool for Measuring Readability," *Journalism Quarterly* 30 (Fall, 1953) pp. 415-33.

50. Roy K. Bartoo, "The Effect of Cumulative Context upon Cloze Test Performance of Tenth Graders," doctoral dissertation, State University of New York at Buffalo, 1975.

51. John R. Bormuth, "The Cloze Readability Procedure," *Elementary English* 45 (April, 1968) pp. 429-36.

52. E. F. Rankin and J. Culhane, "Comparable Cloze and Multiple-Choice Comprehension Test Scores," *Journal of Reading* 13 (December, 1969) pp. 193-98.

53. Donald O'Brien, "An Investigation of Relationships Existing Between Cloze Form Measures of Reading Comprehension and Behavior Determined by the Reading Inventory Technique and Standardized Reading Test," doctoral dissertation, State University of New York at Buffalo, 1973.

54. Janet L. Prange, "An Investigation of the Relationships Obtaining Between Cloze Test Measures of Reading Performance and Measures of Critical Reading, General Reading, Intelligence, and Sex," doctoral dissertation, State University of New York at Buffalo, 1973.

55. Kathleen T. McWhorter, "The Influence of Passage Organizational Structure upon Two Estimates of Readability," doctoral dissertation, State University of New York at Buffalo, 1974.

56. Richard D. Robinson, *An Introduction to the Cloze Procedure* (Newark, Del.: International Reading Association, 1972).

57. Roy Bartoo, *The Effect of Cumulative Context upon Cloze Test Performance*.

58. M. S. Johnson and R. A. Kress, *Informal Reading Inventories* (Newark, Del.: International Reading Association, 1965).

59. Jerry L. Johns et al., *Assessing Reading Behavior: Informal Reading Inventories. An Annotated Bibliography* (Newark, Del.: International Reading Association, 1977).

60. C. Selltiz et al., *Research Methods in Social Relations* (New York: Henry Holt and Co., 1959).

61. Victor Noll, *Introduction to Educational Measurement*, Second Edition (Boston: Houghton Mifflin Company, 1965), pp. 139-56, passim.

62. R. L. Ebel, *Measuring Educational Achievement* (Englewood Cliffs, N.J.: Prentice-Hall, Inc., 1965).

## SUPPLEMENTARY SOURCES

Blanton, William E., Roger Farr, and J. J. Tuinman, Editors. *Measuring Reading Performance.* Newark, Del.: International Reading Association, 1974.

Buros, O. K. *Reading Tests and Reviews.* Highland Park, N.J.: Gryphon Press, 1968.

Farr, Roger, Editor. *Measurement and Evaluation of Reading.* New York: Harcourt, Brace and World, Inc., 1970.

Farr, Roger. *Reading: What Can Be Measured?* Newark, Del.: International Reading Association, 1969.

Johns, Jerry L., et al. *Assessing Reading Behavior: Informal Reading Inventories,* An Annotated Bibliography. Newark, Del.: International Reading Association, 1977.

Johnson, M. S., and R. A. Kress. *Informal Reading Inventories.* Newark, Del.: International Reading Association, 1965.

Klare, George R. *The Measurement of Readability.* Ames, Iowa: Iowa State University Press, 1963. Also, "Assessing Readability." *Reading Research Quarterly* 10 (1974-75) pp. 62-103.

Robinson, Richard D. *An Introduction to the Cloze Procedure,* An Annotated Bibliography. Newark, Del.: International Reading Association, 1972.

Seels, Barbara, and Edgar Dale. *Readability and Reading,* An Annotated Bibliography. Newark, Del.: International Reading Association, 1971.

Viox, Ruth G. *Evaluating Reading and Study Skills in the Secondary Classroom.* Newark, Del.: International Reading Association, 1968.

# III

# READING INSTRUCTION

# EIGHT

# Fundamentals of Reading Instruction

*The secondary developmental reading program is concerned fundamentally with the continued refinement and development of the more mature aspects of the self-same types of abilities that were being refined and developed in the elementary school.*

Guy and Eva Bond

*Overview*  Chapter Eight is concerned with basic reading instruction as it should be executed in developmental and corrective reading settings, and as it may be employed incidentally in content classrooms and in adjusted forms in supplementary service situations. The chapter presents eight guidepoints for effective reading instruction, a model for reading instruction, a structure for teaching specific reading behaviors, the major tasks of developmental reading instruction, and seven broad approaches to developmental reading instruction utilized in middle, junior, and senior high schools: basic reading series, neobasic reading series, component reading systems, multiple-skills programs, autoinstruction, language-experience instruction, and individualized reading. These fundamentals of instruction serve to coordinate the operational use strategies of secondary reading development presented in Chapters Five and Six with the tactics for improving specific reading behaviors presented in Chapters Nine through Twelve.

## IMPLEMENTING READING INSTRUCTION

A brief review of the differential functions of reading education, reading instruction, and developmental reading instruction will place the concepts presented in this chapter in better perspective.

*Reading education* includes any short- or long-term experience which contributes usefully to learning those general and specific behaviors needed to deal effectively and satisfactorily with the essential printed sources of one's cultural situation. Reading education may take place informally as well as formally; semiconsciously, incidentally as well as through conscious, systematic exposure. The reader is indebted to the whole of his life fabric for the sources of his reading education.

However, it has been our experience that a series of unorganized informal incidents of reading education do not produce a society capable of reading printed language. And we come to realize that it takes more than six years of consciously planned school reading–learning experiences to produce the reading competence and maturity necessary for the survival of the individual with a complex society and perhaps for the survival of that society.[1] To this end, this text recommends that *formal reading education* provide every secondary pupil with planned experiences in four essential areas of reading: systematic instruction in the essential developmental behaviors of reading, instruction and guidance in content area reading, extended independent reading, and reading evaluation and assessment. In addition, pupils with special needs will need supplementary reading–learning services.

The concept *reading instruction* when unaccompanied by some further delimitation refers to planned teaching and reinforcement of reading behaviors—knowledges, attitudes, and skilled performances—wherever they may occur within the school setting. This will include such reading instruction as conducted within the content area classroom to facilitate content area learning and application. When successful, all such instruction contributes to the reading development of the pupil, in the sense that it helps him progress toward reading maturity, regardless of whether it occurs in developmental, corrective, or remedial situations. Much of the content of this chapter, as well as Chapters Five and Six, applies to the reading instructional circumstances wherever it occurs in the secondary school.

*Developmental reading instruction* will be used to refer to those class or center situations administratively targeted to carry major curricular responsibility for the ongoing development of essential behaviors of reading as determined by the scope and sequence of the reading curriculum and the learning needs of the pupil.[2] The premises and practices of general reading instruction certainly apply to developmental reading instruction, and adjusted developmental reading instruction serves as the core of most corrective, remedial, and compensatory reading programs.

Reading behavior develops along a general continuum toward that level of maturation evidenced by our better readers and thinkers. This reminds us, in the words of Bruner, that "instruction is, after all, an effort to assist or shape growth" and that "intellectual development depends upon a systematic and contingent interaction between a tutor and a learner."[3] To this end, the teacher and pupil benefit from structure in the form of a scope and sequence of curriculum.[4] Instructional materials and established procedures can exert negative as well as positive influence upon pupil development; for that reason, they need to be chosen and used selectively to implement the objectives of the program, the unit, and the lesson.

The improvement of specific skilled behaviors is a vital responsibility of developmental reading instruction, but hardly the whole of it. A balanced, meaningful program of instruction in developmental reading will find as much use for general strategies of utilizing and structuring the purposeful reading of text (Chapters Five and Six) and for broad developmental approaches of systems (this chapter) as it does for the techniques of improvement of specific reading behaviors (Chapters Nine, Ten, and Eleven).

## Guidepoints for Effecting Reading Instruction

Human learning being the product of many variables, no rule of instruction is without its exceptions. Yet some conditions of instruction bear so consistently upon the nature and degree of the learning product that they deserve careful consideration by teachers. Classroom experience augmented by research reveals that certain teaching factors do increase the effectiveness of reading instruction.[5] Other conditions seem to inhibit instructional success. The following guidepoints or working principles are worthy of special recognition when planning or carrying out instruction in reading. It should be noted that most of these guidepoints are relevant to secondary reading education, wherever encountered.

*1. A direct and continuing relationship should exist between the objectives, the content and procedures, and the evaluation of reading instruction.* Objectives are essential to productive instruction; they motivate, guide the selection of materials and teaching procedures, and serve as criteria for evaluative feedback to the pupil and to the instructor.[6] Too often, the purposes for developmental reading lessons or specific reading activities are defined too vaguely to serve instructional-learning needs. It may be useful to "read the selections in the book" in serial order or to assign the "next three pages" in the workbook—but much will depend largely upon how these selections and exercises are instructionally handled and whether those materials meet the specific learning needs of the pupils involved.

Growing professional concern is being focused upon the need to determine instructional objectives in a more advantageous manner. One major issue is to develop classroom teachers' recognition of their responsibility for the development of viable specific instructional objectives which are melded with instruction and evaluation into a continuous coordinated process.[7] A key point in this concern is to get teachers to differentiate between teacher behavior (e.g., to teach the vocabulary of a selection) and desired pupil behavioral outcomes (e.g., to recognize the form and to understand the meaning of the target words in the selection); that is, the teacher's own instructional operations are the enabling means, while the identified learning objectives consist of the specific concepts, skills, or attitudes to be mastered by the pupil as a product of those teacher operations. Similarly, course and curriculum developers need to state broader learning objectives in terms of the specific behaviors for which the pupil should demonstrate terminal mastery.[8]

The specific relationships among objectives, instruction, and evaluation are depicted later in this chapter, as are major objectives or continuing functions of developmental reading instruction. The general and specific behaviors of mature reading presented in Chapter Three are converted readily to terminal behavioral objectives pertinent to basic reading instruction.

*2. The usefulness of a reading instructional approach or activity is determined by how well it helps the pupil master the immediate function of the lesson while contributing to the pupil's long-range reading development, reading attitudes, and personal well-being.* Reading instructional activities should be planned, executed, and evaluated on a pragmatic basis. They will include those general approaches, specific methods, and instructional materials which best satisfy ultimate and immediate instructional goals. There are numerous instructional activities which can be employed in the reading teaching situation. The teacher will need to choose those which provide greater instructional utility.

Neither research nor practice has established the "one best way" to handle reading instruction. Other things being the same, the most successful programs in reading instruction will give appropriate and systematic attention to each of its major functions, will be flexible and eclectic in instructional strategy, and will employ those specific tactics, activities, and materials which best accomplish the targeted objectives. Reading instruction in the secondary school may be implemented successfully by a variety of program formats and specific instructional activities.

However, some instructional activities are better choices for a particular situation in that they: (a) provide a greater probability of success with a wider range of pupil ability; (b) provide a greater probability of success for pupils with special learning needs; (c) are more readily adapted to a variety of instructional objectives; (d) satisfy multiple reading or learning objectives; (e) are more readily understood or independently handled by the pupil; (f) are more efficiently prepared and effected by the teacher; (g) require less in the way of expensive materials and equipment; (h) are more economical of pupil time and energy; (i) require less specialized training on the part of the teacher; and (j) contribute to the pupil's ongoing motivation to read and to learn to read.

Some approaches, methods, and materials will meet these criteria more often than others. Moreover, some of these criteria should be weighted more heavily in some situations than others. There is no adequate substitute for intelligent, experienced teacher judgment in determining the usefulness of a reading instructional activity in the specific learning situation. These criteria should facilitate instructional choices among several possible activities.

*3. The pupil learns to read through reading activity, and whenever appropriate, reading instruction should be conducted so that the pupil spends the majority of instructional time in direct contact with print.* This principle often has been ignored.[9] Cohen cites evidence that over half of reading instructional time in some elementary school settings is spent in pupil listening to oral reading or to teacher verbalization.[10] Observation of those secondary teaching settings where reading serves as a pivotal mode of learning (e.g., literature classes) reveals that the great majority of class time is consumed in nonreading activity.[11] Classroom and school routine mechanics and teacher susceptibility to verbalization have an insidious way of usurping reading instructional time. Moreover, this lack of contact with printed language usually is accentuated for those who most need it—the less able and reluctant reader.

Basic reading instruction should be dominated by active pupil participation in purposeful, meaningful silent reading. This does not suggest that the ideal reading lesson consists of continuous, intensive, or monotonous involvement in independent reading or worksheet practice. Reading learning is facilitated by teacher explanation and demonstration, by pupil questioning and discussion, as well as by a number of group and individual reading-related activities. Good instructional planning provides for pacing in reading activity: reading activity interspersed with nonreading learning activity, high-intensity reading interspersed with less stressful reading activity, short- with longer-term reading tasks, and independent individual reading with whole-class and special-group reading activities.

Segmented skills instruction is susceptible to the isolation of reading instruction from meaningful reading activity. The perfection of performance on specific subskills of reading has its place in developmental and general reading instruction, depending upon the needs of the pupils, but it hardly should be treated as a singular or dominant program emphasis. Materials, exercises, and instructional procedures aimed at the development of specific reading behaviors are necessary factors of reading instruction. But such experience should be incorporated in or correlated with meaningful silent reading of interest, as well as with applicational reading in which the particular skill serves a useful function.

Moreover, contact with printed material is not a sufficient condition of reading instruction in itself. The learning conditions under which the pupil has contact with print in the instructional circumstances are of considerable importance, as we have seen. There are many useful ways and settings by which this instructional interaction with printed material can be offered. Improved teacher planning and administration of the reading instructional period, controlling the size and selection of instructional groups, and providing for sufficient number and variety of reading instructional materials are key factors in increasing reading activity in reading instruction.

*4. Structure in the form of preparation, guidance, and reinforcement of learning is vital to the development of those skills, knowledges, and attitudes which comprise the essential operations of mature reading performance.*[12] Failure to recognize the difference between independent personal reading and reading instruction explains the indifferent results of laissez-faire forms of reading programs. Even "individualized" approaches to reading instruction provide for teacher-pupil interaction.[13] Instructional intervention may be effected in different ways: direct teacher interaction with pupils, study guides, worksheet exercises, structured extended reading assignments, programmed learning materials, automated devices, the use of teacher aides, etc. In this, the advice of Ernest Horn is particularly cogent: "There is no substitute for the teacher, either in stimulating and guiding the student's efforts or in correcting and perfecting the ideas that he forms."[14]

A corollary to this guidepoint also deserves recognition: *the mastery of specific reading behaviors will involve direct and specific provision for original learning and overlearning [retention] of those behaviors.* This corollary carries two implications sometimes overlooked in the reading instructional situation. The first is that the specific behaviors of reading interpretation, reading flexibility, study application, and the like are not learned automatically from nontargeted, generalized reading activity. These specific processes require direct and sequential instructional attention to make sure that every pupil can understand and use them. The second implication is that such instructional intervention goes beyond initial introduction and guidance of the skill or knowledge. Adequate provision for corrective feedback and learning reinforcement must be provided to bring the specific behavior to a point of likely retention. This usually requires provision of delayed reinforcement as well as immediate use in meaningful learning situations.

*5. The execution of reading instruction should recognize the existence of individual pupil differences in learning ability, needs, and interests.* Individual differences in potential, learning patterns, and performance exist in all areas of pupil behavior, and they are readily evident in pupil reading performance. Unfortunately, actual classroom adjustment to individual differences in learning has lagged behind verbal recognition that such differences do exist, particularly at the secondary school level.[15] Many traditional instructional practices have been forged by classroom experience into reasonably useful unilevel instructional tactics, but they may not be appropriate to all pupils at the same moment of instruction. Instructional adjustment to pupil differences in learning potential, experiential background, and stage of reading development admittedly takes planning and activity not required by whole-class instructional approaches. Differentiated reading instruction is not beyond the competence of the sincere secondary teaching professional, however. Principles and strategies for differentiating reading instruction are discussed in Chapter Thirteen.

*6. Reading instruction should incorporate a variety of instructional activities, materials, and reading situations.* Judicious use of diversity in reading instruction contributes to a number of reading-learning objectives. (a) It stimulates pupil involvement; a monotonous routine is deadly to pupil motivation. (b) Variety is essential to the differentiation of instruction needed for adjustment to individual differences. (c) Learning transfer is facilitated by reading instruction which reflects the varied uses of reading in school and life. (d) Different learning objectives are satisfied by different instructional approaches and tactics.

Close teacher guidance of pupil reading of a textbook or workbook selection may be an excellent vehicle for accomplishing some instructional purposes, but not all. The learning of locational skills should involve the use of dictionaries, newspapers, encyclopedias, etc. The teaching of critical reading skills calls for the guided reading of written sources of opinion, propaganda, and advertising. It may include researching the past publishing record of an author, a journal, or a company; or it may involve multimedia presentations, e.g., comparing the effect of the same speech on videotape, an audiotape, and in written form.

Variety in reading instruction begins with the development of the curriculum and the selection of instructional materials. After this, instructional variation is achieved through the planning and execution of the reading lesson. There will need to be a certain core of consistency in instructional organization and procedure, of course. But in the long run, daily lessons should reflect a judicious balance of reading approaches and resources selected to implement the ultimate and immediate instructional objectives of the program. Inflexible reliance upon a particular ready-made commercial reading program reflects educational naiveté and/or insecurity in teaching. An unstructured hodge-podge of incidental, teacher-made exercises and activities is hardly preferable. Reading instructional diversity should be generated naturally by the varied purposes and tasks of reading instruction.

*7. The reading materials employed in reading instructional activity are pivotal to the success of that activity.* The experienced reading teacher finds ways to modify available instructional reading materials or otherwise adapts them through instructional procedures to meet the needs of the instructional situation. Pupils are capable of a certain amount of tolerance where instructional materials are concerned. But there are certain limits to such adaptation by pupil and teacher. Generally, the long-term and immediate objectives of basic reading instruction are more readily accomplished when the materials used meet three criteria: (a) the content holds some topical value and interest for the pupil; (b) the pupil can decode the basic meaning of the material; and (c) the structure and substance of the material are appropriate to the reading behaviors to be developed.

*Materials of appropriate difficulty.* Each bit of reading done by the pupil in the instructional set-

ting provides an opportunity to add to his accumulative competence in attacking printed content in a meaningful manner. How well the pupil understands the meaning of that content will exert some influence upon how well he learns the skills developed in that lesson. Consider a lesson which is concerned with developing the interpretive ability to detect sequence in a writer's argument. To carry out the processes of the lesson, the pupil first must read a short selection containing an argumentative sequence. The next step of the activity involves reading five statements in disarranged order which paraphrase the five key points of the writer's argument. Finally, the pupil must arrange them in the argumentative sequence employed by the writer. Unless the pupil gains a basic understanding of both the selection and the five statements, it is unlikely that he will profit from this lesson, and he may leave the lesson with a misconception of this particular interpretive skill. The general processes of reading, as well as the specific lesson objectives, are losers when instructional materials are beyond the pupil's present reading capabilities.

Teachers and writers of instructional materials typically underestimate the difficulty such materials can engender for the average and below-average pupil.[16] Teachers would do well to consciously compensate for this tendency. This does not mean that instructional materials must be bereft of conceptual substance and structure. There are many readable materials with enough substance to serve as interesting sources of instructional content.

*Relative and functional criteria of material difficulty.* How much difficulty can be tolerated in the reading material of a reading lesson will depend in part on how we use that material. In this regard, experienced reading professionals have found it useful to employ the general concepts of "independent," "instructional," and "frustrational" levels of reading difficulty, discussed in Chapter Seven, in selecting materials employed in the educational situation.[17]

How much difficulty can be handled will depend upon the reader's tolerance to anxiety, his strength of motivation for reading that material, and how we employ that material for instructional purposes.[18] Thus, if the reading lesson involves extensive reading of a self-directed nature, the material should serve some extrinsic or intrinsic need of the pupil and should approximate independent-level reading difficulty for that pupil. However, if this same material were to be read under teacher guidance, the teacher can assume some responsibility for motivation and can aid the pupil with some of the reading problems. Thus, the criteria of difficulty can be set at the instructional-level acceptability. This increase in difficulty is possible since it is assumed that teacher preparation for and guidance during the instructional reading of the material will result in higher levels of reader performance than if the pupil were on his own.

Some special and short-term reading instructional situations may employ materials more difficult than indicated by instructional criteria. For example, practice exercises in the use of word analysis techniques probably would face the learner with limited-length context in which unfamiliar words pertinent to analysis by those techniques would appear more frequently than would be desirable in general instructional context of an extended nature. As another example, the teaching of a reading-study attack procedure for dealing with a content area reading assignment might use textbook-type materials (usually more difficult than instructional criteria) to achieve realism and learning effect, i.e., to demonstrate how such a system can improve the reader's interpretive powers on materials of typical textbook organization and difficulty.

*Materials pertinent to the lesson objective.* Finally, the written content of a reading lesson or exercise should be selected to meet the objectives of that lesson. Beyond being readable enough that the pupil can grasp the concepts and generalizations presented, the content should be conducive to teaching the competency stressed in that lesson. If the lesson is concerned with teaching outlining as an interpretive behavior, the material should lend itself to an outline organization. If the lesson deals with the identification of propaganda techniques,

the instructional material should contain uses of those techniques. Too often, teachers attempt to use general narrative to teach interpretive skills more appropriately developed through expository or argumentative nonfiction. In this, everyone loses—the author, the pupil, and eventually, the teacher.

*8. The development and active use of a reading curriculum guide to organize the secondary program in basic reading instruction is advisable.*[19] Indiscriminate choice in and chance combination of specific instructional activities does not sustain efficient continuity in learning, nor does it assure balance in meeting the developmental functions of basic instruction. The construction and ongoing revision of a curricular plan for the coordination of instructional programs should help to provide needed scope and sequence in learning activity.

Such a curriculum for developmental reading instruction in the secondary school should be devised so that it: (a) articulates with other levels and phases of the reading program, (b) recognizes the evaluated needs and abilities of the pupils for whom the program is planned, and (c) draws upon and contributes to the instructional resources of the broader secondary school setting. It may be useful to model the curriculum upon a general plan devised by the state or by the central school system in order to get the program underway. In any case, it is beneficial to teacher education, staff cohesion, and program viability to systematically revise the plan, biennially if not yearly.

Whether original or adapted, the plan should give first attention to the identification of the major objectives of the program. It should show how these major outcomes are underpinned by enabling behavioral objectives. Recommended materials, general strategies, and illustrative specific procedures for the instructional implementation and evaluation of these objectives will increase its use and success. It would be advantageous for such a reading curriculum guide to account for the other components of the secondary reading program, in addition to detailing the developmental reading instructional effort.

A reading curriculum guide provides considerable instructional support to the less experienced teacher of developmental reading instruction. It should help the experienced teacher maintain a balance in instructional objectives and procedures. A reading guide helps to coordinate the instructional efforts of personnel in multiple-staff and multiphase programs. While a curriculum for developmental reading instruction should prevent idiosyncratic mismatch of instructional objectives, procedures, and materials, it should allow reasonable flexibility for the adjustment of instruction to pupil needs, for making use of relevant emergent instructional situations, and for creativity in teaching.

Suggestions for developing the reading curricular guide are offered in Chapter Fourteen.

## A General Model for Reading Instruction

The probability that learning will occur and be reinforced is increased significantly when basic reading instruction is guided by an instructional plan which coordinates the essential elements of instruction into a teaching-learning sequence. Kibler, Barker, and Miles have reported a model of instruction which is helpful in identifying the major dimensions to be considered in basic reading instruction.[20] The model, as revised in Figure 15, suggests that the component sequence which the teacher should consider in planning and effecting reading (or content) instruction should include: (1) the determination of *objectives* to be satisfied in that particular unit of instruction—preferably in the form of pupil behaviors to be learned and reinforced; (2) the use of tests and other *preassessment procedures* to determine (a) the present status of pupil mastery of the objective, and (b) pupil readiness to learn in terms of contributing skills, motivation, and learning capability; (3) the selection and activation of a sequence of individual/group learning *procedures*; (4) the *evaluation* of pupil mastery of the targeted behavioral objectives of the lesson through direct and indirect assessment procedures;

and (5) the use of that evaluation to provide *feedback* in the form of (a) reinforcement of effectively learned behavior, (b) modification of original objectives, (c) reassessment of pupil readiness, and/or (d) revision and reinstitution of a new instructional sequence to effect the original or modified objectives.

In this general plan, direct teaching activity consists of but one, albeit an important, component of instruction. Moreover, this instructional procedures component usually involves a combination of activities which call for teacher planning and action: (a) locating, selecting, or perhaps devising the necessary pupil learning materials; (b) preparing the pupils for learning by developing motivation and background; (c) clarifying pupil understanding of the desired behavioral outcome through such procedures as teacher or pupil demonstration, use of audiovisual aids, or an example product; (d) monitoring pupil learning activities—eliciting, guiding, assessing, modifying, reinforcing pupil learning responses through personal interaction or structured learning devices; and (e) providing for immediate and delayed practice or use of the behavior or learning product.

The type and number of instructional procedures or activities will vary with the complexity of the lesson objective and the instructional setting. The amount and degree of specific point-by-point instructional guidance needed will depend upon the present achievement and capability of the pupil or pupils. In general, prevailing school instructional practices underestimate the pupil's need for a cognitive grasp of the skill to be learned and for careful and specific guidance through the entire instructional sequence, including reinforcement beyond initial mastery of the skilled behavior.[21,22]

This model of instruction helps place basic reading instruction in broad perspective. The model and its component functions readily will be perceived as applicable to instructional units targeted on the learning of specific behaviors and involving direct and relatively short-term learning sequences (e.g., the sight recognition of certain words, identifying the topic idea of a paragraph, or using a book

*Figure 15    Instructional procedures component of general model of instruction.* [After R. J. Kimbler, L. L. Barker, and D. T. Miles, *Behavioral Objectives and Instruction* (Boston: Allyn and Bacon, Inc., 1970), p.17.]

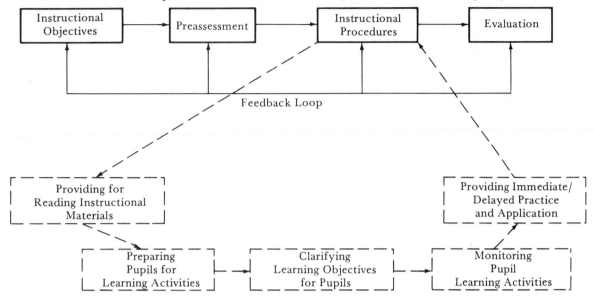

index to locate specific information). However, the usefulness of the model for implementing larger instructional sequences and longer-term multiobjective reading instructional units should not be overlooked. The components of the generalized instructional model are as applicable to guiding the reading of a selection (Chapter Six) as they are to developing a specific reading behavior (Chapters Nine through Twelve).

This model of instruction, then, serves as a general strategy for implementing reading instruction. The strategy holds: (1) that objectives and pupil capability should shape the choice of instructional materials, methods, and evaluation, not vice versa; (2) that the focus of instruction should be upon guidance of pupil learning activity rather than upon teacher verbalization; (3) that the guidance of pupil learning involves a planned methodological sequence of activities with more extended teacher-pupil interaction than one-shot instructional sessions; (4) that instructional procedures are drawn from a bank of possible teaching tactics in order to assure sufficiency, variety, and individualization of pupil learning involvement; and (5) that evaluation of pupil learning is an integral part of the instructional sequence, not a post hoc judgment of pupil worth.

## DESIGNATED DEVELOPMENTAL READING INSTRUCTION

The nature and place of designated developmental reading instruction as a component of the comprehensive secondary reading program were discussed in Chapters One and Four. Our concerns here are to review the major tasks or continuing functions of designated developmental reading instruction and to overview some of the more common general approaches used to package and deliver developmental instruction in grades seven through twelve.

## Major Tasks of
## Developmental Reading Instruction

Developmental reading instruction, as viewed in this text, refers to that strand of reading educational experiences in which instructional priority is given to the learning, retention, and application of the fundamental competencies of reading—those skilled behaviors, knowledges, and attitudes which form the essence of reading development as they are accumulated and integrated by the reader, and which enable him or her to cope with conventional varieties of written materials appropriate to present stage of maturity. The cruciality of these competencies, as necessary elements of successful reading behavior, argues for a designated responsibility for sequenced, direct instruction and practice to bring them to a state of mastery, as supplemented by those developmental reading learnings which accrue from effective reading instruction in the larger school experience.

> Studies of school progress of youth show conclusively that development in ability to read is continuous throughout elementary, high school and college years.... Furthermore, experience shows that satisfactory growth in and through reading occurs, as a rule, only when appropriate stimulation and guidance are provided in all school and college subjects that require reading.[23]

With the considerable number of reading competencies to be developed and with the unfortunate prevailing tendency to see reading as a series of separate skills, it is quite easy for the program of developmental reading instruction to be narrowly conceived in emphasis and lost in specifics. One way of counteracting this tendency is to step back and take the broad view of reading instruction—to identify those continuing objectives of reading instruction which serve the pupil's long-range development and which provide a base for building a structure of operational, specific, and shorter-term behavioral objectives.

For convenience, the major tasks of secondary reading development are restated here. These are the primary concern of developmental reading instruction, but they are appropriate to reading instruction in any setting. It will be understood that each task involves a cluster of reading competencies which the pupil should master. These fundamental tasks with their implication for developing corresponding pupil competencies identify the essential behaviors which comprise the scope of designated developmental reading instruction. Each should be incorporated in the planning and delivery of any developmental reading instruction curriculum.

1. To contribute to ongoing reading development by providing guidance in increasingly sustained purposeful reading in materials of "instructional" level difficulty.
2. To extend independence in the decoding processes by increasing sight vocabulary and by improving word- and sentence-reading competencies.
3. To deepen understanding of the writer's meaning by increasing competency in the various interpretive behaviors of reading.
4. To develop competency in the specific applicational and assimilative behaviors of reading which facilitate learning, problem solving, and creative activity.
5. To improve flexibility and efficiency in purposeful reading interpretation and thoughtful reaction.
6. To contribute to ongoing reading development by providing opportunity to engage in sustained independent reading in materials of independent-level difficulty.
7. To expand the pupil's range of reading interests and to establish habits of extended personal reading.
8. To develop sensitivity to and appreciation of honest and powerful literary sources which add to the reader's insight, inspiration, and fulfillment.
9. To contribute to the general mastery of language usage and, wherever feasible, to integrate the use of writing, listening, and speaking with reading activity.

*10.* To promote self-understanding and adjustment, and particularly to increase understanding and acceptance of reading, of school and other work-learning situations, and of others.

The degree of emphasis placed upon each will depend somewhat upon the needs of the individual or group and the nature of the broad reading education effort in that school. Ordinarily, the first five functions would receive some greater in-class developmental instructional priority. Responsibility for the second five functions would be shared with other strands of the secondary reading effort— reading utilization, extended independent reading, and reading evaluation. However, in schools where relatively little is offered in reading education other than in developmental or remedial instructional settings, notable provision within the basic instructional setting will need to be made for all of the functions. This, of course, places an awesome load upon the shoulders of the teacher of designated reading instruction. And this is why the comprehensive, all-school secondary reading program is needed for the development of reading maturity.

## Approaches to Developmental Reading

Reduced to its operational essence, reading instruction consists of helping pupils use written materials in such a way that they understand those materials and, at the same time, develop the competencies needed to handle those and other conventional sources in an increasingly mature and independent manner. Effective reading instruction makes use of various media of communication and learning, of course. Nevertheless, any realistic discussion of reading instruction must recognize the critical, even determining, role played by the written materials involved. What materials are employed and how those materials are employed largely determine whether reading instruction is effective or ineffective.

### Material-Oriented Approaches

In his overall reading development, the secondary pupil should have contact with and make meaningful use of a wide assortment of printed content. Illustrative here are textbooks, newspapers, encyclopedias, magazines, novels, telephone books, dictionaries, short stories, technical manuals, biographies and autobiographies, tabular and graphic representations, and verse. Many of these, such as the newspaper, in themselves provide variety of written content and related reading experiences. Each pupil experience with print is an opportunity to extend reading development, whatever the setting in which it occurs. The planned provision for meaningful use of a wide range of printed materials is a responsibility shared by all strands of the comprehensive secondary reading program. Certainly, acquaintance with and instruction in the purposeful use of varied written sources is a necessary element of developmental reading instruction.

While it is possible to build a curriculum of reading instruction geared entirely to the use of collateral reading selections, such an approach requires a considerable amount of instructional time, energy, and experience.[24] Two major problems encountered in collateral reading-centered instruction consist of (1) controlling the developmental scope and sequence of competency mastery, and (2) providing extended opportunity to read continuous text of an appropriate level of reading difficulty.

The intimate relationship which exists between the organization and procedures of reading instruction and the instructional materials available or employed to that end is not surprising. In the first place, reading instruction should be geared to preparing and guiding pupils in the materials they are reading. Less obviously, teaching theory and practice tends to be shaped by the instructional materials that are available.[25] The influence of instructional reading sources and their related manuals upon reading instructional approaches should not be underestimated.[26] Moreover, the influence of materials is felt in specific aspects of instruction as well as in general approaches, as the following quote from the Harvard-Carnegie survey of reading practices in the United States illustrates: "Many teachers devote the major part of each reading class to...activities...requiring answers which can be found in the text rather than those which call for reflective reading on the part of the readers."[27]

Reading instructional materials pertinent to the secondary school tend to fall into certain broad classifications. The most notable of these approaches includes instruction based upon or developed around: upper strands of basal-reader series; reader series of special orientation; published multimaterial reading systems composed of component strands; multiple-skills development programs; and to a lesser extent, the programmed instructional, individualized, and language-experience approaches.

Discussion is limited here to the general characteristics of each approach and the general nature of materials so utilized. However, an annotated bibliography of instructional materials is presented in Appendix D, and the association of an approach and the published materials which may be used to implement the approach can be made. Many of these materials also are useful in teaching the specific reading behaviors treated in following chapters.

Perhaps it should be noted that most of the approaches discussed below are not recommended as programs of developmental reading instruction in themselves. In the opinion of this writer, none is sufficient to encompass the ten major functions of developmental instruction, as identified earlier in this chapter. The various approaches of their component materials can be combined, however. When done so consciously and judiciously to meet instructional objectives, their strengths can be augmented, while the limitations of each can be minimized. Moreover, many of these materials, like those targeted for developing specific reading behaviors, can be adapted to support more than one approach or instructional objective.

### Basal Approach

Basal readers have been used extensively in elementary reading instruction since the mid-1800s.

Since McGuffey's day, the graded reading textbook has expanded into the modern basal-reader series with its correlated instructional materials and methodology. Surveys report that roughly 90 percent of current elementary reading instruction is oriented around basal readers, although other approaches to reading instruction have gained some greater recognition in the last decade.[28] Some basal-reader series extend upward to the eighth grade. While not as dominant as in elementary reading instruction, basal patterned reading texts are used in secondary reading instruction, particularly in seventh- and eighth-grade developmental reading programs, reading-literature core classes, and with special-interest instructional groups. Indirectly, basal-reader series and their instruction have exerted a large influence upon developmental reading materials and instruction at all levels. Thus, they deserve some particular consideration in this overview of approaches.

*Nature of basal-reader materials.* Whipple observed several decades ago that comparison of published basal-reader programs revealed notable variation.[29] That generalization continues to be valid. However, most major basal-reader programs are comprised of similar general components of instructional materials, even though these components may differ in content and emphasis. These include: (1) the *pupil's reader*, composed of instructionally oriented reading selections; (2) the *pupil's workbook* of learning exercises—some of these may introduce or guide the reading of the particular selection, but largely, they provide supplementary vocabulary and skills practice; (3) the teacher's *manual* or guidebook—which usually provides detailed suggestions for directing the reading of the selection, for using the supplementary materials, and for providing additional reading-learning activities; (4) *reading assessment aids* for placing pupils in appropriate readers, evaluating performance and progress, and diagnosing pupil difficulties—particularly as related to the basal-reader program; and (5) a variety of optional *supplementary instructional materials*, including wall charts, audiovisual aids, additional practice materials and games, and reading selections and books for independent, extended reading experience.

***Instructional theory.*** The theory of basal-reader instruction is founded in the concept that pupils develop reading competency as they are guided progressively through the reading selections and related activities of each basal reader. The fundamental instructional strategy is to "teach the reader selections," for which most series employ a systematic procedure much like that of the "guided reading lesson," discussed in Chapter Six of this text. One of the conditional assumptions of this approach is that the pupil should be "placed" in a reader which is appropriate in difficulty (instructional level). As traditionally practiced, the teacher does this placing, determines the reading selection assignment, and takes personal responsibility for directing the instruction.

Some modern basal series divide the six- or eight-grade program into a series of reader (reading text) levels to encourage within-class individualization and multigrade sequencing of reading material difficulty and instruction. Vocabulary and reading skills are introduced gradually according to the master plan—throughout each reader and throughout the series as a whole. Theoretically, the pupil matures in reading competency as he sequentially "reads" (with teacher guidance) his way upward from the readiness materials and preprimers of first grade to the sixth- or eighth-grade levels of materials. If a cobasal or supplementary reader system is employed, the pupil may read in more than one strand of readers at each level, as needed.

***Advantages and disadvantages.*** One can hardly evaluate materials for reading instruction without evaluating how they are used in instruction. The almanac, the newspaper, or a comic book are not prime materials for general reading instruction by some criteria; but as used by creative teachers for appropriate purposes, they can be highly useful. So it is with basal readers. Their strengths and weaknesses depend in large part upon how they are used

and upon whether one accepts the teacher-centered structure which is commensurate with the plan of most basal series.

Advantages frequently cited for the use of basal-reader series include: (1) reading materials of defensible quality treating varied topics and of reasonable interest to most pupils meeting the developmental norm for that reader level; (2) controlled introduction of vocabulary, syntactical structure, and related components of readability, leading to a gradual scaling of reading difficulty throughout the series; (3) a planned scope and sequence in the development of fundamental reading skills; (4) good articulation between instructional materials and instructional procedures; and (5) considerable instructional support provided in the teacher's guidebook and in the availability of supporting tests and materials. It is the combination of these advantages which explains the popularity of basal series.

Disadvantages associated with use of the basal reader relate both to its content and to its methodology. Some criticism has been directed at the literary quality of the reading selections, the social philosophies implicit in the content of the stories, the predominance of narrative, and the exclusive use of standard American cultural referents and language patterns. Recent basal revisions reflect attempts to adjust to these areas of critical reaction.

Methodological criticism of the basal-reader program includes its susceptibility to pupil boredom through repetition; its lack of flexibility; its emphasis on controlled development rather than on pupil self-selection of personal reading; its orientation toward group rather than individual instruction; its underdevelopment of advanced interpretive and work-study skills; the inclination of some series to tie their programs to a specific methodology; and, in some recent editions, the tendency of some series to overwhelm the teacher with a superfluity of instructional paraphernalia and direction.

All instructional materials have weaknesses, and the basal reading series is no exception. However, some of the criticisms of basal-reader instruction are directed more appropriately at those who use them. Basal readers and their accompanying materials need not be employed as rigidly as some criticism indicates. The teacher can use them in flexible groupings, as individualized reading materials, or in unit/problem study. Some recent basal editions provide correlated strands for independent and content-oriented reading usage. Basal series can be combined with other series (cobasal approaches) to provide greater variety in content, level, and skills instruction. Basal readers can be supplemented by a variety of independent reading materials, skill practice materials, and content-oriented materials. Reading educational authorities do not accept the basal-reader series as a substitute for a total program in basic reading instruction, let alone a total developmental reading experience at any school level.

*Basal-series extensions.* Most of these advantages and disadvantages apply as well to the seventh- and eighth-grade extensions of the basal series. There are some differences, however. Vocabulary and general readability are controlled less easily when dealing with more sophisticated content. The range of reading performance in a heterogeneous secondary class may extend seven to ten reading-grades, with pupil maturity and level of interest much above the content of lower basal levels. Hence, the advantages of controlled readability and appropriate instructional placement are less easily effected at the upper end of the program, although it is not impossible to find reasonable matches for most pupils if multiple levels of cobasal series are employed. Nevertheless, instructional grouping for greater individualization of basal instruction, so workable at the primary-intermediate levels, becomes more tenuous when the teacher works with a total of 100 to 130 pupils in four to six classes a day for forty or fifty minutes—a not uncommon scheduling practice in developmental reading among departmentalized junior and senior high schools. Also pupils who have had a steady diet of basal readers in the elementary grades may have developed some motivational resistance to their format and traditional approach by later middle and junior high years. That problem can occur with

the continuous use of any reading approach or materials, of course.

Recent basal-series editions have made greater provision for independent reading, content-oriented reading, and literary interpretation in their middle-upper grade programs. It is quite doubtful that such materials, in themselves, can provide either the breadth of content or range and reinforcement of specific-skills development needed by maturing readers. But it is not necessary that they do so. Responsible authors of basal-reader programs have resisted pressure to sell basal-reader series either as a total program or as a reading cure-all. Basal readers can be used effectively as the developmental core of instruction for some pupils and as supporting instructional materials for others. It will be recalled that 30 to 50 percent of junior high pupils will need instructional materials of a fourth- through eighth-grade reading difficulty.

*Special-function series.* A growing number of neobasal or semidevelopmental materials are being published for use in secondary reading situations. These tend to provide some developmental sequence in reading difficulty, content selection, and skills development. Several patterns may be identified: higher-interest-controlled, lower-difficulty readers; special-interest or special-group readers; and content-oriented readers.

As a rule, these special-function series do not meet rigorous criteria and should not be considered as equivalent to "basal" series. They do not provide the amount and range of reading content, the total program organization, or the degree of instructional support in teacher guidance or supplementary materials as will be found in the basal series. Most provide little systematic development of general reading skills. In others, vocabulary development is limited or inconsistent. Most do not provide for extended reading.

These reader collections may serve a useful place in basic reading instruction if their deficiencies are recognized and compensated. They provide useful supplementary reading or special instructional materials. Some are written in a highly interesting manner or are directed at the needs of special pupil groups. Frequently, the difficulty of these "readers" is controlled to mid-elementary grade levels. Thus, they can be valuable in getting problem readers or disadvantaged pupils to do sustained reading at instructional or independent levels. Some comprise literary-oriented reading-textbook miniseries and provide some useful compromise for English classes which combine reading development with more traditional English course objectives. A somewhat similar pattern consists of sequenced levels of reading-study instructional workbooks geared to one or more of the traditional content fields.

### Component Reading Systems

Component reading systems, as the label implies, include those somewhat comprehensive approaches to secondary reading instruction which are composed of the combination of relatively self-sufficient instructional elements; elements which may be used independently and usually targeted on the development of certain reading behaviors. Although a school or a teacher may develop the materials for a component system, usually they are purchased. Like hi-fi's, the component system may be purchased as a total package from a particular publisher, as selective combinations from a single publisher, or as components from several publishers and combined as program objectives dictate. Component systems share some of the same broad objectives and types of learning experiences as basal-reader series, except that they are less centrally organized and provide greater variety in types of reading materials and instructional formats.

The component reading systems approach is more adaptable to the larger secondary reading instructional setting than basal readers. The materials of the components usually have been developed with the instructional needs, reading levels, interests, and behavioral characteristics of the upper-school learner in mind. Component reading systems usually place greater emphasis upon multimedia aids and automated instructional hardware in delivering instructional experiences. The more comprehensive of these systems will include separate instructional components in listening, word perception and analysis, sight vocabulary, controlled continuous fluent reading and comprehension, selective flexible reading techniques and study skills, extended reading in graded-level paperbacks, and an instructor's manual for organizing facilities and coordinating instruction.

***Advantages and disadvantages.*** Like other approaches, these "systems" have some instructional weaknesses. Although they sometimes are sold as total programs of basic instruction at the middle, junior, and senior high school levels, most fall short of meeting total developmental program objectives. Published component programs, like other instructional materials, vary in quality. Treatment of interpretive and study skills is far from comprehensive in scope, and some systems tend to stress isolated, short-span reading instruction. The articulation between the instructional components or strands may be casual. The emphasized use of instructional hardware (projectors, tape recorders, etc.) focuses pupil attention upon mechanics rather than meaning, calls for adequate pupil sensory resources, and requires personnel with mechanical operation and repair skills. Depending upon which and how many components are used, they are expensive to purchase relative to other instructional materials.

On the positive side, component reading systems are adaptable to many instructional settings and organizations: whole-class groups, small groups, open-classroom centers, individualized instruction, and laboratory setups. They can be employed for both developmental- and remedial-designated groups comprising fairly wide ranges of reading-learning abilities. The reading content, the variation in instructional approach, and the greater independence of pupil reading and learning activity cater to the needs and motivation of reluctant readers. Selected components of such systems can be used to supplement other programs or can be combined with other reading materials and instructional activities to form an eclectic system of developmental instruction. Since the individual components usually have been developed to meet instructional objectives in certain areas, they are amenable to programs and approaches geared to specific behavioral objectives and performance criteria.

### Specific-Skills Programs

A number of publishers have produced materials which can be used to combine instruction and practice in two or more areas of specific reading behaviors. Most frequently, the competencies stressed include: vocabulary and word skills, comprehension or interpretation skills, reading rate and flexibility, and selected study skills. Usually these are packaged as boxes of graded and sequenced individual exercises, reproducible master copies of exercises, or in textbook-workbook form. The enterprising teacher or program director can form such combinations from separately published skills-development materials, of course. Multiple-skills development materials may be employed as an intact approach. They are used more defensibly as supplementary aids to instruction in specific skills.

Even when combined selectively and purposefully, the multiple-skills approach cannot be considered an adequate program of developmental reading instruction in itself. It fails to provide sufficient developmental reading experiences in many of the major tasks of basic reading instruction. The most notable deficiencies in this respect are lack of sequential guidance of developmental reading, extended independent reading, and composite transfer of reading skills to realistic problem-solving situations.

When skills-centered materials are not used as a component of or supplement to a broader instructional approach, they are susceptible to monotonous, isolated skills practice, which is not conducive to meaningful learning and application. Some multiple-skills development programs provide diagnostic placement tests, exercises at multiple levels of difficulty, and a built-in sequence of skills development. Most do not.

### Programmed, Computer-Based, and Automated Reading Instruction

The educational utopia envisioned by the most ardent supporters of the "new media instruction" a decade or more ago has not been realized. Nevertheless, programmed, computer-assisted, and automated instruction have made a place for themselves in progressive secondary schools.[30] They join textbooks, workbooks, films, slides, television, and chalkboards in the teacher's arsenal of available instructional resources.

*Programmed reading instruction.* Programmed instructional materials directly concerned with the teaching of reading have been developed in workbook, scrambled text, and machine-housed forms, but in far fewer numbers than more traditional reading instructional materials. Most of these "programs" have been targeted for less mature readers. Programmed reading instruction at secondary levels never gained the brief popularity enjoyed by programmed content area textbooks. Programmed reading instruction does represent a useful innovation in secondary reading, particularly as a teaching model or adjunct source of instruction, and deserves consideration in our present survey of approaches and materials of basic reading instruction.

Schramm has developed a succinct description of programmed instruction, as conceived by Skinner or Crowder:

> By programed instruction I mean the kind of learning experience in which a "program" takes the place of a tutor for the student, and leads him through a set of specified behaviors designed and sequenced to make it more probable that he will behave in a given desired way in the future—in other words, that he will learn what the program is designed to teach him.... The *program* is the important thing about programed instruction. It is usually a series of items, questions, or statements to each of which, in order, the student is asked to make a response. His response may be to fill in a word blank, to answer a question, to select one of a series of

multiple-choice answers, to indicate agreement or disagreement, or to solve a problem and record the answer. As soon as he has responded to the item, he is permitted to see the correct response so that he can tell immediately whether his response has been the right one. But the items are so skillfully written and the steps are so small between them that the student practices mostly correct responses, rather than errors, and the sequence of items is skillfully arranged to take the student from responses he already knows, through new responses he is able to make because of the other responses he knows, to the final responses, the knowledge, it is intended that he should command.[31]

Pressey views autoinstructional learning in a broader sense: it involves larger, more meaningful units of learning, permits the learner greater choice in response, and is considered to be an adjunct system of instruction.[32]

*Computer-assisted instruction.* The use of computers carries certain methodological and curricular implications for reading instruction. Neither programmed instruction (Skinner) nor autoinstruction (Pressey) should be considered as synonymous with the concept of computer-based instruction. The latter generally refers to the use of electronic data processing to aid teachers in selecting instructional activities for individual or group learning objectives. It involves the preidentification, categorization, and codification of resource units (instructional activities, content, and materials) which are recorded on computer tapes and retrieved selectively according to the instructional purposes of the teacher or instructional needs of the pupil.[33] Computer-based instruction is a matter of curriculum planning and effecting as well as an instructional procedure or activity. Computer-assisted reading instruction has been limited largely to the development of content area reading units.

*Automated reading instruction.* The purchase and use of reading instructional hardware provoked notable controversy among reading professionals a

decade or two ago, and some differences of opinion still exist.[34] *Hardware* in this instance includes the instructional use of mechanical or electronic devices for improving speed and accuracy of short-term perception (tachistoscopes, flashmeters); for presenting instructional information about reading and for skills practice (slide and strip film projectors); for improving reading rate and flexibility (reading films, controlled readers, individual reading pacers); and for improving reading-related language, listening, and word analysis competencies (record players, tape recorders, cassettes).

Much of the controversy over the use of machines in reading is associated with and confounded by professional attitudes toward narrow approaches to reading-rate improvement. The issue is raised here because such devices do appear with increasing frequency in the modern secondary classroom and do figure in developmental reading instruction, particularly in multimedia reading instruction and component reading systems. In themselves, mechanical devices and related procedures cannot fulfill the broad functions of basic reading instruction as viewed in this text.

Are they useful as supplementary aids? General reviews of research reveal that the use of machines to improve specific reading skills has produced equivocal results when compared to the use of assorted printed materials for such purposes.[35] They may do as well, however, for the improvement of visual and auditory perception and reading rate.[36] When used judiciously, they can motivate learners and provide the teacher with opportunities to vary and individualize instructional procedures. The purchase and use of reading instructional hardware should be decided by the same criteria employed in judging the value of any instructional aid.

In any case, we need not confuse the use of hardware with the end goal of reading instruction nor be confounded by our own views of social change. The technology of our age subtly permeates our lives. The educational sector of our society has dragged its heels in the utilization of technological advances which are readily accepted in business, govern-

ment, military, library, and even industrial operations. In time, no doubt, these will play a larger role
in reading as in other areas of instruction. Illustrative here is the presently neglected but potentially
powerful resource of computer-assisted instruction.[37]

***Judicious use according to purpose.*** Programmed learning, computer-supported instruction, and automation deserve consideration in
developmental reading instruction. Empirical evidence does not now suggest that they produce better
learning of secondary reading than the effective use
of other instructional approaches or materials.[38]
However, they do provide reasonable alternatives in
organizing and implementing basic reading instruction.

Programmed learning and automated instructional materials may be used effectively as additional ways to individualize reading instruction and
to facilitate more effective use of teacher instructional time and energy. To date, programmed
learning materials for reading instruction tend to
emphasize the teaching of vocabulary, decoding,
and the more basic interpretive and study skills.
Automated instructional devices and programs
have been useful in supporting a wider range of
reading instruction objectives. The use of each
presumes their selective adjunct instructional role
and the careful preparation of the pupil in how to
use them. The criteria for the use of either programmed learning or automated instruction are
much the same as for other materials and approaches to reading instruction.

### Language-Experience Approaches

Language-experience approaches consider reading to be but one part of language behavior and
development, and thus incorporate reading instruction within a larger structure of language instruction.[39] Most of the variant forms of this approach
draw heavily upon some common experience which
the group has shared (or the individual divulges) as
a basis for oral language interaction. The teacher,
teaching aide, or some designated student makes a

written record of all or selected elements of the
verbal productions of the individual or group. This
record, in turn, serves as the vehicle for reading and
rereading instructional activities. The assumed
basic instructional sequence therefore becomes: (1)
generating or evoking the memory of an experience, (2) stimulating thoughtful analysis of the
experience, (3) eliciting oral statements about the
experience, (4) recording these statements in print,
(5) utilizing this written record for reading practice,
(6) filing and reusing the record for independent
rereading and as the basis of vocabulary and skills
development. There are a considerable number of
language-related experiences which may be drawn
upon for such instruction.

As a developmental approach, the language-
experience approach is most commonly encountered in the early stages of reading and it gives way
to book-based reading instruction as soon as the
pupil can make this transfer. Lee and Allen[40] and
Stauffer,[41] among others, have published volumes
which present well-developed structures of theory
and practice for utilizing the language-experience
approach in this manner. As a developmental approach to early reading instruction, the pupil benefits from the easy transition from general activity to
meaningful use of language and the amount of
attention given to listening, speaking, and writing.
As a singular approach, it encounters such disadvantages as difficulty in control of scope and sequence of vocabulary and reading skills development, the heavy load it places upon the classroom
teacher for organization and evaluation of learning
experiences, and the early boredom of better readers with the mechanics of the process and the limited substance and quality of pupil-constructed
reading materials.

There are two plausible ways in which the language-experience approach to reading might be
used in the secondary school. First, as a supplementary or incidental approach to developmental instruction, it provides a ready vehicle for creative
writing-reading activities, for development of concepts in preparation to reading a difficult selection,
and for structuring organizational-critical thinking

skills lessons. Second, it lends itself to adaptation for compensatory reading instruction with disabled or disadvantaged readers. Fernald developed a variation of this procedure nearly forty years ago for use with pupils who were seriously blocked in mastering words and sentences.[42] Edwards has called attention to its compensatory value in instructing the culturally deprived,[43] and Becker[44] has discussed its use with Job Corps trainees. Abrams and Marshall have cited similar therapeutic and communication values of the method in teaching delinquent children.[45]

### Individualized Reading Approaches

Individualized approaches to reading instruction are applicational extensions of the concept that pupils learn best in terms of their own needs, characteristics, and development time clock.[46] The literature contains reports of a number of attempts to bring a somewhat systematic structure to developmental reading instruction at the individual pupil level.[47] Generally, these fall under one or another of three rubrics: "individualized reading," individually "prescribed" skills instruction, and "case study" diagnostic-therapeutic reading instruction for severely disabled readers. Since these approaches are discussed as approaches to aiding the different reader in Chapter Thirteen, only the major elements will be treated here.

*Case study instruction.* One-to-one *case study* reading instruction, in the fullest sense of the approach, consists of a microversion of the developmental reading program directed at the reading needs of the individual pupil.[48] Based on thorough individual diagnostic assessment and close teacher supervision, it attempts to provide for all of the continuing functions of the developmental reading program as adjusted to the resources and learning capabilities of the reader. It often assumes a clinical or special resource-center setting and is handled by a teacher trained and experienced in diagnosis and remediation.[49] As such, it becomes a relatively expensive instructional provision which secondary schools usually feel is justified only by the most

severe pupil reading-learning adjustment problems.

*Individually prescribed instruction.* Individually *prescribed* reading instruction covers a number of strategies for targeting reading instructional methods and materials to the specific momentary reading-learning needs of the pupil. The key elements consist of: (1) identifying individual pupil weaknesses on one or more of the competencies stressed in the instructional program; (2) "prescribing" needed learning experiences in terms of exercises and other activities geared to the needed behavior; (3) assisting the pupil, if necessary, in carrying out those learning activities; and (4) monitoring the pupil's progress in those and other needed skills. The varieties of individually prescribed reading instruction range from the broad operational structure and tenets recommended by Strang to the specific association and reinforcement of reading behaviors through programmed or semiprogrammed reading approaches.[50] The goals and principles of individually prescribed instruction can be transferred to the classroom reading situation. As can be seen, they are readily adapted to criterion-based reading instruction. Individually prescribed reading instruction tends to neglect the broader functions of developmental reading for specific skills development. It requires considerable planning and teacher ability.

*Individualized reading.* Of the three general patterns, *individualized reading* is the most widely recognized as a general classroom approach to reading instruction. In 1970, Sartain indicated that more than six hundred references had been published concerning its various manifestations.[51]

In its purest form, individualized reading is a conscious attempt to break away from teacher-dominated, instructional-materials-oriented reading instruction. It places considerable faith in the developmental learning power of reading as reading. The fundamental procedure stresses pupil self-selection, self-direction, and self-pacing in individual reading of a wide variety of materials. Usually, such plans call for teacher-pupil contact by means of the individual conference. Some variations call for short-term "ad hoc" skill instructional groupings based on the discussions and evaluations of these conferences. Other variations would call for a parallel program of systematic skills instruction. Individualized reading also may be employed as a strand or period of personal-recreational reading which supplements more directly the developmental teaching of reading through other approaches.

Support for the individualized-reading approach comes from its encouragement of positive associations with reading instruction and reading, the greater amount of actual reading done by the pupil, and the development of personal pupil responsibility for learning. Criticism has most often focused upon the overwhelming teacher workload in classes of average size; the inefficiency of classroom operations; the lack of scope and sequence in the development of vocabulary, concepts, and skills of reading, and lesser long-term learning progress when compared to more systematic approaches. There are a number of useful publications which present the pros and cons of "individualized" approaches to reading instruction.[52,53]

### Multiple Approaches to Secondary Reading Instruction

Eclectic or combination approaches to reading instruction are becoming more common at the secondary level.[54] Most authorities recommend a combination of the best features of group and individual procedures for reading instruction.[55] In some instances, instructional combinations are opportunistic: the product of administrative mergers or extensions of separate programs of instruction. One would expect some transfer, exchange, and general sharing of instructional strategies and materials to result from these coalitions.

More recently, eclectic approaches to reading instruction in upper schools are being initiated on a preplanned basis. To some extent, this is the result of a more dynamic role for the school reading coordinator.[56] In some instances, it is the product of team teaching combinations of reading and content area instruction. One of the most ambitious of these multiple-thrust efforts is Singer's report on a USOE project which involved a combination of approaches to the teaching of reading in junior high content areas: project-theme approaches to unit instruction; use of vocabulary, reading, and reasoning guides; language-experience utilization and enrichment; self-selection of paperback reading, and cross-ability or paired-pupil teaching.[57]

## A Structure for Specific Reading Instruction

Specific reading instruction as used here refers to the controlled teaching and reinforcement of such specific reading behaviors as locating needed words in the dictionary, identifying the implied (unstated) topic idea of a paragraph, or recognizing inconsistent use of facts to support a generalization. The improvement of specific reading performance is an essential element of secondary reading education wherever it may be encountered — in the developmental reading class, in corrective reading groups, in individualized remedial treatment, in the reading center, in the instruction of exceptional and disadvantaged learners, and in the content-oriented classroom. The general model of instruction presented in Figure 15 serves appropriately for structuring the teaching of specific reading behaviors. An adaptation of that model is presented here as a sequence of instructional phases.

The sequence is consistent with the psychology of learning and should be observed in most instances of specific reading instruction. However, it is not intended as an inflexible mechanism. The time and emphasis given to each step or phase, for example, should vary with the behavior to be mastered and the response of the learners. In creative instruction, the steps may be modified and telescoped. For example, if some pupils demonstrate mastery of the specific competency during the early phases of the instructional procedure, later steps can be shortened or eliminated. The final phases of providing for delayed reinforcement and application of the specific behavior should not be overlooked.

A number of teacher tactics and a variety of materials have proved useful in implementing each step. How many activities and the degree of stress placed upon them will vary with how readily pupils profit by that stage and upon the teacher's broader plan and personal teaching style. In general, varied implementation of each step will avoid repetitive monotony and should increase probable adjustment of the instructional step to individual learning differences, as well as greater transfer of the specific skill to wider-use situations. As in all aspects of instruction, nothing is more important than teacher experience, professional judgment, and creative impulse to make specific reading instruction interesting and effective.

The eight steps or phases comprising the organizational structure for teaching a specific reading competency are presented below. Each is followed by a brief identification and some general activities typically used to effect the step. Specific activities and exercises which illustrate ways to implement the instructional sequence for specific reading behaviors are provided in Chapters Nine through Twelve.

*1. Identify the specific competency [or competencies] which will serve as the target of the instructional sequence.* Whenever possible, state these in terms of pupil performance outcomes, e.g., "To be able to write a sentence accurately summarizing the topic idea of a short reading selection." Identification of the particular competency may be guided by a taxonomy of reading behaviors, a statement of course objectives, a "skills" scope and sequence presented in a curricular guide, or in the instructional materials accepted as a curricular guide. Or it may emerge from teacher observation of pupil need or difficulty in other learning activities.

*2. Preassess the present competence of pupil performance in using the targeted behaviors.* Differentiation of instruction begins here. Some pupils may demonstrate mastery of the specific reading competence and may be moved forward even to step 8 where emphasis is placed upon problem-

oriented independent application of the behavior. Other pupils will reveal such difficulty with the task that the teacher will need to provide instruction in those contributing knowledges, attitudes, and skills which comprise necessary readiness to perform the targeted competency. The preassessment of the specific competency should be as efficient as possible and take a form which is identical or nearly identical to the use of that behavior in actual reading circumstances. Chapter Seven suggested a number of general strategies which can be adapted to reading preassessment. Other specific assessment procedures may be adapted from exercises and activities presented in Chapters Nine through Eleven.

*3. Develop readiness to learn the competency.* Particular emphasis here should be placed upon pupil understanding and motivation. Terms may need explanation. Pupils should be made aware of the operational form of the competence and its several values and uses in school and life tasks. One advantage of developing specific reading behaviors as an adjunct of the guided reading lesson, of a content-related project, or of a problem-oriented reading unit is the rather natural way in which readiness for skill learning can emerge or be induced from this larger reading focus. Good instructional materials and curricular guides usually provide suggestions or activities for skill-learning readiness.

Preassessment (step 2) usually benefits pupil readiness, especially if the teacher is careful to explain the preassessment form, its meaning, and results to the pupil.

Readiness activities may include a review of essential contributing subskills necessary to performance of the specific targeted behavior. For example, in instructing how to outline the content of a short expository selection, the teacher should make sure that pupils are familiar with outline form and outlining principles as well as being able to differentiate main ideas, supporting ideas, and details in the selection. In any case, the instructor should not take for granted that pupils are ready and should supplement existing readiness as needed. Step 3 (readiness) leads quite naturally to step 4 (demonstration), and in many cases the two steps may be melded.

*4. Demonstrate the mechanics and operational use of the specific competency.* The beneficial impact of cognitive grasp of a behavior or of the principles which bear upon a behavioral performance has been reaffirmed by nearly fifty years of psychological research.[58] Unfortunately, too many teachers and prepared programs of instruction assume that the operational mechanics of performing a specific reading competency are self-apparent or self-explanatory. A whole-part-whole demonstrational "walk-through" of how to carry out the competency should give most pupils the understanding necessary to guide the development of skilled response. The teacher should be wary of depending too heavily upon verbal description to provide understanding of skilled processes. Iconic or enactive demonstration often is clearer and more efficient for these purposes.

The provision of a simple, step-by-step skill-execution guide by which pupils can follow and carry out the teacher's explanation and direction will aid "demonstration" activities. Another direct method takes the form of cooperative exploration; the teacher might say: "Here is how I go about locating a topic in an encyclopedia. You follow my actions and my thinking [given aloud] as I do it. Then, together we will see if we can identify and summarize on the board the most important steps in this process. After that, I will ask one or two of you to demonstrate how you would use those steps in locating information on another topic in the encyclopedia." Some commercial instructional materials provide creative activities for explaining and demonstrating the mechanics and uses of basic skills. A few companies have developed films, filmstrips, transparencies, tapes, and other multimedia aids which serve the needs of this step to some specific reading behaviors. (See Appendix E.) Creative teachers and departments have found it valuable to videotape selected demonstrations of those reading competencies considered significant to the curriculum and not supported by commercial aids.

*5. Provide guided practice in the performance of the competency.* This should follow *immediately* upon the completion of steps 3 and 4 to assure maximum initial success. Close teacher supervision and open communication between the teacher and pupils are essential here to avoid reinforcing an association between the task stimulus and an inappropriate behavioral response. A worksheet or study guide which structures the performance into easy operational steps will facilitate both classroom control and learning. It is most important that the pupils be able to concentrate upon the competency to be learned; thus, the reading-thinking tasks to be performed should not be proliferated beyond those absolutely necessary to the performance, and the reading difficulty of the materials employed should be on the independent side of instructional level for the pupils involved. Some pupils may need more than one guided experience in using the targeted behavior.

*6. Reinforce initial learning of the competency with independent practice in its use.* This should follow as soon after step 5 as possible to ensure efficiency in learning and greater retention. There are a number of ways in which such practice may be provided. A substantial segment of commercial instructional programs provide a variety of practice materials from which the teacher may select ready-made exercises which fit instructional needs. Some companies provide student materials to implement the entire skill instructional sequence. (See Appendix D for a selected listing of published materials which lend themselves to the practice and use of specific reading behaviors.) However, skills instruction should avoid dependency upon commercial exercises or programs.

Teacher or departmentally developed worksheets, study guides, practice exercises, and application activities provide reinforcement possibilities. They can be quite creative and are readily adapted to local pupils, local programs, as well as to the reading materials at hand. Frequently, such practice can be supplied in the form of group or individual games and puzzles to heighten motivation and to add variety. Using graded tests for such practice should be avoided, for it inhibits pupil exploration, limits pupil-teacher and pupil-pupil communication, and shifts attention from the process to be learned to the grade label assigned to the product. Feedback in the form of acceptable responses and discussion of encountered problems is necessary and should be available during or shortly after the completion of the practice activity.

7. *Assess pupil mastery of the competency after sufficient learning and practice opportunity has been provided.* One purpose for such assessment is to identify those aspects of the skilled behavior which are troublesome for a significant number of the class and which require some further large-group instruction and practice. A second purpose of this assessment is to identify those pupils with serious difficulty in learning the skill. Such serious difficulty may imply the need for reassessment of the pupil's state of readiness to learn the skill. It may suggest the need for a different approach to reinstructing the competency in individual or small-group settings. This assessment need not be formal; indeed, the teacher who works closely with an instructional group on the previous steps of the sequence has a good basis for evaluative judgment of pupil performance. If more structured assessment is desired, an alternative form of the preassessment test will provide a basis for determining group or individual growth.

8. *Build systematic delayed practice and transfer application of the competency into functional reading- or content-learning tasks.* Initial learning of a knowledge or skill seldom assures retention for later use.[59] Ordinarily the most efficacious pattern for providing delayed reinforcement is to make use of the competency regularly for the first several days after initial mastery and then to increasingly space the reinforcement sessions. The provision of additional practice and application is not limited to maintaining the early stages of mastery; most pupils can improve upon their accuracy, and all can improve upon the efficiency with which they employ the competency. Moreover, transfer of the use of the competency to broader problem situations usually requires instructional stimulus and guid-

ance. We may accept that the pupil nears mastery of a specific competency when he accurately, efficiently, and selectively employs it on a self-determined basis in repeated appropriate situations.

This structure for specific reading instruction serves as an appropriate conclusion to this chapter. In the past four chapters we have traced the issues of reading instruction from broader to ever more specific concerns: from improving the conditions whereby reading is utilized in any setting, to guiding pupil reading of larger text in any setting, to the conditions and approaches to developmental reading instruction, and now to a structure for teaching a specific reading behavior in any setting. The following chapters are concerned with tactics for improving various key specific behaviors of secondary reading. Such methods as suggested in those chapters are more meaningfully employed within the above structure for specific instruction.

## REFERENCES

1. Guy and Eva Bond, *Developmental Reading in High School* (New York: The Macmillan Company, 1941) p. 54.
2. R. J. Kibler, L. L. Barker, and D. T. Miles, *Behavioral Objectives and Instruction* (Boston: Allyn and Bacon, Inc., 1970).
3. Jerome S. Bruner, *Toward a Theory of Instruction* (Cambridge, Mass.: Harvard University Press, 1967) pp. 2 and 6.
4. G. W. Ford and L. Pugno, *The Structure of Knowledge and the Curriculum* (Chicago: Rand McNally & Company, 1964) p. 2.
5. Constance M. McCullough, "What Does Research in Reading Reveal About Practices in Teaching Reading?" *English Journal* 58 (May, 1969) pp. 688-706.
6. E. F. Lindquist, *Educational Measurement* (Washington, D.C.: American Council on Education, 1955).
7. Kibler, Barker, and Miles, *Behavioral Objectives and Instruction*, p. 3.
8. Robert F. Mager, *Preparing Instructional Objectives* (Palo Alto, Calif.: Fearon Publishers, 1962) p. 13.
9. Edward L. Thorndike, "Reading as Reasoning: A Study of Mistakes in Paragraph Reading," *Journal of Educational Psychology* 8 (June, 1917) pp. 323-32.

10. S. Alan Cohen, *Teach Them All to Read* (New York: Random House, Inc., 1969) p. 187.

11. James R. Squire, "Reading in American High Schools Today," in *Reading and Inquiry*, J. A. Figurel, Editor, International Reading Association Conference Proceedings 10 (Newark, Del.: International Reading Association, 1965) pp. 468-72.

12. Jerome S. Bruner, *Toward a Theory of Instruction* (Cambridge, Mass.: Harvard University Press, 1967) p. 41.

13. Harry W. Sartain, "Research on Individualized Reading," *Education* 81 (May, 1961) pp. 515-20.

14. Ernest Horn, *Methods of Instruction in the Social Studies* (New York: Charles Scribner's Sons, 1937) p. 150.

15. Russell G. Stauffer, "Individualizing Reading Instruction—A Backward Look," *Proceedings of the Thirty-ninth Annual Education Conference,* University of Delaware (1957) pp. 3-11.

16. A. Sterl Artley, *Trends and Practices in Secondary Reading* (Newark, Del.: International Reading Association, 1968) pp. 82-84.

17. E. A. Betts, *Foundations of Reading Instruction* (Cincinnati, Ohio: American Book Company, 1957) pp. 445-54.

18. Margery Bernstein, "Relationship Between Interest and Reading Comprehension," *Journal of Educational Research* 49 (1955) pp. 283-88.

19. Mary Austin and Coleman Morrison, *The First R: The Harvard Report on Reading* (New York: The Macmillan Company, 1963) p. 55.

20. Kibler, Barker, and Miles, *Behavioral Objectives and Instruction*, p. 17.

21. James B. Stroud, *Psychology in Education* (New York: Longmans, Green & Company, Inc., 1956) p. 337.

22. H. F. Spitzer, "Studies in Retention," *Journal of Educational Psychology* 30 (1939) pp. 641-56.

23. The Committee on Reading, *Reading in High School and College: Forty-seventh Yearbook,* Part II, of the National Society for the Study of Education (Chicago: University of Chicago Press, 1948) p. 3.

24. Paul Witty, "Reading Instruction—A Forward Look," *Elementary English* 38 (March, 1961) pp. 158-59.

25. Ernest Horn, *Methods of Instruction in Social Studies* (New York: Charles Scribner's Sons, 1937) p. 30.

26. Ralph C. Staiger, "How Are Basal Readers Used?" *Elementary English* 35 (January, 1958) pp. 44-46.

27. Austin and Morrison, *The First R*, p. 41.

28. Austin and Morrison, *The First R*, p. 54.

29. Gertrude Whipple, "Desirable Materials, Facilities, and Resources for Reading," in *Reading in the Elementary School,* Forty-eighth Yearbook, Part II, of the National Society for the Study of Education (Chicago: University of Chicago Press, 1949) p. 151.

30. Edward T. Brown, "Programmed Reading for the Secondary School," *High School Journal* 49 (April, 1966) pp. 327-33.

31. Wilbur Schramm, *Programed Instruction: Today and Tomorrow* (New York: The Fund for the Advancement of Education, 1962) pp. 1-2. Reprinted by permission of the publisher.

32. Sidney L. Pressey, "Teaching Machine and Learning Theory Crises," *Journal of Applied Psychology* 47 (1963) pp. 1-6.

33. R. S. Harnack, C. F. Toepfer, and J. K. Sullivan, *Computer-Based Curriculum Planning*, Third Revision, Center for Curriculum Planning, State University of New York at Buffalo (1974) p. 4.

34. Emery P. Bliesmer, "Overview of National Reading Conference Research Reviews," in *Changing Concepts of Reading Instruction*, International Reading Association Conference Proceedings 6 (Newark, Del.: International Reading Association, 1961) pp. 217-18.

35. Artley, *Trends and Practices in Secondary Reading*, p. 75.

36. George D. Spache, "A Rationale for Mechanical Methods of Improving Reading," in *Significant Elements in College and Adult Reading Improvement*, Seventh Yearbook of the National Reading Conference, O. S. Causey, Editor (Fort Worth, Tex.: Texas Christian University Press, 1958) pp. 115-32.

37. Robert S. Harnack, "Guidelines for Using Computers to Improve Instruction," *Impact* 4 (Spring, 1969) pp. 10-14.

38. Artley, *Trends and Practices in Secondary Reading*, p. 75.

39. Lillian K. Spitzer, *Language-Experience Approach to Reading Instruction*, An Annotated Bibliography (Newark, Del.: International Reading Association, 1967).

40. D. M. Lee and R. Van Allen, *Learning to Read Through Experience* (New York: Appleton-Century-Crofts, 1963).

41. Russell G. Stauffer, *The Language-Experience Approach to Teaching Reading* (New York: Harper & Row, Publishers, 1970).

42. Grace Fernald, *Remedial Techniques in Basic School Subjects* (New York: McGraw-Hill Book Company, 1943).

43. Thomas J. Edwards, "The Language-Experience Attack on Cultural Deprivation," *The Reading Teacher* 21 (April, 1965) pp. 546-51.

44. J. T. Becker, "Language Experience Approach in a Job Corps Reading Lab," *Journal of Reading* 13 (January, 1970) pp. 284-91, 319-21.

45. Jules C. Abrams and Gordon Marshall, "Teaching the Delinquent Child in a Residential Situation," *Journal of Reading* 12 (March, 1969) pp. 471-78.

46. Helen K. Smith, Editor, *Meeting Individual Needs in Reading* (Newark, Del.: International Reading Association, 1971).

47. Harry W. Sartain, *Individualized Reading*, An Annotated Bibliography (Newark, Del.: International Reading Association, 1970).

48. T. M. Trela and G. J. Becker, *Case Studies in Reading*, An Annotated Bibliography (Newark, Del.: International Reading Association, 1971).

49. G. M. Della-Piana, *Reading Diagnosis and Prescription: An Introduction* (New York: Holt, Rinehart and Winston, Inc., 1968).

50. Ruth Strang, *Diagnostic Teaching of Reading* (New York: McGraw-Hill Book Company, 1964).

51. Sartain, *Individualized Reading*, p. 1.

52. Sam Dukor, *Individualized Reading: An Annotated Bibliography* (Metuchen, N.J.: Scarecrow Press, 1968).

53. N. Dean Evans, "Individualized Reading—Myths and Facts," *Elementary English* 39 (October, 1962) pp. 580-83.

54. Artley, *Trends and Practices in Secondary Reading*, pp. 34-62.

55. Paul Witty et al., "Individualized Reading—A Summary and Evaluation," *Elementary English* 36 (October, 1959) pp. 401-12.

56. Lois A. Badar, "The Reading Coordinator: Key to an Effective Program," in *Reading in the Middle School*, G. G. Duffy, Editor (Newark, Del.: International Reading Association, 1974).

57. Harry Singer, *Preparation of Reading Content Specialists for the Junior High School*, Final Report, U.S. Office of Education OEG-0-70-1732-721, pp. 14-15.

58. Stroud, *Psychology in Education*, pp. 336-37.

59. Spitzer, "Studies in Retention."

## SUPPLEMENTARY SOURCES

Kennedy, Eddie C. *Methods in Teaching Developmental Reading*, Chapters 6 and 13. Itasca, Ill.: F. E. Peacock Publishers, Inc., 1974.

Kibler, R. J., L. L. Barker, and D. T. Miles. *Behavioral Objectives and Instruction*. Boston: Allyn and Bacon, Inc., 1970.

McCullough, Constance M. "Balanced Reading Development." In *Innovation and Change in Reading Instruction*, H. M. Robinson, Editor, The Sixty-seventh Yearbook of the National Society for the Study of Education, Part II, Chapter IX. Chicago: University of Chicago Press, 1968.

Sartain, Harry W. *Individualized Reading*, An Annotated Bibliography. Newark, Del.: International Reading Association, 1970.

Spitzer, Lillian K. *Language Experience Approach to Reading Instruction*, An Annotated Bibliography. Newark, Del.: International Reading Association, 1967.

# NINE

# Developing Word Power

*The meaning of language symbols is similarly aroused by way of the responses which have become associated with them in the past. The pages of a book are brought to life largely through the reader's capacity to identify with the word picture which the author has drawn.*

Irving Anderson and Walter Dearborn

***Overview***   With Chapter Nine we begin a series of chapters on the instructional development of the specific reading behaviors which implement the integral reading act. More particularly, Chapter Nine is the first of two chapters that focus upon the improvement of word power in reading. The first major section of this chapter considers the more specific tasks of word power assessment and includes a survey instrument — the Analytic Checklist of Pupil Word Power — which teachers may use to review the broad range of word behaviors that comprise word reading competency at the upper grade levels and/or to organize the specific appraisal and development of pupil word behaviors. The second general section treats the development of sight vocabulary and its efficient recognition. It presents an instructional format to guide this development and a number of illustrative activities and exercises for teaching and reinforcing sight recognition of words.

The essential natures of the word behaviors employed to implement the reading decoding processes were discussed in Chapter Three. The decoding of the writer's literal or stated meaning usually is a prerequisite to the purposeful interpretation of his functional, larger, and/or implied meaning. And the ability to deal with words — the integration and application of those knowledges, attitudes, and skills necessary to the association of meaning with and/or the derivation of meaning from graphic symbols — is necessary to success in decoding.[1] But important as word power is to general reading power, the program and the teacher should remember that it is a *means* to the end of reading interpretation and reaction, not an end in itself.[2] Word power performance in the upper grades is distributed across a broad continuum of achievement; most secondary pupils are in need of further instruction and are capable of continuing improvement.[3]

# WORD POWER
# ASSESSMENT

For purposes of general description and assessment, word power may be subdivided into three interrelated components of contributing word behaviors: (1) *sight vocabulary*—the ability to associate denotative and connotative meaning with the printed word form; (2) the quick *recognition* of known or familiar word forms; and (3) *word attack*—the studied analysis of unfamiliar word forms—to arrive at their meaning directly, or, if necessary, indirectly through arriving at their pronunciation. The correlated improvement of meaning vocabulary is implied, of course.

Word power involves the effective use of syntactical and general meaning clues as well as being able to process individual word cues. Indeed, the use of context may be the most efficient, the most frequent, and perhaps the most essential element of word power employed by the mature reader in arriving at the appropriate meaning, the quick recognition, and the efficient analysis of words encountered in his reading material. The effective use of context needs to be combined with the perception of individual word cues. In addition to context, individual word recognition draws heavily upon selected letter cues and general visual patterns; word analysis draws upon the use of context as well as upon the analysis and synthesis of word structure, phonic associations, and the use of word references.

## Sources of
## Word Assessment

The evaluation of word power should draw upon and collate multiple sources of assessment.[4] Some of these were discussed earlier in connection with other instructional or assessment matters: e.g., the pupil's elementary school reading record; vocabulary test or subtest scores obtained as part of general school or reading achievement testing; performance on material-referenced informal word inventories; and oral reading performance, particularly as assessed on the oral strands of informal reading inventories. Other sources of word assessment include standardized vocabulary tests, special word lists, standardized survey tests of word skills, word skill tests included in published instructional materials or programs, informal or teacher-constructed word power survey or criterion word skill tests, and analytic checklists.

It is advisable for the school to do a general screening assessment of word power as pupils enter secondary school—preferably at the beginning of seventh grade. Reading teachers should make a periodic assessment of word power, since the extension of word power is a continuing developmental concern. English and content teachers will need to be aware of pupil word power as it relates to use of course materials and independence in using the technical vocabulary of the content area. Corrective and remedial reading instruction will give continuing attention to the assessment of pupil weaknesses and evaluation of progress in total word power as well as in specific word competencies.

## *Professional Deficiencies in*
## *Word Assessment*

Word power assessment and related instruction have been susceptible to a number of errors.[5,6] Professional practice too often tends: (1) to be myopic (to restrict evaluation to a particular word skill, such as phonics, or to a particular word test); (2) to confuse symptoms with causes (e.g., to assume that the excessive number of word errors manifested on frustrational-level reading material is representative of the pupil's true recognition and analysis capabilities); (3) to overemphasize the significance of the phonetic (grapheme-phoneme) analysis of individual words in upper-grade reading; (4) to underestimate the significance of contextual and structural analysis of words; (5) to overlook the significance of word meaning in the effective learning and use of word recognition and word analysis techniques; (6) to overstress mechanics of precise linguistic rules and to understress the combined use of those word abilities necessary to associate meaning with the words; and most notably, (7) to place greater value upon the mastery of specific, isolated word skills than upon the functional and efficient use of coordinated word abilities in the reading act.

## The Analytic Survey of Word Power

One means of placing word assessment and related instruction in balanced perspective is to use an analytic survey of word power to coordinate the word assessment data obtained from various tests and observations. Such a survey or checklist as the one offered below also provides a global view of word power of which the teacher, especially one involved in reading assessment, should be cognizant.

---

### ANALYTIC CHECKLIST OF PUPIL WORD POWER

DIRECTIONS: This checklist provides a means for collating data derived from various word power assessment sources. It may be simplified to meet a particular instructional situation. Part I is used for summative evaluation and ready reference and usually is completed after the analyses of Part II are finished. The following suggested rating code may be used for those behaviors which call for an evaluative rating: ( + + ), consistent, efficient competency; ( + ), usually accurate, but inefficient use; ( √ ), frequently inaccurate in use; ( √√ ), rarely accurate in use; ( √√√ ), incompetency confounded by learning blocks and motivational problems. Adding descriptive commentary, the source of assessment, etc. improves the usefulness of the checklist.

    I. *Summary*

       A. *Composite Rating:* Fluent and Flexible Use of Total Word Power _____

       B. *Summary Rating:* Major Components of Word Power

          ____ 1. Word meaning and reasoning

          ____ 2. Sight vocabulary bank (size and depth)

          ____ 3. Quick word recognition accuracy (perceptual skills)

          ____ 4. Analysis of unfamiliar words

          ____ 5. Word readiness factors

    II. *Word Power Component Ratings and Problems*

       A. *Word Meaning and Reasoning*

          ____ 1. General vocabulary mastery

          ____ 2. Ability to learn new word concepts

          ____ 3. Denotative accuracy

          ____ 4. Connotative flexibility

          ____ 5. Word meaning manipulation

              ____ a. derivatives

              ____ b. synonyms

              ____ c. antonyms

              ____ d. analogies

B. *Sight Vocabulary Bank* (learned word form–meaning associations)

_____ 1. Proficiency in reading conventional materials

_____ 2. Proficiency in reading content area sources

    _____ a. Literature

    _____ b. Social studies

    _____ c. Applied or technical areas

    _____ d. Science

    _____ e. Math

_____ 3. Learns words readily from contextual reading

_____ 4. Learns words readily from instruction

    _____ a. Word learning rate (per lesson) _____

    _____ b. Word retention rate (per lesson) _____

    _____ c. Employs common modes of association (visual-visual, auditory-visual, kinesthetic-visual, etc.)

C. *Fluency and Flexibility in Combined Use of Word Attack*

_____ 1. Gives meaning of message higher priority than word pronunciation

_____ 2. Uses most efficient approach to arrive at needed meaning of words in print

    _____ a. Recognizes rather than analyzes known words

    _____ b. Uses phonic synthesis only when more efficient analysis is inappropriate

_____ 3. Demonstrates ability to combine context, recognition, and various analysis clues in dealing with challenging content

_____ 4. Demonstrates balanced mastery of word analysis techniques (e.g., context, structural analysis, phonic analysis)

_____ 5. Can use word resources (dictionary, glossaries, thesauri, indexes) accurately to get word information, but uses only when necessary

D. *Adequate Use of Sight Recognition Cues*

_____ 1. Is accurate in recognition of known words

_____ 2. Recognizes individual words efficiently (in 1/3 to 1/5 second)

_____ 3. Readily fits recognized words into syntactical mean unit, e.g., fluent reading of phrases

_____ 4. Is free from persistent word recognition errors; check notable recognition error difficulty ( ✓ ):

    _____ a. Small words (single-syllable)

    _____ b. Larger words (multisyllable)

    _____ c. Persistent location of error

        _____ word beginning elements

        _____ word ending elements

        _____ medial word elements

        _____ reversal of parts

_____ d. Persistent phonemic error patterns (letters, phonograms, syllables); list: _____

_____

_____ e. Overgeneralizes from configuration

_____ f. Overgeneralizes from context

E. *Adequate Use of Word Analysis Technique*

_____ 1. Produces meaning for word analyzed

_____ 2. Synthesizes (blends) word parts into total word pronunciation

_____ 3. Inductively generalizes unknown word from similar known words (derivatives, variants, etc.)

_____ 4. Effectively uses word structure elements in analysis

     _____ a. Compound words

     _____ b. Prefixes

     _____ c. Roots

     _____ d. Suffixes

_____ 5. Effectively uses phonic elements to analyze unknown words

     _____ a. Syllables

     _____ b. Phonograms

     _____ c. Vowels

     _____ d. Consonants

_____ 6. Makes use of typographical aids to analyze unfamiliar words

_____ 7. Is familiar with functions of and can use common word sources to gain word information

_____ 8. Profits from instruction in word analysis technique

F. *Demonstrates Inadequate Word Readiness;* check notable and limiting weakness in word power ( √ ):

_____ 1. Very limited listening vocabulary

_____ 2. Minimal attention span

_____ 3. Lacks sensitivity to or interest in words

_____ 4. Inadequate visual perception

     _____ a. Discrimination (beginnings, endings, middles)

     _____ b. Memory

     _____ c. Synthesis of parts

_____ 5. Inadequate auditory perception

     _____ a. Discrimination (sounds)

     _____ b. Memory

     _____ c. Synthesis (blending)

_____ 6. Poor use of oral context

_____ 7. Orientation problems (left-to-right)

_____ 8. Lacks knowledge of letters (capital/small)

        _____ a. Cannot name

        _____ b. Cannot identify

        _____ c. Cannot match

III. *Factors Associated with Notable Difficulty*

    _____ 1. General or composite reading performance

        a. Standardized test _____ norm result _____

        b. Functional reading levels: Instructional: _____

                              Independent: _____

    _____ 2. English-language competency: _____

        _____

    _____ 3. Intelligence or mental ability

        a. Group test _____ norm result _____ IQ_____

        b. Individual test _____ norm result _____ IQ_____

    _____ 4. Physical impairment (visual, auditory, other _____)

    _____ 5. Unusual general perceptual/learning/transfer difficulty: _____

        _____

    _____ 6. Motivational factors

        _____ a. School: _____

        _____ b. Personal reading: _____

        _____ c. Reading instruction: _____

        _____ d. Word skills instruction: _____

IV. *Major Assessment Sources Employed*

    (Give name of test and date. Attach results or summary thereof. Possible sources employed include standardized achievement, reading, and vocabulary tests; standardized diagnostic tests; informal reading and word inventories; cloze reading tests; oral reading analysis; teacher checklist or rating sheet; informal word analysis inventory; and listening tests.)

## DEVELOPING SIGHT VOCABULARY

The reader's *sight vocabulary* consists of that reservoir of graphic words with which he can associate the appropriate referential and/or linguistic meaning in one-third to one-fifth of a second. The considerable contribution which sight vocabulary makes to total reading power, comprehension, and reading fluency has been well established.[7,8] In turn, the development of sight vocabulary benefits from general language competency, word recognition and analysis behaviors, extended personal reading, and, of course, planned instruction and reinforcement of a direct nature.

It would be unrealistic to assume that specific reading instruction at the secondary school level should assume singular responsibility for developing sight mastery of all words which the maturing reader is likely to encounter in school, let alone those needed for a lifetime of reading print. Instructional time is not sufficient to meet this gargantuan task. Moreover, the attempt would require such continuous, intensive instructional effort that it would inhibit attention to other significant aspects of reading development, and very likely would drive both teacher and pupil to the brink of rebellion.

Thus, it is essential that maturing readers learn to employ the writer's context, word analysis skills, and word resources to enable them to deal with many of the essential new words encountered. Establishing habits of extended personal reading will increase the pupil's accumulated word experiences and should contribute notably to the development of sight vocabulary—especially of those vocabulary items of personal value which are encountered with some frequency.

## Sight Vocabulary Instruction

Even so, increasing the size and depth of the pupil's sight-reading vocabulary and general word power becomes one necessary function of reading and content instruction at the secondary school level. Any notable increase in meaning and sight mastery of words with high frequency of use will make materials more readable, and understanding those terms that represent more complex concepts will aid the accuracy, fluency, and level of pupil reading interpretation.[9,10]

### Teaching Words of Greater Utility

Certain words have greater utility than others, and their development should be assured through planned specific instruction. These include: (1) that sight vocabulary necessary to understand the written materials employed in developmental reading lessons; (2) those words representing key concepts of the several content areas and those words crucial to understanding specific materials currently employed in content area study; (3) that basic sight vocabulary which appears with high frequency in conventional reading materials encountered by the secondary pupil; and (4) those words which lend themselves to the development of power in word analysis, e.g., words which illustrate the use of key roots, affixes, and derivations which serve to form models or from which the reader can generalize to independently expand his vocabulary.

Direct, structured development of sight vocabulary as a specific instructional task is a responsibility shared by every reading, English, foreign language, and content subject teacher. Most of the discussion in this section deals with direct instructional implementation. However, the teacher may contribute importantly to sight vocabulary proficiency through choice of instructional sources, by helping pupils develop independence in analyzing unfamiliar words, and by encouraging the independent word-learning efforts of pupils.

### Structuring the Teaching of Sight Vocabulary

The ability to recognize individual words by sight is a specific reading behavior; a graphic stimulus-response, word-meaning association which can be developed through direct reading instruction. The model and sequence suggested in Chapter Eight for teaching specific reading behaviors is adapted below for the development of sight vocabulary.

*1. Select or otherwise identify the words which need to be taught.* This selection should be guided by certain criteria: (a) the cruciality of the word/concept in understanding current reading selections or content-learning materials, (b) the projected frequency with which the word will appear in school-life reading materials (priority appearance on vocabulary lists and in content glossaries), (c) the special difficulty or interest the word currently holds for pupils, and (d) the probability that sufficient, sustained instructional attention can be given to the learning and reinforcement of the words selected.

*2. Assess pupil mastery of both the meaning and quick recognition of the target words.* This may be handled in a number of ways: worksheets, informal tests, quick visual exposure techniques, pupil self-selection card sorts, checklists, oral reading, etc.

When possible, it is useful to assess pupil mastery of the word with and without contextual support.

*3. Place instructional emphases upon the words with which pupils [individual and/or group] reveal difficulty or notable insecurity.* Adjust the number of words taught per learning session to pupil learning-retention span. Eight to twelve words is a reasonable word-learning load for the typical secondary reader; top-level learners may handle as many as twelve, and three to five words may be maximal for pupils with reading difficulty. Usually, it proves more effective to divide and conquer, i.e., to concentrate upon eight words each of five vocabulary learning segments rather than to try to teach forty terms in one mind-blowing session.

*4. Develop pupil readiness for learning the words.* Any of a number of activities may be employed here. Preassessment often promotes learning readiness, but cannot be assumed as sufficient in itself. A critical readiness task is to develop an understanding of the meaning or meanings of the words to be taught. Also, pupils should be prepared for unfamiliar instructional procedures, use of word resource tools, or word skills which will be employed in activities of the instructional sequence.

*5. Form a psychologically clean and vigorous associative connection between the graphic form of the word, its meaning, and its pronunciation.* Ordinarily this is best handled by close personal teacher direction, although the use of tape recorders (teacher input and pupil response), programmed learning materials, autoinstructional devices, and pupil teams can be used to this end. Attention should be focused upon the graphic form of the word while its meaning(s) are reviewed and its use illustrated in simple oral and written context. Multiple associations should be formed: e.g., the pupil pronounces the word, underlines it in context, identifies it among other word choices, writes the word, and/or analyzes the structure and meaning of the word. A key element of this step is to obtain a check upon the accuracy of this initial pupil association and to correct erroneous associations before they are reinforced.

*6. Provide for immediate, then extended, practice to reinforce the appropriate associations.* A considerable range of instructional activities may be employed for this purpose. Such practice should involve reading and self-testing the word in meaningful context. Practice exercises and worksheets should use varied format and require different pupil responses, e.g., underlining, matching, labeling, and using the word in written sentences. The number of such reinforcements needed will vary with the pupil and the word. Typically, teachers underestimate the number of meaningful reinforcements needed for words which, in themselves, are not colorful, unique, or of particular personal importance to the pupil.

Kennedy has recommended a useful series of steps for directly teaching word meanings and sight vocabulary through the use of affixes which illustrates how instruction and reinforcing use can be combined.

*a.* Study the word, discuss its meaning, and write it into a sentence.

*b.* Break the word into its parts—prefix, root word, and suffix—and find how the total meaning of the word is dependent upon its parts.

*c.* Select other root words and add the same prefixes and suffixes in order to build words with different but related meanings.

*d.* Have pupils construct words in which the prefixes and suffixes are used. Discuss the words and write sentences in which they are used.

*e.* Help students analyze new words containing prefixes and suffixes to find how the meanings can be derived.

*f.* Have students examine the words in context to find if their analytical definitions are correct.[11]

Successful rereading of the word in different and interesting content is essential. One of the advantages of developing reading vocabulary as a part of the guided reading of instructional selections written for vocabulary development purposes (basal, literary, or content-oriented readers which have exerted control over the vocabulary employed) is that the pupil will encounter the target word a number of times in his reading and rereading of the content. Since sight vocabulary words should be quickly "recognized" rather than "analyzed," some part of reinforcement practice should include quick exposure-recognition response (e.g., flash cards, tachistoscopic presentations, timed contextual reading, etc.).

The developmental, corrective, and content teachers of reading also may contribute to the development of sight vocabulary through less direct instructional procedures. These include:

*1. Employing textbooks and other instructional sources which give careful attention to the development of vocabulary.* Vocabulary and concept development are important considerations in the choice of instructional materials. They should be examined for careful pacing in the introduction of new terms in context, the extent to which words are defined and reinforced in context, their provision of word-learning aids in the text or in supplementary workbooks. The inclusion of a glossary and the quality of the index are factors which should be assessed in a secondary text.

*2. Helping pupils develop independence in dealing with unknown words.* These include teaching and providing practice in the use of the glossary, index, general dictionary, and the technical dictionary and word sources of the area; teaching the frequently used affixes and roots of words commonly used in the area, and reviewing the general patterns of context clues which can be employed in identifying unfamiliar words. Pupils with serious deficiencies in phonetic and structural word analysis should be referred to the reading specialist if the content teacher cannot provide this help.

*3. Encouraging the independent word-learning efforts of pupils.* There are many ways in which this may be accomplished. One is to show pupils how to develop a file of word cards and how to use the file both for word reference and for content review for tests. A part of the reading or content notebook can be set aside for significant vocabulary. Periodic checking of the notebook by the instructor does wonders in maintaining sincerity in this effort. The bulletin board may serve as a showplace for word puzzles, interesting etymologies, or significant

words in current events. Word games may be collected in centers for pupil independent or small-group use.

The sources cited at the end of the chapter contain a number of references dealing with the teaching of vocabulary. Appendix D presents a selected list of instructional materials which place particular emphasis upon the development of reading vocabulary.

## Illustrative Instructional Activities

### Readiness-Introductory Learning Activities

*1. Word location activities.* The locational use of text and word resources to provide readiness or initial learning and practice with vocabulary words is an appropriate and efficient way to develop sight vocabulary and also provides practice with locational skills. No instructional activity should be used slavishly, and these locational activities may be modified in many ways to avoid monotony. Some variety in word reference sources may be employed, e.g., general dictionary, content area dictionary, basic and special text glossary, book index, dictionary of American idioms, etc. Two or more of these sources may be used for comparison of findings. Duplicated pages or mock-form pages from such sources may be developed if multiple copies of the sources are difficult for class members to obtain. Also, the word locational task can be varied. The teacher, a pupil committee, or individual pupils may identify the stimulus words to be located. The task response may involve locating denotative meaning, connotative meaning, pronunciation, synonyms, antonyms, homonyms, roots, derivatives, etymology, or linguistic function.

*2. Word survey committees.* A variation of word location activity which combines pupil cooperative involvement, differential instruction, practice in scanning-skim reading, vocabulary development, and instructional efficiency is the use of word survey or "word prep" committees. A committee of pupils is formed to survey a text chapter or section of a chapter to identify the key words and concepts which need special attention before the chapter or selection is read. Generally, it is best if the selected pupils work individually and then meet to form their composite list. The committee should be formed of pupils of varied reading ability. The composite list may be divided into sections—by priority of use, difficulty level, associated meaning, etc. It should be duplicated for class use. Individuals, additional committees, or the class as a whole may then set about identifying the meanings and other vital aspects of the selected words. As a variation, the better readers and learners of the class may take on the task of working these terms or concepts into an advanced organizer—in written context, outline, or flowchart form. This, of course, can also be done as an assignment by individual pupils.

*3. Miniunits on word function or malfunction.* At regular intervals, a session or combination of sessions can be spent in concentrated study of significant word characteristics or their common misuses so that pupils can become sensitive to generalized word characteristics and responses such as synonyms, antonyms, homonyms, and idioms. Such a unit should incorporate most of the instructional steps identified earlier. Here the primary objective is to stress the nature of the particular word function or malfunction. Individual words employed during such a unit would serve as examples or illustrations. Although they may be learned incidentally, that would not be a major instructional concern.

One such miniunit might focus on malapropisms, the ludicrous misuse of words through confusion of sound and form. The pupils might be introduced to Sheridan's character Mrs. Malaprop in the play *The Rivals* and to some of her wilder word misuses. The pupils, individually or as groups, may develop a list of examples with which they are presently familiar or which they encounter in the next week. (One class wryly labeled this list "Malapros and Cons.") The use of malapropism in literature or performing arts to convey humor, unusual ideas, character descriptions, satire, or propaganda can be discussed. Some pupils may search for examples in the works of selected authors, e.g., Shakespeare (Falstaff), Mark Twain, Damon Runyon, and Irving S. Cobb. Others may view a week of selected situation comedies, such as "All in the Family," for examples and related implications. As a culminating activity, the teacher may develop a worksheet or informal test in which pupils can identify malapropisms in context, match given malapropisms with their correct word form, or even engage in a little "malapropagation" of their own.

*4. Newspapers and magazines as word activity sources.* Recent and current publications provide rich sources for word study. They are easily available to most pupils, are readily related to pupil interests and knowledges, and lend themselves to a variety of word-learning activities. (a) The teacher may use several photos which are likely to stir pupil emotion and verbal response to move pupils, collectively or individually, to recall, recognize, or write words they would use to describe the picture. (b) A variant tactic would involve asking the pupils to write sentences which describe feelings or ideas which the magazine or newspaper photos stimulate and which use at least one word from those presently under study. (c) Or the teacher can make a bulletin board display of ten photos or graphic advertisements along with a list of key vocabulary words, with the challenge to form single word-picture associations. (d) Another activity might involve having pupils "search and clip" sentences from the printed media in which typographical errors change significant meaning or in which selected key vocabulary or technical concepts are utilized. (e) A more complex activity would involve making a week's comparative study of vocabulary usage in different sections of the newspaper, e.g., the front or news page, sports section, editorials, want ads, and comics. Such a study might be restricted to certain terms under present study or it might be an open-ended search for special terms of common use; it could be extended to include analysis of the use of modifiers, the length of sentences, and other linguistic functions. The use of newspapers, magazines, and other print media as sources of word study dovetails nicely with activities intended to extend pupil independent and personal reading contacts, with locational skills, and with various interpretative tasks.

## Word Learning and Reinforcement Activities*

*1. Creative response word-learning activities.* Although sight vocabulary properly functions as a quick recognition response in actual reading situations, activities which require pupil recall and creative involvement with significant terms usually strengthen word form-meaning relationships—a prerequisite of sight recognition use. Such activity should be meaningful and stimulating; drill-type writing and rewriting of isolated words should be avoided!

Perhaps the most easily administered of such activities is to have pupils write sentences, paragraphs, or anecdotes which make use of the target terms. There are many ways to add variety to such use: (a) small-group writing of television commercials where the term is the product to be plugged, and therefore used repeatedly; (b) using the words in paragraphs emulating distinct writing or speaking personalities; (c) using the words in free verse or in developing limericks; and (d) developing one-sentence definitions in a whole-class effort to construct a cumulative unit-by-unit content area glossary of key terms.

This creative response need not be limited to contextual writing. Word combinations and derivations may be formed. Words may be illustrated by drawings and other creative media. (e) Pupils can use the words in cartoons or as dialogue from a sequence from their favorite comic strip. (f) Pupils

*The activities in this and later sections will contain directions only where the nature of the involved items would not be obvious.

may create word puzzles which are to be solved by other members of the class. (g) A group word tree can be constructed: the teacher places a key word or words on the bulletin board. During the next week each class member adds one new word which uses either the root of the original word or which serves as a derivative (or synonym or antonym) to the list or tree. (Initialing bulletin board contributions adds personalization and motivation to an otherwise anonymous activity.) In addition to stimulating creative activity and language usage, pupil creative response to words provides a means by which the teacher can compile a file of instructional materials for later use—simply by filing the best pupil products.

*2. Target vocabulary activities.* Some instructional activities center on the identification, learning, and practice of specific vocabularies. These might consist of ongoing collections of terms vital to content area study, personal vocabulary lists, or predetermined lists of words essential to basic or functional literacy. The activities pertinent to this vocabulary study may be handled independently by the pupil, systematically directed by the teacher, or some combination of independent study supplemented by teacher-stimulated learning activity. Generally, the teacher has three basic responsibilities in this word-learning approach: (a) identifying the key words the pupil is to learn or helping him develop a system for identifying his own list of words; (b) teaching the pupil a system for independently mastering the list of words (a modification of that structure presented earlier in this section should be adequate for this purpose); and (c) providing activities for supplementary practice, periodic testing, and individual support and guidance.

Suggesting or insisting that pupils have a word file or a special place for keeping the words to be studied is beneficial to mastering target vocabulary. The words can be reviewed more readily and the task itself serves as a concrete reminder to maintain word study efforts. A notebook or part of a notebook can be set aside for this purpose. There are some particular advantages to using 3 × 5 cards for this purpose and filing them alphabetically (or according to some linguistic or content meaning system) in a box. The word may be printed on one side of the card; the back of the card may be used for writing the meaning or meanings, synonyms, antonyms, phonetic pronunciation, or several examples of use in context. (If such a word file is collected under teacher guidance, each of these backside fillers can become a separate activity for reinforcing word usage.) Writing only the word on one side facilitates self-testing, various card matching or sorting procedures, as well as paired or small-group flashcard recognition practice. Some teachers have pupils divide their word files into three parts: those words mastered, those words not yet mastered, and those words targeted for current study and use.

*3. Word puzzles.* Most pupils seem to enjoy word puzzles as long as they feel it is possible to solve them. Word puzzles which reinforce selected words under study are more helpful than generally published puzzles. Some reading and vocabulary development materials provide ready-made puzzles emphasizing basic vocabulary. The teacher can construct puzzles and duplicate them for members of the class or place them on the bulletin board. Pupils can be encouraged to make their own puzzles, and these can be duplicated or exchanged with other members of the class.

Crosswords and crostics are the most common forms of such puzzles and can be developed into a variety of patterns. The following illustrate how the word puzzles can be adapted to content area concept development.

---

DIRECTIONS: Fill in the word (concept) which we have studied in this unit on measurement and which is defined by each of the numbered statements. The selected word should fill the blank spaces exactly. When you are finished, the letters in the box should form a related concept we have studied recently.

1.    [V] E L O C I T Y
2.    [O] R D I N A L
3.    K I [L] O G R A M
4.    C [U] B I C
5.    D I [M] E N S I O N
6.    M [E] T R I C

1. Rate of position change in relation to time.
2. A number to indicate order in a given series.
3. One thousand grams.
4. Having three dimensions; having volume.
5. A physical quantity; measurements in length, width, or depth.
6. System of measurement based on the meter and gram.

Depending upon the pupils and study objectives, such puzzles can be made easier by providing a list of words which includes the correct responses. They can be made more difficult by using a longer base word, by restricting correct word choices to supporting concepts, or by increasing the complexity of the puzzle form, e.g.:

---

```
 1.             IN V E S T E D
 2.            P O L I T I C A L
 3.         R I G H T
 4.     C I T I Z E N R Y
 5.             R E G I S T R A T I O N
 6.                 Q U A L I F I C A T I O N
 7.         S T A T U T E
 8.                 A G E
 9.         P O L L
10.         R E S I D E N C E
11.                 T A X
12.         P A R T Y
```

---

Puzzles may take forms other than crosswords, crostics, or anagrams. A simple device for turning an exercise into a puzzle involves numbering the word responses and the stimulus items. The pupil knows he has resolved the puzzle correctly when the cumulative sum or product of the response–item numbers added to or multiplied by stimulus–item numbers is the same as the given "grand total."

*4. Word games.* Games present an excellent tactic to engage pupils in motivated, intensive reinforcement practice, and words are readily adapted to game formats. Almost any card or parlor game or sport can be converted to word use format. The four "classics" given below are illustrative of the many possibilities. One note of caution: pupils with reading, language, or general learning difficulty sometimes feel insecure in game situations and may be reluctant to enter competition or will overreact to the outcome. Such anxiety can be lessened if the pupil plays against the teacher, his past record, or is teamed with other pupils who accept him.

*a. Wordo.* This is played in the manner of bingo. Pupils use tablet-sized oak tag cards with twenty-five or thirty-six squares, each square with a word written on it. Each player's card will differ in the location of these words. The caller draws word cards from a box containing the total vocabulary under study. The winner is the first pupil to have filled five connected word squares—horizontally, vertically, diagonally. A more advanced form of this game is Defino or Concepto, in which the caller reads definitions drawn from the master box and the players must identify the word or concept defined. Any manageable number can play.

*b. Rummy variations.* A number of instructional games can be fashioned out of the rummy format. One small-group variation involves the use of key words or word "demons" along with their antonyms and synonyms. Twenty-six key words are written twice (the second may be a variant form) on small index cards. After shuffling, seven cards are dealt to each player and the remaining cards are placed face down in a deck. Each player takes his turn at matching the up card with one in his hand. To gain a point, the player must define or give a correct synonym or antonym for the word match. A dictionary is used to check challenges. (Correct challenges gain two points.) Winning the game can be a set number of points or the voiding of one's word cards. Incorrect challenges cost the challenger one point.

c. *Silent password.* Instructional games and particularly word games can be developed as adaptations of currently popular television game shows. Silent Password is played like TV's Password except that clue words are written instead of spoken, and the number of clues is limited to five. Key-concept words or demon words serve as the target words. The class may be divided into groups of five, two teams of two pupils and one MC to provide the words and serve as referee. A correct solution on the first clue is worth 5 points; 4 points on the second clue, and so forth.

A whole-class variation of this game can be played. The class is divided into pairs (it is good to team strong readers with weaker readers). Each contestant sits with back to the chalkboard and his clue-writing partner faces it. The teacher places one of ten keywords on the board at two-minute intervals. In the two minutes, the partner writes his clues (maximum of three) and the contestant writes his choice. Winners are those teams with the largest number of correct words.

d. *Word football.* With a little ingenuity, many sports can be converted into word games. In this version of Word Football, played by two players or teams, oak tag is used to lay out a 100-yard field. The teacher selects approximately 150 words of variant difficulty. These are arranged on a list in order of approximate difficulty, and each is given a different yardage value: e.g., for the word "differ," a running play is worth 3 yards; a passing play, 5

yards; a place kick, 15 yards; a punt, 35 yards; and a kickoff, 40 yards. (Easier words would get less yardage; more difficult words, greater yardage.) The words are printed on cards and their various yardage values for the playing options are given on the back. The players flip a coin for kick or receive to start the game. The word cards are placed in a covered box. The kicker picks one and if he can pronounce it, the football marker is moved the designated number of yards for kickoff. The receiver takes the next card and if he can pronounce it, moves the number of yards listed for kick return. Thereafter, the offensive team player calls his play and draws a card. If he cannot pronounce it, he fumbles and the defense has an opportunity to recover through pronouncing the word correctly. However, if the offense can pronounce the word, the defense can nullify the gain by giving a synonym or a definition of the word. Punts and place kicks cannot be nullified. Place kicks with adequate yardage are considered good.

## Representative Vocabulary Exercise Forms

Worksheet practice exercises provide a solid fare for the learning and reinforcement activities of an instructional sequence. Often, the teacher can find commercially published exercises which meet the instructional need or which can be adapted to class use. Practice exercises developed by the teacher are more readily adjusted to pupil need, currency of content, and the planned learning sequence. The master copy of these exercises may be filed for future use. The same cautions should be observed in developing and using practice exercises as have been recommended for any independent reading assignment. Most word exercises can serve also to reinforce reading-thinking processes. A few representative examples of vocabulary and sight-recognition exercise formats are given on the following pages. For reinforcing skills learned, more than one type of form or skill may be combined for study purposes—as long as the pupils understand the procedures to be followed.

## MATCHING FORM

DIRECTIONS: Each of the key words in column I can be paired with its antonym in column II by drawing a line connecting the two, as in the following example:

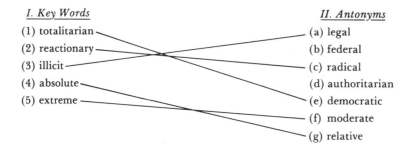

| *I. Key Words* | *II. Antonyms* |
|---|---|
| (1) totalitarian | (a) legal |
| (2) reactionary | (b) federal |
| (3) illicit | (c) radical |
| (4) absolute | (d) authoritarian |
| (5) extreme | (e) democratic |
| | (f) moderate |
| | (g) relative |

## COMPLETION FORM

This is one of the simplest exercise forms for the teacher to construct. However, since it requires a rather precise response from a number of possible responses, it can be a task which is time consuming, frustrating, and operationally disruptive for some pupils. Some of this difficulty can be alleviated by providing structure for guiding the search and the response. The use of context, the identification of sources and procedures for responding, combining completion with other response forms, and the provision for discussion of alternative responses are several techniques by which the completion form can be enhanced.

DIRECTIONS: From the ten terms listed below, choose the one which best completes the meaning of each of the sentences and write that word in the blank. After completing the ten sentences, decide whether the meaning of the word selected was denotative or connotative and write D or C after the sentence to indicate your choice. Use your dictionary and our class word list as necessary.

*Word choices:* cold-blooded, debatable, elected, forehanded, grab, politician, referee, sniping, tripped, victorious.

*Items*

1. At midseason, the strength of our team was (debatable). (D)

2. The coach (elected) to use John as team captain. (C)

3. As team captain, John soon proved he was a clever (politician). (C)

4. As the team began to win, the (sniping) of the fans decreased. (C)

## MATCHING–COMPLETION

DIRECTIONS: Listed in column I is a list of descriptors we have studied. Following each descriptor are two blanks. In the first blank, write the letter of the most appropriate synonym given in column II. In the second blank, write the name of the person, place, or thing in Jack London's short story *The Strength of the Strong* best described by that term. Later we will discuss the exercise in our small groups, so be prepared to defend your choices!

|  *I*  |  |  | *II* |
|---|---|---|---|
| 1. able | (d) | Little-Belly | a. sullen |
| 2. disdainful | (g) | Deer-Runner | b. peaceful |
| 3. ferocious | (f) | Old Boo-oogh | c. organized |
| 4. giddy | —— | ———— | d. clever |
| 5. humble | —— | ———— | e. careful |
|  |  |  | f. violent |
|  |  |  | g. haughty |

## TRUE–FALSE (AGREE–DISAGREE) FORM

DIRECTIONS: Each of the following sentences contains an underlined word. If the sentence provides an accurate or consistent use of that word, write a (C) in the blank provided. If the underlined word is inconsistent with the meaning of the sentence, write down an (I).

 __I__ (1) The two armies charged together in a furious <u>disengagement.</u>

 __I__ (2) The victors began to divide their <u>respite.</u>

 __C__ (3) The rebels <u>harried</u> the occupation forces with hit-and-run attacks.

 __I__ (4) <u>Belatedly,</u> the royal forces struck back at the best possible moment.

## BEST–ANSWER MULTIPLE–CHOICE FORM

DIRECTIONS: Each of the following items presents an underlined term in context followed by four answer choices. Mark with an X that choice which *best* describes the meaning of the underlined word as it is used in the stem of the item.

(1) They proved to be an <u>adaptive</u> people.

_____ a. They were quite clever in the use of tools.

 __X__ b. By changing their behavior, they were able to survive.

_____ c. As a people, they had no strong beliefs.

_____ d. They made considerable changes in their environment.

## ALTERNATE–ASSOCIATION FORM

DIRECTIONS: Listed below are twenty pairs of words. Read each pair to determine whether the pair are synonyms, antonyms, homonyms. Mark synonyms (S), antonyms (A), and homonyms (H). Mark words which have no relationship to each other with an (N).

 __A__ 1. placid — excitable

 __N__ 2. wary — weary

 __S__ 3. incident — happening

 __N__ 4. launch — midday meal

 __H__ 5. staid — stayed

## MULTIPLE–DISCRIMINATION FORM

DIRECTIONS: Listed below are twenty-five items. Each item consists of four words. Three of the words have very similar meanings. Draw a line through the word which does not have the same meaning.

1. opinion; belief; judgment; ~~evidence~~
2. deceive; mislead; ~~debate~~; betray
3. ~~support~~; superb; splendid; superior
4. patient; ~~fatigued~~; enduring; calm

## CLASSIFICATION FORM

DIRECTIONS: Given below are a list of descriptive words which were used in the last two of the series of poems we have studied in this unit. (1) List each word under the category of human condition or behavior to which it ordinarily (or literally) would relate. (2) After you have classified the words, reread these two poems to see how the author used the words. (3) What generalizations can you form about the use of descriptive words and literal meaning in the writing of poetry?

*Descriptive words:* able; arched; berating; commending; devoted; hulking; inhabiting; judges; knocked; lulling; manipulate; nervy; puzzling; scrape; solution; thick; and verbal.

| *Physical* | *Mental* | *Emotional* | *Social* |
|---|---|---|---|
| (arched) | (able) | (berating) | (inhabiting) |
| (hulking) | (puzzling) | (devoted) | (judges) |
| etc. | etc. | etc. | etc. |

## ASSOCIATION BY ANALOGY

DIRECTIONS: You will remember that an analogy consists of an inference about the generalized similarity of two things which share a common characteristic. The basic form of a word analogy is A:B as C:D, or A is to B as C is to D. For each of the following problems, (a), (b), and (c) are given. Your task is to complete the analogy by marking the most appropriate choice for (d).

1. (a) general: (b) army as (c) king:
   _____ theocracy
   _____ royalty
   (d) monarchy

2. (a) ruler: (b) carpentry as (c) sextant:
   _____ oceanography
   (d) navigation
   _____ drama

## MULTIPLE COMPLETION FORM

DIRECTIONS: Listed below are ten foreign terms which appear often in English writing. Using the foreign expressions section of your dictionary and your personal word file as necessary, supply: (a) the language from which the term comes, (b) the literal meaning of the term or phrase, (c) one or two English connotations or a common English definition of the term, and (d) write a sentence using the term.

1. *coup de grâce*

   a. (French) _____

   b. (stroke of mercy) _____

   c. (end, wipe out, death blow) _____

   d. (Losing her purse delivered the coup de grace to her summer hopes.)

2. *de facto*

   a. (Latin) _____

   b. (from the fact) _____

   c. (existing unofficially) _____

   d. (The vigilantes served as a de facto police force.)

---

### Quick Recognition Practice

A word cannot be considered as part of the secondary pupil's sight vocabulary until he can recognize it as a unit of meaning upon an initial perceptual fix; that is, in approximately one-third of a second or less. Most adequate secondary readers usually quickly recognize a learned word when given enough opportunity to encounter it in print. However, this process can be facilitated by practice in the quick recognition of words. Such practice adds to the reinforcement of the basic form association and can contribute to some greater efficiency in reader reaction to print. There are a number of ways by which pupils can improve quick recognition of words. Most of these involve short-exposure procedures or timed exercises.

*1. Flash cards.* Perhaps the simplest quick recognition practice procedure is to use flash cards on which the word (or word in brief simple context) is written. The pupil can administer these to himself by rapid card-sort procedures on a timed or self-counting basis: familiar words in one pile, unknown words in another, and unsure responses in yet a third pile. This procedure can be handled by pairs of pupils. Or the teacher can flash the cards (about half a second exposure) and pupils have ten seconds to: (a) find their own matching card; (b) mark one of four or five grouped words on lists on a worksheet (for that particular exposure); or (c) write the perceived word on a blank.

Flash cards also can be converted into *quick recognition games*, such as a variation of Slap Jack. Two pupils each have a set of identical word cards. After shuffling their separate card decks, each simultaneously rolls the top card to expose it. If the two words on the cards are identical, the first pupil to cover them with his hand gets them. Covering an unmatched pair loses those cards to the opponent. The winner is the pupil with the most cards at the end of ten minutes.

*2. Tachistoscopes.* A somewhat more controlled flash exposure can be obtained by constructing or having pupils construct a *hand tachistoscope* for self or paired practice (see Figure 16). This usually consists of an elongated, open-ended "holder" formed by folding a 7½- by 11-inch piece of oak tag into three overlapping parts and taping it. A ½- by 2-inch exposure slot is cut into the single side. Words are typed or printed at double-spaced intervals on sheets of oak tag (roughly 2¼ by 12 inches) and inserted in the sleeve or holder. By drawing the sheets through at a steady pace, the words are exposed at roughly ½ to ⅓ second. (If desired, a shutter can be made by cutting a 1½-

**Figure 16**    *Hand tachistoscope.*

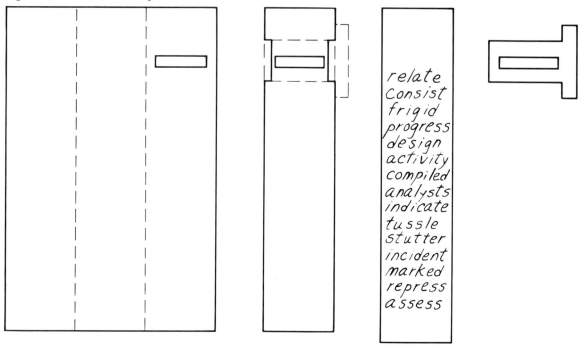

relate
Consist
frigid
progress
design
activity
compiled
analysts
indicate
tussle
stutter
incident
marked
repress
assess

inch slot in the edges and constructing and inserting the shutter, which when moved up or down exposes the word for ¼ to ⅕ second.)

*3. Commercial exposure devices.* More elaborate quick exposure devices are available from commercial sources. These include: (a) hand–held "flash-meters," (b) strip–film or overhead projectors fitted with timing shutters, (c) specially designed word tachistoscopes with accompanying visual materials,

and (d) 6-mm films constructed to provide quick perception practice of words and context. Such hardware is included in the bibliography of instructional materials in Appendix D.

*4. Timed exercises.* Quick recognition practice can also be provided by a series of timed exercises over which the pupil may determine his progress in speed and accuracy. Following are two examples:

A. DIRECTIONS:  For each of the following items, draw a line through each word which is the same in form as the first word in the series. Time yourself and note the number of seconds it takes you to complete the 15 items. Add one second for each incorrect response.

1. <u>notate</u>: notable; dictate; ~~notate~~; noting; denotate; no rate; ~~notate~~; notating

2. <u>through</u>: ~~through~~; though; ~~through~~; thorough; thought; throw; ~~through~~

B. DIRECTIONS: For each item, draw a line through each word in the series which has the same *root* as the first word in the series. Using the wall clock, determine the number of seconds it takes you to complete the exercise. Add one second for each incorrect response.

1. marker: maker; ~~remarked~~; necker; ~~markedly~~; ~~demarcate~~; masking; marred

2. labor: neighbor; ~~laboratory~~; ~~laborer~~; arbor; ~~elaborate~~; ~~belabor~~; Labrador; ladder

---

# REFERENCES

1. Irving H. Anderson and Walter Dearborn, *The Psychology of Teaching Reading* (New York: The Ronald Press Company, 1952) p. 177.
2. Eddie C. Kennedy, *Methods in Teaching Developmental Reading* (Itasca, Ill.: F. E. Peacock Publishers, Inc., 1974) p. 213.
3. Paul Witty, "Current Role and Effectiveness of Reading Among Youth," in *Reading in the High School and College*, Forty-seventh Yearbook, Part II, of the National Society for the Study of Education, N. B. Henry, Editor (Chicago: University of Chicago Press, 1948) pp. 15-19.
4. Roger Farr, *Reading: What Can Be Measured?* (Newark, Del.: International Reading Association, 1969) p. 81.
5. Kenneth S. Goodman, "A Linguistic Study of Cues and Miscues in Reading," *Elementary English* (October, 1965) pp. 639-43.
6. Rozanna A. and Robert B. McCall, "Comparative Validity of Five Reading Diagnostic Tests," *Journal of Educational Research* 62 (March, 1969) pp. 329-33.
7. Frederick B. Davis, "Fundamental Factors of Comprehension in Reading," *Psychometrika* 9 (1944) pp. 185-97.
8. E. L. Thomas, "Movements of the Eye," *Scientific American* 219 (August, 1968) pp. 88-95.
9. George R. Klare, *The Measurement of Readability* (Ames, Iowa: Iowa State University Press, 1963) p. 15.
10. Frederick B. Davis, "Psychometric Research on Comprehension in Reading," *Reading Research Quarterly* 7 (Summer, 1972) pp. 662-63.
11. Eddie C. Kennedy, *Methods in Teaching Developmental Reading*, pp. 225-26.

## SUPPLEMENTARY SOURCES

Bond, Guy L., and Miles A. Tinker. *Reading Difficulties: Their Diagnosis and Correction*, Chapter 12. New York: Appleton-Century-Crofts, 1967.
Dawson, Mildred A., Compiler. *Teaching Word Recognition Skills*. Newark, Del.: International Reading Association, 1970.
Deighton, Lee C. *Vocabulary Development in the Classroom*. New York: Teachers College Press, Columbia University, 1959.
Herber, Harold. *Teaching Reading in Content Areas*, Chapter 6. Englewood Cliffs, N.J.: Prentice-Hall, Inc., 1978.
Kennedy, Eddie C. *Methods in Teaching Developmental Reading*, Chapter 9. Itasca, Ill.: F. E. Peacock Publishers, Inc., 1974.
Thomas, Ellen L., and H. Alan Robinson. *Improving Reading in Every Class*, Chapter 2. Boston: Allyn and Bacon, Inc., 1972.

# TEN

# Bolstering Competency in Word Attack

*...the pupil who has a limited reading vocabulary or has difficulty in word recognition is handicapped in all phases of reading comprehension....upper grade pupils will be found whose techniques are more or less seriously defective and whose reading...suffers...from difficulties in dealing with unfamiliar words during the reading process.*

Arthur I. Gates

***Overview***   Chapter Ten continues the discussion of developing maturity in word-power behaviors initiated in Chapter Nine. The focus here is placed upon the upgrading of competency in attacking unfamiliar, unrecognized words in isolation or in context; the polishing of such specific behaviors as phonic analysis, structural analysis, contextual analysis, and the use of word references. General instructional strategy is related to the general model of instruction presented in Chapter Eight. Further recommendations and specific techniques are provided for the assessment of pupil word attack proficiency, particularly in the form of an Informal Survey of Word Attack Skills. Illustrative activities and exercise forms are included for preparing, teaching, and practicing these word attack behaviors.

# SECONDARY INSTRUCTION IN WORD ATTACK BEHAVIORS

*Word attack* refers to the reader's collective competency in analyzing an unfamiliar word — regardless of whether it is encountered in isolation or in context. The ultimate objective of learning word attack skills and knowledges, as in learning other specific reading behavior, is to enable the reader to obtain the needed meaning of the writer's message. The reader attacks an unfamiliar word either by analyzing its meaning more or less directly — or if necessary, by systematically synthesizing its component parts into the pronunciation of the word and then associating that word pronunciation with the word as it occurs in his listening vocabulary.* As Gates indicates, word attack proficiency is essential to general reading proficiency and deserves attention in secondary developmental, corrective, and remedial instruction.[1] The fundamental language and decoding processes contingent to word attack were discussed in Chapter Three.

## Significant Word Attack Behaviors

The usual major classifications of word attack behaviors pertinent to assessment and instruction at the secondary level consist of phonic analysis, structural analysis, contextual analysis, and the use of word references. As the reader matures, these behaviors should be coordinated into a single flexible attack whose immediate function is to decode the basic meaning of the message.[2] Upper-grade instruction should emphasize the combination of these skills in contextual reading as well as provide

---

*The fact that linguists, psychologists, and reading scholars differ in their views of the role of subvocalization in the quick recognition of words or word parts need not concern us in matters of instructional application of word attack at the secondary level. Such subvocalization occurs as a latter stage of development as an internalized psycholinguistic response which is instantaneous and generalized from more basic word competency.

review and practice in those particular behaviors in which the pupil is deficient. Most secondary pupils can profit from help in selective, efficient use of word attack behaviors in order to develop and maintain efficient interpretation of content. Illustrative of this higher-level use of word skills is the fact that recognition of familiar words may draw upon many of the same structural and syntactical cues employed in the studied analysis of an unfamiliar word.[3] The difference lies in how they are used — more rapidly, selectively, and subliminally in word recognition. In the same sense, pupils should utilize a word reference while in the act of reading only when other more efficient means of attack are insufficient.

The specific tasks relating to the learning of word attack competencies amount largely to being able to: (1) select and form associations of cue components of the word — with the word, the sentence, or the word resource, (2) synthesize these cues into a whole-word gestalt, which can be (3) associated with a meaning appropriate to its use in that contextual setting. The difference between the types of word attack behaviors lies largely in the mode of cue-response association formed.

## Phonic Analysis and Synthesis

*Phonic analysis* is concerned with graphemic-phonemic associations — the connection of appropriate sounds with individual letters and combinations of letters (phonograms) and the blending of these to produce the subvocal pronunciation of the whole word. The use of "phonics" requires a further association of this subvocal production of the word with its meaning (previously learned as part of the pupil's listening or general vocabulary). In mature reading situations, phonic analysis is of limited value unless (1) the word is part of the reader's listening and understanding vocabulary, or (2) the reader can generalize the meaning of the word from context and thus begin to form an association between the pronunciation and meaning for later use. Phonic analysis is less efficient and less frequently useful to the mature reader than other word attack abilities. It plays a more significant role in early reading instruction, where the pupil is learning to master the basic reading act and where his listening vocabulary is considerably larger than his reading vocabulary. For these reasons, intensive reteaching of phonics need not be stressed in the program aimed at the broad run of secondary readers.

### Structural Analysis and Synthesis

*Structural analysis* makes use of cues provided by the word structure parts of multiple unit and compound words. The reader may associate either pronunciation or meaning with these word units. If he associates and blends the pronunciation units to arrive at the whole-word pronunciation, he must then convert that pronunciation into meaning, as in phonic analysis. The direct association and synthesis of word-part meaning is the more efficient level of structural analysis and has the advantage of arriving at the meaning of words not presently a part of the reader's general or listening vocabulary. Most secondary pupils, particularly during the junior high period, can profit from systematic instruction and practice in the meaning analysis of word structure. The essential word components employed as cues in structural analysis consist of prefixes, roots, suffixes, variant forms, and general similarities to known words.

### Use of Context

The effective use of context draws heavily upon the pupil's general language proficiency and is a goal of instruction in basic interpretation as well as in word attack. Contextual analysis in word attack consists largely of: (1) utilizing general sentence meaning to trigger the quick recognition of familiar words or to anticipate the probable meaning of unfamiliar words, and (2) utilizing linguistic and typographical cues to analyze the contextual function of a difficult nonreferent word. Use of contextual meaning is the most frequently used word attack behavior of the mature reader. It is a complementary word attack skill, in that additional word-form cues are needed to confirm or pinpoint the particular word and meaning the writer used.

(Otherwise the reader would be "guessing" at the word from context — a perilous practice.)

### Use of Word References

The use of word references is as much a function of locational reading as it is of word attack. Where word attack is concerned, instruction and practice is limited primarily to the use of such word references as general and special dictionaries, the content glossary, the thesaurus, and in special circumstances, the book index. The focus of such word attack instruction is to obtain the meaning, pronunciation, and usage of the word or words in question.[4] If such instruction also improves the pupil's locational reading proficiency and vice versa — nothing is lost and much is gained.

## Teaching Word Attack Behaviors

Word attack behaviors — skilled responses, knowledges, and attitudes — contribute subtly to the overall proficiency of the basic reading act at any level, and they become essential to removing the impediment to meaning imposed by unfamiliar words or by familiar words used in an unfamiliar manner. In spite of the fact that most elementary approaches to reading instruction place a relatively heavy emphasis on word skill instruction,[5] many secondary pupils are capable of greater proficiency in word usage.[6] Such instruction may be incidental as well as planned. Normally, it will receive less stress than the development of vocabulary, interpretation, reaction, and extended personal reading. The emphasis of such instruction should be placed upon the efficient use of structural meaning clues, context, and word references.

### Structuring the Teaching of a Word Attack Behavior

Since word attack proficiency consists of the mastery of specific behaviors and their selective, versatile application in the integral reading act much as other specific reading behaviors, the major steps in a structure for teaching word attack behaviors would include:

*1. Identifying the specific word attack competence targeted for mastery learning in terms of the desired pupil behavioral outcome,* e.g., "to be able to blend (synthesize) unfamiliar words of two and three syllables into an accurate pronunciation of the word."

*2. Preassessing present pupil competence in the targeted behavior and, if necessary, in its contributing behaviors.* This may be accomplished through the use of a formal or informal diagnostic survey of word attack skills at the beginning of the course of instruction. Or it may be done just prior to beginning the initial instructional sequence by means of a group informal test, a test accompanying commercial instructional materials, or through individual pronunciation tests and oral reading analysis. Examples of contributing subbehaviors which may need to be assessed for the target behavior identified in step 1 above would include the ability to pronounce separate syllables, the ability to blend separate syllables, and the knowledge of the most fundamental syllabic rules and phonic generalizations. Of course, if these recently have been pretaught as prior components of a sequential program in word instruction, separate testing of contributing skills may be unnecessary.

*3. Developing readiness to learn the targeted specific word attack behavior.* The three major readiness tasks most often needed for secondary instruction in word attack are: (a) to motivate the pupil—to gain and hold the pupil's attention during explanation and to involve him in the execution of instructional and practice activities; (b) to bring the pupil to cognitive grasp of the nature and application of the targeted behavior in the typical reading act; and (c) to teach those necessary enabling behaviors which he has not mastered. Utilizing words which appeal to pupils or which have caused difficulty in prior instruction usually facilitates motivation and grasp of the functions involved.

*4. Demonstrating the mechanics and operational use of the word attack behavior.* Pupils with a history of word attack confusion and/or reading diffi-

culty will profit from an unhurried whole-part-whole demonstration of the processes involved—perhaps several times. The teacher may use a number of examples and inductively bring pupils to the generalized behavior. He may articulate the generalization and provide several examples and then ask the pupils to supply and demonstrate additional examples of the behavior. Or he may combine these approaches.

The use of the chalkboard, overhead projector, prepared worksheets, taped lessons, selected workbook pages, and other means that provide visual-aural associations and direct attention to the significant components would seem essential in demonstrating word attack behaviors. The use of some of the better commercially prepared film strips and transparencies dealing with word attack behavior provides possible alternative approaches. When possible, the demonstration and explanation stage should be handled with smaller groups of pupils so that the teacher can readily identify pupil confusions, and pupils can be encouraged to ask questions and to take an active part in the lesson interaction.

*5. Providing guided practice in using the targeted behavior.* The first reinforcement practice should follow immediately upon step 4 and should be done under close teacher supervision to detect pupil confusions and to confirm successes. Independent practice may consist of the second stage of the guided practice or may be handled as a take-home assignment or part of the next class meeting. The selection of words for immediate and delayed practice is of some importance. Generally, the progression of words used should be from familiar words to unfamiliar words, from simple applications of the behavior to more complex applications, and from word items which confirm the generalized word behavior to those words which reveal exceptions to the rule.

*6. Assessing pupil mastery of the targeted word attack behavior.* A separate testing exercise on the particular behavior may not be necessary where the teacher has had close contact with smaller groups of pupils during instruction and where sufficient evidence of performance adequacy is available from practice exercises and observation of behavior on practice activities. More mature pupils should be encouraged to keep their own skill progress records and make self-diagnosis of their success and difficulties. Small-group and/or individual appraisal should be scheduled for pupils having difficulty mastering the targeted behavior. It can be useful to do periodic testing of earlier taught behaviors in order to assess the retention of those behaviors after intervening instruction has taken place.

*7. Encouraging retention and transfer of the learned word behavior through systematically delayed practice and application in reading situations.* A number of activities which may be used for ensuring retention and transfer are suggested in the later sections of this chapter. The judicious selection of words for these activities and exercises will facilitate the function of this step—i.e., selecting words which have proved troublesome in recent lessons, selecting words which play a significant role in upcoming reading lessons, and selecting words from targeted vocabulary lists—either high-frequency general vocabulary lists or technical vocabulary of content area courses.

## Some Guidelines for Word Attack Instruction

The place, manner, and degree of emphasis to be accorded word attack instruction periodically has become a controversial issue in beginning and primary-grade reading instruction.[7] This is less true for secondary-level reading instruction, because word attack is more readily perceived as enabling behavior in the broader pursuit of meaning. Also, fewer secondary teachers have been indoctrinated in word-dominated teaching theory, and the pupils have had prior exposure to most of the word attack behaviors.

It has been suggested that most junior high or late middle school pupils could benefit from review instruction and efficiency practice in the more advanced word attack behaviors, and that some may need systematic reteaching in fundamental word attack behaviors as part of a corrective and remedial effort. It would be unfortunate if such instruction should be overemphasized and misapplied, for that would create more problems for the reader and the program than could be justified by resulting benefits. It may be helpful, therefore, to present some practical principles to guide instruction in word attack.

*1.* Word attack behaviors should be taught in the perspective of the integral reading act and the total reading program. Both pupil and teacher should recognize that word skills are means to the end, which is the understanding of content. It is the development of interpretation and reaction behaviors which requires the greater instructional emphasis in most secondary school learning situations.[8]

*2.* It will be counterproductive to the learning, motivation, and the reputation of the secondary reading program to ask all pupils to follow slavishly a total program in reteaching the fundamental word attack behaviors. Many secondary pupils can profit from some review of word attack behavior—when the thrust of instruction is the development of greater efficiency and flexibility in the use of word attack, or when it is geared to the learning of new or troublesome words. The reteaching of specific word attack skills is most efficiently handled on a selective basis as the result of preassessment surveys and diagnostic testing.

*3.* Upper reader word attack deficiencies are more probable in structural analysis and word reference behaviors. Usually, they have not received instructional emphasis at earlier levels. Also, structural analysis and word reference learning and usage require greater reading and language maturity.

*4.* Instruction in specific word attack behaviors should not be limited to reading instructional situations. Word analysis behaviors are germane to all areas of language usage. The precise use of phonics, structural analysis, and word references is more a requirement of encoding, as in writing and speaking, than in silent reading. Some reading authorities recommend that primary responsibility for the teaching of specific word attack behaviors should be placed in the spelling-writing curriculum.[9]

*5.* The use of word attack behaviors in personal or instructional reading situations should stress efficiency in obtaining necessary meaning. If an unfamiliar word cannot be readily identified by a combination of word perception behaviors, pupils should be encouraged to attack it systematically on an efficiency priority basis, i.e., first the use of context plus structural analysis, then add phonics, and finally, word reference when necessary. Likewise, developmental and content reading of selections should not be interrupted for word attack lessons. It is better for the teacher to supply the pronunciation and/or meaning of the word causing the pupil difficulty, to add this word to a list in the margin of the teacher's text or notes, and to include these words in later separate vocabulary and word attack instructional sessions.

*6.* Word attack behaviors should be taught within a context of meaning. Whenever feasible, unfamiliar words to be analyzed should be presented within meaningful oral or written context. The word product of word analysis–synthesis activity should be associated with or tested for meaning. Provision should be made for using such word products by reading them in context or by using them in writing/speaking activities.

*7.* Care should be taken not to teach word part behaviors in isolation. This is a particularly important guideline for those word behaviors which stress phonic or structural analysis of word parts. Analysis of words should be followed by their synthesis or blending to arrive at the articulation of the whole word.

*8.* Structural rules, phonic generalizations, and technical terms should be introduced only when they will aid the pupil. Owing to Celtic-Anglo-Saxon-Roman-American contributions to English, it is not a phonetically or structurally consistent language. Word elements take on different sounds and/or meanings in different words; different words have similar pronunciations; and similar word forms take on different pronunciations and/or meanings in different language contexts.

Moreover, the verbalizing of elaborate rule systems often carries little correlation with effective recognition and analysis of words in the actual reading situation, as remedial teachers soon learn when working with older disabled readers who have been immersed in years of phonics reteaching.

*9.* A secondary pupil's deficiency in phonics or any other set of word attack behaviors cannot be safely attributed to a lack of opportunity to master these behaviors nor can one presume that this deficiency will be readily mitigated by the provision of instruction in that behavior. It is the more likely case that this pupil has had much reteaching in this word deficiency, especially if phonics related, and that this has led to reinforced confusion and negativism in this area. It may be wise to stress alternative approaches to word attack and sight recognition of whole words for such pupils until they have developed greater confidence in their word attack skill.

*10.* Persistent, serious word attack deficiency can be the result and/or concomitance of general reading difficulty or basic learning disability. The assumption that reading difficulty is the simple product of word analysis problems has led to many useless and deadly hours of remedial programs dominated by word-focused instruction. Word recognition and analysis problems can be and usually are no more than a part of the more general syndrome of reading disability. Words and word behaviors are more readily learned and applied when the pupil is not confounded by other problems in handling the reading act. The assessment and prescriptive remediation of serious deficiency in fundamental behaviors in learning and dealing with words should be handled with a broader diagnostic assessment of the pupil's general reading performance, language proficiency, learning potential, emotional stability, and auditory-visual perception.

### The Teaching of Phonics

The position taken in this text is that instruction in phonic analysis and synthesis should be made available to those pupils who exhibit both notable difficulty in the use of phonics and an ability to profit readily from such instruction. The majority of secondary pupils will need no more than a quick review and some practice in flexibly and efficiently using phonic analysis in conjunction with other word skills. For most secondary pupils, word behavior instruction is more productively centered in the development of vocabulary, the quick perception of words, the efficient use of word references, and the selective use of structural analysis.

In any case, the teaching of phonics should be conducted pragmatically.[10] A number of elaborate phonic systems have appeared upon the market, and the secondary school and teacher would be wise to avoid becoming entangled in such morasses of inconsistent rules and overelaborated specifics. Instructional controversies and differences in educational philosophies have combined to convince naive teachers that the accurate and precise use of phonics is a crucial reading behavior. It is not, at least in the upper grades! The vast majority of mature readers make relatively little use of phonics, and when they do, tend to utilize a few of the most generalized form-sound associations. Elaborate phonic systems are not consistent with the minimal number of perceptual-cognitive cues needed by the adequate reader for receptionally processing graphic representations of meaningful language. Many of the same cautions can be expressed about the intensive shaping of reading instruction around any of the various linguistic "theories" which currently are fashionable in language circles. In these matters, the secondary reading teacher would do well to consider Durrell's observation of some years ago concerning the deifying of word systems in reading instruction: "Areas of ignorance always produce highly emotional crusaders for picayune details which they consider matters of great moment."[11]

The selective teaching of phonic analysis and synthesis is defensible for secondary pupils with inhibiting deficiencies in form-sound association, when conducted on a pragmatic basis as recommended in prior discussion. In this respect, Burmeister has published a comparative review of seven studies on the utility of phonics generalizations and has identified those which have broad enough application to be considered useful.[12]

*Consonant sounds*

1. "C" followed by "e," "i," or "y" sounds soft; otherwise, "c" is hard (omit "ch"). (certain, city, cycle; attic, cat, clip; success)
2. "G" followed by "e," "i," or "y" sounds soft; otherwise, "g" is hard (omit "gh"). (gell, agile, gypsy; gone, flag, grope; suggest)
3. "Ch" is usually pronounced as it is in "kitchen," not like "sh" as in "machine."
4. When a word ends in "ck," it has the same last sound as in "look."
5. When "ght" is seen in a word, "gh" is silent. (thought, night, right)
6. When two of the same consonants are side-by-side, only one is heard. (dollar, paddle)

*Vowel sounds: single vowels*

1. If the only vowel letter is at the end of a word, the letter usually stands for a long sound (one-syllable words only). (be, he, she, go)
2. When "consonant + y" are the final letters in a one-syllable word, the "y" has a "long i" sound; in a polysyllabic word the "y" has a "short i" (long e) sound. (my, by, cry; baby, dignity)
3. A single vowel in a closed syllable has a short sound, except that it may be modified in words in which the vowel is followed by an "r." (club, dress, at, car, pumpkin, virgin)
4. The "r" gives the preceding vowel a sound that is neither long nor short. (car, care, far, fair, fare) [single or double vowels]

*Vowel sounds: final "vowel-consonant-e"*

When a word ends in "vowel-consonant-e" the "e" is silent, and the vowel may be long or short. (cape, mile, contribute, accumulate, exile, line; have, prove, encourage, ultimate, armistice, come, intensive, futile, passage)

*Vowel sounds: adjacent vowels*

1. Digraphs: When the following double-vowel combinations are seen together, the first is usually long and the second is silent: ai, ay, ea,

ee, oa, ow (ea may also have a "short e" sound, and ow may have an "ou" sound). [main, pay; eat, bread; see, oat, sparrow, how]

2. Diphthongs (or blends): The following double-vowel combinations usually blend: au, aw, ou, oi, oy, oo ("oo" has two common sounds). [auto, awful, house, coin, boy, book, rooster]

3. "io" and "ia": "io" and "ia" after "c," "t," or "s" help to make a consonant sound: vi*cio*us, par-*tia*l, musi*cia*n, vi*sio*n, atten*tio*n (even o*cea*n).

*Syllabication: determination of a syllable*

Every single vowel or vowel combination means a syllable (except a "final e" in a "vowel-conso-nant-e" ending).

*Syllabication: structural syllabication*

These generalizations take precedence over phonic syllabication generalizations.

1. Divide between a prefix and a root.
2. Divide between two roots.
3. Usually divide between a root and a suffix.

*Syllabication: phonic syllabication*

1. When two vowel sounds are separated by two consonants, divide between the consonants but consider "ch," "sh," "ph," and "th" to be single consonants. (assist, convey, bunny, Houston, rustic)

2. When two vowel sounds are separated by one consonant, divide either before or after the consonant. Try dividing before the consonant first. (Consider "ch," "sh," "ph," and "th" to be single consonants.) [alone, select, ashamed, Japan, sober; comet, honest, ever, idiot, modest, agile, general]

3. When a word ends in a "consonant-l-e" divide before the consonant. (battle, treble, tangible, kindle).

*Accent*

1. In most two-syllable words, the first syllable is accented.

    a. And, when there are two like consonant letters within a word the syllable before the double consonant is usually accented (begin-ner, letter).

    b. But, two vowel letters together in the last syllable of a word may be a clue to an accented final syllable (complain, conceal).

2. In inflected or derived forms of words, the pri-mary accent usually falls on or within the root word (boxes, untie). [Therefore, if "a," "in," "re," "ex," "de," or "be" is the first syllable in a word, it is usually unaccented.]

Although instruction in phonics ordinarily will not occupy a priority emphasis in the secondary school, teachers of corrective and remedial reading programs will find it useful to gain a better grasp of the specifics of such instruction before becoming involved. In this respect, a number of sensible treatments have been published which will extend the teacher's understanding beyond the general principles and illustrative developmental proce-dures to which this chapter has been limited. These useful professional references have been listed at the end of Chapter Ten.

# ASSESSING WORD ATTACK BEHAVIORS

Word attack assessment serves several purposes in word attack instruction: surveying pupil strengths and weaknesses in word attack behaviors to identify instructional objectives and priority among such objectives, preassessing present competency in an instructionally targeted word attack behavior, identifying deficiencies in enabling skills and abili-ties upon which instruction in word attack behavior is dependent, providing formative assessment and feedback to the pupil concerning accuracy of her learning response, and supplying summative evalu-ation concerning mastery or progress made in word attack skills and knowledges.

Appraisal of word attack competency should be an integral part of thorough reading assessment; it is especially important in cases of notable reading disability.[13] Knowledge of word skill deficiency often provides insight concerning inadequacy in larger reading performance, while assessment of silent and oral reading performance helps to place word strengths and weaknesses in proper perspective.[14] The close relationship between word abilities and general reading performance was discussed in Chapter Seven and is readily illustrated by the nature and functions of the cloze procedure, the informal reading inventory, and word sample pronunciation tests. The interdependence of word attack assessment, vocabulary assessment, and the survey of pupil word power were emphasized in Chapter Eight.

The word assessment instruments upon which the developmental and corrective reading teacher at the secondary level may draw fall into two classifications: published group word ability tests or batteries and informal word assessment surveys and tests. With appropriate training, the teacher may also employ individual reading diagnostic batteries which include specific word skill tests and word error diagnosis through oral and silent reading appraisal.

## Published Group Word Tests

Published tests which may be of use in the secondary program include group tests which incorporate or focus upon word skill measurement. Typically, these are batteries consisting of tests or subtests which measure two or more of such word abilities as reading vocabulary, accuracy of word perception, structural analysis, and phonic analysis of various types. Sometimes these are labeled, rather ambitiously, as "diagnostic" reading tests. Raw scores obtained on these tests can be converted into norms, or more meaningfully, into a profile of performance on differentiated word abilities. Some reading survey test batteries include subtests of vocabulary and related word skills.

The advantages of published tests include professional skill in development, efficiency of measurement, norms and diagnostic profiles, and associated aids for interpretation and use of results. The majority of these tests require silent rather than oral

response from the pupil, although the teacher or examiner may read some stimulus items aloud for the phonic sections of the test. Some test developers argue that this silent analysis and response makes these group tests more realistic. The group-silent assessment conditions place some restriction upon the number and specificity of the behaviors assessed. Standardized tests are not easily geared to particular instructional objectives, and groups do not encourage close observation of the pupil's method in arriving at his correct or incorrect word response.

Most group word ability batteries are intended for screening purposes at upper elementary and middle school use, with norms developed on those grades. While word performance tests developed for such populations can provide some insight concerning the capabilities of upper-grade pupils to handle the tasks involved, these, like other criterion assessments, will need to be interpreted on face performance (e.g., the pupil correctly identifies short-vowel usage with 90 percent or better accuracy). However, it is no more correct to use norms with upper-grade pupils which are developed on lower-grade pupils for word skill tests than for any other type of test.

In fact, there are few published group word ability tests that extend into secondary school. Rarely are such tests normed for the entire upper-grade range because there has been relatively little school demand for them.

In general, published group word ability tests are better used for screening pupils early in the secondary years and for broad diagnostic purposes with selected pupils evidencing notable word difficulty thereafter. These published survey tests of word abilities will need to be supplemented by criterion-oriented measures. Diagnosis of word attack difficulty usually requires individual assessment. Some of the more pertinent published individual diagnostic reading batteries with word assessment subtests or components are identified in Appendix A. Generally, these are assessment sources best employed by specialists and experienced reading teachers.

## Informal Assessment of Word Attack

Classroom assessment is necessary to bring evaluation in juxtaposition with instructional objectives and to fill in the gaps of information left by standardized testing. This applies as much to the assessment of word power as it does to other significant areas of reading assessment. Reading instructional materials often include vocabulary and word skill tests or workbook exercises which can be used directly or can be modified to meet the assessment needs of a class or individual pupil. The teacher with some understanding of word power should be able to devise other measures and situations to assess specific criterion word behaviors.

Reading teachers may construct their own diagnostic inventory of analysis skills to screen pupils for operational deficiencies or to supplement information gained from other sources. Such measures are criterion-oriented—they attempt to determine whether the pupil has mastered the particular competency or needs aid with specific components of the word analysis task. Informal word attack measures are more useful when the teacher is familiar with how the parts of the test relate to independence in word analysis, when he or she has experience with test results, and when word attack performance is compared with other observations of the pupil's reading and word ability.

An example of such a screening measure, the *Informal Survey of Word Attack Skills*, is presented on the following pages. The writer has found this survey useful both as a practical individual screening of secondary pupil competency in word analysis and as a means of illustrating the applied functions of these behaviors to secondary teachers who may have little background in such matters. It samples pupil word attack behavior in five key areas: use of context, individual word synthesis, structural analysis of words, phonic analysis of words, and word readiness skills. The total test and the separate subtests are arranged to test from greater to lesser competency. This informal survey, like any such informal test, does not assume to be a complete assessment of word power, but can be used as a quick direct check on suspected difficulty with the more essential word attack behaviors. It may be used as part of a more thorough reading diagnostic effort. It should be used to complement other assessment data from standardized and informal tests of vocabulary, oral reading performances, use of word sources, and reading interpretation and study skills.

---

### INFORMAL SURVEY OF WORD ATTACK SKILLS

NOTE: This individual survey contains 12 functional tests which sample pupil competency in five areas of word analysis performance: Part I, Contextual Analysis: Part II, Individual Word Synthesis; Part III, Structural Analysis of Words; Part IV, Phonic Analysis of Words; and Part V, Word Readiness.

For screening purposes, the examiner should start at the level estimated that the pupil can handle and move forward and/or backward as needed. The survey is arranged so that the several parts, and the tests within each part, appear in order of word attack sophistication and frequency of use among maturing readers. This increases efficiency in general screening, since strong (accurate and fluent) performance on Parts I and II or on the first tests of Parts III or IV suggest little need to check on the contributing behaviors measured in the later tests.

The examiner should be as cognizant of the pupil's general confidence and successful attack in an area as on a specific test behavior. Experience indicates that approximately

90 percent or better accuracy on a particular test is an indication of competency in that area. An accuracy of 75 percent or less suggests need for further analysis or instructional help in that skill. An accuracy of 50 percent or less indicates serious difficulty and suggests that the pupil has some deficiency on the more basic skills contributing to that test.

### Part I: Contextual Analysis

The ability to use context to arrive at the quick recognition of known words or in conjunction with the studied analysis of unknown words is one of the most useful word attack behaviors for mature readers. Among the more common of such context clues are direct definition, synonym or restatement, comparison and contrast, familiar expression or experience, summary, and mood or tone. Test A samples the pupil's ability to arrive at the correct recognition/analysis of a key word by use of context and selected word parts. Correct spelling or pronunciation of the word is not necessary if the response can be identified as correct in meaning.

### Test A: Use of Context and Word Parts

DIRECTIONS: Read each of the following sentences and supply the word which is incomplete.

1. The boys were angry. T_____ yelled and stomped.
2. We entered the old warehouse at dusk. The machines stared down like silent mon_____rs.
3. They were a very different pair; he was old and slow while she was young and spr_____ly.
4. Someone appointed to take care of parentless children is known as a g_____-ian.
5. The c___pli___ted plan confused me.
6. Gazing at the sky that night, we could see five c_____t_ll_t_____s.
7. A house d_____ against itself cannot stand.
8. Take that sick child to a p_____tri_____n.
9. Why do I say she is e___t___t_cal? She is vain, selfish, and insensitive!
10. Only a few came to the mission the first year. But in four years it took a new building to hold the con_____n.

### Part II: Individual Word Synthesis

Test B checks the fluency with which the pupil can combine word cues (primarily structural elements) to arrive at the fluent pronunciation and meaning of largely unfamiliar words. The examiner is concerned with three types of assessment: (1) Does the pupil readily and accurately pronounce the word in a confident, efficient manner? (Mark it *P*.) (2) Does he arrive at a reasonable meaning by studied analysis of the word? (Mark it *M*.) (3) Can he arrive at a fluent pronunciation of the word by studied analysis? (Mark it *A*.) If the pupil appears to be quite familiar with most of these words, it probably indicates that he has read considerably and has general word power strength.

## Test B: Reading and Defining Words

DIRECTIONS: First read and pronounce each word and then give a reasonable meaning for it. If you are not sure of the pronunciation or of the meaning, take time to analyze it.

| | | |
|---|---|---|
| 1. fortifier | 6. bilaterally | 11. polyphony |
| 2. deflation | 7. nonchromatic | 12. interdigital |
| 3. subserving | 8. irreverency | 13. autointoxicating |
| 4. promisee | 9. superfluity | 14. circumlocutional |
| 5. reflectance | 10. predicating | 15. comatose |

## Part III: Structural Analysis of Words

The major concern of the three tests in Part III is to check on pupil competency in using word structure clues (prefixes, roots, affixes) to analyze words. Classroom observation or difficulty experienced in Test B may have raised questions about the pupil's accuracy and fluency in this significant aspect of mature word recognition and analysis. The most efficient structural analysis produces word meaning directly. A second level of structural analysis produces efficient word pronunciation for which meaning is associated by aural recall. It is useful to assess the pupil's ability to handle both types of structural analysis—accurate pronunciation and meaning. Test C assesses the ability to meaningfully combine affixes and roots. If the pupil performs strongly (90% or better), there may be no need to administer Tests D and E. Test D assesses the pupil's knowledge of quite common prefixes and suffixes. Test E measures a more basic skill of structural analysis—the abilities to pronounce the word and to distinguish the prefixes, roots, and suffixes of these multistructural words.

## Test C: Combining Roots and Affixes

DIRECTIONS: Select the needed word parts (prefixes and suffixes) from the lists given which make it possible to build the root into a longer word with the meaning given for the item. (Correct answer given in brackets).

| I. Meaning | II. Root | III. Response |
|---|---|---|
| (Example) to erect again | build | _re_ build_ing_ |
| 1. poisonous | eat | ____eat_____ [uneatable] |
| 2. one who examines | spect | ____spect_____ [inspector] |
| 3. an exciting happening | vent | ____vent_____ [adventure] |
| 4. substitute | place | ____place_____ [replacement] |
| 5. unusual | stand | ____stand_____ [outstanding] |
| 6. not free | pend | ____pend_____ [dependent] |
| 7. wrong | take | ____take_____ [mistaken] |
| 8. something thrown | ject | ____ject_____ [projectile] |
| 9. courageous manner | fear | fear____ _____ [fearlessly] |
| 10. foolish, imprudent | creet | _____ _____creet [indiscreet] |

*Prefixes:* ad, be, de, dis, in, mis, out, pro, re, sub, un

*Suffixes:* able, ed, en(n), ent, ile, ing, less, ly, ment, or, ure

### Test D: Meaning of Common Affixes

DIRECTIONS: Identify the letter of the prefix (word beginning) or suffix (word ending) in List I which has the same meaning as the numbered word or phrase given in List II, and fits the example word given. (Correct letter of response is given at the right of the item.)

|  | | | *List II* | |
| --- | --- | --- | --- | --- |
| *List I: Affix* | | *Meaning* | *Example* | |
| a. | ad— | 1. under | ____soil | (o) |
| b. | —an | 2. two | ____plane | (c) |
| c. | bi— | 3. before | ____pare | (l) |
| d. | con— | 4. belonging to | urb____ | (b) |
| e. | dis— | 5. again | ____charged | (m) |
| f. | —en | 6. condition of | boy____ | (g) |
| g. | —hood | 7. without | blame____ | (i) |
| h. | —ing | 8. apart | ____sect | (e) |
| i. | —less | 9. act of | jump____ | (h) |
| j. | —ness | 10. after | ____script | (k) |
| k. | post— | | | |
| l. | pre— | | | |
| m. | re— | | | |
| n. | —some | | | |
| o. | sub— | | | |
| p. | —ty | | | |
| q. | —ure | | | |

### Test E: Distinguishing Roots and Affixes

DIRECTIONS: First pronounce the word to yourself. Then in the blank following the word, write the root of the word, the number of prefixes, and the number of suffixes it has. (Correct response provided in brackets to right.)

| *I. Word* | *II. Response* |
| --- | --- |
| (Example) replayed | ____(1) play (1)____ |
| 1. guilty | _____ [guilt (1)] |
| 2. protester | _____ [(1) test (1)] |
| 3. uncertain | _____ [(1) cert (1)] |
| 4. bicycles | _____ [(1) cycle (1)] |
| 5. enchantment | _____ [(1) chant (1)] |
| 6. prelease | _____ [(1) lease] |
| 7. maladjusted | _____ [(2) just (1)] |

|  |  |  |
|---|---|---|
| 8. superstructure | _____ | [(2) struct (1)] |
| 9. nonextending | _____ | [(2) tend (1)] |
| 10. oddity | _____ | [odd (2)] |

## Part IV: Phonic Analysis and Synthesis

Part IV consists of five short pronunciation tests (Tests F through J). The tests in Part IV require individual pupil testing. However, this should prove no great problem; only selected pupils will need to be assessed in the behaviors in Part IV, and the individual tests take little time. Also, Tests F through J are arranged in decreasing order of composite phonic unit. Thus, it is unnecessary to administer the later tests in the sequence when the pupil demonstrates solid competency (90% accuracy) on an earlier test.

### Test F: Syllable Blending

DIRECTIONS: Have pupil pronounce these syllable groups aloud as if they were words. The concern here is with the pupil's ability to *blend* together the total pronunciations of the individual syllables. If he seems to have difficulty with individual syllables, have him take Test G. Say to the pupil: "Read these aloud as if they were words. Read them across the page."

| | | | | | | | |
|---|---|---|---|---|---|---|---|
| tergo | nevor | bigat | eldow | lidate | gastu | lewpi | forbrine |
| subary | tilerete | lopunack | ripelee | denerous | trindolar | kismetoot | |

### Test G: Syllables

DIRECTIONS: The purpose is to assess ability to deal with common-form syllables independently. Alternate vowel sounds are acceptable in a number of cases. If pupil has trouble or lacks fluency in the sounds, have him take Test H. Say to the pupil: "Read these aloud, look at it carefully and say it again."

| | | | | | | | | | | |
|---|---|---|---|---|---|---|---|---|---|---|
| int | oke | ler | pud | eed | ane | ack | nul | shu | pir | ile |
| ust | ging | dils | chit | zurp | cred | thart | brot | whin | | |

### Test H: Phonograms

DIRECTIONS: "Pronounce these as they should sound. Read them across the page. Pause between each set."

| | | | | | | | |
|---|---|---|---|---|---|---|---|
| lo | ra | en | ud | ip | fu | er | ir |
| st | th | br | ch | sp | wh | cl | bl |
| ai | oa | oo | aw | ay | oi | ow | ea |

### Test I: Giving and Blending Sounds

DIRECTIONS: Pupils can have difficulty with phonograms (Test H) because they cannot synthesize or blend the two sounds involved. Test I checks this ability. The pupil takes one combination at a time, sounds each letter, then produces the blend. Alternate vowel sounds are acceptable. Say to the pupil: "Give the sound of each letter, then blend them into one sound."

r—a    i—p    u—l    d—e    w—o    a—s—p
o—r—k    n—i—t    v—e—r    b—r—u    b—a—n—t
j—o—r—y    f—l—d    y—u—m—p    s—h—e—v

### Test J: Letter Sounds

1. Vowel Sounds (Long and Short)

DIRECTIONS: "Give two different sounds (long and short) for each of the following letters."

i    o    u    a    e    y

2. Consonant Sounds

DIRECTIONS: "Give a sound for each of the following letters."

t    m    d    k    b    r    w    f    j    h
n    g    v    z    q    p    x    c    s    l

### Part V: Word Readiness

Occasionally a secondary pupil will have word attack problems because he cannot draw upon certain foundational word skills. Visual discrimination and association (Test K) and auditory discrimination and association (Test L) are the two most probable bases of such word deficiency. If a secondary pupil evidences difficulty on Tests J, K, or L, he should be examined more thoroughly for perceptual, learning, and/or language difficulties.

### Test K: Small–Letter Names

DIRECTIONS: Use a mask or hand tachistoscope and give the pupil no more than ½ second for his first response. Give him longer if he errs. Say to the pupil: "Say the name of each letter."

w    r    b    m    t    s    d    x    k    c    f    v    g
h    j    n    z    l    q    p    e    o    u    i    y

### Test L: Auditory Blending

DIRECTIONS: This is an auditory, not a visual, test; the teacher gives individual sounds at 1-second intervals, then the pupil blends the sounds. Say to the pupil: "I will say some separate sounds. You say the word they make."

n—o    i—t    a—m    c—r—y    th—ing    h—e—n
p—o—d    m—a—n—y    br—an—ch    b—ir—d
h—i—l—t    t—u—s—k    h—un—gr—y
pl—an—t—ing    p—ar—d—ner

# ILLUSTRATIVE ACTIVITIES FOR WORD ATTACK INSTRUCTION

## Phonic Analysis Activities (Form–Sound Association)

*1. Inductively teaching a form-sound association.* Most reading authorities suggest the use of a planned sequence for teaching pupils to identify and pronounce significant word parts.[15] Inducing pupils to form accurate general responses often proves more effective than catechismic repetition of teacher-given association. Five fundamental steps for inductively teaching a form-sound association are presented below. With modification, the procedure also can be used to teach the form-pronunciation association of prefixes and suffixes.

*a. Determining that pupils can distinguish the sound of the element to be taught.* The teacher may pronounce sounds in pairs, one which contains the sound to be associated, and ask pupils to tell when the sounds are different or similar, generally progressing from gross difference to fine, e.g., "ile—art; ile—lap; ile—ile; ile—ale; ile—ile; ile—la," etc. Next the teacher may pronounce a group of words with a sound element in common and ask pupils to identify that element—e.g., "mile," "file," "while"—and then ask individual pupils to pronounce other words which have the same common sound element. Some instructional audiotapes provide for this element for small group and individual practice.

*b. Determining that pupils can distinguish the form of the word element to be associated.* The teacher may write three or four words on the board and ask a pupil or pupils to underline their common element, e.g., m<u>ile</u>, f<u>ile</u>, p<u>ile</u>. When that element is identified, pupils may be asked to identify the element form in other words presented on a study or exercise sheet.

*c. Establish the association.* The teacher pronounces or asks pupils to pronounce the words written on the board, emphasizing the sound and form each has in common. Pupils suggest addi-

tional words with the same sound, and the pupil or the teacher writes them on the board and underlines the common element, e.g., t<u>ile</u>, r<u>ile</u>, sm<u>ile</u>, etc. Individual pupils are asked to pronounce one word from the board while the class audits accuracy, or the group pronounces the various words in unison as the teacher points to them. Such practice should include provision for using the word in context or otherwise dealing with its meaning to make sure pupils make an appropriate association, e.g., filed rather than filled.

*d. The association is immediately reinforced.* The immediate practice may involve whole group activities: e.g., the teacher flashes cards with the element and words containing the element along with previously taught elements and their example words, and the pupils pronounce them or identify the differences. Such immediate reinforcement also may be handled through pupil worksheets completed under teacher guidance. Another common form of such reinforcement is for the pupil to use letter or phonogram cards to form words the teacher pronounces which employ the element.

*e. The association is further reinforced, extended, and distinguished.* Any number of group and independent activities, games, and worksheet exercises may be used to provide delayed practice and extension. Wherever possible, such activities should be meaningful and employ oral or written context. After the basic form-sound association is established, practice with accompanying explanation and instruction should be extended to include variants (filing, miler, compile, isle.) Finally, the now established association is distinguished from confusing associations, e.g., ile, ill, le, el, etc.

*2. Search and study.* An activity which can be used either as an introductory study of a phonogram or as a reinforcement exercise involves asking pupils to locate five to ten words in the evening newspaper (or text chapter) which contain the targeted element. The next day a composite class list is formed from this collection. (The teacher should be prepared to add as many as necessary to arrive at a total list of fifteen or twenty. If the phonogram is capable of taking two or more pronunciations, such as *augh* (laugh, taught), the group (individually or collectively) may classify them according to alternate sounds. The dictionary may be used to determine or verify pronunciation. The activity may be concluded by asking pupils to write sentences using five words for each of the different sounds for the phonogram in the same sentence. (The best of these sentences may be saved to use in later discrimination exercises.)

*3. Reconstructing or writing limericks.* If the pupils are not familiar with limericks, the teacher may develop a study sheet with several examples and discuss their significant characteristics — change in rhyme and rhythm (meter). The following block form may then be used so that pupils may change the rhyme (and meaning). This may be restricted to words with certain sound elements or it may be left as an open rhyming task. Interested and capable pupils should be encouraged to create their own limericks. The activity can be varied to include other forms of light verse, such as Graham's "Little Billy," Housman's "Infant Innocence," Ogden Nash's "The Turtle," etc.

> There was a young teacher of (<u>verse</u>)
> Who rhymed while he sat with a (<u>nurse</u>).
> At the end of his (<u>tryst</u>)
> A voice came through the (<u>mist</u>)
> Get a doctor if you become (<u>worse</u>).

*4. Game practice.* Like sight vocabulary, word attack lends itself to a variety of game forms which can be used for motivated reinforcement of sound-form associations and discrimination.

*a. Spin the blend wheel.* Out of cardboard or oak tag, cut a wheel disc with a diameter of 9 inches (for small groups) or 18 inches for the class. Around the edge of the wheel print the letter blends which have been learned to date (e.g., *bl*, *ch*, *cr*, *fl*, *sp*, etc.). Fashion a spinner or pointer, which is then fastened at the center of the wheel. The group is divided into two teams, and each member takes a turn at spinning the pointer. One point is earned for pronouncing a word that contains the blend indicated by the pointer. A second point is earned by correctly using the word in an oral sentence. If the pupil spinning

the wheel fails on one of these tasks, volunteers from the other side may pick up those points by supplying the correct answer.

*b. Phonic bingo.* This is a variation of word bingo, described earlier. In this case, cards are constructed with either phonic elements or words which have key phonograms *underlined* and written in the squares (in different random order for each card). The caller pronounces sounds and an example word containing that sound, and the players cover the word or word element on their cards which represents that sound. First player with five contiguous squares covered wins.

*c. Letters and answers.* This game can be played independently as a riddle-solving activity or between individuals or small groups as a game. It also can be related to content area study. A set of envelopes is collected. On each envelope a question is asked or a riddle stated which can be answered by one word. Inside the envelope are placed cut-up cards or oak tags, each with a printed letter or phonogram which, when arranged in the proper order, will give the answer to the question or riddle. Examples:

> A sticky-footed cop. ( G u m s h o e )
> The happiest state in the union.
> ( M a r y l a n d )
> Like father, like son. ( c a s t e )
> Environmental rip-off. ( p o l l u t i o n )

*5. Worksheet exercise forms.* There is a considerable amount of published exercise material dealing with word attack, much of which emphasizes phonic analysis or sound-form association. A good deal of this material has been written for elementary pupils, but that does not preclude its use for secondary pupils who need considerable instruction and practice in basic phonics. These prepared exercises and phonic programs should be used selectively, and they may need modification to fit class circumstances and abilities. There is no lack of available models of learning and practice exercises for the teacher who makes a serious effort to locate them. The following are simply representative of the range of such exercises.

## MATCHING HOMOPHONES

DIRECTIONS:  Each of the words in column I can be matched with its homophone in column II. Write the letter of the matching word in the blank before the number. A homophone, you will remember, is a word which has the same pronunciation as another word, but which has a different form or is spelled differently.

|     | I | | II |
| --- | --- | --- | --- |
| (c) | 1. pail | | a. bare |
| (a) | 2. bear | | b. dear |
| (d) | 3. cite | | c. pale |
| (b) | 4. deer | | d. sight |
|     | etc. | | etc. |

## RECOGNIZING SILENT LETTERS.

DIRECTIONS: Twenty-five words are listed below. Identify the twelve words with silent letters by underlining the silent letter. Some may have more than one silent letter. Use your dictionary if you have doubts. After identifying, write a rule or generalization which would fit these examples. Remember—consonant blends and vowel digraphs are considered as making a combined sound, not a silent letter.

1. photo            5. concern

2. kneel            6. wreck

3. lack             7. ghost

4. chance           8. islet

## WORD CHANGING

DIRECTIONS:  Listed below are twenty words. Each of these words can be made into one or more new words by adding or inserting one vowel. In the blanks following the word, write the one vowel you plan to use, and then write the word or words you have created. Remember—you cannot change the order of the letters of the given word!

1. bad  (e)  bade   bead

2. mit  (e)  mite   emit

3. led  (a)  lead

## VOWEL CLASSIFICATION

DIRECTIONS: Here are fifty words, each with a long vowel sound. Make five columns and label each with one of the vowels. Under each vowel heading, list the words that contain that long vowel sound and underline the letter or letters producing that long vowel sound.

| A | E | I | O | U |
| --- | --- | --- | --- | --- |
| ace | eel | height | noble | ewe |
| stain | buddy | lye | woe | new |

## SYLLABICATION

DIRECTIONS: Listed below are eighteen words which were hyphenated at the end of a line on the school page in last week's issue of our local newspaper. Consult your list of basic rules for syllabicating a word, and identify those which were hyphenated incorrectly. After each of those words indicate with a dash the correct hyphenation.

1. polic-eman    (police/man)
2. plann-ed      (plan/ned)
3. loc-al        (lo/cal)
   etc.

## SENTENCE COMPLETION

DIRECTIONS: Fifteen sentences are given below. Each has two key words above it and each has a word missing in its context. Your task is to fill in a word which begins with the same letter(s) as the first word and which rhymes with the second word. Remember, the word must help the sentence make good sense.

1. climb — trap

   Suddenly, there was a (<u>clap</u>) of thunder.

2. strong — played

   By morning, she had (<u>strayed</u>) far from camp.

---

### Structural Analysis Activities

*1. Direct instruction of affixes.* Structural analysis largely consists of recognizing, understanding, and synthesizing prefixes, roots, and suffixes to arrive at the meaning of unfamiliar words. Since there are a limited number of frequently employed affixes and a rather unlimited number of roots, the teaching of structural analysis pivots largely upon pupil learning and ready use of affixes in word attack. Most of these are meaningful units and can be taught in much the same manner as sight vocabulary. The remainder, plus those which seem to cause some individual confusion, may be developed by the inductive system of teaching, suggested previously for the teaching of phonograms. The teaching of word roots is largely a function of vocabulary development, although adjunct reinforcement of roots may occur during instruction and practice in structural analysis.

Many pupils will have mastered a good number of the most common affixes by the time they reach seventh grade. Thus, it is important to preassess to identify those affixes and those pupils needing direct reinstruction. As in the teaching of vocabulary, it is important to keep the number of prefixes and suffixes taught within pupil learning load. Owing to their varied application and appearance, sometimes with contradictory meaning changes, affixes are not mastered as readily as free–form words. One to two affixes per week make a challenging learning load for many pupils, especially if the teacher is concerned with developing discriminate functions and illustrative application of the affix. Most pupils who have learned to use an affix in studied analysis of unknown words can profit from practice in quick recognition of the affix.

Many word development materials published for high school and college provide instruction and practice in the use of structural analysis, particularly affixes. A few place major emphasis upon developing vocabulary through synthetic structural analysis. Structural analysis can, with other approaches, contribute to vocabulary development. More significant to reading, however, is to use word structure for the ready recognition of complex words and the analysis of unfamiliar words that lend themselves to structural analysis.

2. *Developing a target vocabulary of affixes.* Usually, it is helpful for the pupil to have a ready source of affix reference and practice. Keeping a notebook, a notebook section, or a card file of affixes, much as suggested earlier for the development of a basic sight vocabulary, generally satisfies this need. An affix card file lends itself to more versatile use, particularly in card sorting, matching, and self–testing activities. Such a file is best developed under teacher direction, the teacher determining the affixes to be studied and providing class time and guidance in the development of the file. For older pupils, the file can be handled as a largely independent and long–term assignment, with the pupil adding affixes, their meaning, language origin, and an example (general and special content area word usage), according to a systematic plan of study or as he encounters difficulty with them in his reading. Since many pupils will be familiar with a fair number of affixes, it usually is more efficient for the teacher to start pupils with a predetermined base list of affixes such as the starter list presented below. The pupils can be tested on these; and as a first priority, set about learning those they do not know. If a considerable number are unknown, the teacher may help the pupil determine priority sets. To this basic list can be added new affixes introduced in reading instructional materials or as problem affixes encountered in general reading and content study.

## An Affix Starter List
## for Secondary Readers

### *Prefixes*

| *Prefix* | *Meaning* | *Example* |
|---|---|---|
| a | not; lacking | atypical; apostasy |
| ab | off; from | ablution; abstain |
| ad | to; toward | adhere; advisable |
| ante | prior | antechamber; antetype |
| anti | against | antiaircraft; antithesis |
| com (con) | with; jointly | compound; conspire |
| contra (con) | against | contraband; contest |
| de (di) (dis) | separation; away; down; fail | depart; divert; disagree |
| en | in; within; cause | enable; encompass |
| epi | upon; above; additional | episode; epifocal |
| eu | good; advantage | eulogy; euphony |
| inter | between | intermural |
| il (im) (in) | inward; toward | illuminate; into |
| mis | wrong; badly; not | mistake; miscast; mistrust |
| mono | alone; one | monoplane; monologue |
| neo | new | neophyte; neopaganism |
| non | not; modified negative | nonfat; nonhuman |
| ob | before; toward | obligatory; obvert |
| para | above; beside | paramount; parapet |

## An Affix Starter List for Secondary Readers (*continued*)

| Prefix | Meaning | Example |
|---|---|---|
| pre | prior; before; superior | prepare; prefix; preeminent |
| proto (pro) | first; in front | protocol; proton |
| re | again; anew | readmit; recheck |
| retro | behind; backward | retrograde; retroactive |
| sub (suf) | under; after; less | submarine; suffix; subpar |
| syn (syl) | accompanying; together | synod; syllogism |
| trans | across; beyond | transmigration; transfigure |
| un (in) (im) (ir) | negative; opposite; reverse | unable; ineligible |

*Suffixes*

| Suffix | Meaning | Example |
|---|---|---|
| al (an) | belonging to; pertaining to | final; Republican |
| ance (ence) | act of; state of | penance; presence |
| ar (ary) | connected with; one who | beggar; nuclear |
| ate | official | potentate; tribunate |
| able (ible) | capable of | retainable; sensible |
| ee | recipient of action | employee; trainee |
| er | one who; that which | player |
| er | comparative form | better; finer |
| est | superlative form | best; finest |
| et (ette) | diminutive | minuet; statuette |
| fy (ify) | to form; to make | signify; beautify |
| geny | beginning; origin | progeny; biogeny |
| ice | condition; quality of | service; novice |
| ing | act of; product related to | knocking; a painting |
| ish | like; urging on | devilish; leftish |
| ize | action of | deputize; pulverize |
| less | without | useless |
| ment | process or quality of | argument; placement |
| or | one who does; quality of | counselor; error |
| ory | place of; act of | salutory; oratory |
| ous (ious) (ose) | having; filled with | rebellious; frivolous; comatose |
| ry (ery) | quality of; conduct | jewelry; bakery |
| tion (ion) | condition of; result of | relation; correction |
| ure | being; act of | investiture; tenure |

---

*3. The dictionary as an affix reference source.* It would be both impractical and educationally insufficient for the teacher to plan to provide pupils with all needed information concerning affixes. Thus, the applied use of the dictionary becomes essential to affix study. One or two guided lessons will help pupils learn how to locate affixes in the dictionaries available to them and what type of information can be expected. Most dictionaries will provide a basic entry with origins, definitions, and variant uses. In addition, some dictionaries provide a separate listing of the most common root combinations with that affix.

Structured use of the dictionary as an affix reference may be provided. As an initial or introductory affix study activity, the teacher may assign each pupil one prefix and one suffix. The pupil's task is to use a dictionary (preferably an unabridged) to gain the vital information about the meaning of the affix. In addition, he should identify two or three interesting words making use of the affix as well as making a quick count of the number of words using the affix. (Some dictionaries provide these as special listings; otherwise, it is better to restrict such counts to the prefixes.) The counts, of course, provide the pupils with an idea of the relative frequency with which the affix occurs in English. Such data can be assembled and collected on a 3 × 5 card. The cards are turned in, and a special committee of pupils may be assigned to compiling a master list of affixes which is duplicated and given to the entire class.

*4. Affix wheels.* For pupils who need intensified independent practice in recognizing and using prefixes and suffixes, affix wheels can be made or provided (see Figure 17). Affix wheels can be constructed in different ways, but they usually provide for variable combinations of prefixes or suffixes with selected root words (usually roots previously learned or currently under study). The usual method of construction is to cut two oak-tag disks which turn independently when fastened at the center by a pin. On the smaller top disk, one or more prefixes (or roots) may be printed adjacent to a radial slot(s). Root words or suffixes are written on the larger wheel so they appear within the slot when the disk is turned. A more complex pattern calls for the use of three disks of different sizes superimposed so that the inner disk presents prefixes, the middle disk provides roots, and the largest disk supplies suffixes. Some combinations of the three-disk pattern may not be appropriate, but this, too, provides practice in discrimination

*Figure 17    Affix wheels.*

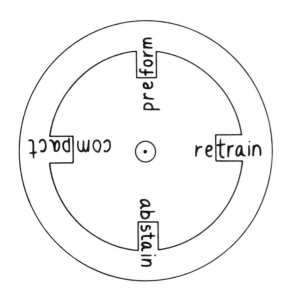

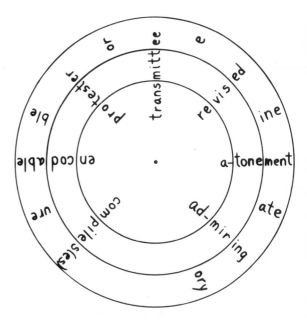

through error identification. For more structured assignments, the affix wheels may be labeled with Roman numerals and the various entries numbered and lettered. The assignment requires the pupil to secure the affix wheel from the activity table, reading file, or similar collecting place, and answer the questions in the assignment, e.g., "a secret plot": (III; b–12–2) or (con–spir–acy).

*5. Speeded recognition of structural parts.* Practice in the quick recognition of structural cues has several values for the maturing reader. The first is that structural cues, especially prefixes and suffixes, are the most efficient word elements to combine with context meaning for rapid, fluent word recognition. The second is that it is the nature of the maturing reader to read at increasingly rapid rates at the same time he encounters structurally more complex words. As a consequence, he is more sus-

ceptible to recognition errors of suffixes particularly, e.g., <u>ion</u> for <u>ine</u>, <u>er</u> for <u>es</u>, etc. Short exposure practice with the recognition, discrimination, and synthesis of affixes promotes both the reinforcement of affix learning and accurate, efficient reading. Such practice can be provided by means of flash cards, tachistoscopes, electronic projection, and timed worksheet exercises—as in the development of sight vocabulary.

*6. Practice exercises.* A number of exercise forms lend themselves to improving structural analysis. Such practice should be concerned with the meaningful learning of structural cues, their quick recognition, and their synthesis into bound or combined forms. The following are illustrative; the innovative teacher should develop variant forms more appropriate to instructional objectives.

---

### PAIRING AFFIXES AND MEANING

DIRECTIONS: From the list of prefixes and suffixes listed at the bottom of the sheet, pick that affix which when added to the root word given in each item, will satisfy the definition of that item. If the figure (2) appears after the definition, you will need to use both a prefix and a suffix to obtain the answer word.

| Definition | Root | Answer |
|---|---|---|
| 1. to lower value | base | (debase) |
| 2. a place for making things | fact | (factory) |
| 3. thinking over again (2) | consider | (reconsidering) |

*Prefixes:* a; ad; con; de; im; mono; pre; pro; trans

*Suffixes:* an; ar; ence; ing; ment; ory; tion; ure

### DISCRIMINATING AFFIX FUNCTION

DIRECTIONS: Circle the letter of the word which best satisfies the definition given in the item.

1. Lack of faith in
   a. atrust
   b. detrust
   c. distrust
   d. contratrust

2. Act of making lawful
   a. legalment
   b. translegal
   c. legalance
   ⓓ legalize

## IDENTIFYING PRONUNCIATION SHIFT

DIRECTIONS: Listed below are ten word pairs. The second word in each pair is an affixed variant of the first. You have four tasks: (1) Syllabicate both words of each pair. (2) Mark the long vowels in each syllable of both words of each pair. (3) Mark the major and minor syllables accented in each pair of words. (4) When finished, write one or more generalizations about what affixes do to the pronunciation of a word. Use the dictionary as necessary.

1. perspire     perspiring     perspiration
2. reverse      reversing      reversal
3. ration       rationing      rational
4. confirm      confirming     confirmatory
5. money        monied         monetary
6. squeak       squeaking      squeakiest

## FITTING WORD STRUCTURE TO SENTENCE STRUCTURE

DIRECTIONS: Below are ten groups of three sentences. Complete each of the following sentences with the most appropriate of the four words which follow it. Note how the sentence determines which form of the word is appropriate.

1. a. The two girls thrived on their (<u>rivalry</u>).
      rival — rivaling — rivalry — rivaled
   b. There was nothing to (<u>rival</u>) the king's palace.
      rival — rivaling — rivalry — rivaled
   c. There is nothing (<u>rivaling</u>) it in the world.
      rival — rivaling — rivalry — rivaled

## WORD CONSTRUCTION

DIRECTIONS: Here are five terms we are studying in this unit on sound. By adding or subtracting prefixes and suffixes which appear on our master list, see how many word variants you can develop from each term. Obtaining five each is above average. Ten each is excellent. Use your dictionary to check the accuracy of your word constructions.

| *pulse* | *phone* | *audio* | *tense* | *note* |
|---------|---------|---------|---------|--------|
| pulsate | | | | |
| pulsating | | | | |
| pulsation | | | | |
| impulse | | | | |
| repulse | | | | |

## Contextual Analysis
## Activities

Although word clues can be obtained from illustrations, headings, paragraphs, and other typographical units, it is the sentence—its meaning, linguistic structure, and function—which provides the major source of word attack clues outside the word itself. It is not surprising, therefore, that most contextual analysis instruction often is difficult to distinguish from practice in sentence interpretation. Sentence interpretation and contextual analysis can be developed simultaneously. However, such practice selectively should reinforce instructional objectives, and not degenerate into repetitive sentence-reading activity.

Published reading programs provide explanation and practice in the use of context clues. If the instructional materials employed do not explain and illustrate the various types of contextual clues for working out the meaning of unfamiliar words (summary, definition, comparison, contrast, synonym or restatement, mood or tone), the teacher may develop these by individual, group, or class activity. One objective of this activity is to develop pupil sensitivity to the use of a context of any type to analyze unknown words. The second objective is to bring the pupil to recognize and understand the different types of clues which are used. No more than two contextual clue patterns should be introduced and practiced at a time.

*1.* One approach is to do *group analysis of sentence clues*. The teacher reads orally and/or duplicates on a study sheet a series of sentences representing a common context pattern, and in which one word is left blank or in which a highly unusual but accurate synonym is substituted. (These words and/or sentences should be written on the chalk board if oral context is used.)

---

1. At first we were impressed, but later we became cy____l. (cynical)
2. Increasingly he engaged in projection; he saw in others his own particular guilts, and he felt that others had to believe as he did.

---

The teacher defines the context clue and demonstrates how it is used in the first sentence. The pupils, individually or as a group, are challenged to identify the key word in each of the remaining sentences. Beginning- and ending-letter clues may be added to the word blank as necessary. From these examples, generalizations about *how* to recognize the sentence clue may be constructed through teacher-directed discussion.

*2.* As a variant procedure, the teacher may present a set of sentences with one difficult word or blank, all of which utilize a common context clue pattern. Through group or class interaction, the pupils arrive at the appropriate missing word and then *induce the common context element* (clue) *used* in the sentences which enabled them to arrive at the correct word. The clue type is labeled and the pupils are given a worksheet exercise of ten sentences, each of which requires the use of comparison or contrast clues to identify the one unknown word.

*3.* A follow-up activity which generates interest and reinforcement is to section off part of a *class bulletin board* with oak tag or string and a heading like "Word Mysteries and Context Clues." After each of the context clues has been taught, a committee of pupils is selected to place on this board area the names, definition, and three examples of the use of that context clue the teacher identified.

*4.* Another instructional objective is to develop pupils to be fluent in their use of different sentence clues. After all basic context clue patterns have been introduced and practiced, the pupils should engage in *timed exercise practice* using an intermix of clue patterns to recognize unknown words. The teacher should be alert to examples arising in general class reading and point them out during this period. Later the clue patterns can be used to introduce new vocabulary.

5. Some pupils will exhibit considerable difficulty in the use of sentence context to analyze unknown words because they do not grasp the reading of sentence context. When such is the case, the teacher should give prior attention to *the development of oral language patterns and basic interpretation of sentences,* as presented in the next chapter.

6. The teacher may find it helpful to start a group of language-limited pupils with a form of a language-experience reading in which a picture or an object serves as a stimulus, and each pupil is asked to make one oral statement about that object. The teacher writes these in the form of a series of kernel sentences. (If a pupil gives a compound sentence, the teacher converts it into two or more kernel sentences.) These sentences are read aloud by individuals or the group and may be copied in their notebooks. Instructional attention is given to identifying the noun phrase and verb phrase. Later, the teacher introduces various markers—negatives, question forms, conjunctions, and connecting words to "transform" these kernel sentences and to build kernel "strings." When the group has mastered this stage enough to feel comfortable with the transforming process, sentences from the text, newspapers, and other sources may be presented, and pupils can analyze how the sentence structure dictates the functions of markers, verbs, nouns, etc.

7. For limited readers, perhaps the best means of providing practice in the use of sentences for gaining basic meaning and its complementary objective of improving use of context clues is to get the pupil *to read extensively* at his independent reading level. In recent years, a greater amount of adolescent-level interest material which is written in relatively simple vocabulary and sentence structure has become available in the form of remedial reading series, disadvantaged reader series, or occupational materials for the illiterate adult. Some of the sources for locating such materials are presented in Appendix B.

8. *Illustrative sentence-decoding exercises.* Practice exercises or worksheets involving the interpretation of sentences remain the best controlled instructional means of developing power in contextual word analysis. These exercises may be used to reinforce content or general vocabulary and basic interpretation as well as word analysis. A sampling of ways to vary the form of such practice exercises is given below.

---

### USING AND IDENTIFYING SENTENCE CLUES

DIRECTIONS: Use the clues in the sentence and the given letter clues to write the appropriate word in the blank for the fifteen items below. If you finish before the others in the group, identify from the sentence clue patterns we have studied, the one which helped you get the answer. Write it at the end of the sentence.

1. In order to purify crude oil, it must be sent to a r(<u>efiner</u>)y. (restatement)
2. Although the population trend is away from the city, some people prefer to live in m(<u>etropolita</u>)n areas. (synonym)
3. A p(<u>arasit</u>)e lives on or in another species without helping and sometimes harming its host. (definition)
4. "Loveliest of trees, the cherry now is hung with bloom along the bo(<u>ugh</u>)." language experience)

## INTERPRETING PHRASES

DIRECTIONS: Each of the sentences below consists of a sentence with an underlined phrase followed by four answers. First, read each sentence and mark an *S* in front of that answer whose meaning is nearly the same as that of the underlined phrase. Then read the sentences a second time and mark an *O* in front of that choice whose meaning is most nearly the opposite of the meaning of the phrase in the sentence.

    1. They were <u>conforming exactly to</u> regulations.

        a. somewhat tangential to

(O) b. quite indifferent to

        c. causing resurgence of

(S) d. agreeing perfectly with

## IDENTIFYING THE CORE MEANING OF SENTENCES

DIRECTIONS: Fifteen sentences are listed below. Your task is to identify the basic noun cluster and the basic verb cluster in each sentence. Underline the noun cluster once and the verb cluster twice in each sentence. What you have underlined should give the core meaning (the source and action) of the sentence. Some of the longer sentences may have more than one noun cluster and verb cluster.

    1. <u>The French boat</u> <u><u>will leave</u></u> port tonight.

   10. I'm afraid that <u>the good general</u> <u><u>must wait</u></u> patiently, but <u>his sturdy soldiers</u> <u><u>may push ahead</u></u>.

## IDENTIFYING FUNCTION WORDS

DIRECTIONS: In each of the sentences below, two function words are identified. In the blanks following the sentence you must identify the particular function of that word. Remember that the function words may serve as noun markers, verb markers, negatives, intensifiers, conjunctions, question indicators, phrase markers, and clause markers.

    1. She <u>is</u> pretty and is <u>unusually</u> talented.
        <sub>(a)</sub>         <sub>(b)</sub>

    (a) <u>(verb marker)</u>

    (b) <u>(intensifier)</u>

    2. They are <u>not</u> trying, <u>and</u> we will lose the game.
           <sub>(a)</sub>     <sub>(b)</sub>

    (a) <u>(negative marker)</u>

    (b) <u>conjunction</u>

---

## Word Reference Usage
## Activities

    The use of the dictionary and other word references is likely to occur in three overlapping aspects of reading instruction: as sources used in conjunction with vocabulary development and other word attack behaviors; as sources used in conjunction with the teaching of locational reading behaviors; and as a means of resolving immediate problems of meaning or pronunciation during the reading act. It is the third of these instructional areas which concerns us in this discussion, although it would be impossible to isolate either procedure or learning product of one of these instructional areas from the others. Thus, the teacher can expect the use of word reference sources in vocabulary and word analysis exercises, or in general locational reading tasks, to extend and reinforce word attack reference use, and vice versa.

For several reasons, some direct attention to using word references as part of word attack competency should be provided in the program of secondary reading instruction. Although most elementary programs will have included instruction and practice in the use of dictionary skills, not all entering secondary pupils will have mastered these fundamentals; this is particularly true for pupils who have experienced developmental retardation in learning to read. Beyond this, most secondary pupils can benefit from practice in the selective and efficient use of word references, especially since the use of word references to analyze an unknown word is usually the least efficient and most disrupting of the word attack behaviors. Third, secondary instruction in word reference usage should provide the pupil with knowledge and firsthand use of the variety of word references available, particularly abridged general dictionaries, unabridged general dictionaries, content textbook glossaries, content-oriented or technical area dictionaries, thesauri, and special language references which focus on idiom, slang, and common foreign words and phrases.

The instructional program should make planned provision for review of dictionary fundamentals and direct instruction and practice in extending word reference proficiency. However, much of the reinforcement of these behaviors can be incorporated in other word development, locational, and interpretational reading activity. Prepared instructional and practice materials in the use of word references are provided as part of most upper elementary reading programs as well as in some published secondary reading materials. (See Appendix C.) Some activities pertinent to developing and practicing word reference usage are provided here.

*1. Assessment of word reference competency.* A standardized or informal test of current pupil competency in using word references can serve several instructional purposes: as an introduction to a word reference study unit, as a review of basic understandings and skills, as an identification of pupils needing considerable instruction in fundamental locational skills, as an identification of reference-use weaknesses by notable numbers of the class or group, as part of a pre-post comparison of performance growth, and as a reference point for later instruction and practice. Such a survey assessment measure should sample the four major areas of word reference behaviors: (a) how to locate a needed word; (b) how to use the pronunciation guides (particularly syllabication, accentuation, and symbol keys); (c) how to obtain needed meaning from the entry (definitions, speech-part labels, etymology, inflected and variant forms, synonyms and antonyms, and idiomatic usage); and (d) when to use word reference sources other than the common abridged dictionary. Some published instructional materials include reasonable survey tests of this type. Otherwise, the teacher can use subtests of standardized work-study or reading measures (e.g., the Directed Reading subtests of the 1973 *Iowa Silent Reading Tests*). Practice exercises provided in workbooks and other commercial programs may serve as models which can be adapted for testing purposes.

*2. Use of films and filmstrips for instruction.* Basal-reader series, some independent programs of pupil reading materials, and some independent instructional media companies have produced films and filmstrips which explain the use of the dictionary and related word usage skills. While the teacher usually needs to incorporate these aids into a broader instructional sequence which includes preparation, discussion, and follow-up practice, they offer an alternative instructional approach, as well as a means whereby individuals or groups of pupils can independently review the essential processes and nature of word references.

*3. Development and use of wall charts.* The

learning and practice of complex skills is facilitated by the appropriate placement of visual aids to which the pupil can refer for guidance and review. Attractive wall charts dealing with dictionary aids have been commercially produced which teachers can purchase. Often the cooperative development of such aids by the class or small groups produces more effective learning and ensures more effective use of the charts as a reference aid. This may be done in the fashion of developing any group experience chart, or it can be handled as the culminating project of small-group study.

These charts can take a variety of forms or substance and can be used simultaneously for a week or two of intensive impact or can be used serially for a longer developmental sequence. The most common forms of such charts involve a blowup of sample pages of a dictionary or a blowup of an individual word entry or both. These may be accompanied by labels which are attached to appropriate aspects of the entry by colored string, e.g., "the pronunciation," "the definition," "the word origin," etc. Another version is to color-code, number, or letter the significant elements of the enlarged dictionary page or word entry, to which are attached a list of use questions and answers: e.g., Which part of the entry gives you a synonym for the word? Which part of the page quickly tells you whether the word "infirmary" appears on it?

If the classroom houses a master or unabridged dictionary, a pupil-developed wall chart can be placed above it which (a) provides a list of review steps for efficiently locating an entry, or (b) provides a table of contents or list of significant dictionary parts for locating information other than the basic word entries. Examples of other pertinent topics for wall charts would include "Five Basic Steps for Recognizing an Unfamiliar Word" (in which use of the dictionary appears after the recommended use of rereading the context, comparing to similar word forms, identifying roots and affixes, and phonic analysis). Another chart might be developed under the title When to Use and Not Use the Dictionary.

*4. The development of special content glossaries.* Nothing provides better insight into the workings of a process than the act of creating or recreating it. The development of special content glossaries or dictionaries as a collective group or individual ongoing activity not only provides useful development and reinforcement of special vocabulary and concepts, but adds to word reference understanding if appropriate dictionary format is followed. Such a special glossary can be introduced as a total group effort in which key words may be preidentified by the instructor. The end product is a small dictionary of special terms which can be duplicated for all members of the class. As an ongoing project, entries are entered alphabetically on pages of a looseleaf notebook or are entered on cards in the pupil's card file system.

*5. Use of word references as elements of the guided reading lesson.* Vocabulary and word attack activities are readily built into the systematic, directed instruction of the reading of a selection, as we have seen (Chapter Six). This places word learning within a meaningful setting and furnishes a vehicle for ongoing, paced development of word behaviors. The use of the dictionary and other word reference sources can implement various phases of the guided reading lesson: as a tactic for clarifying key vocabulary during the readiness phase, as a vehicle for clarifying interpretation of content, and as part of the extension of skill performance in the reaction phase of the lesson. The form of this practice should be varied to include group search and discussion, individual exercise practice, and creative response activities.

*6. Practice exercises.* Controlled practice is necessary to improve accuracy and efficiency in the use of the dictionary and other word references. Such practice may include simulated parts (duplicated worksheet pages or individual entries) of word references. Whenever possible, the instruction and reinforcement activity should require use of the actual word resource to increase both the reality of the practice and transfer of the learning. Illustrated exercise forms appear on the following pages.

## ALPHABETICAL ORDERING

DIRECTIONS: Listed below are twenty words which could serve as entries or items in a dictionary, glossary, index, or other word reference. They presently are in random order. Place them on the numbered lines according to their correct alphabetical order. The first and last words are given.

*Items:* brooch, cough, indelible, along, nicety,
counsel, materialize, nostalgic, quoted,
urgency, fistic, notify, aromatic, border,
corrupt, permeate, quota, rancid, vestal,
normative

1. along
2. ____
3. ____
    •
    •
    •
20. urgency

## IDENTIFYING DICTIONARY LOCATION

(A number of exercise forms can be developed for practicing the location of word items in dictionary format. The first concern is with understanding and accuracy; later, the exercises should be timed to increase speed in location.)

(1) DIRECTIONS: Listed below are twenty words. In the blank after each word, identify which quarter of the dictionary you would open to locate that word quickly. For example, *butler* would be in the first quarter while *sustain* would be in the last quarter. To aid you, the letter spreads for the four quarters are given below.

1st quarter, A-F;    3rd quarter, N-S
2nd quarter, G-M;    4th quarter, T-Z

| 1. universe | 4 | 11. reverse | 3 |
| 2. humane | 2 | 12. estimate | 1 |

(2) DIRECTIONS: Listed below are twenty words. Also given are the guide words which appear at the top of the pages of your class dictionary. Your task is to identify the page number on which you would locate the listed word. Mark the number of that page on the blank after the word. You should do this in less than 2 minutes. Forty-five seconds or less is excellent time for accurate responses.

| *Page* | *Word Guides* |
| --- | --- |
| 541 | nandin — narcotherapy |
| 542 | narcotic — natality |
| 543 | naval — neo |

| *Page* | | *Word Guides* | |
| --- | --- | --- | --- |
| 544 | | neoclassic — nerving | |
| 545 | | nervous — nester | |
| 1. Neptune | 544 | 11. narcissus | 541 |
| 2. nearby | 543 | 12. Nazi | 543 |
| 3. neon | 544 | 13. navigation | 543 |

(3) DIRECTIONS: Here is a list of fifteen words. When you are told to begin, locate the page in your dictionary on which that word appears and write it after the word. When you are finished, look at the digital clock timer and determine the number of minutes and seconds it took you to complete the exercise. Then check your answers against your partner's and recheck those on which you disagree. (Words should reflect pupil skill.)

## CONFIRMING SYLLABICATION AND PRONUNCIATION

Several approaches to complementary use of the dictionary to extend word attack skills were presented in the activities of prior sections. Here are several for using the dictionary to confirm syllabication and pronunciation.

(1) DIRECTIONS: Examine the twelve words presented below and divide them into syllables according to the rules you have learned. When finished, check your accuracy by locating each word in your dictionary and then noting how it was syllabicated. (Illustrative words: equivalent; noble.)

(2) DIRECTIONS: You should read the ten statements given below and determine whether the statement makes sense. If it does, mark it (S); if it does not, mark it (NS). One or more words in each sentence are written according to the pronunciation key of your dictionary. First, try to respond on the basis of reading the sentence and sounding out the coded words. If you are unsure, check the pronunciation and meaning of the word in your dictionary.

    1. A (sär′jant) is (sen′yar) to a (jen′ar al). (NS)
    2. The Women's Prison has a new (da rek′triss). (S)
    3. His spirited (per′a rā′shan) instilled (n′spa rā′shan). (S)

(3) DIRECTIONS: Look up the following words in your dictionary. Using your pronunciation key as a guide, write two different sentences that reveal that you understand two different pronunciations and the related usage for each word.

    content, desert, object, attribute, present, buffet, address, quiver

    1a. (If we escape, I shall be <u>content</u>.)
    1b. (We must examine the <u>content</u> of this law.)

## LOCATING APPROPRIATE MEANING

Several exercise forms for providing dictionary practice in determining word meaning are suggested here. Others have been presented in the sight vocabulary section. The resourceful teacher can develop many other forms.

(1) DIRECTIONS: Below are pairs of words which are frequently and incorrectly interchanged in conversation and writing. Check your dictionary to determine the meaning and pronunciation of each pair to reflect their pronunciation differences. Then write one sentence for each word which reveals its correct use.

| | |
|---|---|
| 1a. illicit | 4a. bazaar |
| 1b. elicit | 4b. bizarre |
| 2a. ascetic | 5a. respectively |
| 2b. esthetic | 5b. respectfully |
| 3a. marital | |
| 3b. martial | |

(2) DIRECTIONS: Each of the fifteen sentences below contains an underlined word. On the first line following each sentence, write a synonym or two for the word as you understand its contextual use. Then look up the word in your dictionary; select the appropriate definition from those provided, and on the second blank line, write the number and definition of the word which is most appropriately used here.

a. The desk had been rifled.
1. (searched, robbed)
2. (rifle; #2 to ransack)
b. The riot was used as the leader in the morning edition.
1. (main story or report)
2. #9 (Journalism) the leading or first column article; the headlined article

(3) DIRECTIONS: Use the classroom or library thesaurus to locate a synonym for the word in the first column which also rhymes with the word in the second column.

| I | II | Choice |
|---|---|---|
| 1. prosper | strive | (thrive) |
| 2. elucidate | remain | (explain) |
| 3. stratum | weigher | (layer) |

## DETERMINING APPROPRIATE WORD REFERENCE

DIRECTIONS: Each of the numbered statements presents a situation for which you might need to use a word reference. Choose the best reference for that purpose from those listed at the top of the page and mark the letter of that reference in the blank after the statement.

| | |
|---|---|
| a. Abridged dictionary | d. Book index |
| b. Unabridged dictionary | e. Content glossary |
| c. Encyclopedia | or dictionary |
| | f. Thesaurus |

1. To quickly identify the etymology of a word. (b)
2. To locate some appropriate antonyms for a word to be used in a report. (f)
3. To find whether an author has dealt extensively with a specific topic. (d)

# REFERENCES

1. Arthur I. Gates, *The Improvement of Reading*, Third Edition (New York: The Macmillan Company, 1950) p. 205.
2. Earl A. Taylor, "The Fundamental Reading Skill," *Journal of Developmental Reading* (Summer, 1958) p. 21.
3. Miles A. Tinker, *Bases for Effective Reading* (Minneapolis, Minn.: University of Minnesota Press, 1965) p. 22.
4. William S. Gray, *On Their Own in Reading* (Chicago: Scott Foresman and Company, 1948).
5. Robert C. Auckerman, *Approaches to Beginning Reading* (New York: John Wiley & Sons, Inc., 1971) p. 509.
6. Ira E. Aaron, "Comparison of Good and Poor Readers in Fourth and Eighth Grades," *Journal of Educational Research* 54 (1960) pp. 34-37.
7. Jeanne Chall, *Learning to Read: The Great Debate* (New York: McGraw-Hill Book Company, 1967) p. 7.
8. Ruth Strang and Charlotte Rogers, "How Do Students Read a Short Story," *English Journal* 54 (1965) pp. 819-29.
9. Donald D. Durrell, *Improving Reading Instruction* (Yonkers-on-Hudson, N.Y.: World Book Co., 1956) pp. 267-68.
10. George D. and Evelyn B. Spache, *Reading in the Elementary School*, Third Edition (Boston: Allyn and Bacon, Inc., 1973) pp. 268-70.
11. Durrell, *Improving Reading Instruction*, p. 231.
12. Lou E. Burmeister, "Usefulness of Phonic Generalizations," *The Reading Teacher* 21 (January, 1968) pp. 352-55. Reprinted by permission of the author and the International Reading Association.
13. George D. Spache, *Diagnosing and Correcting Reading Disabilities* (Boston: Allyn and Bacon, Inc., 1976) Chapter 8.
14. Eldon E. Ekwall, *Diagnosis and Remediation of the Disabled Reader* (Boston: Allyn and Bacon, Inc., 1976) Chapter 3.
15. Paul McKee, *Reading* (Boston: Houghton Mifflin Company, 1966) p. 97.

# SUPPLEMENTARY SOURCES

Dawson, Mildred A., Compiler. *Teaching Word Recognition Skills*. Newark, Del.: International Reading Association, 1970.

Dechant, Emerald. *Reading Improvement in the Secondary School*, Chapter 6. Englewood Cliffs, N.J.: Prentice-Hall, Inc., 1973.

Durkin, Dolores. *Strategies for Identifying Words*. Boston: Allyn and Bacon, Inc., 1977. 135 p.

Heilman, Arthur W. *Phonics in Proper Perspective*. Columbus, Ohio: Charles E. Merrill Publishing Company, 1964.

Wilson, Robert M., and Maryanne Hall. *Programmed Word Attack for Teachers*. Columbus, Ohio: Charles E. Merrill Publishing Company, 1968. 63 p.

# ELEVEN

# Sustaining Interpretive Competence

*Furthermore, recognition and knowledge of meaning of words do not insure adequate understanding of the text.... When word recognition and meaning are adequate for what is read, instruction should be directed toward obtaining the literal meanings. As soon as students can recall details, identify main ideas, and see their relationships, other literal meanings along with implied meanings may become the focus of attention.*

Helen M. Robinson

***Overview*** Reading interpretation, as the purposeful, flexible search for meaning in written sources, is dependent upon the decoding of words and sentences and, in turn, is necessary to appropriate reader reaction. In that sense, instruction in the fundamental competencies of interpretation should not be considered as isolated incidents, but as a supplementary aspect of content reading usage and the broader instructional strategies identified in Chapters Five, Six, and Eight. Some attention to the development of the specific behaviors of interpretation is needed, however. Chapter Eleven suggests guidelines and presents illustrative activities and exercises for implementing development of selected specific behaviors of two essential levels of secondary reading interpretation: basic, which subsumes literal and functional reading tasks; and analytical, which is concerned with the meaning of idea relationships as conveyed through the writer's organization.

## READING INTERPRETATION
## AND ITS INSTRUCTION

The fundamental issue in the teaching of second-ary school reading is to prepare pupils to indepen-dently, purposefully, and flexibly interpret the meaning of the writer's message.[1] Reading, and thus interpretation, is a holistic process, and any division of the interpretation behaviors is necessar-ily arbitrary. Yet it can be useful to do so to facili-tate explanation, instruction, and program plan-ning.[2] For our purposes, it is instructionally useful to separate the interpretive behaviors of reading into three groups: (1) *basic*, those which are pri-marily concerned with understanding the stated literal meaning of the writer's message and which include those *functional* competencies which satisfy minimal real-life reading requirements; (2) *analyt-ical*, those interpretive behaviors necessary for academic competence in the upper school, which call for somewhat higher-level thinking processes and are concerned with the concepts, generaliza-tions, and arguments the writer intended to convey by the way he constructed and arranged the state-ments of his message; and (3) *evaluative* or *critical* interpretation, the objective assessment of the writer's stated and implied facts, ideas, and argu-ments to determine their pertinency, validity, and quality.

It should be remembered, however, that inter-pretation is not a unilateral behavior, even though the teacher's or pupil's purposes may be specific and the processes of interpretation rather directly implemented.[3] As Robinson indicates, this interde-pendency of interpretation must be taken into consideration when implementing reading instruc-tion.[4]

### General and Specific
### Approaches

The improvement of reading interpretation benefits from the combination of general and specific reading instructional strategy and experi-ences.[5] It is not very likely that most secondary pupils will learn and employ such particular behav-iors of interpretation as identifying the function of a paragraph, recognizing an author's argumentative pattern, or analyzing the writer's use of propa-ganda—unless these behaviors become the objec-tives of specific instructional sequences.[6] Even the more fundamental tasks of decoding the literal meaning of functional messages will require direct instructional attention when secondary pupils are unable to handle them in an adequate manner.

But such specific instruction may be handled more meaningfully, purposefully, and efficiently when incorporated within such larger structures for guiding the content assignment and directing the reading lesson as presented in earlier chapters. The illustrative activities and exercises for improving functional and analytical interpretation in this chapter and the extension of evaluative and flexible interpretation of Chapter Twelve should be consid-ered as means to implement or to supplement broader reading instructional strategies. Many of the published materials of reading instruction presented in Appendix D provide general or specific practice exercises in reading interpretation.

Once again, the general instructional sequence for teaching a specific reading behavior provides a useful structure for organizing the instruction. It will be recalled that the stages of the general instructional sequence were: (1) identify and articu-late the behavioral objective of the instructional sequence; (2) preassess pupil competence in the targeted objective; (3) develop readiness for learn-ing; (4) demonstrate the mechanics essential to carrying out the behavior; (5) provide immediate supervised, guided practice and assessment in use of the behavior; (6) provide independent practice; (7) assess pupil retention of mastery in the behavior; and (8) implement delayed practice and transfer of the behavior through application to developmental, functional, or content area reading–learning tasks.

### *Some Supplementary Guidelines for*
### *Teaching Interpretive Behaviors*

When the teaching and reinforcement of a speci-fic type of reading interpretation is not conducted within the larger structure of a guided reading of a selection, the teacher should consider the following additional guidelines.

*1.* The first order of concern in teaching a specific skill of interpretation is to select, modify, or otherwise prepare the material (or pupil) so that the learner can comprehend the basic meaning of such material at a minimal level of 70 to 75 percent accuracy. Such material includes a wide range of reading form and content: sentences, paragraphs, selections, creative and expository writing, nonfiction and fiction. This criterion for reading accuracy extends as well to the accompanying written matter of the activity, study guide, or exercise (e.g., directions, questions, outlines, etc.). In effect, the first step in teaching a specific interpretive behavior is to assure adequate basic understanding and appreciation of all reading material employed in the lesson.

*2.* A second important consideration is that the pupil understand what is expected of him in the interpretive activity or exercise. Much of the advice given for improving the assignment in Chapter Seven applies usefully here. Generally, explaining the purpose, giving clear directions, providing examples, plus giving pupils ample opportunity to raise questions as they initiate the activity or exercise will resolve most pupil difficulties with the instructional procedure.

*3.* Attention should be given to whether the pupil has mastered the necessary contributing processes of the interpretive skill to be learned. For example, a pupil will have difficulty writing a summary of an article if he is unable to differentiate the significant generalizations (main ideas) of the selection from other detailed exposition. Observing a planned scope and sequence of instructional program, pretesting, and subdividing classes for specific instruction help prevent this too common error of instruction. Interrupting the instructional activity to teach the needed preliminary skills is not a desirable alternative.

*4.* If the initial learning and practice exercise or activity calls for the use of an independent source of reading content (e.g., textbook, magazine article, newspaper editorial page, etc.), the teacher should make sure that sufficient copies of these sources are immediately available for pupil use! Pupil independent location of such sources may be appropriate as an extended reading activity or as a locational practice exercise, but not when the instructional objective involves the immediate teaching or reinforcement of specific interpretive behaviors.

*5.* It is best to focus an activity or exercise whose function is the initial teaching and reinforcement of a particular interpretive behavior upon that one interpretive skill or process. However, a first reading of the selection to obtain a basic understanding of its content and to reinforce interpretive behaviors learned previously presents no difficulty as long as such review or practice activity does not divert the attention of the pupil from the new behavior to be learned. Thus, the combined interpretational exercise which asks the pupil to respond to multiple types of interpretive questions or to do multiple processes is useful as a practice or reinforcement exercise, but not for initial learning.

*6.* Whenever possible, certain instructional sequences should be implemented in the teaching and practicing of specific interpretive behaviors. These include:

*a.* Progressing from using the interpretive behaviors in shorter selections to longer selections.

*b.* Progressing from simpler context or that where the desired response is reasonably obvious to more complex context where the appropriate response requires greater discrimination.

*c.* Progressing from a recognition of correct interpretive response to recall of correct response to an application of response.

*d.* Progressing from untimed use of the interpretive behavior to time-limited (faster or more efficient) use of that interpretive behavior.

*e.* Progressing from teacher or writer identification of needed interpretive behavior (i.e., questions or study guides calling for the performance of the interpretive task) to pupil self-identification of the need to implement the interpretive behavior in order to understand, enjoy, or to apply the meaning to a larger problem.

### Five Implications of Purpose
### for Teaching Interpretive Processes

The significance of active purpose strategies in effective interpretation was identified many years ago by Thorndike and has been corroborated by a good deal of later research.[7,8]

At the most fundamental level, the general purpose of the reader to make sense of the writer's message provides a basis for associating meaning with the individual words and sentence word strings encoded by the writer. This assumes that the reader has sufficient decoding skills, language competency, and experience background. This is the first implication of purpose for instruction in interpretation:

*1. The pupil must be sufficiently motivated to attend to the written context, decode the writer's statements into literal meaning, and to check the acceptability of that meaning by linguistic and cognitive sensibility.*

But writers usually manage to pack more than literal statement meaning into their messages. Thus, another level of interaction between writer-reader purpose and reader purpose interpretive response is created: the reader must differentiate and react to a variety of meanings which may be conveyed by the writer. From this, three additional implications for instruction in interpretation are generated.

*2. Over a sufficient period of instruction, the pupil needs to understand the possible mental manipulations which a writer may employ.*

*3.* In turn and at an appropriate time, *the pupil must learn to respond accurately to each of these varied interpretational tasks* under instructional direction. That is, he must be able to handle the language and thought processes specific to the interpretational task, when it is identified for him.

The mature reader, however, is a dynamic person in his own right. He or she has many needs to fulfill through reading—to enjoy, to gain a general impression, to escape, to be stimulated, to find a specific answer to a personal need—which involve the varied use of selective, self-directed interpretive behaviors.[9] Sensitive writers understand and accept this reader independence. Once when asked why readers have many different understandings of *Mary Poppins,* P. L. Travers, the author, replied: "A book has two parts—the writer and the reader."[10] Thus:

*4. The reader must learn to transfer learned specific interpretive responses to new reading situations*—to identify the cues in the written material or reading situation which trigger off the appropriate learned interpretive response.

Moreover, specific interpretive needs, time and situational pressures, the topic, the style of the writing, all argue for the selective reading of the message to satisfy the reader's priorities. This evokes one more implication for instruction in interpretation:

*5. The pupil needs to be taught to be selective, flexible, and efficient in the application of his interpretational behaviors.*

## INCREASING COMPETENCY
## IN BASIC FUNCTIONAL
## INTERPRETATION

It should be clear from the previous discussion that the mastery of reading interpretation is an open-ended challenge. Certainly it needs twelve school years, or more, of instructional guidance. Each teacher, of course, will need to take each pupil from his present level of competency in interpretation and move him as far as possible toward the mastery of these purposeful functions in interpretation. Education is much as Robert Frost described it: "getting someone from where they are to where they ain't."[11] For some secondary youngsters, the reading "where they ain't" is the development of an adequate sight vocabulary plus minimal proficiency in those word attack, decoding, and functional interpretation behaviors which will enable these pupils to begin to enjoy the world of books, to gain the most essential understanding from school assignments adjusted to their present ability, and to prepare them to cope with those functional, utilitarian reading situations which Bormuth has described as "real-world reading tasks" and which Wilson has identified as "survival" reading.[12]

Our accumulated experience with both developmental and remedial instruction indicates that it would be unwise to limit the development of basic or functional reading competency to isolated instruction and practice in selected basic interpretive behaviors. Basic reading interpretation becomes operational in the decoding of words, phrases, sentences, questions, directions, and context of a literal, instrumental nature. Thus, instruction directed toward the establishment of competency in functional interpretation should include appropriate aspects of vocabulary development, word recognition, word analysis, and the guided decoding of general meaning in developmental reading lessons, regardless of the label attached to the program or instructional setting.

Nevertheless, the functionally borderline secondary reader, as well as those more adequate readers demonstrating irregular profiles of proficiency in basic interpretive behaviors, will benefit from supplementary instruction and practice in such basic interpretive behaviors as:

1. Interpreting sentence literal meaning with accuracy and efficiency.
2. Purposefully locating and recalling essential factual details presented in text of limited length.
3. Recognizing basic intertextual relationships such as: (a) understanding and following directions, (b) identifying the topic idea in paragraphs and shorter selections, and (c) selectively identifying and relating significant details which support topic ideas.
4. Gaining familiarity with and becoming competent in selective use of such fundamental sources of real-life information as: (a) the telephone directory, (b) the newspaper, (c) mail-order or discount-house catalogs, (d) the state driver's manual, and (e) the dictionary.
5. Purposefully interpreting and reacting to such representative survival-type situations involving reading as: (a) signs; (b) bus and plane schedules; (c) city and state maps; (d) medicine labels; (e) job applications; (f) recipes for cooking and preserving food; (g) restaurant menus; (h) financial billing statements from banks, businesses, and utilities; (i) credit card and loan applications; (j) directions for sewing, assembling, and contructing projects; (k) instructions for operating of household equipment and tools; and (l) sales and lease contracts and insurance policies.

The following pages present some representative activities and exercises for supplementing instruction in basic or functional reading interpretation. A few activities and exercises are included which have the basic interpretational needs of the more capable secondary school reader in mind.

## Supplementary Instructional Activities

*1. A sentence attack system.* Pupils with limited reading ability usually will not persist in attempting to understand sentences which confuse them. Learning a system for attacking problem sentences often increases reading confidence as well as sentence insight and keeps the pupil involved in actual reading. Such a system can be developed inductively by putting several representative difficult sentences on the board and soliciting suggestions from the group on how they deal with difficult sentences. (The teacher may contribute to this as needed.) These suggestions are listed on the board, and the group can determine their order in terms of efficiency of attack. When completed, the system can be duplicated so that each pupil has a notebook copy and the system can be placed on a wall chart for ready in-class reference.

1. Read the rest of the material to see if it explains the meaning of the sentence.
2. Review the main idea and purpose in reading the paragraph or selection.
3. Reread the sentences which come just before and after the unknown sentence.
4. Is the sentence meaning confusing or important enough to understanding to interrupt the reading further? If so:
5. Compare the sentence to the basic sentence model: Who (what) did what? To whom or what? How? Why? When? Where?
6. Restate the sentence in your own words.
7. Read the sentence aloud.

*8.* Underline any unknown words in the sentence and (a) analyze them by structure or sound, (b) if necessary, look up the meaning in your personal dictionary, and (c) reread the sentence substituting the meaning.

*9.* Ask for help from others concerning the meaning of the sentence.

(It should be noted that many of these steps are worthy subjects of instructional and practice activities in themselves.)

*2. Personal dictionaries and related activity.* Properly employed, much of the locational, vocabulary, and word attack activities which make use of the dictionary and which have been described earlier can aid in the improvement of basic interpretation. Such activity will be more useful if each pupil can have a personal dictionary on his own level of reading ability. For many pupils with problems in functional interpretation, one of the dictionaries developed for middle-grade pupils will be more appropriate than the typical high school or college abridged dictionary. Pupil defensiveness about using these simpler dictionaries can be avoided by glueing opaque vinyl over the cover. This makes the paperbacks last longer and lets pupils select their own dictionaries on the basis of immediate usefulness with later option for exchange. School or pupil investment in personal dictionaries can be well worth the expense, as Fader and McNeil have reported.[13]

*3. Language-experience reading.* In Chapter Eight, the language-experience approach to teaching reading was described as a method particularly useful with pupils with limited reading ability and/or English-language competence. This approach has particular value in developing basic listening-writing-reading control of sentences and simple organization. The procedure, it will be recalled, can be used with classes, groups, or individuals.

*a.* In essence, a secondary-level adaptation of the approach involves: (1) the identification of an interesting experience or functional task by individuals or group; (2) the development of a limited series of dictated oral statements about the experience (descriptive, sequential, emotional reaction, etc.); (3) which are written on the board by the teacher or written in a notebook by pupils; (4) which are read critically by partners or the group to check for sentence meaning, sentence form, and to select the sentences to be used and to be adjusted to fit the appropriate organizational pattern (a summary, a set of directions, a narration, a sequence of events or process); (5) which is revised and rewritten by each member of the group; and (6) which is used in follow-up practice or creative activities (e.g., a personal diary or a group problems book).

*b.* The experience selected may be derived from many sources: a class trip, a school or class event, a subject area demonstration, a film or filmstrip, listening to a tape, a visiting speaker, a short story or selection read by the teacher, a content area-related assignment, or a life-use reading task such as ordering materials from a catalog to carry out a project.

The language-experience approach can serve usefully in dealing with functional reading tasks. One teacher used this procedure with a class of seriously disabled adolescent readers and produced a pupil rewritten, simplified version of the state driver's manual. The teacher and pupils consulted with driver training personnel to identify the most useful parts of the manual for the driver applicant. Pupil committees were formed and selected the section of the manual they were to rewrite. The members of each group, aided by the teacher, read the section, identified and discussed its significant points. Technical questions were discussed with the driver training teacher, who became quite interested in the project. When the group felt that it was ready for the rewriting stage, it used a recorder to tape the oral restatements volunteered by the group members. These were rewritten by individuals of the group and subjected to group correction and revision. The original section and the pupil revision then were presented to the whole class for suggested improvements. The final revision of each group was collated into the simplified manual. The teacher later used the manual as a basis for several reading interpretation exercises. This language experience culminated by taking a state-type multiple-choice driver's test which had been constructed by the driver training teacher. Yes, the large majority of the class obtained a passing score (75 percent accuracy) on that test. Of greater educational importance was the wealth of vocabulary, writing, and reading interpretational experience gained by the class. The language-experience approach can be usefully modified in many ways.

*4. Sentence stringing and transforming.* Constructing sentences can help even the more adequate pupil gain insight about reading them. Many variations of group and individual learning activities or practice can be developed from this format. Here is an example. The teacher places on the board (or on a worksheet) four or five kernel sentences dealing with the same general topic. To make sure that the pupils can read them, vocabulary is controlled, and the teacher or individual pupils may read the sentences aloud. The noun and verb phrases of each are underlined, and the meaning of each of these is paraphrased. As a group or individual assignment, the pupils are asked to:

1. Generate two meaningful compound sentences by stringing two of these kernel sentences together by use of connective function words (and, but, or, although, etc.).
2. Generate two negative sentences by the use of negative function words and transforming the kernel sentence involved.
3. Convert one kernel sentence and one kernel string (compound) sentence into questions by use of interrogative function words and by transforming the sentences as needed.
4. Expand two of these kernel sentences by modifying either the noun phrase or verb phrase.
5. Conclude the activity by asking the pupils to construct a meaningful paragraph by using some of the above transformations. These may be exchanged among members of the group for comparative reading.

*5. Analyzing sentence demons.* The individual members of the class or group are assigned the task of bringing to class five sentences from the current text assignment which caused considerable personal difficulty in interpretation. The teacher takes a random series of these from pupils and writes them on the board. Through class discussion, the teacher leads the group in an inductive analysis of some of the ways in which sentences can cause interpretive difficulty: unknown words, unknown word referents, length of sentence, complexity of sentence structure, inconsistent writing, and inability to use context clues. The possible difficulties are listed on the board (or in notebooks) for ongoing reference classifications. The example sentences are reorganized into kernel sentences. In smaller groups, the pupils discuss and analyze the sentences they have brought and compare the factors which made them difficult to those reasons previously identified. Groups may report or add to the list of factors producing sentence interpretation. The activity culminates with each pupil identifying the kernel sentences and then the noun-verb phrases in his own sentence demons, as well as paraphrasing those difficult items into more meaningful statements. A variant introduction of this activity is to start with one or more sentences selected from newspaper or magazine copy which the pupil feels to be poorly written or intentionally ambiguous.

*6. Microunits of sources of functional information.* The directed or guided reading of such informational sources with "real-life" utility as telephone directories, mail-order catalogs, popular magazines, and the local newspaper can be particularly useful in teaching the functionally incompetent secondary reader. In addition to gaining familiarity, confidence, and efficiency in the use of the source, it presents an excellent opportunity to teach vocabulary, locational, and basic interpretational skills as well as providing supplementary reading-related practice in language and math usage. One practical advantage to the teacher is that each pupil can be provided a copy with little or no expense to the school, since most are free for the teacher's asking or can be readily obtained from pupil homes.

The telephone book, particularly the larger metropolitan version, is excellently suited to functional reading instruction. The basic listings, of course, can be used for practice in alphabetizing and accuracy of quick locational skills. The yellow advertising pages can be "finger-walked" to satisfy a wide assortment of practical scanning, skim reading, and locational reading tasks. The special ads in the yellow section can be used for basic and critical reading exercises. And the introductory front matter contains information which is readily converted to instruction and practice in reading and using indexes, maps, and rate tables, as well as a wealth of descriptive interpretation and direction-following exercises.

*7. Direction reading activities.* Reading directions lends itself to a wide variety of exercise-based instruction and practice. The need to teach a general strategy for dealing with directions and the need to acquaint pupils with a variety of direction forms often are overlooked in reading instruction.

*a.* Utilizing two or three sets of directions as a basis for stimulating interest and drawing generalizations, the teacher may lead the pupils to develop or induce a basic set of rules for using a set of directions. Here is an example.

1. What is the purpose? What will be the outcome? How will the product look?
2. Read the complete set of directions.
3. Which of the steps or items are difficult to understand?
4. What is the correct or best order for carrying out the directions?
5. What tools or materials are needed? How should these be arranged for ready use?
6. Begin with the first direction and carry out each in its proper order.

*b.* Construct a class looseleaf notebook of direction types by having each pupil bring in one or two examples which he or his parents encounter during daily home or work operations. The goal here is variety in selection—from how to prepare for a backpacking trip to how to operate a computer. Many secondary pupils find such a notebook intriguing leisure reading activity. It also serves as a source of stimulating extended personal/vocational reading and as the means for developing later practice exercises.

*c.* Another version of (b) is to collect a notebook of directions used by teachers in the school—for handling assignments, taking tests, performing demonstrations, constructing projects, using the library, etc. While these may be less intriguing to the pupil, they serve very nicely to prepare pupils for handling the operational reading tasks of school life.

*8. Readability study.* Since readability is a matter which seriously affects the pupil's daily life and which focuses upon factors of basic interpretation (with words and sentences), an activity which can interest and enlighten secondary pupils of varied reading strength is the conduction of a readability study.

*a.* The nature of readability is discussed with the class with emphasis placed both on the use of words and sentences in estimating readability and upon those aspects of reading not measured in such formulas. Usually it is easy to generate curiosity about the difficulty of local newspapers, high school texts, popular magazines, etc. The next step is to teach the pupils to use one or two simple formulas or graphs for estimating readability such as those presented in Chapter Nine and to pair or group them for assessing certain target materials chosen by the class. Results are collected and compared as a group or class project. The resulting discussion should place emphasis upon the function and interrelationship of words and sentences in basic reading difficulty.

*b.* A variant of this activity is to have pupils read four short selections of 150 to 250 words of known different readability. Each pupil is asked to identify the number of sentences in each selection which causes him difficulty. The readability of each selection then is assessed (by individual pupils, groups, or whole classes), and the pupil, group, or class compares the number of sentences presenting difficulty with the results of the readability survey.

*9. Cloze testing.* Quite frequently, the cloze test procedure (described in Chapter Seven) of exact replacement measurement for accuracy produces notable argument by pupils for allowing synonyms to count as correct responses. This interest can be used for generating several different forms of contextual clues instruction and practice.

*a.* An every-fifth-word cloze test is constructed over a text chapter segment. It is scored by the exact-word method. Then it is scored by the synonym method — but only after the group develops a list of acceptable synonyms or alternate word answers.

*b.* The teacher develops three cloze test versions of the same text selection; one "clozes" every third word, one "clozes" every fifth word, and one "clozes" every seventh word. The class is divided randomly into three groups to take one of the tests and to score it on an exact-word basis. The comparison of group results will provide a good opportunity for emphasizing the significance of frequency of unknown words in causing sentence difficulty. (The accuracy of every fifth or seventh word deletion should be notably greater than every third word deletion.)

*c.* The teacher chooses a short selection (about 200 words) and develops two alternate cloze forms — one which deletes every fifth noun or verb and one which deletes every fifth language marker or modifier word. The class is divided into two groups of approximately equivalent reading ability to take the resulting cloze test. In addition to filling in the missing word, each pupil is given a five- to ten-question test over the concepts of the selection. The results of the two groups are compared. Then the groups exchange forms and answer the questions a second time. Resulting discussion may focus on which type of words are most important to general meaning (referents) and which for specific meaning (markers and modifiers).

## Illustrative Exercises for Basic Interpretation

Many examples of the simpler, traditional exercises for developing basic interpretive behaviors may be found in the workbooks and other instructional materials listed in Appendix D. The concern here is to illustrate some varieties in supplementary exercise types which relate to the basic-functional interpretation behaviors described earlier. Caution always should be exerted to fit the vocabulary of the exercise and its directions to that appropriate for the group intended. When possible, the exercise should reinforce vocabulary previously taught. In instances of very limited readers, it is wise both to limit the length of the exercise to their work-attention span and for the teacher to read the directions aloud and to work several examples with the group. Pupils with extremely limited vocabularies and decoding skills should receive considerable guided reading and rereading of short stories and selections to develop an adequate independent vocabulary and control over basic decoding procedures. Context exercises, such as those presented in Chapter Ten, also serve as means of practicing the more basic decoding interpretational behaviors.

---

**READING SIGNS**

DIRECTIONS: Read the ten common signs which are given at the bottom of the page. Then read each of the ten statements and write the letter of the sign which best fits that statement.

   <u>i</u> (1) You should slow down.

   <u>d</u> (2) You should not smoke.

   <u>f</u> (3) It tells when you can get in.

| d. | Danger:<br>Explosives | i. | Dangerous<br>Curve<br>Ahead | f. | Daily Hours<br>M–F: 8–4<br>Sat.: 9–5 |
|---|---|---|---|---|---|

## CARRYING OUT SIMPLE DIRECTIONS

DIRECTIONS: Read each of the directions given below and do what it tells you to do, using the drawings presented at the bottom of the page.

(a) Draw a line from the tool to the chair.

(b) Write the number seven in the smallest circle.

(c) Divide the larger square into four parts.

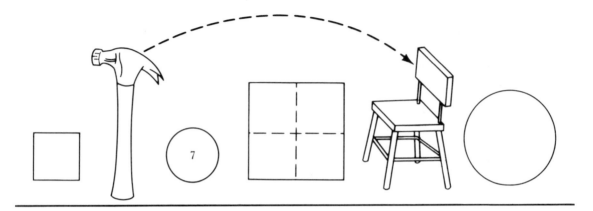

## UNDERSTANDING DIRECTION FORMS

DIRECTIONS:  Read each of the ten statements given below and do what it tells you to do.

(a) Write your name in the blank following this statement.

_____

(b) Write the month, day, and year of your birth. _____

_____

(c) Put an X in the blank which states how many years of schooling you have completed. 6 ____ 7 ____ 8 ____ 9 ____ 10 ____ 11 ____ 12 ____.

## SENTENCE–QUESTION MATCHING

DIRECTIONS: Below you are given a list of ten questions in Part A and a list of ten sentences in Part B. Your job is to identify the sentence which best answers each question and write the letter of that sentence in the blank before its matching question.

A

__d__ (1) How will we know when to start?

__b__ (2) Who has been chosen?

**B**

(a) Bill runs the bike shop.

(b) Mary is the Spring Dance Queen.

(c) The house has been painted.

(d) I have my watch with me.

## FUNCTION OF SENTENCE ELEMENTS

DIRECTIONS: Read each sentence and decide which of the "question words" the underlined part of the sentence answers. Sometimes the underlined part answers two question words. Write the letter(s) of that question word in the blank before the sentence.

(a) Who?          (d) Where?

(b) What?          (e) Why?

(c) When?          (f) How?

 _d_ (1) We decided to chase the horses <u>into the woods.</u>

 _c_ (2) <u>Before the sun is hot</u>, we can catch fish from the shore.

 _f, d_ (3) He lifted it <u>by using a pulley tied to a limb.</u>

## IDENTIFYING SENTENCE SIMILARITIES

DIRECTIONS: Ten paired sentences are given below. If the two sentences in each pair have the same or nearly the same meaning, mark that pair with an *S*. If the two sentences have quite different meanings, mark that pair with a *D*.

Our guards hog the ball.

 _D_ (1)

This team really works together.

We agreed to wait for the result.

 _S_ (2)

We would stay until the outcome was known.

## IDENTIFYING SENTENCE CONSISTENCY AND INCONSISTENCY

DIRECTIONS: Read each of the following sentences. If the statement is consistent with itself (makes sense), write a *C* at the end of it. Otherwise, write an *I* (inconsistent). Time yourself with the wall clock to see how long it takes you to do the exercise. Write that time to the nearest half-minute at the bottom of the exercise. (Difficulty of exercise can be adjusted by difficulty of vocabulary and sentence complexity, as illustrated.)

(a) Twenty is less than a dozen. _I_

(b) An average performance is not exceptional. _C_

(c) I find it difficult to believe in those things which seem stupid. _C_

(d) Since no risk was involved, we must describe his act as highly courageous. _I_

## READING ADVERTISING

DIRECTIONS: Read the following ad for general understanding. Then read it again, using the key question words we have studied: What? Who? How? When? Why? Then answer the true-false statements below, using a *T* for True and an *F* for False. (This exercise can be modified by asking the student to write in the key information in a blank following each of the key question words.)

COULD YOU USE
EXTRA MONEY?

Family grown, free time? Try telephone sales,
selling maintenance agreements. Part-time.

Openings for evening work.
5 to 9 P.M.
Apply in person, 9 to 11 or 1 to 3
**Mon.-Fri.**
Personnel Office

SAWBUCKS AND REARS
500 North St.

An Equal Opportunity Employer

  _T_  (1) This ad announces job openings.

  _F_  (2) These jobs will provide full-time employment.

  _T_  (3) You must have evenings free.

  _F_  (4) Only older men are wanted.

  _F_  (5) You must call for an interview.

  _F_  (6) You must apply between 5 and 9 P.M.

  _T_  (7) The Personnel Office is located at 500 North Street.

  _T_  (8) People presently holding a job can apply.

  _T_  (9) These jobs will involve selling by phone.

  _F_  (10) You must have previous maintenance experience.

## UNDERSTANDING LABELS

DIRECTIONS: Read the label given below and answer the following questions by marking *T* for True, *F* for False, and *N* for questions not answered.

*FORMULA #10.* FORMULA #10 was developed especially to provide hours of relief from minor aches and pains in the muscles of the body and head due to colds, arthritis, and headaches. *Dosage:* Recommended use is two tablets at bedtime and after breakfast, followed by one tablet every four hours thereafter. Do not exceed taking more than 8 tablets in any 24-hour period. Not recommended for those under 12 years of age. *Caution:* Should not be continued if nausea and swelling occur. If pain persists for more than a week, consult a doctor.

  _F_  (1) This label would be found on a soft drink bottle.

The label for FORMULA #10 tells you:

_T_ (2) What it is used for.

_T_ (3) Who should use it.

_T_ (4) How it should be used.

_F_ (5) FORMULA #10 is good for stomach aches.

_F_ (6) You can give it to your 9-year-old sister by breaking the tablets in half.

_N_ (7) You can use it for a toothache.

_F_ (8) You must have a cold to use it.

_F_ (9) It will cure an injured knee.

_T_ (10) FORMULA #10 is a pain killer.

## INTERPRETING NEWS SELECTIONS

DIRECTIONS: Following are five paragraphs, each followed by four questions. Read each and identify the number of the sentence which best serves as the topic statement of the paragraph (the sentence which identifies the main idea or states the generalization which the other sentences support or illustrate). Then locate the sentences which answer the three other questions following the paragraph. (For better readers.)

(1) A little old lady in a midwest village carefully bolts all her doors and windows. (2) A young businessman in Miami takes a cab to travel two city blocks to his hotel. (3) Violence in modern America is as common and feared as in the Middle Ages. (4) Probably no one factor explains why this is so. (5) Among those conditions which have been associated with this problem are rapid increases in population, the development of large cities, the influence of television and other media, the desire for shared political power, and economic disadvantagement. (6) Others believe it results from a lessening of religious beliefs and the deterioration of belief in law and personal responsibility.

_(3)_ a. Topic statement (main idea)

_(4)_ b. Why haven't we solved this problem?

_(6)_ c. Which sentence suggests a moral basis for the problem?

_(5)_ d. Which sentence suggests that the problem has a number of causes?

## AUGMENTING ANALYTICAL INTERPRETATION

Analytical interpretation is concerned with the meaning the writer intended to convey through the use and arrangement of facts, concepts, generalizations, and the textual structures of his message. In purposeful reading situations, the behaviors by which analytical interpretation is implemented intermix with and are dependent upon those needed for accurate decoding and basic interpretation.[14] At the same time, it is unlikely that evaluative interpretation could function effectively without incorporating some of the behaviors of analytical interpretation.

As in the instruction of other reading behaviors, instruction in analytical interpretation will take advantage of opportunities provided by directed reading of developmental selections and other larger systems for structuring the reading of content. In such situations, it and other higher interpretive behaviors are best developed through the rereading and reacting stages of the lesson; that is, after a general understanding of the content has been achieved in the initial directed reading of the selection. [15]

The development of the specific behaviors of analytical interpretation will need to be supported by activities and reading exercises which can clarify and reinforce understanding, accuracy, and efficiency of response. One particular advantage provided by such supplementary instruction is that materials can be selected which represent different writing styles and organizations which call for analytical interpretation.

The teacher should select materials for activities and exercises so that pupils do not encounter so much difficulty in the decoding and basic interpretation of the content that they cannot give attention to the writer's organization of ideas. Thus, the exercise content is best selected within the "independent-instructional" difficulty range, and/or the teacher should prepare and guide the first reading of the exercise content much as he would for a short reading selection. Since many selections appropriate to the teaching of analytical interpretation will consist of larger, multiparagraph text, the guided first reading of the selection is an instructionally appropriate step. Moreover, it provides a good opportunity to clarify and polish those behaviors of decoding and basic interpretation which have been taught previously.

The remainder of this section presents some illustrative activities and representative exercises by which instruction in the following analytical interpretational behaviors can be supplemented:

1. Identifying concepts.
2. Recognizing levels of generalization.
3. Extending understanding of paragraph structure.
4. Inferring unstated ideas and details.
5. Identifying various paragraph functions.

6. Determining sequence.
7. Understanding common textbook organization.
8. Recognizing expository-argumentative patterns.
9. Analyzing the structure of selections.
10. Restructuring printed information to serve reader need.

Many of the workbooks, texts, and boxed practice materials listed in Appendix D will provide additional exercise models for improving analytical interpretation. The secondary-level sources tend to emphasize the more traditional organizational skills. Some of those materials included within the college section may be used directly or modified for instruction in higher-level analytical thinking.

## Illustrative Instructional Activities

*1. Headline or heading hyping.* Because news headlines or text headings are contracted sentence forms employed to catch attention, they serve as useful vehicles for instruction in title-content and idea relationships. Some illustrative activities which may be generated from this base are presented here.

*a.* The teacher can bring five to ten examples of current news headlines to class. Using the chalkboard or overhead projector, each headline is presented and different interpretations of meaning are solicited. The teacher then may read aloud enough of the article or story to place the headline or its key word in perspective. Following class or group direction, the teacher writes a more complete sentence which contextually explains the headline. The two versions are compared as pupils analyze what sentence functions usually are retained for headlines or headings.

*b.* Pupils are asked to find and bring to class three newspaper articles with headlines, magazine leads and articles, or headings from one of their texts in which one or more words lend themselves to more than one meaning: e.g., "Cuba Attacks U.S.

Position" (in UN debate); "Baby Market Depleted" (companies adapting their production to youth and elderly markets); "Weather Is Wearing" (the influence of climatic conditions upon personal behavior). The pupil task is to identify the key ideas presented in the article and rewrite the headline or heading to give it explicit referential meaning. These headlines and their improved versions also may be collected and duplicated for use as a class exercise in which the pupils attempt to identify the topic statement which goes with the headline or heading.

*c.* The teacher provides the class with duplicated copies of a short magazine article minus its heading. (Several different articles of different reading levels may be used, if a notable range of reading ability exists in the class.) The pupil task is to write a topic sentence which summarizes the main idea of the article, and then, further reduce the topic sentence into a three- to five-word title or heading. (As a variation, certain short segments of the content area text could be used in place of the duplicated articles.)

*d.* If the teacher employs a classroom reading center or bulletin board for stimulating interest and incidental practice in reading, a series of brief paragraphs or articles can be numbered and pinned to the bulletin board. Surrounding these in random order would be a circle of headings (each labeled with a mark or letter). The display can be titled something like "Heads Up," with a challenge to match the heading with its article. At the end of the week, the teacher, a pupil committee, or individual pupils can use different colors of yarn to connect the headings and its appropriate article. (Sometimes it is more productive to use such feedback as a class activity and thus generate discussion, including argument, of why one heading–article lash-up is preferred to another!)

*2. Paragraph function activities.* The recognition of the function a paragraph may serve in the total selection involves an analytic task which goes beyond paragraph meaning or paragraph internal-idea structure. After pupils have had initial lessons in the nature and recognition of each of the most common expository paragraph functions (i.e., *introductory, definitional, explanatory, illustrative, transitional, summary,* and *mixed function*), activities such as the following may be modified to provide further learning and reinforcement in the recognition of paragraph function.

*a.* The teacher finds a number of interesting articles composed of four to eight paragraphs which represent several (not necessarily all) of the basic paragraph functions. These are reproduced, and the paragraphs of each separate article are coded according to the teacher's key, separated, and placed into envelopes (also coded to facilitate teacher checking and re-sorting and regrouping). The envelopes are given to a group or to individual pupils, according to their general level of reading competency. The task of each group or pupil is to place the paragraphs in a meaningful order (as in the original order) and to write down the function served by each paragraph. Response may be made on a sheet included within the envelope (or it can be recorded on the board.) Groups may exchange envelopes as a means of checking accuracy and to provide additional practice. To provide feedback, the teacher or the group recorder can write the correct answers on the chalkboard or they can be provided by a dittoed answer key.

*b.* The class, group, or individual is given an article of appropriate readability from which a paragraph serving the functions of introduction, summary, or transition has been omitted. The task is to read the selection and to write a paragraph which fulfills the function of that paragraph omitted. After writing this paragraph, it may be compared with the original and both critiqued for strengths and weaknesses.

*3. Argumentive-structure activities.* Most pupils need continuing reinstruction and reinforcement in identifying and following argumentive structure. At the upper secondary level, this includes the less obvious patterns of *induction* and *deduction*, as well as that *mixed form* of educational prose in which the paragraph or selection combines *explanation* and *illustration* with argument. After each form of organizational structure is reviewed and practiced separately in exercise form, they may be intermixed in exercises which require identification and analysis of multiple types and parts.

*a.* If the instructional materials do not provide examples readily available to pupils, the teacher should. The structural label, its major characteristics, one or two examples outside regular context, and several examples of the structure as it appears in narrative or expository text (with the key points of the argument underlined and conclusions double-underlined) should be duplicated for each pupil to keep in his notebook. These should be taught or explained like any other lesson material.

*b.* Part of the reading bulletin board or activities center may be used as the "Argument of the Week." Examples of written discourse are clipped and placed on the board or in the activities-center folder, and pupils are challenged to identify the argumentive form and sign their name to the checksheet. Pupil interest is increased if these are picked from treatments of significant national or local controversies—in sports, politics, school-related news, crime, etc.

*c.* Pupils may be asked to search through a current magazine or newspaper and bring to class one example of each of the argumentive structures previously identified. The pupil should label the article with the name of the argumentive form, check in the margin the major generalization or conclusion, underline each supporting detail or premise, and underline the generalization involved.

*d.* After the nature of the typical mixed paragraph and chapter argumentive style has been identified and practiced in exercises, selected textbooks used in the content classes may be brought to class (if not a part of regular classroom or center library or equipment). In groups or whole-class situations, pupils may identify certain sections or paragraphs in which the idea structure was difficult to follow. With the aid of the instructor, the group or class can read those segments (with the overhead projector if all students do not have copies of the text) and identify the type and elements of the structure.

*e.* A variation of this activity would involve bringing to class texts from a number of different content areas. Students may be grouped, according to the content area of their interest, to randomly sample ten or twenty pages to identify the type of organizational structure employed. A large chart—with the name of the texts by content area set down the left side and the various argumentive structures labeled across the top to form columns—is placed on the board. Each group or individual responsible for a text writes the number of examples of each structure found in the sample in its appropriate slot. Probably the mixed function textbook pattern will be most common, but the comparison provides practice and gives pupils some special insight about textbook writing and reading.

*f.* A problem pertinent to the content area or of current student interest is or has been discussed in class. Each pupil is asked to role-play as a member of an organization (e.g., the Sierra Club, the Consumer's Aid Agency, the Newspaper Guild) which supports a particular position. As such, he is to write short, separate paragraphs supporting that position: by inductive argument, by deductive argument, by analogy, and historical trend.

*g.* All upper secondary pupils should have some work in distinguishing sentences in paragraphs which serve as coordinate (equal-weight ideas) or subordinate relationship (supporting) sentences. Advanced students may be challenged to analyze the use of coordinate and subordinate structure in statement-support textbook paragraphs from four or five content areas and to present the results of their comparative findings to the class as a whole. One generalization likely to result is that many textbook paragraphs mix these patterns regardless of whether the obvious organization is sequential, comparison-contrast, statement-support, or whatever.

*4. Study-related organizational activities.* An informational article or selected pages of a content area textbook may be used as the reading base for the analysis of organization (content or structure pertinent to a number of study learning tasks).

*a.* Pupils may be asked to underline the key points or to develop a marginal outline (key outline points are marked in the margin opposite their text statement), as they might use these as aids to memory or for study review. The teacher then shows (by overhead projector) the underlining or outline pattern he or she would use.

*b.* A variation on the above procedure is to ask the pupils to construct those questions whose answers they feel capture the significant points of the article or chapter segment. Questions may be exchanged for answering by other pupils. A considerable amount of learning takes place when the pupils compare their questions to those of other pupils or to those presented by the teacher as the items he would ask on a test over the material.

*c.* Secondary pupils often enjoy participating in surveys or experiments related to the topic of study. The class is divided into groups. Each group reads a selection and takes a test of ten or fifteen objective questions. Then each group is assigned the task of developing a set of notes by a different system — e.g., summary, underlining, outlining, raising and answering questions, etc. A second test is given which not only includes the first set of questions but also an additional ten or fifteen questions. The class can participate in the comparison of its pre-post test scores on the same questions as well as the comparison of performance among groups using different study-notational systems. The follow-up discussion should emphasize the key generalization of *differentiated rereading* as an aid to interpretation and study.

*d.* A committee of pupils may be asked to read the next text assignment in advance of the class. Their job is to develop an advanced reading–study organizer in the form of a summary, a flowchart, an outline of key related terms, or a list of questions which will be duplicated for use by the remainder of the class. Some teachers consider this an ongoing instructional procedure, with the membership of the "advance committee" changing in a systematic manner, and leaving one or two experienced members always to aid the new committee.

*5. Purposeful reorganization of written materials.* The reorganization or restructuring of printed materials is a common work or study task which draws heavily upon analytical interpretation. Ordinarily, instructional activities in the *re*organization of materials will not be utilized before the individuals in the group or class have mastered basic read-

ing and noting processes such as listing, outlining, and writing summaries.

*a.* Individual pupils (or small groups) are paired by approximate reading ability. One member of the pair is given a sheet of directions in traditional listed format. The task of that individual or group is to rewrite those directions, to incorporate them in an interesting short descriptive article or selection such as one would encounter in a guidebook, a manual, a textbook segment, or a magazine article. The other half of the paired individuals or groups is given a short article which includes a set of implied directions and has the task of abstracting these directions and listing them in appropriate sequential form. The two individuals or groups work independently and, when finished, share their results with each other. A good deal of insight and some fun occurs when the paired individuals or groups recognize that they have been working on the same original material or its appropriate listed directions when they compare the results of the two processes.

*b.* Using a short videotape, a filmstrip, a portion of a film without sound, a series of coordinated still pictures, or just one complex picture as a base experience, the teacher asks the members of a group or class to write a one-page summary of what they have seen in the form of a newspaper article, with its heading, its interest-catching lead paragraph, and the body which answers the basic reportorial questions of "who, what, when, where, and how." The descriptions are interchanged (or four or five chosen from volunteers) for comparative analysis. The source is presented again as a means of rechecking accuracy.

*c.* Pupils are given a reading selection with the direction to mark certain sentences which, when abstracted, will provide the best summary of the selection itself. The progression in such exercises should move by gradual steps from short (two- or three-paragraph selections) with quite apparent key points to longer (five-page selections) with less obvious structure.

*d.* Present the members of the class with three or four pages describing a product, a process, an administrative unit, or an organization which can be bought or whose services can be leased. The first pupil task is to construct some magazine or newspaper advertising copy which will call the attention of prospective customers to the product or services. The second task of the individual or group is to develop a one-page summary of the essential nature as well as positive and negative aspects of the product or services as it might appear in a consumer's magazine or better business department report. (Copies of pertinent advertising, magazine articles, and reports may be analyzed by the class for their style elements prior to undertaking this activity.)

*e.* Relatively short (5- to 10-page) biographies of interesting figures in such visible fields as sports, entertainment, politics, and religion are read by the pupils. Converting these into one-page personal vitae or resumés often stimulates a good deal of interest (or amusement) while providing practice in writing and reading such resumés.

*f.* The class may be divided into a number of teams. Each team is provided a different set (one or two pages) of random data pertinent to a topic. The first task of each team is to identify the central topic. Then each group reorganizes the data in a different manner: time order, pro-con analysis, classification analysis such as outlining, cause-effect relationship, and narrative summary. Members of the group are encouraged to interact and help each other. Team competition in completing the task may be encouraged.

*g.* Two or three selections dealing with the same topic are duplicated and presented to the members of the class or group along with an outline in which selected major or first steps (I, II, III, IV, etc.) and selected second steps (A, B, C, D, etc.) are given. The task facing the pupil is to complete the indicated blanks on the outline and to add those representing step three (1, 2, 3, 4, etc.) by selectively drawing information from the several selections. (This activity can be adjusted to pupil ability by the number and difficulty of selections, the detail required, and the number of steps completed on the original outline form.)

---

## Representative Exercises in Analytical Interpretation

### RECOGNIZING CONCEPTS

DIRECTIONS: Following are fifteen sentences. Underline the one or more concepts contained in each. Remember, a concept is a term which represents a grouping of items according to some factor or quality they have in common. The first two sentences are marked as examples.

(a) I prefer <u>beans</u> to other <u>vegetables.</u>

(b) <u>Reporters</u> take <u>pleasure</u> in <u>baiting</u> the <u>candidates.</u>

### DISCRIMINATING BETWEEN PARTICULARS AND GENERALIZATIONS

DIRECTIONS: Following are ten pairs of statements. In each pair, mark the one which represents a statement of a detail (a particular) with a *P*. Mark the one which states a generalization (presents a relationship between two or more concepts) with a *G*. The first two pairs are marked to guide you.

a. <u>G</u> Football injuries are at an all-time high.

<u>P</u> All-Pro Buck James had surgery for a broken arm.

b. __P__ Nine people failed the spelling quiz last week.

__G__ Spelling is not a good example of abstract reasoning.

## DIFFERENTIATING LEVELS OF GENERALIZATION

DIRECTIONS: Each item of this exercise consists of three statements of differing degree or level of generalization. In each group of three, mark that statement with a *B* which is the broadest generalization. Mark that statement with an *L* which is the least generalized (or most specific) statement. Two examples are marked.

A. __L__ 1. Jim threw the pass to Bill.

_____ 2. Football is a popular pastime.

__B__ 3. Sports are common to all peoples.

B. __B__ 1. Rainfall is a problem in most of Africa.

__L__ 2. The Sahara desert covers hundreds of square miles.

_____ 3. Seasonal heavy rains wash away important minerals in some areas.

## IDENTIFYING IRRELEVANT STATEMENTS

DIRECTIONS: This exercise consists of five groups of four statements each. Three of the four statements in each cluster support a common topic or idea. Check that statement which is irrelevant (does not support the common topic or idea.)

A. _____ 1. Use the metro bus to get to work with less strain and cost.

_____ 2. Nonstop flights from Chicago to Seattle take three hours.

__X__ 3. The new snowmobiles are more powerful than last year's models.

_____ 4. The trucking industry touches every city in the nation.

B. _____ 1. Sunlight is the basic source of metabolic energy.

__X__ 2. Enzymes regulate activity within cells.

_____ 3. Respiration releases the chemical energy from digested food.

_____ 4. Photosynthesis provides the basis by which plants can manufacture food.

## INFERRING TOPIC IDEAS AND SPECIFICS

DIRECTIONS: Read each of the following paragraphs; then answer the questions following it. The questions deal with information which may be implied but not directly stated by the writer. Mark the statement __I__ if it can be defended as an inference intended (implied) by the writer. Mark it __F__ if it cannot.

In May 1607, the days were warm, the nights, cool. Life was stirring in the wilderness and nature had been generous, the colonists thought. There were fruits, abundant timber, deer and other animals for food, and a not too numerous native population. The hot, humid weather of midsummer and the snow, ice, and emptiness of winter were not in evidence. The choice of a site for settlement was both good and bad. The anchorage for ships at Jamestown was good. The island had not then become a true island and had an easily controlled dry land isthmus connection with the mainland. As the river narrows here, it was one of the best control points on the James. It was not used by the Indians; and it was a bit inland, hence somewhat out of range of the Spanish menace. Arable land on the island was limited by inlet and "guts." The swamps were close and bred mosquitoes in abundance and, with contamination so easy, drinking water was a problem. All of these facts became evident to these first English Americans as the months went by.

__I__ 1. The paragraph describes the Jamestown site.

__I__ 2. Early summer was one of the better times of the year.

__F__ 3. Relations between the natives and the colonists were relaxed.

__F__ 4. The island was easily cultivated.

__I__ 5. Living conditions would worsen in the months following.

## DETERMINING SEQUENCE

DIRECTIONS: A group of four statements is presented below. Each sentence is part of a set of specifics, but the sentences of each group are presented in jumbled order. In the first five, the process or central sequence which the sentences represent is identified, and your job is to number the statements as they should appear in the proper sequence. In the last five, you must also identify the topic or major function which the statements serve.

A. Topic: Planning a Wilderness Canoe Trip

__4__ When you have gathered the other information and supplies, choose a canoe which best meets your need in terms of weight, toughness, and size.

__3__ Make a list of essential supplies, then select them for minimal size and weight.

__2__ Laying out the route will include consideration of distances to be covered, water conditions, and the number and length of portages.

__1__ Everything else is dependent upon obtaining a good detailed map of the area to be covered.

B. Topic: [*The Emergence of American Taxation*]

__3__ But during the Revolutionary War, power was withheld from the Continental Congress to levy taxes.

__1__ Many colonists came to the new land to escape oppressive levies by landowners and government.

__2__ In the early days, the colony had to collect some revenues from settlers to pay the expenses of a small militia and necessary supplies.

__4__ Not until 1787 did the Constitutional Convention include a section which gave Congress the "power" to levy and collect taxes, duties, posts and excises.

## IDENTIFYING PARAGRAPH STRUCTURE

Each of the ten paragraphs given below has one of the five common organizational patterns or argumentive structures which we have studied. Read each paragraph and identify its major pattern of structure by labeling it with the appropriate letter. To refresh your memory, the five common structures are given below:

A = *Analogy.* Association of two events or concepts with the inference of likeness in all their particulars; used in argument and creative expression.

D = *Deduction.* An argumentative form of logic which arrives at (deduces) a conclusion by means of the syllogism, i.e., (1) accepted major premise, (2) reasonable, related minor premise, and (therefore) (3) conclusion.

E = *Explanation.* The use of description, definition, or illustration to inform about the nature of the topic.

S = *Statement-Support.* An argumentative process in which particulars are presented to support a generalization or a reasoning process in which a generalization is induced from a series of particulars.

T = *Time Order.* Information representing a time, event, or procedure relationship.

(T) 1. New Haven, settled in 1638, is the seventh oldest city in the United States. It was laid out in nine squares and is considered the first American city to have a city plan. The central square was set aside as a market place and public ground. Many later cities followed this plan. New Haven grew from a handful of settlers to a population of 8,000 at the time of the American Revolution. After some 220 years of gradual and pleasant growth, New Haven, in less then fifty years, lost much of its beauty and acquired most of the slums it is now removing. From 1860 to 1910, the population expanded from 40,000 to 134,000.

(A) 2. Once again the column was set in motion. Trucks, guns, and mobile armor humped and jerked like a giant rounded snake over hills, down valleys, and across streams. Slowly, surely, it slid toward the defenseless sleeping city.

(D) 3. Now few Americans would seriously question that a member of Congress is, indirectly, a representative of the American people's will. Yet here we have a congressional member who refuses to support legislation overwhelmingly wanted by the people, as expressed in opinion polls. Isn't this, in fact, a most serious irony—an apparent severing of administrative responsibility to the electorate?

(T) 4. In order to get rid of silica, we add limestone to the ore and coke which we dump into the furnace. In the furnace, the limestone changes to calcium oxide because of the high temperature. The calcium oxide then unites with the silica to form slag. At the high temperature in the furnace, the slag is a liquid which drips to the bottom of the furnace. Since it has a lower density than iron, the slag floats on top of the liquid iron at the bottom.

(S) 5. Purification of ritual pollution is effected in various ways. Common among the methods are fasting, shaving the hair and cutting the nails, crawling through cleansing smoke fumes produced during an elaborate ritual, passing between fires or jumping through fire, washing with water or blood, and cutting or gashing the body so as to let the evil out with the rushing blood. If an unclean spirit haunts a community or enters a man or woman, it may be expelled by introducing a more powerful spirit whose presence will be cleansing.

## INTERPRETING PARAGRAPHS

DIRECTIONS: Each of the fifteen exercises in this section consists of a paragraph followed by five questions. Answer the questions only after carefully reading the paragraph. Reread the paragraph, if necessary, to clarify your answers. The first three questions are true-false and concern particulars stated or implied in the paragraph. The fourth question requires identification of the organizational pattern of the selection. The fifth item asks for a statement of the main idea of the paragraph.

A. Oil burners are of two kinds: vaporizing and atomizing. Vaporizing burners premix the air and oil vapor. The pot-type burner is vaporizing and consists of a pot containing a pool of oil. An automatic valve regulates the amount of oil in the pot. Heat from the flame vaporizes the oil. Air enters just above the pool of oil either by natural draft or by means of a small fan. A pilot flame ignites the oil pot when heat is required. There are few moving parts, and operation is quiet. Some pot-type burners can be operated without electric power.

   <u>T</u>  1. The pot-type oil burner premixes air and oil vapor. (T or F)

   <u>F</u>  2. The pot-type burner is a complex mechanism. (T or F)

   <u>F</u>  3. The pot-type burner requires a fan draft. (T or F)

   <u>c</u>  4. Basic organization structure: (a) analogy; (b) deduction; (c) explanation.

      5. Main idea: (<u>The pot-type oil burner operates by a vaporizing process.</u>)

## ANALYZING THE STRUCTURE OF SELECTIONS

DIRECTIONS: This is a review practice exercise. It consists of paragraphs followed by five questions that measure your understanding of organization. First, you identify the best summary of the selection. Questions 2 through 4 concentrate on the structural pattern, purpose, function, or topic ideas of the individual paragraphs. Question 5 asks you to identify the organizational pattern of the selection.

I. In nineteenth-century rural America, it was difficult to see ahead. On February 28, 1848, an Indiana schoolmaster (who was also a farmer, a candlemaker, and a cooper), Jethro Mace by name, made an entry in his journal. He wrote it with a buzzard-quill pen by the light of a tallow candle of his own manufacture, using homemade brown ink on handmade paper. In the margin he noted in his fine script, "A busy day." The entry reads: "Tended fire of dry kiln, made a bench hook of wood to hold staves and such things, planed out staves for a bleacher...tore down brickwork in cabin by new house, put up shelves in the hut by the sink, sawed blocks for bedstead. Busy."

II. Did Jethro Mace suspect, even faintly, that the next century would bring ballpoint pens and electric lights, and that millions of wheels would be turning out millions of barrel staves, hooks, kitchen cabinets, and orthopedic mattresses? Probably not. "I would give a trifle," he wrote, "to know what my grandfather 100 years ago was occupied in doing. Who knows but some person may feel the like curiosity 100 years hence to know what this writer has been doing." A world where men have come together in order to pool their manpower and exchange their services simply did not occur to old Jethro.

III. A combination of men and machines, together with freedom and individualism that acted as a spur, has made such a world possible. Since 1900, output per man-hour has risen more than 200 percent. In 1950 the average worker produced more than three times as much as his grandfather did in 1900. Today, the value of goods and services in the United States is about $3 trillion. If output per man-hour were to keep expanding, as it has expanded in the past, by 3 percent a year, the total value of goods and services by 1985 would be staggering.

1. Which of the following is the best summary of the selection? __b__
   a. During the past one hundred years the American way of life has become easier and more dependent.
   b. Industrialization, specialization, and exchange of services have had a tremendous impact on our way of life during the past century.
   c. The United States has demonstrated a consistent trend toward an increase in the value of goods and services through a combination of American initiative and natural resources.

2. Which of the following best states the function of paragraph I? __d__
   a. It summarizes nineteenth-century American life patterns.
   b. It emphasizes the busy nature of life one hundred years ago.
   c. It illustrates the self-reliance required of the rural American living a century ago.
   d. It introduces the selection and provides a base for demonstrating technical advances of the last century.

3. What is the key idea of paragraph II? __c__
   a. Men frequently have been curious about life before and after their times.
   b. It would have been difficult to anticipate the changes in American life that have taken place in the last century.
   c. The technical pooling and exchange of services have produced a great impact on American life.
   d. Civilization progresses a great deal in a century.

4. What is the main topic of paragraph III? __b__
   a. Progress made in the United States.
   b. Increase in man-hour output in this century.
   c. A social revolution in America.

5. What is the organizational pattern of this selection? __a__

    a. Chronological comparison of a century's change in U.S. production patterns.

    b. Description of daily life and thought in nineteenth-century America.

    c. Deductive proof of the limitations of man's personal perspective.

    d. An explanation of the per man-hour principle.

## REFERENCES

1. Helen M. Robinson, "Corrective and Remedial Instruction," Chapter XX in *Development in and Through Reading*, Sixtieth Yearbook, Part I, of the National Society for the Study of Education, N. B. Henry, Editor (Chicago: University of Chicago Press, 1961) pp. 357 and 360.
2. Theodore Clymer, "What Is Reading: Some Current Concepts," Chapter I in *Innovation and Change in Reading Instruction*, Sixty-seventh Yearbook, Part II, of the National Society for the Study of Education, Helen M. Robinson, Editor (Chicago: University of Chicago Press, 1968) pp. 27-29.
3. John B. Carroll, "The Nature of the Reading Process," in *Theoretical Models and Processes of Reading*, Second Edition, H. Singer and R. R. Ruddell, Editors (Newark, Del.: International Reading Association, 1976) p. 14.
4. Robinson, "Corrective and Remedial Instruction," pp. 357 and 360.
5. Olive S. Niles, "Comprehension Skills," *The Reading Teacher*, 17 (September, 1963) pp. 2-7.
6. Mary C. Austin and Coleman Morrison, *The First R* (New York: The Macmillan Company, 1963) pp. 222-23.
7. Edward L. Thorndike, "Reading as Reasoning," *Journal of Educational Psychology* 8 (June, 1917) pp. 323-32.
8. Eleanor J. Gibson and Harry Levin, *The Psychology of Reading* (Cambridge, Mass.: The MIT Press, 1975) pp. 477-79.
9. David Russell, *The Dynamics of Reading*, R. R. Ruddell, Editor (Waltham, Mass.: Ginn-Blaisdell, 1970) pp. 15-17.
10. P. L. Travers, interview on the *Today Show*, December 11, 1975.
11. Robert Frost, lecture at the University of Cincinnati, March, 1955.
12. John R. Bormuth, "Reading Literacy: Its Definition and Assessment," *Reading Research Quarterly* 9 (1973-74) p. 12.
13. Daniel N. Fader and Elton B. McNeil, *Hooked on Books: Program and Proof* (New York: Berkley Publishing Co., 1968) pp. 82-85.
14. Christian Gerhard, *Making Sense: Reading Comprehension Improved Through Categorizing* (Newark, Del.: International Reading Association, 1975) p. 163.
15. Russell G. Stauffer, *Directing the Reading-Thinking Process* (New York: Harper & Row, Publishers, 1975) p. 94.

## SUPPLEMENTARY SOURCES

Carsetti, Janet K. *Literacy Problems and Solutions: A Resource Handbook*. College Park, Md.: American Correctional Association, 1975.

Dawson, Mildred A. *Developing Comprehension Including Critical Reading*. Newark, Del.: International Reading Association, 1968.

Gray, William S. "Increasing the Basic Reading Competencies of Students." In *Reading in High School and College*, N. B. Henry, Editor, Forty-seventh Yearbook of the National Society for the Study of Education, Part II, Chapter VI. Chicago: University of Chicago Press, 1948.

Green, Richard T. *Comprehension in Reading*, An Annotated Bibliography. Newark, Del.: International Reading Association, 1971.

Henry, George H. *Teaching Reading as Concept Development: Emphasis on Affective Thinking*. Newark, Del.: International Reading Association, 1974.

Kelly, L. "Survival Literacy: Teaching Reading to Those with a Need to Know." *Journal of Reading* 17 (February, 1974) pp. 352-55.

Russell, David H. *The Dynamics of Reading*, Chapter 7. Waltham, Mass.: Ginn-Blaisdell, 1970.

# TWELVE

# Extending Maturity in Interpretation and Reaction

*...the mature reader must do more than get the literal meaning of a passage. He must be able to interpret the author's thought, and to make critical judgements, evaluations, and inferences. This is "reading between the lines." "Reading beyond the lines" involves drawing conclusions, forming generalizations, and applying ideas gained from reading.*

Ruth Strang

*It is apparent that any reader's rate is greatly affected by his purpose in reading.*

Frederick B. Davis

***Overview*** Chapter Twelve attends to the instruction and general development of those behaviors which enable the secondary and adult reader to move beyond functional reading competency in school and life into reading maturity. It reviews the nature of mature reading and its components of evaluative interpretation, flexible reading efficiency, and extended personal reading. This chapter presents the need for the secondary school to correct its benign neglect of these more advanced but essential reading behaviors, and emphasis is placed upon their extension through content classroom and reading program implementation. A number of representative instructional activities and exercises are included to illustrate how the reading, English, or content teacher can supplement published materials of instruction in these significant behaviors.

# TOWARD MATURITY
# IN READING

The ultimate major objective of the upper-school reading program is to move as many readers as far along the developmental continuum toward reading maturity as possible. Reading maturity presumes the development of the fundamental competency in reading—a sufficient sight vocabulary, proficiency in word recognition and analysis, the ability to derive necessary meaning from decoding the literal meaning of sentences, and the purposeful analysis of the fundamental relationships among the various units of the writer's message structure—needed to negotiate occupational and school reading tasks. But it requires more than this. Mature reading involves reading "between and beyond" the lines, as Strang has suggested.[1] In our society and times, it requires flexible efficiency—an effective rate of comprehension as determined by reading purpose.[2] And all of this means little if the mature reader does not read, selectively yet extensively, with personal satisfaction and successful application for mature purposes.

## The Gray–Rogers Study of
## Reading Maturity

To gain a broader understanding of the dimensions of reading maturity in our society and a better understanding of the challenge the secondary school faces in developing mature readers, we need to consider one of the most intensive investigations of mature reading behavior in our culture—the Gray-Rogers study.[3]

In 1956, William Gray and Bernice Rogers published *Maturity in Reading*, an account of their efforts to identify and delineate the significant characteristics of reading maturity and to develop a scale for evaluating the developmental degree of maturity achieved in reading by American adults. After a review of the available empirical evidence, they arrived at six major categories needing investigation: (1) interest in reading, (2) purposes in

reading, (3) nature of material used, (4) comprehension of what is read, (5) thoughtful reaction to and use of the ideas, and (6) personal adjustment to reading. After tryout and analysis, these categories were revised into five subscales, each depicting five incremental levels of maturity, which were combined to form the total scale. This scale was utilized in three case study investigations of the reading behavior of 80 adults.

The study produced stark evidence of an inadequate level of reading maturity among the products of our school system—evidence which has not been reversed in more recent, but less intensive, studies.[4] The following Gray-Rogers findings carry particular implication for secondary schools and secondary reading education: (1) the greater majority of adults sampled in the pilot and main studies demonstrated relatively low levels of reading maturity on the five subscales—indeed, a specially selected sample of highly educated subjects had to be located to validate the more mature levels of the scale, since subjects of the pilot and main study failed to reach them; (2) generally, a low level of competence in reading interpretation and reaction was revealed by these adults; (3) interpretive skill in reading alone does not satisfy reading maturity, but should be complemented by breadth and depth of reading interests, purposes, and types of materials used—i.e., the way one habitually *uses* one's reading competence; and (4) high school graduates demonstrated but limited superiority over grade school graduates on these assessments. Artley considered the latter point as clear evidence for the need for stronger developmental reading programs in the secondary school.[5]

### *Implications for Personal Reading Habits*

As the third Gray-Rogers finding indicates, adult immaturity in reading is revealed in personal reading habits over and beyond competency in interpretation and reaction. The investigation included evaluation of reading interest, reading purposes, and materials read as reported by these adults. Interest was assessed in terms of enthusiasm for reading, time spent in voluntary reading, and breadth of reading interests. Purposeful reading appraisal included the variety, personal growth value, and self-awareness of purposes for which reading was or might be done. Materials read were evaluated in terms of intellectual challenge, quality of treatment, and the originality and significance of ideas they presented. The Gray-Rogers subjects revealed a disturbing lack of breadth, intensity, self-direction, and quality in their personal reading practices.

In this respect, Artley argues that much of the responsibility for enhancing reader motivation and personal reading habits must be accepted by secondary school personnel—librarians, reading, English, and content teachers.[6] Informal teacher interaction may be as potent a source of effecting this change as planned formal programs. In this respect, available evidence of restricted teacher habits in their own personal and professional reading is disheartening and suggests that teacher training and in-service programs may need to be concerned with more than teaching mechanics.[7,8]

## SHARPENING EVALUATIVE INTERPRETATION AND REACTION

Evaluative reading interpretation and reaction are related to "critical reading," a traditional term which has been used rather loosely in the professional literature.[9] Instructionally, *evaluative interpretation* encompasses teaching the attributes and processes of objective analysis of evidence and argument. The function and behaviors of evaluation in the integral reading act were identified in Chapter Three.

Evaluative interpretation involves a good deal more than teaching pupils to be critical of materials and writers. In the first place, specific evaluation-oriented interpretation behaviors are extensions of other interpretive processes—organizational, inferential, and logical.[10] Second, evaluative reading goes beyond particular interpretive response and involves other reader interpretation and reaction behavior, including appreciation and application. Third, evaluative reading performance is quite dependent upon personal reader factors—particularly upon the intellectual, the experiential, and the affective characteristics of the reader. Finally, evaluation interpretation and reaction should depend to some extent upon the nature of the material under consideration.[11]

The development of evaluative interpretation is not a short-term instructional issue. It may begin with the development of fundamental evaluational processes in the primary grades (for example, differentiating sensible from nonsensical language, nonfiction from fiction, and fact from fancy in literature).[12] In all probability, refining one's evaluational reading processes is a lifelong reading task.[13] Certainly, the development of critical thinking, as such, and as applied in reading, is not the sovereign responsibility of the reading teacher. All teachers, all content areas of instruction, share in the general development of this behavior. Beyond this, each content field—particularly in literature, social studies, the general sciences, and the applied subjects—includes special applications of critical thinking and evaluative reading which are taught best within that content instructional setting.

Beyond the analyses of the organizational structure of ideas and details discussed in Chapter Eleven, the key specific learning tasks of evaluative interpretation (and reaction) tend to support one or more of three major objectives:

1. Developing and maintaining an objective reading set, including:
   a. Understanding how personal factors can influence accuracy of interpretation and reaction.
   b. Recognizing one's own particular bias or biases.
   c. Identifying written appeal to reader personal needs.
   d. Suspending judgment and qualifying one's conclusions in lieu of adequate evidence.

2. Determining the relevance of written content, including:
   a. Ascertaining whether the specific content or general source is pertinent to reader's task or personal objectives.
   b. Examining the currency of the publication and the data it contains.
   c. Differentiating fact and opinion.
   d. Evaluating the quality of argument—identifying the sufficiency and precision of evidence, and whether it employs a rational or emotional style of writing.
3. Verifying the validity of written content, including:
   a. Checking factual evidence against authoritative external sources.
   b. Analyzing specific content and generalizations for consistency within the source or selection.
   c. Identifying the writer's intent.
   d. Identifying the fallacious use of argument, i.e., in the use of historical, inductive, deductive, and statistical support of generalizations and conclusions.
   e. Recognizing common propaganda techniques.
   f. Checking the credibility of the writer, the publication, and the publishing house.

It matters little whether the focus of this training is in developmental reading or content area instruction; the secondary grades are a time when considerable emphasis should be placed upon the teaching and practice of evaluative reading—critical thinking behaviors.[14] During the secondary years, most pupils begin to accrue the mental development, the general and school experiential background, and the mastery of fundamental reading behaviors which facilitate the learning and use of evaluative reading. Adolescence generally brings a greater awareness and personal concern with those aspects of societal interaction which lend themselves to, indeed which require, the use of careful, objective evaluation. Also, the instructional materials, tasks, and objectives germane to the broad second-ary curriculum draw heavily upon evaluative reading and critical thinking. For those pupils not going beyond the secondary school in formal education, grades seven through twelve may be the only real chance to receive instruction in these processes.

Most of the principles and recommended conditions of instruction which improve the general use of reading and the development of interpretive reading processes presented in earlier chapters also hold for instruction in evaluative reading. As in the development of literal and analytical interpretation, the larger developmental or content area guided reading activity lends itself to the development of evaluative reading, particularly in the rereading and application phases of the lesson. One important observation needs to be made here. Critical thinking deserves a worthy target. The pupil must read propaganda, advertising, materials which deal with controversial subjects, and other life-like sources of writing to create realistic conditions for the learning of these crucial reading processes. The use of sterile, pedagogic reading materials, or a classroom climate dominated by authoritative attitudes, is not likely to encourage effective objective evaluation (although they may stimulate suppressed emotional reaction).

Increasingly, published instructional materials such as those presented in Appendix D include units and exercises which aid in the development of critical reading performance. As useful as these are, the teacher and school will need to go beyond these sources and the practice they provide to sharpen pupil critical or evaluative interpretation. The following activities and exercises suggest the nature and direction of specific instruction both reading and content teachers may employ to improve evaluative reading behavior.

## Representative Instructional Activities

### Investigating Reader Factors Which Influence Interpretation

Following are several of many ways in which teachers may help pupils become aware of how personal interests, attitudes, and emotions may influence reading interpretation.

*1.* Interests serve as a useful beginning to the awareness of reader differences in reaction to material as well as in the self-analysis of reading behavior. The teacher can direct a committee in conducting a reading "interests" survey of fellow class members. Pupils may respond to this anonymously, depending on the questions in the survey. Such a survey may include items of reading attitudes and habits (frequency and types of materials) as well as general personal likes and dislikes. If such survey data are signed, it will be useful for teacher analysis or guidance. But whether personally identified or not, the committee can summarize the findings in a report and the results can be analyzed by the class. During such discussion, modal patterns and differences should come to light and serve as a basis for later instruction and exercises as well as a means of revealing personal differences which can influence how one critically or creatively reacts to written material.

*2.* The teacher may develop a fictitious paragraph or short selection on a topic or about an individual which is likely to interest most pupils (e.g., dropping sports from the high school program or the arrest of a rock star). The selection builds to a climax, and each student is asked to write a one- to three-sentence ending to the selection. After this is done, representative pupils may read aloud their endings, which may be classified on the board according to general type: comedy endings, tragic endings, moral endings, constructive endings, fanciful endings, etc. After the differences are noted, the teacher should stimulate or take advantage of pupil analysis of what may have influenced the way they reacted to the content, e.g., prior attitudes, emotional state at the moment, or nature of the material.

*3.* Each class member is asked to bring in five written advertisements which appeal to him or her. The class may be divided into groups of four or five to analyze and summarize the patterns reported, and a follow-up class discussion can examine the patterns identified by each group, e.g., the subject content of the item, the style of the advertisement, where it appeared, etc. The end goals of such an activity are: (a) to bring pupils to be aware of a writer's conscious appeal to their needs, and (b) to identify our most common primary and secondary needs and how they can influence interpretation and reaction to material read.

*4.* The teacher may find or write a short description of an event in which a certain ethnic or socioeconomic group of youths (Group A) had a conflict with another group of a different ethnic background, neighborhood, or socioeconomic class (Group B). (Although the teacher must employ both sensitivity and sensibility in the nature and timing of the use of controversial materials, activities of this nature work best when they touch on areas of some pupil sensitivity.) The facts presented in the basic story are objectively identified by the teacher—much like a good newspaper reporter's description of something that happened or is alleged to have happened. Three versions are prepared, all using the same basic facts: one control version which uses innocuous names and group identities; a second, identical form which employs two ethnic or political groups labeled in ways to obtain an emotive pro-con response from this class of pupils; and a third form which exactly reverses this labeling. The class is randomly divided into three groups, each reading one of the three versions and responding to a question as to whether the reader (a) believes, (b) disbelieves, or (c) is unsure that Group B was wronged and Group A should be held responsible. Ordinarily, the findings will differ on these three stories, which are identical except for group names. The real nature of the experiment should be explained—and the class discussions led into how one's own identifications and feelings influence his perceptions of a conflict situation.

*5.* As a class or special group assignment, members are asked to examine texts in general psychology to locate and report on those primary and secondary human needs identified by the various authors. Through class or small-group discussion, these are collated into one common listing. Class members are asked to bring in examples of written materials which appeal to one or more of these needs. These can be shared with the class, and master examples compiled in a class booklet as a culminating project.

### Determining the Relevance of Written Content or Sources

*1.* A miniunit of study dealing with "Useful Sources of Information" may be developed as a frontal attack on this objective for classes with minimal knowledge in such matters. The unit may be introduced by a filmstrip or film, a presentation by the school librarian, a pretest, or an assignment which poses problems in identifying useful sources of information. Several pupil committees may be formed—to investigate availability of useful reference sources in the classroom, the school library, the local library, and any special resources such as a local historical society, an area college or university, etc. Each committee will submit a class report, and a master list or chart is constructed of the references available—by type, and where located. The class may then be divided into groups; each group analyzing one general type of information source (dictionaries, encyclopedias, textbooks, selected primary sources, and government data references) to list the type of information best delivered by that source and/or illustrative reading purposes for which the source would be useful. A summary or outline report may be presented for class discussion and personal use.

As a related class project, the teacher may pose one or more questions, hypotheses, or topics to be researched for some purposes. Each group would be responsible for reporting how their resource would contribute to this task. The unit may conclude by having a student committee or the class compile a resource booklet containing the general table of references and location, each group's resource summaries, selected problems illustrating the use of the sources, as well as an index of the total report. If desired, a final test over the nature and preferred uses of the sources studied may be administered.

*2.* The teacher may locate three or four different textbook presentations of the discovery of the New World—e.g., the Columbus, the Ericson-Viking, the land-bridge hypothesis, and/or Heyerdahl's primitive sailing thesis. These are used to stimulate discussion of problems of evidence needed to support hypotheses and to compare changes in position in history texts written at different periods of time. (If the problem is chosen judiciously, most content areas can produce other notable changes in textbook conceptions of that area in a 1915 to 1975 span.)

*3.* A newspaper or magazine article is located which suggests possible and controversial developments which carry significance for three or four different groups of people—e.g., the prospective building of a large industrial plant on the edge of the city's lake or river. Through class discussion, identify the types of people most affected—e.g., sports people, local business owners, labor unions, ecologists, and the local chamber of commerce. Divide the class into voluntary groups which identify with one of these groups or role-play its position. The task of each group is to (a) assemble arguments for or against this development, and (b) locate the sources of information needed to gain information for strengthening or modifying the group's position. (This may include group visits to the agencies involved for interviews or supportive data.)

*4.* The encyclopedia tends to be one of the more commonly used references by secondary pupils and adults, and frequently it is given an unreasonable amount of credibility. An activity which is easily adjusted to any secondary course involves the selection of a little known topic which is rather vaguely presented in the text. As a group, the class may raise five or six questions dealing with that topic. Next, the teacher may assemble appropriate volumes dealing with that topic (Americana, Britannica, Colliers, Funk and Wagnall, World Book) and ask individuals or groups to develop comparative-contrastive answers to these questions, as provided by the different encyclopedias. As an interesting variant, the presentation of a particular topic in various editions of the same encyclopedia may be compared by different groups of pupils to show how encyclopedias change with the advance of knowledge over the years of their existence.

### Checking the Validity of Content

*1.* There are several commercially produced films, filmstrips, and tapes which deal with selected understandings of this area, e.g., the accuracy of perception and report, the use of propaganda techniques, etc. Some larger school systems have these in their libraries. Most can be ordered from regional school or university educational media centers. These are quite effective for stimulating discussion, introducing a topic study, or for implementing a specific instructional lesson for the poorer readers. At the other end of the reading distribution, Altick's *Preface to Critical Reading* or Hayakawa's *Language in Thought and Action* will serve to stimulate the better learners in this area of reading and competency.[15,16]

*2.* Differentiating between real and legendary figures (Johnny Appleseed, King Arthur, Robin Hood, Uncle Remus) and differentiating between real and legendary acts of historical figures (George Washington, Davy Crockett, Jesse James, Benedict Arnold, Benjamin Franklin) can be used to stimulate evaluative reading at many different levels. The teacher may bring to class several treatments of the same figure, one factual and the other fanciful or folk legend in nature, which students may read and contrast, using rules of evidence and checking writer publication evidence as a basis for evaluation. A group of advanced students may choose a legendary figure such as King Arthur to investigate the origin of the legend, the prevailing theories concerning his possible existence, and reasons why the legend has survived (its psychosocial appeal). Students may select some current or recent figure, investigate the factual evidence available, and through manipulative writing develop an account which treats the personality as a legendary hero or villain a century later.

*3.* A local freelance writer (one who makes a living writing and selling different articles to a number of different magazines and journals) may be invited to class to discuss how he or she would adapt the same basic article to appeal to the editors and/or readers of several quite different magazines. A variant activity would involve inviting a local newspaper writer to visit class to demonstrate the difference between responsible and irresponsible writing of a related news story and to discuss the way an objective reader should approach reading a news story.

*4.* For more adequate readers, the teacher may take a current national issue producing considerable polarization of opinion and emotion and secure current news accounts and editorials from three or four newspapers or newsmagazines representing different views of this issue. Comparison of the evidence and opinions presented between the news stories and the editorials provides an excellent vehicle for comparing the editorial position of different publications as well as comparing the news selection and reporting patterns of these sources. An analysis of why these papers and magazines might differ in their position and style should be helpful to the budding critical reader.

*5.* A number of good books and journal issues have dealt with the control of the news media by government and private sources. Some of the more capable high school readers may choose one or more of these for an independent study project. If the school area is served by a newspaper which is owned by a national syndicate, a group of pupils may wish to conduct a personal study of that syndicate, e.g., the number of papers and other news media controlled, the nature of the ownership, the editorial policies, the political–social bias of the owner, whether it is part of a corporate conglomerate, etc.

*6.* After the pupils have been introduced to various propaganda devices for slanting information, a class survey may be conducted to determine the frequency of encounter with these techniques over a period of a week—in advertisements, in editorials, and like sources. (This activity may be simplified by developing a checklist with the type of device listed in rows and the days of the week as columns. The student merely checks the appropriate square when he encounters the device.) At the end of the week, a class summary report or tabulation may be developed to gain an idea of the relative frequency of use of propaganda devices. Notable examples may be presented by individuals to stimulate discussion and reinforcement.

7. After the various ways of slanting information have been taught, a topic currently under study or of current school or local interest can be assigned to or chosen by the pupil. His tasks concerning that topic are: (1) to write an objective, factual report on the topic, 200 to 300 words in length; (2) using one or more of designated propaganda devices, to write a second 200- to 300-word article supporting a particular but unstated bias; and (3) to write a third article of similar length which uses different techniques and which supports a second bias, preferably in opposition to that expressed in the second article. The three articles may be exchanged with a classmate or the teacher may elect to show samples with an overhead projector for the class to read and discuss. The tasks of the reader are to differentiate the objective selection from the two biased ones, to identify the direction of the bias, and to detect the type of propaganda technique employed. (Usually, it is helpful for the teacher to first write models and to then guide the class in developing these arguments.)

## Illustrative Exercise Patterns in Evaluative Interpretation

### RECOGNIZING EMOTIONALLY CHARGED WORDS

DIRECTIONS: In each set of three words presented below, underline the word which most qualifies (delimits or decreases) the impact of the sentence. Then draw a box around the word which most exaggerates (extends, magnifies) the emotion of the sentence.

    a. I think Jane is (attractive — <u>nice</u> — voluptuous ).

    b. His dog is (wild — <u>untrained</u> — vicious ).

    c. This (amazing — <u>unusual</u> — weird ) man came forward.

### INFERRING MEANING FROM IDIOMATIC EXPRESSION

DIRECTIONS: Certain words carry particular meaning in any language. Words which refer to the body, such as "heart," "head," "back," and "hand," figure frequently in idiomatic expression. In this exercise, for each of these key words: first find five synonyms for it in the thesaurus and then match the idiomatic expressions given with its implied meaning.

    A. Heart

(Synonyms: <u>vascular pump, center or core, essence, courage, love or feeling</u>)

| Idiom | | Meaning |
|---|---|---|
| (1) to lose heart | 4 | a. consider seriously |
| (2) change of heart | 5 | b. show your emotions |
| (3) at heart | 1 | c. become discouraged |
| (4) take to heart | 2 | d. revise one's judgment |
| (5) your heart on your sleeve | 3 | e. fundamentally |

## DIFFERENTIATING BETWEEN STATEMENTS OF FACT AND OPINION

DIRECTIONS: Here are 15 pairs of statements dealing with the same subject. Mark that member of the pair which is factual with an *F*. Mark that statement which is opinionated with an *O*.

    __O__ a. These problems are causing me to lose weight.

    __F__ b. I have lost five pounds in ten days time.

    __F__ c. Our team won four games and lost six.

    __O__ d. We had a terrible team this year.

## RECOGNIZING QUALIFIED AND UNQUALIFIED STATEMENTS

DIRECTIONS: Listed below are 10 statements. Using the points we discussed concerning the use of modifying words and phrases in generalized statements: (a) mark an (X) in front of those statements which are unqualified; (b) rewrite the unqualified statement so it is more qualified; and (c) in the qualified statements, underline the sentence part which tends to qualify a statement.

    __X__ 1. That is a baldface lie.

        (That statement has more room for the truth.)

    _____ 2. The evidence <u>at this time suggests</u> that Gumshoe Co. is polluting Clear River.

    _____ 3. <u>Within the limits set</u>, the city has met its budget.

    __X__ 4. At nine in the evening, the police arrested the guilty parties. (took the suspects into custody)

## IDENTIFYING PERTINENT SOURCES OF INFORMATION

DIRECTIONS: For each of the problems given below, put an (X) before the source which would be your best (most direct or most complete) source of information.

    A. You need to locate a synonym for the word "marathon" as in "the soldiers gave a marathon effort."

        _____ (1) *Webster's Dictionary*

        _____ (2) *Encyclopedia Americana*

        __X__ (3) *Webster's Thesaurus*

        _____ (4) Library card catalog

    B. You would like to find the name of the fastest marathon runner in the world.

        _____ (1) *World Book Encyclopedia*

        _____ (2) *Random House Dictionary*

        __X__ (3) *Guinness Book of Records*

        _____ (4) *Believe It or Not by Ripley*

C. You need a detailed description of the events surrounding the first marathon run.
_____ (1) a dictionary
_____ (2) an encyclopedia
_____ (3) a world history text
_X_ (4) a book dealing with Greek and Roman history

D. You want to read how it feels to run the marathon. Your best source would be:
_____ (1) an encyclopedia article
_____ (2) a book on the heroes of ancient Greece
_____ (3) a report on the Olympic Games by Howard Cosell
_X_ (4) a magazine article by a recent winner of the marathon

E. What would be the quickest way to locate a magazine article about the marathon run?
_____ (1) Ask the librarian.
_____ (2) Look in the card catalog.
_X_ (3) Look in the *Reader's Guide to Periodical Literature*.
_____ (4) Ask the coach.

F. Who would be likely to write the most objective account about the shootings which occurred at the 1972 Olympic Games in Munich?
_____ (1) A PLO leader
_____ (2) The captain of the Munich police
_X_ (3) A Scottish newsman attending the games
_____ (4) A Zionist athlete

## RECOGNIZING THE USE OF OPINIONATED CONTENT

DIRECTIONS: We have learned how certain techniques and words will produce stronger reader reaction. You will remember that superlatives are adjectives or adverbs which exaggerate the degree of the description or action—usually, but not always, in a positive manner. Critically read the three paragraphs below—first to identify the major point the writer would have you believe, and then to *underline* each notable use of a superlative in its context. An example of the frequent use of superlatives is given below.

*Example:* And h..e..r..e..'s ED MCMAHON! Watchers of the "Johnny Carson Show," that masterpiece of <u>sly</u> inventiveness which may have the <u>greatest</u> spontaneity of anything on the air, recognize Ed as <u>more</u> than just a number two man when plans and scripts go awry—as they often do. Ed <u>really</u> is a <u>great</u> stylist in his own right, who <u>gallantly</u> supports Johnny in all ways and situations. But Ed McMahon is a <u>master</u> showman in his own right, ready to handle <u>any</u> circumstance with the <u>greatest</u> of ease and <u>unusual</u> competence. So have no fear concerning his <u>most</u> <u>personal</u> advice concerning your investment in this <u>marvelous</u> opportunity.

*Writer's Key Point:* (*Ed McMahon is a talented person, so you can believe him when he recommends this investment.*)

## DETERMINING BASIS FOR READER RESPONSE

DIRECTIONS: In this exercise, you are given five short selections drawn from varied sources. Read each selection critically to determine to which of the reader's major drives or secondary motives the writer is directing his appeal. He may use more than one. Mark the number(s) which apply.

| *Drives* | *Motives* |
|---|---|
| 1. Hunger | 6. Acceptance |
| 2. Thirst | 7. Achievement (adequacy) |
| 3. Pain avoidance | 8. Companionship |
| 4. Activity | 9. New experiences |
| 5. Sex | 10. Freedom and independence |
| | 11. Security |
| | 12. Aesthetic satisfaction |

A. To gain more work surface in the kitchen, Bill bought a Butcher Block Cart. Its six square feet of solid hardwood surface can be used for cutting or holding hot, greasy pans, yet resists stains and marring. Knives are handily housed in a side rack, and bowls and pans can be stored in its cabinet. When dinner is ready, its free-wheeling locking casters permit Bill to whisk piping hot food from the oven to the dining center. The beautiful inlaid hardwood top of variated grains makes a showy stage to display unusual dishes for admiring friends.

   Drives (1 and 4)

   Motives (6, 7, 8, 9, 10, 11, and 12) (It's a "block" buster!)

## IDENTIFYING PROPAGANDA TECHNIQUES

DIRECTIONS: We have discussed the propaganda devices and how frequently they are employed in advertising. Listed below are the most common propaganda techniques of commission, followed by fifteen major leads used in magazine ads. For each advertisement lead given, write in the letter identifying the propaganda technique it illustrates.

| a. Bandwagon | d. Loaded Words (Bad and Glad Names) |
|---|---|
| b. Card Stacking | e. Transfer |
| c. Plain Folks | f. Testimonial |

  _d_ (1) SKINNY SCARECROW? Use Upem Body Builders!

  _f_ (2) If Leather Goods satisfy John Wayne...

  _b_ (3) Can a Granada match a Cadillac or Mercedes Benz?

  _d_ (4) So good, it's the only main line—Bell System.

  _c_ (5) In this hard, cold world—YOU know what YOU need.

  _a_ (6) More calm businessmen stay at Holiday Inn.

## IDENTIFYING THE WRITER'S INTENT

DIRECTIONS: Read the following selection twice: First to understand and enjoy it, and a second time to critically evaluate how the writer has used language, implication, and argument to influence the reader and get across his intent. Answer the questions after you have completed your second reading. You may reread again to answer the questions, if you wish.

*Mephitis mephitis*

I.  I have had about a dozen unsought meetings with this greatly dreaded, seldom befriended, but much-talked-of creature. Most of them are moonlight scenes—pictures of dimly lighted, shadow-flecked paths—with something larger than a cat in them. It stands stock-still or moves slowly toward me, black and silvered down its back in the pale light, appearing to grow larger where the shadows lie deepest. These memories are filled with a faint scent of oddity and chill feelings of close escape.

II.  I have learned something of *Mephitis mephitis,* and he is no epicure. The matter of eating his family has never struck him as unusual. He does not ask—Is it good form? Or even—Will it digest? Rather, the supreme question is—Can this thing be swallowed? I have caught him stripping sugar corn ears in stalk after stalk of an isolated patch. For downright barnyard destruction, he outdoes even the fox. Reynard has something of the sportsman about him—a cleverness and a sense of honor. Mephitis is a poacher and goes straight to his prey, successful but without style.

III.  Yet, like every other predatory creature, this beastie more than balances his debt for corn and chickens by his credit for destroying obnoxious pests. He feeds upon insects, mice, rats, and moles by digging out their nests and destroying the young. In this way, a single Mephitis rids his territory of thousands of man's hated vermin. But the farmer forgets his debt when the chickens disappear, no matter how few he loses.

IV.  Shall we never learn to say, when the redtail swoops among the pigeons, when the rabbits get into the cabbage, when the robins rifle the cherry trees, and when a skunk helps himself to a hen for dinner—"So be it, for it is the natural way of things"? Shall we ever learn to love and understand the fitness of things out-of-doors enough to say, "But then, poor beastie, thou maun live"?

1. What or who is *Mephitis mephitis?*

_____ a. the devil

_____ b. a legendary creature

__X__ c. the skunk

_____ d. the fox

2. What is the significance of the title?

_____ a. It is a scientific term.

_____ b. It intends to catch the reader's interest.

_____ c. It contains a humorous implication.

__X__ d. All of the above are true.

3. What is the writer's major purpose in paragraph I?

_____ a. to frighten the reader

_____ b. to amuse the reader

__X__ c. to catch and hold the reader's interest

_____ d. to bring home the basic point of his argument

4. What is the writer's major purpose in paragraph II?

_____ a. to turn the reader against Mephitis

_____ b. to tell it like it is

_____ c. to set up the reader for the counterargument

_____ d. both a and b

__X__ e. both b and c

_____ f. all of the above

5. In terms of its function in his argument, paragraph II is best represented by which of the following folk sayings?

__X__ a. Honesty is the best policy.

_____ b. A penny saved is a penny earned.

_____ c. A stitch in time saves nine.

_____ d. Waste not, want not.

6. What is the writer's main point in paragraph III?

_____ a. Mephitis does not do damage.

_____ b. Mephitis does some good.

__X__ c. Mephitis aids man as well as annoying him.

_____ d. Mephitis is not remembered.

7. What is the major function of paragraph IV?

_____ a. It summarizes the selection.

__X__ b. It states the writer's primary message.

_____ c. It adds further support to paragraphs I and II.

_____ d. It provides a smooth ending.

8. Which of the following would best represent the writer's primary intent in the entire selection?

_____ a. Strange things occur after dark.

_____ b. Man must be ready to protect himself.

_____ c. There are no destructive animals.

__X__ d. Nature's way should be understood.

9. Assuming that you knew the occupation of this writer, which of the following occupations would lend greatest strength to his argument?

_____ a. a noted adventure writer

__X__ b. a noted naturalist

_____ c. a well-known TV personality

_____ d. a well-known social dissenter

10. Who is most likely to agree with the writer's main argument?

__X__ a. ecologists

_____ b. hunters

_____ c. women

_____ d. farmers

## GENERATING FLEXIBLE
## EFFICIENCY

A reexamination of the discussion of Chapter Three will clarify the performance relationships between reading flexibility and reading efficiency. Reading flexibility and reading efficiency both are significant objectives of mature reading. Although interrelated in performance, there are some differences between these concepts in the way the reader uses them. While both are products of effective reading, each deserves attention in secondary reading instruction. However, the position taken in this text, and one supported by many authorities, is that reading efficiency should be used and taught within a structure of flexibility.[17]

It will be recalled that reading *flexibility* is a broad ultimate objective of mature reading: the mature reader adjusts his decoding-interpreting-reacting approach to his purposes, to the material, and to the conditions under which he is operating. Flexibility is concerned with (1) needed meaning and (2) efficiency in obtaining it. A reader is *efficient* when he satisfies his *reading purposes* in the minimal amount of time required to satisfy *that* particular reading task.

Rational analysis and empirical research have produced certain premises to guide the planning of specific instruction in improving reading efficiency.[18]

1. Reading efficiency becomes significant because we live in a time-limited world; thus, interpretation per unit of time is just as crucial, particularly in the out-of-school world, as is interpretation per unit of material.
2. Reading efficiency is a contributing characteristic of reading flexibility just as flexibility aids the development of reading efficiency.
3. Reading efficiency is applicable to all modes of flexible reading; that is, one can learn to scan, skim-read, rapid-read, read critically, and study-read more efficiently. Thus, reading efficiency is not synonymous with the "speed" reading concern of commercial reading enterprises.

4. Interpretation must remain the premier component of the reading act; in the broad spectrum of school and life reading situations, however, understanding in terms of one's purpose is no more dependent upon slow reading than it is upon fast reading.
5. Secondary pupils will manifest a wide range of differences in reading efficiency, as they do in other reading characteristics.
6. Most secondary pupils, and particularly the better readers, can profit from direct instructional attention to improving reading efficiency—within a framework of flexibility.

The following pages treat some instructional guidelines, activities, and exercises pertinent to the generation of flexible reading efficiency. Appendixes D and E contain references to instructional hardware and software which may be purchased to aid in the development of reading efficiency.

### Instructional Considerations

Reading efficiency, as a vital component of reading flexibility, can and should be developed as part of the larger developmental or content reading instruction. For example, developing greater efficiency in rereading for selected purposes lends itself nicely to the use of the Guided Reading Lesson. The benefits derived from extensive personal reading should include greater fluency through the polishing of basic reading skills. And the practice of most any specific reading behavior—from the recognition of individual words to the identification and analysis of the writer's argument—should be extended to using such behaviors flexibly and efficiently. The development of reading efficiency is likely to be more effective if considered an ongoing goal achieved by degrees of improvement and integrated with other reading instruction, whenever reasonable to do so.

Nevertheless, direct and specific instruction in reading efficiency is useful, and specific instructional sessions, units, or minicourses directed at the generation of flexible reading efficiency have a place in the broader secondary reading program.[19]

Most of those guidelines which have been recommended for the teaching of reading, generally, and particularly for the improvement of interpretation, will serve the improvement of reading efficiency. Some which bear more directly upon instruction in reading flexibility and efficiency are presented below.

*1. It is particularly important to assess the pupil's reading resources prior to an instruction and practice unit in reading efficiency.* Some pupils are slow readers because they have an inadequate grasp of basic reading skills. In identifying such problems, the teacher can prevent the pupil from being exposed to undue difficulty and can guide him into more fundamental areas of instruction and practice. A few pupils may have physical or emotional problems which are worsened by time-pressured situations. Pretesting reading rate and flexibility provides evidence for making individual pupils aware of their need for improvement and establishes a pretest base by which improvement can be measured. When such assessment is considered with other reading data, it helps to determine group and individual objectives, needed materials, and possible instructional groupings. All tests which have time limits are, in effect, rate tests. Some tests which produce direct measures of rate and flexibility are listed in Appendix A.

*2. The pupils should be provided with a meaningful rationale to guide their understanding of reading efficiency.* Many pupils will have misunderstandings about the nature of reading efficiency. Others will have misgivings about developing different approaches to reading. In particular, the pupils should understand the concept of reading flexibility; the nature and uses of the modes employed by a flexible reader—scanning, skim reading, rapid reading, analytical–critical reading, study reading, and personal choice reading; the general relationship between rate and comprehension—particularly that the reader's purposes should influence both, and that one may read too slowly or rapidly for satisfactory comprehension; that important differences exist between rapid silent reading and fluent oral reading; and that by developing greater reading efficiency they should be able to cope better with the tasks of secondary school, college, and life.

*3. A unit aimed at generating reading efficiency will give particular, but not singular, attention to improving rapid reading.* Rapid reading deserves attention because it is not likely to have been taught or taught effectively, and because it is an important contributing element of flexibility and mature reading. There are good reasons for not dealing with rapid reading in isolated instruction.[20] The development of scanning and skim reading behaviors establishes a selective and purposeful reading attack which helps many pupils break out of their staid, overly careful approach to reading—an attitude shift which is necessary to effective rapid reading. Also, dealing only with rapid reading can become boring, too intensive, and can encourage misunderstanding of its place and use.

*4. In the initial phases of generating reading efficiency, the nature and difficulty of the practice reading materials are very important.* The materials should be easier than the student's instructional level; that is, he should have very few word difficulties, feel at ease with the content, and have better than 75 percent comprehension. The materials should be lucid, neatly organized, on topics of interest, but not requiring special background or information. If the pupil has considerable difficulty comprehending, he is very likely to resist reading at faster rates. These recommendations are even more significant for materials read under mechanical pacing (group projected or individual pacing) since these are pressuring experiences in themselves.

*5. The early portion of rate improvement instruction may need to jolt the reader out of sluggish reading reaction habits.* The four basic elements of this attack are: (a) instruction in the rationale of flexible reading rate; (b) demonstration of procedures; (c) controlled guided practice (here, mechanical devices are useful, though not essential); and (d) immediate transfer to timed but uncontrolled reading practice.

*6. After the initial phase of establishing new patterns, the direction of instruction and materials should move in graduated steps*: (a) from easy to more difficult content; (b) from shorter to longer selections; (c) from comprehension tasks of general overview to identification of main ideas, to summary organization of the major structure, to specific recall and critical analysis of content; and (d) from instructor-provided purpose to pupil identification of purpose. As more efficient reading habits become established, the instructor should include practice in flexible adjustment of reading attack to a variety of materials and purposes.

*7. Motivation is important, since the student is being asked to change deeply grooved behavior.* To this end, frequent individual conferences, periodic testing, variety in instructional procedures, reading selections of interesting content, the keeping of personal progress records, and a personable, energetic teacher are quite helpful.

*8. Periodic reinforcement of reading flexibility and reading efficiency will be necessary.* This is especially necessary if these behaviors have been taught through special, intensified units of instruction. Opportunities to reinforce tactics of flexibility and efficiency arise naturally in the varied and multiple reading situations of developmental reading lessons and content-oriented reading study. Even so, spaced reinforcement in the form of classroom tests and timed exercises should be a part of the planned development of these essential behaviors.

## Representative Instructional Activities

While many secondary pupils will recognize the advantages of being a more flexible and efficient reader, even these may be unable to convert that wish into smooth, conditioned efficient reading responses.[21] Some pupils will cling tenaciously to the security of old, unvaried reading patterns. Others will overreact: e.g., they will use a scanning approach to all content, regardless of whether that mode is pertinent to their interpretive purposes. Instruction in flexible reading efficiency should include components of motivation, teaching of basic principles, and provisional tryout practice with feedback, reinforcement, and application. Improving flexible reading efficiency—whether

packaged into an intensive unit, minicourse, or interspersed with other reading lessons in the developmental program—takes some planning and time.[22] Following are some ways in which this instruction can be implemented.

*1. Introductory activities.* Like the readiness stage of other instructional units, these introductory activities are concerned with motivating, preassessing performance, and gaining pupil understanding of the objectives/processes of flexible and efficient reading.

*a.* After the pupils have developed a general understanding of the definitions of reading flexibility and reading efficiency, they might keep a week's log of the situations in which they wished they could read more efficiently or felt a need to read in a different manner. A variation on this procedure might involve pupils in conducting an interview/questionnaire survey of the ways their teachers and chums approach different reading tasks. These approaches may be brought together in discussion and summarized on the chalkboard. A committee might develop a table of common situations requiring greater reading efficiency; this table could be duplicated and distributed to all pupils.

*b.* A timed reading test may be given to gather baseline information on pupil rate and comprehension. Each pupil should record his results for comparison with the results of similar tests given later. The teacher may record these on two parallel frequency distributions (high to low scores) to show the class how members vary on rate and comprehension measures. If the teacher makes a scattergram of these scores (a two-dimensional chart with low to high comprehension represented along the left vertical axis and rate measures running left to right along the base axis, where each individual's rate and comprehension is represented by an X at the point of intersection), the class also may observe that those pupils with the higher and lower comprehension scores have varied rates of reading—thus giving lie to the myth that slow readers comprehend best.

*c.* To demonstrate the value of using different modes of flexible reading, the pupils may be divided into three groups. These are given the same four- or five-page selection to read. Each group, however, is given a different direction for reading, with its corresponding set of questions to answer: Group 1—scanning to locate particular facts and terms; Group 2—skim-reading to identify the topic idea of the selection and the topic sentence or idea of each paragraph; and Group 3—rapidly reading to answer ten general questions over the content. The time it takes to complete the different interpretive tasks is recorded by each pupil and averaged for the group by the group leader. These group averages are placed on the board and should generate some ego-involved statements that one group had an easier task than another. Bingo! One key instructional generalization has been induced! Very likely, some pupils of the rapid-reading group will assert that their group understood more. The sly teacher then produces a set of twenty questions requiring analysis of additional specifics, inferred ideas, argument, and writer technique. The pupils must answer these without reexamining the original selection. In all probability, the rapid-reading group will average a better comprehension score, but one far from perfect. When some pupil claims that the rapid-reading group had more time and a better purpose—a second key instructional generalization has been made! If one or more pupils do not suggest that rereading to answer the questions would improve their score (easily elicited if the teacher acts as if this final score is to be used in pupil evaluation), they may be permitted to do so. Rereading scores are compared with the previous test score and improvement noted. Follow-up discussion should bring out the summary generalizations of the relation of different modes of reading to different relative rates and types of interpretation, the usefulness of specific purpose to specific comprehension, as well as the advantages of a different type of rereading.

*d.* The group or class may undertake to make a large table on oak tag or drawing paper which summarizes essential characteristics for each of the modes of flexible reading—scanning, skim reading, rapid reading, recreational reading, analytical

reading, and study reading. Columns may be developed under such headings as relative speed in time, basic nature, illustrative interpretive purposes, school tasks where needed, etc. If pasted on the wall, the chart will make a useful instructional referent for pupil and teacher, as well as a ready point of reinforcement.

*e.* A similar teacher-guided, group-developed summary may be employed for reading efficiency (see Figure 18). This may first take the form of a language-experience lesson, the product of which is duplicated so each pupil may have a copy to place inside his notebook or reading folder. It can be developed in form of a checklist, with five to ten columns corresponding to the weeks over which the period of instruction or unit runs. On a selected day (e.g., Friday of each week) the pupil assesses himself on the points on the checklist.

*f.* If work on reading flexibility and efficiency is to be effective, it should be extended over a period of time and include enough instructional practice sessions to produce and reinforce notable change. One means of maintaining pupil motivation and structuring this ongoing and interspersed instruction is to provide each pupil with a folder and a set of progress charts for each mode of reading to be practiced—scanning, skim reading, rapid reading, filmed reading, etc. On each of these, the pupil can develop twin line graphs to note improvement in rate and accuracy. The folder also can be used to hold any summary instructional materials, other records, tests, etc.

*2. Selective reading activities.* For many, meaningful improvement in flexible efficiency pivots upon whether the pupil can learn to be selectively purposeful in his reading tasks. For this reason, it often is fruitful to begin work with the selective reading modes and let that set transfer naturally to rapid reading when it is introduced. Many of the activities and exercises which are used to develop locational and locational interpretational skills can be converted to scanning and skim-reading practice simply by limiting the amount of time to do the task or by timing how long it takes the pupil to accomplish this task.

**Figure 18**  *Reading efficiency checklist.*[a]

| This week: | Date | | | | |
|---|---|---|---|---|---|
| | 10/24 | 10/31 | | | |
| 1. I believe I can increase my reading efficiency. | ? | X | | | |
| 2. I analyze my reading purposes for a particular reading task. | X | X | | | |
| 3. I use the mode(s) which best serve my reading purposes. | ? | I | | | |
| 4. I have used scanning at least once per day. | ? | X | | | |
| 5. I have skim-read to preview nonfiction materials. | ? | I | | | |
| 6. I have skim-read to preview/review text assignments. | ? | X | | | |
| 7. I have self-tested my rapid reading _____ times. | 2 | 2 | | | |
| 8. I have selectively read a newspaper _____ days. | 1 | 3 | | | |
| 9. I have selectively read one magazine. | No | X | | | |
| 10. I have read _____ pages of a book. | 35 | 50 | | | |

[a]X, yes; ?, not sure or questionable performance; I, improving.

*a. Dictionary race.* The class is divided into teams. Fifteen words are placed on the board, and the teacher notes elapsed time in five-second intervals. The pupils locate the dictionary page for the word (or write the pronunciation, the origin, etc.). As each pupil finishes, he marks his time on his paper and on the board under his team's name. The race continues until all pupils are finished. The team wins whose total membership finishes first. Papers are exchanged and checked for accuracy. Each inaccurate response adds 5 seconds to team total time. Variations can be employed using out-of-date telephone books, a textbook index, different volumes of an encyclopedia, etc.

*b. Heading search.* Each pupil obtains or is provided with a copy of the same issue of the local newspaper. The teacher selects ten or fifteen headings which are rewritten into questions. These questions should contain leads to the section in which the heading is likely to occur—national, local, sports, financial, etc. The pupil must scan to locate the head (noting the page and column) and then skim-read the article to write the answer to the question. The pupil records his time to complete both tasks for the ten or fifteen questions. Example:

> What are small investors buying now?
> (Head: "Change Noted in Small Investment Pattern")
> Answer (p. 13, columns 2 and 3): Municipal bonds

*c. Product order.* Provide each group with a copy of three different mail-order catalogs and a list of ten products needed, with a stipulated maximum total cost to be paid for the ten. The groups then compete to find the product, list its name, maker, and price and then total the cost. A variant form of this activity involves placing the catalogs in the class or reading center and making the assignment an exercise to be completed during the school day.

*d. Paper trace.* Select a prominent newsmaker or group (e.g., the President or the Supreme Court).

Pupils are asked: (1) to scan certain copies of the classroom or school library newsmagazine to identify the number of articles in which the individual or group figured, and (2) to skim-read the articles to find the key topic or activity in which the group figured. During a political year, this activity can be used to trace the reported speeches of a stumping candidate—where made, audience type or group, and topic. More advanced students can plot a chart of the topic frequency and inconsistency in reported messages or news stories.

*e. "Beheading" quiz.* To practice skim rereading, pupils may be given a timed test in which they take each question given at the end of the chapter and scan and skim-read the chapter to locate the subheading of the section or paragraph which contains the answer to the question. The page and the column of the heading are noted. A follow-up activity involves discussion of the answer to the question after rereading that segment.

*f. Topping the text.* Place ten varied subject content texts of moderate difficulty on a table for four pupils. On a given signal, each pupil is to locate one text of his choice, skim-read the table of contents, skim-read the book summary, then skim-read the chapter summaries until twenty minutes have been used. Then the pupil has ten minutes to write a list of the major topics that he can remember without reexamining the text.

*3. Timed reading practice.* Reading rate tests and timed reading selections figure frequently as a reading efficiency activity. Certain practices will improve the administrative ease or learning value of these activities.

*a.* The teacher should develop a system for timing these exercises and explain the procedure to the pupils. There are two basic patterns employed: amount limit and time limit. Amount limit involves letting the pupil read until the selection or task is completed. By using the wall clock, his wristwatch, or the teacher's digital clock, he compares his time on finishing with that at beginning the selection to determine how many minutes and fractions of a minute it took him to complete the task. He determines the number of words per minute (wpm) read by dividing time taken into the total number of words in the selection. Amount-limit testing is realistic, administratively convenient, and meaningful. In time-limit testing, the pupil reads for a given number of minutes, and then is told to mark the line he was reading at the teacher's signal. In time-limit rate testing, he then completes the selection at his own rate. In both patterns, the pupil answers the questions on an untimed basis and without reexamining the content. To increase validity of measurement, the rate test or exercise should approach 2,000 words and the time limit set at three or more minutes when the pupils are ready for longer selections.

*b.* True-false, multiple-choice, or occasionally, short-answer questions are given following the selection. This provides an opportunity to practice interpretation and helps the pupil to be realistic about his rate. These questions should deal with key ideas and the more general aspects of the plot or argument, since these are realistic purposes for rapid reading. The pupil should record both rate and comprehension. Rereading to improve the comprehension score contributes to interpretation or flexibility and makes the pupil feel more confident in his attempt to improve his rate.

*c.* For rate improvement practice, the selections chosen for initial rate improvement should be quite readable in both interest, language difficulty, and organization. It is better to start with shorter, easier selections and later increase their length and difficulty.

*d.* Rapid reading may be used as a prereading, interpretive reading, or rereading activity of the guided reading lesson in the general instructional reading situation.

*e.* In addition to class work, pupils should be encouraged to read one selection or story in a book or magazine of modest difficulty each evening. In this effort, pupils can time themselves, determine the approximate number of words, and write a one-paragraph summary as a word check.

*f.* Another technique for providing home practice is for the teacher to purchase five or six of the rate improvement exercise books on the market. These are separated into individual exercises and filed in folders by difficulty level, length, or topic.

Pupils may check such exercises out for in-class or home practice exercises.

*4. Mechanical/electronic aids.* A number of mechanical or electronic pacing devices have been produced to aid in sharpening quick perception and/or rate improvement. The three major classifications of these are tachistoscopic or short-exposure devices, controlled rate and/or spaced fixation reading films, and individual pacers. A list of available mechanical/electronic reading improvement devices is included in Appendix E.

A professional teapot controversy once swirled around the use of such aids in reading instruction.[23] As in other reading materials, their values and disadvantages depend upon how they are used and other resources available in the program. The major disadvantages seem to be that their expense in relation to the cost of other useful reading instructional materials is disproportionate (i.e., What did the program forgo to buy these?); that they contribute little to other aspects of reader development; that they distract the pupil from interpreting and enjoying reading selections; and that they increase reader anxiety.

These need not be serious problems if the mechanical/electronic device is employed judiciously to meet specific purposes in the balanced reading program. Their purchase and use can be justified if the school can afford them without stinting on good instructional softwear, assessment tools, and recreational reading materials, and if the teacher employs them selectively along with other instructional activities.

Such devices do provide motivation, variety, and a source of independent practice. They are particularly helpful as a crutch for those pupils with well-reinforced rigidity in reading style. Of the three, the tachistoscope seems to produce less transfer to actual reading situations. The individual pacer can be employed with most text materials and is more easily adapted to the needs of the individual pupil. A teacher or a school can develop efficiency in reading without such hardware, as most of this section has attempted to demonstrate.[24]

### Illustrative Exercise Patterns

Timed reading selections, or reading films, or individual reading pacers—each with its accompanying comprehensive check—form a significant part of instructional activities aimed at generating greater efficiency in content reading, as such. In addition, many exercises aimed primarily at the development of decoding, locational, or interpretational behaviors may be converted to reading efficiency exercises merely by adding a timing or time-limit condition. The following are illustrative:

---

### SPEEDED RECOGNITION OF WORD FORMS

DIRECTIONS: This is the first of ten exercises. These exercises consist of fifteen lines, each consisting of a key word followed by 4 or 5 words. Underline the key word each time it appears after the colon. Use the second hand on your watch or the wall clock to determine how many seconds it takes you to complete the exercise. Reexamine the exercise to determine the number of words you missed or incorrectly marked. Add five seconds for each word error. Keep a chart or graph of your improvement from exercise to exercise.

    a. detrain:  .deplane; insane; <u>detrain</u>; decline; <u>detrain</u>

    b. thorough:  <u>thorough</u>; thought; thought; <u>thorough</u>; through

## SPEEDED UNDERSTANDING OF WORDS

(*Note:* This type of exercise uses the same pattern and directions as the previous exercise, with the exception that the pupil must identify words that *mean* the same as the key word. To save time, the teacher can include both synonyms and antonyms and use the same exercise twice—once to identify synonyms and a second time (later) to identify the antonyms.)

    a. execute:   <u>kill</u>; curse; save; help; <u>effect</u> (syn.)

    b. generous:   notable; <u>greedy</u>; liberal; <u>grasping</u> (ant.)

## SPEEDED UNDERSTANDING OF PHRASES

(*Note:* The directions are much the same as in previous exercises, except that the pupil must check those phrases which either mean the same as (or the opposite of) the underlined phrase in the given sentence.)

    a. We must take <u>a significant step</u>.

        <u>(ant.)</u> (1) no important action

        _____ (2) notice of him

        _____ (3) a calm run

        <u>(syn.)</u> (4) this vital approach

## QUICK IDENTIFICATION OF SENTENCE PURPOSE

(*Note:* The directions are similar to those of the previous exercise patterns. Here, depending upon which pattern is employed, the pupil either identifies the sentence which answers the question (type A) or the question which captures the essence of the sentence meaning (type B). Ordinarily, five such items is adequate length for such an exercise.)

Type A

1. Are most people good "credit risks"?

    a. Without credit, most people could not afford to buy a home or new car.

    b. A good name with the credit bureaus is a great asset.

    (c.) Ninety-five percent of credit users pay their bills on time.

    d. The best way to have a good credit rating is to pay cash.

Type B

1. Will Rogers' wit frequently stuck its barb into politics, but down deep he considered politics the greatest show in America.

    a. What was Rogers' talent as a performer?

    (b) How did Rogers feel about politics?

    c. Where did Rogers learn about politics?

    d. Why did Rogers go into politics?

## SCANNING AND SKIM READING FOR RELEVANT INFORMATION

DIRECTIONS: This is a timed exercise to determine how quickly you can locate information in your text which answers each of the ten questions given below. To do this exercise, you will find it helpful to select key words from the question to enter in the text index, which is arranged alphabetically by topic and subtopic. After scanning the appropriate index pages to locate the probable text page or pages, skim-read those text pages until you identify the answer. Then provide the number of that page, that paragraph, and those lines within the paragraph in the space following the question. The key words and answer are given for the two examples to make sure that you understand the exercise. You will have five more exercises like this upon which to improve your speed of scanning and skim-reading.

A. In which <u>direction</u> do the <u>rivers</u> of <u>Siberia</u> flow?
   (p. 72; paragraph 1; lines 5-8.)
B. What major <u>textiles</u> are <u>manufactured</u> in modern <u>Japan</u>? (<u>p. 339; paragraph 3;</u>
   lines 1-2.)

## SKIM-READING, RAPID-READING, AND REREADING SELECTIONS

DIRECTIONS: You are to read the following selection four times using skim-reading, rapid-reading, and rapid-rereading techniques. The selection contains ten numbered paragraphs and approximately 1,800 words. Using the wall clock (or the teacher's digital clock), you are to mark the time in minutes and/or seconds that it takes you to accomplish each reading task. (Any reasonable selection will serve as long as it satisfies the criteria for efficiency improvement materials mentioned earlier.)

Starting time _____:_____:_____

Task I.   Skim-read to identify the topic paragraph of the selection, _____.
          Paragraph _____; time needed _____.

Task II.  Skim-read to identify the number of the sentence in each paragraph which
          serves as the topic sentence.
          1_____; 2_____; 3_____; 4_____; 5_____;
          6_____; 7_____; 8_____; 9_____; 10_____.
          Time _____.

Task III. Rapidly read through the selection and determine the time it took.
          Time _____.

Task IV.  Answer the ten questions given on the page attached to the selection.
          Rapidly skim and reread as necessary to be sure your answers are correct.
          Determine the time taken for this task. Time _____.

Task V.   Determine the total time it took to complete the four readings of the selec-
          tions. Time _____.

Ending time _____:_____:_____.

# STIMULATING INDEPENDENT READING

One of the major premises of this text has been that maturity in reading is determined eventually by the extent to which the dependent reading *pupil* can be transformed into the independent reading *student* without the loss of accuracy, efficiency, and flexibility in reading performance. The development of successful independent reading at the secondary-adult level is dependent upon maturation of the integral reading act. Thus, the potential for independent reading is effected, in part, through the mastery of the decoding-interpretive-reactive behaviors treated earlier. Even so, the extension of independent reading requires direct attention to the development of positive reading attitudes and the establishment of broader reading interests, contacts, and habits.

## A Total Program Concern

Extending the independent reading habits of secondary pupils carries notable implication, both directly and indirectly, for developing mature readers, and that is why it should be considered a major objective or component of the total secondary reading effort.[25] The direct implication is that we need to develop a society of more literate readers. Available evidence, extending from the Gray-Rogers study to the most recent investigations, indicates that we have failed in this objective. A good many American adults do demonstrate competency in short-term, functional reading tasks. But relatively few do extended reading, on a regular basis, in a broad selection of materials of better quality, to satisfy purposes which involve higher-level interpretation and reaction. Indirectly, general reading performance is enhanced by extensive and varied reading.

To these ends, the reading program needs to promote a school-wide reading awareness as well as to improve school conditions and resources related to independent reading. Teachers, both of developmental reading and content instruction, need to implement specific activities to encourage extended reading behaviors. We have seen how some of these can be handled through in-class developmental and content reading instruction—that is, through the teaching of reading-study systems for attacking larger content, the conditioning of more sustained reading through SSR procedures, and the guided reading of significant content sources. But the broadening of pupil contact with varied personal reading materials and establishing pupil habits of reading voraciously for personal satisfaction will need more teacher-school involvement than has been evidenced.

## *Improving the School-Wide Personal Reading Effort*

Much can be done to broaden contact and increase student interest in personal extended reading. Some guidelines which should aid secondary personnel to shape more vigorous pupil involvement in independent pupil reading are presented here.

*1. Correcting inhibiting misconceptions.* A number of myths held by school personnel, pupils, and parents need to be dispelled, if real action to expand personal reading among secondary pupils is to be generated. Some pains have been taken in earlier text discussion to deal with the most pivotal of these misconceptions: i.e., that personal reading is a rather insignificant facet of the educational process. Other erroneous assumptions which retard school thrust include these misbeliefs: that most students do engage in a notable amount of personal reading from a broad selection of types and levels of printed sources; and that stimulating personal reading in the secondary setting is the singular responsibility of the English (literature) teacher.

*2. Initiating an emphasis on personal reading.* The individual reading teacher or English teacher can stimulate some pupils to greater and wider personal reading, but any notable impact upon the personal reading habits of pupils will require a continuing cooperative effort of most, if not all, of the professional staff. In addition to classroom teachers, the involvement of library, administrative, pupil personnel staff, and representative pupil leaders would seem necessary. This effort consists of one aspect of the charge to the school reading committee, discussed in Chapter 14, or it may be started informally by a few concerned staff and be broadened through informal or formal in-service education efforts. The initial effort should include generating a survey of pupil reading patterns, making a study of notable sources of personal reading available within the school and community, completing a survey of teacher attitudes and practices pertinent to personal reading, and compiling practical recommendations which can be implemented by the administrator, the librarian, and the individual teacher.[26]

*3. Increasing the availability of personal reading sources.* The concern here should include increasing variety as well as quantity of printed materials. Moreover, it implies increasing the pupil's opportunities to make use of the resources presently at hand.

A concerned and emancipated library staff is crucial to the extension and personalization of pupil reading as well as to the success of the total reading effort.[27] The school library or the materials resource center serves as a key to the broadened reading attack. Among other things, this should include an analysis of the quantity and type of reading sources presently housed in the library or materials center, the budget restrictions and establishment priorities for purchase of library materials, and the philosophy and policies of the library regarding pupil opportunity to use and withdraw sources for personal use and teacher opportunity to withdraw multiple sources for classroom use.

Attention should not be limited to the library or school resource center in this matter. The reading laboratory or center often has a viable collection of materials, many oriented toward reluctant readers, which are underemployed. The guidance center and individual classroom or content department libraries are other sources of personal reading materials which could be made available to a wider range of pupils.

Nor should this effort be limited to the usual school resources. Many community libraries are not used effectively by pupils or school programs. Especially with the trend toward open secondary schools and divided or modular scheduling, some attention should be given to arrangements to bring the community library resources within easier reach of individual pupils (e.g., opening the town library during morning hours, busing pupils to the library on a regular schedule, and rotational loans of selected library materials to the school resource center). The home should not be overlooked. Many nonimpoverished homes have a large number of paperbacks, magazines, and other reading resources which collect dust or take up vital storage space, and which readily would be loaned or given to the school, if the need were known. In our abundant society, the unavailability of reading materials to the secondary pupil should be considered an educational immorality![28]

*4. Gaining the personal involvement of the classroom teacher.* The reading and content area teacher can do much to deepen and broaden the pupil's reading interests and contacts. In general, the classroom teacher can extend pupil personal reading by sharing his or her own personal reading experiences with pupils, by arranging for pupils to share personal reading interests with each other, by bringing pupils in contact with interesting printed sources pertinent to course topics or revealed areas of pupil interest, by providing within-class opportunity to read or to search for personal reading sources, and by incorporating personal reading with the acceptable learning tasks of the course. These uses perhaps border upon extended instructional reading. The difference may not be highly significant and would hinge upon how much the choice were given to the pupil to pick among recommended or pertinent content sources and to read to satisfy his own motives.

*5. Making time available to read.* Lack of time is one of the major reasons offered by secondary pupils and adults for inadequate personal reading. In spite of present tendencies toward more liberal evaluation, many secondary pupils remain snowed under by course assignments. Even the adequate and conscientious reader would find it difficult to cover adequately all assignments for all classes. One by-product of the proliferation of course requirements is the depletion of the pupil's contact and psychic energy where personal reading is concerned. Providing time in class to read may seem sacrilegious to the compulsive content area or reading teacher, but that might be our best chance for encouraging personal reading. Also, the opportunity to read during free periods, study periods, or lunch can be enhanced by making both reading sources and areas to read available to pupils.

6. *Stimulating pupil interest through special projects.* A number of classroom tactics which serve as aids to pupil motivation to read are presented later in this section. A wide range of related projects is possible. At the school level, special-interest clubs, Great Books groups, special reading emphasis weeks, between-class competitions, filmed versions of great novels, speeches by local or visiting writers, competitions to discover pupil writing talent, group readings of plays, the development of an in-school bookmobile service are illustrative of such possibilities. None is likely to be an answer in itself, but each contributes to the school reading climate.

7. *Providing for the problem reader.* The foregoing recommendations have value for enhancing personal reading among all secondary pupils — for the good, adequate, indifferent, and the poor reader. The task is easier for those who like reading, generally, and even for those reluctant readers with competency in the basic reading act. The objective of broader personal reading is not impossible even for the pupil with serious reading and language deficiencies, however. It will require a more concentrated effort, one which assumes that personal reading is a key program objective.

Getting the disabled reader involved in highly interesting materials at his independent-instructional reading level has been a key tenet of remedial reading theory for several decades.[29] More recently, Fader has argued persuasively that "hooking" impoverished pupils on books through *saturation* of materials in the learning setting and their *diffusion* by teacher intermediaries may be one of the last

possibilities we have for salvaging these pupils from illiteracy and personal defeat.[30] Cohen has made much the same argument for aiding the disadvantaged reader through the high-intensity reading laboratory program.[31] Thus, instead of avoiding the issue of personal reading as many teachers do with poor readers, there is a good basis for arguing that it should become the focus of the reading effort. It may not be easy, but there may be no reasonable alternative. A bibliography identifying sources of recommended personal reading for the less than adequate secondary reader is presented in Appendix B. Higher-interest series are listed in Appendix C.

## Classroom Activities for Stimulating Personal Reading

1. A free reading table, shelf, or classroom "center" may be established at which a good collection of varied sources pertinent to the course or to the current unit or topic is made available for browsing. Some of the shorter selections might be reserved for in-class use; others can be checked out for longer periods. It is important that such a collection undergo some continuous change to maintain interest. Pupils should be encouraged to contribute sources or recommendations of sources they found useful or about which they are curious.

2. A bulletin board may be designated for personal reading purposes. It is useful to locate this near the personal reading shelf or table, if possible. Such a bulletin board should be attractive but not rigidly controlled. Pupils should feel free to contribute to it at any time. It can be a revolving pupil committee responsibility. The content of the bulletin board may be a wide variety of materials: duplicated pages of pertinent reading sources; reviews of books and articles — by pupils, the teacher, or content professionals; or creative reactions or interpretations by pupils to the sources.

3. A voluntary content area interest club may be formed. Experience reveals that such clubs are most successful when one or more teachers of that area take a continuing vigorous interest in it. The activities of the club should be varied and probably will stress films, trips, and projects; but book reviews

and related personal reading discussions are also viable club activities.

*4.* A "contact" checklist may be given to the class or placed on the bulletin board. Such a checklist may take a number of forms, and the form should be changed from time to time to avoid monotony. Basically, it consists of a voluntary search of key content sources pertinent to the current unit of study, e.g., to identify personalities, quotes, or to locate and answer specific questions.

*5.* Pupil creative response to content or content sources can be encouraged. If feasible, such efforts should be shared with the group. Creative responses to content reading can take many directions: the description of a personal observation, an experiment performed, a skit developed by a group to portray some event described in the literature of the field, or a "book" of cartoons.

*6.* Visits by or taped interviews with local content area writers or authorities may be arranged. Copies or examples of the written work of such people may be put on display.

*7.* There are a variety of games which can be converted to broaden interest in the content area and to increase contact with a rich range of reading sources. The "contact" checklist can be converted into a treasure hunt (and it will be helpful to team less able readers with able readers for competitive activities). The development of a pupil-composed content-related riddle sheet or the inclusion of riddles on the bulletin board can stimulate pupils to check reading sources to find the answers.

*8.* Sampler box collections of selections from significant reading sources have been commercially published. These can be purchased where available. As a longer-range project, the staff of a content area may build its own collection.

*9.* The adolescent's interest in trivia and competitive spirit can be used to expand contacts in personal reading. To initiate this activity, several students with an inclination in this direction are asked to develop a trivia question based on their personal reading and to post it on a special bulletin board. The source where the answer may be found is given with each question. The object is for a second student to post the answer next to the question. Best questions may remain for quite some time. Motivational sources to prompt this type of recreational reading, such as *Guinness Book of World Records* and the New York Times's *Famous First Facts and Records*, should be available in the classroom.

*10.* A reading time line may be used to stimulate pupil reading for a particular historical period pertinent to instruction in social studies, literature, or science. A strip of wrapping paper about one foot wide is pinned the length of one wall of the room, with the years, decades, or centuries marked off in appropriate units. Each pupil is encouraged to add the name of an author who wrote in that period, or a short story, book of fiction or nonfiction, or informational article which appeared during that period. The author and title should accompany each entry.

*11.* An activity based somewhat upon the "individualized reading" procedure discussed in Chapter Ten is the personal reading contract system. The teacher and student jointly decide upon a specific area in which the student has a sufficient interest to do some independent reading. The teacher then helps the student develop a list of available titles appropriate for that student's level of reading. Next, the pupil checks those titles that he or she will read. A contract is then developed which stipulates that the student will read certain titles within a reasonable period of time and will write a *brief* reaction concerning his feelings, criticisms, and thoughts about the source read. Pupils may be grouped by common interests, and the teacher should meet periodically with the group or individual to discuss problems and to encourage pupil interaction. Upon completion of the contract, the pupil may pick a new area of interest to pursue.

*12.* A bulletin board area given over to pupil-choice reading reports can be enlivened in many ways. One is to emulate a journalistic style of reporting. Newspaper-type headlines with a short journalistic exposé encourage creativity as well as making other pupils aware of the possibilities of a particular book. Examples of how headlines in newspapers and magazines appeal to one's interest can be discussed and pupils encouraged to create their own for the books the class is presently reading. For example, "HESTER GETS AN 'A' IN LOVE" with a short *Time* magazine-style paragraph can motivate more than a few high school students to get into or finish *The Scarlet Letter*.

*13.* Stimulating outside reading by use of a book club is enhanced when the teacher is a member and arranges the initial process. Teachers can obtain application forms and promotional materials to distribute to students. A few minutes of classroom time devoted to discussing new titles will interest a number of students to read outside the classroom. Teachers can do the ordering for the students who want to join. Some commercial book clubs or organizations may be drawn upon. The Mystery Guild, the Arrow Book Club, the Junior Literary Guild, Library of Science Young Adult's Division, and the junior version of the Great Books association are just a few. Lists of clubs can usually be obtained from local public libraries.

*14.* Forming groups to attack specific problems through reading is yet another approach. The teacher can capitalize on student interest in science fiction by arranging a debate on which is stranger— true happenings in the field of science or fictitious accounts? Both science fiction and true science materials can be provided for both groups. Authors such as Bradbury, Serling, Asimov, Lovecraft, and Heinlein can be used as examples of good literature in science fiction. Nonfictional accounts can be found in many trade books as well as in *Scientific American*, *National Geographic*, and *Science World*. Momentary interests can be utilized in this way. For example, a tenth-grade class became greatly involved in an argument over the true nature of sharks after seeing the movie *Jaws*. A paperback version of *Jaws* was brought by some pupils, and this was compared with Jacques Cousteau's book *The Shark*, provided by the teacher. Before the debate was finished, the related literature consulted included encyclopedias, zoology texts, and articles from commercial and sports fishing magazines.

*15.* Developing a classroom library for general- or specific-interest areas is possible through the purchase of paperbacks for the developmental reading or content area classroom. The increasing use of paperbacks in secondary instruction is encouraging. They are economical, versatile to use, accepted by pupils, and lend themselves to a variety of reading uses.

It can be seen that the approaches to broadening personal-choice reading interests and activity are limited only by the ingenuity of the staff and the resources of the school and community. The essential conditions are availability of a varied selection of materials, time to explore and use them, and guidance by teachers. This is a highly valuable way of increasing both reading performance and content background.

## REFERENCES

1. Ruth Strang, "The Reading Process and Its Ramifications," in *Invitational Addresses, 1965* (Newark, Del.: International Reading Association, 1965) p. 50.
2. Frederick B. Davis, "Measuring Improvement in Reading Skill Courses," in *Problems, Programs, and Projects in College-Adult Reading*, Eleventh Yearbook of the National Reading Conference, E. P. Bliesmer and R. C. Staiger, Editors (Milwaukee, Wis.: Marquette University Press, 1962) p. 30.
3. William S. Gray and Bernice Rogers, *Maturity in Reading—Its Nature and Appraisal* (Chicago: University of Chicago Press, 1956).
4. Amiel T. Sharon, "What Do Adults Read?" *Reading Research Quarterly* 9 (1973-74) pp. 148-69.
5. A. Sterl Artley, "The Development of Reading Maturity in High School—Implications of the Gray-Rogers Study," *Educational Administration and Supervision* 6 (October, 1957) pp. 321-28.
6. Artley, "The Development of Reading Maturity."
7. Doris L. Mueller, "Teachers' Attitudes Toward Reading," *Journal of Reading* 17 (December, 1973) pp. 202-5.

8. Harold H. Roeder, "A Comparison Between Leisure Reading Habits of Female Teachers and Other Women of the Same Social Status," in *The Psychology of Reading Behavior*, Eighteenth Yearbook of the National Reading Conference, G. B. Schick and M. M. May, Editors (Milwaukee, Wis.: National Reading Conference, Inc., 1969) pp. 55-60.

9. William Eller and Judith G. Wolf, *Critical Reading: A Broader View*, An Annotated Bibliography (Newark, Del.: International Reading Association, 1969) p. 15.

10. Robert H. Ennis, "A Concept of Critical Thinking," *Harvard Educational Review* 32 (Winter, 1962) pp. 81-111.

11. W. Weiss, "Emotional Arousal and Attitude Change," *Psychological Reports* 6 (1960) pp. 267-80.

12. Willavene Wolf and Bernice D. Ellinger, "Teaching Critical Reading: An Observational Study," in *Critical Reading*, Martha L. King, Bernice D. Ellinger, and Willavene Wolf, Editors (Philadelphia: J. P. Lippincott Company, 1967) pp. 434-45.

13. Lee O. Thayer and N. H. Pronko, "Factors Affecting Conceptual Perception in Reading," *Journal of Genetic Psychology* 61 (July, 1959) pp. 51-59.

14. Helen M. Robinson, "Developing Critical Readers," in *Dimensions of Critical Reading* 11, Russell Stauffer, Editor (Newark, Del.: University of Delaware, 1964) pp. 1-12.

15. Richard D. Altick, *Preface to Critical Reading*, Third Edition (New York: Henry Holt and Co., 1956).

16. S. I. Hayakawa, *Language in Thought and Action* (New York: Harcourt, Brace and Co., Inc., 1940).

17. Lawrence W. Carrilo, "Developing Flexible Reading Rates," *Journal of Reading* 8 (April, 1965) pp. 322-25.

18. Walter Hill, "Applying Research Findings in Rate of Reading," in *Forging Ahead in Reading*, J. A. Figurel, Editor, International Reading Association Conference Proceedings 12, Part 1 (Newark, Del.: International Reading Association, 1968) pp. 620-26.

19. Paul Witty, "Rate of Reading: A Crucial Issue," *Journal of Reading* 13 (November, 1969) pp. 102-6, 154-63.

20. M. H. Dembo and D. A. Wilson, "A Performance Contract in Speed Reading," *Journal of Reading* 16 (May, 1973) pp. 627-33.

21. James D. Brandt, "Internal Versus External Locus of Control and Performance in Controlled and Motivated Reading Rate Improvement Instruction," doctoral dissertation, Ohio State University, 1974.

22. Oneta R. Furr, "Improving Flexibility in Reading for the Advanced Student," in *Meeting Individual Needs in Reading*, Helen K. Smith, Editor (Newark, Del.: International Reading Association, 1971) pp. 124-32.

23. Emery P. Bliesmer, "Overview of the National Reading Conference Research Reviews: Rate and Comprehension, Eye Movements, Use of Machines," in *Changing Concepts of Reading Instruction*, International Reading Association Conference Proceedings 6 (Newark, Del.: International Reading Association, 1961) pp. 214-223.

24. Miles A. Tinker, "Devices to Improve Speed of Reading," *Reading Teacher* 20 (April, 1967) pp. 605-9.

25. Dennis L. Hagenson, "The Role of Interest in Improving Reading Skills," *Elementary English* 37 (April, 1960) pp. 244-46.

26. Helen K. Smith, "Evaluating Progress in Recreational Reading," in *New Horizons in Reading*, Proceedings of the Fifth International Reading Association World Congress in Reading, J. E. Merritt, Editor (Newark, Del.: International Reading Association, 1976) pp. 208-14.

27. Grace Shankin, "The Role of the Librarian in the Total Reading Program," in *Libraries and Children's Literature in the School Reading Program* (Hempstead, N.Y.: Hofstra University, 1967) pp. 24-28.

28. Nancy Larrick, "The Paperback Bonanza," in *Reading Interaction*, L. Courtney, Editor (Newark, Del.: International Reading Association, 1976) pp. 101-5.

29. Albert J. Harris, *How to Increase Reading Ability*, Fifth Edition (New York: David McKay Company, Inc., 1970) p. 283.

30. D. N. Fader et al., *The New Hooked on Books* (New York: Berkley Publishing Co., 1976) p. 46.

31. S. Alan Cohen, *Teach Them All to Read* (New York: Random House, Inc., 1969) p. 246.

## SUPPLEMENTARY SOURCES

Berger, Allen, and James D. Peebles. *Rates of Comprehension*, An Annotated Bibliography. Newark, Del.: International Reading Association, 1976.

Carrello, Lawrence W. "Developing Flexible Reading Rates." *Journal of Reading* 8 (April, 1965) pp. 322-25.

Eller, William, and Judith G. Wolf. *Critical Reading: A Broader View*, An Annotated Bibliography. Newark, Del.: International Reading Association, 1969.

Gerhard, Christian. *Making Sense: Reading Comprehension Improved Through Categorization*, Chapters 4,

7, and 9. Newark, Del.: International Reading Association, 1975.

Gray, William S., and Bernice Rogers. *Maturity in Reading—Its Nature and Appraisal*. Chicago: University of Chicago Press, 1956.

King, Martha L., Bernice D. Ellinger, and Willavene Wolf, Editors. *Critical Reading*. Philadelphia: J. B. Lippincott Company, 1967.

Labuda, Michael, Editor. *Creative Reading for Gifted Learners*. Newark, Del.: International Reading Association, 1974.

# IV

# EXTENDING SECONDARY READING EDUCATION

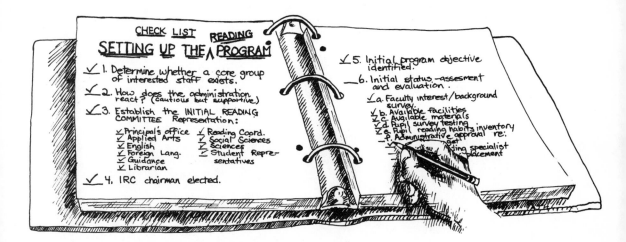

# THIRTEEN

# Aiding the Different Reader

*As regular class instruction becomes successfully adapted to individual needs, the differences between developmental teaching of reading on the one hand and corrective and remedial instruction on the other become smaller and smaller.*

Albert J. Harris

***Overview*** The nature of inter- and intrapupil reading differences at the secondary level was introduced in Chapter One, the developmental pupil factors which contribute to those differences were presented in Chapter Two, and many other chapters carried indirect implication of pupil differences for general reading instruction and use. Chapter Thirteen presents a number of approaches for adjusting secondary reading instruction to the different reader. The second half of the chapter considers program implications for those pupils whose reading is different enough to mark them as "problem readers." The nature of reading difficulty, functional incompetency, and the several patterns of reading disability are examined to sharpen the secondary teacher's perception of differences among problem readers and to broaden the concept of supplementary reading program tasks.

# ADJUSTING CLASSROOM INSTRUCTION FOR READING DIFFERENCES

Although we use some measure or description of central tendency in pupil performance, such as "median," to facilitate professional communication, there is no typical reading behavior which adequately captures the reading performance of secondary school pupils. Rather, an extended, continuous range of individual differences in secondary reader performance exists in classes supposedly composed of high uniform ability and among those with obvious problems in learning and using reading.[1] Such differences should influence secondary reading instruction and classroom utilization. We need to give them special recognition.

Individual differences are a developmental fact of life. Children are born with varied genetic potential for maturation and learning.[2] The environment into which they are born and the learning experiences they encounter interact with this potential to form countless possibilities for resultant personal development and behavior. Sometimes the life and school experiences of the child compensate for lesser potential to learn. More often, such learning experiences tend to reinforce and extend existing pupil differences in school performance and general behavior.[3]

The general nature of pupil differences as they are reflected in reading development have been described earlier in this text. As a brief review, it was noted: (1) that differences in reading potential are observed prior to initial school attendance; (2) that between-pupil differences in reading performance are observable during the first year of instruction and tend to increase every instructional year thereafter; (3) that acceptable instructional practices are more likely to increase rather than decrease these pupil differences; (4) that variation in pupil performance for a typical class will extend approximately as far above the average performance for a class as they extend below; and (5) that within-pupil variation in reading development also is notable for most pupils.[4,5]

In short, the evidence seems clear that individual differences in reading exist and do not go away. Differences in pupil reading performance levels in typical secondary classrooms are quite extended: for example, levels ranging from third to thirteenth reading grade equivalents in a heterogeneous eighth-grade class are not uncommon. Reading performance in many "tracked" or homogeneously selected classes also will show marked variation.[6] The better readers as well as the less able readers of a secondary class will reveal profiles of irregular mastery in the specific competencies of mature reading. Recognition of the existence of such differences would seem advisable for any secondary learning situation in which reading is used. Finding ways to deal reasonably with individual reading differences becomes another dimension of structuring reading learning.

## General Considerations

There is, perhaps, no perfect way to adjust reading instruction to individual differences. But there are better ways of aiding each pupil to grow toward his potential through adjusted instruction. Five factors which improve the probability of such adjustment include: (1) teacher understanding of reading behavior and familiarity with reading educational strategy, (2) teacher acceptance of the normality of pupil differences and of the need to adjust instruction to them, (3) a program of reading evaluation which enables the identification and assessment of between- and within-pupil reading differences, (4) a plentiful selection of classroom reading materials, instructional and general, wide enough to meet the needs and interests of these pupils, and (5) teacher familiarity with various strategies for organizing instruction to meet these differences.

### A Pupil Information Base

Effective adjustment of reading conditions and/or instructional strategy to meet significant variance of pupil reading performance and needs begins with knowledge of these pupil reading differences. The development of a systematic plan of reading evaluation and assessment as described in Chapter Seven should provide much of that needed information. Most of those reading behaviors and reader characteristics identified in Part One of this text deserve consideration in structuring reading learning through adjusted instruction, but several are particularly pertinent. These would include identification of: (1) pupil "instructional" and "independent" reading levels; (2) approximate instructional reading–difficulty levels of assigned and recommended reading materials; (3) pupil competency in the general and behavioral objectives targeted for instruction; (4) combinations of persistent inhibiting pupil characteristics which contribute to difficulty in decoding, interpretation, and/or study; (5) pupil reading interests, attitudes, and habits; (6) pupil English-language competency; and (7) current pupil learning potential (general scholastic aptitude).

## Realistic Perspective and Compromise

Adjusting instruction to individual pupil differences in reading at the secondary school level needs to be placed within realistic perspective. Some authors write of procedures which will "solve" the instructional problems associated with pupil differences with the fervor and intuitive leaps one associates with religious revivals or political rallies. The arguments for extremist positions on the individualization of reading instruction often seem self–contradictory. They suggest that the method rather than the individual learner is the significant integer of instruction. Well-intended but rigid plans of individualization often reduce the personalization of learning. Moreover, it is questionable whether methods of individualization which provide little structure for teaching and reinforcing developmental competencies really recognize the individual learning needs of the many pupils in a class who need structure and who profit from group interaction in reading-learning activities.[7]

Learning, indeed, is an individual matter. However, learning involves changes in behavior, and changes in those complex behaviors which characterize mature reading seldom occur by chance contact or good intention. Rather, it is a pragmatic matter of adjusting the reading–learning situation, doing what is reasonable to bring the pupil, with his present reading-learning resources, within learning range of the new behaviors he needs to master. In some instances, this may involve raising the pupil's resource potential by increasing motivation or supplying needed experience. In other cases, this might be achieved by reducing the level of learning material or simplifying the complexity of the behavior to be learned. In yet other instances, adjusted instruction might consist of reducing the rather long learning leap between present pupil status and the learning objective by a series of graduated learning steps, each of which the pupil can master with his present capabilities through structured guidance.

Improving adjustment of reading instruction to pupil differences involves some compromise between the largely undifferentiated secondary instruction currently evidenced and the dream of complete individualization of instruction. Where this point of compromise is located depends upon the ability of the teacher, the nature of the pupils, the learning setting, the instructional resources available, and the learning objectives. For teachers doing very little in the way of such adjustment, experience suggests that small beginnings (e.g., dividing the whole class into two learning groups, or selecting one or two pupils for extra instructional aid, or using two or three levels of differentiated group assignments) initially are more workable than launching into a complex system of individualized prescription for every pupil. Like other aspects of instruction, adjustment to individual needs in reading instruction improves with teacher opportunity to work at it. A significant operational beginning is to make the break from a totally formal classroom structure. But as Loban, Ryan, and Squire observe, an increase in the flexible use of methods and materials need not exclude some commonality in pupil learning needs and instructional modes.[8]

## Strategies for Instructional Adjustment

Some of the more common instructional and administrative strategies for adapting instruction to pupil reading differences are described on the following pages. These include broad school administrative adjustments, within-class grouping, programmed and semiprogrammed instruction, individualized reading, individually prescribed reading, and differentiated large-group instruction. Each has its advantages; none is without its weaknesses. No single strategy is recommended here as an answer or near-answer to the instructional problem of pupil learning differences. As far as reading class instruction is concerned, the recommendation of McKim and Caskey to work toward a flexible combination of instructional approaches — individual, special-group, and whole-class — seems very sensible.[9]

### *Broad School Administrative Adjustments*

These approaches include a varied mixture of organizational and administrative structures and practices which involve attempts to prescribe minimal curricular standards, to control pupil performance ranges within classes, to increase flexibility of teacher assignment, and to provide special teachers or resources for facilitating personalized instruction. The success of administrative adjustment varies with type of strategy and how it is implemented. Promotion-retention policies and attempts at homogeneous grouping have proved least effective, while team teaching and provision of supplementary instructional services generally have proved useful.

Grade retention and course failure policies have proved ineffective as means of improving pupil reading performance or in reducing the range of pupil reading differences at later school levels.[10] Current attempts to rigidly prescribe minimal learning standards for all pupils at any specific school level (competency based learning programs notwithstanding) may prove to be equally discouraging. A school may shape pupil behavior, but it seldom succeeds in dictating it! In a similar vein, assignment to reading classes on the basis of general academic performance or reading test scores may reduce initial ranges of pupil reading differences — but not enough to eliminate need for in-class instructional adjustment. A considerable disadvantage of attempts at homogeneous grouping is that it tends to collect the academic "losers" into a single class or section — a situation which usually proves horrendous to teacher personal adjustment and pupil development.

Greater adjustment of learning opportunity is the major objective of the special services component of the school program. Too often this objective becomes lost in administrative machination or sinks under inadequate or inappropriate staffing. Broadly speaking, special services involving diagnosis and remediation are ways of adjusting reading instruction for the pupil with notable reading problems and usually make a useful contribution when the school adequately implements these services. One sometimes overlooked benefit gained from special services in reading is the manner in which it frees the classroom teacher to deal with the less extreme individual differences of other pupils. Two other areas of the reading service component which carry particular potential for broadening the school's responsibility to the different reader include the development of compensatory programs for the experientially and linguistically different and for the gifted. The former has received considerable attention.[11-14] Concern for the gifted and creative student reader largely has been limited to the professional literature.[15,16]

Team teaching plans encourage flexibility in instructional setting, utilization of teaching personnel, and pupil grouping — all of which can contribute to individualization if so used. The results are more encouraging when: the team effort is coordinated through planned organization; the team effort is adjusted through experience; one team member, at least, is well prepared in reading education; a sufficient selection of adequate reading materials is readily available; and when reading instruction receives significant consideration as a team objective.

Perhaps the most useful contribution a school administration could make to the individualization of reading instruction largely is ignored in modern secondary schools — the reduction of class sizes. It is not a popular administrative concept in these days of accelerating school costs and taxpayer revolt, of course. But arguments that class size has little to do with pupil progress smack of rationalization based on questionable research. Smaller classes should improve the interpersonal contacts of teacher and pupil, and they should improve learning effectiveness. And if they do not, the instructional dynamics of the teachers of those classes deserve close and critical examination.

### Within-Class Grouping

Organizing the pupils within a class into various smaller-number groupings for reading instruction has been a popular and effective approach to adjusting reading instruction to pupil differences at the elementary school level.[17] It has not been employed as extensively at the secondary level, where the greater maturity and work independence of the pupils should facilitate its operation. Grouping does not necessarily imply that the members are regularly collected in close physical proximity, of course. At the secondary level, pupils grouped by assignment to the same level of instructional text need not "get together," although this can be advantageous.[18] Other foci of reading groupings include common reading skill needs, similar reading interests, specific content reading assignments, and teamwork on certain research problems. Such groupings may be fixed (moderate-term) or flexible (changed frequently to meet short-term needs). Like other approaches to reading instructional individualization, within-class grouping has theoretical and functional weaknesses which the teacher should consider.[19,20]

Subdividing the class into instructional or interest groups provides an administrative vehicle for the teacher to more nearly differentiate reading assignments according to reading abilities, needs or inter-

ests, and to provide more personalized assignment, more immediate guidance, and ready feedback. Assignments to groups by instructional reading level carries an additional advantage of narrowing the range of reading performance levels within the group.

The teacher can form as many groups by reading level as he is capable of handling and as can be implemented by classroom instructional materials of differentiated levels. Inexperienced teachers might start with two groups — the high-average and better readers, who can work rather independently after the initial phases of the guided reading lesson or instructional assignment have been accomplished, and the low-average and below readers, who now can be given more intimate attention at all phases of the lesson.

As the teacher develops confidence with grouping, these two initial groups can be subdivided. This may involve four different levels of material or two different instructional approaches to each of two levels of material. Most teachers find it difficult to fit more than four instructional-level groups into the time available in secondary schedules. Moreover, the administrative complexities of differentiated assignment and instruction for four or more successive group levels can increase teacher planning and executive load significantly, especially if such grouping involves a separate additional guided reading lesson or its instructional equivalent for a different level or type of material. Grouping by instructional levels contributes to individualization, but it would be unrealistic to assume that any teacher can develop as many instructional groups as needed, since a secondary class is likely to span six or more instructional reading levels.

Because they require extended and sequential instructional exposure and learning impact, reading-level groups ordinarily are fixed or semifixed groups. Fixed grouping has been criticized for becoming too rigid to meet emerging pupil needs and for reinforcing negative attitudes among poorer readers. This depends considerably upon the way they are handled and the prevailing emotional dynamics of the classroom. The use of coexisting, flexible (changing, short-term) groupings which cross other instructional group memberships to work on skills development, cross-level groupings by reading interests or problems, the concomitant use of whole-class instruction, and/or the additional use of individualized personal choice reading lowers the emotional profile of level groups and also helps provide for greater personalization of reading development. Finally, group composition should not become typed; the pupil should be assigned to another level group whenever that new group better meets his learning needs.

### Programmed and Semiprogrammed Instruction

It will be recalled that programmed instruction usually is implemented by "programs," the specified learning materials in which the units of learning are presented in a controlled sequence of stimulus-response items, with provisions enabling the student to determine the accuracy of his responses and to move forward in the learning sequence at his own pace. Most commonly, these programs are delivered via teaching machines, programmed textbooks, or "scrambled" textbooks and workbooks.[21] The number of truly programmed learning materials pertinent to secondary basic reading instruction is somewhat limited, as we have seen. More plentiful are semiprogrammed materials which provide a looser autoinstructional sequence in learning. In reading, these may draw upon automated instructional devices or they may be contained in workbooks and other "software."

The pros and cons of programmed instruction as a general vehicle of learning have been debated roundly in the professional literature. Obviously, any set of learning materials which the pupil can use rather independently, with which he can proceed at his own learning rate, and which meet some of the key objectives of basic reading instruction will contribute to individualization directly. They may contribute indirectly by freeing the teacher to give personal instruction to other pupils.

A number of semiprogrammed instructional approaches have been employed in the teaching of reading. Most of these require teacher direction or monitoring, but they do provide a prescribed set of learning objectives and a sequential set of learning experiences which the pupil may handle in a semi-independent manner. Illustrative of the diversity here are basic reading systems, criteria behavior curricula, computer-based reading units, systematic programs of reading practice exercises, any workbook series which provides sequential instruction and reinforcement in reading skills development, even guided reading lessons and reading-study systems.

The degree to which programmed or semiprogrammed materials contribute to individualization of instruction will depend upon how they are employed. If the teacher can set them into a learning sequence so that the pupil, with or without the teacher's guidance, can assume larger responsibility for: (1) determining his learning behavioral needs, (2) self-administering the instructional sequence to learn and practice that behavior, (3) assessing his own mastery of the behavior, and if necessary, (4) reframing his learning experience to correct any deficiencies — that should contribute to individualization of reading instruction. It requires sufficient materials, adequate facilities, and a teacher with administrative acumen. Generally, programmed and semiprogrammed instruction should be viewed as a supplementary or supporting facet of the basic reading curriculum rather than as a self-sufficient curriculum in itself. Some secondary and college reading-skill centers have switched their emphasis from group to semiprogrammed instruction. Semiprogrammed instruction makes such approaches as the "high-intensity" reading centers and composite reading systems possible.

### Individualized Reading Instruction

Broadly speaking, any reading instruction which is tailored to better meet the learning needs of any particular pupil is individualized. In that sense, many of the strategies and tactics presented in this chapter contribute to individualization of reading instruction.

For several decades, the term "individualized" has referred connotatively to the use of one or more variations of a particular approach to reading instruction. The *individualized reading approach* calls for the structuring of largely independent sets of reading-learning experiences for each member of the class—such experiences serving as the major segment of the program of basic instruction of a developmental nature. The essential elements of this approach consist of: (1) the collection of a wide selection of reading materials of varied literary and print forms, topics, and difficulty levels; (2) pupil self-selection of the materials he wishes to read; (3) pupil self-determination of purposes and self-pacing of reading; (4) the guidance of vocabulary development by the teacher, if the pupil is unable to handle this independently; (5) the use of individual teacher-pupil conferences once or twice a week to monitor what and how adequately the pupil has read since the previous conference and to identify and clarify any special reading problems he has encountered.[22] Some reading authorities recommend that individualized reading instruction works best if the teacher exerts subtle control in selection of materials and activities and if it is supplemented by whole-class language activities and small-group systematic instruction in skills development.[23] Others suggest that it is better used as a personal reading strand of the program which supplements basic instruction of a more traditional nature.[24] The distinction between individual *prescribed* reading instruction and individual *personalized* reading instruction has been made by Hunt.[25]

In its purer forms, the individualized approach to reading serves to exemplify both the ideals and the difficulties of any attempt to adjust instruction to individual pupils. When the pupil is taken out of the lockstep of uniform-group or formalized whole-class instruction, he may benefit from an increase in intrinsic motivation, wider and more extensive reading, greater acceptance of personal responsibility for learning, and more intimate interaction with the teacher. However, pure-form individualization shuns the use of basal readers and like systematic instructional materials with their sequential program of instruction in vocabulary and skills development. This exposes the pupil to somewhat inconsistent developmental learning experiences and places critical stress upon the creative and organizational skills of the teacher. Providing for individual developmental programs for a class of twenty-five or more pupils can become mentally, emotionally, and physically overwhelming for the conscientious teacher.

The more individualized basic reading instruction becomes, the more critical the requirements of teacher competence, a wealth of reading materials, smaller class size, pupil maturity, and practical systems for class management, pupil assessment, and record keeping. There may be easier ways to gain the advantages of individualized reading without paying its substantial price in teacher time and uncertain development of essential reading skills and knowledges. One such way is to utilize the general structure of individualized reading in a strand of personal-choice reading as an adjunct of rather than a substitute for basic reading instruction.

### Individually Prescribed Reading Instruction

Notable differences exist between pure-form *individualized* reading and *individually prescribed reading instruction*.[26] The former is concerned with extending and personalizing reading, whereas the latter in its various forms contributes directly to competency development tasks of basic reading instruction. The common elements running through the forms of individually prescribed reading instruction include: (1) pupil reading assessment, leading to (2) identification of pupil learning needs, leading to (3) assigned prescriptive reading activities, drawing upon (4) a wide variety of reading instructional materials and activities.

Three general patterns of individually prescribed reading instruction deserve identification in a discussion of general approaches to basic reading instruction. The first consists of diagnostic teaching of reading as advocated by Strang.[27] A developmental extension of corrective-remedial instruction, it consists of continuous teacher identification of pupil reading difficulty or developmental need through formal and informal assessment and observation and effected in individual or small-group instruction or in prescribed independent-reading activities. Such diagnostic teaching can occur incidentally in any basic reading instructional situation. It can be utilized more systematically when the teacher plans individual pupil "interviews" or reading analysis sessions on a regular basis for class members.

The second form of individually prescribed reading instruction came to the secondary school by way of college reading improvement centers. It works best in a reading facility in which sufficient instructional materials can be permanently located, preferably in "stations" according to function, and where pupils can "walk in," i.e., come individually or in small groups to work. This approach begins with a reading assessment and pupil interview in which the diagnostic results and the initial prescriptive program are explained to the pupil. The location and independent use of the instructional materials and equipment are explained. Each pupil has a personal folder in which his diagnostic analysis, prescriptive assignments, progress charts, and current work materials are kept. He comes to the center, locates his folder in the file, and works independently at his prescribed reading-learning activities. At periodic intervals, and as he makes progress and completes activities, prescriptive programs are revised and extended. Direct teacher instruction may or may not be employed in conjunction with this approach.

A variant version utilizes a skills center attended by whole classes daily or for regularly assigned periods of work. It is essential that such a facility be large enough to handle a mobile group of pupils. The general procedure is much like that of the "walk in" center, except that work stations become expanded to meet larger-group usage. Where typical-sized classes are concerned, it is useful to divide less mature pupils into smaller groups for controlled introduction to the workings of the individually prescribed reading instruction center. In this version, some group testing probably will be necessary to initiate and maintain sanity of opera-tion while more individual prescriptions are being developed.

To facilitate such an intensified group approach to individually prescribed reading instruction, an instructional management system is recommended. As recommended by Cohen, such a system would employ a bank of predetermined and behaviorally defined objectives.[28] For each of these, a criterion test is developed and a corresponding set of prescriptive activities are catalogued. The teacher, teacher aide, and pupils learn this system and how to locate and use the personal recording system, the tests, the instructional sequence, and any autoinstructional devices employed. Pupils work continuously at a set of (ten) reading criterion tasks, which are changed periodically as the pupil masters them. The system also makes provision for personal-choice pleasure reading of an extended nature and provides a self-administered guided reading lesson pattern to be used in semidevelopmental reading sources.

Perhaps it should be added that individually prescribed reading instruction draws upon a number of general strategies of basic reading instruction. The guided reading lesson and the differentiated reading assignment discussed earlier can contribute to this. So also does the teacher who remembers the interests or needs of a particular pupil and finds library books or constructs a skill game to meet those interests or needs.

### Differentiated Large-Group Instruction

Regardless of whether the school or teacher brings any of the above strategies to bear upon the individualization of reading instruction, the teacher can implement certain procedures to achieve greater personalization of basic instruction within large-group or whole-class settings. Most of these are no more than good instructional tactics, but they serve well in the adjustment of instruction to pupil needs. The most notable of these include: (1) placing the pupil in reading materials reasonably approximate to his instructional and independent performance levels; (2) adjusting the steps of the guided reading lesson to the needs of individual pupils, i.e., varying the amount of readiness and personal guidance during reading and reaction phases; (3) providing differentiated worksheets and study guides for independent reading assignments so that all levels of readers can feel satisfaction in accomplishment, yet work at personally challenging tasks; and (4) adjusting reading tasks so the lesser reader can achieve at reasonable learning levels — e.g., by limiting the number of interpretive tasks to those which first satisfy an understanding of the key and explicit meanings of the material, by dividing the whole of the selection into a series of small sequential units which are read to answer specific questions, or by utilizing recognition-response answering techniques.

Whole-class or large-group instruction has a vital contribution to make to the socialization and general expansion of the experiential background of pupils. Pupils learn from pupils. Lesser achievers learn from the more accurate responses, insights, and work systems of better achievers. Better students gain insight about learning, interpretation, and background differences of other pupils. Moreover, appreciation and enjoyment of a common story or article often transcends intellectual and skill goals. Whole-class instructional situations can contribute to feelings of belonging.

As important as the adjustment of instruction to individual needs may be, it should not lead to depersonalized, laboratory-type total-learning programs for basic instruction. Adjustment of instruction to pupil differences is a significant facet of any defensible reading program. And personalization is a significant facet of individualization. An eclectic combination of approaches to reading instruction seems most likely to serve these various goals best.[29]

## THE PROBLEM READER

There is a plethora of terminology used to identify and classify pupils with reading problems. Some of these terms are empty labels. Some otherwise useful classifications are employed loosely or inconsistently. Until such time when the profession clarifies its terms, all references to the inadequate reader need careful consideration.[30] Too often, "problem reader" is a label applied to pupils whose reading, among other characteristics, causes "problems" for the teacher or administrator. Some secondary pupils do exhibit unusual problems in learning and/or using reading. These may be short-term or situational. Or they may be of a blocking, persistent nature.[31] Even when the label "problem reader" is used to designate those with persistent reading difficulty or disability, it remains a broad classification which includes a number of more functional patterns.

In this section, we shall examine some of these patterns. Our concern here is with the differentiation of concepts which relate to these patterns and which carry particular implication for the secondary school program, pupil, and teacher. This discussion assumes that all reading instruction, regardless of its setting, is concerned with reader learning, which is essentially developmental.

### Reading Difficulty and Reading Disability

There is some professional confusion concerning the concepts of reading difficulty and reading disability. They are related but are not identical. *Reading difficulty* is a descriptive term which denotes unsuccessful reading performance wherever and however it may occur. *Reading disability* is a general diagnostic-administrative classification, a particular condition of reading difficulty. The nature and implication of these two concepts will be discussed on the following pages and will lead to a suggested system for the classification of persistent reading problems at the secondary school level.

### *Reading Difficulty*

Reading difficulty can be identified normatively. When viewed in this manner, "difficulty" is defined as relatively poorer test performance which places the pupil at the lower end of the distribution of reading scores — generally below some arbitrary point of differentiation, e.g., below the second decile, below the fifteenth percentile, third stanine and below, etc. Such an identification or definition has some notable weaknesses. One of these is that a pupil may place at the lower end of the distribution owing to unusual conditions which prevailed at that particular testing. Another weakness of test score definition of reading difficulty is that a pupil scoring at the lower end of a distribution of test scores may be making good learning progress according to his own potential after getting off to a belated start in reading—perhaps exhibiting better reading growth than some pupils who score higher on the criterion test or tests. A third problem raised by this definition is that of relativity. At what point does reading difficulty end and normality begin? The first percentile? The tenth? The fiftieth? Illustrative of the weakness here is that test distributions vary with school population; advantaged suburban school pupils placing near the twenty-fifth percentile for their school may be substantially better readers than those scoring near the median of reading scores for inner-city metropolitan schools.

But perhaps the greatest weakness of normative test placement identification of reading difficulty is that it seldom tells us anything useful about the nature of the difficulty or what the school should do about it. Survey reading tests usually are limited to use of generalized reading behavior. Normative test scores may be useful in screening large pupil populations, but they are insufficient for precise identification or functional classification of reading difficulty.

*A functional definition of reading difficulty.* Based upon twenty years of diagnostic reading experience, this writer has found it more useful to identify reading difficulty in a pragmatic manner: reading difficulty is *any reading situation in which the reader cannot make effective use of printed sources [including the derivation of literal and implied meaning] to solve his present needs, interests, and development.*

Reading difficulty can be *short-term* and *situational.* All of us have experienced this kind of diffi-

culty to some degree. It may occur when personal factors such as fatigue, lack of motivation, or inhibiting emotional circumstances interfere with our generally adequate reading attack. Or it can occur when our background of concepts and vocabulary are not adequate to deal fluently and meaningfully with specific materials, e.g., a graduate text in statistics.

While any short-term reading difficulty is annoying or even momentarily frustrating, it is *persistent* reading difficulty which is our greater concern in the secondary school. This may be situational, as when the pupil will not attempt to read poetry, cannot understand a social studies or science text, or is unable to use library aids to locate needed information. From a specific learning and instructional view, this is serious enough, and each teacher must strive to ameliorate such problems.

*Generalized persistent difficulty.* Of larger school implication is *generalized persistent reading difficulty* of a defeating nature in instructional and personal reading situations. Often this reflects seriously inadequate development or malfunction in handling the integral reading act. It is this generalized persistent inhibition in reading which requires special administrative and instructional consideration, at least to the extent of identifying and adjusting reading-learning situations to pupils with some degree of reading blockage. Such adjustment, however, should recognize that persistent reading difficulty can occur in different forms, at various levels, and arise from different sources or conditions.

A hierarchy of reading difficulty as it could be evidenced among the pupils of a large secondary school is given below to illustrate the relative nature of reading difficulty. The probability of such difficulty increases with the numerical order of the item. Inability to satisfy a particular functional level probably denotes greater difficulty at following levels.

1. The pupil has little command of basic English usage and cannot use oral-aural language

background as a means of learning fundamental reading words and processes.

2. The pupil has not mastered a minimal basic sight vocabulary (250 words which he can recognize and understand) and has difficulty in adding to his sight vocabulary.

3. The pupil cannot use word attack skills to unlock the pronunciation and/or meaning of simple, known but unrecognized words.

4. The pupil has not progressed from the oral recoding stage (vocal pronunciation of words) to purposeful silent decoding of meaning of relatively simple context.

5. The pupil does not demonstrate competency in reading and reacting appropriately to sources of survival-type real-life information. (The pupil is functionally illiterate.)

6. The pupil cannot gain an acceptable literal understanding from adjusted content classroom materials when reading under the guidance of the teacher.

7. The pupil independently cannot gain an acceptable understanding from a short assignment in the regular classroom text.

8. The pupil cannot utilize study and research behaviors to handle larger classroom learning tasks or projects requiring location and purposeful use of collateral sources.

9. The pupil does not read efficiently, flexibly, and with appreciation in materials appropriate to his general level of interpretive accuracy.

10. The pupil does not react to instructional and argumentive material with purposeful and evaluative interpretation, problem solution, or creative response.

*Possible sources of reading difficulty.* Chapter Two stressed that reading is a composite human behavior and that persistent serious reading difficulty or disability generally indicates the presence of more than one inhibiting pupil condition. The varied nature of reading difficulty can be further demonstrated by examining certain sources or conditions which have some probability of contributing to pupil reading difficulty.

Wiener and Cromer, in a conceptual analysis of the literature and research pertinent to reading difficulty, identified four different "assumptions" used to account for reading difficulty and its etiology.[32] These patterns or conditions which *may* explain the existence of pupil reading difficulty are identified as defect, deficiency, disruption, and difference.

*Defect* operates where some permanent personal malfunction occurs in the sensory, neurological, or cognitive processing necessary to the reading act, e.g., severe mental retardation or borderline blindness. Since the defect cannot be ameliorated to any great extent, the implication for treatment is to adapt or change instructional procedures altogether so that the pupil may learn by other modalities or processing, e.g., to use the tactile modality to teach Braille reading. Also, there is a clear implication that pupils with reading difficulty emanating from sources of defect should not be evaluated by the same norms as other pupils, since the condition generally is not correctable. These pupils, however, should receive adjusted instruction to the end of maximizing their functional development in the use of reading.

*Deficiency* implies that the reading difficulty is attributable to the absence of some function or process needed for reading, such as a limited sight vocabulary or not being familiar with the inductive pattern of argumentive writing. Deficiency assumes that such conditions can be treated—generally by instruction. Indeed, the assumption of deficiency seems to serve as the basis for many corrective or remedial reading efforts in elementary and secondary school. Since the other three major sources of reading difficulty will interfere with reading learning if they occur during the instructional years, there may be some justification for assuming the presence of deficiency, whatever the cause. However, efforts at the remediation of deficiency may be wasted if adjustment is not made to counter the influence of causal sources when present.

*Disruption* assumes that the reading difficulty can be attributed to something present which interferes with the pupil's use of his reading or reading-learning processes. Perhaps the form of disruptive causality which appears most frequently in the research and clinical literature is emotional disturbance. The treatment implications here involve the removal of the disruptive factors, and if this cannot be readily attained, then to mitigate and circumvent the disruptive source as much as possible in the course of instruction. When serious reading difficulty has existed for some time, it quite frequently generates a by-product of reading-situational emotional disturbance. This may explain why developmental group reteaching of reading so seldom is successful in remediating serious, long-term reading difficulty.

*Difference* refers to issues of reading difficulty which are attributable to "mismatches" between the pupil's mode of learning and response, which may be quite adequate in nonschool or noninstructional situations, and those required to profit from formal reading instruction as usually practiced. Perhaps the best current example of the operation of difference as a plausible contributor to reading difficulty is that of the discontinuity between the vocabulary and oral-language usage patterns of pupils from "nonstandard English"-speaking homes and that used by most writers and teachers. Another level of such difficulty by way of difference is the case of the ninth-grade pupil who is capable of dealing effectively with a text of roughly eighth-grade readability, but who cannot understand the assigned text which approximates eleventh-grade readability. There are two implications for dealing with reading difficulty generated or accentuated by difference: (1) to situationally minimize the effect of the mismatch by adjustment of instruction, while (2) working to reduce or eliminate the discontinuity by helping the pupil develop the needed behaviors and background.

***Functional illiteracy and basic reading competency.*** Functional illiteracy and its secondary school counterpart, incompetency in basic or survival reading behaviors, are operationally defined reading difficulty. The definition here is criterion-oriented, though that may not make it a more realistic conception. The nature and instructional recommendations for teaching survival or real-world reading proficiency were discussed in Chapter Eleven. The significance of this form of reading difficulty deserves some further attention, however.

Estimates of the amount of illiteracy among youth and adults in the United States tend to be general, transitional, and seem to vary with the criteria of literacy employed and for the population to which they are applied.[33] Even though we need a more precise data base on functional illiteracy, such evidence as we have is disturbing. The Harris surveys and the American Library Association report approximately one-tenth of our adult population as illiterate.[34] The latest U.S. Census data indicate that roughly 20 million Americans over the age of 15 have not completed six years of school. Bormuth argues that such grade completion figures greatly underestimate functional illiteracy; for example, he found that 67 percent of sixth graders and 35 percent of twelfth graders could not comprehend adequately a representative sample of eight news articles.[35]

More realistic and more critical evidence has been developed from studies of how youth and adults handle functional reading-related tasks. The following selected findings from Northcutt's extensive national survey of adults aged 18 to 65 are illustrative of the severity of the problem: 36 percent of the sample could not use data from a W-4 form to enter the correct number of tax exemptions; 44 percent (an estimated 52 million adults) could not use help-wanted ads well enough to correctly match personal qualifications to job requirements; 60 percent could not use catalog advertising to correctly fill out a mail-order form; and 29 percent could not accurately order a meal for two from a restaurant menu.[36]

The issue of functional illiteracy is most directly felt in economic self-sufficiency. Moreover, the double jeopardy of illiteracy and unemployment strikes disproportionately at disenfranchised minorities, language handicapped, and others with the least resources to combat them.[37] The U.S. Office of Education estimates that approximately one-half of unemployed youth are functionally illiterate.

The problem worsens. Not because of a deterioration in reading instruction: most evidence of a rigorous comparative nature reveals comparable if not better current school reading achievement when present test scores are compared with the past.[38] Rather, the crunch comes from the fact that we live in an era of knowledge explosion and rapid technological advancement. Marginal and sublevel reading power carries with it greater socioeconomic disadvantagement than in prior periods. Beyond the present, the influence of parental literacy levels on reading success of their children being what it is, this is a whirlpool which draws in the yet unborn.[39]

Probably there is some immediate short-range value in developing stopgap programs of instruction in reading which are targeted on the survival reading needs of those senior high pupils who do not demonstrate such competency. The goal is socially acceptable and the attempt should be made, even if experience in remediating seriously disabled readers suggests that the objective is overly ambitious for short-term instruction. We have little empirical evidence to support the assumption that severely retarded readers can be taught to read with adult-level effectiveness without several years of excellent quality remediation. After all, reaching such competency must encompass substantial growth in vocabulary meaning and recognition; word attack; decoding literal meaning; attention span and purposeful interpretation; locational and organizational skills; transfer, recall, and simple problem solving; integration of reading with writing and math; and considerable broadening of background in the functional processes and subjects to be read about.

A more realistic approach to the problem of functional literacy in youth is to begin as early as seventh grade to administer criterion testing in all aspects of functional literacy (e.g., applied writing; math, economic, social, scientific knowledges and behaviors; as well as reading) and to incorporate instruction in the needed or deficient competencies through developmental instruction in the pertinent

curricular areas from seventh grade on. Who knows, maybe all secondary pupils will be motivated by the opportunity to read, learn, and do something practically related to their present and later lives. It could blow a fresh stream of instructional air through what has become a stuffy, academically archaic secondary school curriculum.

At the very least, general corrective and remedial instruction at the secondary level could incorporate more realistic, functionally oriented reading-learning tasks. Three to six years of compensatory literacy learning can make a difference, even to those with primary-level reading skill, minimal general ability, and little motivation. But a one-semester or one-year crash program will be remarkable if it accomplishes the task—if one assumes that developing functional reading competency involves improving reading by three or four grade equivalencies and results in coping successfully and independently in a socially and technically complex society such as ours.

### Reading Disability

In the introduction to this section, the term "reading disability" was identified as a diagnostic-administrative classification. It need not be an arbitrary or senseless label or classification, although it has been so employed in particular school situations. Unfortunately, the term "reading disability" is used rather inconsistently in general and professional literature, although not quite as loosely as the term "dyslexia."[40] Nevertheless, the term "reading disability" does have operational value—if its basic conditions are observed and its use for identification, diagnosis, and program classification is modified to fit the particular school or school system.

*Differential conditions of reading disability.* To be logically consistent and administratively sensible, the classification of reading disability should include only youngsters who exhibit a generalized persistent degree of reading difficulty and/or learning-to-read difficulty. The purpose of identifying pupils as reading disabled is to provide special diagnostic and treatment services so that they, in time, can make normal progress in the general instructional program according to their learning potential.

Thus, the reading disability classification usually assumes that the pupil has generalized persistent difficulty in reading and also is *underachieving in reading*, i.e., his prevailing level of reading performance falls below his reading potential (frequently interpreted as his verbal mental ability or his general scholastic aptitude) to a degree considered significant in that school setting. If the school or teacher has no intent or resources to provide these special services or instruction, nothing is served by classifying pupils as reading disabled. It would be just as useful to identify them as "pupils" or "readers" or perhaps "pupils with persistent reading difficulty."

How much the pupil with reading difficulty needs to underachieve in reading in order to classify as reading disabled is a matter which varies widely in the research and clinical literature. Perhaps this is just as well, since such a decision should be oriented to factors in the school situation. Among the more important of these school factors would be: (1) the range of reading underachievement in the school; (2) the number of pupils with reading disability at various criterion levels, e.g., one year underachieving, two years underachieving, etc.; (3) the availability of teachers or specialists trained to help disabled readers; (4) the availability of facilities and the funds needed to provide special and supportive services; (5) the degree to which content classroom teachers are capable of and willing to provide for individual differences in reading ability; and particularly, (6) whether developmental reading class teachers can provide the special aid needed by the disabled reader in an adjusted instructional setting.

The nature of individual differences is such that underachievement is present to some degree in all school populations. In most secondary schools, the amount or frequency of reading disability decreases with the stringency of the criteria for underachievement and associated factors of disability. Thus,

perhaps no more than 5 percent of a stable, middle-class suburban high school would be disabled if the criteria of disability included three or more years underachievement in reading with no notable presence of inhibiting emotional, language, or physiological problems. By comparison, perhaps 50 percent of some inner-city schools in blighted metropolitan areas drawing pupils from bilingual and socioeconomically disadvantaged homes might be underachieving one or more years (assuming one could find a culture-fair intelligence test to assess reading potential). Fifty pupils out of a 1,000-population school can be individually treated by one capable remedial reading specialist. One thousand pupils of a 2,000-population school make individual remedial reading aid quite unlikely; it would be more realistic to modify the developmental reading or English program so that it incorporates corrective-remedial approaches to instruction.

***The identification of reading disability.*** The most common school practice is to identify reading disability in terms of criteria of underachievement, as we have discussed. Some school programs combine degree of underachievement with the seriousness of the functional reading difficulty exhibited by the pupil. Yet others add certain qualitative criteria to the selection of pupils for special services: evidence of recent reading progress or the lack of it; the amount of "limitation" the reading difficulty imposes upon self-development in reading or survival in school; the absence or presence of serious inhibiting emotional, linguistic, experiential, or physiological conditions; and the extent to which reading disability is a concomitant of generalized learning disability.

*Underachievement*, itself, usually is determined in terms of school years or grade levels of reading retardation. There are any number of formulas which have been employed for this purpose and which any good text in reading diagnosis will describe in detail.[41-44] One approach commonly employed is to compare the pupil's reading performance obtained on a well-developed standardized reading test with his verbal aptitude obtained through the administration of an individual intelligence test.

Another professional practice for determining the amount of underachievement is to utilize individual standardized or informal reading tests constructed of selections equivalent to successive-level reading instructional materials. Selections of parallel difficulty are read by the pupil and read to the pupil. Questions are asked over the content. The highest level to which the pupil can listen to a selection and yet obtain 75 percent accuracy on the related comprehension test is his *listening level*. The highest level the pupil can read with reasonable fluency and obtain 75 percent accuracy on the comprehension test over the selection is considered his *reading level*. Subtracting the reading level from the listening level (usually a higher level) produces a functional measure of reading underachievement.

These, of course, are rather simple, direct means of defining underachievement. Diagnostic reading specialists may use multiple measures and more complex equations or formulas in the process. Usually, the tests are administered individually, and the diagnostic analysis of the reading problem may be more important than the enumeration of underachievement.

***An operational classification of reading disability.*** Reading disability varies in degree, specific nature, and concomitant or associated conditions. Experience indicates that a differential program for the treatment of reading disability usually is more effective and economical than a broad, undifferentiated program. Such differentiation has certain pragmatic or operational implications for the identification and subclassification of reading disability.

The subclassification of reading disability should take into consideration the more efficient means of reeducation as well as the underachievement, reading level, and skills confusion of the pupil. It should be understood (1) that all reading-disabled pupils do not fall neatly into such classifications, and (2) that all schools or school systems do not

need nor can they provide separate program provision for all of the subclasses identified below. There are three major divisions in the following classification system, each with its general implication for instruction or treatment: *basic reading disability, reading-learning dysfunction,* and *concomitant reading disability.*

*Basic reading disability.* This broad category appears in varying degree and frequency in all school settings. The implicit reading difficulty largely emanates from reading "deficiency," although some degree of "disruption" and more generalized school deficiency occurs with the greater degree of the disability. Operationally, this classification may be subdivided into "corrective" and "remedial" disability.

*1. Corrective reading disability* includes pupils with a significant but lesser degree of limitation in reading. The pupil has mastered the basic reading act, but has notable difficulty in handling reasonable secondary school reading assignments. While he presents more than minor adjustment problems in reading situations, he can make ready progress with well-motivated, adjusted, smaller-group instruction in either the developmental class or special class setting. He may need intensive corrective work on certain deficient skills, or broader developmental instruction at his present level, or both. The major pragmatic issue is this: he can profit from adjusted, reasonably short-term reinstruction in reading in larger group situations.

*2. Remedial reading disability* includes pupils whose developmental progress in reading has been blocked or inhibited for some time and whose difficulty with the fundamental reading processes is severe enough to require regular individualized reading instruction in group settings of five or fewer pupils. Because these pupils present special motivational problems and require ongoing diagnosis and continually adjusted basic instruction in reading processes, remedial reading needs to be conducted or closely supervised by reading specialists. The normal general learning modes and processes are intact, however. The amount of underachievement will vary with the pupil and school level, but a three- to five-year discrepancy between reading potential and achievement levels is not uncommon by high school entry. While no learning "defect" is involved, it is likely that the pupil has accumulated some greater degree of emotional disruption and a more generalized condition of learning deficiency, particularly in school language usage. Extreme cases of remedial reading disability might fare better when included in "reading-learning dysfunction" classes.

*Reading-learning dysfunction.* This classification includes those pupils whose reading disability and related school learning problems are so severe as to recommend their inclusion in small, daily, multiple-period classes staffed by reading specialists or by reading specialist-concerned classroom-teacher teams. These are the pupils who Doll and Mills have identified as "interjacent," neither meeting the criteria for traditional programs in exceptionality (e.g., mental retardation, physically handicapped, etc.) nor being currently able to profit from normal classroom instruction supported by corrective or remedial assistance.[45] Often, they are seriously disabled in language skills and those academic areas highly dependent upon reading–writing competency. They may arrive at this generalized state of disability through the accumulated effects of early and persistent disability and/or because of situational disruption or learning differences. The purpose of the classification is to provide a controlled core setting for integrating adjusted instruction in reading with other language-skills learning and study in foundational subject areas. These pupils would take general elective classes with other pupils, especially where normal secondary reading study performance is not expected or rigorously enforced. Instruction may emphasize basic literacy and life-oriented skills for senior high pupils with immediate vocational aspirations.

*Concomitant reading disability.* Usually, learning defects, disruptions, and differences contribute to reading difficulty, as we observed earlier. These conditions also can result in reading disability, even though the pupil's immediate learning potential is retarded or inhibited. Youngsters in this classification need special instructional attention in reading as a part of a broader adjustment in the school's curriculum or in exceptional education. They need compensatory education beyond remediation in reading. The function of the classification is to increase the probability that these pupils will receive appropriate program and instructional adjustment to their broad learning needs. Some of the diverse circumstances or conditions include severe cultural and language disadvantagement, neurological impairment, mental retardation, physical handicaps, or generalized emotional disturbance. These pupils should receive reading instruction of a remedially adjusted developmental nature in instructional settings which incorporate other essential academic study and which are adapted particularly to their learning adjustment needs.*

***Using a differential classification of reading disability.*** The use of a differential system for classifying reading disability implies its adaptation to a particular school or school system. Its relative and operational intent should be communicated to all involved, so that the disadvantages of "labeling" are minimized. The primary advantage of such a classification system is that it encourages differentiated treatment of disabled readers. It provides a consistent framework for diagnosis and treatment decision. But it should be used with certain assumptions: (1) that such placement is merely an initial try; (2) that shifts and adjustments will be made for pupils who do not profit from a particular placement; (3) that the school or school system can combine its resources for such differentiation; (4) that the treatment of pupils with the most severe

---

*The writer is fully aware that these recommendations run counter to the presently popular concept of "mainstreaming" educationally different pupils. The recommendations are made from pragmatic grounds; even nonexceptional problem learners do not receive adequate individualization of instruction in current secondary settings. Time will tell whether "mainstreaming" is more than a socially cosmetic and economically escapist educational theory.

reading difficulty/disability conditions will require greater intensification of diagnosis and individualization of instructional treatment; and (5) that disabled pupils with common reading-learning needs and operational patterns are more efficiently aided when placed within the same treatment setting.

## Instructional and Assessment Implications

Surely, teaching problem readers does require an understanding of their reading-learning strengths and weaknesses, adjustment to present level of competency, specific guidance and reinforcement of competencies to be learned, sensitivity to anxieties, and provision for motivation and success. But such concern should apply to every pupil. With sensible modification, most of the assessment and instructional strategies suggested throughout this text will work with problem readers. It is more a matter of "how" than "what."

The point emphasized here is that secondary developmental reading and/or content teachers, for whom this text is written, should find the following suggestions for education of the problem reader to be of applicational value for their normal instructional assignments. It should add to their understanding of the problem reader and the work of the reading specialist. For those interested in pursuing deeper understanding of diagnosis and treatment of problem readers, sources written specifically for that purpose are identified at the end of this chapter. Enrollment in supervised training programs is recommended for those who wish to become reading specialists.

### Some Operational Premises

*1. All reading learning is developmental.* Unless the problem reader has some rare condition of sensory or neurological defect, he will need and should be able to master the same reading competencies as the "normal progress" reader. He may reveal a greater irregularity in his mastery of these reading competencies, and his present generalized

levels of reading performance will be developmentally retarded. But if he has the potential to learn, he will need to have those developmental learning experiences which will move him along the continuum of reading maturity. Because he has some developmental ground to regain, the reading underachiever needs to participate, like the achiever, in the four essential phases of the reading educational program. This can be effected in the classroom, in a special center, or by combination of the two.

*2. The decision to provide services or maintain a pupil in a special service setting should be made on the best available evidence that he can profit from such activities.* The special reading services should not be employed for the purposes of "dead-end referral," i.e., as a dumping ground for mentally retarded, emotionally disturbed, or socially recalcitrant pupils with whom classroom teachers and administrators cannot cope. These pupils need help, but beyond the provision of diagnostic and reading educational prescription, they need help in programs designed to meet their more general personal and educative problems. Moreover, pupils with reading disability should be maintained in the program only as long as they reveal reasonable progress in terms of the severity of their difficulty and disability, desire to stay in the program, are receptive to the services, and do not inhibit the learning opportunities of other pupils.

*3. Corrective and remedial placement, objectives, and instruction should be guided by what is known of the client's learning behavior and capacity.* Current reading levels, learning potential and patterns, profile of specific reading skill strengths and weaknesses, reading attitudes, and interests comprise the basic core of needed information. Performance in content-related reading tasks is a related area of needed information. More severe and persistent cases of blocked and retarded reading development, particularly when the disability is generalized to other language usage, will require diagnostic language assessment as well as investigation of physical health and social-emotional adjustment. Of all of these, identifying the levels of materials at appropriate levels for instruction and independent reading—i.e., "instructional" and "independent" levels of difficulty as determined through appropriate assessment techniques—is most important.

*4. Reading diagnosis is an enabling activity, not an end in itself.* Reading diagnosis is not testing nor does it end with reporting test results or compiling case studies. It is a question-raising, information-gathering, and decision-making process. It is a means to an end—the improvement of pupil reading performance and school adjustment through instructional prescription and recommended treatment. The scope and intensity of diagnosis depends upon the pupil and the extent and type of problems that he or she manifests. Generally speaking, the greater the degree of disability, the more obscure the factors contributing to the difficulty, and the more generalized the difficulty—the more intensive and extensive the needed initial diagnosis. Individual diagnosis is an expensive process, in terms of pupil and specialist time, and thus it should be employed judiciously. The most thorough diagnosis, the reading case study, should be reserved for the most serious pupil problems. Reading diagnosis is ongoing; it is continued through daily/weekly instructional interaction. Whenever possible, reading diagnosis should be a cooperative process— including the contributions of the classroom teacher, the pupil, and possibly the parent, as well as the reading specialist.

*5. Special reading programs for disabled readers are flexible, yet they do have a planned scope and anticipated sequence.* The general plan for group instruction or the plan for individual pupils should be guided by objectives geared to pertinent developmental pupil needs. Instructional activities should be selected as they aid the pupil in progressing toward these objectives. Artificial and isolated drills are to be avoided. Usually they do not produce effective learning, and they further detract from the disabled reader's small reservoir of motivation. However, the day-to-day and the within-period plan is flexible enough to permit variation in task, learning procedure, and revision of enabling objectives. Although advantage should be taken of "hot" periods of learning and breakthroughs in understanding, it should avoid the haphazard ongoing instruction of an "emerging" nature. Usually, the daily/weekly plan should include activities which provide for: (a) guided, reasonably continuous reading in interesting materials of independent-instructional difficulty, (b) the extension of sight vocabulary, (c) the improvement of word attack skills, (d) work on particularly deficient and inhibiting skills and understandings, and (e) practice in applying reading to content-oriented learning-study situations.

*6. The more severe the reading difficulty or the more stressful the reading disability, the greater the need for continued individualized instructional provision.* Basically this will be of developmental nature, but adjusted to pupil level and deficiency. Compared to the program for the normally progressing reader, the corrective or remedial program generally will need to make greater provision for: (a) assessment of status and progress, (b) readiness and preparation for the learning task, (c) individual guidance and demonstration, (d) overlearning of specific skills, (e) extensive application of the total skill, and (f) use of extrinsic reward of learning. Pupils with more severe and more generalized disability, such as cases of reading-learning dysfunction, will need even greater attention to these matters. Pupils with minimal disability or difficulty in mastering a few specific skills of reading should be able to progress with properly adjusted and differentiated instruction in regular developmental reading classes. Remedial treatment is primarily a matter of reeducation. Remarkably quick cures are rare among truly deficient readers. Remediation of severely disabled secondary readers should be started as early as possible. The more disabled the reader, the longer it will take to extinguish deficient learning patterns and establish and reinforce new behaviors to the point of continued retention of skill.

*7. Special consideration needs to be given to the personal-school adjustment and motivation of seriously disabled readers.* Pupils with an extended history of reading difficulty usually have experienced little school success and, understandably, may have damaged educational/reading-related self-concepts which may be expressed in resistance to try anew, overreaction to failure, latent hostility, withdrawal tendencies, and/or overdependency. The establishment of a positive learning dynamic and trusted interaction between the remedial or classroom teacher and the disabled reader is an important objective of the early phase of treatment. Some treatment rules of thumb which have proved helpful in improving pupil motivation, adjustment, and learning involvement are listed below.

*a*. The remedial program or class should avoid embarrassing labels and other unnecessary conflict. Rather it should encourage the aura of privileged consideration. No pupil should be forced into special reading service situations. However, he or she should have the advantages of participating in the program explained and be encouraged to give it a provisional try. Remedial aid should not be scheduled in place of school activities which the pupil needs or which are enjoyable to him.

*b*. Cooperative relationships and effective communication should be established between the remedial teacher and other teachers, counselors, social agencies, and parents, who also are involved in the pupil's learning and development. A combined and coordinated effort toward the amelioration of pupil difficulty is more likely to produce effective results. Independent efforts may present conflicts of interest and process. Such a cooperative approach provides the reading specialist with an excellent opportunity for in-service education of teachers and other personnel.

*c*. The disabled reader's predisposition to frustration should be taken into consideration in planning the remedial educational effort. Since attention span is short and stress usually high for disabled readers, a forty-five minute period of instruction may need to be subdivided into work at three or more different learning activities. Intense, high-effort activities should be interspaced with less taxing release activities. Wherever possible, cooperative assessment and program planning between the teacher and pupils should be effected.

*d*. The instructional and independent reading materials used with disabled readers should be chosen with particular care. The materials need to be interesting, but of a readability level which permits the pupil to read them in a fluent meaningful manner. Unfortunately, many adolescents with a history of learning difficulty are particularly sensitive to being "put down" by elementary school texts, even if they are of appropriate difficulty. The teacher can work to change this attitude, of course, and an increasing number of higher interest–lower difficulty books are being published. Also, secondary instructional materials are being packaged more attractively.

*e*. The nature of remedial instructional procedures should give due consideration to the motivational problems of the pupils involved. The intrinsic merit and understanding of learning activities should be cultivated. When possible, the relationship of the learning activity to the learning objective should be explained. Problems and projects should be employed as reading-enabling settings. Reinforcement (overlearning) activities can be transformed into a variety of learning games. Summary records of remedial instructional sessions should be kept and analyzed to plan further work. The pupil can aid in this. Progress can be dramatized by colorful charts and client-acceptable demonstrations. Many of the instructional suggestions included in Chapters Five through Twelve may be adapted to or used directly in the remedial situation as well as in the developmental reading or content classroom.

## Some Tools and Concerns for Diagnostic Assessment

Reading assessment always benefits from training and experience in the administration and interpretation of reading tests and other sources of assessment. Despite test advertisements, the task of making instructional adjustments, devising prescriptive activities, or effecting remedial programs still will need to be done.

Any tool of reading assessment can be misused, and such misuse can lead to unfortunate educational circumstances. There are some reading and reading-related assessment tools which require special training to administer and interpret because of their complexity or their social-personal implication. These include individual reading tests with diagnostic implications, vision and hearing screening tests, intelligence tests, and personal adjustment measures. A number of these tests are discussed briefly here because they do figure in diagnostic reports and professional discussion of pupils with serious reading difficulty, and all secondary professionals should be aware of their existence, nature, and general use.

*Individual diagnostic reading tests and batteries.* Most of these were developed for use with elementary school populations, but can be helpful in the diagnosis of serious secondary reading retardation. Although they have administrative manuals, these measures assume an examiner of special experience in reading diagnosis and corrective-remedial instruction. Special caution needs to be exerted in the administration, the interpretation, and the communication of findings, since their reported results tend to carry special, if somewhat unwarranted, implication of importance. There are three general patterns of tests involved here: (1) standardized oral reading tests for diagnostic interpretation, (2) standardized versions of the informal reading inventory, and (3) individual diagnostic batteries combining oral reading, silent reading, word skills, and readiness subtests. Representative diagnostic reading tests are listed in Appendix A. 4.

*Assessment of reading-related physical conditions.* In Chapter Two, those physical conditions with some possibility of exerting negative influence upon reading and learning-to-read behavior were identified. Except in unusual circumstances, the identification of these conditions usually is more critical during the early elementary school period. There is a good probability of detection and treatment before the pupil reaches secondary school, with the possible exception of pupils from lower socioeconomic backgrounds or of recent immigrant status.

There are several areas of physical condition for which secondary personnel need to maintain some

alertness—not only because they influence reading-learning performance, but because they figure in the pupil's general well-being. These are vision, hearing, glandular balance, fatigue, and malnutrition. They increase in frequency with the physiological, anatomical, and life-style changes which accompany early adolescence.

In general, the assessment function of the professional (classroom teacher, reading specialist, or counselor) is to identify possible presence of the inhibiting condition through observation of pupil behavior and referral to school health personnel or parents for trained examination by specialists. The symptoms identified in Chapter Two should be of aid in this. This is no small charge, nor an insignificant one. Teacher observation during small-group instructional situations or study periods may be the closest benevolent scrutiny some adolescents are privileged to have.

Some educational specialists, like reading clinicians and speech therapists, have had training in using such visual screening instruments as the Keystone Telebinocular, the Bausch and Lomb Orthorater, or one of the several screening audiometers available. While far superior to such gross procedures as the Snellen vision chart or the "whisper" or "watch-tick" tests, these special instruments should be considered as screening for referral tools.

*Intelligence testing.* Intelligence tests have been considered useful measures of general scholastic aptitude for fifty years. We have examined the crucial role of mental ability in the learning, retaining, and thinking processes of reading, as well as the relatively high, positive correlations which exist between intelligence test scores and reading achievement. The major diagnostic implication is that intelligence testing can be used in arriving at a general estimate of reading "potential," i.e., how well the pupil could read if he received appropriate learning opportunity.

Functional reading potential involves more than intelligence. Nevertheless, valid intelligence test results are one useful means of estimating a pupil's reading aptitude, which when compared with present reading achievement enables the school to identify the presence and degree of pupil reading underachievement or reading disability. This, in turn, facilitates decisions about appropriate program placement and type.

The fly in this educational ointment is that intelligence tests carry far-reaching legal, personal, social, political, as well as educational, implication. If care should be exerted in obtaining and communicating any aspect of pupil evaluation — then the utmost caution should be exerted in obtaining, interpreting, and reporting intelligence test results.

In addition to the usual chance and momentary-situation errors of measurement, several conditions tend to spuriously lower the intelligence test scores of pupils with serious reading difficulty — that is, are likely to erroneously depress the problem reader's obtained intelligence test score below his true or valid score. One of these conditions is inadequate reading ability itself, if the intelligence test requires the pupil to read words, sentences, or larger units of material. Another is language or general experiential background deficiency, if either has contributed significantly to the pupil's present state of reading difficulty. Yet another is anxiety or test-related anxiety, which many problem learners experience.

No practical, effective way has yet been discovered to eliminate the influence of language-experiential deficiency or personal anxiety from intelligence testing. It can, of course, be recognized as a probable contributing influence by an experienced psychometrician, and the test results can be reported in a properly qualified manner. Reading influence on intelligence scores, as such, can be minimized by the use of nonreading or individual intelligence tests. Individual intelligence testing also provides less biased, though by no means unbiased, estimation of reading aptitude for pupils with culturally or linguistically different backgrounds.

There are acceptable standardized group intelligence tests, such as the *Cooperative School and College Ability Tests* and *Lorge-Thorndike Intelligence Tests,* which are useful for school surveys or screening of general intelligence and which deliver valid and reliable scores for the broad run of adequate readers with mainstream cultural backgrounds. The use of individual intelligence tests such as the *Peabody Picture Vocabulary Test,* the *Revised Stanford-Binet,* or the *Wechsler Intelligence Scales,* as administered by personnel properly trained in intelligence testing, is advocated in the diagnosis of serious reading disability.

***Assessment of personal adjustment.*** There is some empirical evidence to support the logic that personal adjustment is related to reading achievement, as we have seen. Thus, it would seem that personality assessment should play a significant role in the prediction and diagnosis of reading difficulty. Except for research uses, this has not been common, however.

The uncertain status of personality assessment in reading evaluation may be explained by a number of factors. While the relationship of adjustment to reading performance is empirically discernible, it is neither perfect nor simple. Some poor readers have strong self-concepts and are well accepted by others, while some good readers have serious personal and social difficulties. Even where personal maladjustment is clearly present in problem readers, it is difficult to determine which is the cause, which is the effect, whether they are mutually reinforcing, or whether both are concomitants of some other influencing factor or factors. Moreover, there is some good evidence that pupil personal adjustment difficulties often are related to the school or reading situation, rather than general in nature, and that the problem lies more in coping with the task, the content area, the instructional environment, or the teacher than with whole-school or nonschool matters. Finally, factors of a more operational nature — which qualify widespread school dissemination of personality assessment — include the recognition that personality assessment is an imperfect art, that relatively few school professionals have the highly specialized training to administer and interpret personality tests, and that the assessment of personal adjustment is considered a questionable educational and social practice by a significant number of parents and school patrons. There are acceptable functional ways of identifying reading-related adjustment problems, however.

For the purposes of this review of special assessment tools, it is convenient to classify the more common sources of personality assessment according to the general approach they implement: (1) pupil self-description (interviews, autobiographies, biographical data blank, interest inventories, problem checklists, temperament-adjustment-personality inventories, and attitude questionnaires); (2) ratings by others (letters of recommendation, questionnaires-opinionnaires, rating scales, nominating techniques, and sociograms); (3) observation of behavior (situational tests, observational rating systems, role-playing activities, and anecdotal records); and (4) personal measures of perception and interpretation ("objective" personality tests and "subjective" projective tests).

The use of personality assessment in secondary reading evaluation is best implemented by those functional and benign instruments such as reading interest inventories, school and study problem checklists, systematic observation of reading and study behavior, and confidential interviews. Personality testing as such should be done by those professionals with proper training. The pupil's and/or parents' permission should be obtained for any unusual or classified examination. Results should be reported in a professional, qualified manner and treated as highly confidential data. Labels (a "paranoid") and subjective generalizations ("has a sex hang-up" or "a maladjusted personality") should be avoided like a polluted stream.

### Labeling and Learning

Perhaps an appropriate way to conclude this chapter is to reemphasize two basic considerations. The first is that labels, although essential to communication and classification for administrative purposes, must be used with understanding and caution. Pupils labeled by their classification may become "locked" into a program or group by teacher perception and administrative mechanics. Also, labels have a habit of accumulating onerous associations which further inhibit the pupil's self-concept, school adjustment, social acceptance, and drive to learn and improve. Illustrative of this problem is an experience I have had in too many diagnostic situations. In getting the normal or bright disabled reader to become a co-member in the diagnosis through self-analysis of his own reading difficulties, one not uncommon reply is "I'm just MR" (mentally retarded). Many times the pupil really believes this. Here is educational damnification compounded. Such side effects of classification labels may never be eliminated completely, but teachers and administrators can do much to educate pupils, parents, and society as a whole to the functional and temporal purpose of the classification and to avoid contributing to the unnecessary humiliation of the individual.

The second premise has been stressed throughout this text. This is the empirically based belief that all pupil learning is, for that pupil, developmental in nature—regardless of the instructional setting in which he participates.[46] Thus, all pupils, with or without problems in reading, need an opportunity to engage in a full or comprehensive program of reading experiences. Moreover, the issue lies not in "can the pupil learn," in the great majority of cases, but in how effectively we adjust the instruction to his developmental status and needs.

## REFERENCES

1. Albert J. Harris, "Diagnosis and Remedial Instruction in Reading," Chapter V in *Innovation and Change in Reading Instruction*, Sixty-seventh Yearbook, Part II, of the National Society for the Study of Education, Helen M. Robinson, Editor (Chicago: University of Chicago Press, 1968) p. 161.
2. Bernard Berelson and Gary A. Steiner, *Human Behavior: An Inventory of Scientific Findings* (New York: Harcourt, Brace and World, Inc., 1964) p. 217.

3. James B. Stroud, *Psychology in Education* (New York: Longmans, Green & Co., Inc., 1956) p. 273.

4. M. Powell and K. M. Parsley, "The Relationships Between First Grade Reading Readiness and Second Grade Reading Achievement," *Journal of Educational Research* 54 (February, 1961) pp. 229-33.

5. Guy Bond and Miles Tinker, *Reading Difficulties: Their Diagnosis and Correction,* Third Edition (New York: Appleton-Century-Crofts, 1973) pp. 46-55.

6. Robert Karlin, "What Does Research in Reading Reveal About Reading and the High School Student?" *English Journal* 58 (March, 1969) pp. 386-87.

7. L. Gail Johnson, "Organization, Methods of Instruction, Achievement, and Attitudes Toward Reading in Selected Elementary Schools," Doctoral Dissertation, University of Oregon, 1964, pp. 157-8.

8. Walter Loban, Margaret Ryan, and James R. Squire, *Teaching Language and Literature*, Second Edition (New York: Harcourt, Brace and World, Inc., 1969) p. 386.

9. Margaret McKim and Helen Caskey, *Guiding Growth in Reading*, Second Edition (New York: The Macmillan Company, 1963) pp. 24-5.

10. Walter W. Cook, *Grouping and Promotion in the Elementary Schools* (Minneapolis, Minn.: University of Minnesota Press, 1941).

11. J. Allen Figurel, Editor, *Better Reading in Urban Schools* (Newark, Del.: International Reading Association, 1972) 78 p.

12. Jerry L. Johns, Editor, *Literacy for Diverse Learners* (Newark, Del.: International Reading Association, 1974) 120 p.

13. Helen K. Smith, Editor, *Meeting Individual Needs in Reading* (Newark, Del.: International Reading Association, 1971) 149 p.

14. Eleanor W. Thornis, *Literacy for America's Spanish Speaking Children* (Newark, Del.: International Reading Association, 1976) 69 p.

15. Paul W. Witty, Editor, *Reading for the Gifted and Creative Student* (Newark, Del.: International Reading Association, 1971) 63 p.

16. Michael Labuda, Editor, *Creative Reading for Gifted Learners* (Newark, Del.: International Reading Association, 1974) 121 p.

17. Helen M. Robinson, Editor, *Reading Instruction in Various Patterns of Grouping*, Supplementary Educational Monograph 89 (Chicago: University of Chicago Press, 1959) 212 p.

18. Harold L. Herber, *Teaching ·Reading in Content Areas* (Englewood Cliffs, N.J.: Prentice-Hall, Inc., 1978) pp. 207-10.

19. Theodore Clymer, "The Structured Reading Program," in *Controversial Issues in Reading and Promising Solutions,* Supplementary Education Monograph 91 (Chicago: University of Chicago Press, 1961) pp. 79-80.

20. Dayton G. Rothroch, "Heterogeneous, Homogeneous, or Individualized Approach to Reading," *Elementary English* 38 (April, 1961) pp. 233-35.

21. A. deGrazia and D. A. Sohn, Editors, *Programs, Teachers, and Machines* (New York: Bantam Books, Inc., 1964) 309 p.

22. Edward R. Sipay, "Individualized Reading: Theory and Practice," 1964 College Reading Conference Proceedings (Providence: Oxford Press, 1964) pp. 82-93.

23. N. Dean Evans, "Individualized Reading—Myths and Facts," *Elementary English* 39 (October, 1962) pp. 580-83.

24. W. Paul Blakeley and Beverly McKay, "Individualized Reading as a Part of an Eclectic Reading Program," *Elementary English* 43 (March, 1966) pp. 214-19.

25. Lyman C. Hunt, "Updating the Individual Approach to Reading: IRI or IRP?" in *Meeting Individual Needs in Reading,* Helen K. Smith, Editor (Newark, Del.: International Reading Association, 1971) pp. 43-51.

26. Harry W. Sartain, "Research on Individualized Reading," *Education* 81 (May, 1961) pp. 515-20.

27. Ruth Strang, *Diagnostic Teaching of Reading* (New York: McGraw-Hill Book Company, 1964) pp. 8-9.

28. S. Alan Cohen, *Teach Them All to Read* (New York: Random House, 1969) pp. 224-30.

29. Albert J. Harris and Edward Sipay, *Effective Teaching of Reading*, Second Edition (New York: David McKay Company, Inc., 1971) pp. 203-5.

30. Roy A. Kress, "When Is Remedial Reading Remedial?" *Education* 80 (May, 1960) pp. 540-44.

31. Margaret Early and Harold Herber, "Redefining the Right to Read," *Journal of Reading* 14 (January, 1971) p. 220.

32. Morton Wiener and Ward Cromer, "Reading and Reading Difficulty," *Harvard Educational Review* 37 (1967) pp. 620-43.

33. David Harmon, "Illiteracy: An Overview," *Harvard Educational Review* 40 (May, 1970) pp. 226-40.

34. Louis Harris et al., *Survival Literacy Study* (Washington, D.C.: National Reading Council, 1970).

35. John R. Bormuth, "Reading Literacy: Its Definition and Assessment," *Reading Research Quarterly* 9 (1973-74) pp. 10-11.

36. W. Norvell Northcutt, "Functional Literacy for Adults," in D. M. Nielson and H. F. Hjelm, Editors, *Reading and Career Education* (Newark, Del.: International Reading Association, 1975) pp. 43-49.

37. Marilyn Lichtman, "The Development and Validation of R/EAL, an Instrument to Assess Functional Literacy," *Journal of Reading Behavior* 6(2) (1974) p. 168.

38. J. Tuinman, M. Rowls, and R. Farr, "Reading Achievement in the United States: Then and Now," *Journal of Reading* 19 (March, 1976) pp. 455–63.

39. Walter Hill, "Key Problems in Developing Reeducational Programs for Semi-Illiterates," in *Reading and Inquiry*, J. A. Figurel, Editor, International Reading Association Conference Proceedings 10 (Newark, Del.: International Reading Association, 1965) pp. 435–37.

40. Albert J. Harris, "Diagnosis and Remedial Instruction in Reading," *Innovation and Change in Reading* (1968) p. 159.

41. Bond and Tinker, *Reading Difficulties: Their Diagnosis and Treatment*, Chapter 4.

42. Albert J. Harris, *How to Increase Reading Ability* (New York: David McKay Company, Inc., 1970) pp. 208–16.

43. George D. Spache, *Diagnosing and Correcting Reading Disabilities* (Boston: Allyn and Bacon, Inc., 1976) Chapter 1.

44. Strang, *Diagnostic Teaching of Reading*, Chapter 11.

45. Robert Mills, "The Interjacent Student," in *Junior College and Adult Reading Programs*, Sixteenth Yearbook of the National Reading Conference, G. Schick and M. May, Editors (Milwaukee, Wis.: National Reading Conference, Inc., 1967) pp. 185–89.

46. Ruth Strang, *Reading Diagnosis and Remediation* (Newark, Del.: International Reading Association, 1968) p. 152.

## SUPPLEMENTARY SOURCES

Bond, Guy L., and Miles A. Tinker. *Reading Difficulties: Their Diagnosis and Correction*, Chapters 7 and 10. New York: Appleton-Century-Crofts, 1973.

Bormuth, John R. "Reading Literacy: Its Definition and Assessment." *Reading Research Quarterly* 9 (1973–74) pp. 7–66.

Fader, D. N., et al. *The New Hooked on Books*. New York: Berkley Publishing Co., 1976.

Johns, Jerry L., Editor. *Literacy for Diverse Learners*. Newark, Del.: International Reading Association, 1973.

Kennedy, Eddie C. *Classroom Approaches to Remedial Reading*, Chapters 4 and 8. Itasca, Ill.: F. E. Peacock Publishers, Inc., 1971.

Robinson, Helen M. "Corrective and Remedial Instruction." In *Development in and Through Reading*, N. B. Henry, Editor, The Sixtieth Yearbook of the National Society for the Study of Education, Part I, Chapter XX. Chicago: University of Chicago Press, 1961.

Robinson, Helen, Editor. *Reading Instruction in Various Patterns of Grouping*, Supplementary Educational Monograph 89. Chicago: University of Chicago Press, 1959.

Smith, Helen K., Editor. *Meeting Individual Needs in Reading*. Newark, Del.: International Reading Association, 1971.

# FOURTEEN

# Implementing the Comprehensive Program

*School-wide reading programs, built and conducted through the cooperative efforts of all teachers, are the only sound means for assuring maximum reading growth of every student.*

Paul A. Witty

**Overview**    Chapter Four identified the significant dimensions of the comprehensive or all-school secondary reading program. It is appropriate that this final chapter address the secondary reading effort. This chapter discusses these elements of developing the comprehensive program: planning, initiation, administration, evaluation, staffing, the role of the reading center, and the public relations effort.

Witty's prescription for the development of effective secondary reading programs was published three decades ago.[1] In the intervening years, the number of secondary schools providing some form of reading at some level has increased greatly. Trained secondary reading professionals have appeared in a growing number of schools. Instructional reading materials pertinent to the needs and interests of secondary pupils have been published. A growing body of research applicable to secondary readers, processes, and education begins to accumulate. Special funds have been funneled into upper-grade reading efforts. Progress has been made. But the effective, comprehensive secondary reading program envisioned so many years ago by Bond, Gray, and Witty exists in too few secondary schools.[2]

Implementing a comprehensive, integrated reading education effort in secondary schools is not an insurmountable task. But neither is it an insignificant challenge. School administrators cite certain persistent inhibitions to the development of more effective secondary reading education: absence of an organized plan of attack, inadequate preparation and reluctance of the general staff for personal involvement in the reading effort, an insufficiency of trained reading specialists, inadequate funding, limited facilities and materials, and scheduling and curricular complications. Sometimes these problems have been exaggerated. They are not insolvable.

Nevertheless, the implementation of a comprehensive secondary reading effort should be viewed realistically. It takes commitment, time, funds, strategy, persistence, and patience. There are few universal and no simple solutions. Some administrative wisdom has accumulated which can be helpful, if applied selectively to the particular school situation. Several sources dealing with the administration of reading programs which may be useful to those particularly concerned with problems of this nature are Carlson, *Administrators and Reading*[3]; Fay, *Organization and Administration of School Reading Programs*[4]; Otto and Smith, *Administering the School Reading Program*[5]; and Strang and Lindquist, *The Administrator and the Improvement of Reading*.[6]

# TOWARD THE INTEGRATED PROGRAM

Good educational programs are not instant mixes. They evolve through experience, good problem solving, and dedication. Some years ago Artley suggested that the development of a defensible secondary reading program, one which goes beyond setting up isolated specialized services, would involve a sequence of actions: (1) assumption of leadership, (2) creating staff interest, (3) organizing the staff, (4) putting the program into operation, and (5) evaluation and modification of the program.[7] Experience indicates that it may take as long as three years to get a new program functioning in a proficient manner, and it requires rather continual modification to keep it that way. But it is unfortunate that more secondary schools did not heed the advice of Artley.

The implementation of the comprehensive secondary reading program does require that the administration and at least a solid core of teaching staff believe strongly enough to persist in its evolution. It is well worth the effort. It improves the total-school educational climate and product as well as pupil reading development. The emergence and evaluation of such programs are dependent upon administrative and faculty acceptance of personal involvement. The latter can be encouraged through planning and orientation, democratic implementation, and ongoing evaluation and adjustment.

## Planning and Orientation

The two major operational goals of this phase are: (1) to increase general staff understanding of reading and its development, and (2) to get the program ready for implementation under the most optimal conditions possible. The initial planning and orientation phase can begin once the need and the feasibility of establishing a comprehensive secondary reading program in a particular school are accepted by a group of faculty and staff members. Enabling objectives of this phase include establishing a positive, productive professional climate; determining needs and priorities; building a general program plan; and fixing initial operational responsibilities. This period of program development may take a year or longer, depending upon the nature of the school and its staff. Since staff, school circumstances, and the reading program undergo continual change, program orientation efforts should be ongoing.

### Typical Enabling Functions

There are a number of enabling functions to be effected during the orientation phase of program development. The priority and specific nature of these will vary from school to school. The following include those of probable value in most settings. The implied sequence should be varied as needed.

*1. Adding to the initial cadre of interested staff members.* If possible, this should be done by a voluntary, informal group. The initial purpose of these sessions is to determine whether the school need and circumstances are such that making a run at a broader secondary reading program warrants reasonable probability of success. Succeeding purposes are to generate staff involvement and to share information and opinions.

*2. Gaining administrative involvement.* This is of such significance to the long-run success of the effort that reasonably active participation by significant administrative representatives in orientation efforts should be considered essential. The administrator can provide invaluable advice and smooth initial operations. Such participation carries weight with some faculty. And without some administrative commitment to future support of the program, the orientation phase can become little more than in-service education.

*3. Establishing the initial Reading Committee.* The function of this committee is to oversee the development of the program through the orientation phase, although it may continue into later phases, and certain members may become the core of the permanent committee. The initial committee should include some of the more involved of the initial cadre of concerned faculty.

This committee is of critical importance, and its composition will require some thought and compromise. It should be small enough to arrive at and effect decisions, but it should be large enough to be representative. Since the committee membership serves as an excellent avenue for broader dissemination of information and attitudes to the staff, it will be useful to include representatives of the administration and each instructional and pupil services department, department heads whenever possible. While the committee should operate democratically, it is not sensible to include members hostile toward the general program concept at this tenuous stage of development. Staff members with some background in reading education should be encouraged to volunteer for the committee. No member should feel coerced to participate.

A chairperson should be selected, preferably one respected by committee members, with leadership qualities and some understanding of reading education. This could be the school principal or an administrative representative, if he or she operates democratically. Generally, it is not wise to choose a reading specialist to head the committee, for it tends to inhibit the acceptance and broad dissemination of responsibility for program development. From the time the inital Reading Committee is formed and chaired, it should serve as the source of all orientation-phase decisions.

*4. Arriving at tentative general objectives of the anticipated program.* The emerging program concept and its related orientation-phase activities will need some organizing direction. Tentative general objectives (or hypotheses, problems, or questions) serve to provide this direction without inhibiting spontaneity, objectivity, and creativity. It is very likely that these tentative objectives can be fashioned from the collective wisdom of the Reading Committee. It may be helpful to review pertinent literature of comprehensive secondary programs and their development or to pick the mind of a visiting consultant. However, care should be taken not to "borrow" the program of other schools or adopt wholesale the suggestions of a consultant. Every school situation is unique, and one school's bonanza can become another school's drywell. Moreover, uncritical parroting can stifle such crucial elements of successful reading program development as the creative self-concept of the program and the emergence of an in-group identification with the program and its product.

*5. Assessing and evaluating the reading-related needs and resources of the school.* Program development, like classroom instruction, is most efficacious when it is based on solid evidence of the present status of things. This assessment should employ a variety of tools, both formal and informal. Generally, it will be concerned with pupil reading achievement and needs, the status of current school reading education efforts, staff knowledges and attitudes about reading and reading education, instructional and recreational reading materials presently available, and general administrative adjustments, and staffing pertinent to the implementation of the program. Some of these data will be available and some will require the construction of instruments and collection of new data. All of it will need to be collated, reported, and evaluated in terms of the tentative program objectives.

*6. Developing the initial plan for implementing the program.* The evaluation of reading-related needs and resources of the school should provide a realistic basis for confirming or modifying the tentative general progam objectives developed earlier. These revised objectives should now be arranged in a hierarchy according to their cruciality, their feasibility, their enabling relationships to each other, or some combination of these. (Sometimes an objective of lesser ultimate significance may be given a more immediate priority, because it can be readily and successfully accomplished and thus serves to develop program momentum as well as facilitate other, more significant, longer-term objectives.)

A set of operational steps to implement each objective should be included in the plan, although some flexibility may be allowed for emerging conditions and innovative solutions. The initial program plan should recommend the means by which the program will be coordinated, administered, and staffed as it enters the stage of implementation.

The tentative program plan should be put in written form and approved by a clear majority of the total initial Reading Committee. Unless the Reading Committee has been established on a representative departmental staff basis, the initial program plan may need to be referred to various departments for their suggestions and edification. The resulting revised plan should be submitted to the administration for approval.

While it is possible to implement a comprehensive school reading effort without such a basis, its long-term success is dubious. Copies of the final program plan should be given to all faculty and other pertinent personnel. This does not assure that the staff as a whole will understand or identify with the plan. It is simply a framework for communication — a starting point. Much remains to be done.

## Program Implementation

Although it is useful for the Reading Committee, the school administration, and the school staff to arrive at a commitment to activate plans for a broader program of reading education, some anticipatory activities can begin during the orientation period. Ordinarily, any earlier established reading instructional activity would be continued during the orientation; it might be incorporated, modified, or phased out during the period of implementation. Undoubtedly some of the orientation activities will have contributed to general staff understanding of reading and reading education. In a broad sense, the implementation activities of the program never end. Through evaluation and daily experience, the dynamic program undergoes continual change with the consequence that orientation, implementation, and evaluation intermingle in a natural manner.

In a narrower sense, the implementation period consists of activating the plan developed during the orientation period. Any good game plan incorporates flexibility to improvise and expand. Fundamentally, effecting the program plan consists of carrying out the operations which were specified for each of the program objectives in their order of priority. With modification, the general functions listed below will figure in the program implementation of most schools.

1. *Setting up the permanent Reading Committee.* Program implementation, particularly in larger schools, operates best under the sponsorship of a representative reading committee. It may be decided that the initial Reading Committee of the orientation period will continue to function intact. If the committee is reconstituted, it is important that enough members carry over to provide continuity. The Reading Committee membership may be expanded and subcommittees set up to deal with specific aspects of the program, e.g., staff communication and public relations, developmental reading instruction, content area reading instruction, the in-service program, and facilities and materials, among others.

Some change in the committee personnel from time to time is needed to introduce new ideas, to keep the actions of the committee directly related to school needs and responsive to staff concerns. Since membership on the Reading Committee comprises an excellent in-service educational opportunity itself, gradual change and/or expansion of membership is desirable. It can be useful to add some parents and/or pupils to the committee. Strategically, it is important that a solid majority of the committee consist of experienced and informed holdovers so that the program maintains its continuity and the committee does not digress into rediscovery of the reading wheel.

2. *Obtaining needed personnel.* Just as an effective comprehensive reading program cannot be accomplished by hiring reading specialists and relegating the total responsibility to them, neither is it realistic to assume that the school can expand its reading education efforts substantially without backing it with trained human resources. The priority of personnel needs should have been determined earlier. Sometimes it is wise to attach the recruitment of personnel to administrative

approval of the program. In some school situations this would be unwise or unnecessary.

With time and an effective in-service education program, certain personnel support can come from the increased know-how and motivation of the general faculty. This would be particularly true for the content area reading component of the program. Also, some present staff members may already be trained in reading education, and if willing, may be shifted into different or greater program responsibilities. However, the committee and/or the school administration should not lightly decide to solve personnel needs with untrained faculty. Pressing literature teachers reluctantly into service as reading specialists has killed more than one secondary reading effort! Present staff members selected for implementation activities as reading teachers per se should meet certain criteria: (a) voluntary involvement, (b) successful experience as a secondary teacher, (c) good understanding of reading and reading education, and (d) willingness to obtain professional training to develop needed competence. The school should provide these individuals with the means to obtain such training, should provide them with expert supervision, and should adjust their instructional and program responsibility to their present state of competence.

Very likely, the school will need to employ trained reading professionals. The qualifications of such professionals are elaborated in the next section of this chapter. Usually the school will get what it needs in terms of what it is willing to provide. Unless evangelistic by nature, a top-quality reading consultant will expect top professional pay *and* a working environment with a reasonable probability of developing a very successful program. The committee and administration should be suspicious of any reading professional who will do it for less.

3. *Instituting in-service education.* Most reports of successful secondary reading programs place considerable emphasis upon the essential role of staff development.[8] There are at least three functions which in-service education can fulfill in the implementation of the comprehensive reading program: (1) the generation of staff awareness,

concern, and general familiarity with secondary reading behavior and comprehensive secondary reading education; (2) providing information and developing general competencies in effecting better reading utilization wherever it may be encountered; and (3) developing competency in developmental reading education germane to the staff member's particular instructional or service responsibilities.

Some in-service reading activities will contribute to all of these functions, but ordinarily the most successful in-service activities are those which are targeted for a particular function and an appropriate professional audience. In-service activity of the first type or function probably begins indirectly during the orientation period, by bringing staff into such committee actions as evaluating school reading needs and resources.

The development of an effective in-service education program is an applied administrative science in its own right. Some in-service approaches are effective for some purposes and not so effective for others. There are pitfalls to be avoided. A poor in-service education program can set the program back just as a good in-service program can be of inestimable value. The in-service program needs careful planning and execution, and it requires time. The functions identified for the orientation and implementation phases provide a framework assuring greater success for in-school professional development in reading, and one which will help the program avoid some of the more serious weaknesses. McHugh,[9] Otto and Smith,[10] and Robinson and Rauch,[11] among others, have published useful treatments of in-service education in reading.

Most authorities recommend that the in-service reading program be related as specifically as possible to the concerns of the staff and the problems of the pupils, and that it be integrated with the development of the program over an extended period of time. Hill[12] and Schleich[13] have described integrated in-service program development approaches which made good use of staff involvement in pupil evaluation and diagnosis. This writer has found the use of a summer in-school program combining development-content reading laboratory opportu-

nity for problem readers with teacher training to be an effective, albeit intensive, vehicle for in-service education. This works best when the structure is carefully planned in advance, and the inexperienced-in-reading teaching staff is gradually shifted from observer and supplementary aide roles to total instructional responsibility roles under close support from experienced reading personnel.

Many combinations of the more traditional approaches to in-service education are possible: lectures, films or videotapes, demonstrations, special-interest or subject-area work groups, select problem workshops, planned and coordinated interschool or interprogram visitations, released-time teacher participation in the Reading Center, even encounter or problem-raising sessions. The use of visiting in-district or outside consultants with special expertise will be improved if their efforts are geared to the objectives to be accomplished, are based upon some familiarity with the particular school situation, and their presentations are preceded and followed by classroom visitation and individual or small-group interaction.

Some operational rules of thumb frequently recommended for in-service sessions include: (1) required attendance by both administrators and teachers, (2) in-service credit participation, (3) release time rather than late afternoon or weekend sessions, (4) close personal contact with presenters and active follow-up, (5) building presentations around teacher responses to pretests and questionnaires, and (6) wide participation in planning and evaluating the in-service effort. However, in-service education activity, like the program development effort itself, should be conducted as a mature professional responsibility and should avoid gamesmanship and power struggle overtones.

*4. Developing the reading program guide.* There are at least four advantages to be realized from developing a curriculum guide for the comprehensive reading program. Most obvious is that such a visual record can help structure the efforts of each component and coordinate the total program effort. A second benefit is that it aids in the orientation of new staff to the program. Third, the guide serves as a basis for evaluating and modifying the program. Finally, there are values accrued from the act of developing the guide—particularly the enhancement of teacher understanding and a closer identification with the program and fellow staff members.

The program guide may take any form and utilize any content which is meaningful to the particular school situation and which facilitates program operation. Ordinarily, such guides contain a brief statement of the philosophy of the total program and the major functions of its several components; a listing of the key operational objectives of the program; an outline or taxonomy of the reading behaviors to be developed; a summary of the curriculum or major emphases of each program component, service, or facility; identification of available tests and recommended procedures by which pupil reading competencies may be evaluated; identification and perhaps illustration of useful instructional strategies and tactics; a bibliography of available instructional materials and resources; and a bibliography of useful sources for further professional development.

The development of key aspects of the guide probably will be undertaken during the orientation phase, e.g., program philosophy, major objectives, and fundamental operations of those instructional segments to be undertaken rather immediately. But it generally is wise to let the more detailed statement of the guide emerge from the implementing experiences. Since the program itself should remain adaptable to changing circumstances and open to improvement, a major revision should be undertaken every two or three years. To keep the program flexible, some authorities recommend that the guide take a looseleaf rather than bound form; however, unilateral individual or departmental changes in the guide can produce much confusion in interstaff communication and record keeping when it takes this form. Perhaps the master copies of the guide should be bound; and those currently used by the staff may take a less fixed form.

*5. Assembling instructional materials and resources.* The survey of instructional resources taken during the orientation phase should serve as a realistic basis for identifying the additional materials needed for implementing the various components of the program. Some resources and materials will need to be purchased, if this is a typical secondary school. Solicitation from other schools in the system, from county resource centers, or from commercial companies can produce some surprising rewards. A number of useful resources can be improvised, and both teachers and pupils are capable of quite creative efforts once needs are identified.

It is important that instructional materials and resources not be perceived too narrowly. Workbooks, textbooks, and teaching devices have a place in the program, but a functional reading program should reflect the wide variety of reading materials and their usages of the larger society.

After a belated entry, publishers now are producing an increasing quantity of very useful materials in secondary reading instruction. Since program funds usually are limited, the following criteria may be helpful in making selections: (a) pertinency to instructional objectives; (b) functional readability in terms of anticipated ability of pupils; (c) feasibility of continuing use by teachers of varied experience; (d) versatility of use; and (e) cost in terms of per pupil usage, upkeep, and durability.

Finally, some plan for cataloging, placing, and retrieving these materials and resources should be executed so that maximum use by a maximum number of pupils in a maximum number of teaching situations is obtained. Some logistic control needs to be exerted, but the materials should not be locked away from pupils and teachers. One possibility is to place as many as possible within the library or instructional resources center. Another is to house them in the Reading Center, where they can be used or checked out by teachers and pupils.

*6. Arranging suitable instructional time and facilities.* Fortunately much of the comprehensive secondary reading program can be conducted in regular class settings. The most important element of these classrooms, as far as reading instruction is concerned, is that they can be flexibly arranged and that needed instructional and collateral reading materials are available. A Reading Center or Laboratory can serve a number of program needs, not the least of which is to provide a physical location for the administration of the comprehensive reading effort. Designated reading facilities are discussed later in this chapter.

Fitting reading instructional activities into an existing full schedule can pose problems, although these are lessening with the increasing use of modular scheduling and open school planning. The problem occurs, of course, more frequently in connection with finding time and places for designated developmental reading instruction and supplementary services than with the other components of the program. Schools have used a number of adroit adjustments to meet this need. The following are illustrative: (a) shortening class periods to create an additional reading period per day; (b) using the homeroom as a developmental reading setting; (c) utilizing the study hall or library period for voluntary reading classes; (d) setting up developmental reading–content area core classes; (e) adjusting team teaching or teacher aide situations to release teachers and pupil groups for instruction; and (f) extending the daily or yearly schedule with voluntary or required reading classes before school, during lunch hour, after school, or during the summer.

*7. Initiating reading program operations on a priority basis.* The primary goals of the secondary reading program are to advance all pupil reading behavior along the continuum of reading maturity and to aid pupils in utilizing reading more effectively to satisfy their personal interests and school learning needs. These involve testing, individual and group instruction, consulting and advising pupils and teachers, as well as priming special program services. The ideal eventual form is the integrated five-component secondary reading program. It is not necessary that program implementation undertake all of this at once. Indeed, it would be unwise to do so.

The priority with which the specific program components and activities are implemented will vary with what the school has in the way of program and services, the most critical needs identified by the Reading Committee, and the practical feasibility and strategic advantages associated with certain choices. For example, in a secondary school in which reading instruction has had a long association with remedial reading treatment, it might be advantageous to initiate a few voluntary classes in reading rate and/or college reading study. These classes are readily implemented with little trouble. They should provide useful aid to the pupils involved at relatively little cost. But more importantly, they tend to capture pupil and teacher attention and serve to broaden the concept of the secondary reading effort. Such classes of limited objectives usually draw the better pupils and tend to be popular and produce successful results in terms of their limited goals. This a pragmatic strategy. The classes can be made operative while more significant objectives requiring longer-term implementation with less dramatic results (for example, aiding content teachers to improve content reading circumstances) are gradually being implemented.

## Evaluation and Continuing Adjustment

Any reading program, but especially the comprehensive secondary reading program, remains useful only as long as it meets pupil and school needs in a satisfactory manner. To remain flexible and dynamic, the program must continue to improve upon its efforts. This requires evaluation. The essential components of reading program evaluation are much the same as pupil reading evaluation.[14,15] In fact, the two are inextricable.

### Significant Factors in Program Evaluation

Whether accomplished by internal or external agencies, evaluation of the reading program needs to be objective, constructive, systematic, and periodic. One way or another, it should involve the school reading staff in order to increase the reception and dissemination of evaluation data and decisions and to avoid unnecessary morale problems. Rauch states that "the purpose of evaluation is to take a comprehensive, unbiased and cooperative look at the program and to decide what modifications or changes, if any, should be made to improve the program."[16]

The basic data for the evaluation should consist of that descriptive-comparative pupil performance evidence generated by those criterion- and normative-referenced sources of assessment discussed in Chapters Seven and Thirteen. This will need to be supplemented by observation of instruction, operational logistics, and interviews, questionnaires, or reports from representative individuals who have been involved with the program: school administrator, reading program personnel, content teachers, school counselor or psychologist, pupils, and parents.[17] The resulting evaluational product should be written, quantified wherever possible, and concerned with present status, changes since initiation or last evaluation of program, major factors which have influenced program operation and development, and recommendations for further improvement.

### The Assessment of Reading Development

Change in pupil behavior is the school's premier responsibility. In the long run, such change is classified as educational development. The ultimate objective of reading development consists of that composite of purposeful, flexible, interpretive, and reaction behaviors which are termed "reading maturity." The pupil should make some progress along the developmental continuum of reading for every year of collective experiences in reading instruction and personal reading usage. The rate or amount of such development will differ among pupils according to their learning potential, reading habits, and instructional experiences. The developmental pattern for each pupil will be less than regular, and will vary with the pupil's present stage of reading mastery and the particular reading behavior under concern.

The assessment of developmental reading change is a major responsibility of the reading evaluation effort at any school level. This follows implicitly from the acceptance of reading development as a key school objective. More recently, the professional significance of the assessment of reading change has been heightened by extrinsic pressures in the form of public concern with functional and academic literacy, from conditions attached to external funding, and by criteria imposed through contracts and other versions of accountability.[18]

The assessment of change makes use of the same referents as the assessment of existing status. Reading growth or change may be identified as mastery of additional performance tasks on a developmental taxonomy of criterion behaviors. In a related manner, it may be depicted in material-referenced terms—either as the improvement of reading on materials of established difficulty or the maintenance of acceptable performance on materials of increased difficulty. But the normative referent is most commonly used, particularly the comparison of results from periodic administrations of standardized reading tests.

### Some Attendant Problems

Some of the problems attending the assessment and evaluation of the status of reading performance have been discussed. The assessment and evaluation of reading progress or change adds further complication. Complexity in the assessment of change arises from three major sources. One is the nature of behavioral development itself, particularly the normal irregularity of learning for any individual and the considerable spread of individual reading differences among pupils. A second is a result of imperfect means of measurement—the imperfect validity and reliability of individual tests being exaggerated by the problems engendered by comparing results on two administrations of the same test, two forms of the same test, or between two different tests. The third source of difficulty lies in the inconsistent phenomena of behavioral change and the difficulty of finding acceptable but uncomplicated ways of assessing change itself.

Although school-level practice has lagged behind professional awareness in these matters, some notable advancement has been made in the past decade. Teachers and administrators grow increasingly wary of untrained administration of informal or diagnostic tests; of subjective evaluation unsupported by objective measures or precontrolled observational structure; of using the same test for pre-post comparisons; of using antiquated tests and tests standardized on different populations for pre-post comparisons; of using raw scores, percent of increase, percentiles, and stanines as measures of growth; and of the phenomenon of "mean regression error," that chance tendency of those who score low on first testing to score higher on second testing and for the opposite to occur to those who score high on the first testing—unless some adjustment is made through a "residual gains" procedure such as those suggested by Davis[19] or Tracy and Rankin.[20]

In his excellent chapter on assessing growth in reading, Farr has suggested the following guidelines to aid the practitioner in evaluating growth.[21]

> 1. The practitioner should carefully define the reading skill or skills being taught and select a measuring instrument or several instruments that are operational definitions of these skills.
> 2. If test norms are used for comparisons, the test user should be sure that the norm group matches the group being tested on all important factors related to growth in reading. Developing local norms is, for most purposes, the best procedure.
> 3. Measurement procedures should be used under conditions as closely approximating those of the teaching situation as possible. If instruction has been designed to produce a generalization of the skills, testing should be done under those conditions to which this skill will generalize.
> 4. If students have been selected for a reading program on the basis of their performance on the lower extremes of test score distribution, some procedure, such as the residual gain score, should be applied to remove regression effects.
> 5. Evaluation of change scores should be interpreted cautiously. The irregular growth curves of individuals indicate that reading improvement is uneven and that measurement in reading always involves some error.

There may be no way to avoid some contamination of results in assessing reading change either as the improvement gain from specific programs of instruction or of longer-term reading growth. Some awareness of the problems involved should minimize the larger errors concomitant with the oversimplification of the process. Professionals will be aided in this by the insightful discussions of Bliesmer,[22] Congreve,[23] Farr,[24] and McDonald,[25] as well as by sources previously identified. Unfortunately, some professionals tend to use the presence of tactical complexity as a rationalization. Those so inclined should be reminded that the short-run problems attendant to finding defensible methods for assessing change are minimal in comparison with the long-run problems of not assessing change or of assessing it simplistically.

***Useful pupil data.*** Listed below are five tasks of the pupil reading assessment effort which should implement the major functions of pupil reading evaluation and thus contribute to program evaluation in turn.

1. Description of the current status of pupil reading-learning development in terms of normative referenced comparisons of pupil with pupil, pupil with group, and group with group; such descriptions including reference to measures of:
   a. Central tendency (i.e., mean, median, and mode).
   b. Distribution (e.g., range, standard deviation, percentiles, and stanines).
   c. Relationship with other pupil variables (e.g., through correlation coefficients, score profiles, and case reports).
2. Analysis of the current status of typical and variant pupil reading development in terms of mastery of program criterion-referenced target behaviors and learning objectives.
3. Identification of progress made in reading development by individuals, groups, and program population through comparison of results on systematic, periodic measurement of reading performance:
   a. Sight vocabulary.
   b. Word recognition and analysis.
   c. Decoding sentences (basic reading act).

d. Basic interpretation levels (independent and instructional criteria).

e. Analytical interpretation of content.

f. Reading flexibility.

g. Reading efficiency.

h. Reading-study attack and skills.

i. Interpretive competency in major content area instructional materials.

j. Extended personal reading habits.

4. Collection and analysis of individual or group data on such reading-related variables as:

a. Reading aptitude.

b. General language competency.

c. Attitudes toward reading, instruction, and study.

d. Interests—reading, general, vocational.

e. Socioeconomic background.

f. Physical and emotional well-being.

5. Provision for efficient screening, identification, and diagnosis of pupils with persistent problems in reading performance or development, including:

a. Persistent situational reading difficulty.

b. Difficulty associated with physical, emotional, and mental handicapping.

c. Difficulty associated with severe experiential and language disadvantagement.

d. Difficulty approaching basic illiteracy.

e. Disability of significant magnitude.

**Other useful program evaluation data.** Program evaluation will require on-site observation and interviews, as well as appropriate records pertaining to specifics of the following general operation factors:

*Organization and administration*

1. Has a program master plan been developed? Quality?

2. Who is responsible for program administrative decisions and execution?

3. How is the program articulated with the K-12 reading effort?

4. How is the reading program integrated with total school program?

5. What is the nature of program line-staff responsibilities, authority, and personal relationships?

6. Is provision made for supervision of the program?

7. Is provision made for systematic program evaluation and modification?

8. Is teacher in-service vital and ongoing?

9. What degree of familiarity and commitment with the program is evidenced by the chief school administrator?

10. How effective is program-related communication? Within staff? Among school staff? Public relations effort?

11. Does the program have a separate budget? Is it realistic with regard to needs?

*Curriculum*

1. Does a curriculum guide exist? How was it developed?

2. Has provision been made for scope and sequence of instructional objectives and related content?

3. How comprehensive is the program effort? At what grade levels and for what proportion of pupils are the five major components provided?

4. How and when is the curriculum adjusted to emerging need?

*Instruction*

1. How many weekly contact hours of reading instruction do pupils receive in various phases of the instructional program?

2. What are the pupil-teacher ratios in the various instructional components?

3. Is instruction appropriate to objectives and abilities?

4. Is instruction planned and executed efficiently?

5. Is instruction pupil-conscious?

6. What type of teacher-pupil dynamics exist?

7. Are instructional procedures and materials varied?

*Materials*

1. Does the program control a sufficient number of instructional and personal reading materials?

2. Are materials organized and administered in a way to assure maximum availability to teachers and pupils?

3. Do materials have appropriate variety? Level? Type? Behaviors taught? Interest areas? Individual as well as supervised nature?

*Personnel*

1. Does the program have sufficient staff? Program administrator, coordinator, supervisor? Diagnostic-remedial specialists? Developmental reading teachers? Content teacher consultants? Aides, secretaries, and other auxiliary staff?

2. How adequate is staff training and experience? Does preparation meet IRA specifications for assigned responsibilities?

3. How effectively are personnel utilized?

4. What affective dynamics exist among personnel? Interprogram relationships? Relationships with nonprogram personnel? Attitudes toward pupils and parents? Identification with program objectives?

*Support services*

1. What support services are available to the reading program and its personnel? Counselors and school psychologist? Health personnel? Media-center personnel? District reading administrator? Library and its personnel? School evaluation and computer services?

2. Are the school librarian and head counselor adjunct members of the reading program staff?

3. Does the program have funds available for non-school support services and consultancy fees?

## STAFFING THE COMPREHENSIVE READING PROGRAM

Every member of the secondary school faculty is part of the staff of the truly comprehensive secondary reading program. Useful single-component programs may be developed with a restricted number of active faculty, but by definition and operation, the success of the broad school reading effort is dependent upon the degree to which content teachers, administrators, counselors, librarians, as well as reading personnel, accept an active role in facilitating those program objectives which fall withing their professional purview.

### Content Area Teachers

There can be little doubt that the comprehensiveness, the all-school quality of the reading program, pivots upon the amount and quality of content-related reading instruction and utilization which is generated by content teachers. It is pivotal in three senses. It is the significant extension of the secondary reading effort beyond the usual developmental and special services program. It is the means by which all students can receive continuous attention in reading improvement. And as things now stand, it is the weakest link in the secondary reading operation and most in need of improvement.

The kingpin is the individual content area teacher. More particularly, the success of the content-reading component, and thus of the broad school reading effort, turns upon: (1) the competence and confidence the teacher has in instructional matters, generally; (2) the sagacity of content-related reading theory and practice which can be delivered to this teacher; and (3) the extent to which he or she is personally flexible enough to make better use of reading in the regular class situation. Preservice education is a significant factor here, and the trend is toward requiring some professional training in reading for secondary certification. However, the majority of present secondary school teachers have little background in reading-related education.[26] The task of providing practical help and changing attitudes thus falls heavily upon in-service education.

### English Teachers

The English teacher has played two roles in the secondary reading effort, both misinterpreted. The duality probably arises from the ambiguity which has developed about the priorities of English instruction: Do English teachers teach literature or English-language skills? As teachers of literature, they fall within the content area reading classification. Surprisingly, there is little empirical evidence that English teachers teach or utilize reading any more effectively than other content teachers.[27] From a developmental reading viewpoint, teachers of literature are suspect not only in teaching pupils *how to read* literature, but in bringing pupils *to like to read* literature of merit.[28]

Secondary administrators have assumed that as teachers of language competency, English teachers should be able to handle reading classes or to develop reading competency as a part of general instruction in English. This has proved to be something of an overestimation of both the English teacher's professional background and his or her motivation.[29] More recently, some leaders in English education have argued that developmental instruction in reading is a definite and notable responsibility of English instruction, and this, in time, may become the position of the English education field.[30] As things now stand, prospective English teachers do not get the thorough preparation in reading education they need. Moreover, this will not be satisfied by a content-reading-methods short course, although this could aid considerably in the utilization of reading in the study of literature.

Developmental reading instruction, whether a correlated segment of the English class or handled through separate developmental reading classes, should consist of a planned scope and sequence of direct instruction and reinforcement of skilled reading behavior. This requires reasonable sophistication in the theory and practice of reading instruction. Training in English-language education does provide a good background for reading education, but it needs to be supplemented by solid training in developmental reading instruction. But this is not likely to succeed if the English teacher does not accept the role of developmental reading instructor as something professionally meaningful and personally satisfying.

### The School Administrator

Reading programs with limited objectives may survive without the support of a good local school administrator, but it is nigh impossible for an effective, broad school program to develop without such aid. If the principal moderately or strongly supports this concept, if he has reasonable resources at his disposal, if he is fairly adroit in personal relations and is respected by most of his faculty — then there is a good chance that the total-school secondary reading education will emerge and strengthen. If he opposes it, or gives weak support to it, then it is quite unlikely that the program will succeed. This is not to saddle the chief school officer with the total responsibility for the existence, nature, and success of the secondary reading program; the faculty also shares much of the credit for the success or failure of secondary reading programs.

Secondary school administrators are not so ill-informed or unconcerned about pupil reading needs as many teachers like to think.[31] The tasks of administration are more complicated (particularly the balancing of program demands against resources) than nonadministrators realize. The development of a comprehensive school reading effort is no insignificant matter — and carries long-term, if not immediate, implications for budget, facility utilization, personnel adjustment, curricular change, scheduling niceties, obtaining support from the central office or school board, as well as positive public relations. No small wonder that administrators are hesitant. However, good administrators can be influenced by faculty members they respect, and most will be willing to take on the extra workload — if they feel the faculty will fulfill their own responsibility toward the program.

The secondary school administrator by training and professional experience differs from the elementary school principal, and it is somewhat unrealistic to expect him to have an in-depth background in reading education. However, as a chief school officer, a former teacher, and someone concerned with the learning needs and adjustment of his pupils, it is not too much to expect him to develop some background in reading and its development and to help in program execution.

Operationally, the administrator can facilitate the development of an effective reading program by: (1) stimulating and participating in program planning and in-service reading activities; (2) developing personal familiarity with the nature and variation of pupil reading performance in his school; (3) establishing a positive school learning climate — for staff as well as pupils; (4) obtaining an adequate budget for reading education; and (5) hiring the best instructional personnel available — reading *and* classroom teachers who are knowledgeable, dedicated, pupil-oriented, flexible, and personally well adjusted. The most effective reading programs are found in the best secondary schools.[32] Beyond the specific direct assistance he gives, the principal aids secondary reading education most by fashioning a strong total secondary school situation.

### The School Counselor

School guidance personnel and school psychologists are perhaps the most underused potential staff resources the secondary reading program has. In larger part, this is the product of separate professional training experiences and dichotomized special school responsibilities. Strang has observed: "It is astonishing that two fields so closely interwoven in actual practice as are guidance and reading should be so completely separated in the literature."[33]

There are a number of areas in which the well-trained school counselor can provide special assistance to the secondary reading program. One such contribution is in pupil and program evaluation, particularly the selection, administration, and interpretation of measures of scholastic aptitude, personal adjustment, and interests. Helping teachers understand the dynamics of teacher-learner relationships, generally, and the problem student, particularly, is another. The counselor may serve as an in-house consultant or team member for those aspects of the program specifically directed at treating the seriously disabled or disadvantaged pupils.[34]

And he can incorporate an understanding of reading and its related behavioral dynamics in his direct counseling of pupils; this may be as useful for potential college students as it is to potential dropouts.[35]

The counselor, in turn, benefits from active participation in the secondary reading program. He can gain a better understanding of reading-learning-study behavior which will facilitate his interaction with teachers and pupils. He can add to his understanding of pupil learning and adjustment problems; reading difficulty frequently figures as a part of the syndrome of pupil-school conflict, delinquency, and attrition.[36] He can extend his competency in assessment and evaluation by becoming familiar with special reading assessment procedures.

Ordinarily, it is not wise to expect the school counselor to be a reading teacher or to assume the responsibilities of reading program supervision, unless he has the motivation, special training, and release time to do so. However, the counselor's major concern should be pupils (not guidance office red tape), and he should be a part of the planning and execution of programs which can be of particular value to those students. Hopefully, the professional training of counselors will include greater preparation in reading — especially in the nature of reading behavior and development, reading assessment, and reading disability. One survey course in secondary school reading theory and practice and some supervised laboratory work with secondary problem readers would seem a minimal expectation for graduate certification in secondary counseling.

### The School Librarian

Chisholm's statement is dead center: "A fine library and an outstanding reading program are so mutually involved in achieving identical goals with respect to student objectives that it is inconsistent to consider one without the other."[37] A trained librarian is a key member of the committee for planning and effecting the broad reading program, and also should be an active member of the reading education effort. There was a time when the preparation and daily responsibilities of school librarians and reading teachers ran in parallel but separate functions. This is changing as each becomes more aware of the total reader and his developmental needs.

The librarian independently may contribute to pupil reading development in a number of ways, but both instruction and library usage are enhanced when they are a part of a coordinated plan or if the librarian and reading teacher work as an informal team.[38] The librarian may contribute to instruction directly by teaching and otherwise helping pupils learn to locate needed resources. The librarian can conduct library-skills instructional sessions in the library or classroom. A more natural learning situation is created when such orientation or instruction is part of a cooperative plan and when the library learning and usage is an outgrowth of a reading or content area study problem. The library is a good place to identify pupil reading behavior under more natural reading circumstances, and the observant librarian can aid in the identification and referral of pupils having persistent reading difficulty. The librarian can provide useful information about group reading interests and group study skill deficiencies.

However, the librarian helps the reading program most by doing what she is trained to do—locating, collecting, organizing, and delivering those reading sources needed for instruction, research, and enjoyment. School libraries have widened the range of types, topics, and difficulty levels of available materials in the past decade. Popular magazines and quality paperbacks as well as general resource references, subject-oriented resources, and the broad run of good literature make the library a powerful source of reading stimulation and practical utilization. Beyond this, the librarian's knowledge of literary sources and expertise in ordering and organizing materials should be utilized in building classroom collections and special resource-center libraries. There is some greater efficiency and economy to be gained if all school reading materials are ordered and organized as part of the central library system and then assigned to

special reading program functions on a semipermanent basis.

The librarian in turn can profit from participating directly in the broader secondary reading program. Beyond the advantage of selling the library and its services to all teachers, the librarian thus can gain a better understanding of total reading behavior, of pupil reading differences, of readability and its measurement, of special reading instruction and independent reading resources, and the objectives and workings of the reading program. The librarian may contribute usefully to any component of the comprehensive reading effort, but a good school library—whether located in special collections, centralized, or a part of a multimedia resource center—is essential to those pupil experiences leading to extended independent reading.

### Reading Personnel

A secondary school reading program of any type needs trained personnel. In this writer's opinion, reading personnel at the secondary school level need to be better trained than elementary school reading teachers: the developmental reading behaviors to be taught are more varied and complex, the conditions often are not conducive to productive instruction, and dealing with serious pupil reading difficulties often is confounded by numerous years of reinforced error and negativism. The type of reading personnel needed will depend upon the size and objectives of the secondary program. The smaller school which institutes a broad-purpose reading effort with a limited staff will need better and more broadly trained personnel than a larger program, which can provide specialized assignment and in-service training for its reading personnel.

The International Reading Association has identified four classifications of reading specialists, along with minimal criteria for their professional training: reading supervisor, reading consultant, reading clinician, and special teachers of reading.[39] These were conceived in terms of system-wide reading activity and with particular reference to the elementary school, where all teachers, supposedly, are teachers of developmental reading. Such criteria are not completely transferable to the secondary school situation. With the exception of the reading supervisor — usually a system-wide coordinator of the reading program at all school levels, and whose relationship with the particular secondary school program is largely administrative and advisory — the reading personnel with which we are concerned here are in-school, and are more functionally described as the *secondary reading consultant,* the *reading services specialist,* and the *developmental reading teacher.*

Whether a secondary school fills each of these reading personnel lines, and how many it employs of each, depends upon the size of the school, the adequacy of its budget, the priority it gives to reading development, and the breadth of its program objectives. The identification of these separate professional entities does not suggest that they should operate independently or that there should be no overlap or interchange of their duties or responsibilities. It may be feasible or necessary to merge the functions of such personnel to meet budgetary or staff limitations, but if such is done, the pupil load and program operations should be reduced correspondingly. The comprehensive reading program in any school of moderate size will have need of all three classifications. The general functions and minimal recommended preparation of these reading staff members are summarized below.

*Secondary reading consultant.* The *secondary reading consultant* (or SRC) is a full-time, thoroughly trained, in-school reading professional. He or she is primarily concerned with stimulating and coordinating the broad secondary reading effort. Administratively, the SRC is responsible to the school Reading Committee and the system reading supervisor (who should be an active member of that committee). In turn, the SRC serves as the supervisory head of all other in-school reading personnel, insofar as their reading program functions are concerned. Robinson and Rauch identify seven key roles of the reading consultant: (1) reading resource person (materials, methods, program operations); (2) reading adviser (to administration, staff, and parents); (3) reading in-service leader (organizes, implements, and participates); (4) reading instigator (of innovation and experimentation in program-related matters); (5) reading diagnostician (conducts, interprets, and tutors teachers in the diagnosis of pupil reading difficulty); (6) reading instructor (to teachers generally, and occasionally to pupils); and (7) reading evaluator (of pupil performance and program progress).[40]

Where the broad secondary reading effort is concerned, perhaps the most challenging responsibility of the reading consultant is to activate dynamic content area reading instruction and utilization throughout the school. Ideally, this calls for a general understanding of content area instruction (objectives, approaches, conditions, and problems) as well as a thorough understanding of reading strategy and its practical application to content learning. It sometimes requires the personal characteristics of both a saint and a sinner. This responsibility for effecting content reading in conjunction with organizational and administrative responsibilities to the total reading effort most distinguishes the consultant's professional role from that of the special services or developmental teacher. The consultant should be capable of working directly with pupils, especially for demonstration purposes, but it should be obvious that the consultant cannot carry much of a teaching load and do an effective job of his or her other responsibilities.

The implication of these critical and varied responsibilities is that the good SRC needs to be a very special combination of experience, professional training, and personality. It would be desirable for the consultant's professional experience to include content area teaching at the middle or secondary school level as well as developmental and remedial reading instruction. The IRA minimal specifications for professional training include a second year of graduate work with emphasis upon advanced course work in diagnosis and remediation, developmental reading programs, curriculum development and supervision, public relations, and field experience under a qualified reading supervisor. Otto and Smith stress that these are minimal requirements and that additional training and experience are desirable.[41] Beyond reading, professional areas in which the SRC should have adequate background include language learning and development, measurement and evaluation, personality and adjustment, guidance and counseling, and basic principles of research.

*Reading specialist.* The *secondary reading specialist* (or RS) is an experienced professional, well-trained in those competencies needed for organizing and directly implementing reading instruction and reading-related treatment which go beyond developmental reading instruction. The RS serves as the core staff member of the supplementary services component of the broad reading program. Very likely this will consist of activities related to the identification, diagnosis, and adjusted instruction of the problem reader, although it may include individual or group work of a special nature for average or better readers.

In contrast to the secondary reading consultant, the RS interacts primarily with pupils and secondarily with teachers. Consultation with other staff members usually centers upon matters pertaining to the special services program or to reading-study problems of specific pupils. The RS may supervise that part of the in-service training of developmental teachers which takes place in the reading center or special facility and which focuses upon reading assessment, diagnosis, and corrective instruction for pupils with learning and adjustment difficulties. Under the leadership of the reading consultant, the RS takes part in developing the comprehensive reading program, and should participate in team case study of pupils with unusual learning difficulty.

The RS should have training and successful experience as a general classroom and a developmental reading teacher. It is preferable that he or she have secondary-level teaching experience. While not expected to be as broadly or deeply

trained as the secondary reading consultant, the RS will have a year or two of graduate training leading to special competency in the diagnosis and remediation of reading and reading-related learning problems, in the organization and administration of reading centers or laboratories, in a wide variety of reading instructional procedures and materials, and in working with pupils, teachers, and parents. In addition to general preparation in the theory and practice of reading instruction, this preparation should include courses and appropriate practice in measurement and evaluation, achievement testing, reading case study, programs for disadvantaged learners, intelligence testing, adolescent personality and development, and guidance and counseling.

*Developmental reading teacher.* It seems entirely inconsistent that school administrators and English educators should complain about the quality of developmental reading instruction at the secondary school level while maintaining that any teacher should be able to do it with no more than one general college course in reading or perhaps some loosely constructed in-service training. Pupil developmental reading experience at the secondary school level can be efficiently and effectively accomplished in classes or units emphasizing direct instruction and reinforcement of essential reading behaviors, *if* handled by teachers adequately trained in developmental reading and in learning situations conducive to such instruction. Some teachers, aided only by ingenuity, determination, and trial-and-error experience, can become effective developmental reading teachers. With rare exception, this takes several years of experience and often is accomplished at the expense of the pupils who served as the instructional guinea pigs.

There is need to establish definite criteria for the developmental reading teacher at the secondary school level which goes beyond classroom teacher certification. In addition to the general survey course in secondary reading theory and instruction, which should be required for the certification of any secondary school teacher or administrator, the teacher of developmental reading needs additional immersion in reading educational theory and supervised reading practica. This should include an understanding of maturing reading behavior; the adolescent reader; the organization and administration of the secondary reading program; principles, approaches, and materials of general reading instruction; tactics and materials for developing specific reading behaviors; strategies for adjusting instruction to individual reading differences; functional techniques for assessing and evaluating reading performance and reading materials; ways to adapt developmental instruction to problem readers and disadvantaged learners; and strategies for stimulating independent reading. It would be helpful if the developmental reading teacher also has some supervised experience in teaching reading in developmental or corrective situations. Other useful background would include language development and education, literature for children and youth, personality adjustment, and learning theory.

Developmental reading instruction in the form of developmental reading classes, English courses, or units is a well-established secondary school entity. It needs to be strengthened and extended, since it is presently the most efficient way we have to provide all pupils with the opportunity to extend their competency in essential reading behaviors. The best way to strengthen developmental reading instruction at the secondary school level is to strengthen the teacher of developmental reading.

# THE READING "CENTER"

The *reading center* (or *laboratory* or *clinic*) is an established operational component of many secondary school reading programs. A recent survey of 200 secondary schools revealed that nearly 75 percent of those schools with organized reading programs had such a designated reading facility.[42] In approximately three-fifths of these schools, this facility was responsible for handling the majority of the secondary program. Another one-third reported that the center primarily provided supplementary reading instruction and services. The results indicated that such facilities were equally popular and highly similar in function in junior and senior high schools.

Individualized developmental instruction and remedial treatment were reported as the most frequent pattern of center instructional activity, although each of the previously described components of the broad reading program were represented. Other frequently reported center functions included diagnosis (95 percent), program administration (72 percent), counseling (62 percent), inservice education (49 percent), and public relations (37 percent). The centers in larger schools provided more diagnostic services, and inner-city school centers were more frequently associated with special programs or services for "disadvantaged" pupils. The general pattern reflected here corroborates the viability of the reading center concept in secondary reading education and probably represents center operations in much of the United States.

## Patterns and Functions of Designated Reading Facilities

The titles "center," "laboratory," and "clinic" have been associated with secondary reading facilities. Once the title may have reflected something of the particular focus of the facility, but that no longer seems to be the case. Colleges and universities established special reading laboratories during the 1910 to 1940 period. Functions served by these laboratories included research, diagnosis and treatment of referred elementary and secondary pupils, reading improvement classes for college pupils (rate, comprehension, and study skills), and teacher or specialist training. The concept was transferred to the elementary setting during the 1930 to 1940 period and caught on in the secondary school soon after. The term "center" is more commonly employed today, perhaps because it reflects the combined or generalized functions of the facility and avoids some of the less appealing associations of "clinic" and "laboratory." More recently, designated reading facilities in some schools have developed as part of broader-function "Learning Centers," which also include special instruction and services in other school behaviors, e.g., math, writing, various content areas, etc.

*Functions of the reading center.* The reading center may serve one or more of the following functions in the secondary school:

*1. Reading evaluation resource* (administration of school reading-evaluation program, administration of supplementary group reading testing, screening identification of pupils with reading disability, diagnostic referral source for pupils with suspected reading-learning difficulty, evaluation of reading instructional activity, and cooperative participant in team case study).

*2. Reading reeducation resource for problem readers* (corrective classes, individual or small-group remedial instruction, team treatment programs for severe learning problems and maladjusted pupils).

*3. Developmental reading instruction* (assigned classes, rotating classes, individually prescribed laboratory instruction).

*4. Voluntary group or individualized reading improvement instruction* (reading rate and flexibility, study and library research, advanced interpretation, vocabulary enrichment, college preparatory skills).

*5. Reading in-service education resource* (incidental on-request aid to individual teachers, topical or departmental units, demonstrations, team-taught content or developmental classes on rotational schedule, release-time teacher training in instructional and diagnostic procedures).

*6. Reading materials and equipment collection and dissemination facility.*

*7. Reading program coordination facility* (administrative and staff offices, instructional resources, Reading Committee function).

How the reading center does function in a particular school will reflect the interaction of certain conditions: the concept of the reading program in the school (its significance and its breadth), the role of the center in that program, the training and orientation of the reading center staff, and the physical setting and resources of the center, itself.[43,44]

### The Reading Center in the Comprehensive School Effort

The reading center (which includes the physical facility, the associated staff, and the related program and functions) can contribute usefully to the comprehensive reading program. As a pupil activity facility, it adds directly to (but does not comprise all) the supplementary services component of the program. The trained staff members of the center can aid immensely in the planning, the actual implementation, and the in-service education effort of the comprehensive program. The materials and other instructional equipment collected for reading center activity can be utilized for broader program instructional functions or can be used as a core around which other instructional resources can be ordered or developed.

Ironically, the most successful reading centers may inhibit the initiation and implementation of the comprehensive school effort. The truth of the matter in most secondary reading settings is that the reading center cannot handle logistically all of the supplementary reading services needed, let alone satisfy the responsibilities of developmental instruction, extended personal reading, and reading evaluation. Quite obviously, the special reading center is not the most appropriate setting for content area reading instruction and utilization.

To counter the view of secondary reading as a specialist-center program, some well-meaning educators have taken an anti-reading center stance. Not infrequently, this "get rid of the reading center" argument is accompanied by the dubious assumption that content area teachers are ready to assume total responsibility for secondary reading education. Why not improve on the operations of the existing center? Widening the functions of an existing center can serve as a base from which the broader program can be developed. In fact, establishing a center where one does not now exist can serve usefully in accomplishing some of the goals of the broader program.

The two key issues here lie in planning and in administrative relationships. Realistic objectives and related enabling activities of the reading center need to be defined in terms of relationship to the objectives of the total program. The reading center administrator and/or staff members (as reading specialists) must be a part of the total program development and operation. But for a number of reasons, this staff should be responsible to a reading consultant who coordinates the whole of the secondary reading program.

## THE PUBLIC RELATIONS EFFORT

Public relations has been defined by Marston as "the management function which evaluates public attitudes, identifies the policies and procedures of an organization with the public interest, and executes a program of action and communication to earn public understanding and acceptance."[45] The term "management" here may be translated to mean responsibility for the product. Three key elements of public relations implied in the definition are research, action, and communication. The major goals of public relations are (1) to inform, and through the communication of pertinent information and cogent reasoning, (2) to persuade.

In a complex and highly mobile society, there is hardly a legitimate enterprise which does not need and deserve some good effort at public relations. If the existence of that enterprise is dependent upon the acceptance and support of the general public or certain specific publics, a solid public relations program becomes essential. However, if that enterprise must change traditions or overcome a residue of negative attitudes, a strong public relations effort becomes essential.

The comprehensive reading program in the secondary school does bump against fifty years of curricular tradition, and it does need to overcome the negative associations, personal insecurities, and general professional inhibitions identified in Chap-

ter One. Establishing a strong public relations effort in support of an effective secondary reading effort should not be viewed as an ancillary post-factum selling job. It is an essential aspect of program implementation (constructive action and support), and of program evaluation and modification (information and communication).

### The Publics

We have been conditioned to believe that the "public" of public relations is the large, amorphous crowd ("Hey there out in television land"). Public relations has both "inner" and "outer" components. Service industries (for example, Bell Telephone, American Airlines, and Walt Disney Enterprises) have recognized for some time that informing and persuading their own employees concerning the value of their product and the importance of the employee to that production is necessary to the success of the broader public relations effort.

Experienced public relations representatives usually attempt to direct the public relations effort toward specific target publics. The secondary reading program needs to be cognizant of the need to inform the general public. Ironically, perhaps, its more immediate task is inner-directed explanation and persuasion. In any case, it should recognize the need to gear its research, action, and communication activities with certain specific publics in mind: the school faculty, pupils, parents, local professionals, influential citizens, and even the local, regional, and state school administrative officials.

### All Means—Great and Small

The effective public relations effort, like the effective secondary reading program, is rooted in the motivation of its key personnel. If this is positive, all contacts are likely to be positive potential public relations acts. Thus, the personality characteristics, the social skill, and the professional ability of those most intimately associated with the program become significant matters in its public relations. Unhappy or uninformed staff members can thwart the development and acceptance of even the well-planned secondary reading program. Much of the "selling" of the secondary reading effort consists of the composite impact of day-to-day interactions with individual teachers and pupils.

There are structured avenues for informing and persuading the various publics of the nature and merits of the reading program.[46] Authorities with both knowledge and personal appeal can be utilized as consultants during the orientation and implementation phases of program development. In-service sessions should be planned with the personal reaction of the general faculty in mind. The content, explanation, and dissemination of the reading program plan (in any of its possible forms) serves as an excellent vehicle for public relations. Clear and interesting "release"-type explanations of the objectives and operations of the program, written specifically for pupils, parents, or other noneducationist publics, can be of considerable value. So are program releases for the media, and these also need care in their construction. Well-prepared staff presentations and demonstrations at school orientation meetings, at parent-teacher conferences, at school board meetings, before social organizations, etc. can do the program a great deal of good. Attractive bulletin board displays and an open door to an attractive reading center or facility are ready means of developing public relation contacts.

Of course, the services (basic and special) provided through the program itself are the most natural and perhaps the best of public relations opportunity. The content teacher who finds teaching more fulfilling because he has learned ways to get pupils more involved in the class reading assignments, the improving reader who brings a buddy to the remedial group "because he needs help," the prospective college student who argues for his admission to a short-term rate improvement class — all are indicators that the program is selling itself. This success can be extended through voluntary reading improvement courses for parents, faculty, and general public.

### Integrity and Gentle Persuasion

Communication is necessarily involved in indoctrination. The message sender nearly always is motivated by a desire to influence as well as to inform the receiver; otherwise it is unlikely he would go to that effort. Those who participate in the secondary reading program effort cannot be devoid of a belief in the values of the program, and it is the express purpose of the public relations effort to improve the image of the program and to inform those who can benefit from these values.

Surprisingly, teachers, who every day, consciously or semiconsciously, set about the task of indoctrinating their pupils, sometimes find themselves inhibited in selling their product to other professionals or to the general public. There is, of course, a difference between benign propaganda and malignant propaganda. There is a difference between dishonest manipulation and the presentation of valid useful information. And there is a difference between the flagrant hard sell and persistent gentle persuasion!

The prime requisite of the public relations effort must be accuracy. Foremost, this is a matter of conscience. But it is also a matter of pragmatics. If the integrity of those supporting the program is in doubt, it soon clouds reaction to the program itself. This need not keep the public relations effort from accentuating the positive and explaining the negative. Indeed, schools as a whole too often find themselves suffering from poor public relations because they didn't get there "fustest with the mostest" — that is, because they didn't take a preventive step of straightforward explanation while there was still someone interested in listening.

In this, the secondary reading program should realize that good public relations also depends upon effective two-way communication: little problems can be identified early and the snow-balling effect is prevented, and of course, a soft answer (or a desire to parley) frequently does turn away wrath and misunderstanding.

There is always some need for a public relations effort where the secondary reading program is concerned. There is a greater need for the broader all-school effort, because it is a change from the traditional school pattern, and it affects more people. There is an inverse correspondence between the amount and type of faculty-directed public relations effort needed and the general professional enlightenment of that staff. A school climate which is shaped by a positive, competent, pupil-concerned staff is not going to require a total effort at persuasion. It will need to be kept informed about reading program matters. Also, by careful orientation, democratic implementation, and honest evaluation of the secondary reading effort, the comprehensive program can do much to put its public relations on a natural and readily maintained course.

Persuasion is the much preferable (and usually more successful) alternative to coercion. The major advantages underlying the need for the secondary reading program also serve as the key premises of its public relations effort: (1) all secondary pupils need and are capable of developing toward reading maturity and (2) the school, the content teacher, and society (as well as the pupil) benefit from such a program. Under such circumstances, it may be forgiven if the public relations effort also takes advantage of circumstances to inform and persuade: "Look at the progress we are making," "How fortunate we are to benefit from this program," and "How can we be of help to you?"

## REFERENCES

1. Paul A. Witty, "Current Role and Effectiveness of Reading Among Youth," Chapter II in *Reading in the High School and College*, The Forty-seventh Yearbook, Part II, of the National Society for the Study of Education, N. B. Henry, Editor (Chicago: University of Chicago Press, 1948) p. 26.
2. Walter Hill, "Characteristics of Secondary School Reading 1940-70," in *Reading: The Right to Participate*, Twentieth Yearbook of the National Reading Conference, Frank P. Greene, Editor (Milwaukee, Wis.: National Reading Conference, Inc., 1971) pp. 20-29.
3. T. R. Carlson, Editor, *Administrators and Reading* (New York: Harcourt Brace Jovanovich, 1972).
4. Leo Fay, Editor, *Organization and Administration of School Reading Programs*, ERIC and IRA Reading Research Profiles (1971).
5. Wayne Otto and R. J. Smith, *Administering the School Reading Program* (Boston: Houghton Mifflin Company, 1970).
6. Ruth Strang and Donald M. Lindquist, *The Administrator and the Improvement of Reading* (New York: Appleton-Century-Crofts, 1960).
7. A. S. Artley, "Implementing a Developmental Reading Program on the Secondary Level," in *Reading Instruction in Secondary Schools* (Newark, Del.: International Reading Association, 1964) pp. 1-16.
8. Joseph Loretan, "Reading Improvement in New York City Public Schools," in *Changing Concepts of Reading Instruction*, International Reading Association Conference Proceedings 6 (Newark, Del.: International Reading Association, 1961).
9. Walter McHugh, "Stimulating Professional Staff Development," in *Administrators and Reading*, T. R. Carlson, Editor (New York: Harcourt Brace Jovanovich, Inc., 1972) Chapter 8.
10. Otto and Smith, *Administering the School Reading Program*, Chapters 8 and 9.
11. H. Alan Robinson and Sidney J. Rauch, *Guiding the Reading Program* (Chicago: Science Research Associates, Inc., 1965) Chapter 5.
12. Margaret Keyser Hill, "Organizing the Reading Program in the Secondary Schools of Dubuque," *High School Journal*, 39 (November, 1955) pp. 106-11.
13. Miriam Schleich, "Groundwork for Better Reading in Content Areas," *Journal of Reading* 15 (November, 1971) pp. 119-26.
14. Mary Austin et al., *Reading Evaluation* (New York: The Ronald Press Company, 1961).
15. Walter Hill, "Reading Testing for Reading Evaluation," in *Measuring Reading Performance*, W. B. Blanton, R. Farr, and J. J. Tuinman, Editors (Newark, Del.: International Reading Association, 1974) p. 12.
16. Sidney J. Rauch, "How to Evaluate a Reading Program," *The Reading Teacher* 24 (December, 1970) p. 244.
17. Walter Hill, "Evaluating Secondary Reading," in *Measurement and Evaluation of Reading*, Roger Farr, Editor (New York: Harcourt, Brace and World, Inc., 1970) p. 134.
18. Thomas P. Hogan, "Reading Tests and Performance Contracting," in *Measuring Reading Performance*, Blanton, Farr, and Tuinman, Editors, pp. 51-65.
19. F. B. Davis, "The Assessment of Change," in *Phases of College and Other Adult Reading Programs*, Tenth Yearbook of the National Reading Confer-

ence, E. P. Bliesmer and A. J. Kingston, Editors (Milwaukee, Wis.: Marquette University Press, 1961) pp. 86-95.

20. R. J. Tracy and E. F. Rankin, "Methods of Computing and Evaluating Residual Gain Scores in the Reading Program," *Journal of Reading* 10 (March, 1967) pp. 363-71.

21. Roger Farr, *Reading: What Can Be Measured* (Newark, Del.: International Reading Association, 1969) p. 148. Reprinted by permission of the author and the International Reading Association.

22. Emery P. Bliesmer, "Evaluating Progress in Remedial Reading Programs," *The Reading Teacher* 15 (March, 1962) pp. 344-50.

23. W. J. Congreve, "Implementing and Evaluating the Use of Innovations," Chapter VIII in *Innovation and Change in Reading Instruction*, Sixty-seventh Yearbook, Part II, of the National Society for the Study of Education, H. M. Robinson, Editor (Chicago: University of Chicago Press, 1968).

24. Farr, *Reading: What Can Be Measured*, Chapter 4.

25. Arthur S. McDonald, "Some Pitfalls in Evaluating Progress in Reading Instruction," *Phi Delta Kappan* 46 (April, 1964) pp. 336-38.

26. L. S. Braam and J. E. Walker, "Subject Teachers' Awareness of Reading Skills," *Journal of Reading* 16 (May, 1973) pp. 608-11.

27. James R. Squire and Roger K. Applebee, *High School English Instruction Today: The National Study of High School English Programs* (New York: Appleton-Century-Crofts, 1968) pp. 156 and 257.

28. Richard S. Alm, "Goose Flesh and Glimpses of Glory," *English Journal*, 52 (April, 1963) pp. 262-68.

29. Braam and Walker, "Subject Teachers' Awareness of Reading Skills," pp. 608-11.

30. Margaret Early, "Changing Content in the English Curriculum," Chapter 7 in *The Teaching of English Preschool to College,* Seventy-sixth Yearbook of the National Society of the Study of Education, J. Squire, Editor (Chicago: University of Chicago Press, 1977).

31. Hill, "Characteristics of Secondary School Reading: 1940-70."

32. Hill, "Characteristics of Secondary School Reading, 1940-70."

33. Ruth Strang, *Guidance and the Teaching of Reading* (Newark, Del.: International Reading Association, 1969) p. vii.

34. Ruth Strang, "The Relation of Guidance to the Teaching of Reading," *Personnel and Guidance Journal* (April, 1966) pp. 831-35.

35. M. D. and J. A. Woolf, *Remedial Reading: Teaching and Treatment* (New York: McGraw-Hill Book Company, 1955) Chapter 7.

36. Ruth C. Penty, *Reading Ability and High School Drop-outs* (New York: Bureau of Publications, Teachers College, Columbia University, 1956).

37. Margaret Chisholm, "The Role of Libraries, Media Centers, and Technology in the Reading Program," in *Administrators and Reading*, T. R. Carlson, Editor (New York: Harcourt Brace Jovanovich, Inc., 1972) p. 137.

38. Grace Shakin, "The Role of the Librarian in a Total Reading Program," in *Libraries and Children's Literature in the School Reading Program*, D. Shepherd, Editor (Hempstead, N.Y.: Hofstra University, 1967).

39. International Reading Association, *Reading Specialists: Roles, Responsibilities, and Qualifications* (Newark, Del.: International Reading Association, 1968).

40. H. A. Robinson and S. J. Rauch, *Guiding the Reading Program* (Chicago: Science Research Associates, Inc., 1965) pp. 1-3.

41. Otto and Smith, *Administering the School Reading Program*, p. 161.

42. Walter Hill, "Secondary Reading Programs in Western New York," *Journal of Reading* 19 (October, 1975) pp. 13-19.

43. C. Reichlin and J. M. Stanchfield, "The Joy of Reading Rediscovered," in *Ivory, Apes, and Peacocks*, S. Sebesta, Editor (Newark, Del.: International Reading Association, 1968) pp. 123-36.

44. Carl B. Smith et al., *Establishing Central Reading Clinics: The Administrator's Role* (Newark, Del.: International Reading Association, 1969).

45. J. E. Marston, *The Nature of Public Relations* (New York: McGraw-Hill Book Company, 1963) p. 5.

46. Otto and Smith, *Administering the School Reading Program*, Chapter 6.

## SUPPLEMENTARY SOURCES

Carlson, Thorsten R., Editor. *Administrators and Reading.* New York: Harcourt Brace Jovanovich, 1972.

Draba, Robert E. "Guidelines for Viable Inservice Education." *Journal of Reading* 18 (February, 1975) pp. 368-71.

Harker, W. John. "Instructional System for Reading: Program Model." *Journal of Reading* 16 (January, 1973) pp. 301-5.

Otto, Wayne, and Richard J. Smith. *Administering the School Reading Program.* Boston: Houghton Mifflin Company, 1970.

Rauch, Sidney J. "How to Evaluate a Reading Program." *The Reading Teacher* 24 (December, 1969) pp. 244-50.

Robinson, H. Alan, and Sidney J. Rauch. *Guiding the Reading Program.* Chicago: Science Research Associates, 1965. 120 p.

Smith, Carl B., Barbara Carter, and Gloria Dapper. *Establishing Central Reading Clinics: The Adminis-trator's Role.* Newark, Del.: International Reading Association, 1969.

Zalewski, Ann Marie. "How to Present a Reading Program to the Administration." *Journal of Reading* 18 (May, 1975) pp. 610-14.

# APPENDIX A

# Upper-Grade Reading Assessment Sources

# 1. STANDARDIZED READING ACHIEVEMENT TESTS

| Test and Publisher [a] | Level | Grade Range | Vocab- ulary | Compre- hension | Rate | Flexi- bility | Study | Reading Total/Power | Alter- native Forms | SS | PR | STA-9 | GE | Time (min) | Date |
|---|---|---|---|---|---|---|---|---|---|---|---|---|---|---|---|
| California Achievement Tests: Reading (CTB) | 4 | 6–9 | • | • | | | | • | 2 | • | • | • | • | 50 | 1970 |
| | 5 | 9–12 | • | • | | | | • | 2 | • | • | • | • | 50 | 1970 |
| Cooperative English Tests: Reading (AW) | 2 | 9–12 | • | • | | | | | 3 | %ile bands | | | | 40 | 1960 |
| | 1 | 12–14 | | • | | | | | 3 | %ile bands | | | | 40 | 1960 |
| Davis Reading Test (PC) | 2 | 8–11 | | • | • | | | | 4 | • | • | | | 40 | 1962 |
| | 1 | 11–13 | | • | • | | | | 4 | • | • | | | 40 | 1962 |
| Gates–MacGinitie Reading Test (PC) | E | 7–9 | • | • | • | | | | 3 | • | • | • | • | 45 | 1965 |
| | F | 10–11 | • | • | • | | | | 2 | • | • | • | • | 45 | 1965 |
| Iowa Silent Reading Tests: 1973 (PC) | I | 6–9 | • | • | • | • | | • | 2 | • | • | • | | 93 | 1973 |
| | II | 9–12 | • | • | • | • | • | • | 2 | • | • | • | | 86 | 1973 |
| | III | 11–12 | • | • | • | • | • | • | 2 | • | • | • | | 56 | 1973 |
| Iowa Tests of Basic Skills: Reading (HM) | ML | 3–9 | • | • | | | | | 2 | • | • | • | | 62 | 1971 |
| McGraw–Hill Basic Skills: Reading (MH) | ML | 11–14 | | • | • | • | | • | 2 | • | • | • | | 70 | 1970 |
| Metropolitan Achievement Tests: Reading (PC) | ADV | 7–9 | • | • | | | | • | 3 | • | • | • | | 50 | 1970 |
| Nelson–Denny Reading Test | ML | 9–16 | • | • | • | | | | 2 | • | • | • | | 40 | 1973 |
| Sequential Tests of Educational Progress (AW) | | | | | | | | | | | | | | | |
| Reading 1 | I | 13–14 | | • | | | | | 2 | • | • | • | | 45 | 1969 |
| Reading 2 | II | 9–12 | | • | | | | | 2 | • | • | • | | 45 | 1969 |
| Reading 3 | III | 6–9 | | • | | | | | 2 | • | • | • | | 45 | 1969 |
| SRA Reading Achievement (SRA) | ML | 4–9 | • | • | | | | | 2 | • | • | • | | 77 | 1972 |
| Stanford Reading Test (PC) | ADV | 9.5 | • | • | | | | | 2 | • | • | • | | 55 | 1973 |
| Tests of Academic Progress: Reading (HM) | ML | 9–12 | | • | | | | | 1 | | • | | | 50 | 1966 |

[a] Publishers' names are given parenthetically in abbreviated form; complete names and addresses appear in Appendix F.

## 2. GROUP TESTS FOR SUPPLEMENTARY ANALYSIS

| Test and Publisher[a] | Grade Range | Reading Assessment Areas | Total Time | Date | Forms |
|---|---|---|---|---|---|
| Adult Basic Reading Inventory (STS) | Functionally illiterate | Reading and listening vocabulary; context reading; word skills | Varies | 1966 | |
| Botel Reading Inventory (FEC) | 1–12 | Word recognition (individual); phonics, reading and listening levels | Varies | 1970 | 2 |
| California Phonics Survey (CTB) | 7–16 | Varied phonic analysis measures | 40–45 | 1963 | |
| Diagnostic Reading Tests (Upper) (CDRT) | 7–13 | Survey; vocabulary; comprehension (silent and auditory); rates; word attack | Varies | 1967 | 2 |
| Diagnostic Reading Tests, Pupil Progress Series (Advanced) (STS) | 7–8 | Use of sources, index, table of contents, word meaning, comprehension, rate | 65 | 1970 | 2 |
| Doren Diagnostic Reading Test of Word Skills (AGS) | 1–9 | Varied word recognition and analysis measures | 180 | 1964 | |
| Durrell Listening–Reading Series (Advanced) (PC) | 7–9 | Listening vocabulary; reading vocabulary; listening comprehension; reading comprehension | 80 | 1969 | 2 |
| Iowa Tests of Educational Development (SRA) | 9–12 | Includes: vocabulary; content area reading; use of sources | Varies | 1972 | |
| McCullough Word–Analysis Tests (PP) | 4–6 | Varied word analysis measures | 70 | 1963 | |
| McGraw–Hill Basic Skills System: Reading (MH) | 11–14 | Rate, flexibility, retention; skimming and scanning; comprehension | 70 | 1970 | 2 |
| SRA Reading Record (SRA) | 8–12 | Rate, paragraph comprehension; sentence reading; vocabulary; locational reading | 30 | 1959 | |
| Silent Reading Diagnostic Tests (LC) | 3–8 | Word recognition; phonic analysis; structural analysis | 90 | 1970 | |
| Stanford Diagnostic Reading Tests (Level II) (PC) | 4.5–8.5 | Comprehension; vocabulary rate; syllabication; phonics; auditory skills | 90 | 1973 | |
| Stanford Diagnostic Reading Tests (Level III) (PC) | 9–13 | Comprehension, vocabulary, word analysis, rate; skimming, scanning | 96 | 1976 | |
| Watson–Glaser Critical Thinking Appraisal (HBJ) | 9–16+ | Inference; recognition of assumptions; deduction; interpretation; evaluation of arguments | 60 | 1964 | |

[a] Publishers' names are given parenthetically in abbreviated form; complete names and addresses appear in Appendix F.

## 3. READING–STUDY ASSESSMENT MEASURES

| Test and Publisher[a] | Grade Range | Assessment Areas | Type | Time | Date |
|---|---|---|---|---|---|
| California Study Methods Survey (CTB) | 7–13 | School attitudes; study mechanics; planning; verification | Test | 35–50 | 1958 |
| EDL Reader's Inventory (EDL–MH) | 9–13 | Reading–study skills, attitudes, physical conditions | Inventory | 20 | 1968 |
| Iowa Tests of Basic Skills: Work–Study Skills (HM) | 3–9 | Use of maps, graphs, tables, references, index, dictionary | Test | 55 | 1971 |
| McGraw–Hill Basic Skills System: Study Skills Test (MH) | 11–14 | Problem solving; underlining; library information; study information and habits | Test/Inventory | 45–60 | 1970 |
| SRA Achievement Series: Work–Study Skills (SRA) | 4–9 | Use of references and charts | Test | 76 | 1972 |
| SRA Youth Inventory (SRA) | 9–12 | Attitudes toward school, self, peers, family, home, health | Inventory | 30–45 | 1960 |
| Study Skills Counseling Evaluation (WPS) | 7–16 | Study planning, conditions; note taking; examinations; study attitudes | Inventory | 10–20 | 1962 |
| Survey of Reading/Study Efficiency (SRA) | 9–16 | Comprehensive survey of reading–study habits and attitudes | Inventory | 30 | 1967 |
| Survey of Study Habits and Attitudes (SSHA) (PC) | 7–14 | Study habits; attitudes toward teachers, school | Test | 25 | 1967 |

[a]Publishers' names are given parenthetically in abbreviated form; complete names and addresses appear in Appendix F.

## 4. INDIVIDUAL READING TESTS[b]

| Test and Publisher[a] | Reading Range | Assessment Areas | Time | Date | Forms |
|---|---|---|---|---|---|
| Classroom Reading Inventory (Silvaroli) (WCB) | 2-8 | Word recognition; oral accuracy; comprehension; functional reading levels; listening levels | Varies | 1976 | 3 |
| Gilmore Oral Reading Test (PC) | 1-8 | Oral reading: accuracy, comprehension, rate | 25 | 1968 | 2 |
| Gray Oral Reading Test (BM) | 1-16 | Oral reading: accuracy, rate, comprehension; reading level | Varies | 1967 | 4 |
| R/EAL Reading/Everyday Activities in Life (CPI) | 1-5 | Functional reading tasks of everyday life | Varies | 1973 | 1 |
| Spache Diagnostic Reading Scales (CTB) | 1-8 | Word recognition; oral and silent reading; phonics; functional levels | Varies | 1963 | 1 |
| Standard Reading Inventory (McCracken) (KPC) | 1-7 | Word recognition; oral accuracy; oral and silent reading and listening levels | Varies | 1966 | 2 |
| (Sucher–Allred) Reading Placement Inventory (BYU) | 1-9 | Word recognition; oral accuracy; comprehension; functional placement | 30 | 1973 | 1 |
| (Woods–Moe) Analytical Reading Inventory (CM) | 1-9 | Word recognition; oral accuracy; comprehension; functional placement | Varies | 1977 | 3 |

[a]Publishers' names are given parenthetically in abbreviated form; complete names and addresses appear in Appendix F.
[b]Best results obtained by those trained in administration and interpretation of individual tests. Used more appropriately at upper-school levels for individuals with notable reading retardation.

# APPENDIX B

# Bibliographies of Readable Materials for Secondary Readers

## 1. General Indexes and Bibliographies

Ahrendt, K. M., and D. V. Hoover. *A Resource Unit of Materials Available for High School Reading Centers with Annotations.* Phoenix: South Mountain High School, 5401 South Seventh Street, 1966. (Annotated listing of exercises, essays, and short stories grouped by reading levels.)

ALA, *Vocations in Biography and Fiction.* Chicago: American Library Association, 1967. (Selective annotated listing on careers for readers in grades 9-12.)

Barnes, R. F., and A. Hendrickson. *Graded Materials for Teaching Adult Illiterates.* Columbus: Ohio State University Center for Adult Education, 1965. (Comprehensive listing of easier adult materials.)

Berger, A., and H. Hartig. *The Reading Material Handbook.* Oshkosh, Wis.: Academic Press, Inc., 1969. (Listings of instructional materials, tests, and professional resources for secondary and college reading teachers.)

Bowker Co. *Annual Paperbound Book Guide for High Schools.* New York: R. R. Bowker Co., 1977. (Selective subject-oriented guide to 5,000 paperbacks useful in secondary schools.)

Carlsen, G. R. *Books and the Teenage Reader.* New York: Bantam Books, 1972. (A guide to reading materials differentiated by topics and types of literature.)

Carsetti, Janet K. *Literacy Problems and Solutions: A Resource Handbook for Correctional Educators.* College Park, Md.: American Correctional Association, 1975. (Includes detailed listing of commercial reading instructional materials.)

Dunn, A. E., M. E. Jackman, and R. J. Newton. *Fare for the Reluctant Reader,* Third Edition. Albany, N.Y.: Capitol Area Development Association, 1964. (Annotated and categorized listing of individual books, series, magazines, instructional materials, and booklists for secondary pupils.)

Fader, D. N., et al. *The New Hooked on Books.* New York: Berkley Medallion Books, 1976. (Contains reading list of 1,000 authors for reluctant readers, topically arranged.)

Kuder, G. F., and L. E. Crawford. *Kuder Book List.* Chicago: Science Research Associates, 1959. (Books of 5-11 RL recommended to fit interests on the Kuder Test.)

Los Angeles Schools. *Portraits: The Literature of Minorities.* Los Angeles: County Superintendent of Schools, 1970. (Annotated bibliography of literature by and about minority groups; organized by literary type for grades 7-12.) .

National Council of Teachers of English. *Good Reading.* New York: Mentor Books, 1969. (1,000 books recommended for college preparation; arranged by historical period and type of writing.)

Schick, G. B., and B. Schmidt. *A Guide for the Teaching of Reading.* Chicago: Psychotechnics, Inc., 1966. (Lists of texts, reference materials, and tests for secondary and college reading teachers.)

Shuman, P. *Materials for Occupational Education: An Annotated Source Guide.* New York: R. R. Bowker Company, 1971. (Reading materials on 63 occupational areas.)

Spache, George. *Good Reading for the Disadvantaged Reader: Multi-ethnic Resources.* Champaign, Ill.: Garrard Publishing Company, 1970. (Bibliographies divided according to reading level, interest areas, life-style settings.)

Spache, George. *Good Reading for Poor Readers,* Ninth Edition. Champaign, Ill.: Garrard Publishing Company, 1974. (A rich source of information, bibliographies, indexes pertinent to reader interests, needs, and abilities.)

Spache, George. *Sources of Good Books for Poor Readers,* An Annotated Bibliography. Newark, Del.: International Reading Association, 1969.

Willard, C. E. *Your Reading: Book List for the Junior High School.* New York: The New American Library, 1966. (Annotation of several hundred books which appeal and are pertinent to junior high readers; differential identification of difficulty provided.)

Wilson, J. A., Editor. *Books for You.* New York: Washington Square Press, 1971. (A book list for senior high school prepared by NCTE.)

## 2. Bibliographies of Limited-Difficulty Personal Reading

American Library Association. *Aids in Selecting Books for Slow Readers.* Chicago: American Library Association, 1959. (Annotated bibliographies.)

Barnes, R. F., and A. Hendrickson. *Graded Materials for Teaching Adult Illiterates.* (See B-1 listing above.)

Cramer, W., and S. Dorsey. *Read-Ability Books for Junior and Senior High School.* Portland, Me.: J. Weston Walch, 1970. (Extensive listings of higher-interest materials by readability levels, 1-9.)

Doubleday & Company, Inc. *Books for Reluctant Readers.* New York: Doubleday & Company, Inc. (Catalog of special interest books by type, interest, and reading levels.)

Emery, R. C., and M. B. Haushower. *High Interest-Easy Reading for Junior and Senior High School Reluctant Readers.* Champaign, Ill.: National Council of Teachers of English, 1965. (Listed for a wide variety of topics; interest and reading levels given for each.)

*Golden Books for Students with Reading Problems.* New York: Western Publishing Co., Inc., 1976. (Annotated catalog of books graded for difficulty, elementary through secondary.)

Kingerly, R. E. *How-to-Do-It Books.* New York: R. R. Bowker Company, 1961. (2,300 books on recreational subjects, arranged by reading levels.)

Palmer, J. R. *Read for Your Life.* Metuchen, N. J.: Scarecrow Press, 1974. (Includes 350 pages of annotated book lists, classified by topic, and identified by reading and interest level.)

Reading Center. *A Place to Start.* Kansas City, Mo.: The Reading Center, University of Missouri Branch. (Graded and topically arranged list of 7,500 sources.)

Spache, George. *Good Reading for Poor Readers.* (See B-1 listing above.)

Strang, Ruth, et al. *Gateways to Readable Books,* Fourth Edition. New York: H. W. Wilson Company, 1966. (245 pages of annotated, graded listings for secondary retarded readers.)

*Uncommonly Good Materials for Remedial Reading.* Claremont, Calif.: P.O. Box 8. (Adolescent and adult materials, reading levels 1-6.)

White, M. E., Editor. *High Interest-Easy Reading for Junior and Senior High School Students.* Champaign, Ill.: National Council of Teachers of English, 1972. (Annotated listings by levels.)

### 3. Content-Oriented Listings

American Association for the Advancement of Science. *The AAAS Science Booklist for Children* and *The AAAS Booklist for Young Adults.* Washington, D.C.: AAAS Publication. (Revised periodically. Annotated listings of 1,000 + titles according to topic area.) *Science*

Bowker Company. *Growing Up with Science Books.* New York: R. R. Bowker Company. (Annual annotated listing of easier science reading.) *Science*

Brewton, J. E., et al. *Index to Poetry for Children and Young People, 1964-69.* New York: H. W. Wilson Company, 1972. (Includes contemporary poetry for junior-senior high.) *English*

Carlsen, G. R. *Books and the Teenage Reader.* (See B-1 listing.) *English*

Carpenter, H. *Gateways to American History: An Annotated Grade List of Books for Slow Learners.* New York: H. W. Wilson Company, 1968. (Arranged by historical period.) *Social Studies*

Crosby, M., Editor. *Reading Ladders for Human Relations,* Fourth Edition. Washington, D.C.: American Council on Education, 1963. (Primary to adult difficulty levels.) *Social Studies*

Earle, R. A. *Teaching Reading and Mathematics.* Newark, Del.: International Reading Association, 1976. (Appendix lists high-interest math sources.) *Math*

Fidell, E. A. *Short Story Index: Supplement 1959-63.* New York: H. W. Wilson Company, 1965. (Indexes 85,000 short stories.) *English*

Gott, M. E., and J. R. Wailes. *High Interest-Low Vocabulary Science Books.* Boulder, Colo.: Bureau of Educational Research, University of Colorado, 1970. *Science*

Hardgrove, C. E., and H. Miller. *Mathematics Library: Elementary and Junior High.* Reston, Va.: National Council of Teachers of Mathematics, 1973. (Revised and enlarged annotated bibliography of enrichment books classified by level.) *Math*

Los Angeles City Schools. *The American Way: A Reading List for Grades K Through 14.* Library Division, Los Angeles City Schools. *Social Studies*

Metzner, S. *World History in Juvenile Books: A Geographical and Chronological Guide.* New York: H. W. Wilson Company, 1973. (2,700 titles of fiction and nonfiction for less mature readers; suggested reading levels given.) *Social Studies*

National Council for Social Studies. *American History Booklist for High Schools: A Selection for Supplementary Reading.* Washington, D.C.: NCSS. *Social Studies*

National Council for Social Studies. *Reading Guide in Politics and Government.* Washington, D.C.: NCSS. *Social Studies*

National Council for Social Studies. *World Civilization Booklist: Supplementary Reading for Secondary Schools.* Washington, D.C.: NCSS. *Social Studies*

National Council of Teachers of Mathematics. *The High School Mathematics Library.* Revised. Washington, D.C.: NCTM. (Annotated listing by math categories.) *Math*

O'Neal, R. *Teacher's Guide to World Literature for the High School.* Champaign, Ill.: National Council of Teachers of English, 1966. (Comparative reviews to expand literature program.) *English*

Reid, V., Editor. *Reading Ladders for Human Relations,* Fifth Edition. Washington, D.C.: American Council on Education, 1972. (Selective bibliographies arranged in order of reading difficulty.) *Social Studies*

Rosenberg, J. K., and K. C. Rosenberg. *Young Peoples Literature in Series: Fiction.* Littleton, Colo.: Libraries Unlimited, Inc., 1972. (Evaluative annotations for reading levels 3-9.) *English*

Rosenberg, J. K., and K. C. Rosenberg. *Young Peoples Literature in Series: Publishers and Non-Fiction.*

Littleton, Colo.: Libraries Unlimited, Inc., 1973. (Nearly 6,000 annotated entries for reluctant readers, grades 3–12.)   *English*

Stensland, A. E. *Literature by and About the American Indian: An Annotated Bibliography for Junior and Senior High School Students.* Champaign, Ill.: National Council of Teachers of English, 1973. (Arranged according to type of literature.)   *English*

# APPENDIX C

# Controlled-Difficulty Reading Series*

*Publishers' names are given parenthetically in abbreviated form; complete names and addresses appear in Appendix F.

408

### 1. General Interest Series and Collections

*The Action Series.* (HMC) Twelve paperbacks 3.5-5.5 RL. Supplementary skills workbooks available.

*All-Star Sports Books.* (FEC) Twelve hardback instructive sport areas books. 4-6 RL.

*Be Informed Units.* (NRP) Seventeen units dealing with survival literacy tasks. 3-5 RL. Exercises included.

*Careers for Tomorrow.* (HZW) Fifteen vocationally oriented sources. 6-8 RL.

*Careers in Depth Series.* (RRP) Fifty-nine titles. 9-10 RL.

*The Challenge Readers.* (MMP) Series dealing with self and social understanding. 6-8 RL.

*Checkered-Flag Series.* (FEP) Four stories on hot rods. 2-3 RL.

*Crossroads Series.* (NN) Sixteen paperbacks on various themes. 3-8 RL. Can be grouped in four subseries for skills work.

*Deep-Sea Adventure Series.* (FEP) Action stories. 1-3 RL.

*Everygirls Library.* (LP) Short stories. 6-8 RL.

*Finding Your Job.* (FC) Six units of 5 books each, covering about 300 job descriptions. 3-4 RL.

*Fun with _____ Books.* (RH) Hobbies and activities. 4-5 RL.

*Fun with _____ Series.* (JBL) Craft and hobbies. 5 RL.

*Garrard Sports Library.* (GP) Seventeen titles dealing with prominent sports figures. 4 RL.

*Getting It Together.* (SRA) Three levels of readers about people and their problems. 2-6 RL.

*Hi-Lo Reading Series.* (PP) Twenty titles on contemporary themes. 3-8 RL.

*Interesting Reading Series.* (FEC) Short adventure stories. 3 RL.

*Kaleidoscope Readers.* (FEP) Eight books. 2-9 RL.

*Morgan Bay Mysteries.* (FEP) 2-4 RL.

*My Hobby Is _____.* (CPI) Varied hobby topics. 6 RL.

*Random House Reading Program.* (RH) Multilevel kits of materials to facilitate individualized reading.

*Reading Incentive Series.* (WD-MH) Five adventure stories. 3-7 RL.

*Reading Motivated Series.* (FEP) Short books for teenagers. 5 RL.

*Reluctant Reader Libraries.* (SBS) The upper-level set includes over fifty titles. 5-7 RL.

*Rochester Occupational Series.* (SRA) Combined text and workbook dealing with different occupational areas. 4-6 RL.

*Scholastic Individualized Reading Program.* (SBS) Multi-interest, multilevel kits for individualized reading.

*Signal Books.* (DC) Thirty-six titles of junior-high interest level. 4 RL.

*Sports Illustrated Library.* (JBL) Explanation of various individual and group sports. 5-6 RL.

*Teen-Age Stories.* (LP) Adventure and mystery. 4-8 RL.

*Teen Age Tales.* (DCH) Short selections with accompanying exercises. Books A-C, 3 RL; Books 1-6, 5-6 RL.

*The Way It Is.* (XC) Six paperbacks and related skills. 4-5 RL.

*Triple Title Series.* (FW) Humor and adventure tales. 5-6 RL.

*Winston Science Fiction Novels.* (HRW) 6-7 RL.

*Young Sportsmen's Library.* (TNS) Various sports explained by an expert. 6 RL.

### 2. Minority-Oriented Materials

*Against the Odds* and *Courage Under Fire.* (CEM) Paperback anthologies aimed at inner-city teenagers. 4-7 RL.

*Americans All.* (FEP) (Rambeau and Rambeau) Four titles. Ethnic-oriented biographies. 4 RL.

*Breakthrough Series.* (AB) Six collections of stories centered in the inner city. Teachers manual and exercises available. 2-6 RL.

*Challenger Books.* (HW) Ten paperbacks focusing on blacks and Spanish-Americans. Teachers guides and study cards.

*Contact.* (SBS) Anthologies of stories from *Scope* magazine centering on disadvantaged pupil concerns. 4-6 RL.

*Contact Books.* (AB) Paperbacks, each a collection of articles for inner-city secondary pupils.

*Forty for Sixty.* (BPC) Sports stories about a minority figure. 2-4 RL.

*Trouble and the Police.* (NRP) Young adult topics. 2-3 RL.

*We Are Black.* (SRA) 120 cards on prominent black figures with vocabulary and comprehension questions. 2-8 RL.

*Zenith Books.* (DC) Ten paperbacks on minority groups. 6 RL.

### 3. English/Communication-Oriented Materials

*Galaxy Literature Program.* (SF) 6 texts for pupils slightly deficient in reading, grades 7-12. Can be combined with *Tactics in Reading* kits or workbooks to provide skills development. 6-11 RL.

*Globe Adjusted English.* (GB) *English Everywhere,* 5.5 RL, and *Insight and Outlook,* 5-8 RL. Short stories by known authors.

*Impact Series.* (HRW) Three levels of literature anthologies including reading skills work. Four paperbacks and related skills kits at each level. Level I for 7-9 grades, 4-5 RL. Level II for 8-10 grades, 5-6 RL. Level III for 9-11 grades, 6-7 RL.

*Legacy Books.* (RH) Series treating myths, legends, folk tales. 4-5 RL.

*Making It Strange.* (HR) Four illustrated books for stimulating writing for severely retarded secondary readers.

*New Worlds Series.* (HBJ) Four anthologies of stories on interesting topics by popular authors. 5-9 RL. Respective manuals and readers notebooks accompany series. *Writers Journals.* Four journals to stimulate creative writing. May be used with *New Worlds Series* or independently.

*Pilot Libraries.* (SRA) Kit of short selections from noted literature. Can be used with SRA Reading Labs or independently. 5-8 RL.

*Scope Magazine.* (SBS) Language arts emphasis. 4-7 RL.

*Stop, Look and Write; The Writer's Eye;* and *Pictures for Writing.* (BB) Photographic approach to working with higher interpretive processes and creative expression.

*Short Story Anthologies.* (SS) Variety of exciting fiction. 4-6 RL.

*Signature Books.* (GD) Simple, readable biographies. 5-7 RL.

*Tactics in Reading.* (SF) Kits at each of grade levels 7-12 oriented toward English-reading skills. Reading difficulty slightly below grade placement of kit.

*Turner-Livingston Reading Series.* (FC) Six text-workbooks dealing with work-related skills and information. 4-6 RL.

*Voyager Books.* (HBJ) Paperback fiction and nonfiction by excellent authors. 4-6 RL.

### 4. Adapted Literature and Classics

*The Adapted Classics* series. (GB) 4-8 RL.

*Classics* series. (DC) 4-6 RL.

*Classics Illustrated Junior* series. (GC) Comic book form.

*Everyreader Series.* (WD-MH) 3-5 RL.

*The Literature Sampler.* (LM) Kit of short excerpts. 4-9 RL.

*Pacemaker Classics.* (FP) 2-3 RL.

*Pleasure Reading Series.* (GP) 4 RL.

*Riverside Reading Series.* (HM) 7-12 RL.

*Simplified Classics Series.* (SF) 3-6 RL.

*Supplementary Texts.* (NN) 5-8 RL.

*Yearling Books.* (DP) 5-7 RL.

### 5. Science/Math-Oriented Materials

*About Books.* (MP) Over seventy titles, each a brief book. Most treat science-related topics. 3-5 RL.

*AEP Unit Books.* (XP) Short booklets, many on science topics. 6-9 RL.

*Allabout Books.* (RH) Simple authoritative treatment of science topics. 4-8 RL.

*Capital Adventure Books.* (CPC) Simple text on mature topics, many science-related. 5 RL.

*Dimension Series: Manpower and Natural Resources Kit.* (SRA) 300 short readings. 4-12 RL.

Ewbank, W. A. *A Downpour of Math Lab Experiments.* Birmingham, Mich.: Midwest Publications. A five-book series. 3-5 RL.

*Harper-Row Math Books.* (HR) Meaningful discussions of computers, calculators, number and other math concepts. 5-9 RL.

*How and Why Wonder Books.* (CEM) 4-6 RL.

*Junior Research Library.* (PH) 5-7 RL.

*Junior Science Books.* (GP) Natural and physical sciences. 3 RL.

Kahn, C. H., et al. *Measure Up; Money Makes Sense; Using Dollars and Sense.* (FP) Interesting explanation of math concepts. 5-7 RL.

*Pathways in Science.* (GB) Three paperbounds of easy text nature: "Earth Science," "Biology," "Chemistry and Physics." Each with accompanying workbook. 4-5.5 RL.

*Science: Study Skills Library.* (EDL-MH) Boxed selections and exercises. 4-9 RL.

*Science Readers.* (RD) Similar format to *Reader's Digest Skill Builders,* 3-6 RL.

*Science/Search.* (SBS) Four paperbacks of articles, exercises, and activities of intermediate-grade reading difficulty.

*Science Works Like This Series.* (RP) Mechanics and history of modern sciences. 4-8 RL.

*What Is It Series.* (BP) Forty illustrated texts on science topics; many appropriate for adolescents. 2-7 RL.

*Young Math Books.* (TYC) Over thirty, highly interesting, excellently illustrated books, each dealing with significant math processes or concepts. 4-6 RL.

*Zim Science Books.* (WM) Over sixty titles, each giving thorough explanation and illustration of a science topic. 5-6 RL.

### 6. Social Studies-Oriented Materials

*AEP Unit Books.* (XP) Short booklets, many on social topics and problems. 6-9 RL.

*American Adventure Series.* (HR) Biographies of American figures. 2-5 RL.

*American Heritage Junior Library.* (AH) Dramatic stories of significant times and people in American history. 5-6 RL.

*The Color of Man.* (RH) Kit dealing with factual data and attitudes regarding race, color, and culture. 9-11 RL.

*Craig Reader Programs C to C-5.* (CC) Series of six programs correlated with phases of American development, employing slides and workbooks. 4-9 RL.

*Dimension Series: Countries and Cultures Kit* and *An American Album Kit.* (SRA) Kits of four-page reading selections. 3-9 and 4-10 RL.

*Globe Social Studies Texts.* (GB) Five texts paralleling

typical social studies courses in junior-senior high. 4-6 RL.

*Enchantment of America.* (CP) Illustrated regional books emphasizing geography, history, and people of each area. 6-8 RL.

*Frontier West.* (MC) Stories of westward movement. 5-6 RL.

*Horizon Caravel Books.* (HR) Interesting stories of major events and people in world history. 6-7 RL.

*In America Series.* (MMP) Twenty-volume series on immigrants and their contributions. 7-8 RL.

*Inquiry: USA* and *Minorities: USA.* (GB) Useful as basic text or supplementary reading for social studies; contemporary scene. 5-6 RL.

*Julian Messner Shelf of Biographies.* (JM) Two hundred biographies related to secondary social studies. 6-12 RL.

*Landmark Books.* (RH) Factual accounts of events and people in American history. 4-6 RL.

*Lands and People Series.* (MC) Brief, interesting overviews of countries of the world. 6 RL.

*North Star Books.* (HM) Famous events and people stories. 4-6 RL.

*People of Destiny.* (CP) Sixteen biographies of significant twentieth-century people. 4-5 RL.

*Piper Books.* (HM) Paperback biographies of famous Americans and explorers. 5-6 RL.

*Regions of America Books.* (HR) Description of major geographic areas. 5-6 RL.

*Rivers of the World.* (GP) Pictorial treatment, discussion, and maps of rivers' influences on civilization. 5 RL.

*Search Magazine.* (SBS) Social studies articles and reading-vocabulary exercises. 4-7 RL.

*United States Books.* (WC) Picture storybooks of each of thirty-six states. 4-6 RL.

*Winston Adventure Series.* (HRW) Factually based fiction on great moments in American history. 6-7 RL.

*World Explorer Books.* (GP) Simple, accurate biographies of explorers. 4 RL.

*You Book Series.* (CP) Ten books on major contemporary events and government. 5-6 RL.

# APPENDIX D

# Secondary Reading Instructional Materials*†‡

*In a number of instances, instructional materials could be placed in more than one classification. Vocabulary- and word-skills developmental materials, for instance, can be found in the Multiple-Skills section and in the Basic-Functional Reading section as well as in section 4, Decoding/Vocabulary/Word Analysis Skills.

†Since individual-item prices change frequently on these materials, the following broader cost rating for materials is given in terms of cost per supplying 25 pupils. Most of these materials are reusable.

| | |
|---|---|
| CR: 1 (Less than $50) | CR: 2 ($50 to $100) |
| CR: 3 ($100 to $250) | CR: 4 ($250 to $500) |
| CR: 5 ($500 to $1,000) | CR: 6 ($1,000 or more) |

‡Publishers' names are given parenthetically in abbreviated form; complete names and addresses appear in Appendix F.

## 1. Multiple-Skills Development

*Audio Reading Progress Laboratory.* (EPC) Program of tapes and workbooks in vocabulary, phonics, comprehension, and study skills on two levels: Intermediate (4-6) and Upper (7-8). CR for each lab: 4.

*Better Reading Books.* (SRA) Three levels of books of overlapping difficulty (reading levels 5-8, 7-9, 8-11), each with twenty rate selections and questions over vocabulary and specific comprehension. CR: 2.

*Breaking the Reading Barrier.* (PH) Workbook dealing with vocabulary, rate, and comprehension improvement over reading selections for. slightly limited secondary readers. CR: 2.

*Building Reading Power.* (CEM) Kit of graduated-difficulty study booklets for learning and practice in contextual analysis, structural analysis, and reading comprehension. CR: 1.

*EDL Laboratory 300.* (MH) Program system composed of multimedia components which can be adapted to particular school program. Options include listening, vocabulary, comprehension, word attack, word recognition, fluency, study skills, flexibility, plus supplementary graded reading. CR: 1 to 6.

*Imperial Junior High School Aural Reading Lab.* (IIL) Multimedia approach (tapes, story cards, workbooks) placing developmental emphasis upon word analysis, vocabulary, comprehension, and reading rate. Readability 4-8. CR: 4.

*Kaleidoscope Readers.* (FEP) Seven softbound books increasing from reading level 2 to 10.5; high-interest articles with accompanying exercises on varied reading skills. CR: 1.

*Lessons for Self-Instruction in Basic Skills: Reading.* (MH) Thirty-six skill-oriented booklets of readability 3-9 stressing comprehension, directed reading, and reference usage. CR: 2.

*Pattern for Reading.* (SBS) Reading workbook offering instruction and practice in developmental reading skills, grades 8-12. CR: 1.

*Power and Speed in Reading.* (PH) Exercise book stressing flexibility, rate, and interpretation for the adequate secondary reader. CR: 2.

*Powereading.* (PAR) Four book series providing practice in comprehension, study skills, locational reading, vocabulary, and reading rate with twelve sequential levels of difficulty, 3-16. CR: 2.

*Random House Criterion Reading Materials: Level 5.* (RH) Criterion-referenced tests and instructional materials for developing word and comprehension skills for readers, grades 7-12. Utilizes materials of other publishers, so cost varies with present resources.

*Reading Development Kits.* (AW) Each kit contains 65-80 four-page reading selections with accompanying exercises in word attack, comprehension, and critical thinking; kit B for limited junior high readers, Kit C for adequate junior high readers. CR: 2.

*Reading for Meaning.* (JBL) Books 4-12 of this series correspond to 3-11 RL; each contains short selections with practice exercises stressing vocabulary and interpretive skills. CR: 1.

*Reading Laboratories 3a and 4a.* (SRA) Each kit consists of short Power Builders, Rate Builders, and Listening Skill Builders for individualized reading and practice. Kit 3a reading levels 3.5-11.0. Kit 4a reading levels 8-14. CR per kit: 2.

*Skill Builder Reading Program.* (RDS) Levels 4-6 consist of 18 illustrated Skill Builders and Science Readers. Levels 7 and 8 are Advanced Skill Builders and *Improve Your Reading* text. Includes dramatization tapes and exercises for word skills, comprehension, and rate improvement. 4-10 RL. CR: 2.

*Target Reading.* (LB) Six books gradually increasing from 3.5 to 7.0 reading difficulty, with inductive instruction in vocabulary, comprehension, locational skills, and study skills. CR: 1.

## 2. Interpretation, Fluency, and Flexibility

*Be a Better Reader.* (PH) Nine workbooks corresponding to reading levels 4-12 emphasizing the development of interpretive skills in content area material. CR: 1.

*Controlled Reading Programs.* (EDL-MH) Sets GH through LK are developmentally appropriate for secondary readers; combines filmstrip reading selections with workbook counterparts. Controlled reader speed can be adjusted to fit group for developing fluent rate of comprehension. CR: 4.

*Craig Reading Program B.* (CC) Twenty-four lessons using reading manuals, workbook, Craig Reader, and slides to improve reading interpretive skills and reading efficiency for reader levels 7 through 9. CR: 4.

*Design for Good Reading.* (HBJ) Four workbooks corresponding to reading levels 9-12 for developing interpretive skills, reading rate, and flexibility. CR: 1.

*Developmental Reading.* (PDL) 16-mm films shown through Perceptoscope, supplemented by tests and booklets to develop skimming, scanning, rapid reading, and interpretive skills. 4-10 RL. CR: 5.

*Gates-Peardon Reading Exercises.* (TC) Classic, short, interpretive reading exercises, reading levels 1-7, for limited secondary readers. CR: 1.

*Help Yourself to Improve Your Reading.* (RDS) Books 1-4 provide high-interest selections with interpretive exercises pertinent to grades 7-9. CR: 1.

*Improving Reading Ability.* (ACC) Text stresses interpretation and rate improvement for better secondary readers. CR: 2.

*McCall-Crabbs Test Lessons in Reading-Reasoning.* (TC) Focuses upon reasoning and critical analysis in reading. Challenging to average secondary readers. CR: 1.

*Name of the Game.* (NDE) Total program of thirty-five copies each of student workshop journals, instructional paperbacks and supplementary paperbacks, a record, and a film. Stresses critical thinking and interpretive reading for somewhat limited secondary readers. CR: 4.

*New Modern Reading Skilltext Series.* (CEM) Emphasizes development of interpretive skills through three student texts and accompanying instructional tapes. Reading levels 6-8. CR: 3.

*Propaganda.* (JWW) Work-text stressing reading and critical thinking skills suitable for senior high readers of average ability. CR: 2.

*Reading for Concepts.* (MH) Eight reading and exercise books appropriate for reading levels 2-10, stressing interpretive and study skills. CR: 2.

*Reading for Understanding.* (SRA) Three kits (Junior, RL 3-9; General, RL 4-10; Senior, RL 6-14), each with 400 cards of short paragraphs stressing higher thinking processes in reading. CR per kit: 2.

*Scope/Visuals.* (SBS) Booklets of overhead transparencies and duplicating masters each emphasizing one of seventeen types of specific interpretive reading behaviors. CR: 2.

*Success in Reading.* (SB) Books 1-6 provide sequential development work for grades 7-12 in skimming, scanning, study reading, interpretation, and retention. CR: 2.

### 3. Reading-Study Skills

*Advanced Skills in Reading.* (MC) Three levels of hardbound books providing many study-type interpretive exercises for adequate readers, grades 7-10. CR each level: 2.

*Basic Study Skills Series 9200.* (MM) Ten packages (tape, thirty response booklets, T.G., test), each package treating directed reading-study skills; secondary-level interest with intermediate readability. CR for total series: 2.

*EDL Study Skills Kits.* (EDL) Systematic individualized study methods and application exercise cards for each of reading levels 3-9 for social studies, science, and library skills. CR per kit: 1.

*Graph and Picture Study Kit.* (SRA) Many cards and related exercises in interpreting varied graphic-pictorial materials. CR: 3.

*Map and Globe Skills Kit.* (SRA) Well-organized, reading-related exercises with reading levels of 4-7 and junior high interest. CR: 3.

*Methods and Habits: A Study Manual.* (EPS) Workbook of reading-study skills applicable to senior high content areas. CR: 2.

*Organizing and Reporting Skills Kit.* (SRA) Multiple-exercise materials appropriate for junior high and mildly limited senior high readers. CR: 3.

*Reading Improvement Program.* (WCB) Workbook stressing flexible reading-study tasks for college-bound senior high pupils. CR: 1.

*Study Lessons.* (FEC) Study-methods emphasis in English and social studies unit booklets for limited junior high readers. CR: 1.

*Study Reading College Textbooks.* (SRA) Work-text consisting of reprinted selections from college-level texts with accompanying study questions; for college-bound secondary readers. CR: 2.

*The Technical Reader.* (PAR) Varied reading-study skills-technical vocabulary exercises for above-average senior high readers. CR: 2.

### 4. Decoding/Vocabulary/Word Analysis Skills

*Base.* (EC) Seventeen tapes plus workbook for building vocabulary through structural synthesis; for retarded secondary readers. CR: 3.

*Breaking the Reading Barrier.* (PH) Multiple word-skills practice source for adequate senior high readers. CR: 3.

*Building Reading Skills.* (MMP) Six workbook series for phonic practice. Also in kit form. CR: 1.

*College Word Study.* (PAR) Textbook emphasizing reading-spelling approach to vocabulary development for better secondary pupils. CR: 2.

*Conquests in Reading.* (MH) Workbooks providing practice in phonic, structural, and contextual analysis using Dolch 220 words; for severely limited secondary readers. CR: 1.

*EDL Word Clues.* (EDL) Vocabulary developing kits of self-instructional, programmed workbooks for adequate readers, grades 7-13. Each book has thirty lessons of ten words based on EDL Core Vocabulary. CR per kit: 1.

*Phonics We Use.* (LC) Eight sequential levels of workbooks A-H for reteaching phonic skills for limited secondary readers. CR per level: 1.

*Picto-Cabulary Series.* (BL) Varied-level sets of booklets for basic vocabulary development, combining pictures, context, and exercises. Sets 111 and 222 for limited readers, levels 5-9. CR per set: 1.

*Programmed Vocabulary.* (ACC) Programmed practice book based on the fourteen "basic words" list. CR: 1.

*Reach.* (EC) Twenty tapes and a workbook of feedback exercises for developing phonics/decoding for very limited readers. CR: 3.

*Scope/Skills.* (SBS) Word Puzzles and Word Mysteries

provide independent-practice word games for limited secondary readers. CR: 1.

*Success with Words.* (SBS) Paperback games and exercises stressing secondary content area vocabulary. CR: 1.

*Word Attack Manual.* (EPS) Corrective exercise workbooks stressing phonic and structural analysis. Test booklets and teachers' manuals available. CR: 2.

*Wordcraft/1* and *Wordcraft/2.* (CA) Each program combines tapes, filmstrips, and student study manual to develop vocabulary through stories and practice exercises, WC/1 for grades 4-6 and WC/2 for grades 6-8 vocabulary. CR: 1 or 2.

*Words.* (SRA) Programmed work-text emphasizing word analysis skills for adequate junior high readers. CR: 2.

*Word Study for Improved Reading.* (GB) Advanced word analysis workbook. CR: 2.

## 5. Basic/Functional Reading Development

*Action* and *Double Action.* (SBS) Each is a unit of story books, exercise books, and LP record stressing vocabulary, comprehension, and word attack development for young adults with primary-level reading ability. CR per unit: 2.

*Adult Readers.* (RDS) Series of twelve attractive story-workbook readers from 1.2-4.1 readability; word skills and comprehension exercises. CR: 1.

*Be Informed Units.* (NRP) Seventeen units on survival literary topics and skills for functionally illiterate adults reading at primary-grade level. CR per unit: 1.

*Breakthrough!* (AB) Series of fifteen paperback readers and duplicator worksheets for developing young adult reading skills and vocabulary from nonreader to intermediate levels. CR: 2.

*Clues to Reading Progress.* (EPC) Program for raising nonreaders to intermediate-level reading ability which utilizes instructional, practice, and testing tapes, testing booklets, and motivated reading magazines. CR: 4.

*EDL Learning 100.* (MH) Total instructional laboratory system with numerous multimedia instructional components to develop basic reading ability to intermediate levels for adolescent and adult nonreaders. CR: 6.

*High School and Adult Basic Reading Laboratory B.* (BRL) Total instructional system comprised of programmed texts, supplementary readers, audiotapes, and tests for nonreader to eighth-grade levels in decoding and comprehension. CR: 6.

*Macmillan Reading Spectrum of Skills.* (MC) Boxed series of sequential instructional booklets, guide, and tests for developing decoding and comprehension skills from primary to middle school levels. CR: 3.

*Mott Basic Language Skills Program.* (AEC) Original or semiprogrammed series text. Workbook reading with oral exercises for very limited or linguistically different learners; reading developmental range of 0 to 9th grade. CR: 4.

*Operation Alphabet.* (NN) Series of illustrated lesson and study books geared to adult survival literacy tasks which stress decoding skills at the beginning reading level. CR: 3.

*Point 31 Remedial Reading Program.* (RDS) Program consists of series of high-interest readers, workbooks, and audio tapes to develop sequential decoding and comprehension skills of secondary nonreaders from beginning to middle grade levels. CR: 3.

*Prevocational Orientation and Guidance Program.* (EP) Series of instructional and practice tapes and related workbooks dealing with work-related literary tasks. CR: 5.

*Programmed Reading for Adults.* (MH) Program of eight work-texts to develop basic-functional literary decoding and comprehension skill. CR: 4.

*Reader's Digest Readings.* (RDS) Series of six consumable story-exercise books from readability levels 2 to 4 for independent practice of adolescents with English language deficiency. CR: 1.

*Reading Attainment Kits.* (GEC) Two kits for minimal readers 2-4 and 3-5 reading levels, consisting of 120 four-page selections followed by multiple-skills practice materials. CR: 3.

*Reading for a Purpose.* (FEC) Program for basic illiterates, developing decoding and comprehension skills consisting of text of separate lessons and instructional transparencies. CR: 2.

*Scope/Skills Series.* (SBS) Particularly, *Jobs in Your Future* and *Consumer Sense and Nonsense* which offer readable format for limited secondary readers and provide simulated work-life reading applications. CR: 1.

*Specific Skills Series.* (BL) Sequential series of seven skills development texts involving reading for different comprehension purposes from 2 to 8 readability levels. CR: 2.

*Sullivan Reading Program.* (BRL) Twenty-one programmed texts, audiotapes, supplementary readers, and test booklets to develop basic decoding, comprehension, and spelling skills of nonreading adolescents and adults. CR: 4.

*Supportive Reading Skills.* (DW) Sets of decoding-comprehension skills-reading booklets to supplement *Specific Skills Series* (see above). CR: 3.

*Turner Career Guidance Series.* (FEC) Six workbooks dealing with work-related interpretation and application reading tasks of approximately fifth-grade readability. CR: 1.

# Electronic–Mechanical Instructional Aids *

*Publishers' names are given parenthetically in abbreviated form; complete names and addresses appear in Appendix F.

## 1. Tachistoscopes (primarily, quick exposure of limited text)

*EDL Flash-X* (EDL)   Hand, mechanical; $9, plus vocabulary disks; 1/3 second.

*EDL Tach-X* (EDL)   Electronic; $198, plus vocabulary filmstrips; 1 to 1/100 seconds.

*Keystone Standard Tachistoscope* (KVC)   Overhead; $370, plus slide sets; 1 to 1/100 seconds.

*Language Master* (BH)   Combined sound print; $290, plus cards.

*Tach-Mate* (I/CT)   Electronic; $130–$165, plus varied 35-mm filmstrips; 1/25 second.

*T-ap All-Purpose Tachistoscopic Attachment* (LI)   Converts projector into tachistoscope; 1 to 1/100 seconds.

*Vu-Mate* (I/CT)   Hand, mechanical; $10, plus varied perceptual, reading cards; 1/25 to 1/100 seconds.

## 2. Pacers (individual use with varied types of printed material)

*AVR Reading Ratometer* (AVR)   Moving T-square; adjustable rate. $40.

*EDL Skimmer* (EDL)   Moving bead of light; adjustable rate. $54.

*Shadowscope* (PI)   Moving band of light; adjustable rate and intensity. $94.

*SRA Reading Accelerator* (SRA)   Adjustable rate shutter; mechanical, $49; electric, $69.

## 3. Projectors (film and slides)

*Craig Reader* (CC)   Rear-view projection screen; adjustable speed. $250, plus slides.

*EDL Controlled Reader* (EDL)   Group or individual; adjustable rate; continuing text. Junior, $195. Standard, $260, plus films.

*Guided Reader* (I/CT)   Group or individual; adjustable rate; continuing text; $170, plus films.

*Iowa Reading Films* (UI)   Sixteen sequential rate films for 16-mm projector.

*Projection Reader* (CEA)   For use with filmstrip programs. $295, plus films.

*Tachomatic 500 Reading Projector* (PI)   Flash exposure plus adjustable rate. $325, plus filmstrips.

# APPENDIX F

# Publishers' Key

| | | | | |
|---|---|---|---|---|
| AB | Allyn and Bacon, Inc.<br>470 Atlantic Avenue<br>Boston, Mass. 02210 | | BYU | Brigham Young University Press<br>205 University Press Building<br>Provo, Utah 84602 |
| ACC | Appleton-Century-Crofts<br>292 Madison Avenue<br>New York, N.Y. 10017 | | CA | Communications Academy<br>Box 541<br>Wilton, Conn. 06897 |
| ACE | American Council on Education<br>1 Dupont Circle<br>Washington, D.C. 20036 | | CC | Craig Corporation<br>921 West Artesia Boulevard<br>Compton, Calif. 90220 |
| AEC | Allied Educational Council<br>Box 78<br>Galien, Mich. 49113 | | CDRT | Committee on Diagnostic Reading Tests, Inc.<br>Mountain Home, N.C. 28758 |
| AGS | American Guidance Service, Inc.<br>Publishers' Building<br>Circle Pines, Minn. 55014 | | CEA | Cenco Educational Aids<br>4401 West 26th Street<br>Chicago, Ill. 60623 |
| AH | American Heritage Publishing Co., Inc.<br>1221 Avenue of the Americas<br>New York, N.Y. 10036 | | CEM | Charles E. Merrill Publishing Co.<br>1300 Alum Creek Drive<br>Columbus, Ohio 43216 |
| AVR | Audio-Visual Research<br>1509 Eighth Street S.E.<br>Waseca, Minn. 56093 | | CP | Childrens Press, Inc.<br>1124 West Van Buren Street<br>Chicago, Ill. 60607 |
| AW | Addison-Wesley Publishing Co., Inc.<br>Jacob Way<br>Reading, Mass. 01867 | | CPC | Chandler Publishing Co.<br>257 Park Avenue South<br>New York, N.Y. 10010 |
| BB | Bantam Books, Inc.<br>666 Fifth Avenue<br>New York, N.Y. 10019 | | CPI | CAL Press, Inc.<br>76 Madison Avenue<br>New York, N.Y. 10016 |
| BH | Bell & Howell Co.<br>7100 McCormick Road<br>Chicago, Ill. 60607 | | CTB | California Test Bureau<br>5916 Hollywood Boulevard<br>Los Angeles, Calif. 90029 |
| BL | Barnell Loft Ltd.<br>111 South Centre Avenue<br>Rockville Centre, N.Y. 11571 | | DC | Doubleday & Co., Inc.<br>245 Park Avenue<br>New York, N.Y. 10017 |
| BM | The Bobbs-Merrill Co., Inc.<br>4 West 58th Street<br>New York, N.Y. 10019 | | DCH | D. C. Heath & Co.<br>125 Spring Street<br>Lexington, Mass. 02173 |
| BP | Benefic Press<br>10300 West Roosevelt Road<br>Westchester, Ill. 60153 | | DP | Dell Publishing Co., Inc.<br>1 Dag Hammarskjold Plaza<br>New York, N.Y. 10017 |
| BPC | Bowmar Publications Co.<br>4563 Colorado Boulevard<br>Los Angeles, Calif. 90039 | | EDL | Educational Developmental Laboratories<br>(*see* McGraw-Hill) |
| | | | EP | Educational Projections Co.<br>3070 Lake Terrace<br>Glenview, Ill. 60025 |
| BRL | Behavioral Research Laboratory<br>Box 577<br>Palo Alto, Calif. 94302 | | EPC | Educational Progress Corp.<br>4900 South Lewis<br>Tulsa, Okla. 74105 |

| | | | | |
|---|---|---|---|---|
| EPS | Educators Publishing Service, Inc.<br>75 Moulton Street<br>Cambridge, Mass. 02138 | | HR | Harper and Row Publishers, Inc.<br>10 East 53rd Street<br>New York, N.Y. 10022 |

EPS    Educators Publishing Service, Inc.
75 Moulton Street
Cambridge, Mass. 02138

ETB    Educational Test Bureau
720 Washington Avenue S.E.
Minneapolis, Minn. 55414

ETS    Educational Testing Service
20 Nassau Street
Princeton, N.J. 08540

FC    Finney Company
3350 Gorham Avenue
Minneapolis, Minn. 55426

FEC    Follett Educational Corp.
1010 West Washington Boulevard
Chicago, Ill. 60607

FEP    Field Educational Publications, Inc.
2400 Hanover Street
Palo Alto, Calif. 94304

FP    Fearon Publishers, Inc.
6 Davis Drive
Belmont, Calif. 94002

FW    Franklin Watts, Inc.
845 Third Avenue
New York, N.Y. 10022

GB    Globe Book Co., Inc.
175 Fifth Avenue
New York, N.Y. 10010

GC    Gilberton Co.
101 Fifth Avenue
New York, N.Y. 10003

GD    Grosset and Dunlap, Inc.
51 Madison Avenue
New York, N.Y. 10010

GEC    Grolier Educational Corp.
845 Third Avenue
New York, N.Y. 10022

GP    Garrard Publishing Co.
107 Cherry Street
New Canaan, Conn. 06840

HBJ    Harcourt Brace Jovanovich, Inc.
757 Third Avenue
New York, N.Y. 10017

HM    Houghton Mifflin Co.
2 Park Street
Boston, Mass. 02107

HR    Harper and Row Publishers, Inc.
10 East 53rd Street
New York, N.Y. 10022

HRW    Holt, Rinehart and Winston, Inc.
383 Madison Avenue
New York, N.Y. 10017

HW    Hill and Wang, Inc.
19 Union Square West
New York, N.Y. 10003

HZW    Henry Z. Walck, Inc.
750 Third Avenue
New York, N.Y. 10017

ICT    Instructional Communications Technology, Inc.
Hawk Drive
Huntington, N.Y. 11743

IIL    Imperial International Learning Corp.
Box 548
Kankakee, Ill. 60901

JBL    J. B. Lippincott Co.
East Washington Square
Philadelphia, Pa. 19105

JM    Julian Messner, Inc.
1 West 39th Street
New York, N.Y. 10018

JWW    J. Weston Walch Publisher
P.O. Box 658
Portland, Maine 04104

KPC    Klamath Printing Co.
Klamath, Oregon 97601

KVC    Keystone View Co.
Meadville, Pa. 16335

LB    Laidlaw Brothers
Thatcher and Madison Streets
River Forest, Ill. 60305

LC    Lyons & Carnahan, Publishers
407 East 25th Street
Chicago, Ill. 60616

LI    Lafayette Instrument Co.
Lafayette, Ind. 47901

LLI    Laubach Literacy, Inc.
Box 131
Syracuse, N.Y. 13210

LM     Learning Materials, Inc.
100 East Ohio Street
Chicago, Ill. 60607

MC     Macmillan Publishing Co., Inc.
866 Third Avenue
New York, N.Y. 10022

MH     McGraw-Hill Book Co.
1221 Avenue of the Americas
New York, N.Y. 10036

MM     Media Materials
409 West Cold Spring
Baltimore, Md. 21210

MMP     McCormick-Mathers Publishing Co.
450 West 33rd St.
New York, N.Y. 10001

MP     Melmont Publishers
1224 West Van Buren
Chicago, Ill. 60607

NDE     New Dimensions in Education, Inc.
160 Dupont Street
Plainview, N.Y. 11803

NN     Noble and Noble, Publishers, Inc.
1 Dag Hammarskjold Plaza
New York, N.Y. 10017

NRP     New Readers Press
(*see* Laubach Literacy, Inc.)

PAR     PAR Inc.
Abbott Park Place
Providence, R.I. 02903

PC     Psychological Corporation
304 East 45th Street
New York, N.Y. 10017

PDL     Perceptual Developmental Laboratories
P.O. Box 1911
Big Spring, Texas 79720

PH     Prentice-Hall, Inc.
Englewood Cliffs, N.J. 07632

PI     Psychotechnics, Inc.
Glenview, Ill. 60025

PP     Personnel Press
191 Spring Street
Lexington, Mass. 02173

RDS     Reader's Digest Services, Inc.
Pleasantville, N.Y. 10570

RH     Random House, Inc.
201 East 50th St.
New York, N.Y. 10022

RP     Roy Publishers, Inc.
30 East 74th Street
New York, N.Y. 10021

SB     Silver Burdett Co.
250 James Street
Morristown, N.J. 07960

SBS     Scholastic Book Services
50 West 44th Street
New York, N.Y. 10036

SF     Scott, Foresman and Co.
1900 East Lake Avenue
Glenview, Ill. 60025

SRA     Science Research Associates
1540 Page Mill Road
Palo Alto, Calif. 94304

SS     Simon and Schuster, Inc.
630 Fifth Avenue
New York, N.Y. 10020

STS     Scholastic Testing Service, Inc.
480 Meyer Road
Bensenville, Ill. 60106

TC     Teachers College Press
Columbia University
1234 Amsterdam Avenue
New York, N.Y. 10027

TN     Thomas Nelson, Inc.
30 East 42nd Street
New York, N.Y. 10017

TYC     Thomas Y. Crowell Co., Inc.
666 Fifth Avenue
New York, N.Y. 10019

UI     Iowa Reading Films
Bureau of Audio-Visual Instruction
University of Iowa
Iowa City, Iowa 52240

WC     Albert Whitman and Co.
560 West Lake Street
Chicago, Ill. 60606

WCB     William C. Brown Company
2460 Kerper Boulevard
Dubuque, Iowa 52001

WD-MH    Webster Division
           (*see* McGraw–Hill)

WM        William Morrow & Co.
           105 Madison Avenue
           New York, N.Y. 10016

WPS       Western Psychological Services
           12031 Wilshire Boulevard
           Los Angeles, Calif. 90025

XEP       Xerox Educational Publications
           Education Center
           1250 Fairwood Avenue
           Columbus, Ohio 43216

# Index of Names

# Subject Index